GARLAND STUDIES IN HUMOR
VOL. 5

CHAUCER'S HUMOR

GARLAND REFERENCE LIBRARY
OF THE HUMANITIES
VOL. 1504

GARLAND STUDIES IN HUMOR

STEVEN H. GALE
Series Editor

S. J. PERELMAN
Critical Essays
edited by Steven H. Gale

BLACK HUMOR
Critical Essays
edited by Alan R. Pratt

MARK TWAIN'S HUMOR
Critical Essays
edited by David E.E. Sloane

AMERICAN WOMEN HUMORISTS
Critical Essays
edited by Linda A. Morris

CHAUCER'S HUMOR
Critical Essays
edited by Jean E. Jost

CHAUCER'S HUMOR

Critical Essays

edited by

Jean E. Jost

GARLAND PUBLISHING, Inc.
New York & London / 1994

Library of Congress Cataloging-in-Publication Data

Chaucer's humor : critical essays / by Jean E. Jost.
    p.   cm. — (Garland studies in humor ; vol. 5)
(Garland reference library of the humanities ; vol. 1504)
    Includes bibliographical references and index.
    ISBN 0–8153–0618–0
    1. Chaucer, Geoffrey, d. 1400—Humor.
2. Humorous stories, English—History and criticism.
3. Wit and humor, Medieval—History and criticism.
I. Jost, Jean E.   II. Series.   III. Series: Garland reference
library of the humanities ; vol. 1504.
PR1933.H85C48   1994
821'.1—dc20   94–10193
                                                       CIP

Printed on acid-free, 250-year-life paper
Manufactured in the United States of America

Contents

General Editor's Note   ix

Acknowledgments   xi

Chronology of Major Events   xiii

Introduction   xvii

Part One

A PROLEGOMENON TO DEFINING CHAUCERIAN HUMOR

The Voice of the Past: Surveying the Reception
of Chaucer's Humor
Jean E. Jost   3

The Idea of Humor   ✗
Howard Rollin Patch   23

Excerpt from *Chaucer*
G. K. Chesterton   39

A Vocabulary for Chaucerian Comedy:
A Preliminary Sketch
Paul G. Ruggiers   41

Chaucer and Comedy
Thomas J. Garbáty   79

The Canterbury Tales II: Comedy
Derek Pearsall   101

Part Two

CRITICAL THEORIES WITH THE COMIC TOUCH:
FEMINIST, FREUDIAN, LANGUAGE, SOCIAL,
AND BAKHTINIAN THEORIES

Feminist Theory
Chaucer's May, Standup Comics, and Critics
   Susan K. Hagen   127

Freudian Theory
Chaucer, Freud, and the Political Economy of Wit:
Tendentious Jokes in the *Nun's Priest's Tale*
   R. James Goldstein   145

Language Theory and Freud
Paradoxicum Semiotica: Signs, Comedy, and Mystery
in Fragment VI of the *Canterbury Tales*
   John Micheal Crafton   163

Social Theory
The Comedy of Innocence
   Alfred David   187

Metamorphic Comedy: The *Shipman's Tale*
   William F. Woods   207

Bakhtinian Theory of Carnival
Rough Music in Chaucer's *Merchant's Tale*
   Frederick B. Jonassen   229

Part Three

"GENERIC" HUMOR: LYRIC, POETIC, DEMONIC,
RELIGIOUS, SCATOLOGICAL, AND TRAGIC

The Lyric
Chaucer's Witty Prosody in General Prologue, Lines 1–42
   Charles A. Owen, Jr.   261

The Poetic
Chaucer's Dainty "Dogerel": The "Elvyssh" Prosody
of *Sir Thopas*
    Alan T. Gaylord   271

The Demonic
"Parlous Play": Diabolic Comedy in Chaucer's
Canterbury Tales
    Robert W. Hanning   295

The Religious
The Semiotics of Comedy in Chaucer's Religious Tales
    Daniel F. Pigg   321

The Scatological
The Mind Distended: The *Retraction, Miller's Tale*
and *Summoner's Tale*
    Judith Tschann   349

Chaucer's Creative Comedy: A Study of the *Miller's Tale*
and the *Shipman's Tale*
    A. Booker Thro   379

The Tragic
Felicity and Mutability: Boethian Framework
of the *Troilus*
    John M. Steadman   397

Select Bibliography   425

Index   447

General Editor's Note

Jean E. Jost's *Chaucer's Humor: Critical Essays* is the fifth volume in Garland's "Studies in Humor" series. Each volume in the series is devoted to an assessment of the work of an individual major humorist or group of authors within a specified category and consists of collections of both previously published and original articles on subjects such as S. J. Perelman, Black Humor, Mark Twain, Classical Greek and Roman Humorists, Woody Allen, and American Women Humorists, among others.

The intent behind this series is to supply in a single volume a representative sample of the best critical reactions by the humorist's contemporaries (when available) and from subsequent scholarly assessments. Typically, the contents of each volume will include: a chronology of the author's life and writing; the volume editor's introduction to the writer's canon; reviews (book, play, and/or film); interviews when appropriate; essays focusing on specific works (this section may contain both journal articles and parts of books); general essays treating particular aspects of the humorist's oeuvre; a selected, annotated bibliography; and an index. This structure provides access to essential scholarship (some of which may no longer be easily obtainable) on the most important and best examples of the humorist's work. It also demonstrates popular reactions to that work and allows for comparisons to be made in critical and popular reactions over the course of the writer's career.

Geoffrey Chaucer is considered the first major humorist in English literature. As such, he is of particular interest to scholars in terms of the humor itself because it reflects the work of his predecessors and contemporaries and because it defines the direction of development for subsequent British humor, and in terms of how his humor relates to his overall canon. In her collection Jost has chosen pieces that approach Chaucer's humor from three perspectives: first, scholarly works that define the nature of Chaucerian humor; second, a variety of theoretically based examinations (including feminist, Freudian, Social, and Bakhtinian "Carnival" theory); and third, an examination of the genres of humor that appear in Chaucer's writing (lyric, poetic, demonic, religious, scatological, and tragic). There are eighteen selections included, all by preeminent Chaucerian scholars; ten were written expressly for this volume—including an informative overview of Chaucerian scholarship by Jost herself. In addition, Jost has furnished a comprehensive introduction, a fine selected, annotated bibliography, and an index.

The elements of the critical discourse represented by these essays are brought together in *Chaucer's Humor: Critical Essays* in a way that makes the author's works clearer and more accessible and brings readers a better understanding of the man who created the canon. Among other things, this takes into account the shift from Aristotle's delineation of what constitutes "comedy" to the genre's modern definition. It is especially valuable to be able to see how critical opinions and emphases have changed over the years, as is evident when the selections from the 1930s and the 1970s though the mid-1980s are compared with the variety of approaches evident in the pieces that are being published for the first time in this volume.

Jean E. Jost is associate professor of English at Bradley University. She is the author of *Ten Middle English Romances: A Reference Guide* and numerous articles on *Troilus and Criseyde*, individual tales from the *Canterbury Tales* and other of Chaucer's works (including the piece on Chaucer in Garland's forthcoming *Encyclopedia of British Humorists*) as well as an essay on King Arthur. She is currently working on a critical volume entitled *"Trouthe is the hyeste thyng": Behests and Their Breaking in Chaucer's Canterbury Tales* in addition to transcribing an unedited text of *The Pricke of Conscience*. Jost is also co-editor of the *Chaucer Yearbook: A Journal of Late Medieval Studies*.

Steven H. Gale
Kentucky State University

Acknowledgments

Editing a volume on Chaucerian humor has been an extremely satisfying experience, presenting new concepts, often in innovative and excitingly new critical frameworks. No doubt the creative multivalency of Chaucer's art has rubbed off on these contributors, for their own creative powers have spawned thought-provoking new ideas in re-defining Chaucerian humor, in seeing how it fits into modern critical theory, and in exploring the implications for multiple, sometimes fluid genres. I am extremely grateful and honored by the commitment and willingness of the participants in this project who offered their time and energy to our joint endeavor and gratified by their timely submission of excellent copy.

I would also like to thank fellow medievalists across the nation, those directly involved in the project and those not, for encouragement and warm wishes, pleasure at my delight in the project, and stalwart certainty of its success. Certainly the National Endowment for the Humanities (NEH) has been a major force in my academic development, often in ways unseen and unacknowledged. But the associations resulting from two seminars and an institute sponsored by the NEH have also assisted in concrete projects such as this one: five of the articles were provided by fellow seminarians and three by organizers or visitors to those seminars. I am grateful for the opportunities the NEH-sponsored projects afforded.

I owe the single greatest debt to Bradley University and the English Department headed by Margaret Carter, who offered a teaching reduction, from four to three courses, to make such a project as this even feasible. The Office of Teaching Excellence and Faculty Development at Bradley headed by Ahmad Fakheri and Robert Weinstein has provided a summer stipend for my tireless Graduate Assistant, Alan Williams, without whose computer experience and proficiency I would have spent untold extra hours at the computer. I would like to thank Mr. Williams for his expertise and willing commitment to complete our project and Graduate Assistant David Tyler for helping compile the index.

Additionally, I am grateful to my secretaries, Willie Heberer and Carolyn Rosser, who with much good grace and willing disposition have typed, photocopied, and assisted in any number of ways; to the Interlibrary loan staff at Bradley University's Cullom-Davis Library headed by Marina Savoie; to Ellen Watson and her Information Services staff at Bradley; to Barbara Tunks and other Bradley library staff who have been unfailingly helpful; to Joan Winters and her Milner Library staff at Illinois State University; and to my many supportive friends and my colleagues at Bradley, most of whom are similarly engaged in various research projects.

The cost of permissions to reprint articles is often a major impediment in compiling a critical anthology, and I would like to express my appreciation to the authors and publishers who granted permission to reprint their work without demanding exorbitant recompense.

My general editor Steven H. Gale has been a source of patient support—understanding delays, suggesting remedies, and providing concrete instances for improvement. I thank him for his generosity. This project was his idea, and I am pleased that he invited me to undertake it.

The editors at Garland Press have been unfailingly helpful and encouraging. I would especially like to thank Eunice Petrini, Adrienne Makowski, and Gary Kuris for helping resolve difficulties expeditiously.

As usual, my family has stood by with patience and encouragement, and I am grateful for their support in all things academic.

Peoria, Illinois

Chronology of Major Events

Although chronology is uncertain, John H. Fisher's and Larry D. Benson's editions of Chaucer's works suggest the following:

1340?	Geoffrey Chaucer born to John and Agnes Chaucer in Ipswich, 70 miles north of London
1357	First record of Chaucer: part of Countess of Ulster's household
1360	Chaucer captured and ransomed by King Edward III
1366	February 22–May 24: safe conduct for Chaucer to travel to Spain
	Philippa "Chaucer" granted royal annuity of 10 marks
1367	Chaucer enters King's service and granted royal annuity of 20 marks
1368	Chaucer on mission in France during French war
1369	Writes *Book of the Duchess*
1370	(or before) writes *Romaunt of the Rose*
	June 20–September 29: Chaucer on mission in France
1372	December 1: Chaucer visits Genoa and Florence
1373	May 23: Chaucer returns to London Birth of son Thomas
1374	May 10: Chaucer leases Aldgate and sets up housekeeping

June 8: Chaucer becomes controller of customs

Writes *Parlement of Foules* and
Second Nun's Tale

Chaucer on peace-treaty and marriage
negotiation (between Richard and Anne of
Bohemia) mission in France

1376–1377   Writes *Monk's Tale* and *Anelida and Arcite*

1378   January 16–March 9: Chaucer in France
             negotiating marriage between Richard
             and Princess Marie

             May 28–September 19: Chaucer in Lombardy
             with Bernabo Visconti

1380   Chaucer released from charge of *raptus*
             of Cecily Chaumpaigne

             ? birth of son Lewis

1380 or 1381 Writes *House of Fame*

1381   Deed of Geoffrey Chaucer, London vintner,
             quit claiming his father's house

1381–1385   Writes *Boece*

1382–1385   Writes *Troilus and Criseyde*

1385   October 12: Chaucer appointed Justice of the
             Peace in Kent

1385 or 1386 Writes *Legend of Good Women*

1386   *Canterbury Tales* begun (*General Prologue, Knight's
             Tale*, Part VII), although some tales may have
             been written earlier

             Chaucer elected to Parliament for Kent

             Rented Aldgate house to Richard Forester

1388   May 1: Chaucer surrenders royal annuities
             to John Scalby of Lincolnshire

1389   Writes *Miller's Tale* and *Reeve's Tale*

             Chaucer appointed clerk of the King's Works

1390   Chaucer appointed subforester of North
             Petherton, Summerset

1390–1394   Writes *Wife of Bath's Tale, Friar's Tale, Summoner's Tale, Merchant's Tale, Clerk's Tale,* and *Franklin's Tale*

1394   Chaucer granted new annuity of 20 pounds

1395   Son Thomas marries heiress Maud Burghersh

1398   Chaucer borrows against annuities

             Action for debt against Chaucer

             Letters of protection from King Richard II

1399   October 13: On his coronation day, King Henry doubles Chaucer's annuity

             December 24: Chaucer signs a 53-year lease for tenement in the garden of the Lady Chapel, Westminster Abbey

1400   September 29: last record of Chaucer—quittance given by him for a tun of wine received

             October 25: date of Chaucer's death on tombstone in Westminster Abbey (erected in 1556)

Introduction

When Dryden referred to the splendid variety of the *Canterbury Tales* as "God's Plenty," he might have been anticipating the plethora of divergent critical responses generated by this densely nuanced work. Recent critics such as Dolores Frese emphasize the need for retrospective reading as essential for discovering the full range of Chaucerian brilliance. No doubt such rereading well rewards the careful reader and prompts new and innovative interpretation. The following discussion first explores some ways of categorizing these tales from a retrospective perspective, as they exemplify various comic modes and methodologies; then it summarizes various critical perceptions of comic themes and theories, often with the innovative, retrospective interpretation offered by exploring scholars within this volume's three-part structure.

Comic Categorization[1]

Noting that the "definition of the terms of comic techniques for Chaucer is sparse and ... [attempting] to point up areas of research for others" (193), fifteen years ago Paul Ruggiers nevertheless warned that "clearly no system can do justice to any of the great geniuses of comic writing, their wit and irony, the special flavor of license, their power to challenge staid opinion, that peculiar innocence that allows them to escape defilement even in the relating of the obscene" (194). This is particularly true of Chaucer's works. Derek Pearsall is right that "Comedy of one kind or another is present in a large number of the *Canterbury Tales*, and pervasive in the links between the tales" (125). The Chaucerian canon is justly known for its humorous spirit, sparked, no doubt, by that inimitable, jocular narrator, affable and lovable, who unfailingly pops up, a poppet in anyone's arms, a jovial year-round Santa. A master manipulator of time, place, circumstances, and particularly attitude and mood, this round smiling cherub most often turns his narrative power to comedy.

Both the humorous and the comedic, generously infused into the Chaucerian corpus, are pleasurable. Humorous elements are local—funny, clever, surprising (in reversals and unmaskings), appealingly deceptive, lighthearted, and jovial. They include clever linguistic word-play (puns and double entendres) as well as funny events and occur in plot episodes (rather than the entire plot pattern) and dialogue within the links. Comedic elements are more global, encompassing the whole structure of the tale or story, and culminate in a satisfying resolution of an ending, situation, or milieu. Thus, dark, nonhumorous comedies, sinister, dignified, or painful, but with an ultimately happy ending, may result. Although serious thematic content may permeate the entire gamut of Chaucerian comedy, segments of the canon—the *Canterbury Tales* and some short works—display the humorous strain most representatively. In both humorous and comedic pieces, a triumph over mischance, or an opponent in agonistic or phallic contention, is often the occasion for rejoicing.

Humorous Works of Mirth: "For the Moore Part They Loughe and Pleyde"

Although the Chaucerian canon may be carved into any number of configurations to display its comedy, examining the operation of time (and timing), place (or locus), circumstance (action or plot), discourse (monologue and dialogue), and tone (mood or disposition) offers a practical method to observe Chaucer's comic structure.

Time and Timing

The congruous coalescence of seemingly dissimilar motifs in a surprisingly appropriate confluence is often the source of humor. This congruence of two events at two places occurring simultaneously produces what Susan Wittig calls the "meanwhile-back-at-the-ranch" motif (*Stylistic and Narrative Structures in the Middle English Romances*. Austin, TX: University of Texas Press, and London, 1978, p. 60). The element of surprise is often the result of perfect, or unexpected, timing. According to E. M. W. Tillyard, in the *Miller's Tale*, "The surprise, the sudden union of the two themes is sublime. It is as if, for a fraction of a second, the heavens opened and we saw all the gods watching the trivial and ridiculous human comedy below" (*Poetry: Direct and Oblique*. London: Chatto and Windus, 1948, p. 90). In speaking of the *Miller's Tale*, Joseph Dane finds that it is the sudden coalescing of these identical structures (carpenter John in a washtub awaiting waters of the flood, and the cuckolding Nicholas demanding water to cool his burned bum) and the opposing imagery . . . that lends the denouement the sense of logical inevitability and utter surprise" (216).

Appropriate timing, both slowing down or freezing of time and rapidly accelerating time, can also trigger humor. As David Wallace points out about the *Merchant's Tale*, "Damyan is poised to do business in the pear tree; and yet Chaucer's Merchant finds time to shift his scene with studied (almost elegant) deliberateness. Such a shift undoubtedly gains in comic effect by echoing similarly deliberate transitions at similarly awkward moments in numerous popular compositions" (*Chaucer and the Early Writings of Boccaccio*. Bury St. Edmunds, Suffolk: D. S. Brewer, 1985, p. 148).

Place

In some of Chaucer's works, inappropriate places for certain activities or misplaced objects are funny because of their incongruity or even their ironically surprisingly apt congruity. Ribald humor in the fabliaux often plays on misplaced or well-placed obscenity. Whether or not we accept Laura Kendrick's suggestion that the three washtubs, two round and one long, decorating the *Miller's Tale* represent God's giant "priviee," they nevertheless make a ridiculously funny sight hanging from the rafters. No less humorous is the misplaced kiss Absolon smacked on the wrong end of the laughing Alison, who is unable to resist her "Tee-hee."

In the *Reeve's Tale*, the unbridled horses who escape their harness to the freedom of the meadow inspire humor because of their symbolic reference to the free young clerks who become equally unbridled with the sunset—in the miller's house! When we envision the baby's crib, what T. W. Craik calls a "shifting landmark" (35), moved from the foot of one bed to that of another, we laugh at this unexpected "musical beds" plot device and its complications. Most shocking is the vision of Allen crawling into bed next to the snoring Miller to gloat over his rollicking love-making—with Miller Symkin's daughter. In the *Merchant's Tale*, May and Damien precariously perched in a pear tree, in violently shaking *flagrante delicto*, is so extraordinary as to provoke laughter for its impossible incongruity. Similarly, January's ridiculous dawn song wafting from his bed is matched only by his erect carriage as he springs up to yodel, and in contrast, his wagging, flaccid neck, not unlike the wattle or dewlap of a rooster that waggles under its chin. Which action symbolizes his sexuality is not hard to determine. The marriage bed has become a humorous fiasco, a place of mockery.

Where the Friar in the *Summoner's Tale* finds his buried "inheritance" is so appropriately punitive, but equally unexpected, that the audience must laugh with old Thomas, the perpetrator. In a similar vein, where the Summoner locates those unfortunate Friars who failed to reach heaven (in an undesirable part of the devil's anatomy) is so startlingly repulsive that the jolting image elicits a humorous response. The place where the Pardoner's three rioters find Death, at the foot of a tree that distracts its visitors with its gold bushels, is deadly funny in a perverse sort of way.

More lighthearted in tone is the *Nun's Priest's Tale*, full of the priest's "safe" humor by which he counteracts Harry

Bailly's obscene innuendos that he is a treadfowl fit for procreating. Chauntecleer's feathering his twenty wives on a tree branch is only slightly less jocose than Damien's precariously doing so to Alison in their pear-tree. Pertelote offers her share of mirth, perhaps in exchange for what Chauntecleer dishes out in calling women man's confusion—or is it his bliss and joy? Her retaliation, in the potent laxative she prescribes for Chauntelceer, may be said to have a local effect. But, the humorous vision of him, caught in Reynard's mouth with arms flailing for release, is most powerful, even superseding the fear that we experience for his safety.

T. W. Craik points to the humor of place in the *Shipman's Tale* by envisioning a stage: "The poetic effect is one of stage farce: the unsuspecting cuckold ambles off the stage in one direction, and the bold seducer swaggers in from the other. The effect is to be repeated in reverse almost immediately, for the monk's business with the wife is rapidly dispatched" (63). Proper place and time, then, facilitate the farce.

In addition, proper placing or judicious juxtaposition of events or tales highlights both, adding humorous contrast. Craik says that in the *Miller's Tale*, "Chaucer's object is, of course, the variety which comes from contrast, a 'cherles tale' after a 'noble storie'; but he makes the contrast more amusing by showing why the Miller insists on interrupting the Host's orderly scheme. . . . The comedy results not merely from rebellious drunkenness but also from misunderstanding: the Miller really does believe that his own tale is a worthy counterpart to the Knight's. . . . The contrast and the parody are the funnier because the Miller is unaware of them" (1).

Furthermore, many of the tales gain a comic dimension, perhaps not uproarious jocularity, but a comic satisfaction, by their apropos juxtaposition to contrary or opposing tales. Fabliau quiting tales—the *Miller's* and *Reeve's*, the *Friar's* and *Summoner's*, and even the serious comedies of the *Second Nun's* and *Canon's Yeoman's Tales*—most obviously reveal this phenomenon. Personal invective between the first two pairs heightens their parallel tales; contrasting plot-lines of the last adds to the comic richness by the ironic reverberation echoing in both directions. As Craik notices, "The *Miller's Tale* follows the *Knight's* as a kind of unintentional parody or anti-masque, and for this reason precedes the *Reeve's*" (31). No doubt the *Wife of Bath's Tale* and especially the humorously revealing Prologue generate the irate retort from the Clerk, notwithstanding the intervening paired fabliaux by the Friar and Summoner. An apropos sense of place, either disruptingly congruous or incongruous within and between tales, thus engenders comedy.

Circumstance/Situation

Most often, details of plot or event, apart from character or tone, are simply funny. The action itself is ridiculous, incongruous, surprisingly "on target," or smacks of a sense of superiority in which the audience can join. Chaucer enthusiastically delights in mental gymnastics or clever constructs. Fabliaux action typically exemplifies this type of humor. A. Booker Thro suggests that in the *Miller's Tale*, Nicholas unfolds his design in a step-by-step procedure, gradually creating a structure of apparently irrelevant materials for which we can see no final construct. When the confusion is dispelled, and "the clerk fashions coherence and relevance out of perplexity, our curiosity and bewilderment alter to a profound appreciation" (99). Thus, when foolish John crashes to the floor from his perch in the washtub, the fall and resulting clamor culminate a series of cleverly planned maneuvers and simultaneously parody the fulfillment of both the Annunciation and Noah stories. This recreation of biblical history at the heart of the poem, which Nicholas engineers and John builds, evidences exuberant mental and physical vitality. Thro finds the comic celebration of creativity, the process and product in the *Miller's Tale*, an all-pervasive element, for its ingenious and elaborate mental constructions monopolize our attention (99). Triumphant wit wins. Farce, the expression of destructive impulses and deflation of pretension, plays a secondary role to creative ingenuity.

With somewhat different effect, when the rampant horses escape and gallop recklessly through the *Reeve's Tale*, we are caught up in their chaos and that of the clerks chasing them. In the slapstick denouement, a farcical battle in which the greedy miller is once again undone, this "gnopf" is beaten and humiliated by his wife as well as the clerks. For his stupidity, boorishness, and dishonesty, we greet his noisy demise with our own vocal laughter.

Action in the serious *Knight's Tale* may be funny because of its surprising incongruity. According to Edward Foster, "We cannot avoid the comic irony of the newly victorious Arcite falling off his charger. . . . Even Arcite's funeral pyre is made of wood whose cutting comically dispossesses the woodland gods" (92). Analogously, Chauntecleer of the *Nun's Priest's Tale* falls into the mouth of the teasing fox; as Craik notes, "the cock shuts his eyes when he should keep them open, the fox opens his mouth when he should keep it shut" (71).

Furthermore, certain tales are funny because tellers, or occasionally characters, inadvertently reveal their inner character or motivation. The audience then feels "Let in on the joke, or 'privitee,'" gaining some sense of superiority, as Bergson's theory of comedy describes it, over the naive or unself-aware but self-revelatory person. No doubt the Wife of Bath, the Canon's Yeoman, the Pardoner, and the Merchant unwittingly reveal their secrets in their prologues and tales and in so doing surprise their fellow pilgrims and their audience. The Wife's marital activity—she is truly a WIFE—is humorous in its excess. Her philosophy of unbounded vitality is refreshingly comic: five husbands at the Church door, and welcome the sixth when he arrives. The circumstances of her life with each of them are equally jocose in their vivid, even bombastic, quest for life. Culminating in the slapstick routine with Jankin, when Dame Alice feigns death to frighten her assailant, this incident highlights her dramatic play; she surprises the audience no less than her unwitting competitor. Not without pathos, this rehearsal of the Wife's intimate emotions and her singularly variegated mood transformations leads to a tale of comedic resolution.

In an otherwise serious tale, the Second Nun tells of a young boy who incongruously and inexplicably sits bolt upright after being slain and surprises his awe-struck witnesses with his determined singing. Motivated in a different fashion from January's similar canticle from his bed, the action is yet funny in its unexpected response to death. Equally abrupt is his final expiration when the grain is removed from his tongue, ending the scene in an unceremonious plot conclusion.

Occasionally the circumstance, demeanor, or personality of a character may itself be funny. The Wife of Bath seems, for example, to enjoy her "center stage" role, making fun of herself and inviting the same from others. She parades herself out before the audience for the sheer joy of the attention and basks in the regard they offer. Yet, her portraiture never draws ridicule from her observers, for she simultaneously exudes a dignity emerging from her *sprezzatura*. Edward E. Foster finds the caricature of the Knight equally entertaining: "The description of the Knight's appearance in rusted and spattered armor is the perfect emblem of the way reality intrudes on his ideals but cannot destroy them. If he looks comic, the comedy is the most generous possible, always in a tone of admiring sympathy" (91). For neither character is humor a function of moral or psychological superiority.

The circumstances of the *Shipman's Tale*, as Craik enumerates them, are set up for the fabliau genre: "the merchant so preoccupied with his business that the wife's lover may court her under his nose, the unfaithful wife who offers her favours for sale, the opportunist monk who disregards his vow of chastity" (49–50). When the self-important merchant leaves his wife with his "cosyn" the Monk Daun John, the humorous and seductive banter makes us anticipate and relish the climax. If the Monk seeks sex, the Wife seeks money. Thro finds the wife's persuasion of the monk illustrative of "how Chaucer depicts creativity as a psychologically cogent, realistic life process" (106). Craik discovers "an amusing fitness in her thinking to use [the Monk] for her own convenience, only to find at last that he has used her for his" (59). When Daun John borrows money from the merchant to give to the wife, he never intends to repay it; rather, he shamelessly, but humorously, contrives against her by revealing that she has received the francs. Only her fast-talking excuse saves her from discovery. As she paid the monk off with sex for the hundred francs, so she pays her husband off—for the same hundred francs, and again with sex.

At other times, pilgrims tell tales that reveal much self-consciousness, an awareness that their speech reveals their character or that they consciously intend to be understood humorously. Chaucer the Pilgrim intends a comic tale of mirth when he relates the *Tale of Sir Thopas*, funny in a way different from that of the fabliaux. Here the circumstances—pricking through the forest to seek adventure—and the unusual characters—the fairy queen and Sir Oliphant—are delightfully laughable. The birthday-party setting, jovial and childlike, sets up few expectations for Thopas' valor. The entire setting is jovial, but the circumstances are particularly humorous precisely because they are so anti-climactic. As Walter Scheps indicates, "Chaucer achieves the illusion of action where none is present in two ways; first, by juxtaposing references to future time ... with words or phrases that suggest immediacy, and, second, by enjambment which forces one line into another as though the action were proceeding at a rapid pace" (37).

This sense of timing, that the tale is progressing when indeed it is not, sets up unmet expectations, which, it becomes clear, is intentional. Scheps lists some humorous anticlimaxes as Thopas *climbing* instead of jumping into his saddle; the giant (an elephant!) intends to slay, not Sir Thopas, but his horse, which he cannot do; Thopas does not arm himself until he takes sweet wine and delectables; the narrator fails to tell of battle, chivalry, or lady's love; his promise of deeds, heroic or otherwise never materializes. Comic incongruity, juxtaposing the heroic and bourgeois ethos, results in absurdity: Thopas is fair and gentle *on the battlefield*, not exactly appropriate demeanor there, is born in the mercantile center of Flanders, not a noble habitat, and partakes of the unknightly sports of archery and wrestling. Finally, as Scheps points out, "The tale breaks off with the ludicrous picture of the minuscule knight drinking water continuously" (36). The entire context is established to spotlight that foolish little character. Other comic elements infuse this tale as well, from puns and wordplay to the exaggerated metrics which Chaucer is satirizing. But, the last laugh, as Scheps notes, is Chaucer's: "By characterizing himself as a minstrel who is so unskilled that he cannot retain either the attention or forbearance of his audience, Chaucer enjoys a cosmic laugh at his own expense; by characterizing his knight as a bourgeois hero he enjoys one at the expense of his fellow pilgrims" (40).

Discourse

Both monologues, in an authoritative, or at least individual point of view (including linguistic manipulation and puns), and dialogues, fostering tension between two voices, can evoke the comic spirit. Additionally, Donald MacDonald points to "comic contradiction between authoritative assertions of wisdom and misguided or otherwise inappropriate premises" (465) as a significant source of humor. The inimitable January of the *Merchant's Tale* surveys his friends' opinions about a bride, but accepts only the authority of those with whom he agrees. Justinus, who rightly warns a sixty-year-old not to marry a twenty-year-old, is ignored. Thus, when January meets his fate, a cuckolded old bird, we laugh at his naive expectations that anything else would occur.

Perhaps the most apparent verbal jocularity in the *Canterbury Tales* erupts in the roughhousing, competitive, phallic, and agonistic debate between pilgrims—both good-natured and testy—in the tale-links. According to Craik, "mirth is the prevailing mood of the prologues and epilogues which link the stories together, and the comic tales often derive added power from the way in which they are introduced" (xiii). Some find the interchange between Host and Pardoner the nadir of humorous degradation.

Edward Foster points to the "courtly disputation between Palamon and Arcite, after the manner of Capellanus and the French romances, [which] swiftly degenerates into bickering. Such humor has grim implications since departure from the forms can have brutal consequences" (91). This is pointedly true in the *Knight's Tale*, but elsewhere as well. MacDonald suggests that alone among English authors, Chaucer "recognizes the possibilities for comic incongruity that arise when an expression of ostensible wisdom, which in another context would be highly respectable intellectual coin, is enlisted in support of a flagrantly erroneous premise" (455).

Straight narration or monologue may likewise be broken with witty, clever, ironic, or incongruously funny language. Speaking of wordplay in the *Knight's Tale*, Foster notes the "ambiguous possibilities of the repetition of 'queynte' four times in five lines ... especially apparent since the scene is the shrine of the virgin goddess and Emily is asking that her virginity be preserved.... With these puns in mind it does not take an especially dirty mind to notice the frequency of the word 'harnys,' which does mean *armour* but is also a curiously appropriate complement to the puns on the female organs. Such a pun adds a realistic dimension to the courtly combat Palamon and Arcite plan" (89, 90).

If bawdy puns qualify the idealistic, courtly, chivalric view of *amor*, the humor lies in the tonal disparity between the two registers. Wordplay in the *Shipman's Tale* adds to the fun as well. Craik notes two ironic puns: the departing merchant advises his wife to be pliant and agreeable to all and to take care of the household goods; ironically she complies. His words, in this unexpected context, become humorous. Similarly, Daun John offers well-wishes, promising anything that will do him good. What he gives is the opposite. Thirdly, the merchant begs his wife to tell him "If any dettour hath in myn absence / Ypayed thee," not suspecting Daun John's payment of his own marriage debt (397–98).

In speaking of the *Nun's Priest's Tale*, MacDonald states that "the comic effect of a fable of even the most primitive kind derives from the basic incongruity in the spectacle of animals behaving like humans and, in particular, using human speech; this incongruity is increased in proportion to the degree in which animals not only use the language of humans but, in so doing, display impressive erudition and a mastery of rhetorical forms" (464). In this regard, many pilgrims and their creations vie for the laurels: the smooth-talking Wife, the suave clerks in the *Reeve's Tale*, the carver who solves the verbal crux—how to divide the "inheritance"—in the *Summoner's Tale*, old Mabley with the mouth in the *Friar's Tale*, the Old Man introducing Death in the *Pardoner's Tale*; the list goes on. Chauntecleer and Pertelote, however, win the fast-talking prize.

Comedic Resolution: Joy After Woe

At the end of *Troilus and Criseyde*, Chaucer's "litel tragedye," he announces that he will henceforth recreate comic visions rather than tragic or epic ones. True to his word, from that point on his work veers in a comedic direction, the *Canterbury Tales* being the apotheosis of his plan. A number of tales—the *Knight's*, *Man of Law's*, *Clerk's*, *Franklin's*, *Second Nun's*, and *Wife of Bath's Tales*—properly fit the Aristotelian definition of comedy, serious matter with a successful, happy closure to a difficult dilemma yet lacking humorous or funny incidents. But sometimes this serious matter involves disastrous events affecting characters, who are seen as victims, albeit comic victims. Morton Bloomfield describes the phenomenon this way: "Now, curiously enough, the continual victim tends to arouse not our pity but rather our amusement. There is something funny in a perverse way about victims. The tragedy of victimization always hovers perilously near to laughing comedy. Yet it is always sad and never really comic" (386).

To various degrees, Chaucer's serious tales with successful "comic" resolutions lie in this nebulous intermediary ground between comedy and tragedy. As such, they cannot be ignored in discussions of comedy.

Knight's Tale

This balanced, stately journey through ancient Athens depicts monumental issues of war and justice overriding particular plot issues. Its serious tone and momentous events are so dominant and all-pervasive as to preclude excessive lightness or laughter. And yet, T. W. Craik finds "cheerfulness is always breaking in, the fabric of the whole poem is shot through with Chaucer's characteristic humour and good sense" (x). Edward Foster concurs, pointing to jocular moments, perhaps unconscious, ranging from the bawdy to the grimly ironic. Foster lists the following instances of consciously intended humor: "the Knight's delicate refusal to discuss Emily's whole ritual, the mixture of catastrophe and trivia in the temple of Mars,

Saturn's speech about his qualifications to restore order, the displacement of the woodland gods for Arcite's pyre, and the Homeric comedy in the behavior of the gods" (89). The complications reside in the relationship between Palamon and Arcite, representing love and war respectively, as they vie for Emily, the courtly ideal, who prefers chastity to either of them. This harmoniously structured work, the longest of the tales, matches these seekers with their triad of patrons, Venus, Mars, and Diana, each promising victory. But, only in the winner's death can a resolution occur; although he wins the battle, Arcite does not live to win the prize. After much lamentation and grieving, then, a comedic ending anticlimactically evolves from a fatally tragic encounter. The serious matrimonial denouement between Palamon and Emily follows from a dignified but somewhat humorless epic, for the most part markedly devoid of laughter. Still, this tale qualifies as comedic, for its final resolution is appropriate and even joyful despite its tragic climax.

Man of Law's Tale

This religious narrative extols the virtues of the forebearing Custance who is forced to withstand much anguish and pain, finding victory in survival and reclamation of her lost life. No humorous tone or witty puns enliven the serious matter, or mitigate the unwanted marriage journey from Rome to Syria on which Custance must go. Space and displacement in space function in reverse fashion here—as dangerous and harmful elements—unlike the function of place in the humorous lighter tales of misplacement. Like her male counterpart Job, she is sent travails unending from treacherous mothers-in-law, a would-be rapist, a false accuser of murder, and a cruel sea. Repeatedly cast out to sea, flung first from her home and then from her husband, Custance finds no joy or happiness, no reprieve from her agony. Words, such as "cruel," "unhappy," "woeful," and "iniquity," reinforce the persistently oppressive tone. And yet, as Morton Bloomfield contends, this tale is a comedy, a Christian comedy, because it has a happy ending (388). Lacking all playfulness, it ultimately resolves successfully, adulating an heroic saint, a type of Christ, who never lost faith with her God. Unlike the *Knight's Tale* climax of tragedy, the first climax here is miraculous: supernatural intervention proclaiming the innocence of this steadfast victim. Perhaps the shocking sound of human speech booming from the clouds is humorous in its unpredictability. When the Deity's voice exonerates Custance of the Queen's murder, she is freed from human oppression, offered marriage and security by the widowed Sultan, and bears a son, Maurice. But once again, a wicked mother-in-law casts her net, falsely calling Maurice a devil, and hurling mother and son into the sea. Only the grace of God preserves the pair, returning them to the bosom of the Sultan. Even this anti-climactic rescue after the untold hardship heaped upon Custance is moderated, for we are told that he soon dies, bringing their joy to an end. Only the spiritual success of the steadfast Custance throughout her ordeals can justify calling this tale of weariness and woe a comedy, for even its conclusion offers only qualified happiness.

Clerk's Tale

Likewise ponderous is the story of faithful Griselda, snatched from the poor but loving bosom of her father to the glory of marquise by the ever-testing Walter. This tale of trials offers no comic relief, no humorous dialogue or action, but does provide a comic resolution, however unequal to the protagonist's pain. When Griselda promises complete obeisance to the bullying Walter, she never expects that this will entail submission to the murder of her daughter and then her son. The tone is dramatic and serious, admitting no humor or levity. Audience patience grows thin when Griselda, supplanted by a younger surrogate, is expected to prepare the new bride for her faithless husband. Trial after endless trial this model of submission and faithfulness successfully passes. Her heroic victory that the obdurate Walter must finally acknowledge prompts the return of the children, whose murders were only feigned to test her submissiveness. The conclusion thus celebrates Griselda's steadfast obedience and the reunion of the family, a joyous, comic resolution to a serious, emotional tale.

Franklin's Tale

This Breton Lai contains moments of levity and joy interspersed with those of anguish and indecision, and finally concludes with a satisfying resolution perhaps worthy of the generous Franklin. A joyful wedding begins this fairy-tale story, but the husband Arveragus' departure puts Dorigen in jeopardy. Fending off the would-be lover Aurelius, she playfully retorts that she will accede to his demands only if he makes the treacherous coastal rocks vanish. When they in fact seem to disappear, the shocked, dismayed wife is caught between two promises. Anguishing over her plight, she confesses her dilemma to Arveragus, who generously sends her to fulfill her promise. But magnanimity finds its match, first in the lover who refuses to take advantage of such a generous husband and then, in the magician who refuses to accept payment from the equally generous lover. Although critics have questioned the wisdom and helpfulness of a husband who sends his wife on an unwanted encounter, his motives cannot be impugned. The conclusion is unambiguously happy, for unlike the previous serious comedic tales, this tale depicts no one injuring or taking advantage of another. By kindness and generosity, an harmonious resolution satisfies both characters and audience in a comedic and joyful victory.

Second Nun's Tale

A serious and determined tone marks this saint's legend of a busy St. Cecilia converting her husband, brother-in-law, and citizens of Rome during the persecutions. Little outright laughter breaks the solemnity of this tale, although moments of humor intrude, perhaps unintentionally. The business of conversion is a weighty one and brooks no interference. When in fact Cecilia audibly laughs, her gesture marks the power of God now fortifying her. Cecilia's moral and religious victory is paid for with her life, but the ethos of the tale and its resolution locates it as comedic—a grand celebration—for the souls won to Christ, before her captors end her mission and her life, have gained salvation. Thus, a joyous closure smack in the face of physical death concludes a comic tale of success.

Wife of Bath's Tale

This fairy-tale romance begins with rape and a thoughtful reparation of the damage done to an innocent maid. Throughout the tale, until the culmination, the tone is one of anxious quest and resolute acceptance, not joyful celebration. Although circumstances occasionally are lighthearted—the fairies dancing out of the magical fairy mound—they conspicuously contrast the deadly serious business being enacted. Clearly the rapist-knight feels impending doom if he fails to discover what women most want. The answer from the hag—a woman not pleasantly humorous, but grotesquely so—initiates the turning-point in the story, although not without further anguish for the criminal.

Early Works

Chaucer's early works, the *Book of the Duchess, House of Fame,* and *Parlement of Foules* being the most well-known, are more subtly and gently humorous than the rollicking plot contrivances or comic resolutions of serious narratives. The *Book of the Duchess* is a lament for the deceased Blanche, ostensibly a consolation to her husband John of Gaunt, a sorrowful recollection of her beauty and goodness; but within its parameters are the most striking images which can only be called funny. Envision for example, the shock of a horse patiently waiting in the Dreamer's room, ready for action at his awakening. Further, the Dreamer's ploy to bribe the god Morpheus with a feather pillow so he can get some sleep is a marvelous stroke. His obtuse and painstaking questioning of the Black Knight whom he meets crying by a tree is itself funny. However, none of the humor detracts from the serious and respectful commemoration that this charming poem offers.

The *House of Fame* introduces us to that jolly narrator with a hearty sense of humor. Book II depicts one Geffrey swooped away by a golden eagle with long sharp nails who carries him to the heights in his claws "as lyghtly as I were a lark." The frightened and astonished narrator, finally brought to his senses by a squawking bird, is told that he is a troublesome burden to carry. Fantasizing first his demise and then that Jove will make him a heavenly star, Geffrey is finally distracted by his conversation with the eagle about his love poetry. The humorous construct of visiting the House of Fame is the means to inform this naive eagle-rider.

The *Parlement of Foules* likewise offers a joyful garden setting and humorous interaction between the Valentine's Day participants. As Francis J. Smith says, "The manner and spirit of *The Parliament [sic] of Foules* is light and gay; such a mirthful approach is immediately delivered by the title itself, which is essentially mock-serious, as well as the opening line 'The lyf so short, the craft so long to lerne,' which is, with deliberate comedy, distorted to fit a context of love matters. In other words, Chaucer did not save his fun for the chatter of birds in the last fourth of the poem but only allowed the comedy to rise gradually to a full climax in that part of it" (16–17). The humorously verbose avians arguing among themselves give rise to the orderly Parliament, an attempt at a comic resolution that, however, is forestalled by the formel eagle herself. According to Smith, "the very situation of choosing a mate on a given date is farcical, as silly as the gondoliers in Gilbert and Sullivan's romp of marriage who choose blindfolded or as whimsical as Palamon's contention that Emily is his true love because he saw her first" (20).

Several of the short lyrics are written in a jocular vein, or contain humorous elements, especially those comic requests for patronage such as "The Complaint of Chaucer to His Purse." The "Lenvoy de Chaucer a Bukton" on marriage humorously invites the Wife of Bath to read the poem. In "To Rosemounde," Chaucer claims never was pike more steeped in Galatine sauce than he is steeped in love for the lady, a surprisingly funny image preceding the humorous appellation with which he styles himself—"the second Tristam." Taken together, these short works are one more indication, in yet another mode, of the

Chaucerian sense of humor for which the master is so well known.

Summary

The concept of comedy is complicated and multi-faceted. The most obvious definition, and recognizable characteristic, no doubt includes the humorous and funny, established on a local and limited scale. Time, place, circumstance, and discourse can all be manipulated for effect by one with an ironic or simply wry sense of the world. A second, perhaps more sophisticated aspect of comedy finds embodiment in satisfying closure, denouement, and completion: reestablishment of some social or physical harmonious order. Chaucer uses his wry sense of humor in both ways. As Foster points out, "consistent with his role as human comedian, Chaucer does not stop with the comfort of a philosophical resolution" (93). Such a comic resolution accompanies and reinforces his expansive vision of the ironic, the witty, the incongruous, the surprising. No doubt Andreas is right in calling the *Canterbury Tales* the greatest comic poem in western literature (58). The balance of his corpus, the short works and lyrics, while not principally or exclusively humorous, reiterate the ever-prevalent Chaucerian sense of humor in its wry content, densely reverberating texture, and philosophical resolution. No doubt this jovial poppet of a man, as Harry calls him, like his Troilus, is somewhere out there in the eighth sphere laughing at these mere mortals obsessed with dissecting and evaluating his methodology and categorizing his brands of humor instead of enjoying their comic resonances.

The articles in this volume represent a broad critical spectrum of definitions and approaches to Chaucerian humor, each elucidating the finely spun art of the master of the comic. In Part I, a chronological history of critical reception and a range of sources and definitions from the classical and neoclassical traditions to the present are examined. Considerations of a structural basis demarcating the comic mode spark our awareness of this current topic. In Part II, the *Canterbury Tales* are explored through contemporary critical theory: feminist, Freudian, social, and Bakhtinian approaches, each with a comic edge. In Part III, the authors hone in on specific issues of humor appropriate to each genre: the lyric, poetic, demonic, religious, scatological and tragic. As is often the case, one investigation may span the scope of two or more categories. John Crafton's exploration of the comic impulse simultaneously defines humor and explores it from psychological and modern critical vantage points; thus his article properly fits in Part I as well as Part II. Similarly, Derek Pearsall defines comedy through a genre discussion of the fabliaux and might equally well be positioned in Part III with genre studies. Regardless of position, together these multi-dimensional contributions offer solid insight into and a broad base for further investigation of this rich and variegated Chaucerian topic.

In Part I the early critical reception of Chaucerian humor is explored, along with the nature of Chaucerian comedy, its sources in the Greek tradition, and its utilization of subsequent eighteenth century ideals: control and balance, parody, burlesque and mock heroic epic. Comedic structure is evidenced in situation and character, its stereotypical and pyrotechnic gymnastics; its identifying characteristics include: a familiar setting, a reductive clinical tone, absence of any moral values except survival and appetite, and failure of wit that brings satisfaction. These critics offering an overview of the nature of Chaucerian comedy present a strong cognitive foundation on which the subsequent theoretical scaffolding can be erected.

In "The Voice of the Past: Surveying the Reception of Chaucer's Humor" critical responses to Chaucer as a humorist from contemporaneous to early twentieth-century writers and scholars are chronologically recapitulated. Since the genre of literary criticism had not yet evolved, responses were primarily brief references and appreciative comments rather than source study, critical analysis, or interpretation of types or extent of humor predominated. Earliest remarks acknowledged his reputation, often found in contemporary imitation. Sometimes he was thought remarkable for his scurrilous verse, a poet with a merry but rough wit.

The later eighteenth-century concern with decorum and reserve accounted for some resistance in the neoclassical mind. The "undignified" blend of tones and genres did not satisfy that aesthetic. As the conception of humor as decorous and dignified slowly emerged, Chaucer's reputation grew. Elements of ridicule and satire became recognized. The nineteenth century questioned the decency of Chaucer's humor, and either condemned or partially excused it. Extravagance and licentiousness were thought to mark its style. The Victorians first began critically perceptive evaluation of Chaucerian comedy, especially in his characterization.

Leaving behind the ideal of "high seriousness," early twentieth-century critics found a renewed appreciation, a vivacity and veracity in his all-pervading humor. A limited acceptance marked his reception, perhaps in part because of some embarrassment with fabliau realism. Later critics lauded Chaucer's humor from social and psychological vantage points, noting his "pragmatic" comic society. Changes in the formulation and conception of Chaucerian humor are evident as current enthusiastic explorations prove its nature and function.

In "The Idea of Humor," Howard Rollin Patch disclaims, "I am far from intending to write a discourse on the single theme of humor," and offers what he calls tentative remarks, "not primarily philosophical or systematic" to discover "more of what the poet himself was like." Patch defines humor as "a sense of incongruity, probably between the transitory and the permanent," noting its omnipresence throughout Chaucer's works. For Patch, Chaucer's comedy "consists less in the out-raged ideal than in the spectacle of human nature as we know it," a bond of common weakness with the characters.

G. K. Chesterton finds Chaucer's national contribution to the culture of Christendom to be his English sense of humor: an appreciation of fun, broadening into farce, and becoming "a sort of poetry of pantomime." Comparing Chaucer to Dickens, Chesterton finds in the first something shrewd, sensible, and solid, yet containing an element of irrational humor. He makes fun of people, but not game of them. While valuing his fools and knaves, he wishes to preserve them—in high spirits.

Drawing on Aristotle's definition of character, Paul G. Ruggiers, in "A Vocabulary for Chaucerian Comedy: A Preliminary Sketch," points to discoveries and reversals, comic incidents, suffering, *agon*, and laughter emerging from the content as part of the absurd or comic incidents. Ruggiers notes that some tales center on conflicts in which sex triumphs over an older husband, while others operate more sinisterly. He posits a movement from the old law to the escape from bondage into freedom, from hypocritical deception to revelation of the truth of villainy. Characters are shown to be evil, and their destruction is part of Chaucer's justification of law. For Ruggiers, comedy is a contest between opposing value systems: the traditional maxims, sermons, *sententiae*, and disquisitions on merit, evil, love, and responsibility, and the proofs by which these are tested—oaths, compacts, conspiracies, testimonies, witnesses, ordeals, tests, and laws. Further, Ruggiers points out that Canterbury pilgrims evince the classical traits of the impostor, ironist, buffoon, plain dealer, clown, rustic, and scapegoat, but with more complexity. With psychological acuity and a camera-like eye, Chaucer privileges character over plot, hence eliciting humor from comparisons, debasement, trivializing of experience, and poor decision-making. Both the exemplary and the base produce comedy because both are human.

Thomas J. Garbáty also surveys Chaucer's humor, noting in "Chaucer and Comedy" that the author has been accused of not taking the world seriously enough by those failing to perceive his depth. Although despair and tragedy may be alien to Chaucer's temperament, images of sorrow and pain suffuse his corpus. Yet this is not his worldview, for, as Garbáty points out, "His tragic poems [are] all interrupted, unfinished, or transfigured into celestial comedy. . . . never does he indulge himself, or us, by settling in on the dark side of life." His humor is neither Boethian, nor Dantesque, but Chaucerian—comedies of situation and character type. Garbáty finds that "nowhere is Chaucer's fabliau skill of precision, punning, parody, and punch line demonstrated with such virtuoso technique as in the *Miller's Tale*" where "his feats of controlled verbal and coincidental pyrotechnics" are most effective. The episodic *Merchant's Tale* involves a more bitter kind of humor as the lecherous May uses the back of her blind old husband as a ladder to join her lover in a pear tree. As Garbáty suggests, nuances of speech, vignettes of life, and allegros of parody are funny, but in character sketches Chaucer achieves unqualified greatness. Language unifies the tales into a human comedy of pilgrims, the cause-and-effect links providing the living magic. Moreover, his multifaceted comic perspective contains the running joke of the dumbstruck, frightened Geoffrey, the dimwitted poetaster pilgrim offered by the wise humble man secure enough to venture it. His own greatest comic figure, he delights in appearing in the most ludicrous situations. Garbáty concludes that we respond both intellectually and emotionally to Chaucer's thoughtfully searching humor, his "consistent overall sense of life, one of attained optimism fostered by a genial and tranquil spirit."

In *"The Canterbury Tales* II: Comedy" Derek Pearsall incisively explores Chaucer's six fabliaux, each of which possesses the narrative structure and expectations that stamp the fabliau as a comic genre. Pearsall points to these comic markers: a localized, familiar setting, a reductive clinical tone, and an absence of any secular or religious values except survival and satisfying one's appetite. Not moral justice but failure of wit brings satisfaction. Neither socially normative nor classical nor satirical, in Chaucerian comedy laughter is seen as a renewal of vitality. If in a romance men act in a noble and transcending way, in fabliau they will always act as animals.

Pearsall finds that the comic narrative structure is comprised of a husband, sexually unsatisfied wife, and younger male intruder. The greatest fabliau, the *Miller's Tale*, overflows with high spirits, and includes genial gusto, amorous serenading, and lyricism in an exuberant travesty of courtly language and behavior, along with technical invention. Remarkably, Pearsall claims, a tale as structurally similar as the *Reeve's Tale* "can create such a totally different impression . . . a spirit of meanness and vindictiveness." The *Shipman's Tale* is "a subtle and highly contrived variation on the form that has its own individual character." Speech is politely diplomatic, lacking honesty, rage, scorn, or desire. "The exchange of money seems to legitimize rather than corrupt the encounter" between wife and Monk, a kind of reasonable business transaction. In the ambitious *Merchant's Tale* Chaucer adds lyrical interpolations, rhetorical digressions, a mock-encomium on marriage, and a final mythological episode. The sneering malevolence in the *Reeve's Tale* is here raised to a pitch of stridency about marriage itself. In the *Friar's* and *Summoner's Tales*, non-sexual masterpieces of satirical anecdote, moral outrage is soon swallowed up in laughter, since the tellers prove not that their victims are knaves but that they are pathetically gullible fools. Pearsall concludes that once again Chaucer "seems to prefer complicity with the world of his creatures to moral criticism."

In Part II of *Chaucer's Humor: Critical Essays* there is an exploration of contemporary critical theories—feminist, Freudian, social, and Bakhtinian criticism—examining Chaucerian humor through each of those approaches. Creative virtuosity, often through retrospective reading, opens tantalizing new dimensions to the comic master's work. The net result is one more panoply of ideas, rich individually and collectively, all in the service of a deeper understanding of Chaucer's fine gift of comedy.

Susan K. Hagen, in "Chaucer's May, Standup Comics, and Critics," contends that the *Merchant's Tale* depends on audience comedic response emerging from a sense of community, much like a standup comic discussing personal backgrounds and attitudes; the audience accepts the comedian's marginal status and the mood of comic license that play off assumed but unacknowledged cultural attitudes such as anti-feminism. Thus, the Merchant, functioning as a standup comic, stands before his audience describing nuptial scenes in exaggerated detail and supplying the anticipated punch line: God knows what May thought about it. Hagen claims that "genuine belief in May's innocence precludes any sense of the comic in January's libidinous shenanigans." That we laugh rather than recoil in moral indignation at their inappropriate wedding means that we cannot "trust ourselves when we say we believe in the initial purity of 'fresshe May.'" According to Hagen, "For the humor to work, there must be in this tale a fundamental incongruity between what January espouses about his sexual prowess and about marriage and what we in our more realistic experience know to be true or likely. " The fabliau humor in this tale lies in the mismatched marriage: the disparity between what January imagines he can achieve and what he actually can do. "[V]alidation of January's fantasies, however, might leave as many readers uncomfortable as does the pear-tree incident. The comedy simply depends on proving the prideful, self-deceived braggart wrong."

In his historically and psychologically compelling article, "Chaucer, Freud, and the Political Economy of Wit: Tendentious Jokes in the *Nun's Priest's Tale*," R. James Goldstein notes that only once in Chaucer's career does he directly refer to a contemporary historic event: the chaos at the end of the *Nun's Priest's Tale* is compared to the Great Revolt of 1381, the Rebel's massacre of the Flemings on June 14. Goldstein uses Sigmund Freud's *Jokes and Their Relation to the Unconscious* to answer why "Chaucer chooses to break his characteristic silence about contemporary politics by alluding to the most serious challenge to the social and political order of four-teenth-century England in a joking *comparatio* at the climax of one of his greatest comic tales." Goldstein hypothesizes that Chaucer's "real target that has been repressed by the tale only to be repeated in jocular form is the class of peasant producers. . . . Repression of the class interests of the exploited producers [is] a symptom of the political unconscious of the text." Furthermore, if jokes provide a form of rebellion against critical reason in the political domain, the Nun's Priest also enjoys sharing antifeminist jokes, such as Chauntecleer and Pertelote's debate, with his male audience. His tale challenges the rule of reason in his bid for comic release.

In his rich article, "Paradoxicum Semiotica: Signs, Comedy, and Mystery in Fragment VI of the *Canterbury Tales*," John Micheal Crafton claims that Chaucer's poetic language both asserts and denies the truth of its statements simultaneously, thereby creating a type of double truth. Crafton discusses Chaucer's comedy as a function of the inherent paradoxes of language that ironize the text, forcing us to read it "up-so-doun": part of the humor is in the slipperiness of the notion of truth in Chaucer's hands. "The *Canterbury Tales* does not work so much to exemplify one or more of the *functions* of humor as it does to exemplify the *analysis* of humor in addition to its functions." Further, Crafton "examine[s] comedy as a function of the congruent incongruities of lies and truth as this comedy relates to medieval and postmodern language theory." In Part I Crafton explores Freud's connection between jokes, the unconscious, and sexuality. Crafton then considers Derrida's postmodern notion of undecidability or paradox and oscillating meaning essential for verbal humor.

In Part II the fact that medieval sign theories are not dissimilar to postmodern ones and have been divided into the realist school (of Plato and Aristotle), the moderate realist school (of Aristotelian and Thomistic tradition), and the nominalist or conceptualist school (of Abelard and Ockam) is reiterated. Crafton finds Chaucer's position radically ambiguous, setting nominalism and realism against each other or collapsing them, to produce ambiguity at all discourse levels: the frame, fragment, and individual tale.

In Part III, Crafton claims that in Chaucer's pairing of tales, often a language facility is compared to its deficit, the former pointing out the comedy of the latter. The dualistic view of language as creator and destroyer, the vehicle for and obstacle of truth, reflects extreme versions of realism or nominalism. Crafton concludes that "Chaucer's characterization of language as pun-ridden, as necessarily slippery and duplicitous is not based upon a notion of language as word play for nihilism's sake, but ... on the notion of necessary play in thought, word and deed, which interrupts the system of human construction and allows the divine comedy to exist, the mystical laughter that emanates from paradox, from the coincidence of opposites." Chaucer's caricature of realism and nominalism, then, dialectically cancels out both scholastic methods, suggesting that he would have had a sympathy with modern conceptualism and new humanistic rhetorical attitudes such as the *ars dictaminis*.

In "The Comedy of Innocence," Alfred David's intriguing article, Chaucer's festivity is found to be rooted in saturnalian spirit and folk ritual that generate comic ritual. Hierarchy and the rule of order dominate the *Knight's Tale*, the end of which

xlii   Introduction

"intimates the social comedy that is about to explode." In the clash of estates vying for dominance, the rebel Miller who insists on following the Knight offends against propriety with his indecent story. But, because "The time is right for feasting and for licentious comedy . . . [and] such comedy has the sanction of deep-rooted folk custom . . . [of] parody, burlesque, and mock-defiance of authority," his behavior is tolerated. David surveys folk traditions such as the Boy Bishop's rule, Feast of Fools, Feast of the Ass, Lord of Misrule, and the tradition of medieval parody. The Miller's fabliau is an inversion of the repressive attitudes of medieval Catholicism, the "religion of love," and the chivalric mystic aura that makes a cult of sentiment. The celestial machinery of romance is replaced by Nicholas' astrology. John's muddled Christian doctrine, pagan superstition, and homespun philosophy is ridiculed and proven false. Finally, according to David, in the *Miller's Tale* Chaucer achieves a comic balance between the sacred and profane, an escape from the eternal for the "audience to look briefly at the temporal as if it were all that mattered." Its festive comedy, what Bakhtin calls "the people's unofficial truth," can be taken seriously as "fidelity to the vital principle of life" without turning it into inverted morality.

William F. Woods' fine close reading in "Metamorphic Comedy: The *Shipman's Tale*" finds comic art in formal elements: details of social setting, structure of episodes, and dialectical play. "The dry irony of an insider's tale, the knowing wit that plays upon the small absurdities of merchantry" is the stuff of comedy. As Woods claims, comic levelling reduces or converts everything—social, sexual, or religious—by subordinating it to mercantile exchange. The humor, however, is not confined to the irony of displacement (profit displacing all other values); it extends to how characters' personal and spiritual needs are served. According to Woods, the merchant's world re-orients all needs and values to the profit motive while transforming the social roles of merchant and monk; the wife is transformed "in a profound comic metamorphosis by which exile within the home and social and sexual dependency become, paradoxically, her means of dominating the market and achieving ... a sense of personal worth." Such an ironic inversion creates the baseline for comedy. The mildly pretentious household cheer is undercut by the language, social manners, and lifestyle of busyness and haste where life *is* trade. Here humor is gentle satire, knowing irony, and scrutiny of each other's small failings. The pathos of the merchant's account of his works and days, sometimes mocking hagiographic behavior, is a source of humor. According to Woods, "The monk's role is the broadest, most accessible source of humor in the tale, and this is mainly because his outrageous, amoral sexuality and scheming can be felt as a relief from the artificial merriment and covert economic *Angst* that typify the roles of both merchant and wife."

Frederick B. Jonassen's "Rough Music in Chaucer's *Merchant's Tale*" is an application of Bakhtin's notion of Carnival, a celebration of the material and physical body, "the most significant and emblematic, the source for the parody, humor, and sense of the grotesque." As Jonassen says, "Carnival generated broad humor by bringing all that was abstract, theoretical, and without an anchor in the material world to the level of bodily functions." Juxtaposition of bawdy and sacred, fabliaux and hagiography, *sentence* and *solas*, *ernest* and *game* reflects the Carnival/Lenten dichotomy of medieval culture. Likewise, the folk custom of *charivari*, a serenading parade with "rough music" of kettles, pans, rattles, horns, pipes, cymbals, cowbells, tea-trays, and drums to punish shameful community behavior (marital age disparity, second marriages, or wife dominance) was prevalent in literature and life. Jonassen concludes that the Merchant's description of January's wedding suggests the rough music of the charivari, which the tale in effect becomes. Jonassen also notes that "The wedding music of the *Merchant's Tale* likewise denotes the false heaven by which January is seduced, for the instruments at the wedding promise a stringed sound associated with heaven, but actually produce trumpet blasts, an infernal noise."

In Part III of *Chaucer's Humor: Critical Essays* the focus is on humor in and resultant from specific genres, so aptly and consistently utilized with versatility by Chaucer throughout his career. Through these creatively ingenious investigations the scholars peruse Chaucer's prosody, dramatic and folkloric patterning, religious and hagiographic comedy, scatology, and tragedy as grounds for comic play. Emerging from this collective whole is the oft-repeated dictum that genres are less mutually exclusive, boundaried categories than overlapping umbrellas under which sliding concepts of structure and form, often sharing remarkably interlocking, comparable, or identical components, shuffle restlessly. Within them all, however, erupts the unquenchable, irrepressible, optimistic humor of a sensibility attuned to human foibles and its absurdity.

Charles A. Owen, Jr., in his perceptive article "Chaucer's Witty Prosody in General Prologue, Lines 1–42," broadens the notion of comedy to include witty language use. Owen defines wit as the humorous, ingenious, and unexpectedly patterned, finding that in prosody it depends on context and meaning. Prosodic features such as internal rhyme, run-on lines, heavily feminine rhymes, alliteration, similar rhymes, near-internal rhymes and identicals, and syntax-defining words such as "Whan" and "Thanne" "participate in the underlying ingenuity that weds sound and meaning in the passage." Delight is seen in the celebration of the forces of nature and the power of language to express them—the water, breeze, sun, and zodiac. Owen fastidiously explores verbal and semantic implications, the phonetic reverberations of *en* and *ond* for longing, and the premonitory build-up to the longest word, "pilgrimages." Rhymes striking in their sound, meaning, and position are attention-getters. The second verse paragraph concretizes details of time and place and a tension between passivity and activity. The third verse paragraph, continuing the address to the reader, moves the emphasis from "felaweship" to the diversity of "sondry folk." Owen's ingeniously considered piece carefully explores all aspects of linguistic nuances that Chaucer craftily explored in furthering his comic attitude. He concludes that "Rhetoric, grammar, meaning, all contribute to the witty prosody that marks the first 42 lines of the Prologue and prefigures some of the effects in the portraits."

Alan T. Gaylord argues that we have missed the joke in Thopas' meter and prosody. In "Chaucer's Dainty 'Dogerel': The 'Elvyssh' Prosody of *Sir Thopas*," he notes that only the

Thopas link is not in couplets, for contrast when Thopas gallops off in an entirely different meter and to make restoring the couplets a return to normalcy. Chaucer's peculiar employment of the form (not the form itself) and the prosody (not the meter) are the objects of the satire: "Chaucer's poetic practice is caricatured and then laughed out of court." If the overriding effect of stanza one is of a nursery rhyme, the underriding effect is a comic monotony of metrical pace." *Thopas'* compulsively regular meter accounts for a "certain underlurch and overdrone, which suppresses some of the normal variety and distinctive humanity of the narrator's voice," expectable "from a poet who likes to make fun of his own artistic pretensions." Thus, Chaucer, "in an exceptionally playful and oblique manner, has given us ample measure of both *sentence* and *solas*... exercised his craft, strangely and wonderfully, in bringing us to a brilliant confusion." If the first joke is that Chaucer's wit should seem short and his art negligible, the second is his own arranging his spot before the pilgrims, for he cannot seem to compete with the other story tellers. Appropriately Chaucer uses the tail-rhyme form epitomizing the mingling and confusing of royal romance with the popular idiom, "French wine with English sprouts." With the return of couplets, we "are shocked loose from burlesque, and hauled back into the comedy" of obstreperous humanity.

In Robert W. Hanning's article "'Parlous Play': Diabolic Comedy in Chaucer's *Canterbury Tales*" the critic suggests how comic actions approximate or reflect a diabolic discourse of language and behavior "as the result of a synthesis between theological understanding of the Devil and comic or festive elements of popular culture." Chaucer's exposure to the drama highlighted diabolic discourse—the devil's role as trickster and his status opposing and perverting divine attributes. In the "Abuse-of-Power" theory of Redemption, it is argued that the devil won man when he beguiled him into sin, but when Christ, disguised as man, tricked him back, his power was canceled. According to folktale belief, a malevolent trickster must be defeated at his own game by a beneficent counter, so the diabolic inversion of the Antichrist was developed as an evil parody and competitor of Christ. The effect of most diabolic behavior in pre-Reformation plays was comic, depending on unscripted performances of the Mummer's Play and nonsense-prone servants. The synthesis of the disruptive, parodic release of carnivalesque license and the presence of the diabolic invited audience participation, agonistic spirits, and social tensions. As Hanning notes, such "parlous play" describes Chaucer's adaptation of the drama's diabolic discourse in the comic narratives of the *Canterbury Tales*. For instance, in the *Reeve's Tale* Chaucer assimilates the diabolic by evoking the "trickster tricked" component of the Abuse-of-Power theory, concretized in the proverb "A gylour shal hymself bigyled be," a deliberate attempt to diabolize his antagonist. Additionally, in the *Nun's Priest's Tale* the fable of cock, hen, and fox are paralleled with the story of the Fall, and its teller, "with typically playful malice aforethought, gleefully evokes the narrative of *Genesis* 3–4 as an *auctoritee*." In this revisionist rendering of the Fall, the Eve-antitype already has been tempted, the Adam-type led astray by sexual desire before the devil-antitype (the fox) arrives to tempt the Adam-type. Further, the tale is "Chaucer's self-directed diabolic comedy, in which, using the conventions of the beast fable, he presents himself as *both* counterfeiter and flatterer, cock and fox," both descriptions of the Devil.

Daniel F. Pigg's "The Semiotics of Comedy in Chaucer's Religious Tales" includes a consideration of the complex sense of linguistic comedy in those tales, despite their charged prob-lematic issues. The classics, the mass, the liturgical calendar, and Dante's work are posited as possible sources of Chaucer's comic vision in those works. For Pigg, comedy in the *Man of Law's Tale* rests in "its orchestrations of discourses that at-tempt to establish homologies between human and divine action. . . multi-layering generates comedy from the verbal level." Pigg also claims that the use of apostrophe defamiliar-izes the action, distances the audience, and provokes laughter under doctrinally correct circumstances. Laughter at the anti-feminist diatribe against the sultaness, at the demonic, and at Constance's economy of words (as opposed to the narrator's ver-bosity), are seen as providing "a key to religious comedy." After describing how each of the religious tales is utilized differ-

ently to extend semiotic configuring, Pigg concludes that a sense
of game and play is present in the religious tales as well as in
the fabliaux, perhaps differing only in their implications.
Religious comedy points away from the shadowy reality of
earthly comedy to the quiet, sublime divine one. Overall, the
structure in the *Canterbury Tales* moves toward the immutable
as it refigures comic signs.

Judith Tschann's "The Mind Distended: The *Retraction,
Miller's Tale* and *Summoner's Tale*" is a delightful serio-comic
exploration using Augustine's theory of time (Book eleven of
the *Confession*) in an up-so-doun scatological world: "there is
nothing more real or more fateful or more mindful of the limited
life in the flesh." Associated with interiority and hiddenness,
escape from the body and spirituality, the scatological is used
to connect narrative and death, revealing contrary impulses to
discover and silence the unavoidable temporal end. The
Miller's and *Summoner's Tales* are a response to the agony of
time-consciousness: "a mocking exaltation, an ecstatic fart,
rage, laughter and denial." The Janus-faced *Retraction*, according to Tschann, looks forward to death and backward to the
text, oscillating between certainty and doubt. Chaucer's apology opens possibilities by creating more room for doubt and
invites us to reconsider the tales. The spacial and temporal
roominess of this ploy, and the sense of containers and boundaries expose the complex nature of meaning. If the *Summoner's
Tale* creates inflation (the fart-made-meaningful), the *Miller's
Tale* creates deflation: order and language dwindling into chaos
and noise. This perceptive and fascinating exposition opens up
the tales, forcing them to surrender their private nuances.

In "Chaucer's Creative Comedy: A Study of the *Miller's
Tale* and the *Shipman's Tale*," A. Booker Thro finds the triumph of wit displayed in imaginative creativity and ingenious
construction. Self-conscious, excessive ingenuity in clothing,
play and plot is the source of humor. Cleverness, not cuckoldry,
is paramount in the two fabliaux discussed. According to Thro,
"This posing of creative exercise and its fantastically imaginative solution appear, since they are in excess of plot requirements, to be dictated by Chaucer's enthusiastic delight in mental gymnastics." Nicholas' brilliant contriving, construction of

seemingly irrelevant materials into a profoundly comic edifice, for instance, dominates the action of the *Miller's Tale*. After summarizing critical positions eschewing farce, with its destructive aggressiveness, and irony, with its adulterating, inverting emphasis as predominant comic elements, Thro points to the Chaucerian persistence of human constructiveness as the dominating force.

John M. Steadman's classical, erudite presentation of medieval poetics and genre theory in "Felicity and Mutability: Boethian Framework of the *Troilus*," is an appropriate way to conclude *Chaucer's Humor: Critical Essays*. Since the essential factor determining a comic or tragic genre was the social level of the characters, romance writers might combine love, valor, elegiac, or comic elements without altering the genre of tragedy. Thus, the *Troilus* is tragic despite elements of comedy, elegy, and encomium. Chaucer could include some fine comic scenes within the context of a tragic fable. In *Troilus*, with these rich overtones, "the hero's laughter acquires a force and a relevance that it could not have achieved" elsewhere, thereby strengthening the comic element. Steadman contends that Chaucer, like Dante and Boethius before him, contrasts the fate of the body and soul, "the antithesis between earthly and celestial felicity." Faced with the tension between poetic and philosophical ideas of felicity and misery in a tale moving "beyond the realm of 'faithless' fortune to the 'stable faith' of the heavens, beyond the value of tragic vicissitude to a permanent and abiding felicity," Chaucer exploits that tension for ironic effect. According to Steadman, "though the Trojan war provides a tragic context for the history of the lovers, though their end is tragic and they themselves belong to the rank appropriate for tragedy, much of Chaucer's material . . . was the conventional matter of comedy." Steadman concludes that "though the tragic sense predominates in the plot, it is the comic vision that overcomes in the end."

We hope that this diverse collection of surprisingly unique approaches contributes to understanding the myriad methods by which our extraordinary medieval comedian has executed his wit, humor, and skill in exploring the human condition. Perhaps some of the enjoyment that we have had in creating this modern *compilatio* can be gleaned from its pages. And, perhaps the reader will find a similar enjoyment in pilgrimaging through the meaning of Chaucerian comedy, the critical theory embodying it, and the genres in which humor is displayed so well.

NOTES

1. The interpretive section of this Introduction is derived from my article on Chaucerian Humor in the *Encyclopedia of British Humorists*, edited by Steven H. Gale (New York: Garland Publishing, 1995).

PART ONE

A Prolegomenon to Defining Chaucerian Humor

The Voice of the Past
Surveying the Reception of Chaucer's Humor

Jean E. Jost

"And Chaucer for his merie tales, was well esteemed there."

Richard Robinson, 1574

The Genre and Extent of Early Critical Interpretation

Critical casebooks of the sort this volume represents regularly offer a sampling of the best literary criticism contemporaneous to the author, and from each subsequent century, a running critical commentary of the attitudes and impressions of the topic, in this case, Chaucerian humor. The impossibility of this procedure here, however, is apparent, for extended literary commentary on humor, or in fact on any aspect of the Chaucerian corpus, quite simply does not exist. Literary criticism as a genre had not yet matured in the early centuries following Chaucer's masterpiece; comments on the topic are no more than brief references to humor, considering neither interpretation nor function of the comic mode within his *opus*. In lieu of the expected chronological survey of critical articles, then, this brief overview historically details significant comments and excerpts marking the critical reception of Chaucer as a humorist.

The Extent of Critical Analysis

The surprising neglect of Chaucer's comic talent throughout the centuries following his death may be accounted for in
part by the pejorative attitude toward humor itself shared by
many. As Derek Brewer points out, "Humour is traditionally
related to realism through satire, as in Chaucer's poetry itself,
but though it is clear enough that Lydgate, for example, greatly
appreciated Chaucer's humour, it is not much commented on in
the fifteenth and early sixteenth centuries. . . . In the later seventeenth century and the eighteenth the Protestant interest in
Chaucer lapsed, as he was seen primarily as a humorist"
(*Chaucer: The Critical Heritage*). If humor is seen as a literary
stepchild, no doubt Chaucer would be treated as an orphan.

Yet certainly remarks such as that by Thomas Wharton,
that Chaucer "was the first who gave the English nation, in its
own language, an idea of Humour" ("Of Spenser's Imitations
from Chaucer" in *Observations on the Faerie Queen*," 1754) are a
useful gauge of his largely unexamined, but also undisputed,
reputation. Caroline Spurgeon rightly remarks that "It is not . . .
until well on in the nineteenth century, not indeed until Leigh
Hunt wrote on it in 1846, that Chaucer's humour seems to have
met with any adequate recognition" (*Five Hundred Years of
Chaucer Criticism and Allusion*).[1]

Larry D. Benson concurs, remarking that "criticism of
Chaucer began in this century ('appreciation' rather than 'criticism' characterized earlier scholarship), and was dominated by
American scholars such as Kittredge, Lowes, and Root until the
late thirties or early forties" (*Writers and Their Background:
Geoffrey Chaucer*, ed. Derek Brewer. London: G. Bell and Sons,
1974, p. 340). Even the amount of that "appreciation," such as
Richard Robinson's epigraph that heads this discussion and is
usually limited to acknowledging but not interpreting humor, is
minimal.

Critical analysis as we know it today was simply not done.
Rather, early critics seem to be writing memorials or testaments
to Chaucer's historical position while providing no close readings, discussing no sources of comedy, and offering no analysis;

in short, there is no equivalent criticism for Chaucer comparable to what we have for Shakespeare or later authors.

Further, few of Chaucer's immediate successors revered him for his humor. Still, Spurgeon points to the value and scarcity of humor in Chaucer's time, remarking "That the quality of humour existed in full measure in fourteenth-century England we know by reading Chaucer's Prologue, but we are forced to ask whether it was less common than now, only to be found here and there among men of genius." Presumably its value would increase in a time of paucity. In 1936 C. S. Lewis implies that Chaucer's humor was valued because imitated, but within a narrow range of his composition:

> Chaucer's comic and realistic style is imitated by Lydgate in the Prologue to the *Book of Thebes,* and by an unknown poet in the Prologue to the *Tale of Beryn*; but this is small harvest besides the innumerable imitations of his amatory and allegorical poetry. . . . When the men of the fourteenth or fifteenth centuries thought of Chaucer, they did not think first of the *Canterbury Tales.* Their Chaucer was the Chaucer of dream and allegory, of love-romance and erotic debate, of high style and profitable doctrine. ("Chaucer," *The Allegory of Love,* pp. 204, 205)

In fact, until the seventeenth century, the tragic *Troilus and Criseyde* was considered Chaucer's most worthy, and most discussed work, the merits of the comic *Canterbury Tales* being recognized only subsequently, and marginally. The widening gulf between Middle English and early Modern English, and hence the difficulty in reading Chaucerian texts exacerbated the situation. Pointing out the dormant state of Chaucerian criticism in general, much less discussions on his humor, Benson acknowledges the value of critical commentary and the effect of its absence:

> [W]ithout the help of scholarship—linguistic, textual, critical, and historical—Chaucer would remain, as he was for centuries, accessible only to a few devoted readers . . . By the end of the sixteenth century it was clear . . . that Chaucer required editing. . . . Thomas Speght's edition of Chaucer (1598; rev. 1602; repr. 1667) was the last to appear until the eighteenth century, and . . . Chaucer remained

until the later nineteenth century (in the words of an anonymous writer in the year 1819) "more neglected, less studied, and less known, though none are more talked of" than almost any major English writer. (321–22)

With such a paucity of early critical commentary on Chaucerian humor, only a judicious sampling of quotations by influential scholars and writers rather than complete reproduction of entire critical documents, of which there are none, is possible. Such a summary of comments and opinion follows.

Contemporaneous and Earliest Appreciation of Chaucerian Humor

J. A. Burrow concurs that few contemporaneous documents consider Chaucer's comic strain at any length; in fact, he notes that "From [Chaucer's] own life-time there survive just three compliments, a handful of imitations and borrowings, and no manuscripts of his poetry whatsoever." (*Geoffrey Chaucer: A Critical Anthology.* Middlesex, Baltimore, and Victoria, Australia: Penguin, 1969, p. 19.) The three compliments, from Thomas Usk, John Gower, and Eustace Deschamps, praise his love poetry, philosophical poetry, and his easy style rather than his humor. Francis Beaumont is virtually alone in seeing the poet as "the verie life it selfe of all mirth and pleasant writing." As Brewer recounts:

> None of these early writers [Lydgate and Hoccleve] comments on Chaucer's humour, and indeed the word itself, in the modern sense, did not exist. It is even doubtful whether the concept existed, though of course medieval writers recognised irony and satire. This does not mean that Chaucer's humour was unrecognised. The lightness of tone of Lydgate's *Prologue to the Siege of Thebes* and its self-depreciatory fun, like the references of both writers to the Wife of Bath, show that they responded to various kinds of Chaucer's humour, at times with their own elephantine gaiety. ("Images of Chaucer 1386–1900" in *Chaucer and Chaucerians*, p. 247)

Brewer does point out, however, that "[i]ncreasingly throughout the century writers refer to his 'merriness' or 'pleasantness.' Spenser's friend Gabriel Harvey seems to have taken particular pleasure in Chaucer and notes his comedy." On the other hand, William Thynne's edition of 1532 includes a dedication to Henry VIII in which the author, one Sir Brian Tuke, praises Chaucer's "excellent learning in all kinds of doctrines and sciences," an apparently influential and dominant opinion for two hundred years, but one which ignores or disdains his comedic spirit.

As Caroline Spurgeon points out, although Spenser, Dryden, Pope, Caxton, and Thynne appreciate Chaucer's poetical strength, imagination, and power of expression, "he is looked upon for the most part as a comic poet chiefly remarkable for the scurrility of his verses. This is a view which . . . began to creep in at the end of the sixteenth century." While some condemned him for his supposed coarseness, his lack of seriousness and dignity, others "merely laughed at his 'merie tales.' . . . This attitude of tolerant amusement rapidly gained ground in the seventeenth and earlier eighteenth centuries. . . . Chaucer was a merry wit, but a rough one, for even his humour, the only quality granted him, was not recognized to be the most light and delicate . . . but rather quaint and coarse, fit only for a barbarous age."

In 1595, Sir Philip Sidney noticeably ignores both the rough and comic strains, claiming: "Chaucer undoubtedly did excellently in his *Troilus and Cresseid*; of whom, truly, I know not whether to marvel more either that he in that misty time could see so clearly, or that we in this clear age go so stumblingly after him" (*The Defense of Poesie*).

In 1675, Edward Phillips offhandedly comments in *Theatrum Poetarum, or a compleat Collection of the Poets* that Chaucer "still keeps a name, being by some few admir'd for his real worth, to others not unpleasing for his facetious ways, which joyn'd with his old *English* intertains them with a kind of Drollery." While Chaucer's true value does not inhere in his comic genius, many are nevertheless so entertained, according to Phillips.

Eighteenth-Century Critical Acclaim

No doubt the neoclassical concern with edification and
decorum explains the restrained and reserved acceptance of the
medieval master of the comic. The "undignified" combination of
different tones, material, genres, and attitudes, the indecent and
the devout, the comic and the tragic, would account for some
resistance. Spurgeon's survey of the changing definition and
perception of Chaucerian humor is one of the most insightful;
reservations about it might be explained by that neoclassical
aesthetic of dignity:

> In Chaucer we have a poet whose distinguishing quality of
> mind is a subtle, shifting, delicate and all-pervading hu-
> mour, to which full justice has not perhaps even yet been
> done; yet through all these years of critical remark there is
> until the eighteenth century no reference to the quality as
> we know it . . . [only] a certain recognition among some
> earlier writers of his "pleasant vayne and wit," and his
> "delightsome mirth" . . . by which is probably meant his
> relish of a good story, his sly sense of fun, and the general
> atmosphere of good-humor which pervades his work, but
> there is no hint of appreciation of the deeper and more
> delicate quality alone deserving the name of humor, which
> is insight, sympathy and tender seriousness, all brought
> into play upon the ever-present sense of the incongruous,
> and of the inconsistent in character and life. (cxxxviii,
> cxxxix)

Only does the concept of humour as dignified slowly
emerge. The eighteenth-century definition of "humour" as buf-
foonery," holding something up to ridicule, or "facetiousness,"
connotes the quality of degradation maintained by that era.
While acknowledging Chaucer's "pleasing way of relating
Comical Adventures," in 1700 John Dryden only briefly
mentions the game-playing of the tales:

> Even the Ribaldry of the Low Characters is different: The
> *Reeve,* the *Miller,* and the *Cook,* are Several Men, and dis-
> tinguish'd from each other, as much as the mincing Lady
> Prioress, and the broad-speaking gap-tooth'd *Wife of Bathe.*
> But enough of this: There is such a Variety of Game
> springing up before me, that I am distracted in my Choice,

and know not which to follow. 'Tis sufficient to say according to the Proverb, that here is God's Plenty. (Preface to *Fables Ancient and Modern*, lst ed., 1700. *The Poems and Fables of John Dryden*, ed. James Kinsley, Oxford: Oxford University Press, 1962)

Dryden's discussion is limited to pointing out instances of humor within the tales with little attempt to consider their role or function. And, as Burrow points out, with the passage of time "the chorus of praise grows fainter as Chaucer's language becomes more and more remote and rebarbative" (35). Joseph Addison appreciates his humor, but describes quite well the fate of Chaucer's fame that Dryden notes:

> Long had our dull Fore-Fathers slept Supine,
> Nor felt the Raptures of the Tuneful Nine;
> Till Chaucer first, a merry Bard, arose;
> And many a Story told in Rhime and Prose.
> But Age has Rusted what the Poet writ,
> Worn out his Language, and obscur'd his Wit;
> In vain he jests in his unpolish'd strain
> And tries to make his Readers laugh in vain.

(An Account of the Greatest English Poets, 1694)

In 1700, Samuel Cobb agrees, calling Chaucer "A joking Bard, whose Antiquated Muse / In mouldy Words could solid Sense produce" (*Poetae Britannici: A Poem*). Twenty-one years later, Julia Madan found that "Here [in Britain] Chaucer first his comic Vein display'd, / And merry tales in homely Guise convey'd" (*The Progress of Poetry*). In 1740, *The Gentleman's Magazine* published "In Praise of Chaucer, Father of English Poetry" by an anonymous author who asks "Does [Chaucer] to comic wit direct his aim? / His humour crowns th' attempt with equal fame."

According to Burrow, in the eighteenth century, "[t]he well-bred frankness of the Augustans . . . allowed many people, like the young Addison, to treat Chaucer as a merry and somewhat improper poet who nevertheless somehow failed to raise a laugh . . . this idea of Chaucer as a jovial, even a coarse poet, can be traced in the Elizabethan age" (37). Samuel Croxwell feels the compelling pull of Chaucer's joyful nature, depicting him "With gleeful smile [while] his merry Lesson play'd" (*The Vision: A*

Poem, 1715). The same year, John Hughes comments that Chaucer "first study'd Humour, was an excellent satirist, and a lively but rough Painter of the Manners of that rude Age in which he liv'd" (from an "Essay on Allegorical Poetry" in his edition of Spenser's works). Although John Gay also points only to the jovial and not the coarse poet, claiming "Prior th'admiring Reader entertains, / With Chaucer's Humor, and with Spenser's Strains" (*Verse addressed to Bernard Lintot in Miscellaneous Poems and Translations by several Hands*), Elizabeth Cooper notes the realistic side as well. In 1737, Cooper claimed that Chaucer "encountered the follies of mankind as well as their vices, and blended the acutest raillery with the most insinuating humour" (*The Muses' Library*, I.xi). Moreover, Thomas Wharton claims to have "found what later and more refin'd ages could hardly equal in true humour, pathos, or sublimity." But, Wharton continues, "It must be confest that his uncouth or rather unfamiliar language has deterr'd many from perusing him" ("Of Spenser's Imitations from Chaucer" in *Observations on the Faerie Queen*). The taint of anachronism follows Chaucer in Hugh Darymple's poem as well:

> Old Chaucer, who in rough unequal verse,
> Sung quaint allusion and facetious tale;
> And ever as his jests he would rehearse,
> Loud peals of laughter echoed through the vale . . . [but]
> His tuneless numbers hardly now survive
> A ruins of a dark and Gothic age;
> And all his blithesome tales their praise derive
> From Pope's immortal song and Prior's page.

> ("Woodstock Park: An Elegy," 1761)

Richard Hurd waxes somewhat more enthusiastically, and extensively, in his *Letters on Chivalry and Romance* of 1762. Instead of pointing to uproarious laughter and innocent comedy, Hurd recognizes elements of ridicule and satire, and of impudently funny behavior:

> Dan Chaucer . . . in a reign that almost realized the wonders of romantic chivalry not only discerned the absurdity of the old romances, but has even ridiculed them with incomparable spirit.

His *Rhyme of Sir Thopas*, in the *Canterbury Tales*, is a manifest banter on those books, and may be considered as a
sort of prelude to the adventures of Don Quixote. I call it a
manifest banter, for we are to observe that this was
Chaucer's own tale, and that, when in the progress of it
the good sense of the Host is made to break in upon him
and interrupt him, Chaucer approves his disgust and,
changing his note, tells the simple instructive *Tale of
Melibeus*. . . .

One might further observe that the *Rhyme of Sir Thopas*
itself is so managed as with infinite humour to expose the
leading impertinences only; as may be seen by the
different conduct of this tale from that of Cambuscan,
which Spenser and Milton were so pleased with, and
which with great propriety is put into the mouth of the
Squire. (107–8)

Thirty-seven years later in his *History of English Poetry*, Wharton
commented upon Chaucerian humor in a somewhat more
inclusive fashion. Not only romance, but the entire canon offers
humorous and satiric characterization, almost curiosities,
anomalous for his era. Chaucer is seen as possessing a method, a
pattern of writing, rather than simply expressing his comic
creativity on a given occasion:

Chaucer's vein of humor, although conspicuous in the
Canterbury Tales, is chiefly displayed in the Characters
with which they are introduced. . . . We are surprised to
find, in so gross and ignorant an age, such talents for satire
and for observation on life, qualities which usually exert
themselves at more civilized periods . . . and renders devi-
ations of conduct and singularities of character more immediately and necessarily the objects of censure and
ridicule. These curious and valuable remains are speci-
mens of Chaucer's genius, unassisted and unalloyed.
(I.435)

Less critically, Charles Burney briefly remarks that "for wit,
humour, and other poetical excellences, perhaps not till a much
later period . . . [is] his equal to be found" (*General History of
Music*, 1782).

Nineteenth-Century Critical Acclaim

Derek Brewer notes that in the nineteenth century there is "a question of the decency of Chaucer's humour, though no one gets very excited about it. Sometimes his humor is partially excused as 'broad' . . . or it may be partially condemned . . . [it] is barely analyzed until the very beginning of the twentieth century."

At the beginning of the nineteenth century William Godwin notes that "after the dramas of Shakespear, *[sic]* there is no production of man that displays more various and vigorous talent than the *Canterbury Tales.* Splendour of narrative, richness of fancy, pathetic simplicity of incident and feeling, a powerful style in delineating character and manners, and an animated vein of comic humour, each takes its turn in this wonderful performance" (Preface 1803). Charles Lamb likewise praises Chaucer's fine sense of comedy. In 1811, he notes that William Hogarth's works "resemble the characters of Chaucer's 'Pilgrims,' which have strokes of humour in them enough to designate them for the most part as comic, but our strongest feeling still is wonder at the comprehensiveness of genius which could crowd, as poet and painter have done, into one small canvas so many diverse yet cooperating materials" ("The Genius and Character of Hogarth" in *The Reflector*). Not only humor, but also comprehensiveness and unity are appreciated. In his 1812 Preface to the *Tales*, George Crabb comments briefly on the nature of Chaucerian comedy from an audience perspective, claiming:

> There are in his *Tales* many pages of coarse, accurate and minute, but very striking description. Many small poems in a subsequent age, of most impressive kind, are adapted and addressed to the common sense of the reader, and prevail by the strong language of truth and nature. They amused our ancestors, and they continue to engage our interest and excite our feelings by the same powerful appeals to the heart and affections. (xx-xxi)

William Hazlitt succinctly comments that Chaucer's poetry has "all the extravagance and the utmost licentiousness of comic humour, equally arising out of the manners of the time. In this too Chaucer resembled Boccaccio that he excelled in both styles, and could pass at will 'from grave to gay, from lively to severe' (Lecture II on Chaucer and Spenser). In the *London Magazine*, October 1820, one H. R. claims that Chaucer's "*Canterbury Tales* are full of broad but not deep feeling—replete with humour and wagger." Equally succinct is the unknown writer's comment of 1823 who claimed that Chaucer's work, "a Comedy not intended for the stage, . . . first shewed the way how comedy should be constructed, and its characters grouped and diversified" (from "An Essential Portion of the Authentic History of his Country" in *The Retrospective Review*). Samuel Taylor Coleridge, in a conversation on March 15, 1834, becomes more expansive in his description, focusing on the joy rather than realism commonly touted behind Chaucer's humor. He admits:

> I take unceasing delight in Chaucer. His manly cheerfulness is especially delicious to me in my old age. How exquisitely tender he is, and yet how perfectly free from the least touch of sickly melancholy or morbid drooping! The sympathy of the poet with the subjects of his poetry is particularly remarkable in Shakespeare and Chaucer; but what the first effects by a strong act of imagination and mental metamorphosis, the last does without any effort, merely by the inborn kindly joyousness of his nature. (433)

While the Victorians wrote no treatises on Chaucerian humor, they offered somewhat more critically perceptive comments than heretofore. Leigh Hunt, for example, points to Chaucerian characterization, claiming that "Humour deals in incongruities of character and circumstance . . . Such is the melting together . . . of the professional and the individual, or the accidental and the permanent, in the Canterbury Pilgrims." In conjunction with his appreciative criticism, he also reiterates the previous century's evaluation of the era as coarse, maintaining that:

> When Chaucer is free from this taint of his age [i.e. coarseness], his humour is of a description the most thoroughly delightful, for it is at once entertaining, profound, and good-natured. . . . Chaucer's comic genius is so perfect, that it may be said to include prophetic intimations of all that followed it. . . . The third great quality of Chaucer's humour is its fair play—the truth and humanity which induces him to see justice done to good and bad, to the circumstances which make men what they are, and the mixture of right and wrong, of wisdom and of folly, which they consequently exhibit. His worst characters have some little saving grace of good-nature or at least of joviality and candour.

Hunt thus examines and categorizes Chaucerian humor as a phenomenon or pattern operating throughout his whole corpus, not an individual instance of creative genius. John Ruskin finds another pattern, an awareness of the burlesque and the comedy within evil. In his 1870 *Lectures on Art*, Ruskin declares that:

> There is one strange, but quite essential, character in us— ever since the Conquest, if not earlier; a delight in the forms of burlesque which are connected in some degree with the foulness of evil. I think the most perfect type of a true English mind in its best possible temper is that of Chaucer; and you will find that, while it is for the most part full of things of beauty, pure and wild like that of an April morning, there are even in the midst of this sometimes momentarily jesting passages which stoop to play with evil—while the power of listening to and enjoying the jesting of entirely gross persons, whatever the feeling may be which permits it, afterwards degenerates into forms of humour which render some of quite the greatest, wisest, and most oral of English writers now almost useless for our youth.

That comedy is enmeshed within the sordid and degenerate, and is a corrupting influence on the young, is Ruskin's overriding concern. In the same year, James Russell Lowell remarks that

Chaucer's humor "pervades his comic tales like sunshine, and never dazzles the attention by a sudden flash. Sometimes he brings it in parenthetically, and insinuates a sarcasm so slyly as almost to slip by without our notice. . . . the humor also in its suavity, its perpetual presence and its shy unobtrusiveness is something new in literature" (in *North American Review*, July 1879). Matthew Arnold skirts around the issue of humor with some indirection, and the issue of the difficulty of Chaucerian language with less. Denigrating French romance-poetry, he expounds on Chaucer's virtues and limitations, saying:

> [I]n the fourteenth century there comes an Englishman nourished on this poetry, taught his trade by this poetry, getting words, rhyme, metre from this poetry. . . . Chaucer's power of fascination . . . is enduring; his poetical importance does not need the assistance of the historic estimate; it is real. He is a genuine source of joy and strength, which is flowing still for us and will flow always. . . . His language is a cause of difficulty for us . . . a difficulty to be unhesitatingly accepted and overcome. . . . His superiority in substance is given by his large, free, simple, clear yet kindly view of human life. . . . The substance of Chaucer's poetry, his view of things and his criticism of life, has largess, freedom, shrewdness, benignity; but it has not this high seriousness . . . which Aristotle assigns as one of the grand virtues of poetry. (*The Study of Poetry*, 1880; rpt in *Essays in Criticism*, 1888, pp. 31–32)

For Arnold, not only is comedy not a virtue, it actually detracts from the quality of the poetry since high seriousness is lacking. According to A. C. Swinburne also writing in 1880, "Chaucer was in the main a French or Italian poet, lined thoroughly and warmly throughout with the substance of an English humorist. And with this great gift of specially English humour combined, naturally as it were and inevitably, the inseparable twin-born gift of peculiarly English pathos" ("Short Notes on English Poets," in *Miscellanies*, p. 3).

Early Twentieth-Century Interpretations of Chaucerian Humor

With the turn of the century, Arnold's ideal of "high seriousness" recedes into the background, inviting a renewed appreciation of humor. Sir Walter Raleigh finds Chaucer's:

> Broad and calm philosophy of life, his delight in diversities of character, his sympathy with all kinds of people, and his zest in all varieties of experience—these are the qualities of a humorist . . . Sometimes [Chaucer's humor] breaks out in boisterous and rollicking laughter at the drunken and unseemly exploits of churls; sometimes it is so delicate and evanescent that you can hardly detect its existence. But it is everywhere, even in places where it has no right to be. . . . Chaucer has the true humorist's gift— the gift of the wooden face. . . . only the faintest twinkle in the eye makes one hesitate in believing him serious. . . . Chaucer's best and deepest humour occurs in parts of his work that are dramatic in everything but form. ("On Writers and Writing")

George Saintsbury's 1908 discussion reaffirms, and in fact reinvigorates, previous evaluations of Chaucer's great genius. His astute comments are worth noting at some length. Saintsbury points to:

> The intense, all-pervading and all but incalculable presence of Chaucer's *humour*—a quality which some, even of those who enjoy it heartily and extol it generously, do not quite invariably seem to comprehend. . . . [I]t "works i' the earth so fast" that you never can tell at what moment it will find utterance. . . . mixed and streaked with seriousness and tenderness in an almost inextricable manner. . . . Chaucer is perpetually seeing the humorous side, not merely of his emotions but of his interests, his knowledge, his beliefs, his everything. . . .

> Of this humour, indeed, it is not too much to say . . . that it is the "stuff and substance," not merely of Chaucer's intellect, but of his entire mental constitution. . . . [T]his humour is employed with a remarkable difference. In most great English humorists, humour sets the picture with a

sort of vignetting or arabesquing fringe and atmosphere of
exaggeration and fantasy. By Chaucer it is almost invariably used to bring a higher but a quite clear and achro-
matic light on the picture itself or parts of it. The stuff is
turned rapidly the other way to show its real texture; the
jest is perhaps a burning, but also a magnifying and
illuminating glass, to bring out a special trait more
definitely.... [A] great deal of the combination of vivacity
and veracity in Chaucer's portraits and sketches of all
kinds is due to this all-pervading humour.... it may be,
and probably is, equally present in other places where the
effect is less immediately rejoicing to the modern reader;
and that medieval pedantry, medieval catalogue-making,
medieval digression and irrelevance are at once exemplified and satirised by the operation of this extraordinary
faculty. (*Cambridge History of English Literature*, Vol. 2)

This well-considered judgment and exploration of Chaucer's
comic usage penetrate to the heart of Chaucerian humor, its
goals and successes, more fully than previous appreciative
comments. In 1932, G. K. Chesterton continues to praise
Chaucer's humor more emphatically than critics of the previous
century, claiming "he was in this very exact sense a great
humorist. And by this I do not only mean a very good humorist.
I mean a humorist in the grand style; a humorist whose broad
outlook embraced the world as a whole, and saw even great
humanity against a backdrop of greater things" (*Chaucer*, p. 20).
In becoming more specific about Chaucer's jokes, Chesterton
says of the *Rime of Sir Thopas*, "Chaucer is mocking not merely
bad poets but good poets; the best poet he knows.... The point
is in the admirable irony of the whole conception of the dumb or
doggerel rhymer who is nevertheless the writer of all the other
rhymes; nay, even the author of their authors" (*Chaucer*, p. 21).

But, interestingly, C. S. Lewis would deny some of what
Chesterton and other critics have accepted as comic: "We have
heard a little too much of the 'mocking' Chaucer. Not many will
agree with the critic who supposed that the laughter of Troilus in
heaven was 'ironical'; but I am afraid many of us now read into
Chaucer all manner of ironies, slynesses, and archnesses, which
are not there, and praise him for his humour where he is really
writing with 'ful devout corage' ("Chaucer," *The Allegory of*

Love). In fact, Lewis's position has proven to be in the minority, as critical acclaim for Chaucer's humor has surpassed that of his acknowledged "ful devout corage."

Larry Benson, for one, points to other critics who did appreciate the poet's humor to a limited extent, but nonetheless underestimated its importance. Perhaps a certain embarrassment with the realism of fabliau humor accounts for this diminution:

> Curiously, Chaucer's most realistic works were seldom discussed by those critics who most prized his realism. Certainly they appreciated Chaucer's humour, but even as late as H. R. Patch's *On Rereading Chaucer* (1939), one could write a whole book on Chaucer's humour with only the barest mention of the fabliaux. They are comic and diverting but not, so it was believed, the stuff of literature.
> (*Writers and Their Background*, 345)

Patch's introductory chapter on Chaucerian humor offers an overview worth noting, couched within a comparative evaluation of Chaucer and Shakespeare among others, and is reprinted following this discussion. Charles Muscatine, one of the more appreciative critics of Chaucer's fabliau style, claims:

> The humor of [the *Miller's Tale*] arises from the unequal conflict between fact and the few illusions that unhappily insist on themselves. The devastating victory of the norm is supported, in the manner of comedy, by reducing the "errors" to caricature. The error of religion, to pass over the error of not wedding one's "simylitude" (3228)—is represented by the credulous, illiterate carpenter. His knowledge of Scripture is from mystery plays . . . Faith in Love is the heresy most elaborately dealt with in the poem, and it is most elaborately caricatured. Linguistic analysis has shown how much the Oxford idiom of love is the idiom of English rather than of French romance. It is the native version of the imported heresy that is parodied here. More congenial to the setting, it is also funnier than Continental love would have been, for it is exposed to the laughter of the sophisticated, who know better, as well as of the Miller's kind, who know worse. But it remains crushingly conventional and the stylistic vehicle for the comedy of love is the farrago of convention and naked instinct that is Absolon's courtship of Alisoun. . . .

> [Alisoun's] portrait is comic in the way that Absolon is
> comic. It matches perfectly (to the sophisticated audience)
> the gaucherie of his "love-longynge." This is a small-town
> heroine whose brows *are* plucked, whose eye *is* lecherous,
> whose forehead shines—from washing after work. (226,
> 227, 229).

R. E. Kaske notes that in the same tale the allusions to Canticles
are organized around a broadly comic association of Absolon
with the bridegroom and of Alisoun with the bride. . . . (52) By
1964, R. Neuse becomes a bit more specific about the nature of
Chaucerian comedy, offering perceptive social and psychological
comments worth quoting at some length. Neuse believes:

> It is the specifically pagan elements that become the source
> of much of the [*Knight's Tale*'s] comedy. The Knight has
> his fun in imagining Emily's rites in the temple of Diana, a
> matter he won't go into. "And yet it were a game to
> heeren al" (2286). There is the burlesque scene in which
> the wood-nymphs and other forest deities are unhoused
> and sent scurrying about when the trees of the grove are
> cut down for Arcite's pyre (2925 ff.). And a kind of
> Homeric comedy plays around the epic machinery of the
> gods whose role at times borders on farce. . . .
>
> Over against the symptoms of disorder, however, there
> emerges from the *Canterbury Tales* the idea of what I
> would call a "comic society," whose order is not so much
> conceptual as it is pragmatic, being rooted (as it were) in
> the nature of things. In such a society the control or order
> arises from below, we might say, because nature is a func-
> tion of (the comic) spirit. Men have the freedom to follow
> their natural inclinations, because by doing so they imitate
> the inner drive in all things toward their full being or
> perfection. But in so far as they deviate drastically from
> the norms of a publicly defined good, they are exposed to
> the censorship of laughter. . . . Sociability . . . manifests
> itself in the sense of freedom and *play* which is so promi-
> nent in the *Canterbury Tales* that we might almost speak of
> the poem as viewing not only society but the world itself
> *sub specie ludi* (to adopt a phrase of Huizinga's). ("The

Knight: The First Mover in Chaucer's Human Comedy."
University of Toronto Quarterly 32 [1964], 302, 308)

This brief survey of critical opinion from Chaucer's contemporaries to critics of the mid-twentieth century reveals extensive changes in the formulation and conception of Chaucerian
humor. Although early perceptions were limited in scope, and
often confined to enumerating humorous incidents in his corpus,
twentieth-century examinations begin to probe into the nature of
this comic spirit with more sophistication. Patch's 1939 essay
serves as a bridge linking the early appreciative and the modern,
more critically acute interpretive criticism that examines the
nature and function of Chaucer's comic genius. Truly building
on the shoulders of previous critics, contemporary scholars have
benefitted from cumulative explorations of the fascinating, if
elusive, topic of how Chaucer crafted his comedy.

The balance of this volume, then, examines the various
directions those contemporary scholars have taken to date. The
purpose of *Chaucer's Humor: Critical Essays* is to encourage further philosophical and theoretical exploration of Chaucer's
methods and means, to penetrate into the nature and function of
Chaucerian comedy, to be the springboard for further investigations, and thus to expand the current understanding of that
medieval master of comedy. Caroline Spurgeon believes that as
people evolve, "they grow in refinement, in quickness and delicacy of perception, in sensitiveness and in sympathy, [and] their
conception of what is humorous must grow proportionately."
Let us wish, then, for a substantial growth in the conception of
what is humorous following from a new realization of deeper
perception, sensitivity, and sympathy. Then perhaps we may say
with Wordsworth:

> Beside the pleasant Mills of Trompington
> I laughed with Chaucer; in the hawthorn shade
> Heard him (while birds were warbling) tell his tales
> Of amorous passion. (*The Prelude*, 1805)

NOTES

1. Caroline Spurgeon's *Five Hundred Years of Chaucer Criticism and Allusion: 1357–1900* surveying early Chaucerian criticism—a veritable compendium of commentary on Chaucer through the ages—has been invaluable for the compilation of this article. The nature of its contents: brief notes, comments, and interjections, reinforces the earlier claim that no longer, fully developed discussions have been written about the tenor of Chaucerian humor in earlier centuries.

WORKS CITED

Benson, L. D. *Writers and Their Background: Geoffrey Chaucer*. London: G. Bell and Sons, 1974.

Brewer, Derek. *Chaucer: The Critical Heritage*. London, Henley, and Boston: Routledge and Kegan Paul, 1978.

———. "Images of Chaucer 1386–1900," in *Chaucer and Chaucerians*, ed. D. S. Brewer. London, Edinburgh, South Africa: Thomas Nelson and Sons, 1966.

Burrow, J. A. *Geoffrey Chaucer: A Critical Anthology*. Middlesex, Baltimore, Victoria, Australia: Penguin, 1969.

Muscatine, Charles. *Chaucer and the French Tradition*. Berkeley & Los Angeles: University of California Press, 1966.

Neuse, Richard. "The Knight: The First Mover in Chaucer's Human Comedy." *University of Toronto Quarterly* 32 (1964): 299–315.

Spurgeon, Caroline F. E. *Five Hundred Years of Chaucer Criticism and Allusion: 1357–1900*. New York: Russell and Russell, 1960.

The Idea of Humor*

Howard Rollin Patch

In a classic and nowadays generally unread essay, James Russell Lowell indicated an essential quality in Geoffrey Chaucer when he spoke of him as "healthy." To this he added the word "hearty," which is undoubtedly accurate for certain of Chaucer's moods, although I am not quite so sure of its further application. The health of the poet's spirit is pervasive in all his works, which exhibit nothing that from any point of view may be called morbid, however much they may show stretches arid to modern taste or passages offensive to the excessively puritanical. No strains from the music of the Dance of Death, which pleased certain ears in the Middle Ages and the Renaissance, no rarefied religiosity or unworldly melancholy mar his lines. As we cannot say of Swift or Pope or Sterne, no rancor poisons the spring of his genius; he has less acerbity than Dryden, and unlike many writers he does not pause in his verse for intervals of bad temper. His peculiar trait may perhaps be described by the allied expression "sanity." "Whether Chaucer saw life whole, I do not know," writes Professor Kittredge. "One thing I know—he saw it steadily."

Dryden had the characteristic in mind when he referred to the poet's "good sense." But what I am now moved to inquire is whether it might not equally well be called "good humor." Contrasting him with Dante, whose satire is "like a blast of the divine wrath," Lowell goes on to say that Chaucer's "is genial with the broad sunshine of humor, into which the victims walk forth with a delightful unconcern, laying aside of themselves the disguises that seem to make them uncomfortably warm, till they have made a thorough betrayal of themselves so unconsciously that we almost pity while we laugh." All this applies well enough to writings in this vein, but what about his poetry and prose where satiric purpose seems to be mainly absent? Do we find there the light of the same healthy spirit playing upon the narrative and illuminating its significance? Or perhaps it does not busy itself with significance at all, but simply affords the pleasure that health and humor in themselves are likely to create. Is Chaucer's quality the same thing as sanity after all, in the sense that the term implies the possession of wisdom? And is the humor he shows anything more than the symptom of physical well-being, expressing itself through the instinct of play, restraining him, it may well be, from piercing into those depths of understanding where the tragic note must be heard and high seriousness is perpetually at home?

With some interest in such problems as these I have been reading Chaucer's works for many years, mindful of the advice of a great critic that one must live in the poet's company before one ventures to think one at least partly understands him. Humor there is almost everywhere in his works; I have no doubt of that. But when it comes to a demonstration of the point, the task is supremely difficult. Readers who perceive none here or there will always urge that it is not present, that we are reading things into lines that were meant to be taken at their face value, and doubtless that we are moved by some dark purpose to uncover irony or mirth where none was intended. Concerning the perception of values there can never be argument. Chaucer himself must have found the reader who is lacking in humor particularly hard to manage. Insight into the matter of humor is in any case a delicate faculty, and as it varies from one individual to another so it has differed in intensity from one century to another. In the long history of the appreciation of Chaucer's poetry, as it is spread before us in Miss Spurgeon's *Five Hundred Years of Chaucer Criticism and Allusion,* one may see that understanding of this special feature has been slow in developing. "It is not . . . until well on in the nineteenth century," Miss Spurgeon observes, "not indeed until Leigh Hunt wrote on it in 1846, that Chaucer's humour seems to have met with any adequate recognition." Francis Beaumont, it is true, found the poet "the verie life it selfe of all mirth and pleasant writing," a comment I like to remember. But Samuel Johnson thought the "tale of *The Cock* hardly worth revival," and another eighteenth-century writer regarded it as "foolish, if not worse." They must have assumed, as Addison had written:

> Age has rusted what the *Poet* writ
> Worn out his Language, and obscur'd his Wit:
> In vain he jests in his unpolish'd strain
> And tries to make his Readers laugh in vain.

The *Parliament of Fowls* could survive, I suppose, as a "poet's poem," so to speak; the *Troilus* and the *Knight's Tale* could stand on their feet as straight narrative. Even today there are readers who find the *House of Fame* dull.

Not only in critical writing but in the modernizations one can see the failure to catch the particular flavor of Chaucer's humor. I am not concerned to prove this point, but I may illustrate it by a reference to one of the best modern renderings, written by a poet with exceptional insight. Take the story of Midas in the *Wife of Bath's Tale* and in Dryden's rendering. For my purpose I shall quote only the ending, first as it is in Chaucer. The wife of Midas thus tells her secret:

> "Biwreye me nat, thou water, with thy soun,"
> Quod she; "to thee I telle it and namo;
> Myn housbonde hath longe asses erys two !
> Now is myn herte al hool, now is it oute.
> I myghte no lenger kepe it, out of doute."

D. 974–78

And thus it is rendered by Dryden:

> "To thee alone, O lake," she said, "I tell
> (And, as thy queen, command thee to conceal,)
> Beneath his locks the king my husband wears
> A goodly royal pair of ass's ears:
> Now I have eas'd my bosom of the pain,
> Til the next longing fit return again!"

195–200

Some humor inevitably remains, of course. But the compactness within the line, the pat rhymes, the gasp of relief in the repeated "now," are all missing. Thus in the seventeenth century one had to polish the rough diamond. So Alexander Pope changed what he took from the *House of Fame* for his *Temple*. As Thomas Campbell wrote, "Much of Chaucer's fantastic matter has been judiciously omitted. . . . In Pope, the philosophy of fame comes with much more propriety from the poet himself than from the beak of a talkative eagle." How ill we could spare the bird despite the gain in propriety! With Pope the man of great authority who comes in at the end challenges the dreamer, who concludes the poem with an aspiration:

> "Then teach me, Heav'n! to scorn the guilty bays;
> Drive from my breast that wretched lust of praise;
> Unblemish'd let me live or die unknown;
> Oh, grant an honest fame, or grant me none!"

                                                                521–524

The point is open to dispute, but I am strongly of the opinion that Chaucer's poem, if it was ever completed, did not end that way.

But the question doubtless rises as to what we mean by humor. This we must make clear if ever we are to examine instances in the poet's works and relate our observations to a consideration of his healthy spirit and good sense. It is, I think, based on a sense of incongruity, probably between the transitory and the permanent. This is the essence of Bergson's definition, in the clash he envisages between the mechanical or static and the changing and living. When a man stumbles he may offer a comic appearance; the humor of the episode lies in the incongruity between his normal self as a properly functioning man and the instant interruption of his procedure. We hardly need to decide whether the man is for the moment the victim of the mechanical, or whether such incidents are the result of the play of unreasoning force, which is the evil spirit in Plato's cosmogony. One thing is certain, the effect of the incongruity can hardly be disastrous or humor is replaced by tragic irony. Also it may be insisted that no feeling of superiority is required in the onlooker (though it may indeed be present); humor is allied to the spirit of play.

Fundamentally no doubt the sense of incongruity is based on detachment—perhaps even an awareness of escape—and a sense of proportion; for by a sense of proportion we imply, I think, some insight into the distinction between the transitory and the permanent. By permanent, I hasten to say, we need not mean everlasting or eternal, only that which endures. And the on-looker who perceives the humor of a situation may not only be guiltless of all feeling of superiority but see in a comic episode implications that include appeals to something close to pity and terror. Remember, onlooker, you may stumble, too! *# See lucky it not us!*

But we need not attempt to go deeply into this problem. My purpose here is not primarily philosophical or systematic. I offer these remarks tentatively as I do the observations that follow in the succeeding chapters. We can take pleasure in notic-ing what seems to fall into the class of what is humorous and make many other observations as well. For my hope is really by comment and discussion to reveal more of the meaning of Chaucer than has been perceived hitherto. I have even the desire to find out something more of what the poet himself was like, and certain of the conditions that lay behind the composition of some of his works. In the process I believe there will appear now and then new evidence to support Lowell's dictum, but I am far from intending to write a discourse on the single theme of humor. Much may be turned up in any search by an indirect approach, and in an age when readers inevitably differ on fundamentals aesthetic as well as philosophical, impressionistic criticism is at times our only resource.

Let me not seem, however, to discount a scholarly approach to the subject. Shooting feathered arrows of thought here and there into problems undoubtedly reveals much that is missed by a judicious and logical procedure. But too much has been made of the failure of the scientific method in the field of aesthetics. Especially in the case of writers living in another age than ours, when the language was different and the whole attitude toward writing was on another basis, it is the scholar who has spent long hours training himself in a real sense for Middle English meanings, who has watched the intricacy of borrowing—today we might mistakenly say pilfering—by one poet from another in the process of composition, it is he who can perceive subtle implications in the use of material and who now and then must lead the way in criticism. This is not to maintain that he will always be right in his judgments, but that he has on one side at least a better chance of being right. He knows, let us say, how Deschamps used a theme in one of his works, and thus he catches overtones when he finds Chaucer putting the same ideas in a very different context. In a masterly way Professor Lowes showed the connotation of the phrases in the description of the Prioress which the English poet took from the *Roman de la Rose* and the poetry of Courtly Love. Let me quote from his remarks regarding her smile "simple and coy": There, in the second line, is struck the keynote of the description. The convention didn't belong to the nun at all, as nun. To every one of Chaucer's readers its distinctly earthly rather than heavenly flavor was unmistakable. Moreover the real student will not be misled by modern developments of the word "coy" into thinking that it suggests the affectedly demure.

Such an obvious instance of the scholar's advantage is necessary to cite in view of the fact that he is often suspect the moment he steps out of his role as the hunter of literary sources or the cataloguer of grammatical forms. It was by Mr. Lowes's tireless pursuit of the phrase "simple and coy" in line after line of poetry that he perceived its background and its redolent association. In a fashion almost parallel Mr. Kittredge's study of the *Book of the Duchess* and its French sources enabled him to see that it is French to the fingertips and at the same time highly original: "For Chaucer uses his borrowings with the power of a master, and nowhere in the poem does his originality appear more strikingly than in the description of the Duchess Blanche,— the very place where his indebtedness is most conspicuous." Now we may recall that this description is presumably a portrait and that in this collection, mostly of borrowed lines, fourteenth-century readers could see the lady's actual features. It is an astounding fact, but one that only the scholar could have made clear. Of the poem Mr. Kittredge further remarks: "Never was there a more conventional situation—a dream, a paradise of trees and flowers and birds, a lamenting lover, an incomparable lady. We who wander through the middle ages have seen and heard it all a hundred times." Yes, we may reflect, but it took much thoughtful wandering before these observations could be made. It signifies all the more that years of such study have preceded the conclusions here and elsewhere enunciated in Dr. Kittredge's essay, as he restores the poem to its proper place of dignity in criticism. He is able to detect the conventional by comparison with other poetry of the kind, and he can also indicate in what way "the conventions are [here] vitalized."

One reason why Lowell's essay is to-day commonly unread is that, despite its own delightful quality of freshness, a quality it has assimilated from Chaucer, much of it has passed into common property and is no longer new. Another reason is that in certain points it seems mistaken, as when Lowell observed, ". . . for I think it a great mistake to attribute to [Chaucer] any properly dramatic power, as some have done." But certainly still another reason is that its scholarship is out of date. I am reminded of William Hazlitt's error as he writes: "One of the finest parts of Chaucer is of this mixed kind. It is the beginning of the *Flower and the Leaf*, where he describes the delight of that young beauty, shrowded in her bower, and listening, in the morning of the year, to the singing of the nightingale. . . ." But we now know that he did not write the *Flower and the Leaf.* Isaac Disraeli quotes with approval the statement that "of all poets, Chaucer seems to have been fondest of the singing of birds." But first we must know whether the lines attributed to him about birds are genuinely his. And, if so, did he coldly take them over for reasons that have little to do with their song? For they are found in almost countless passages describing nature; as a student, who has investigated medieval accounts of the seasons, laments: ". . . one cannot hope to be exhaustive when one deals with centuries of 'singing birds.'" The critic is dependent on the scholar and facts must be tested before inferences are made. Thus Disraeli writes: "It was behind the bars of a gloomy window in the Tower . . . that Chaucer, recent from exile and sore from persecution, was reminded of a work popular in those days, and which had been composed in a dungeon,—'The Consolations of Philosophy,' by Boethius. . . . He composed his 'Testament of Love,' substituting for the severity of an abstract being the more genial inspiration of love itself." But, again we are now quite certain that this work was not his, and the discovery of its true authorship was made in time for Lowell to say: "We are thankful that Chaucer's shoulders are finally discharged of that weary load, 'The Testament.'"

But it would be churlish not to recognize the gifts of the critic and merely to list examples of this kind. I simply want to urge that the most valid criticism of at least the older poets will come, to be sure, from one who has an insight into aesthetic values but also from one who has gone through some of the process followed by the scholar. If this provision is allowed, impressionistic criticism is still possible on its own terms. Yet it will be somewhat affected in its procedure—for it should take account not only of the impression a work of art makes on its modern readers but of that which it was intended to make on readers at any time, and here again scholarship will have something to say. Indeed the result will be similar to judicial criticism if the judgments, the prejudices, the principles of the writer, are examined with reference to what he does. While the reader may not share the philosophy of the poet, he must include it in his consideration of artistic values, or he will miss important elements in that emotional pattern which the poet has designed. If he finds fault with the philosophy because it is shallow, he may seem to have left the realm of aesthetic criticism; but his aim quite justly may be to show its weakness in comparison with some other which would have a richer emotional and thus artistic content. For example, he may complain if a writer is so romantic as to set forth only what is remote from life and experience, since an art so little realistic is not the one to move the reader most profoundly in terms of his own experience. If the critic, following Longinus, searches for the "great thoughts" which are the mark of the sublime, he must at some time ponder over the problem of what characterizes the greatness of the thought.

But when a critic thus takes account of something other than mere texture and pigment, if he drags in philosophy and morals, he incurs the risk at once of being denounced as academic. He will probably slip at times into the use of technical expressions. He may at times be systematic and even conscientious. He can reply, of course, that in all such aberrations his purpose is no worse than to illuminate and reveal, but even then he will be regarded with distrust. The Host on the pilgrimage to Canterbury felt he must warn the Clerk:

> "Youre termes, youre colours, and youre figures,
> Keepe hem in stoor til so be that ye endite
> Heigh style, as whan that men to kynges write."

E. 16–18

I think there is a shot here at all fine writing. The only obvious remedy is to avoid the logic of the monograph, and to adopt a method less direct and more casual. This will be an advantage to anyone who sets out to investigate the poet's humor; for such a task involves special difficulties of its own. In being systematic about that a scholar can be far too funny for what he is trying to do, without uncovering the full humor of the original. It is hard to prove that at least a smile is hidden where none has been seen before. It is safer to disclaim the intention of dealing with the subject at all, or at any rate to make it only a subordinate consideration.

I still admire Professor Saintsbury's comments on certain aspects of this "all-pervading" quality in Chaucer. It is one, he quickly and I think cautiously adds, "which some, even of those who enjoy it heartily and extol it generously, do not quite invariably seem to comprehend." He alludes to some readers who seem "destitute of the sense itself." This humor, he continues, "'works i' the earth so fast' that you never can tell at what moment it will find utterance. . . . It is by no means certain that in [Chaucer's] displays of learning he is not mocking or parodying others as well as relieving himself. It is by no means certain that, seriously as we know him to have been interested in astronomy, his frequent astronomical or astrological lucubrations are not partly ironical. . . . His good humour is even more pervading. It gives a memorable distinction of kindliness between *The Wife of Bath's Prologue* and the brilliant following of it by Dunbar in *The Tua Mariit Wemen and the Wedo*; and it even separates Chaucer from such later humorists as Addison and Jane Austen, who, though never savage, can be politely cruel. Cruelty and Chaucer are absolute strangers. . . ." Well, in the sense that Addison and Jane Austen showed their finesse, I am not so sure whether Chaucer's satire was any less mordant. What about the Pardoner and the Merchant in their own stories? But I am now chiefly interested in Mr. Saintsbury's fear that not all readers will find the quality of humor where he does, and that he must expound it for the unseeing. This I fancy is a hopeless undertaking; all that can be done is for those who agree in perceiving it here and there to rejoice together. Disquisitions must be left for more serious business.

Some years ago, when the date of the poet's birth was much discussed, passages in his works which happen to refer to his age were brought forward as evidence that when he wrote a certain poem he was so and so many years old. Thus in the *House of Fame* we read the challenge of the talkative eagle:

> "Wilt thou lere of sterre saught?"
> "Nay, certeynly," quod y, "ryght naught."
> "And why?" "For y am now to old."

993–95

And critics who dated the poem not later than 1386, and perhaps ten years earlier, asked themselves whether the poet if born as late as 1340 or 1346 could have regarded himself as too old at forty-six (or less) to hear something about astronomy. The medieval attitude toward age was studied, and parallels adduced to prove that in those days a man was regarded as old from forty on. But perhaps this poem was written when Chaucer was much younger than that—even at the age of thirty-five, at the prime of life the poet would say and "nel mezzo del cammin di nostra vita" others might urge. Even then there would be point; for in his reply the eagle's victim is only trying to shut off the long edifying discourse to which he has had to listen. And the bird shows his disappointment when he goes on:

> "Elles I wolde the have told,"
> Quod he, "the sterres names, lo,
> And al the hevenes sygnes therto
> And which they ben." "No fors," quod y.

996–99

The eagle manages to accomplish some of this all the same, and Chaucer cannot stop him entirely. The bird shows the pride in his learning that the Canon's Yeoman feels in his knowledge of alchemy, and pours it out with a similar zest. There is no reason at all to look for evidence of the poet's age here unless we choose to miss another point. But there is reason here to suspect that Chaucer saw the humor of a display of this kind, just as he did in the case of Chantecler (Chantecleer) and Pertelote. While it is difficult to prove this interpretation, it is nonetheless important not to miss it lest we suppose that the poet wore his own learning simply as a badge of honor.

But the skeptical may well ask why, if humor was so long in coming to its fruition, as we infer from Miss Spurgeon's survey of Chaucer criticism, there is any likelihood that it flourished or was understood in the fourteenth century. Would the poet, no matter how well endowed himself with this faculty, write in terms which his audience or readers of his own time could not possibly appreciate or grasp? Yet there is no possible doubt that humor, irony, wit, and satire were widely understood and relished in the Middle Ages. The animal epics show it; the student songs have now one now another of these qualities; the development of comedy leading to the *Second Shepherds' Play* of the Towneley Cycle proves the point; wit and sometimes even humor touch the allegories of the Court of Love, as, for instance, in the Church service of the birds in Jean de Conde's *Messe des Oisiaus.* Chaucer's contemporaries, Gower and Lydgate, were not strong in this type of appeal, that is certain; but there is a touch in the *Tale of Florent* and something more in *Bycorne and Chichevache.* Chaucer got some of his material in this vein from Deschamps. His Envoys to Scogan and to Bukton and to Sir Philip la Vache show that there were some people to enjoy his subtlety. I think his reference to Gower in the Introduction to the *Man of Law's Tale,* when he says that he himself never wrote of Canacee (of such cursed stories he says fie!), and his allusion to moral Gower at the end of the *Troilus,* were both meant to be humorous (or something like it) for others than just himself. He makes fun of others as he makes fun of himself, and he gives every impression that his fun was meant to be shared. How high the general average of humor was in the period he wrote, it is hardly possible to determine here. Yet considering the elements in Chaucer's works which are generally accepted as humorous in purpose, we may say that the poet found a contemporary spirit that prompted him to the full expression of this talent, and an assurance in his world that his fullest inspiration in this sort of writing would meet a response. It remains to inquire whether the highest type of appeal can ever be made in writing of this sort. Even today there are readers who regard humor as trivial, as if comedy must always be an interlude, and mirth a little lower than the dignity of the angels; we have it on high authority that jesting and foolish talking are sometimes inconvenient. Chaucer can reach the heights in realism, yes, and, if he can step elegantly enough, in the romantic; but can the sublime be achieved through humor? To answer this question at once we have only to recall the great examples. I have said that humor implies a sense of harmless incongruity between the transitory and the permanent, and this whatever its overtones is found in the scene of the knocking at the gate in *Macbeth*. For many this scene long had nothing better than the meaning of the irrelevant. But in a subtle way that is its very point. DeQuincey taught criticism its deeper meaning, the incongruity lodged in the porter's silly speech contrasted with the knocking of a world demanding admittance to tragedy. While the episode as a whole has its own grim irony, the porter's speech is harmless enough; by its use the humor is lifted to sublimity. Or if it be maintained that by this process the humor is transmuted into something else, there is always the scene of Falstaff and Hal, where the Prince issues his challenge. The Hostess has quoted the rascal's boast that the Prince owes him a thousand pounds:

> *Prince.:* Sirrah, do I owe you a thousand pound?
> *Falstaff:* A thousand pound, Hal? A million!
> Thy love is worth a million; thou owest me thy love.
>
> *I Henry the Fourth*, III, iii, 153–157

Wit there is here in the quick turn no doubt, and pathos as well, but they serve the dominant humor. It is to this expression of love between the two great characters that the later rebuke emotionally points back, when Hal says: "I know thee not, old man. Fall to thy prayers." (*II Henry the Fourth*, V, v, 51)

In fact, I find that the sublime may be achieved in humor in various ways. In such illustrations as those just considered it is mainly in terms of human character. The same is true with *Don Quixote* perhaps; together with wit this is what we find in most satiric writing. The weaknesses or the deeps of human nature are made visible, and the operation is effected with less pain than with tragedy. The range of opportunity, all the way from grossness to the intellectual laughter of high comedy, follows the infinite variety of human nature itself. But there is another kind of sublimity in humor, which is familiar with authors who put the emphasis elsewhere. I find it in Moliere, who is witty and ironic and also humorous, as in the famous scene when Monsieur Jourdain is provoked to observe that his opponent does not fence according to the rules: ". . . tu me pousses en tierce avant que de pousser en quarte, et tu n'as pas la patience que je pare" (*Le Bourgeois Gentilhomme,* III, iii) I find it even more where Mme. Jourdain rebukes her husband for cultivating the nobility, and he replies: "Lors que je hante la noblesse, je fais paroitre mon jugement; et cela est plus beau que de hanter vostre bourgeoisie." Here, I think, we find the dramatist likes his leading character for the moment. But the predominating interest of Moliere, I think, is less in the values of human nature which he displays than in the situations and indeed the forces that serve to expose them. This possibly is just another way of saying that as an artist he seeks to produce his effect chiefly in his design; he cares more about the pattern than the elements of emotion and human character that compose it. Unlike Shakespeare, who in Falstaff shows many kinds of traits, Moliere strings his characteristics on one thread: the avaricious, the hypocrite, and so on. The universality implicit in this concern is a step removed from that which has to do with the general significance of human nature itself; it deals rather with elements in some kind of cosmic plan that discovers human beings to one another or to themselves.

There is, however, at least another kind of sublime humor, and this is more difficult to describe. It is, I believe, the particular quality of the poet whose imagination at once expresses itself symbolically, in a rich profusion of figures of speech dramatically personified or set forth in allegory because literal statement is inadequate. Its stuff, of course, is ultimately human nature and ordinary experience, but transformed into poetry by the intensity of the artist's insight into abstract meanings. This may be found in Aristophanes, in *The Frogs* for example; it also appears in Bottom's translation in *A Midsummer Night's Dream*. It furnishes exquisite notes to *The Tempest* in the person of Caliban as well as in that of Ariel; the whole play, in fact, may be said to be on this level. I can imagine the claim made with good reason that in humor of this type there is something mystical; occasionally its overtones are without doubt celestial. But the mystical may also be present in that of the first and second types. Sufficient belief in the magnificence of human nature (apart entirely from the problem of whether it is fallen from grace, which is another matter) will radiate this quality in humor of the first type. In Moliere's comedy the power of life to reveal implies something of almost the same illumination.

But perhaps I must revert to the question whether it is the humor in the instances I have cited which is in itself exalted. The argument on that score I am afraid must depend on the extent to which the reader feels its power. Arnold could not find high seriousness in Chaucer. He has been answered with references to the Epilogue of the *Troilus*, but another critic has shrewdly pointed to part of the speech of the Wife of Bath about herself. Let me quote it:

> But, Lord Crist! whan that it remembreth me
> Upon my yowthe, and on my jolitee,
> It tikleth me aboute myn herte roote.
> Unto this day it dooth myn herte boote
> That I have had my world as in my tyme.
> But age, allas! that al wole envenyme,
> Hath me biraft my beautee and my pith.
> Lat go, farewel! the devel go therwith!
> The flour is goon, ther is namoore to telle,
> The bren, as I best kan, now moste I selle;
> But yet to be right myrie wol I fonde.
> Now wol I tellen of my fourthe housbonde.

D.469–480.

"The positive quality of such a passage as this," wrote Professor Neilson, "its vividness, its zest, its penetration to the very marrow of life, and the informing of every phrase and accent with vital energy, have much more to do with the production of a highly exalted poetic enjoyment than seriousness of treatment or theme." No, sublimity is not a matter of solemnity but rather of vitality, of life itself in its fullness and with all the disturbing implications that accompany it. Religious pictures may or may not show it in the greatest abundance; it may appear also in Rembrandt, or, say, in the smiling cavalier of Franz Hals.

So far in the discussion I have used the word "humor" in the modern sense without apology. But some student, who remembers the old physiology with its humors, or its temperaments based on one or another of these, and who is aware of the sense of the word in the title of certain of Jonson's plays, may reproach me with ambiguity. It is now relevant to point out how this expression, when it assumed anything like the modern meaning, had special reference to human character. One probably thinks of the old use of the term when one reads again the description of the Canterbury pilgrims, although immediately their richness of temperament, their power to escape classification in this way, will strike the analyst. A sense of the incongruity in certain elements of human nature is, I suspect, the first and most elementary form of humor among the types that I have been discussing. The second and third types are more sophisticated, perhaps the production of a fuller insight into life, perhaps only that of a greater creative power of expression. The first, few would deny, is often found in Chaucer. Commenting on the more earthy passages in the *Canterbury Tales,* Mr. de Selincourt suggests "that if such things are comic they are only comic from a sense of incongruity, and that their whole humour depends ultimately upon that ideal which they seem to travesty or to outrage," and further ". . . the Wife of Bath's philosophy of life is only amusing to you insofar as you do not share it." Here the perception of the distinction between the transitory and the permanent is plain enough, and the suggestion has its value. But I would urge that the humor consists less in the outraged ideal than in the spectacle of human nature as we know it and in part share it. We do not feel the humor of these pilgrims in so far as they are unlike us; on the contrary we have a bond in our common weaknesses. This is not to say, I hasten to add, that these weaknesses, though they make the whole world kin, must in every way or at all times possess us. But I think we enter most fully into the play when we know them from experience, and when we feel perhaps a kind of personal release we have longed for in the blunder or exposure or slip of someone besides ourselves. Does not Freud suggest something of the sort in his explanation of laughter? There can be no doubt that what Chaucer represents is an assortment of traits characteristic of mankind at large.

But does he show any other sort of humor? As the question is put I find the shadow of academic halls upon me, and I confess it irks me and hampers speech. I cannot list the types of humor again and catalogue instances. Some day when the technique of science has revealed all the truth available in literature, this will be done. All possible types of humor will be set down and the examples subjoined in proper and graded order, and one can then turn to the special case one desires or see in the graphical outline appended the general trend of development. We shall be able to prove perhaps that when Chaucer left the Custom House his humor increased for a season, or again that the daily pitcher of wine awarded to him served more to sadden than to cheer. On the other hand, it may be evident that when his verse was at its merriest he was most bored with life. But I cannot offer a contribution to such a study except by the attempt to make his meaning clearer or to suggest certain qualities in his nature or to say what I suppose to be his intention here and there. If these remarks are modified by readers who come closer to that great and pleasant genius, I can only be the happier. For, as everyone will agree, it is more important to know what Chaucer meant than it is to enjoy what the critic says.

NOTES

*Reprinted with permission from *On Rereading Chaucer*, Cambridge, Mass.: Harvard University Press, 1939, 1967.

Excerpt from *Chaucer**

G. K. Chesterton

And the greatest of [Chaucer's virtues] is something that neither Puritanism nor the Public School has contrived to kill; he is generally fond of a joke. His great national contribution to the culture of Christendom has been that quality. It is the English sense of humour, like the Spanish sense of honour or the French sense of right reason. It is true that a certain sort of pompous ass like Sir Willoughby Patterne or Mr. Dombey has been exhibited as an Englishman; but he has generally been exhibited by Englishmen. Podsnap would not have been so absurdly English, if Dickens had not been an Englishman. True, there is only one Dickens, but there are a million Dickensians; a great many more Dickensians than there are Podsnaps. On the whole, the prevailing spirit of the English is an appreciation of this sort of fun, especially when it broadens into farce. Indeed, when it is properly understood, there is something in it that breaks out beyond the limits of mere farce, and becomes a sort of poetry of pantomime; a climax of anti-climax. Dickens is full of wild images that would be nothing if they were not funny. They would be not merely nonsensical but non-existent, if they were not (I say it with some firmness) so damned funny. Mrs. Todgers's wooden leg; Mr. Swiveller's gazelle who married a market-gardener; the toothpick of the gentleman next door, which if sent to the Commander-in-Chief would produce some marked results; the effect of Henry the Eighth's little peepy eyes on Mrs. Skewton's view of history; these are things that would simply cease to exist in a really rational universe. They are not symbolic; they are not really satiric. They are upheld by an invisible power and lifted without support upon the wings of laughter; by a power more unanswerable and more irresponsible than pure beauty.

Now compared with the fun of Dickens, there is certainly something altogether shrewd, sensible and solid about the humour of Chaucer. He was, as has been said already, only the seed of that separate growth; but it was growing separate and it was soon to be growing wild. We shall note elsewhere the way in which the medieval common sense of Chaucer differs from the almost maniac laughter we sometimes hear from the Elizabethans, even from Shakespeare. But for all that a frontier had been crossed, and there is already in Chaucer an element of irrational humour, which is not the same as the old rational humour. The old humour had been a form of satire. Chaucer often sounds satirical; yet Chaucer was not strictly a satirist. Perhaps the shortest way of putting it is to say that he already inhabits a world of comicality that is not a world of controversy. He makes fun of people, in the exact sense of getting fun out of them for himself. He does not make game of them, in the actual sense of hunting them down and killing them like wild vermin or public pests. He does not want the Friar and the Wife of Bath to perish; one would sometimes suspect that he does not really want them to change. Anyhow, a softening element of this sort has got into his satire, even if he really meant it for satire. But, with this step, he is already on the road to the Dickensian lunatic-asylum of laughter; because he is valuing his fools and knaves and almost wishing (as it were) to preserve them in spirits—in high spirits. In a hundred other ways his humour is English, and not least in this, that he often uses flippancy to avoid an argument and not to provoke it.

NOTES

*Reprinted from *Chaucer*, New York: Pellegrini and Cudahy, 1949, pp. 197–99.

A Vocabulary for Chaucerian Comedy
A Preliminary Sketch*

Paul G. Ruggiers

I am attempting in this essay to lay out a vocabulary for handling the complex subject of comedy in Chaucer. I have leaned heavily on Aristotle's definitions of character in the *Nicomachean Ethics* and the *Rhetoric*, upon the *Coislinian Tractate*, and upon Lane Cooper's attempt to recreate an Aristotelian theory of comedy.[1] It has been fairly clear that we are generally more comfortable with the vocabulary for romance and tragedy than we have been for comedy, perhaps because of formalistic tendencies in these modes of experience and because there has been a more definable tradition for them. I have wedded several schemes: one a series of headings under general rubrics representing the categories needing illustrations; another system resulting from Aristotle's suggestion in the *Rhetoric* about the sources of laughter, and finally, a series of topics borrowed from the *Coislinian Tractate*.

I will restrict my discussion mainly to considerations of plot and character,[2] trying to avoid the complicated question of Chaucer's ironical point of view regarding the human condition, and avoiding as much as possible considerations of the larger movement of the *Canterbury Tales* as a whole, the placement of the tales in the frame, and the relations between tellers and tales.

Much of what we suggest here will seem obvious to sensitive readers of Chaucer; it seems justifiable on the grounds that definition of the terms of comic technique for Chaucer is sparse and that such an attempt as this one may serve to point up areas of research for others. If it does nothing more than to demonstrate that there is a universal language of comedy and that there are affinities between comic writers of any age, then nothing will have been lost. There is always a danger that a theory of comedy will aridify the subject more than can be justified. In all classification there is the inherent sin of imposing system upon art and therefore of making that art appear mechanical. Clearly no system can do justice to any of the great geniuses of comic writing, their wit and irony, the special flavor of license, their power to challenge staid opinion, that peculiar innocence that allows them to escape defilement even in the relating of the obscene. This said, let us move on.

The Problem of Definition

There are certain critics who believe that it is not possible to define comedy on the ground that no definition will in any way illuminate our experience of it. There is not much point in repeating the terms of the debate. Yet, Chaucerian comedy, which everyone takes for granted, rarely finds its way into discussions of comedy, the omission being explained away on the ground that theory of comedy is mostly dramatic anyway. What, in fact, is there to explain? Accepting the tradition of the comic tale, what are the criteria by which to understand it? And what tales in Chaucer's canon shall we generalize from?

If we set aside the prose tales, the saints' lives (*Man of Law's Tale, Clerk's Tale, Prioress' Tale, Second Nun's Tale*), the clear romances (*Knight's Tale, Squire's Tale, Franklin's Tale*, though the latter qualifies as comic in some of its elements, and the *Wife of Bath's Tale*, a romance with strong comic infusions that need to be taken into account) what remain are comic structures of one sort or another: the *Miller's Tale, Reeve's Tale, Cook's Tale, Shipman's Tale, Merchant's Tale, Friar's Tale, Summoner's Tale, Canon's Yeoman's Tale* and the *Pardoner's Tale*. To these we must add the *Nun's Priest's Tale* and *Sir Thopas* as burlesque or parody, and the *Wife of Bath's Tale* as a mixed form. Obviously these are not all the same kind of structure; laughter is not the key to all of them. Some of them are more "serious" than others, having weight given them by the presence of thought-provoking matter in them; some seem lighthearted, others manage to convey either by their position in the *Canterbury Tales* or their assignment to their narrator certain unpleasant levels of emotion.

The definition of comedy given to the Knight, the result of a long historical tradition going back to Theophrastus, developed simultaneously with tragedy as an action beginning in misery and ending in prosperity.[3]

> As whan a man hath been in povre estaat,
> And clymbeth up and wexeth fortunat,
> And there abideth in prosperitee.
> Swich thyng is gladsom, as it thynketh me. . . .

> (II.3965–3968)

The definition leaves something to be desired. No one can object to the general term "gladsom"; it implies an entire attitude towards experience—one intends something to be received as happy; or to put it another way, one is predisposed by clues of character, tone, ambiance, and language to accept the view of experience as nonserious, to see the good things of life trivialized.[4]

The definition is thus useful largely as making a simple distinction between what is basically serious and nonserious, weighty and lightsome. But the definition as given does not fit Chaucer's practice entirely, as we may see from a consideration of the closures of his tales: A protagonist outwits an adversary, arriving at a curious stalemate in the *Nun's Priest's Tale*; a lover triumphs at the expense of another and with considerable pain to himself in the *Miller's Tale*; the most likable character of the *Shipman's Tale* remains duped at the close, and though the wife triumphs, she too has been duped. The summoner of the *Friar's Tale* is carried off to perdition; the rioters of the *Pardoner's Tale* are damned in their own self-annihilating way; the long complications of the *Canon's Yeoman's Tale* must be seen in the context of a losing art; and the knight of the

Merchant's Tale is blind and deceived, even with eyesight. In short the definition can be made to apply only by expansion of its basic terms into considerations of tone, character, and plot; I question whether we find Chaucer's comic tales uniformly "happy" except in their total effect of producing in the audience or reader the general sense that the ending "should be so."

Plot

We will make a distinction at the outset that is obvious to everyone but needs to be set forth early: (a) Half of the comic tales are about conflicts in which the reprisal is a sexual triumph over a conventional, older person. Of these tales, i.e., those of the Miller, Reeve, Merchant, and Shipman, only the *Shipman's Tale* does not tell us about the relative ages of the agents except to imply by the age of the Monk the general age of all; (b) Half of the tales, those of the Friar, Pardoner, Summoner, and Canon's Yeoman, are nonsexual tales, comedies without lighthearted humor; these are, more frankly, unmaskings. They each have some quality of the sinister about them that raises ethical considerations in a way that the first group does not; they describe ugly actions in the process of raising questions about the kind of society that allows them. They are comedies that frankly face up to human concerns: good and evil, life and death. The comedies about adultery, it should be pointed out, may also raise criticisms of a society that tolerates the marriage of youth and age; the *Shipman's Tale*, for example, or the *Merchant's Tale*, both have the capacity to challenge us at levels we have not anticipated. Seriousness is always an implied quality in Chaucerian comedy.

In both types of comedy, the whole tendency of Chaucerian comedy is to move from an old law, stated at the outset (usually as an enchaining marriage or family order in the tales of the Miller, Reeve, Merchant, and Shipman), to a wily escape from its bondage into momentary freedom from its constraints; or in the darker comedies (those of the Friar, the Summoner, the Pardoner, and the Canon's Yeoman's Introduction) to tear away illusion and hypocrisy by building the *agon*, not around the opposition of youth and age, but around demonstrations of conspiratorial behavior destined to be exposed as hypocritical, thievish, or mendacious.

These two types are quite different in their emphasis, the first kind being aimed largely at giving satisfaction through cleverly arranged episodes, suspense, and a sense of something being carefully nudged toward surprise and an unexpected conflation of happenings, like the episode of the misplaced cradle in the *Reeve's Tale*, or the cry of "water, water" in the *Miller's Tale*, which tops all previous surprises. The closing barrage of puns at the conclusion of the *Shipman's Tale* enables the level of comic statement to soar immediately into the dimensions of verbal wit.

In the second kind of tale, (those of Friar, Summoner, Pardoner, and Canon's Yeoman), the emphasis is largely upon describing the ethos of a society or group: something more communal, perhaps a community of demon types, mostly hypocrites and liars, persons wearing masks of one sort or another, who are either exposed or destroyed. In the *Pardoner's Tale*, for example, in the enveloping sermon a scapegoat is made by his own words to unmask himself and to undergo the threat of expulsion (only to be restored in Chaucer's comic generosity); and similarly in the exemplum, the three rioters, one of whom serves as a scapegoat, get what they deserve, being shown as thieves and murderers. It might be noted that the figure of a scapegoat may make for pathos—a mood that Chaucer manages to avoid here—which can destroy the comic tone if carried too far.[5]

In at least two of the tales, the *Friar's Tale* and the Pardoner's exemplum, where the intention is clearly preacherly, the thematic statement is overtly moral and self-righteous; and there is also an elevated moral appendage to the *Canon's Yeoman's Tale* which somewhat distresses a purely comic impulse.

The distinction that may be made between the two kinds of comic structures has to do with a deeper, more serious view of things, a willingness to make comparison between higher and lower norms in the manner of satire and irony. Both types of tales yield their special satisfactions: the closed garden of the

Merchant's Tale has been successfully invaded, the upward mobility of the Reeve's snobbish family has been damaged, the
unwise marriage of unlikes in the *Miller's* and *Merchant's* tales
has been given its "just" due and the guileless simplicity of the
merchant of the *Shipman's Tale* has been confirmed (but he
seems no worse off than before; the other characters seem
faintly shameful). In the others, perhaps because of their
stronger moral and social concerns, the satisfaction derives from
seeing conventions, theological and moral, vindicated.

A writer who vindicates or defends piously held beliefs
is writing comedies of a limited range; but they are not to be
dispraised for being so. For the Christian poet, stripping off the
disguises and masks of villainy precisely in terms of religiously
defined norms and writing comedies about damnation demonstrates that comedy may derive its materials from anywhere;
attitude and tone are all. And obviously comedy does not exclude suffering; it makes capital of it but uses it for its own ends
and with the right tone and attitude.

These two broad types of comedic structures in Chaucer
thus confirm that double perspective which is implicit in comedy generally. One cannot know the merely existing without
testing it against essence, the factual without the ideal, the
life of instinct without the life of reason, body without soul.
The norms which are vindicated in Chaucer's comedies about
adultery are clearly those of nature; in the others, the tension
is clearer in terms of good and evil men and women. Chaucer
does not pretend that his protagonists are not bad men and
women; they are shown to be so, and one has the feeling that
their predictable destruction has been part of a larger justification of law.

Chance, trickery, and improbable possibilities may be
the laws of the first kind or comedies; from the perspective of
the other type, these laws dwindle before an inexorable law. In
the first type, things turn out well for the agents; in the second,
for the audience.

I do not know whether Chaucer's comic structures can be
placed on any scale. Irony of various sorts invests them all. But
of the tales of license and the "adultery" tales, the *Miller's
Tale* is the "happiest," the *Reeve's Tale* less so, because the

somewhat morose and dispeptic disposition of the miller of the tale tends to cast a large shadow over the action; and he has something of the humor about him. The *Shipman's Tale* even less so, perhaps because of the age of the persons involved: they should not behave so lightheartedly, or perhaps we feel that in the tale nothing is held sacred. They are lightweight alongside the *Merchant's Tale*'s somewhat more grandiose style and manner. Essentially, in formal ways they are the same; but they are all different in tone, in characterization, in kind of structure, and in the amount of the serious that has been added to the plot.

The others are ironic-comedies, built around the basic theme of unmasking. In these it is society at large that has profited from the unmasking. If the villains will not mend their ways, then they must go. And their going is justified when we consider the demonic values which they had hoped to impose upon the world. In the outer frame, the Pardoner and the Yeoman stay, the Canon goes; in the tales, the friar is carried off to hell; the rioters die.

Chaucer's range is considerable in its effects: there are tales in which considerations of moral responsibility are totally absent; others in which the question of rightness and wrongness somehow springs into our minds (*Shipman's Tale*—at least it disturbed earlier generations of scholars); still others in which the agents are frankly described as bad persons and so are calculated to rouse feelings of indignation in us.

Some Elements of Plot

Complex Plot: Discoveries and Reversals

In Aristotle's sense, Chaucer's comedies are generally complex; they are actions attended by discoveries and reversals of fortune arising from the structure of the plots. But the plots themselves are built up out of ludicrous incidents upon which the discoveries and reversals depend. Prime examples are afforded by the *Miller's Tale*'s clever alternations of success and failure for Absolon and Nicholas, the deception of Absolon at the window on two occasions and his carrying out of revenge; the swift discoveries and reversals for Absolon and the reversal of fortune for Nicholas when he is smitten by the coulter afford three obvious instances in which laughter is elicited by ridiculous actions. The conclusion of the tale, in which the old husband, fallen and injured, fails to gain an audience for his side of the story, is also a major reversal. In the *Reeve's Tale*, the loosing of the horse leads to a major reversal for the young students; and the positioning of the baby's cradle leads to a series of discoveries (by false inference) and reversals of fortune for the various agents. Similarly, in the *Shipman's Tale*, the wife's fortunes are threatened with a reversal from good to bad fortune when her husband inadvertently reveals to her that she has been duped by the monk; her quick wit produces a reversal for the better, and a threatened continued bad fortune for the unwitting husband.

Comic Incidents

Such discoveries and reversals are part and parcel of absurd or comic incidents: a blind man suddenly regains his eyesight and sees his wife in a tree with her lover; a would-be lover is deceived into kissing his love's nether eye and on a subsequent occasion is farted upon by her lover; a young student, thinking he is getting into bed with his fellow student, gets into bed with the father of the girl he has just swived; a wife bargains her body for quick money from a monk which he subsequently borrows from her husband; a summoner and a demon each demonstrate separately what is legitimate prey, each incident being attended by its own discoveries and reversals of fortune; a friar has his hand farted upon; three rioters find gold and in the process find death; a feckless, gullible priest participates in successful experiments to make silver; a rooster-hero "sings" for his enemy. These are of course only the major incidents from the tales, attended by discoveries and reversals of fortune. There are others.

Seriousness and Cognition

Though Chaucer divides his work into serious and nonserious forms, he has the often-noted tendency to inject serious elements into comic forms as well as the opposite tendency to make jests within the romances. It should not be surprising to discover that Chaucer's comedies always contain something serious against which we measure the absurd. The *Miller's Tale* has its parody of romance, its biblical allusions; the *Reeve's Tale* has its gnomic wisdom, etc. As many critics have noted, everything in a comedy need not be laughable. But what is serious in Chaucer's tales enables us to see the themes in the largest context; we "learn" something in the evolution of the plot, and the cognition confirms what is pleasant to us. Although the *Tractate* states that comedy "has laughter as its mother," serious cognition may transcend the laughter, as in the *Nun's Priest's Tale*, where one has the sense of a sublime Presence laughing at the follies of mankind, and before which mankind shrinks to smallest dimensions; or as in the *Franklin's Tale* where one has a sense of swirling upward out of the confines of a romance into the loving and indulgent view of the human condition, a view that escapes from the latitudes of mere comedy into those of a high moral stance.

Too, some of Chaucer's comedies are "dark" comedies, in which the comic retreats from lightheartedness before the weight of truly serious considerations. The *Merchant's Tale*, *Franklin's Tale*, *Pardoner's Tale*, and even the *Summoner's Tale* with its horrid exempla of power casually used, have the capacity to adduce serious matters for the sake of making heavier kinds of statement. The theology of marriage, the relation of penance to salvation, considerations of destiny, and the betrayal of kindness may all be seen as various levels of serious thematic statement throughout the entire gamut of Chaucerian comedy.

Suffering

In Chaucerian comedy we may expect elements of suffering, either physical or mental, but offered to us in such manner that it will seem ludicrous; or we will not be overly conscious of the pain or ugliness of the situation because of the tone of presentation. The comic tales have a large share of violence, suffering, and discomfiture: broken arms, threats of death, burnings, assaults, beatings, blindness, and mental anguish; all demonstrate that comedy uses what may seem at first glance to be matter not suited to it. Obviously they are not dealt with seriously but are seen as arising out of causes and situations that are established in various ways as comic. Absolon is chagrined and discomfited after the fateful kiss; the merchant's wife in the *Shipman's Tale* has a shock of surprised indignation from which she quickly recovers; and the worse physical effects, the old husband's broken arm in the *Miller's Tale*, the beaten pate in the *Reeve's Tale*, and the threat of death in the *Nun's Priest's Tale*, are treated lightly. Generally husbands remain deceived; the deceivers go free.

In the *Friar's Tale* and the exemplum of the Pardoner, their cautionary preacher's gambit makes death and damnation highly desirable; our satisfaction arises as much from the fate meted out as from the surprise and wonder in watching the plot work out to its conclusion.

Agon

The comic *agon* has been a comic necessity since at least the time of Aristophanes, as a balance to the phallic element which is the "other" content of comedy generally. Though all the tales have an *agon* in the generalized opposition of the main agents of the story, there are several instances of a proposition being debated in the "classical" way: Justinus and Placebo in the *Merchant's Tale* take the sides respectively of the old and new law; Chauntecleer and Pertelote in the *Nun's Priest's Tale* debate the truth of dreams; the old hag of the *Wife of Bath's Tale*, to become more general, offers arguments against the issues of moral recalcitrance in the debating manner; Dorigen weighs the merits of death and dishonor; and there is, too, the great *agon* of the *Canterbury Tales* debated by the narrator in several places, on the question of prudence versus morality, an artistic responsibility versus artistic freedom.

Laughter from Content

The *Tractate* suggests two sources of laughter for comedy, from the "things" depicted and from the diction. The section on action or "things" (roughly content) divides into considerations of plot devices of one sort or another and of ways of depicting the characters as "worse than average" or ludicrous and absurd. These categories pertaining to plot are as follows (the others will be given in the section on character):

Deception

Deception is one of the staples of comedy, along with surprise. All of Chaucer's "clever" comedies exemplify the ingenious, elaborate deceptions, lies, tricks, and stratagems by which husbands are taken in. But deception may be seen equally well in the others, when, for example, the Summoner is tricked into damnation by the demon of the *Friar's Tale*, or the friar of the *Summoner's Tale* is duped into putting his hand down the back of Thomas, or the poor priest in Part II of the *Canon's Yeoman's Tale* is deceived into thinking he can make silver. Some of the deceptions have a quality of the sinister, being allied to the deeper considerations of salvation and death, not only in the *Friar's Tale* but in the *Pardoner's Tale* where the two rioters plot to kill the third, do so, and meet their own unforeseen demise. One thinks also of the elaborate duping of the Wife of Bath's three old husbands, and the fox's deceiving of Chauntecleer in the *Nun's Priest's Tale*.

It is difficult to separate deception from the next category, that of the *unexpected*, since the major deceptions often come to us with an element of surprise. And clearly, too, in word-play there is always an element of the unexpected and of surprised wonder as we take in a clever conclusion. But here we have in mind that sequence of events held together by comic probability by which the poet leads us through sometimes labyrinthine complications to a conclusion that elicits from us a burst of laughter, or a flash of intuition, or a sense of approval. In this category of acts rather than of language belong all the tricks and outwittings, dupings and pretenses, without which comedy cannot exist.

The unexpected is, however, dealt with as a separate category in the *Tractate*, and we see it as one of the chief ingredients of comedy, along with deception and surprise. The verbal agility of the wife at the close of the *Shipman's Tale*; the loosing of the stallion, perhaps; the aftermath of the misplaced cradle in the *Reeve's Tale* when the wife gets into bed with Alan and John gets into bed with the miller; the swift deaths of the Pardoner's exemplum; the demon of the *Friar's Tale* carrying off the summoner with the line, "Thou shalt with me to helle yet to-nyte"—the result of the old woman's statement of repentance as necessary to salvation; the shout of "water, water!" and its aftermath in the *Miller's Tale*; the coupling in the pear tree of the *Merchant's Tale*; the fart exploding in Absolon's face, as well as that other in the friar's hand—all may serve as examples that fit in this category.[6]

Starkie thought that the *impossible* should include "all degrees of unreason, illogicality, unintelligibility, intended to excite laughter," to which Cooper adds only the phrase, "violating the laws of natural sequence."[7] More in keeping with Starkie and Cooper's definition, and linked both to garrulity or disjointed narrative, may be the old man's night spell in the *Miller's Tale* and the elaborate descriptions of processes and lists of elements in the *Canon's Yeoman's Tale*. The whole study of illogic for comic purposes in patterns of rhetoric is surely worthy of further study.

It is simpler to include here only those obvious examples that enable us to see how much comedy depends upon our willingness to move beyond the factual, plausible world we ordinarily inhabit into considerations of persons or devices that either do not exist in everyday life or that do exist but are put to absurd use in comedy. Such examples include the "magic" removal of black rocks in the *Franklin's Tale*, the urbane and articulate demon of the *Friar's Tale*, the physical encounter with Death in the *Pardoner's Tale*; the belief in the alchemist's power in the *Canon's Yeoman's Tale* to convert base metals into gold and silver; the challenge to the young clerics of the *Reeve's Tale* to make by their "philosophy" a large room of his cottage; and—I am tempted to add here—the daring acrobatics in a pear tree of the *Merchant's Tale*, along with a surer example, the marvellous partition of a fart at the conclusion of the *Summoner's Tale*; and that of the old man's belief in a possible repetition of Noah's flood in the *Miller's Tale*.

Loose Structure

The long *confessio* of the Wife of Bath (including the two interruptions by the Pardoner and the Friar-Summoner altercation), along with its connection with the tale she tells; that of the Pardoner with its somewhat free, associational coherence; much of Part I of the Canon's Yeoman's criticism of the profession of his master; and the slowly developed display of the friar's personality in the *Summoner's Tale* all manifest something of the improvisational loose structure that is the ancient inheritance from Greek and Roman comedy, both in dramatic and narrative forms. Not only is the total structure of the *Canterbury Tales* episodic or mechanical; but the tales themselves show a tendency toward developing the comic topic in segments; the lengthy complaint of Dorigen in the *Franklin's Tale*, Chauntecleer's exhausting recitation of dreams, the long discussion of marriage at the outset of the *Merchant's Tale*, even the exempla on wrath in the *Summoner's Tale* and the portraits of Alison and Absolon in the *Miller's Tale* provide fairly obvious examples.

Chaucer was not working inadvertantly towards the effects of disconnectedness. Gothic aesthetics offered a sympathetic option of the processional and sequential as much as the consequential and logical, which goes well with Chaucer's cool reportorial stance and enables him to break the mood of narration, to interrupt its flow, forcing our own increased distance as he calls attention to a particular episode or tells us baldly he is moving on to something else. Robert Jordan calls such moments "recurrent disruptions of illusion."[8] We thus have a double satisfaction—that of participating in a mimesis as a product as well as that of participating in the process of making the illusion work.

Related to the general category of disjointed narrative is that of garrulity. No one would accuse Chauntecleer, Dorigen, the Wife of Bath, the Pardoner, the Canon's Yeoman, or even the Reeve in his Introduction, of being short of wind. In each of these instances, interesting talk, sometimes for its own sake, becomes discursive and associational, and therefore contributes to the general impressions of disconnected narrative.

The Dianoetic Function

Comedy may be seen as a contest between opposing value systems: i.e., between any systems that serve as the two aspects of the *agon*; and struggle for dominance or survival may be regarded as the thematic skeleton of the plot or, more conventionally, its intellectual element. The *Tractate* gives names to the opposed sides: *gnome* or opinion, and *pistis* or proofs and persuasions by which the strength of the *gnome* is tested or opposed. Opinion belongs generally to the older or more conventional members of society, though not always; proofs and persuasions are encumbent upon the opposition. These latter jibe with the forms of proof given by Aristotle in the *Rhetoric* I, 15: oaths; compacts or conspiracies; testimonies or witnesses; tortures or ordeals; and finally, laws.[9]

Opinion

Here we must place all maxims, *sententiae*, extended discussions of values and the worth of things, or descriptions of the qualities of life, etc. One thinks immediately of the set speeches of Arcite and Palamon, those of Theseus, the long speech of the hag in the *Wife of Bath's Tale*, Dorigen's disquisition on evil, as well as the definition of love and friendship earlier in the *Franklin's Tale*, among the romances; among the comedies, the proverbial element of the *Reeve's Tale*, the Summoner's definitions of wrath, the Pardoner's sermon statements (not the exempla, which fall under the heading of testimonies or witnesses), the speeches of Placebo and Justinus in the

Merchant's Tale, the defenses of the values of marriage in both
the *Wife of Bath's Introduction* and the *Merchant's Tale*, the
merchant's discourse on luck in the *Shipman's Tale*, the quotation from Cato in the *Miller's Tale*, to name a few obvious examples. More generally we may see the opening propositions of
the *Shipman's Tale* and the *Merchant's Tale* as the *gnome*
which the remainder of the tale either illustrates or challenges.

Proofs or Persuasions

1. *Oaths:* There are so many oaths in Chaucer that we
shall have to content ourselves with only a few examples. They
have a range from swearing by the name of God, his bones, his
blood, of saints real and imaginary, by Mary, by Jesus, and to
more generalized expressions like "so may I prosper." They are
especially numerous in the *Miller's Tale*. They may serve on a
mundane level as fillers in comic discourse; more seriously they
serve the ends of irony by pungent innuendo especially when
they are part of a compact or conspiracy, or when the oath
itself has a special aptness to the situation.

2. *Compacts and Conspiracies:* Chaucer is replete with
various kinds of collusion. Nicholas and Alison in the *Miller's
Tale*, the two clerks of the *Reeve's Tale*, the Wife and Monk of
the *Shipman's Tale*, the canon and yeoman in the *Canon's
Yeoman's Tale*, the three rioters of the *Pardoner's Tale*, May
and Damian of the *Merchant's Tale*, the summoner and demon
in the *Friar's Tale*—all provide examples of the conspiratorial
part of a comic plot. Much of the satisfaction of comedy arises
from watching the evolution of the compacts, in language rich
in irony, by which the allegiances are crystallized among the
dupers. We remember, too, that the whole *Canterbury Tales*
depends upon the compact laid out for the pilgrims by the Host;
the compact or agreement is made much of in the links.

3. *Testimonies and Witnesses:* Aristotle allows, for ancient testimony, the citing of poets and the use of proverbs, to
which we may add exempla like those of the *Summoner's Tale*,
illustrating sudden wrath, or those of the *Nun's Priest's Tale*, to
support one or the other side of the *agon* on the worth of

dreams. There are, too, many instances of calling upon the authority of old writers, Solomon, Cato, etc.—the *Wife of Bath's Tale* and that of the merchant is especially rich in such witnesses. In a more legal sense, we recall that Nicholas and Alison witness for each other in putting down the protestations of the old husband; Pluto and Proserpine are witness to the episode in the pear tree, each swearing an oath, though not called to give testimony; the canon's yeoman's testimony against his master comprises virtually all of his tale.

4. *Tortures, Ordeals, Tests—mental or physical, by mechanical or other means:* The cartwheel of the *Summoner's Tale* is the most obvious example of a mechanical testing device. The other examples that come to mind are ordeals in the more common sense: Absolon's mental anguish and the use of the hot coulter of the *Miller's Tale*, the weary chasing of the loosed stallion in the *Reeve's Tale*, the Wife of Bath's inquisition of her three old husbands, the merchant's inquisition of his wife at the close of the *Shipman's Tale*, the challenge to May by January in the *Merchant's Tale* which produces her "sincere" protestation of fidelity. We may adduce, too, the long ordeal of Dorigen resulting from the unfortunate compact with Aurelius, the various "tests" in the *Canon's Yeoman's Tale*; the various "ordeals" described in the exempla of the *Summoner's Tale*; Chauntecleer's ordeal of nightmare and the subsequent ordeal of being carried off by the fox; the resting of the three rioters of the *Pardoner's Tale* against the cleverness of death; and lastly the two ordeals, that of the carter and that of old Mabely that make up the structure of the *Friar's Tale*.

5. *Laws:* Chaucerian comedy of adultery begins with an absurdly observed convention of marriage or family held by an older person which the subsequent action subverts. To these we might add other tyrannies inherent in "humorous" comedy, such as that of the dominant passion in the nature of the Pardoner, for example the hypocrisy of the Friar, the *idée fixe* of the friar of the *Summoner's Tale*, and that of the old knight in the *Merchant's Tale*. Chaucer's *Canterbury Tales* is full of references to law, both in the serious and nonserious tales, from proverbs that proclaim it is lawful to put off force with force in the *Reeve's Tale* to the law of Arthur's court in the *Wife of*

Bath's Tale against rape, and the other law imposed upon the young knight by the queen, that he find what it is that women most desire. The *Concordance* to Chaucer gives many instances of "law" in the comic tales alone.

Comic Catharsis

We may make an initial assumption based on Aristotle that something like equanimity is the soul's natural state, and that pleasure is what one feels when one is restored to it. Aristotle says (*Rhetoric* I.2) that pleasure is "a certain motion of the soul, and a settling, sudden and perceptible, into one's normal state." Among the activities of mind that produce this settling into one's natural state are wonder and learning, more particularly the latter, when wonder has been fulfilled in learning. At the close of the chapter he writes: "Since amusement and relaxation of every kind are among pleasant things, and laughter too, it follows that the causes of laughter must be pleasant—namely, persons, utterances, and deeds," though he does not say anything here about the kind of pleasure afforded.

A second assumption we may make is that every kind of art has its own special pleasurable effect; obviously the effect of comedy will not be that of tragedy, though in both some kind of "learning" is going on; and learning is associated with pleasure. But the pleasure yielded by comedy is associated with the worthless, the ridiculous, and the ugly without pain. It is accompanied by laughter often, though laughter is not the only available response, for there is also some sense of satisfaction or elation which serves as well; in the close of the *Odyssey*, for example, though the suitors all die, Odysseus and Penelope are restored to each other, or at the end of the otherwise tragic *Iphigenia Among the Taurians*, all the agents make their escape without mayhem or bloodshed.[10]

Before Aristotle, Plato had pointed out in the *Philebus* (48–50) that in both comedy and tragedy, pleasure and pain are mysteriously intermingled; we laugh while we experience untoward or painful emotions, like envy, desire, sorrow, fear,

love, emulation, etc. Both philosophers hold in common a view
that the emotions are burdensome and that they can be deliberately brought in excess to the surface of the mind by various
arts. Aristotle's famous and problem-ridden statement in the
Politics and the *Poetics* goes farther, making the function of
tragedy the arousal and catharsis of specific emotions. The
state of mind that remains is presumably one of relaxation, of
salutary distance, or a sense of things turning out as they must,
the process being a psychological/physiological one rather
than a moral one.

I am reasonably sure that the contribution of depth psychologists enables us to make application of such a process
intelligently to Chaucer's comic structures. If the psychologists
are correct in their opinion that we are all guided by deep-
seated psychic drives over which we exert little conscious
control, we may add to the consciously perceived emotions a
whole array of suppressed aggressions and desires, many of
them painful and ugly, thronging in the unconscious, which
comedy may allow to surface and to be dissipated. The distortion and exaggeration, as well as a deeper instinct for destruction, desecration, and the vile that we see when we put on the
distorting spectacles of comedy, enable us to reach down into
truths about ourselves.[11] Freud saw this process as fundamentally cathartic, a release, not a stimulant, and cathartic specifically of matter in the soul regarded as obscene.

I do not know whether it is possible to define precisely
the emotions that are released in comedy. Lane Cooper was of
the tentative opinion that "if you succeed in making an angry or
envious man laugh with pleasure, he ceases for a time to be
angry or envious. Thus anger and envy might be said to be
purged away by comedy . . . by something very unlike them."
Frye offers the view that sympathy and ridicule are the emotions that comedy purges. It might be argued more generally,
however, that comedy, being vicarious, gives innocent release
to the untoward pleasure that attaches to even so-called
painful emotions, like anger accompanied by the confident
expectation of revenge. Translated into feeling, consider with
how much satisfaction we watch the discountenancing of
arrogance, want the "bad" characters driven out or chastened,

with what joy we participate in unmasking the knave, in ferreting out the scapegoat, gratifying our cravings for the trappings of wealth in film presentations, losing ourselves in fantasy of whatever sort. Consider our satisfaction and mingled wonder in the working out of certain Chaucerian plots: the carrying off of the vile summoner to hell and the mutual murder of the three rioters, the grimly satisfying "revenge" upon the lying hypocrisy of the pardoner at the hands of the host—from which Chaucer redeems us by the kiss of peace; the ugly satisfaction of watching the Manciple play games at the expense of the drunken cook. In short, comedy makes capital of the emotional endowment we have. Laughter gives us the necessary distance, the ability both to see things from a very low vantage point of human failing and to know by contrast what may lie at the opposite extreme.

Chaucerian comedy has the capacity to make us laugh for a while, indulge pleasure, particularly *unworthy* pleasure and excessive laughter, after which we settle back into equanimity or a sense of well-being. We have the satisfaction of license, trickery, foolishness, even cruelty in punishing a scapegoat or wishing someone dead, or feeling that death was deserved. We have the privilege of making attacks on many piously held moral conventions, of watching the plot work out such attacks on convention, as in the *Miller's Tale* and in the *Merchant's Tale*; or on human stupidity, as in the *Canon's Yeoman's Tale*; or arrogance and hypocrisy, as in the *Summoner's Tale*.

The elaborate stratagems of plot, character, and vocal utterance all coerce us—as we go willingly—into indulgence. For Aristotle, and I believe for Chaucer, this activity, a surrender to lower faculties, is salutary in its ability to give vent to what is deleterious to the serious affairs of life. Chaucer lets us see what is to be affirmed and rejected in the course of the *Canterbury Tales*; what should be rejected must be seen, as in the Palinode of *Troilus and Criseyde*, against the backdrop of eternity and its imperatives,[12] or at the very least as a necessary contrast to the values of romance.

I am led to believe, therefore, that the *Tractate* may mean what it says: that pleasure and laughter are the emotions to be purged in comedy and that there should be a due proportion of laughter in comedy. Such a statement must inevitably sound strange to our ears. Are there really unworthy and excessive degrees of pleasure and laughter?[13] My affirmative answer, admittedly inferential, rests upon Aristotle's discussion of pleasure, which I read differently from those who do not see a kind of restorative power in art of whatever sort and that art can serve the larger ends of civic morality generally. Chaucer, given to making frequent references to self-control, might have felt considerable sympathy towards Aristotle's views on the educative and purgative powers of art.

As we have said, the pleasure of participating in the forms of art is of a special innocent sort; it arises from learning something, from contemplating, and from wonder. Beyond amusement, which Aristotle says (in the *Politics* 1137b 41–133a 21) is as a medicine to the soul (for the emotion created in the soul "is a relaxation, and from the pleasure we obtain rest") lies the higher, intellectual pleasure of music (and of the verbal arts), from which one learns during the complex psychological processes of emotional release. He writes (1340a 17): "Since then music is a pleasure and virtue consists in rejoicing and loving and hating aright, there is clearly nothing which we are so much concerned to acquire and to cultivate as the power of forming right judgments, and of taking delight in good dispositions and noble actions." And in a canny insight he adds (1340a 24): "The habit of feeling pleasure or pain at mere representations is not far removed from the same feelings about realities," reminding us that one benefit from representations of music is purgation (1341b 37), a process by which the soul is "lightened and delighted" (1342a 16).

By way of summary, then, I infer the following:

1. The effect of comedy is pleasure, specifically the pleasure of learning something. (a) This pleasure is a higher pleasure than that of mere amusement, though even mere amusement relaxes and delights. (b) The emotions attached to such representations are very close to the emotions arising from real things and occurrences, and therefore we learn something about ourselves in life.

2. There is a second kind of pleasure which it is the function of comedy to purge; the pleasure arising from participation in ugly, untoward admixtures of emotions arising from watching the trivialized actions of inferior characters.

3. Comedy thus yields two kinds of pleasure, of which the second kind alone is to be relieved or dissipated.

4. A "highest" kind of pleasure specifically attaches to attainment of the life of virtue, the realm of "what is intermediate and best," in which we acquire the ability to make right judgments and experience "delight in good dispositions and noble actions." One of the benefits of art is to enable us to see ourselves in relation to the life of virtue.

The whole matter is, of course, a vexed question: whether we see in Aristotle (and subsequently in Freud) a justification for a theory of catharsis in comedy is of less moment than our realization that the whole movement of the *Canterbury Tales* is purgatorial, inclining finally to a redemptive closure in which the excesses and disproportions of the comic tales are seen from a cooler aesthetic distance, a model of what catharsis should produce in us in the dynamics of the poem itself.

Reader Response

Chaucer "banks heavily on the sanity of his audience," to borrow a phrase from Eric Bentley,[14] their moral sanity as well as their common sense, and the closures of the tales may be attended by a generalized moral tag (*Friar's Tale, Canon's Yeoman's Tale, Pardoner's Tale*) as a constant reminder that human beings live in two worlds, that above and the purgatorial state below. In the one above they will be judged according to virtue; but in the one below, they are interesting for their vices. To throw off the shackles of conscience, to enter into a world with few restrictions, as Lamb puts it, yields us plain pleasure in the sexual tales and releases us from the law court; while in the other unmasking tales, the conscienceless are punished, giving us assurance of an overwhelming presence of law. Thus, it is the interaction between the two worlds (that of instinct and plain pleasure, and that of conscience and the norms of morality) that provides a range of comic response from joy to the larger satisfactions of learning something about the relation between the two, or having something confirmed. At one end of the spectrum the characters verge on the demonic as in the *Canon's Yeoman's Tale* and the *Pardoner's Tale*; at the other, as in the *Franklin's Tale* and the *Wife of Bath's Tale* on the morally transformed (but the latter view of humanity, as Dante complained, is offered by few); and the fact is that we are more comfortable with the former than the latter.

Until his last years—or at any rate until the period of the *Canterbury Tales*—Chaucer seems not to have shared Plato's assumptions[15] that the audience is to be guarded against its tendency to indulge in real life the emotions aroused by literature, though he debates the issue for his own purposes in several places. It is true that some members of an audience are always platonic in their attitudes towards comic experience, and are apt to be distressed by violence, sexuality, and aggression; they are apt to react too sympathetically to hot coulters, broken arms, bashed heads, perhaps because the illusion is too real for them.

But Chaucer demands a surrender to the illusions of a comic world down to the level of buffoonish action and the pratfall, without excessive concern. The conventions of comedy demand such surrender, posit the element of suffering, and do not shrink from ugliness, and if we have been given the clues properly, have the illusion broken for us often enough by one means or another, and have thus learned the proper attitudes of detachment that are part of comic response, we can see the difference between the world of fantasy and the world of action.

If we see this difference, then we can accept the irony that holds up a bad marriage or the union of youth and age, for that special scrutiny which comedy affords: an unblinking look at hypocrisy.[16] Or we may take a more detached view of the son-father rivalry, which is clearly visible in disguised form in Chaucer's sexual comedies. Chaucer avows through the mouth of the Man of Law that he wrote no tales of incest, though there is ground (provided for us by Freud) for seeing the competition for Alison, the Miller's wife, May, and Dorigen as a displaced expression of a perennial theme. This statement must not be taken to mean that the tales in which these agents figure do not involve other thematic considerations, but only that they contain a topic anchored in a tradition going back through Roman to late Greek comedy, a topic so popular it has never gone out of style since Menander. It may be seen at a glance which tales are, in a sense, Roman comedies built around the theme of a *senex* and the successful rebellion against his rule. Sex triumphs; yet, where it does not completely, it is adroitly welded to another drive—money, and thus becomes more "social" in its implications, as aggression moves over from one arena to another. In either case, the themes touch upon universal concerns of the audience of whatever age and time.

The tales that seem more social give this impression because of the emphasis placed upon a single agent, as in the *Summoner's Tale*, or the *Merchant's Tale*, in both of which there is a fairly subtle debate between secular and theological values centralized in a single "humor" upon whom the audience may center its amused animosity. The debate is given a firm secular conclusion which the audience approves no less than the conclusions of the comedies without the quality of good nature, those of the Friar, Pardoner, and the Canon's Yeoman, in which not instinct to survive but will to damnation becomes the prime instrumentality. In either case, the audience experiences a psychic need which the ending gratifies.

Comic Characters

I once offered the view that one may distinguish comic characters from other types on the grounds of their impenitence: if the agents remained recalcitrant, did not change for the better in the course of an action, remained stupid and deceived, or clever and deceiving, continuing in a single-minded course of action, we were dealing with comic characters in a comic structure. These were agents we could not take seriously; they were "no account" deceivers or dupes who figured in complicated stratagems.

A surer way of classifying comic characters is through Aristotle's *Nicomachean Ethics*, *Rhetoric*, and the *Coislinian Tractate*, the reservoirs out of which, for comic theory, a cast of comic characters may be formed. It may be seen from these authorities that the pilgrims of the *Canterbury Tales* evince comic qualities in remarkable conformity with ancient description: pretentious boasters and liars, garrulous men and women, ironists both modest and mock-modest, learned men, buffoons and clowns, boors, men of touchy and choleric dispositions, rude and churlish men, quarrelsome and flattering types, witty and scurrilous speakers—both in the *General Prologue* and links and within the tales. And with the various types go various clues to social level: the humor and laughter of "gentle" persons being different from that of the churls; kind wit being opposed to unkind; and obscenity and license opposed to innuendo. The names of pilgrims in Chaucer's parade of characters leap to mind even as we enumerate the classic characters.

These characters may be subsumed under the headings drawn from our authorities as the impostor (*alazon*); the ironical man (*eiron*); and the buffoon (*bomolochos*), names we would do well to retain as part of the vocabulary of comic theory. These may be modulated to include a number of other types for which names have evolved: the straightforward man or plain-dealer, the various kinds of fools and clowns, a rustic type called by Aristotle agroikos, and the scapegoat or *pharmakos*.[17]

Examples are not far to seek, although we must recognize always that the types merge with each other in accordance with the poet's intuition of them. The host, for example, may be seen as a buffoonish type whose task it is to be master of revels, who functions virtually as a chorus in the links, recalling by his summons to a feast the ancient lineage of comedy from *komos*. But he is also something of an ironist in the links, taking various stances vis-à-vis the pilgrims; and as an impostor, he unmasks himself in a well-known confession about his virago wife. Similarly, the pardoner may be seen as an impostor who manages to speak with ironical contempt for his audience, and who, in the process of demonstrating his great skills as an entertainer, becomes the scapegoat threatened with full disclosure. His role is paradoxically that of mixed blessing: he nurtures in us a kind of quest for truth, while at the same time he functions as a scourge of society. The Manciple, who is depicted as a sly ironist in the *General Prologue*, emerges in his tale as something of a plain-dealer who turns into a malcontent and complainer, railing at hypocrisy in language and in society. The Reeve, an *eiron* to the Miller's posture as loud boaster, is something of a rustic, a refuser of festivities, grouchy and churlish in response.

Within the tales the oppositions of *eiron–alazon* types are clear: Thomas–friar; demon–summoner; canon–gullible priest; old man–three rioters; May/Damian–January; miller–students, etc. But merely to pin such tags upon the various agents does injustice to Chaucer's art. In the dynamics of his poem, both the pilgrims of the outer frame and the characters in the tales become fleshed out in all their variety and values. Particularly in the "serious" comedies they evince, along with their grotesqueries, the capacity to move out of stereotypes into full moral stature. The Wife of Bath, the Pardoner, the summoner of the *Friar's Tale*, and even the Canon's Yeoman have the capacity to raise truly disturbing questions, to challenge us at unexpected moments in the flow of statement or event. Who would have expected from the young scheming Wife of the three good, old husbands the later strain of melancholy courage, the "surprise" of the Canon's departure from the community, the decision of the Yeoman to remain, or the compelling strain of a beneficent religion that flows in a deep substratum beneath the treble of the Pardoner?

Chaucer will not allow his impostors (dim relics of the *miles gloriosus*) to remain comic stereotypes, but rather gives them a complexity far beyond simple role-play. The impostor exists to be unmasked, and part of the interest of the Wife's character, for example, is the result of her steady shedding of earlier roles and masks, and of her realization of the loss of youthful radiance in the passage of time. In the process of unmasking appear the subtler tones of self-depreciation, the implied serious questions (What should one want? What is love? What is honest in human dealings?) of the ironist, the "other" to the *alazon*. The Wife, who has made a travesty of marriage, has profaned a rite, in Cornford's terms, and must kill off the old self. If later in the tale she tells we see something of the wise fool or of the sibyl speaking far more philosophically than we had anticipated through the mouth of the hag, we can estimate something of Chaucer's complex art. Like the clown of later literature who gets slapped, she is the fool who, though beaten, somehow emerges unscathed.

It is not merely psychological acuity that enables Chaucer to make his characters lifelike. He has, to an uncommon degree, the camera eye that sees clearly at various distances. There is always in his descriptions what Virginia Woolf called "the hardness and the freshness of an actual presence."[18] It is obviously people that interest him. He speaks of them unself-consciously, particularly on matters that later ages came to think shameful, and so retains that open candor so necessary to comic license; and his attention to visual physiological detail is part and parcel of that directness and plain utterance essential to the comic mode.

It is Chaucer's clear eye for hard detail that works towards character that dominates plot rather than plot formations to which character is merely subordinate. In general, comedy tends not to be concerned about the relations of plot to character in the same sense as tragedy, where plot becomes the working out of "necessity" or some other law that gives form to human actions. There, character becomes subordinate to the working out of that plot, although the hero's ethos gets revealed in the process of it. But comedy may display character for its own sake, outside the pressures of an inexorable plot movement, as in the *Summoner's Tale*. Thus, too, the characters of the General Prologue are presented, in a sense, as freestanding, operating by the flimsiest of imperatives, to tell tales for a meager prize. Similarly within the tales, character is sometimes presented with directness and flair, often as though each person were a portrait (particularly in the Miller's and Reeve's tales) before being released into actions that are forms of play, chance, and unexpected fortune. We may see a relationship between Absolon's fastidious, squeamish nature, and the surprise blast in his face, but it is not inevitability that produces the blast but the comic spirit, and it is not necessitated by his character.

Thus, unlike tragedy, which in Aristotle's view subordinates character to plot, comedy tends to place its largest emphasis on the characters to the extent that plot may seem merely the showcase for them. Chance, improbability, mischief, what Sypher calls "a tidy arrangement of improbable possibilities"[19] by means of which a character is brought to triumph or is exposed as an impostor, are the casual imperatives, alternates to tragedy's law.

Several of the categories in the *Tractate's* division of "laughter caused by things" have to do with the various ways in which the characters of comedy may be made to appear inferior or ridiculous. They are as follows:

1. From comparisons (implicit or explicit) to what is better or worse:

It will be remembered that comedy tends to represent men, in Aristotle's phrase, as worse than they commonly are. Men and women may be compared downward in the scale of being, to chickens in the *Nun's Priest's Tale*, to denizens of the barnyard and meadows in the *Miller's Tale*, to sparrows, to geldings or mares, to rabbits, to butcher-birds, to snakes and scorpions, all the way down to the demonic world, where they are seen as working devilish actions. The subtle rapprochement between stallion and human being in the *Reeve's Tale* is one of the subtler comparisons, less overt. There is also the assimilation of the Canon to trickster in the *Canon's Yeoman's Tale*, that of the friar of the *Summoner's Tale* to greedy cheat; even an implied comparison of better and worse in the haughty clerical tone that criticizes secular values in the *Merchant's Tale*. The Wife of Bath compares herself to vessels of gold and those of wood, the implied comparison of the wife of the *Shipman's Tale* to Ganelon; of the summoner of the *Friar's Tale* to Judas, to a shrike, and to a juggler; of the fox of the *Nun's*

Priest's Tale to Judas, Ganelon, and to Sinon; the use of such terms as "popelote" and "piggesnye" to "lower" the character of Alison in the *Miller's Tale*—all demonstrate the ease with which Chaucer assimilates character to the worse. It may be noted that the humor here is frequently linguistic as well as comparative.

The comparisons are frequently those of worse to better: as in the Wife of Bath's comparison of her "wood" to gold, that of Alison's face to the newly forged coin; the comparison of the softness of the weasel, perhaps, and to apples laid up in the hay, bring the beauty of nature into the human sphere. There is a subtle interplay between the two kinds of movement in such comparisons, that upward and that downward.

In the largest context of such comparisons, between truth and falseness, for example, consider the satisfaction we feel in the *Manciple's Tale*, in getting things straight: a whore is only a whore, not a dear lady, and a brigand is a brigand, not a great captain; or between honor and dishonor in the *Merchant's Tale*, when the wife defends herself (just prior to her assignation with Damian) as being a woman of honor; or between higher and lower loves in the implied relationship of Pardoner and Summoner in the General Prologue.

In some of these examples, the effect is not always that of laughter, but rather that of irony and occasionally ethical import, particularly in the parodies of high style strewn throughout Chaucer's work; for example, when Pertelote is compared to the bereaved wives of Roman senators, and when Dorigen compares herself with the various wives and virgins of antiquity. Something of a a more casual, more insolent comparison is inherent in naming the Pardoner "beel amy."

2. *Debasing the personages:*

This category is related to the previous one in which there is a comparison either implied or stated with things above and below in the scale of being. Cooper's translation of the Greek phrase makes the distinction clearer: "fashioning the personages in the direction of the worthless."[20] Thus, depicting the husband of the *Shipman's Tale* as obtuse, the wife as conniving and sexually irresponsible, and the monk as opportunist demonstrate the poet's practice of debasing not the total person, but only one aspect of his character, the one necessary to plot. Similarly, Nicholas's handiness, Absolon's squeamishness, the Reeve's admission of the vices of old age, the miller's (in the *Reeve's Tale*) defensiveness and angry nature, his wife's stupid haughtiness, the daughter's resemblance to her father, the headstrong nature of the two young clerics, Damian's crouching in a bush, May reading her billet-doux in the privy, the closing line of the *Cook's Tale*, the summoner's vicious control of the young of the diocese, the Wife of Bath's scorn for her first three husbands and her anti-intellectual battle with Jenkin—all provide examples, from one vantage or another, of debasing the persons. It should be noted that though comedy requires the lowering of character towards the worthless, the characters may be seen as likable and therefore as drawing our sympathies. Equally they may be seen as despicable. In any event, what happens to them is to be felt by the audience, at the close, as psychologically satisfying.

3. *Having a choice and choosing the worthless, passing by what is worthwhile and fastening upon what is trivial:*

I am tempted to say that all comedy depends upon the deliberate trivializing of experience or upon reducing the view of experience from graveness; and that the choices made by the agents in the course of any action must support the inner law of trivialization. Thus, the characters of comedy habitually choose courses of action displaying mean-mindedness, malice, bad nature, or more simply make choices that bring about a sequence of increasing complications. The badinage between the Miller and Reeve in which the Miller provokes the Reeve, then offers a disclaimer, may be seen as a kind of bad choice that demonstrates sly malice. The Reeve subsequently makes a firm decision to requite the Miller, though earlier he avows only that he could, if he wanted to, tell a story about a Miller.

Even his platitudes on old age have a somewhat trivial air, though raised up by powerful imagery.

Absolon's decision to go back to Alison's house (in the *Miller's Tale*), the miller's release of the clerics' horse (in the *Reeve's Tale*), the wife's reliance upon the monk (in the *Shipman's Tale*), old January's determination to marry and his subsequent willingness to believe his wife's protestations (in the *Merchant's Tale*), the rioters' resolve to seek out Death (in the *Pardoner's Tale*), the summoner's assumption of a profitable alliance with the demon-yeoman (in the *Friar's Tale*), the friar's belief that he has talked Thomas into giving him money (in the *Summoner's Tale*)—all serve to demonstrate the dependence of comedy upon bad decisions as a source of comic satisfaction.

There are good decisions, too, that raise comedy to a more thought-provoking dimension: that of the Canon's Yeoman not to go off with his master, and that of the young knight of the *Wife of Bath's Tale* to leave a major decision to his wife. This latter example may test for us, in part, the degree to which the *Wife of Bath's Tale* is predominantly a romance, with comic overtones.

Probability

The final test by which we come to know an artist's skill is in his handling of the probable and necessary. We almost never question probability unless violations are so bald as to elicit either mild anger in us or a laugh at ineptness in developing the inner coherence of a literary form. In tragedy, where we come into the action close to the end of a previous sequence of events (in which there may have been elements of the fortuitous or the merely sequential), we expect the final action, regardless of the number of complications it contains, to be the consequence of all the antecedent actions, including those recalled by the protagonist as memories. The tragic writer thus in depicting the final act of a larger action reaching far back in time enables us to see an inexorable order or law working itself out both in terms of events and character, this law overriding all the accidents and chance occurrences that might have intervened between cause and effect. We may have thought the events were merely sequential, but now we see that, far from being so, there are parts of a pattern rooted in character or fate.

But Chaucer, even in his serious tales, allows the accidental and the merely sequential into the actions as normal means of developing both his serious and nonserious plots. The more the accidental and fortuitous become parts of the presented actions, the closer we are to the accepted norms of comedy and realism, where we are interested less in the ways in which human beings are made to conform to law or obey an inexorably developing pattern, than in the quixotic, the unforeseen, the merely sequential, and the frankly absurd.

The opposition of the vocabularies of providence and fortune tells us a good deal about the experiential mode in which Chaucer is writing, and often about the degree of irony in the manner of presentation. It is instructive to look at such verbal practices in the *Concordance* to help penetrate the mystery of that peculiar largeness of mind and complex world view which deliberately conflates modes usually kept separate from each other (at least in the classical Greek drama that has come down to us).

Chaucer's humorless comedies, particularly the Pardoner's exemplum and the *Friar's Tale*, imitate the rigorous "law" of the most serious forms of literature: character is made clear as fate, and an unsmiling presence is felt overseeing the inevitable catastrophe which comes as the necessary consequence of character-in-action, a preacher's conviction about an inevitable relationship between morality and action. There is a similar alliance with the serious tonalities of probability in both the *Merchant's Tale* and the *Nun's Priest's Tale* where a host of imperatives from dreams to destiny are playfully brought to the foreground, left momentarily to reverberate their potentially tragic overtones and then withdrawn in favor of codas stating existential truths, not of a corrected ethos but only of a manipulative rationality.

And this manipulative rationality is what is left in the "pure" comedies: Absolon and Nicholas working to solve problems of gratification and revenge as quickly as possible by immediately available means; Alan and John moving in obedience to plot trickery into actions controlled by chance and misunderstanding; and the merchant's wife and best friend wittily squeezing personal advantage out of their circumstances, casually buying and selling love, solving problems seen finally to be as trivial as the blast of hot air which is the catastrophe of the *Summoner's Tale.*

If thus we eliminate from human actions the larger considerations of an inevitable relationship between micro- and macrocosms, cut off so to speak from the transcendental dimensions of love, fidelity, and truth-to-word, what is left is man-in-a-middle-world, with the limited possibilities therein, in which providence gives way to fortune and the penalties of temporality: lineality, witty judgment, and the warp of time. And so, when we are dealing with inferior agents whom we watch moving through their designed stratagems, the imperatives we see demonstrated are not those of the human race's moral nature, but rather those of their mere humanity: survival, gratification, and winning.

What does one do to win? To put it simply, anything, in the order the poet deems best. And will we "believe" in the sequence in which the events are made to occur? Of course we know from tragic tales about inevitability and necessity; comedy conditions us to take satisfaction either in the parody of their function or in the outright suspension of their function, substituting for them gratuitous choice and absurd results, the possible with an inconsequential sequel.[21]

And therein lies the clue: Chaucer, like any comic writer, invents the degree of plausibility or probability which we define here as the relation of events entirely internal to the work. Though the entire tale may be a mimesis of a clearly improbable or impossible action (as in the *Nun's Priest's Tale* and *Friar's Tale)* the events within the tale have their own relatedness. Even when a cause-and-effect sequence is interrupted by what appears to be accidental, we do not question that it could happen so. The coherence imposed upon it is that which the character or the situation necessitates. Thus, a Chaucerian comic action, even when sequential as in the

Reeve's Tale, is not *merely* a sequence of events imitating the events of history, but evolves under the imperatives of an entirely inner probability and convinces us precisely because of our understanding that given the microcosm of the poem, the events might have taken place just so. They make, not any sense, but the sense that only this concatenation yields, a mimesis of what might be. This is not to be taken to mean that life is being imitated in a mechanical way, but rather that the poet's plastic power imposes a pattern equally upon the absurd or accidental and upon the factual, thus demonstrating a relationship between life and art by making intelligible wholes of life's great range of possibilities.[22]

Chaucer's genius, as many scholars have pointed out, sees both sides of human nature, the lower as well as the higher imperatives. Both sides of human nature can be made to produce convincing depictions in literature because both are human, and because, in the final analysis, we believe in both.

NOTES

*Reprinted with permission from *Medieval Studies in Honor of Lillian Herlands Hornstein*, ed. Jess B. Bessinger, Jr., and Robert R. Raymo (New York: New York University Press, 1976), pp. 193-225.

1. Lane Cooper, *An Aristotelian Theory of Comedy with an Adaptation of the Poetics and a Translation of the 'Tractatus Coislinianus'* (New York: Harcourt, Brace, and Company, 1922). A classic study that has influenced much comic theory is Francis Macdonald Cornford's *The Gin of Attic Comedy* (New York: Doubleday, 1961), and that of Northrop Frye, *Anatomy of Criticism* (Princeton: Princeton University Press, 1957).

2. I have omitted "laughter arising from diction" from this paper for reasons of length, though much needs to be done in studying the ways in which Chaucer manipulates language for the sake of laughter or special effects. His comic style is an interesting mixture: he bristles with similitudes and metaphors, along with other devices which have received good treatment by Janette Richardson, *Blameth Not Me: A Study of Imagery in Chaucer's Fabliaux* (The Hague: Mouton, 1970); and two

dissertations have given considerable insight into Chaucer's imagery, that of Elizabeth Rudisill Homann, "Kinesthetic Imagery in Chaucer" (Berkeley: University of California, 1948), and William A. Tornwall, "Studies in Chaucer's Imagery" (Baton Rouge: Louisiana State University, 1956). Verbal as well as dramatic irony has been given ample treatment in numerous works, notably the pieces of Earle Birney, and doubtless there will be more articles on the subject with regard to individual topics and loci; level of delivery has received good impetus from E. T. Donaldson's "Idiom of Popular Poetry in the *Miller's Tale,*" *English Institute Essays*, 1950, ed. A. S. Downer (New York: Columbia UP, 1951), pp. 116–40.

Puns have been collected and their role assessed in a number of articles, notably Paull F. Baum, "Chaucer's Puns," *PMLA*, 71 (1956): 225–46, and *PMLA*, 73 (1958): 167–70; and Helge Kökeritz, "Rhetorical Word-Play in Chaucer," *PMLA*, 69 (1954): 937–52. Chaucer's familiar names, his Latin and French terms sprinkled through the comic tales, the pertinence of oaths, word-play (homonyms, synonyms, paronyms), periphrases and circumlocutions, euphemisms, the occasional nonce word, distortions of words, and the Chaucerian habit of style of compounding, particularly nouns and adjectives, all need further investigation.

In omitting the most tempting aspect of diction, style, I am passing by an important consideration of ascents and descents into grandiloquence, apostrophes, jargon, garrulity, travesty, etc., which are part and parcel of the texture of Chaucer's comic style, and these, of course, involve considerations of manner of delivery and gesture.

3. J. W. H. Atkins, *English Literary Criticism; The Medieval Phase* (Cambridge: Cambridge University Press, 1943), p. 32.

4. Susanne Langer, *Feeling and Form: A New Theory of Art* (New York: Scribner's Sons, 1953). She writes, p. 331, that the comic vision deals with man's capacity to triumph "by art, luck, personal power, or even humorous, or ironical, or philosophical acceptance of mischance."

5. Elder Olson, *The Theory of Comedy* (Indiana University Press, 1968), pp. 52–54. It happens that these two classes of tales jibe loosely with a part of the scheme evolved by Olson for dramatic forms. The second group represent his "plots of folly . . . in which the agent acts in error," for whatever reason; the first group corresponds to his "plots of cleverness . . . in which the stratagems of the agent produce the comic action." The agents are rewarded or punished according to their deserts; according as the agent is well- or ill-intentioned, we respond. The agents themselves, those that fall into the class of the ridiculous, may be of three types: (a) morally sound but intellectually deficient; (b) morally deficient

but clever; and (c) deficient both intellectually and morally. Moreover, the agents may act from good or bad motives.

Olson's scheme, illustrated from a simple archetype (p. 53), is as follows:

> Plots of Folly: well-intentioned fool;
> outcome must be successful.
> Plots of Folly: ill-intentioned fool;
> outcome must be failure.
> Plots of Cleverness: well-intentioned cleverman;
> outcome must be successful.
> Plots of Cleverness: ill-intentioned cleverman;
> outcome must be failure.

In this scheme the friar of the *Summoner's Tale*, the summoner of the *Friar's Tale*, the three rioters of the *Pardoner's Tale*, and the Canon of the *Canon's Yeoman's Tale* may be seen as ill-intentioned fools, for whom the outcome must be failure; in the cleverness plots, the wife and monk of the *Shipman's Tale*, the pairs of young men in the Miller's and Reeve's tales, Damian and May of the *Merchant's Tale*, because they succeed in their various ways, must—to preserve the scheme—be seen as well-intentioned. This constitutes a definition of terms that strains our belief in the applicability of the theory to Chaucer's tales. Obviously much hangs upon our definition of "well-intentioned." One has to adopt a rather special perspective to see the agents in this light, that is, as well-intentioned with reference exclusively to their own interests.

6. Cooper, p. 243: "... every ludicrous accident to which an author carefully leads up with a view to surprising us into laughter has the nature of a deception; and similarly the outcome of deception is unexpected."

7. W. J. M. Starkie, *The Acharnians of Aristophanes* (London: Macmillan & Co., 1909), p. lxiv; Cooper, p. 224.

8. Robert M. Jordan, *Chaucer and the Shape of Creation* (Cambridge: Harvard University Press, 1967), p. 8.

9. Northrop Frye, p. 116. Frye defines the opposition as roughly "the usurping and the desirable societies respectively," the action of comedy being like "the action of a lawsuit, in which the plaintiff and defendant construct different versions of the same situation, one finally being judged as real and the other as illusory. This resemblance of the rhetoric of comedy to the rhetoric of jurisprudence has been recognized from earliest times." It should be reiterated that opinions and various

proofs may be uttered or offered by *any* characters in any situation. The description given above is archetypal.

10. Cooper, pp. 60–62.

11. Wylie Sypher, *Comedy* (New York: Doubleday, 1956), p. 222: "Tragedy has been called 'mithridatic' because the tragic action, inoculating us with large doses of pity and fear, inures the self to the perils we all face. Comedy is no less mithridatic in its effects on the self, and has its own catharsis. Freud said that nonsense is a toxic agent, acting like some 'poison' now and again required by the economy of the soul. Under the spell of this intoxication we reclaim for an instant our 'old liberties,' and after discharging our inhibited impulses in folly we regain the sanity that is worn away by the everyday gestures. We have a compulsion to be moral and decent, but we also resent obligations we have accepted. The irreverence of the carnival disburdens us of our resentment and purges our ambivalence so that we can return to our duties as honest men." And he adds: "From license and parody and unmasking—or putting on another mask—come renewed sanity and responsibility, a confidence that we have looked at things from a lower angle and therefore know what is incorruptible." See also Cooper, p. 67 and Frye, p. 177.

12. I have explored elsewhere what the moral implications of the position are for Chaucer: *Art of the Canterbury Tales* (Madison: University of Wisconsin Press, 1965), pp. 23–41, 34–40, 146–47, 248–49.

13. Elder Olson writes, p. 45, "Why anyone should want to get rid of pleasure or be pleased by getting rid of pleasure, or how he can get rid of pleasure and still have it [the *Tractate*] fails to say." And earlier, p. 36, [comedy] ". . . has no catharsis, since all kinds of the comic—the ridiculous and ludicrous, for example—are naturally pleasant." But see in particular, Cooper, pp. 70–78, on the dual effects of comedy.

14. Eric Bentley, *Life of the Drama* (New York: Atheneum, 1964), pp. 221–22.

15. "Poetic representation . . . waters the growth of passions which should be allowed to wither away and sets them up in control, although the goodness and happiness of our lives depend on their being held in subjection." *Republic* X, p. 606.

16. Chaucer is without interest in the family and its vices or virtues; Virginia of the *Physician's Tale* comes to mind, as does the love-hungry Molly of the *Reeve's Tale*, the little girl under the "yerde" of the merchant's wife in the *Shipman's Tale*, the various levels of domesticity in the *Clerk's Tale*, the *Summoner's Tale*, and even the gracious atmosphere of upper class households in *Troilus and Criseyde* in which

Criseyde is ensnared and victimized. In none of these is the family itself the subject under comic examination; perhaps his instinct told him that the family generates "drama" rather than comedy. But his view of marriage will serve to demonstrate the range from bemusement to something like sardonic contempt.

17. A full discussion of these types is to be found in Frye, pp. 171–76.

18. Virginia Woolf, "The Pastons and Chaucer" in *The Common Reader*, 1st series (Hogarth Press, 1925), p. 26.

19. Sypher, p. 209.

20. Cooper, p. 250.

21. Several remarks by Cooper are of interest here: "It is clear that the sequence of incidents in comedy must often run counter to the laws of necessity and probability. Yet it is equally clear that the comic poet must keep in mind the law of a necessary or probable sequence, and must suggest it, in order to depart from it in the right way for the ends of comedy, showing that he observes the law by his method of violating it. . . . the stress [for Aristophanic comedy] clearly must be, not the relation of one incident to another. . . . [Aristotle] thinks of "probability" less (as we commonly and vaguely do) with reference to things in general, and more with reference to specific antecedent and consequent within the limits of a particular play or tale. In other words, the poet is not a historian" (pp. 187, 191). And finally: "Comic incidents affect us most when we are not expecting them, if at the same time they are caused, or have an air of being caused, by one another; for we are struck with more amusement if we find a causal relation in unexpected comic occurrences than if they come about of themselves and in no special sequence; since even pure coincidences seem more amusing if there is something that looks like design in them. Plots therefore that illustrate the principle of necessity of probability in the sequence of incident are better than others" (p. 194).

22. Eva Schaper, *Prelude to Aesthetics* (London, 1968), pp. 93–101.

Chaucer and Comedy*

Thomas J. Garbáty

Geoffrey Chaucer is our "owene maister deere" of English comedy, and he has been identified with this genre of literature as completely as he has mastered it. But England's greatest medieval author has also been faulted, as we know, for not taking the world seriously enough, and this view unfortunately clouds the understanding of many today, especially those who watch the stage or see the movies but never read a book. Hot coulters, bare bottoms, and swyved wives—Chaucer represents the teller of dirty tales, the agent of bawdy comedy. Ah, Geoffrey, forgive us these trespasses!

In principio, let there be clarity: Chaucer's view of the world is quite serious enough; it just happens never to be a tragic one, for to describe such a world with its final despair was alien to his temperament. If we look at the whole corpus of his work, we see his tragic poems all interrupted, unfinished, or transfigured into celestial comedy.

It would be interesting to know whether Chaucer wrote with a comic theory of his own. It appears so, but only implied in opposition to his well-known Boethian definition of tragedy that occurs in the Prologue to *The Monk's Tale*:

> Tragedie is to seyn a certeyn storie
> As olde bookes maken us memorie,
> Of hym that stood in greet prosperitee,
> And is yfallen out of heigh degree
> Into myserie, and endeth wrecchedly.[1]

(*CT* VII.1973–77)

The Knight interrupts the Monk's endless list of fallen men, and protests:

> I seye for me, it is a greet disease,
> Whereas men han been in greet welthe and ese,
> To heeren of hire sodeyn fal, allas!
> And the contrarie is joye and greet solas,
> As whan a man hath been in povre estaat,
> And clymbeth up and wexeth fortunat,
> And there abideth in prosperitee.
>
> (*CT* VII.2771–77)

This view coincides with that of Lydgate in his *Troy Book* (2.847): "A comedie hath in his gynnyng ... a maner compleynyng, And afterward endeth in gladnes," wherewith we should point out that a Lydgate statement on literary theory usually originated with Chaucer anyway, as a Wordsworth comment often did with Coleridge.

Of course in a theological and medieval sense, any punishment of evil, any justice, or final bliss in heaven constituted comedy, divine according to Dante. As has been ably shown, under these liberal conditions all of Chaucer's finished works can be defined as comedy.[2]

But it would be meager fare for our modern, mundane world, if we were left with this. Nor are we. Surely Chaucer has known the "smiler with the knife" and enough of "sorrow" to describe it well:

> For whoso seeth me first on morwe
> May seyn he hath met with sorwe,
> For y am sorwe, and sorwe ys y.
>
> (*BD*, 595–97)

The images of the Temple of Mars in the *Knight's Tale*—the burned town, the corpse murdered in the bush with cut throat, the pig chewing up the baby in the cradle reflect war time experiences he could not have gained from books. But never does he indulge himself, or us, by settling in on the dark side of life, whether with his Pardoner, his Black Knight, or his Troilus. *In extremis*, as with Troilus, he may pull in heavenly bliss for a deathbed conversion into comedy, but generally, he provided us with laughter closer to home. Indeed, Chaucer ends up laughing at himself as a representative of witless Mankind, and that is a kind of funny comedy which is neither Boethian, nor Dantean, but Chaucerian, the complete embodiment of Meredith's Comic Spirit: "Men's future upon earth does not attract it; their honesty and shapeliness in the present does. . . ."[3]

Yet Chaucer was also the great master craftsman of this genre. He was its student, as well as its teacher. He drew from the greatest traditions of the past, and he initiated some of the most penetrating concepts of the future.

Basically, Chaucer reworked tradition as he used it. His debt to the French fabliaux has been adequately discussed elsewhere. These comedies of situation, stories of intricate sexual jokes involving coincidences, contrivances, and manipulations seem to have been preferred by romance audiences in the Middle Ages, with Boccaccio their best-known advocate. But nowhere is fabliau skill of precision, punning, parody, and punch line demonstrated with such virtuoso technique as in Chaucer's *Miller's Tale*. Humor of situation was ever one of the poet's strengths.

Nor did he neglect the tradition of character type. Chaucer's famous wandering Wife of Bath, and his equally peripatetic Pandarus were both well-known confidants and intermediaries in the Roman comedies. But there they were stereotypes, and Alisoun is seen again as such in Juan Ruiz's Trotaconventos, and the later famous Celestina. After Chaucer, Pandarus went into a well-known, and dramatic, decline. Both characters received their humanity with Chaucer, which had not been given them before, nor since. But more of that anon. We must not sentimentalize Chaucer, for our poet belongs in other aspects of his multifaceted comic genius to the tradition of the eighteenth century. A gently satiric outlook on life was surely part of Chaucer's nature, and irony its method of expression. His General Prologue to the *Canterbury Tales* is written in heroic couplets, but it does not ever portray the waspish mind of Pope; it bares the soul of contemporary society without succumbing to the misanthropy of Swift. Control and balance are

the disciplines of Chaucer's comedy, whose bounds his inter-
preters may transgress, but the poet never does.

The tradition of ironic and satiric verse was not invented
by Chaucer (nor even by Petronius), but the English poet undoubtedly fathered this form of humor in Britain, and it is today one of the hallmarks of the national temper. But Chaucer
also leaves his own earnest age behind when he discovered his
genius for parody of literary styles, combined with burlesque of
social conventions. We must leap the centuries to rediscover the
mock heroic, and even here Chaucer goes Pope one better, comedy on top of comedy. *The Rape of the Lock* mocks an epic situation, but the contestants are still only poor mortals, eighteenth-
century gallants. Chaucer's heroes are, after all, chickens, for
the *Nun's Priest's Tale*, perhaps his comic *chef d'oeuvre* (in
spite of Dr. Johnson who felt that "The tale of The Cock seems
hardly worth revival" [by Dryden in his Fables]), is a double
hit, a compound burlesque, of beast fable as well as classical
epic. And, finally, we must leap over to the twentieth century
to find for him in Max Beerbohm a worthy match in parody.

To place Chaucer in a continuing tradition, however,
skews the perspective on his art. Chaucer is the master of every
form of comedy, and as such he even has a personal signature on
all his creative endeavors, a private joke that runs from youth
to age throughout the totality of his works. This is the dumbstruck and frightened "Geffrey" of the *House of Fame*, the dim-
witted poetaster pilgrim called "Chaucer" in the *Canterbury
Tales*; it is the narrator in all his works. No one in English
literature has achieved such a lifetime of personal but shared
comedy. Only a supreme artist could have accomplished this
feat, only a wise and secure man could have afforded it, only a
humble man would have ventured it.

But this brief descriptive survey of Chaucer's comedy
should not mislead anyone into misunderstanding the poet's
motives. As royal servant to three kings, Edward III, Richard
II, and Henry IV, and occasional poet to the royal family,
Chaucer could not afford to be openly didactic, nor did he ever
judge. But he teaches as he delights; his "sentence" is often
implied as clearly as his "solaas" is explicit.

The most striking aspects of Chaucer's comic genius are undoubtedly seen in his fabliaux, his comedies of situation. "Sentence" seems to go begging here (or perhaps we lack the *caritas* to notice it), but we have "solaas" enough. The *Miller's Tale*, if not also the tales of the Reeve, the Shipman, and the Merchant, is surely known to everyone who has ever heard the name of Chaucer. These are the tales, after all, which have made our poet among the populace such a jolly good fellow, that nobody can deny. But in what specifically lies their brilliance? At their best, of course, they are feats of controlled verbal and coincidental pyrotechnics. Standard motifs of folklore and literature: the *senex amans*, the ill-matched marriage, the shrewd lover, appear again and again. The jealous and/or niggardly husbands are cuckolded by crafty clerks, by sly monks, or by boisterous students. There are no heroes and no villains. Nanny Morality has taken a day off and left the children to their own devices. The beautifully contrived and directed turbulence that ensues is at times awesome to watch. Indeed, we find ourselves rooting for the action rather than the actors. In the *Miller's Tale*, Chaucer combines two plots: that of the old story of Noah's Flood, often staged by the miracle plays, and the folkloric tale of the misdirected kiss. The old carpenter hangs in a tub from the ceiling, awaiting the deluge while the clerk is "swyving" the wife underneath. A second precious lover, armed with a coulter to avenge a previous slight, approaches the window and is met by the bare bottom and fart of the clerk. The hot coulter is rammed, the clerk cries "water" in anguish, the old carpenter thinks the flood is at hand and cuts the rope. The rest is hullabaloo. It is as simple as that, and yet I know of no one who has equalled Chaucer in this technique.

Not all of the fabliaux, of course, reach this supreme achievement of situational comedy. The Reeve's tale is more episodic, less genial in the "justice" executed by the two students on husband, wife, and daughter for an attempted trickery, than the Miller's tale. But in all this the tale fits the Reeve's thin, rusty, choleric personality. The Shipman's story is based on an old folklore anecdote called "the lover's gift regained" as here, where a wife receives money from a "loving" monk who in

turn had borrowed it from her husband. She requites her lover
in bed, and he later tells the husband that the loan had been
repaid to the wife. When questioned, she admits getting the
money and spending it, having thought that it had been given
outright, in friendship. But she would repay her husband: "Fro
day to day, and if so be I faille, / I am youre wyf; score it upon
my taille" (*CT* VII.415–16), and the poem ends, "Thus endeth
now my tale, and God us send / Taillynge ynough unto our lyves
ende" (*CT* VII.433–34). Tale, tail, and tally, Chaucer's triple
puns are part of the dextrous humor in these harmless stories.
Not quite so harmless or kindly, however, is the comedy in the
Merchant's Tale with its famous pear tree episode. The picture
of a lecherous May using the back of her blind old husband
January as a ladder to join her lover in a pear tree is bitter
humor, even though the pit may laugh loudly when "sodeynly
anon this Damyan / Gan pullen up the smok, and in he throng"
(*CT* IV.2352–53). To some it is always funny, I suppose, when
they don't wear pants, even in the southern parts of Lumbardye.

However, if this is the only aspect of Chaucer that
makes some people think him jolly, then indeed they do deny
him. True, the fabliaux are filled with nuances of speech,
vignettes of every day medieval life, allegros of parody, and
deft character sketches which defy description but demand
personal acquaintance. They are elegant and polished pieces in
spite of their earthy content, but they don't pretend to probe
much below their surface. If we critics do so, we tend to find
what is perhaps not meant to be.

When Chaucer himself gets interested in a character,
however, he achieves unqualified greatness. And this is what
obviously happened with Alisoun, the Wife of Bath. Geoffrey
liked her so much that he had her appear in and out of the
Canterbury Tales. Aside from her description in the General
Prologue, her long introductory dramatic monologue, and her
tale, she is mentioned by the Clerk in the *envoi* to his tale and
by Justinus, a character *in* the *Merchant's Tale!* The apparent
paradox of this last appearance, reality entering into fiction, is
easily resolved when we remember that Alisoun was the *primum mobile* of many thoughts, of the sequence of tales called
the "Marriage Group," and of the Clerk's sarcastic outburst.

Why then could she not also enter into the Merchant's imaginative process? Indeed, Chaucer mentions her again in his later poem, the *Envoy to Bukton*, à propos the latter's ensuing marriage.

Alisoun is definitely the grande dame of the pilgrimage, and probably also of Chaucer's literary life. She is his great creation, whom he dearly loved, along with Criseyde, though the Wife of Bath is a comic character, where Criseyde is not. But why is the Wife of Bath so intriguing? Because she openly talks about sex, her urges, and the trials and tribulations she caused her first three husbands? I think not. Not for this did Chaucer admire her. Rather, I suspect, it was because she, like himself, understood well enough the seriousness of life, that she had suffered anguish and heartache and personal misfortunes, as he may have done, but in spite of this, her outlook on life was not a tragic one, her optimism was unassailable, as she pilgrimaged forth with the rest, ready for an adventure, good or bad, with a sixth husband. No man can create but what is in himself; both the light and the dark are part of him. In the Wife of Bath Chaucer reflected the great sympathy he had for mankind and mirrored the strength of his own comic view of existence.

She did not, of course, jump out of his head like Athena out of the mind of Jupiter. Her forebears were ancient, evil and benign witches, spinners, matchmakers who knew the remedies of love and hustled for others when they could no longer go it alone. The Grimm fairy tales are full of them, and they have spun and woven the fates of men from the beginning. They are not lovable women because their motives and machinations remain a mystery to us. But Alisoun makes herself understood, even beyond her intent. Her rambling, naively blithe confession of how it was she who laid her husbands low: "As help me God, I laughe whan I thynke / How pitously a-nyght I made hem swynke!" (*CT* III.201–02), of her prowess in carping, her vanity, and greed could easily be passed off as being no more than a clever exposition of the medieval antifeminist tradition, did not her romantic tale, which yearns for youth and beauty and *gentilesse*, give her character a roundness and her personality a psychological depth of which before we had received only hints: "But, Lord Crist! whan that it remembreth me / Upon my yowthe, and on my jolitee / It tikleth me aboute myn herte roote. . . . / But age, allas! that al wole envenyme, / Hath me biraft my beautee and my pith" (*CT* III.469–71, 474–75). The *Wife of Bath's Prologue* was one, I suspect, that Chaucer was loath to finish.

Alisoun's male counterpart is Pandarus in the *Troilus and Criseyde*. They have the same ancestors and lineage, except that Pandarus is unsuccessful in love and thus his emotional life is a vicarious one. Here too a sadness lurks in the background, and his bustling efforts on behalf of his niece and friend have become suspect through the action of time. But Chaucer's Pandarus is not yet tainted. He moves the action with zest and joy in the hunt. He huffs, and puffs, and sweats through the streets of Troy; he carries letters, stuffs them down the breast of the unwilling receiver, organizes a series of complex rendezvous worthy of the efforts of our best P. R. men, which involve scores of people and feigned motives, in order to attain a brief secret meeting, and finally tears the shirt off the fainting lover and "into bed hym caste." Admittedly, his values are surface ones compared to those of Troilus. Pandarus would hold with the lower birds in the *Parlement of Foules* rather than with the courtly eagles. But it must be remembered that Pandarus never knew love, whereas Troilus had tasted it to the full. Pandarus therefore never got over his concern about the basic need for sex; a starved man can not wait for gourmet food. However, these considerations could lead us into an area that is not necessarily comic and there is no need to pursue them here. I have mentioned them, and Alisoun's complexity, only in passing, to show that Chaucer produces a comedy that is human and compassionate, truly humane.

But "Awak!" It is not always human. Among the greatest comic figures that Chaucer produced, the Wife of Bath and Pandarus, we must not forget his birds! Perhaps the most astonishingly delightful of all of Chaucer's comic characters is the enormous golden "Egle" that appears at the end of Book I of the *House of Fame* and is the main actor in Book II. The eagle is at first a fearsome animal as he swoops down to pick up Geffrey in his claws. Diverse thoughts, of Dante, of the rape of Ganymede, even of the terrible bird Roc in the Arabian Nights pass through our mind, and possibly Chaucer's as he is swooped up, and the poet fears that he perhaps might join other dead notables among the stars: "'O God!' thoughte I, 'that madest kynde, / Shal I noon other weyes dye? / Wher Joves wol me stellyfye?'" (*HF* 584–86). But as it turns out, the eagle is a kindly, if authoritative teacher, who shows his hapless burden the world from the skies, initiates him into the mystery of the law of sound, as they behold beneath them fields and plains, valleys and forests, and ships sailing in the sea. The Egle would even have shown Chaucer the stars close up, had not the poet demurred, pleading his age and danger to his eyesight. The avian guide will lead Chaucer to the House of Fame, to hear tidings of love, but the more he talks, the less the poet dares to answer. In fact, this preceptorial eagle is enthused with his ability and the opportunity to teach a student of little mind, as Geffrey appears to be. Like any good teacher who wishes to establish rapport, he has addressed the poet by his first name, and he even asks for "student feedback," delighting already in his assured success:

> Telle me this now feythfully,
> Have y not preved thus symply,
> Withoute any subtilite
> Of speche, or gret prolixite
> Of termes of philosophie,
> Of figures of poetrie,
> Or colours of rethorike?
> Pardee, hit oughte the to lyke!
> For hard langage and hard matere
> Ys encombrous for to here
> Attones; wost thou not wel this?"
> And y answered and seyde, "Yis."
>   "A ha!" quod he, "lo, so I can
> Lewedly to a lewed man
> Speke, and shewe hym swyche skiles
> That he may shake hem be the biles,
> So palpable they shulden be."

(*HF*, II.853–69)

If I might enter into this discussion with a personal remark, I would say that for me Chaucer's Egle represents one of
the high points of his comedy, truly funny for many complex
reasons, of which the most important probably are the lovable
pedantry of the bird and the author's identification with his
own persona; the "lewed man" in the eagle's claws is "Geffrey."
Also, in spite of the eagle's obvious enthusiasm for his own
wisdom, he is a powerful teacher, an enormously learned, and
eccentric bird of a man. It seems only natural to identify him
with an individual we know through legend, perhaps a great
professor. As a Chaucerian, impressed, admittedly, only by
hearsay, the Egle has always seemed to me like a huge, flying
George Lyman Kittredge, and how apt (or ironic?) that he
should be teaching Chaucer.

Eagles also appear in the *Parlement of Foules*, although
there they are of lesser interest than their "lower class" counterparts. Notwithstanding that there is much doubt of the exact meaning of this poem, with its debates on love and common
profit, there is no question that it is one of the finest small jew-
els in Chaucer's collection of gems. The poet's sympathy here
clearly lies with the rabble in their impatience with the
courtly love ritual of the noble birds of prey, the stultifying
debate of the "tercels" who woo a shy "formel" lady eagle.
They too have their humor, but it is the cuckoo, the goose, the
duck, and turtledove who really get this show on the road. The
representatives of water, seed, and worm fowls have their say
in no uncertain terms:

> The goos, the cokkow, and the doke also
> So cryede, "Kek kek! kokkow! quek quek!" hye
> That thourgh myne eres the noyse wente tho.
> The goos seyde, "Al this nys not worth a flye!"
>
> (*PF*, 498–501)

The goose's advice is simple: If she won't love him, let him
love another, to which the sparrow hawk replies with open
contempt, "Lo, here a parfit resoun of a goos!" The duck reacts
scornfully to the turtledove's romantic idea of everlasting love:
"'Wel bourded,' quod the doke 'by mye hat!'" What a silly
idea! "Ye quek!" There are more stars in heaven than a pair.

But this remark angers the falcon: "Now fy cherl! . . . Out of
the donghill cam that word ful right!" reminding us that we
are very much part of a class society. But there is so much of
earnest absurdity shown by the members of this parliament or
congress of birds, all of which leads to no resolution, that to
look for underlying symbols or meaning here is to take the edge
off the comedy. It is enough to have the duck swear by his hat
(which he would not do if he did not wear one) and to envision
this bird with a headdress taken from the Ellesmere MS illustrations. Perhaps a Flemish beaver hat might stand him well,
since he supposedly represents the merchant class. However,
we must never forget that he is but a duck.

Nor must we forget that Chauntecleer is but a cock! For
the mock-heroic beast fable of the *Nun's Priest's Tale* is the
most delightful marriage story of them all, and wifely
Pertelote's long helpful speech from VII.2907–8 (after her mate
has awakened from an ominous dream of death by a hound-like
beast) runs a very human gamut of rhetorically noble outrage at
her caitiff, coward of a husband, to wise counsel on humors and
dreams, and finally to the truly basic, solicitous advice to
"taak som laxatyf." Earnest thoughts, which surely have over-
extended the knowledge of Pertelote as no situation ever had
before, she who was used to listen meekly to the endless crow-
ings of her noble lord and master. To all of which her husband
patronizingly answers, smiling condescendingly through his
beak: "Madame, . . . graunt mercy of youre loore." And then we
are launched into fine rhetoric, great speeches, which never
seem to stop, the upshot of which are ". . . I seye forthermoor, /
That I ne telle of laxatyves no stoor. . . ." Truly, Chauntecleer
is a magnificent cock, in his own eyes certainly like to Ozy-
mandias, king of kings, of the barnyard, and equally unstable of
perch.

The Beast Fable of the continent, with its Reynard and
Ysengrim and various fowls, was, like the fabliaux, not too well
known in England. Here, as everywhere, Chaucer took the roots
of material from foreign soil, fertilized the ground with new
genius, and let the plant flower. Chauntecleer is literature's
greatest rooster. He is as long-winded as the Egle, but he is less
lovable, for he lacks the Egle's ingenuous enthusiasm for teach-

ing and concern for his student. Chauntecleer, we remember, is so superior to all, that he will indulge himself in a private joke, with no one around to understand it, except (perhaps) himself:

> For al so siker as *In principio*
> *Mulier est hominis confusio,*
> Madame, the sentence of this Latyn is,
> "Womman is mannes joye and al his blis."
>
> (*CT* VII.3163–66)

Indeed, such pride goeth before a fall. But, although much of the rooster's glory is but a sham, though he is at times so infuriating that one would love to call him a pompous ass if he were not a bird (and indeed such a one would by his very inflated nature hate the undignified thought of laxatives), still, his wit wins out, and all is well in the end. Chaucer's birds follow a definite line of comedy. They are all very talkative (as birds seem to be on an early summer morning), and they pontificate to various degrees. Thus their comedy is a verbal one, and as characters they are not so dimensionally drawn, so deeply probed as Chaucer's human creations. The birds are caricatures; were they more they would be humans masquerading in feathers, and that, of course, is not the point of the game.

Language in general was Chaucer's most effective comic tool. Where his humor appeals to our intellectual sense it is always in the ironic statement, the understated conclusion in many portraits of the General Prologue, the implication in the accumulation of irrelevant material, and the quick-running, highly realistic dialogue of the pilgrims. We recognize many of his portraits in Langland's *Piers Plowman* where this "earnest contemporary of Chaucer's" has included stereotypes and broad comedy of similar individuals: friars, physicians, pardoners. But where Langland cuts with a broadsword, Chaucer pierces with a foil. His Friar is an individual; his name is Huberd. Such a worthy man as he should have no truck with lepers and other unwholesome beings. And the Prioress, a most elegant and truly charming woman! We learn all about her table manners, her dress, her love of dogs, her physical beauty, her jewelry. Forty-five lines of description but not a word of her spiritual qualities or duty. She did sing the divine service well, but then so might have the Wife of Bath or "hende" Nicholas. Everywhere in the General Prologue Chaucer challenges our values, the standards we go by, of getting and spending and laying waste our powers. But he does not judge us, or his pilgrims. Indeed, he defends them, in the guise of his little-witted alter ego, the pilgrim Chaucer. At one point, we remember (*CT* I.183–88), he explains that he had conversed with the Monk, and in this conversation had agreed fully with the Monk's worldly principles. Nor did he do so ironically then, for at the present moment he is telling us, the reader, about this little talk, and even justifies himself to us as to the reason why "I seyde his opinion was good." How, after all, should the world be served! It is here, in the General Prologue, that our enjoyment of Chaucer's comedy becomes an exciting game which involves our own sharpness of mind and appreciation for the most delicate shades of irony. This is intellectual humor. Few of the pilgrims are exempt from the poet's finger. It points at high and low, at religious as well as secular: The Sergeant at Lawe, "Nowher so bisy a man as he ther nas / And yet he semed bisier than he was" (*CT* I.321–22); the Merchant, "This worthy man ful wel his wit bisette: / Ther wiste no wight that he was in dette. . . ." (*CT* I.279–80); the Cook, "But greet harm was it, as it thoughte me, / That on his shyne a mormal hadde he. / For blank-manger, that made he with the beste" (*CT* I.385–87). For most, the trip to Canterbury was indeed a necessary one.

Again, language unifies the various tales into a human comedy of pilgrims. The so-called "links" among the tales, the argumentative chains of cause and effect among the narrators, provide the living magic; for the Miller wishes to "quite" the Knight, and in doing so insults the Reeve whose tale enthuses the drunken Cook—three tales and a fragment thereby tied into unity. The Wife of Bath's brilliant monologue, interrupted by the nervous Pardoner and commented on ironically by the Friar, who provokes the Summoner, leads into a series of six tales. Everywhere there is movement, medieval England on the highway, but the road that is travelled seems never very distant from our own. For if we have not met these people, then our friends have, and indeed some of them are our friends. Worse luck, at times we even see ourselves! This acquaintance with Chaucer's pilgrims, then as today, stems from familiarity with the little touches and gestures of our fallible humanity, as when the Wife of Bath forgets for a moment the point of what she was saying (*CT* III.585–86), or the Friar in the *Summoner's Tale* shows his arrogant familiarity with the house he visits: "And fro the bench he droof awey the cat" (*CT* III.1775). As Dryden said, here indeed is God's plenty, and it is brought about through the word.

But when the word mocks the word, when language makes fun of language, then indeed our sense of humor is cerebrally challenged. And such it is with Chaucer's amazing gift of parody. In this most literate form of comedy, Chaucer was the great innovator in English letters. Here was virgin territory, a new world, and only an independent, uninhibited mind would have had the urge to leave the old world of literary convention, and embark out.

For Chaucer, this old world consisted in the main of the traditional French themes of *amour courtois, service d'amour*, and romance literature. Machaut and Deschamps schooled him in the early days; the *Roman de la Rose* was at his bedside. Thus it was this type of standard noble fare which proved to be grist for Chaucer's satiric mill. Parody and mockery of courtly love themes appear throughout the *Canterbury Tales* and, in fact, form part of the last poem he presented at court, one of his wittiest verbal games, employing double and even triple entendres, the *Complaint to his Purse*.

One can imagine that Chaucer could hardly wait to finish the *Knight's Tale*, so that he could "quite" it with the Miller's. In the latter we find his most pervasive imitation, on a lower and absurd level, of the courtly *descriptio* and painstaking ritual of the game of love previously played by Arcite, Palamon, and Emily. The Miller's wife, Alisoun, is described in eye, brow, mouth, hue, and song, but she is dark rather than fair, and her body is not like to a goddess, but rather a weasel. The parallels to the portrait of Emily are exact in form, but on a lower, animal scale. "Wynsynge she was, as is a joly colt," and class difference is made explicit in the conclusion: "She was a prymerole, a piggesnye, / For any lord to leggen in his bedde, / Or yet for any good yeman to wedde" (*CT* I.3263, 3267–70). Though her first lover, Nicholas, is a handy man, her second, Absolon, woos only by word and mouth. He sings a love song, "Lemman, thy grace, and sweete bryd, thyn oore," chews licorice, and puts a sweet-smelling herb under his tongue to change the odor of his breath. Like a courtly lover, he will languish and pass a sleepless night, but to endure this vigil he must first take an afternoon nap. We have burlesque here and parody, for Absolon addresses his beloved weasel in the words of the Song of Solomon, explaining that she makes him "swete" for love of her. Unfortunately, as we know, his oral tactics backfire, and "His hoote love was coold and al yqueynt!" (On his home court Chaucer's word play is indeed hard to beat.)

Since we find a similar mockery of convention in the *Merchant's Tale*—the secret message, *complaint d'amour*, the rather quick "mercy" of May and illicit assignation in the bower of love (a pear tree), and even a parody of the French Aube in the *Reeve's Tale*: "Fare weel, Malyne, sweete wight! / The day is come, I may no lenger byde. . . ." (*CT* I.4236–37)—it seems clear that one of the main themes of Chaucer's fabliaux is the burlesque of romance tradition and that the joke is always at the expense of the middle and lower class.

This is perhaps best seen in Chaucer's two most brilliant tours de force, *Sir Thopas* and the *Nun's Priest's Tale*. The first is a parody of the endless Middle English tail rhyme romances. A continuous repetition of the rhyme scheme *aab, aab* over a long period of time tends to engender a range of reactions, from sleep to irritation. But it does not ever inspire delight. And yet *Sir Thopas* is a thoroughly delightful piece. Chaucer takes a bourgeois Flemish "knight" who swears by ale and bread, a "doghty swayn" described in feminine terms, white of face, red of lips, and with a "semely nose." He loves an elf queen he has never seen, rides through a forest: "Therinne is many a wilde best, / Ye, bothe bukke and hare," (*CT* VII.755–56) on a war horse that "gooth an ambil in the way." Nothing is sacred in this piece, neither romance style, nor action, nor hero. In the romances, the tail rhyme line, for instance, does have a specific narrative function as transition, or as strong concluding statement. The stanzas should build up to these lines and to the last important line especially:

> Sir Thopas was a doghty swayn
> Whit was his face as payndemayn
> His lippes rede as rose;
> His rode is lyk scarlet in grayn,
> And I yow telle in good certayn,
> He hadde a semely nose.

(*CT* VII.724–29)

The letdown can be heard. The "semely nose" is not only burlesque of noble heroic description, but also parody of the romance stanza, and this double effect is seen throughout a work which is of major importance in English literary history. The poem is a fun house of delight for medievalists, but we are not all too unhappy when the Host puts a stop to it, though we must disagree with his opinion that the pilgrim Chaucer's "drasty rymyng is nat worth a toord."

From a misplaced middle-class burgher in a fairy world of romance, we descend further into the henyard of the *Nun's Priest's Tale*. This simple story of a rooster's dream of death, his abduction by a fox, and his subsequent rescue is the core of an extremely intricate, fascinating, and intriguing web of Chaucer's highest art, especially since many of the poet's major literary and philosophic themes are here tossed about in rapid sequence and apparent wild abandon. The narrative moves from the lowest style of barnyard communication: "Out! harrow! and weyl away! / Ha! Ha! the fox!"—and after him ran Colle the dog, and Malkin with a distaff in her hand—to the highest style of noble rhetoric and lament after Chauntecleer had closed his eyes to the fox who did him "by the gargat hente." "O destinee, that mayst nat been eschewed. . . . O Venus, that art goddesse of plesaunce. . . . O Gaufred, deere maister soverayn . . ."

> O woful hennes, right so criden ye
> As when that Nero brende the citee
> Of Rome cryden senatoures wyves
> For that hir husbondes losten alle hir lyves.

(*CT* VII.3369–72)

Earthshaking is the tragedy of Chauntecleer's fall. He is classed with the great heroes of all time and his enemy the fox with the greatest of biblical, classical, and romance villains:

> O false mordrour, lurkynge in thy den!
> O new Scariot, newe Genylon,
> False dissymulour, o Greek Synon,
> That broghtest Troye al outrely to sorwe!
> O Chauntecleer, acursed be that morwe
> That thou into that yerd flaugh fro the bemes!
>
> (*CT* VII.3226–31)

His Fall is sung in Boethian terms, and it is blamed on the advice of woman in true anti-feminist, or anti-hen, fashion. The glorious romance fury of the cock's outraged sovereign mistress ends with homely advice against constipation. A topsy-turvy world, a spectacular literary production where almost every line turns a new corner, brings new lore divertingly into play, about dreams, references to the medieval Bestiary, saints' legends, and the ways of Fortune. Indeed, this is Big Game. Its true splendor is surely wasted on the newcomer to Chaucer although, unfortunately, the tale is often found on the high school reading list. It is a work that can be enjoyed to the fullest extent only by those who are familiar with the poet, his major themes, and their medieval background. A comic masterpiece like the *Nun's Priest's Tale* occurs but once in English literature. It merits a prepared reader.

When we view this literary wealth of a lifetime, it is hard to imagine that its creator was a man taken to task continually for his ignorance, his dullness, his little wit. Wherever he went or flew, he was treated with impatience by the Black Knight, lectured to by an Egle, yanked out of bed and shoved hither and yon by the Noble Roman Africanus, condemned to talk about endlessly faithful women by the God of Love, and finally told to shut up by the Host of the Tabard Inn. And there is no question about the identity of this hapless individual. His name was "Geffrey" in the *House of Fame*, and "Chaucer" in the Tales. He is a poet, and round of form. This is how Chaucer saw himself and developed himself as the "persona" in most of his works, throughout the vast adventure of his life.

He was himself his own greatest comic figure, and the delight he took in having himself appear again and again, in the most ludicrous of situations, is patent. We can only conjecture on why he took such pleasure in this unusual device, a figure which paradoxically seemed to increase in naivete as Chaucer grew older, and undoubtedly wiser. There are many theories; the subject has been a central debate of our times. Let me say here only that it represents a kind of comedy that issues from the poet's heart. Chaucer's own pose was not an intellectually planned device. In some ways it was traditional, having been used in French literature and in English by Langland and the author of *Pearl*. But Chaucer's persona had a specific name, the poet's, and his own profession. As I have mentioned above, the use of this kind of narrator is revealing. *Ad hominem* humor was alien to Chaucer, though Pynchebeke was a living lawyer, Roger of Ware a cook, and Harry Bailey host of the real Tabard. All of these, however, were portrayed as experts in their work; none was derided as being dim or dull. Chaucer had enough confidence in his name and reputation to be able to point the finger at himself. Rather would he do it so that others would not. But to reason this way is to insert a calculating quality into his humor. It is not there, although Chaucer could not have survived three kings in the English civil service, had he not been capable of diplomacy. His persona may indeed have been a shield, at Court or in affairs, but the symbol it bore represented Geoffrey Chaucer's main characteristic: he was wise to himself, and to his world, and thus he could be no man's fool.

Our mention of the Sergeant at Law at whose writing none could "pynche" (*CT* I.326) brings to mind that we should say a few words about Chaucer's lost humor. Much of the poet's comedy was topical of course. We need new Manlys with their Ricketts to come up with more historical identifications. No doubt there are such. Also, a full understanding of Chaucer's pervasive and complex punning will have to await the "zodiak" or other terminal word of the *Middle English Dictionary*. At present we find many puns where we should not, but overlook, I am sure, even more. Again, the recent stress on the oral presentation of Chaucer's works—but only by himself, I would suppose—must lead us to study cadences and rhythmic patterns of his verse. Perhaps the joke lay in the telling, though possibly Chaucer was as dull a reciter of his own verse as some of our modern poets today.

In the process of rediscovering Chaucer's lost humor, two caveats should be observed. First, we cannot trust any of his specific descriptive references to be merely ornamental; an underlying narrative reason may always be lurking in the bush. Second, we must be careful never to stop looking until we are sure to have reached the basic level of a term. In describing the Reeve in the General Prologue, for instance, Chaucer writes (or reads aloud to his audience):

> Of Northfolk was this Reve of which I telle,
> Biside a toun men clepen Baldeswelle.
>
> (CT I.619–20)

The reference to Norfolk and Baldeswell is meaningless to us today except as it specifies the home of the Reeve, and thus adds to a sense of realism. But it cannot serve as a joke. And yet it did probably provoke chuckles in Chaucer's listeners, for we know today that the provinces sent many immigrants to London at this very time, and most of them came from Norfolk, specifically even from Baldeswell. Their dialect was just on the fringe of comprehension, and their manners quite uncitified. Baldeswell is a topical joke, rediscovered, but, in finding it, the spectre of countless undiscovered others rises before us.

Again, the ugly, disfiguring disease of the Summoner, of whose "visage children were aferd" has been identified in the past as "alopecia," a medieval form of "leprosy," and there the matter was allowed to stand for decades. It added something to the portrait of this cunning and lecherous church warden of social morality: it made him even uglier than he was. But as has been noted, Chaucer rarely wastes words purely for descriptive reasons. When we look a little further and see that in the Middle Ages "leprosy" was a venereal disease, and thus more often than not confused with syphilis, the joke of the Summoner's disease broadens indeed. The face of this corrupt member of the Church's "vice-squad" betrays him to the world. All these are indeed only stones in Chaucer's grand mosaic, but they prove that the reconstruction of this mosaic is incomplete, that much can still be done by scholars, historical or critical, to add to their own enjoyment, and all our benefit.

For Chaucer repays a lifetime of study with a lifetime of ever-increasing pleasure in his works. And it is more than that. Chaucer provides for many that very thing which Matthew Arnold felt he lacked, an essential quality in his work "which gives to our spirits what they can rest upon." This is so because Chaucer's comedy is not of the intellect alone, and here Meredith's thought is incomplete when he writes that comedy laughs through the mind, that it is really the "humour of the mind." But when the critic adds that "the test of true Comedy is that it shall awaken thoughtful laughter,"[4] we would agree, for thoughtfulness is characterized by a searching, a depth of feeling. We respond emotionally to Chaucer's comedy of life, do we not? The Wife of Bath or Pandarus do not affect us on an intellectual plane alone, nor can we react to the complex implications of Chaucer's own portrait throughout his works only on this level. In spite of the poet's frequently discussed relativism of view, and his refusal ever to give a specific judgment, Chaucer does have a consistent overall sense of life, one of attained optimism fostered by a genial and tranquil spirit, which we are taught again and again when we study what he tells us. This sense is not only, as a later author explains, that

> All the world's a stage
> And all the men and women merely players.
> They have their exits and their entrances. . . .
>
> (*As You Like It* II.vii.139–41)

although it may have seemed so to the writer, for, no doubt, he knew his craft well. But life is not really play acting, with each of us set in our predestined comic or tragic parts. Some more useful information about the world would seem preferable, even if the news were bad. I can, for instance, accept the Chaucerian statement that

> This world nys but a thorghfare ful of wo
> And we been pilgrymes, passynge to and fro
>
> (*CT* I.2847–49)

for I know that the man who has recognized this "lytel erthe"
for what it is, can, in spite of such knowledge, continually look
past the sorrow at the world's joy, take cheer in the
pilgrimage, hold the "heye weye" and sustain us as well along
the road.

Those of us who have devoted our lives to the lessons of
this great teacher of comedy, dissimilar as we may at times
appear to be, have been united by his spirit into a unique fellowship, with Chaucer himself as our prime mover and friend.
Like the Host,

> He served us with vitaille at the beste;
> Strong was the wyn, and wel to drynke us leste.
>
> *(CT I.749–50)*

On the pilgrimage, I admit, I have "rested upon" him and
drunk with him often, and he has lightened my mood. Truly, I
cannot imagine for any of us a more happy vocation than the
continuing opportunity to pass this sustaining pleasure on to
others.

Indeed, all things considered, and with all due humility,
I think we Chaucerians are a fortunate lot.

NOTES

*Reprinted with permission from *Versions of Medieval Comedy*, ed. Paul
G. Ruggiers (Norman, Okla.: University of Oklahoma Press, 1977), pp.
173-90.

1. All references to Chaucer's works are from the edition by F. N.
Robinson, *The Works of Geoffrey Chaucer*, 2d edition (Boston: Houghton
Mifflin, 1957).

2. Cf. Helen Storm Corsa, *Chaucer: Poet of Mirth and Morality*
(Notre Dame: University of Notre Dame Press, 1964).

3. George Meredith, "Essay: On the Idea of Comedy and of the
Uses of the Comic Spirit," in *The Works of George Meredith*, Memorial
Edition (New York: Russell and Russell 1968), XXIII, pp. 46–47.

4. Meredith, p. 46.

The Canterbury Tales II: Comedy*

Derek Pearsall

Comedy of one kind or another is present in a large number of the *Canterbury Tales* and pervasive in the links between tales, but we are concerned here with those tales where the narrative structure and expectations are those of comedy as a specific genre. There are six such tales, those of the Miller, Reeve, Shipman, Merchant, Friar and Summoner, and a seventh, that of the Cook, which is left unfinished but which was certainly going to belong to the genre. The fact that we know this, from only fifty-eight lines, is an indication of the general firmness of the initial structure of expectation of Chaucerian comedy, the codifiability of the preliminary ground-rules, whatever strain or defiance those rules may be subjected to in Chaucer's subsequent development of the story. Anticipatory indications of the nature of a particular tale are often given by what we know or suspect of the character of the pilgrim who tells it, and the comic or satirically abusive prologues to five of these tales are important in creating expectation; but even without such clues we should know, from elements built into the narrative structure, the rules of the narrative game we were being invited to play.

The time is the present, and the story is introduced as an up-to-date report on a contemporary "slice-of-life." There is nothing of what "olde stories tellen us" (*Knight's Tale* I.859). The place is the homely known world of town or village, usually in England. The Miller's and Reeve's tales are slily set

101

in or near the two university towns of Oxford and Cambridge (Trumpington is "nat fer fro Cantebrigge": I.3921), as if to give a broad and impartial view of the principal preoccupations and activities of university students, and the *Cook's Tale* is set in London, "our citee" (I.4365). The *Friar's Tale* speaks of "my contree" (III.1301), again communicating that sense of the known and familiar, while the *Summoner's Tale* is set in Holderness, in Yorkshire. The French setting of the *Shipman's Tale* in "Sent Denys," with Paris and Bruges figuring in the action, would have seemed homely enough, and quite different from another French setting, that of the *Franklin's Tale*, near Penmarch, in Brittany, with all its romantic associations. The *Merchant's Tale* is set in Pavia, in Lombardy, which may have had a reputation in English eyes as a "city of sin": whatever the connotations, in this as in other respects the *Merchant's Tale* proclaims itself "different." Apart from these matters of setting, in time and place, there is also a distinctive tone about Chaucer's comic tales which helps to mark them off as a genre, a reductive tone, resembling a clinical analysis of the inhabitants of a zoo. Only in this type of tale would we be told of a merchant "That riche was, for which men helde hym wys" (VII.2) or of the desire of an old man for a wife, "Were it for hoolynesse or for dotage" (IV.1253) or be given an unoutraged description of a wife "that heeld for contenance / A shoppe, and swyved for hir sustenance" (I.4421–22).

More important than any of these features, however, in contributing to the distinctiveness of the sense of genre in Chaucer's comic tales are the assumptions we are asked to share in reading them. In romance, to take a contrasting type of tale, we are asked to accept for the purposes of the story that there are noble ideals of behaviour, fidelity to which is the means through which human existence is validated, through which life is shown to be meaningful. So Arveragus speaks of "trouthe" (V.1479), and Arcite, in dying, of "trouthe, honour, knyghthede" and the other values he admires (I.2789). In religious tales and saints' legends, an equally self-transcending system of values operates, in this case proving the significance of life through the demonstration of its ultimate insignificance in relation to life eternal. Comedy sets all this aside, and asserts

that there are no values, secular or religious, more important
than survival and the satisfaction of appetite. Characters who
may be temporarily under the illusion that things are otherwise, such as Absolon or January, are given short shrift. The
injunction is not "be noble," or "be good," but "be smart."
Our extreme satisfaction in seeing Nicholas, in the *Miller's Tale*,
receive his comeuppance is not based on a perception of moral
justice being done—the idea that he is "scalded in the towte"
(I.3853) because he has committed adultery is too trite for
words—but on the comic justice of "the biter bit." Nicholas
makes himself vulnerable because he ceases to be smart, and
tries to play the same trick on Absolon that Alison has already
played: this is not the behaviour of a cunning animal, which is
what the comic hero is expected to be.

It will be seen that Chaucerian comedy, on this definition
of it, differs markedly from comedy as classically defined, that
is, as a socially normative literary form, working to correct our
behaviour through making us laugh at the ridiculousness of
vice and folly. This is the comedy of dramatists like Jonson or
Molière, or of theorists like Bergson or Meredith.[1] In Chaucer,
though, the social norms are not clearly displayed and moral
norms are often openly subverted, as when the narrator of the
Miller's Tale, after licking his lips over the description of
Alison, comments in conclusion:

> She was a prymerole, a piggesnye,
> For any lord to leggen in his bedde,
> Or yet for any good yeman to wedde.

(I.3268-70)

For the reader to reassert the moral norm by attributing the
neglect or subversion of moral value to the narrator's inadequacy is a trick that has often been tried, but mostly by people
who think laughter unimportant or who have misunderstood
the rules of this particular game. This is not to say, of course,
that satire, done from well-established normative positions is
not present in these comic tales: the complacency and gullibility of John the carpenter, the ludicrous philandering of
Absolon, are classics of satirical comedy. But the tales as a
whole are not satirical comedies: one would have to ask, satiri-

cal of *what?* and Chaucer will not return any simple answer, or
any complicated one for that matter. The case may seem different with the Friar's and Summoner's tales, but even there the
satire is made part of a mutual exchange of abuse and thereby
pushed away from any authoritative moral centre. The
wickedness of summoners and friars remains the theme of the
two tales, respectively, but not their *point.*

At the same time that one rejects moralistic interpretations of Chaucerian comedy, one should not allow one's enthusiasm for immorality to go so far as to encourage an alternative
kind of assertiveness—that the comic tales are a "celebration
of life," a universal subversion of established values, a kick up
the behind for all orthodoxies. The popularization of the
views of Bakhtin in the West has led to a good deal of insistence on the presence of this kind of "festive comedy" in
Chaucer, as in Shakespeare.[2] In a certain basic way, of course,
laughter always offers a kind of psychic release which is as-
sertive of life, especially when we laugh at the blaspheming of
what is revered, the breaking of taboos, the open practice of
verbal obscenity, the explicit depiction of excretory and sexual
functions. There is also release of another kind in the denoue-
ments of these comic tales, where in every case the climax, after much build-up of tension and expectation, involves the final
acting-out of some trick, accompanied by delightful surprise
and reversal. The moments when we realize that Nicholas's
call for water—"'Help! water! water! help, for Goddes
herte!'" (I.3815)—is going to be construed by the carpenter in
his tub as the announcement of the predicted deluge, or that
Aleyn, thinking he has got into bed with his fellow student,
has snuggled up to the miller, are moments of almost cathartic
physical release. Laughter here is a renewal of vitality: it
does not, however, mean anything beyond itself, in relation to
life (as distinct from art), or constitute a "celebration of life,"
that is, of life in its physical functions (as if those functions
were more "real" than intellectual, emotional or spiritual functions). Chaucer's comic tales exist no more to celebrate life than
to criticize immorality: "realism" is not in question, and the
narrative assumptions we are asked to make are no more realistic than those we are asked to make in romance.

It is important at this stage to introduce a distinction between the Friar's and Summoner's tales and the other four (or
four-and-a-bit) tales, and to appropriate the technical term
fabliau to apply to the latter group. The term is often used
broadly for all comic tales of low life involving trickery, but
there is much advantage in restricting it, in discussing Chaucer,
to the tales involving marriage and sex, and setting aside the
Friar's and Summoner's tales for later discussion. The four tales
remaining are capable of quite strict definition as fabliaux, as
tales, that is, in which a bourgeois husband is duped or tricked
into conniving at the free award of his wife's sexual favours to
a clever young man. Such tales are widespread in European tradition, and well known from being included in such numbers in
Boccaccio's *Decameron* or in French collections such as the *Cent
Nouvelles Nouvelles* ("A Hundred New Stories"). There are
very few examples in English: indeed, Chaucer's are almost the
only examples of the genre as more strictly defined. It was long
believed, because of a convenient assumption about social class
and social morality, that the fabliaux could only have been
enjoyed by the lower classes, or the bourgeoisie at best, but this
belief has been shown to be unfounded,[3] and indeed it seems on
the face of it unlikely, given that the pillars of petit-bourgeois
society are constantly the objects of ridicule, and that the humour of the stories often relies on quite a subtle understanding of
the courtly behaviour that is travestied.

In practice, Chaucer blurs this distinctive sense of audience, this sense of a sophisticated courtly group laughing at the
animal antics of their inferiors, perhaps because his idea of his
potential audience in the *Canterbury Tales* is much more generous and comprehensive. He allocates the telling of the tales, by
a shrewd dramatic stroke, to the kind of people that they are
about, suggesting half-playfully a kind of merging of pilgrim-
age-reality and tale-reality (the appearance in the *Miller's
Tale* of a servant who, like the Miller himself (I.3129), is
called Robyn and has a special way with doors (I.3466; cf.
I.550) is the most whimsically audacious example of this), and
subsuming the real audience (us) in the fictional one (the pilgrims). He also apologizes in advance, in the *General Prologue*,
for telling such coarse tales, explaining that, as an honest re-

porter, he must report exactly what was said, however "rudeliche and large" (I.734) he has to speak, and he returns to these tongue-in-cheek excuses in introducing the *Miller's Tale*. It is hard to believe that Chaucer was genuinely embarrassed by what he was doing: it is all part of the fun, and all part of the system of dramatic subterfuges that Chaucer has worked out in the *Canterbury Tales* to give himself the freedom he needs to do what he wants to do as a writer. The freedom, however won, was worth winning, for the four fabliaux are, without exception, amongst the supreme achievements of his artistry.

The association of fabliau with romance needs a word more said about it, since the two literary forms seem to exist in a complementary relationship. Romance asserts the possibility that men may behave in a noble and self-transcending manner; fabliau declares the certainty that they will always behave like animals. The one portrays men as superhuman, the other portrays them as subhuman. Neither is "true" or realistic, though we might say that our understanding of what is true gains depth from having different slanting lights thrown upon reality, so that beneficial shock enrichment, invigoration is given to our perception of the world. Romance and fabliau complement one another, and Chaucer encourages us to look at them thus by setting the *Knight's Tale* and the *Miller's Tale* side by side. Each type of story makes a selection of human experience in accord with its own narrative conventions or rules. Out of the interlocking of these and other different types of story, in the general medieval hierarchy of genres, or in the *Canterbury Tales* as a whole, grows the social relevance of literary forms, the fabliau amongst them.

The narrative structure of Chaucer's four fabliaux has already been briefly described. Before going on to deal in detail with the manner in which he works variations on this structure in individual tales, it may be worth pausing to refine the model a little. The basic ingredients are three, a husband, a wife, and an intruder, though the functions of the last two may be duplicated in more complex plots. The intruder is always a man: it is possible to imagine a modern fabliau in which it was a woman, but not a medieval one. The husband belongs to the petit-bourgeoisie, or, if that term means nothing in the Middle Ages, to the world of successful tradesmen; the *Merchant's Tale* is, as often, exceptional, in that the husband is a "knyght." The wife is younger than her husband, or, if not younger, still with some unsatisfied sexual potential. This is briefly and devastatingly indicated, for instance, in an aside in the *Reeve's Tale*, when John leaps on the good wife: "So myrie a fit ne hadde she nat ful yoore" (I.4230). The wife of the fabliaux is not, it must be stressed, promiscuous, and there is no suggestion that the affair in which she is engaged is a matter of regular occupation. This is not because Chaucer is mealy-mouthed where Boccaccio is (quite often) frank, but because he can thereby increase the amount and quality of the intrigue. The "intruder" is usually younger than the husband or at least, as in the *Shipman's Tale*, explicitly more sexually active. More importantly, he belongs to a different class, being usually a student or other kind of cleric or religious, and therefore more clever, flexible and mobile than those with whom he is temporarily (as lodger or guest) accommodated. He is a member of a classless intellectual elite who, in being shown as a predator upon the conventional marital and materialistic values of the bourgeois, can be brought into an implicit alliance with the aristocracy. The *Merchant's Tale* is once more the exception, and there is no doubt that the nastiness of the tale is much increased by the fact that the intruder is a squire of January's own household, and furthermore one who plays a subordinate part in the intrigue to the wife.

It is not difficult to speak of Chaucer's fabliaux in this way, with the plot-elements and characters abstracted as functions, and it is not a distortion of the nature of the fabliaux to draw attention to the narrative rules upon which they operate. But the success of Chaucer's poetry is in the manner in which he works variations on these set patterns, defies expectation, tests the tolerance of the form and the habitual perceptions of the reader, and creates four poems which are as enjoyable for the ways in which each is unique as for the ways in which they fit a pattern.

The *Miller's Tale* is Chaucer's greatest achievement in the genre, and in many ways the most perfectly accomplished of all the *Canterbury Tales*. It seems to overflow with high spirits, and to convey, despite the nasty and painful events it describes, a sort of genial gusto. It is full of music and amorous serenading, whether Nicholas practising on his "gay sautrie" (I.3213) and singing *Angelus ad Virginem* (thinking, perhaps, of himself as the angel Gabriel and Alison as the prospective "virgin") or Absolon setting about his midnight "gyternynge" (I.3363) at the famous "shotwyndowe." The allusions to music often have a strong sexual suggestion, as when Nicholas turns his attention to his instrument after his exciting interview with Alison:

> Whan Nicholas had doon thus everideel,
> And thakked hire aboute the lendes weel.
> He kiste hire sweete and taketh his sawtrie,
> And pleyeth raste, and maketh melodie.

> (I.3303–06)

The most notable of these allusions, and the one that seems to capture the spirit of the tale, is the brief description of the love-making of Nicholas and Alison after they have tiptoed down from their tubs into the vacant marital bed: "Ther was the revel and the melodye" (I.3652). The little touch of lyricism here is not dissipated by the further musical allusion that follows, when we are told that they went on enjoying themselves "Til that the belle of laudes gan to rynge, / And freres in the chauncel gonne synge" (I.3655–56). A contrast between the two kinds of "music" is implied, but with no more than genial perfunctoriness. The notion that some critics have that the religious reference acts as a reminder of Nicholas and Alison's wickedness is heavy-handed in the extreme. Nicholas and Alison have their "bisynesse," and the friars have theirs: there is no competition. References to the church and the religious life of the community are frequent in the tale, but essentially as part of the unnoticed furniture of everyday urban life and part of the tale's incomparable substantiality. That Alison should go, after being well "thakked aboute the lendes" by Nicholas, to the parish church, "Cristes owene werkes for to wirche" (I.3308), is charmingly inapposite, but to call it "ironical" would be to load the tale with a moral freight it has no purpose to bear.

The quality of lyricism in the tale is further enhanced by its exuberant travesty of courtly language and behaviour. It is a very "literary" fabliau. The elaborate description of Alison, for instance, comes at just the point where the heroine would be described in a romance, and it is a beautifully observed parody of the conventional top-to-toe inventory. In itself, too, it is a subtle mixture of the vulgar and the artfully seductive: bedizened in black and white silk, in the latest out-of-date provincial fashion, and with a brooch planted in her cleavage "As brood as is the boos of a bokeler" (I.3266), she is yet as lithe as a weasel, "wynsynge" like a young colt, and her breath smells, unforgettably, one would think, of apples "leyd in hey or heeth." To try to "contain" such a picture within a moral or satirical frame of reference would be to deny the irresistible impression of animal vitality, indeed of innocence. So too when she acts out her little scene with Nicholas: he is the impassioned lover, ready to "spille" if his desires are not satisfied (I.3278), and she is the coy mistress, threatening to cry out (but not too loud) if he does not remove his hand from her "queynte." She does not thoroughly understand why she should be, even temporarily, under this nice restraint (any more than a colt "in the trave": 3282), but she obliges with a decent if brief show of reluctance.

Absolon, of course, is a more obvious satirical target, and his efforts to play the courtly lover are genuinely ludicrous. He has had some success with the flighty local barmaids, but he is a deal too circumspect for your true courtly lover, who would not expect to have to take a nap in order to prepare for his night's doings (I.3685) nor to chew "greyn and lycorys" (I.3690) to make his breath sweet. When he arrives at the "shot-wyndowe" to devastate Alison with his guitar, he gets everything wrong: the echoes of the Song of Songs (I.3698–3707) are in a good courtly tradition, but not the emphasis on his "sweating" for love nor on his desire for her as that of the "lamb after the tete." He also calls her, twice, his "lemman," which is a coarse form of address, and hilariously inappropriate to his pretensions as a lover.[4]

In addition to the lyricism and gaiety that these allusions give to the tale, there is also an unexpected generosity, as well as a great fertility of comic invention, in Chaucer's portrayal of his characters. John the carpenter is the most notable example: set up at the start as that traditionally licensed victim of satire, the old man who marries a young wife, he is portrayed as richly complacent and gullible. The congratulations he offers himself on his simple honest Christian faith, and the way it has helped him avoid getting into the state Nicholas is in, are unforgettable:

> "I thoghte ay wel how that it sholde be!
> Men sholde nat knowe of Goddes pryvetee.
> Ye, blessed be alwey a lewed man
> That noght but oonly his bileve kan!"
>
> (I.3453–56)

His readiness to accept Nicholas's fantastic story of the coming flood shows another kind of simple faith, and perhaps no great reluctance to be cast in the role of a second Noah. Yet his concern for Nicholas, who has been missing all weekend, is quite good-natured and unselfish, and his first reaction to the news of the flood is to think of his wife: "'Allas, my wyf! / And shal she drenche? allas, myn Alisoun!'" (I.3522–23). There is enough here to give us a twinge of sympathy, but no more. Chaucer's control of our emotional responses of engagement and sympathy, responses such as are totally alien in the tradition of fabliau, is consummate. He allows us the delightful apprehension of a momentary intrusion of feeling, and then resumes his splendid fooling.

The high spirits of the tale are of course best exemplified in Nicholas, who has all the attributes of "our hero," the master of plotting and connoisseur of intrigue. Notice what lengths he goes to in order to secure Alison's company on Monday night when the carpenter has been away in Oseney all the previous weekend. To have sneaked into bed with Alison then would have been, one feels, no challenge. When he is describing the escape from the flood, one senses that he has almost got carried away in the delighted contemplation of his own imaginative creation:

> "Thanne shaltou swymme as myrie, I undertake,
> As dooth the white doke after hire drake.

> Thanne wol I clepe, 'How, Alison! how, John!
> Be myrie, for the flood wol passe anon.'
> And thou wolt seyn, 'Hayl, maister Nicholay!
> Good morwe, I se thee wel, for it is day.'"

> (I.3575–80)

Nicholas's wit and vitality carry all before them, but his downfall comes when he tries to repeat the trick Alison played on Absolon; this is a lapse from the high standard of cunning and inventiveness we expect of him, and he is duly punished. Absolon deserves his moment of triumph. Alison, by contrast, escapes scot-free, and quite properly so, according to the laws of the comic fabliau, not because she has done nothing wrong but because she has done nothing that betrays her nature. Throughout she behaves like the healthy animal she is, quick, alert, high-spirited, where Absolon has fantasies of the various animals he might be—a lamb seeking its mother's teat, or a cat playing with Alison-mouse (I.3347). The ending of the tale, with its catalogue of punishments (I.3850–53), has the air of justice meted out, but it is not a moral justice.

Fertility and richness of invention characterize the tale, but also a high degree of technical accomplishment. The dropping of hints is unobtrusively neat: the mention of Nicholas's skill in astrology and his ability to predict "droghte or elles shoures" (I.3196) and of Absolon's unfortunate squeamishness of farting (I.3338) are delightful anticipations of significances still to be fulfilled. Absolon's certainty that the itching of his mouth is a sign of kissing "at the leeste wey" (I.3680) is one of many prophetic puns that detonate by delayed action. The careful specification of the height above street-level of the "shot-wyndowe"—"Unto his brest it raughte, it was so lowe" (I.3696)—is of course vital to the ensuing action. Most cunningly devised is the long dormancy of the flood-plot, and the reader's sudden realization that Nicholas' cry for water will reactivate it. This is a sublime moment of almost pure aesthetic pleasure. Add to this what Muscatine has called the "overpowering substantiality" of the tale,[5] and one sees the loving care Chaucer has lavished upon it. The density of detail, the sense of town life extending into deep perspective behind the foreground action, is extraordinary.[6] It is present in the architecture of John's house, down to the gable that looks out upon the garden, over the stable (I.3572), in the ramblingly uninformative account of John's whereabouts given by the anonymous "cloisterer" (I.3661); in the nocturnal activities of Gerveys the blacksmith (I.3761), who had to work at night, of course, because the things he was mending were needed by day; and perhaps above all in the series of references to the mystery plays. The bustle and business of the streetplays comes vividly alive in the allusions to the Miller himself speaking "in Pilates voys" (I.3124) and to Absolon playing Herod "upon a scaffold hye" (I.3384)—perhaps in a slightly "camp," effeminate way? And Chaucer hints mischievously at the effect mystery plays might have on the average citizen in describing John's spectacular ignorance of the whole point of the Noah story.

The *Reeve's Tale* has much of this same substantiality, in its account of the Cambridge college background, the activity of flour-milling, the weary chase through the fens after the run-away horse, and above all in the evocation of the darkened bedroom of the night's encounters. It is remarkable, though, how a tale so similar in structure and technique can create such a totally different impression. Gusto and geniality give way to a spirit of meanness and vindictiveness; the only music to be heard is the cacophony of the family snoring (I.4165) and the only "courtly" allusions are in the contemptuous reference to the miller's wife's absurd pretensions to be a lady (I.3942–43). Both the *Miller's Tale* and the *Reeve's Tale* make a stronger impact individually because of the effect of contrast, a measure of Chaucer's skill in juxtaposition in his mature work on the *Canterbury Tales*.

The tale seems to be concentrated on its destructive purpose, and everything serves the Reeve's revenge upon the Miller. Where the *Miller's Tale* began with a seductive description of Alison, the Reeve begins by presenting the miller of his tale as a target to be attacked and destroyed. His violence, his thievery and his pride in his lineage are singled out for attention, and then systematically rebuked and punished in the most painful and humiliating way. He himself is beaten up not only by the students but by his own wife, his ill-gotten flour is restored to the students by his own daughter, and that daughter

herself, of whom he had such hopes, is now thoroughly shop-
soiled:

> "Who dorste be so boold to disparage
> My doghter, that is come of swich lynage?"
>
> (I.4271–72)

Even his hospitality in allowing the students to lodge with
him is given no chance to register sympathetically because of
his sneering remarks about the students' book-learning (I.4122–
6). His wife is portrayed with open contempt, and there is no
hint of affection in the picture of his daughter and her coarsely
nubile charms:

> This wenche thikke and wel ygrwoen was,
> With kamus nose, and eyen greye as glas,
> With buttokes brode, and brestes rounde and hye;
> But right fair was hire heer, I wol nat lye.
>
> (I.3973–76)

The students themselves have nothing of Nicholas about them
and are not attractive in their own right. They are oafish
fellows, and Chaucer takes some care to present them as north-
erners and to have them speak in a passable imitation of fourteenth-century northern dialect: that the miller can be shown
to be outwitted and put down by such bumpkins makes him even
more to be derided.

A particular edge is given to the tale's nastiness by the
manner in which sexual activity is portrayed. Chaucer has removed from the original story, as told in a French fabliau,[7] the
element of sexual attraction that first draws the one student to
the daughter and then the other to the wife. Aleyn and John
act simply out of revenge and because the family snoring is
keeping them awake. There are no musical allusions or lyrical
overtones: they jump on the women like animals: "He priketh
harde and depe as he were mad" (I.4231) and the fact that the
women find they like it impugns only the miller's pride and
virility. The little parody of the *aube*-scene (the lovers must
part because of the approach of day) has Aleyn taking his
leave of the daughter, Malyne, more because he is exhausted, it
appears, than anything:

Aleyn wax wery in the dawenynge,
For he had swonken al the longe nyght.

                                                    (I.4234–35)

His vows of undying fidelity are perfunctorily echoed by
Malyne, who has the grace "almoost" to weep (I.4248), but who
is chiefly concerned to hand over her father's hard-won cake of
flour.

Systematically, it appears, those touches of lyricism and
generosity that graced the *Miller's Tale* have been stripped
away, and the fabliau used as a machine for the Reeve's vindictive purposes. Something of the tale's special tone might be
related to the character of the Reeve, who seems bent on revenge even before he has heard the supposed attack on himself
(also a carpenter) in the *Miller's Tale*. He is the kind of man
who makes a profession of taking offence, and who makes a
slimy pretence of self-righteousness to cover his envious and
suspicious nature. His own prologue is a remarkably disgusting
piece of self-ingratiating self-abasement. In pressing the narrator upon our attention in this way, Chaucer is bound to make us
conscious of him, at least at one level, as we read his tale: certainly the sense of vindictive purpose is strong, and there are
pointed allusions to the quasi-legal sanctions that justify
getting one's own back (I.4181, 4321). But it would be wrong to
make this "the meaning" of the tale: the rumpus in the bedroom
at the end is in the best manner of high-spirited fabliau, and
the most we might say is that Chaucer has given our laughter
an edge of uneasiness by having us share it with the Reeve.
From a larger point of view, one might see the *Reeve's Tale* as
the inseparable companion of the *Miller's Tale*. They are the
Jekyll and Hyde of fabliau; the one necessarily belongs to and
comments upon the other.

The *Shipman's Tale* has no dramatic context in the pilgrimage, and its brevity has often encouraged people to think of
it as "basic" fabliau. It is in fact a subtle and highly contrived
variation on the form which has its own individual character.
At first, by comparison with the Miller's and Reeve's tales, it
seems easiest to characterize by negatives. It has no violence
and no very explicit depictions of sexual activity, no courtly
allusions, no lyrical fantasies, and no one seems very much upset

by what happens. The narrator seems quite happy with the world he inhabits, and there is very little satirical comment, except such as is implicit in reporting such a world without comment.

It is in terms of such blandness that the tale is most acutely characterized. Throughout no one speaks openly or directly or honestly to anyone else, neither in rage, scorn nor desire. Everyone is politely diplomatic, careful not to offend and not to reveal any real purpose or feeling. The scene between the wife and the monk in the garden is a beautifully decorous comedy of manners, with each delicate advance towards mutual understanding carefully planned and signalled. The monk's playful insinuation of her husband's inadequacy in bed (at which he has the grace himself to blush) encourages the wife to speak of her other dissatisfactions; they exchange vows of secrecy; the monk discovers that he has always been waiting for this moment of intimacy; the wife's need of money seals the bond. It is like making love over the counter, and in some strange way the exchange of money seems to legitimize rather than corrupt the encounter. Nothing of this comes out in the open, of course. The wife sees what she does as a perfectly reasonable business transaction, and the monk, though there may be an element of calculation in his carefully regulated tipping of the members of the merchant's household (VII.46), and certainly an accomplished skill in his technique of asking for a loan (VII.269–80), is not portrayed as a scrounger or a predator.

The merchant, however, is the most unexpected beneficiary of the general complacency. He too is treated soberly, even generously. His avarice is not stressed, except by his wife, and he has a careful tedious explanation to his wife of why he has to spend so much time on his accounts:

> "Wyf," quod this man, "litel kanstow devyne
> The curious bisynesse that we have" . . .

> (VII.224–25)

He speaks as if this is not the first time he has had to do this kind of explaining. The same quality of carefully fostered good nature comes over in his response to the monk's request for a loan. It is a generous response, of course, and the hundred francs

are immediately promised. The promise, however, is followed
by the careful qualification:

> But o thyng is, ye knowe it well ynogh,
> Of chapmen, that hir moneie is hir plogh.
>
> (VII.287–88)

He wants to remind the monk that ready money is not easily
come by in the finance business, that it is not a little thing for
him to do, that it is a loan, at the same time that he wants to
appear generous. One recognizes the desire to be thought well
of, or to think well of oneself, and it comes out again in the
merchant's later rebuke to his wife for not having told him of
the return of the loan. He is annoyed because he feels he might
have been thought by the monk to have arranged to meet him
in Paris in order to ask the monk for his money back. We are
specifically told that this was not his intention (VII.338), and
the merchant cannot bear the thought of a generous intention
wasted.

The wife has her own problem when she hears of what
the monk has in fact done—that is, borrow the money from her
husband to give to her (in exchange for a night in bed with her)
so that she can pay her debts. She now owes the money to her
husband too. But sex comes to the rescue again, and she pays her
husband in the same coin as she paid the monk. So the hundred
francs has gone the rounds, and so has the wife, and no one
seems much the worse for the experience. In fact, there is
hardly a ripple on the surface of suburban life. There is a good
deal of insight in this tale into the power of money, into the
nature of sex as a commodity, and into the subterfuges of self-
deception. The tale is coldly exhilarating in its total disregard
of familiar moral decencies.

The *Merchant's Tale* is quite different, and certainly
Chaucer's most ambitious exercise in the fabliau form, so ambitious in fact that it threatens to explode the form into something like a modern "black comedy." It is a more powerful poem
than the *Miller's Tale*, and expands on the technique of that
tale with extensive lyrical interpolations (the marriage ceremony IV.1709–41; January's love song, IV.2138–48), rhetorical

digressions (e.g. IV.1783–94, IV.2057–68), a long mock-encomium on marriage at the beginning, and a mythological episode of Pluto and Proserpina at the end. There are, as in the *Miller's Tale*, many subtle verbal anticipations and echoings: January's comparison of his sexuality to the evergreen laurel (IV.1466) is echoed in the laurel in the garden where he is cuckolded (IV.2037); the wax to which he compares the pliability of the desired wife (IV.1430) is echoed in the wax that the wife uses to make a copy of the key to the garden (IV.2117). The fabliau nucleus is still there, in the episode of the peartree, but is almost an afterthought to a rich and strange performance.

One was aware of a sneering malevolence in the *Reeve's Tale*. Here that tone is continuous and raised to a high pitch of stridency. The opening account of January's desire to get married drips with contempt for such old fools, and the mock-encomium of marriage is openly sarcastic at times rather than mockingly ironical. The description of the marriage ceremony is cynically reductive: the priest comes forth,

> And seyde his orisons, as is usage,
> And croucheth hem, and bad God sholde hem blesse,
> And made al siker ynogh with hoolynesse.
>
> (IV.1706–08)

Not merely this travesty of marriage, but marriage as such, seems to be sneered at, and the same Thersitean voice is heard in the comments on January's energetic imitation of the Song of Songs: "Swiche olde lewed, wordes used he" (IV.2149). The voice throughout is that of the clerical misogynist, and is expressive of that cynicism about sexuality generally which is the legacy of religious celibacy. It is the rhetoric of a disordered and mutilated consciousness, and Chaucer gives to it an extraordinary Swiftian power.

January himself is something more than the traditional *senex amans*. To the disgust traditionally associated with that figure Chaucer adds a lurid physical reality:

> And Januarie hath faste in armes take
> His fresshe May, his paradys, his make.
> He lulleth hire, he kisseth hire ful ofte:

With thikke brustles of his berd unsofte,
Lyk to the skyn ol houndfyssh, sharp as brere.

(IV.1821–25)

The images of sexual possession as eating (IV.1419), the fantasies of prolonged rape (IV.1757–61), the haste, the barrel-fuls of aphrodisiacs (IV.1807), give a partly comic effect, but always with an undertone of disgust and repulsion. It is as if someone were telling a dirty story and insisting on going into detail, materializing every innuendo. The effect is shocking and disorienting, for there seems no centre of consciousness that we can draw to except the one that is disgusted and fascinated by sexuality. What is more, January is granted a kind of deformed moral consciousness, so that he is constantly preoccupied with whether what he is doing is right or lawful. Hence his long debates with his advisers, and with himself, and his pathetically confident explanation to May that what he is about to do to her, previously wrong, is now, by virtue of "trewe wedlok," right: "For we han leve to pleye us by the lawe" (IV.1841). There is no need to be reminded how alien to fabliau is the stimulus to feeling and moral reflection, however perverted, that we are given in the *Merchant's Tale*.

A further strange twist to the tale is given by the portrayal of May and Damian. They would conventionally in a fabliau have the advantage and merit of youth, and some quality of gaiety and vigour would hang about their liaison. But they lack even January's vitality. God knows, says the narrator, what May thought of January's wedding-night performance, suggesting, in his prurient way, the unspeakable horrors of maidenly innocence violated—but then he tells us, with equally characteristic bluntness: "She preyseth nat his pleyyng worth a bene" (IV.1854). The coldness of the appraisal is as shocking as any of January's excesses, and the narrator's subsequent sneering remarks about her "pitee" (IV.1986, 1995), his gratuitous bit of information about the fate of Damian's love-letter (IV.1954), suggest not a healthy animal vitality but a perverted cold sexuality. Damian is no more than a poodle to this lady dog-trainer and it is indeed to a fawning dog that he is compared when he returns to court and smothers January with his obsequious attentions (IV.2014). January's own overheated sexual fantasies come to seem almost natural by comparison. His blindness, too, creates a grudging sympathy in us, and in him a kind of insight, as when he speaks to May of his "unlikly elde" (IV.2180) and his awareness of how he may appear to her. The corrupted understanding seems more and more to be that of the narrator.

The ending restores the lighter and more spirited mood of fabliau, and May's trick is a good one. If the ending suggests that January will do well to cherish the illusion she has put him under, and that happiness is truly the perpetual possession of being well deceived, then that is no more than we expect of fabliau. The sense of trespass, however, in the tale as a whole remains. Chaucer, in suggesting to us all sorts of themes of moral and emotional significance, has violated all the expectations of the genre without creating any alternative order for the understanding of the tale. There is a character called Justinus, whose name suggests that he should represent some point of vantage in the story, some resting-place for the reader's bewildered moral consciousness; but he turns out to be wise only in the cynicism of embittered experience. There is no escape from the horror of sexuality. The attribution of the tale to the Merchant solves no problems, since there is no way in which the tale can be "contained" within what we can legitimately assume about his character. The most we can say about the prologue, and its account of the plight of the unhappily married Merchant, is that it may be part of some process of revision in which this disturbing tale was accommodated to a more conventional complaint against marriage.

The *Friar's* and *Summoner's Tales* lack something of the immediacy of appeal of the fabliaux, since they deal with specialized kinds of medieval corrupt practice, and not with sex and marriage, but they are both masterpieces of satirical anecdote. Though not strictly speaking fabliaux, they operate according to the same basic comic rules, namely, that the criterion by which human beings are judged successful is the extent to which they find means fully to satisfy their appetites and manipulate the world, by their smartness, to their will. What Chaucer has done is to absorb satire of the professional activities of summoners and friars into the dramatic comedy of the exchange of abuse between the Friar and Summoner. Moral outrage at what they describe each other as doing is a proper preliminary response, but it is swallowed up in laughter, since what the narrators try to do is to prove not that their victims are knaves but that they are fools. They know perfectly well that to demonstrate their opponent's success in villainy will cause no wound, since there is nothing to be ashamed of in following one's rapacious nature. To demolish one's victim effectively, he must be shown to be stupid, and both the Friar and the Summoner do this in the same way, by portraying their victims as pathetically gullible. Both the summoner of the *Friar's Tale* and the friar of the *Summoner's Tale* misunderstand things that would be obvious to the meanest intelligence, mistake the surface for reality, the letter for the spirit, and end up destroying themselves through their own stupidity.

The *Friar's Tale* is quite brief. It begins with the expected attack on the fictional summoner, but soon the story takes over, and we gradually forget the pilgrim-Friar and pilgrim-Summoner, engrossed as we are in the summoner's meeting with the mysterious yeoman. The revelation of his identity is gradual, with all sorts of hints and ironies to follow up; the summoner's embarrassment about his own profession, meanwhile, makes him more pathetically contemptible than being accused of robbing a hundred widows:

> He dorste nat, for verray filthe and shame
> Seye that he was a somonour, for the name.

(III.1393–94)

The hilarity of the tale begins when the devil-yeoman reveals his identity. We naturally expect that the summoner will show some sign of apprehension, or at least some sign that he realizes something significant is happening. But no: he seems impenetrable to all understanding, and preoccupied with the devil's skill in shape-changing. He behaves like a con-man who has met a fellow trickster, and is so persistent in his trivial enquiries that the devil begins to show a certain exasperation, as if irritated that he has been sent on a special mission to capture a soul of such banality. Through all the subsequent incidents of the carter who curses his horse and does not mean what he says and the old widow who curses the summoner and does, the summoner remains impervious to any perception but of the grossly literal. Twice invited to think again or to repent (III.1522, 1629), he seems not even to understand what he stands to lose. The joke against the summoner is not that he is snatched off to hell but that he will not even realize where he is when he gets there.

The Summoner's response is violent, and his immediate riposte, concerning the dwelling-place of friars in the nether regions, is appropriately anal. This anality is wittily prolonged into the tale, with puns on "ferthyng" (III.1967), "fundement" (III.2103), and "ars-metrik" (III.2222), and of course the denouement is a great fart. All this may seem very suitable to a man whose diet was all "garleek, oynons, and eek lekes" (III.1, 634). However, the story he tells is not vile and reeking of the sewer, but cool, witty, and precisely judged. The portrait of the friar at his characteristic activities of hypocritical wheedling, and "glosynge" ("Glosynge is a glorious thyng, certeyn": III.1793) takes up the great bulk of the tale, and it is done with superb skill and panache. One notices the accustomed smoothness with which he shoos the cat off the most comfortable seat and takes its place (III.1775), the amorous suggestiveness of his address to Thomas' wife and the little variation he introduces into the fraternal kiss ("and chirketh as a sparwe / With his lyppes": III.1804–5), the air of ascetic self-denial and true Franciscan charity ("But that I nolde no beest for me were deed": III.1842) with which he orders his gourmet dinner. There is even something quite engaging about his quickness of wit in getting out of difficult situations. Suddenly realizing that the household of which he is such a close friend has suffered a bereavement of which he should have apprised himself, he lays on immediately an imaginary funeral service in which he galvanizes the whole brotherhood into activity:

> "With many a teere trillying on my cheke,
> Withouten noyse or claterynge of belles."

(III.1864–65)

The last detail is a shrewd bit of quick thinking: the bells, if they had sounded, would have been heard. So too when Thomas complains that all his gifts to the different friars have done him no good:

> The frere answerde, "O Thomas, dostow so?
> What nedeth yow diverse freres seche?
> What nedeth hym that hath a parfit leche
> To sechen othere leches in the toun?
> Your inconstance is youre confusioun . . .
>
> A! yif that covent half a quarter otes!
> A! yif that covent foure and twenty grotes!
> A! yif that frere a peny, and lat hym go!
> Nay, nay, Thomas, it may no thyng be so!
> What is a ferthyng worth parted in twelve?"
>
> (III.1954–58, 1963–67)

He is a true ancestor of Falstaff, and we are obliged to pay laughing respect, in the very teeth of morality, to such vitality.

Towards the end of the tale, however, the friar seems to "go into automatic." His sermon on Ire is queasily irrelevant, and his demands on Thomas become more peremptory and blatant. He falls over-eagerly for Thomas's trick, and then, ridiculously, seems more put out by the absurdly impossible problem in "ars-metrik" he has been set than by the grossness of his humiliation. All our memory of the quarrel between the Friar and the Summoner, all possibility of morally based satire on the friar, seem swallowed up in the conclusion of the story, in the posing of the puzzle of the divided fart and its fantastically imaginative solution. Humour gets the better of satire, and Chaucer, as often, seems to prefer complicity with the world of his creatures to moral criticism.

NOTES

*Reprinted with permission from *The Cambridge Chaucer Companion*, eds. Piero Boitani and Jill Mann (New York: Cambridge University Press, 1986), pp. 125-42.

1. The essays of Henri Bergson ("Laughter") and George Meredith ("An Essay in Comedy") are conveniently available in *Comedy*, ed. Wylie Sypher (New York: Doubleday, 1956).

2. Mikhail Bakhtin, *Rabelais and his World*. trans. Hélène Iswolsky (Cambridge, Mass.: M.I.T. Press, 1965). For skillful use of Bakhtin in relation to the *Miller's Tale*, see Alfred David, *The Strumpet Muse: Art and Morals in Chaucer's Poetry* (Bloomington, Ind./London: Indiana UP, 1976), pp. 94, 104–5.

3. The traditional view is that of Joseph Bédier (*Les Fabliaux* Paris: Champion, 1893) and is opposed by Per Nykrog, *Les Fabliaux: étude d'histoire littéraire et de stylistique médiévale* (Copenhagen: Ejnar Munksgaard, 1957). For a convenient summary of opinions, see D. S. Brewer, "The Fabliaux" in *Companion to Chaucer Studies*, ed. Beryl Rowland (Toronto/New York/London: Oxford UP, 1968), pp. 247–67. There are important qualifications to Nykrog's view, suggestive of a looser and more heterogeneous audience for fabliau, in Charles Muscatine, "The Social Background of the Old French Fabliaux," *Genre* 9 (1976): 1–19.

4. See E. Talbot Donaldson, "Idiom of Popular Poetry in the *Miller's Tale*," in *English Institute Essays, 1950*, ed. A. S. Downer (New York: Columbia UP, 1951), pp. 116–40; repr. in the author's *Speaking of Chaucer* (New York: Norton, 1970), pp. 13–29.

5. Charles Muscatine, *Chaucer and the French Tradition: A Study in Style and Meaning* (Berkeley/Los Angeles, Ca./London: U of California P, 1957), p. 226.

6. J. A. W. Bennett, *Chaucer at Oxford and at Cambridge* (Toronto: U of Toronto P, 1974), provides ample historical documentation to confirm this critical impression of the *Miller's Tale* and the *Reeve's Tale*.

7. For analogues to Chaucer's fabliaux, see Larry D. Benson and Theodore M. Andersson, *The Literary Context of Chaucer's Fabliaux: Texts and Translations* (Indianapolis, Ind./New York: Bobbs-Merrill, 1971).

PART TWO

Critical Theories with the Comic Touch: Feminist, Freudian, Language, Social, and Bakhtinian Theories

Chaucer's May, Standup Comics, and Critics[1]

Susan K. Hagen

Merely a brief review of the criticism on Chaucer's *Merchant's Tale* reveals a long standing disagreement as to exactly how embittered is the tale's view of matrimony in particular and life in general and exactly to what degree we are to read January as a surrogate for the Merchant himself.[2] But on the whole the critics agree on two points, that the tale *is* funny[3]— whether we are embarrassed by our laughter or not—and that as readers we are initially sympathetic with May in her freshness, that she represents beauty, purity, and youth menaced by January's repugnant hoary lasciviousness. If we are honest with ourselves, though, we cannot reasonably claim to accept both that the tale is funny and that May represents innocence; we cannot hold to a belief in her purity and still laugh, no matter how uncomfortably, at the descriptions of his fantastical sexual ego and the grotesquery of their wedding night. Genuine belief in May's innocence precludes any sense of the comic in January's libidinous shenanigans.

The fact that we laugh rather than recoil in moral indignation "Whan tendre youthe hath wedded stoupyng age" (IV.1738)[4] really renders it quite impossible to trust ourselves when we say we believe in the initial purity of "fresshe May." And if it were not enough that our own amusement belies us, the narrator and the tale's genre actually set up obstacles to such a belief, for one blatantly expresses his intentions to show the cursedness of women and the other takes its form from a complicated mixture of fabliau and anti-romance.[5] In some ways E. Talbot Donaldson makes an admission very much to the point in the opening paragraphs of "The Effect of the *Merchant's Tale*." Having noted that on the one hand B. H. Bronson "lightly dismiss[es] the tale as just 'another high card in the unending Game between the Sexes'"[6] even though recognizing some bitterness on the part of the Merchant, while he, on the other hand, reads the tale as an ugly self-exposure of its highly embittered and misogynistic narrator, Donaldson begins to address the divergency of the two readings by acknowledging, "while we both pretend to be describing the tale objectively, we are in fact describing our reactions to it: we are casting on its persons and incidents a kind of spotlight, to be sure, but one that takes its colouring from our own preconceptions, and these neither of us has troubled to justify to the reader."[7]

Our own preconceptions and how they color our comic reaction to the tale is something we, or at least until recently I, have never troubled to acknowledge. But the basic reality is this: if we did not think that January could neither surprise nor satisfy May sexually, that her appetite, her threshold of pleasure, were not greater, higher, and longer-lasting than his then we would think him truly insidious, not comically ridiculous. We would not be embarking on a funny tale; we would be launching into pathos akin to the *Physician's Tale* with virginal innocence about to be brutally—and clumsily—victimized.

For the humor to work, there must be in this tale a fundamental incongruity between what January espouses about his sexual prowess and about marriage, and what we in our more realistic experience know to be true or likely. Of course the narrative voice corroborates the elderly knight's praise of marriage with such exaggerated claims on his own part that we can hardly be anything but prepared for contradiction. Accordingly, we find the basic fabliau humor of the tale lying in the *senex amans* and the mismatched marriage; in other words, the *Merchant's Tale* is one of what Thomas J. Garbáty calls Chaucer's "comedies of situation."[8] Certainly many have noted the disparity between what old January imagines he is capable of and the relative erotic quality of what it is he is indeed able to achieve, none better than Helen Cooper, who sees "in stark contrast accounts of January's sexual fantasies of his bedding his bride, and the anti-erotic crudity of the actuality."[9]

At first we think we are laughing at the cocksure old knight as he pities the hard work his fresh young wife will have to bear on their first night:

> But in his herte he gan hire to manace
> That he that nyght in armes wolde hire streyne
> Harder than evere Parys dide Eleyne.
> But nathelees yet hadde he greet pitee
> That thilke nyght offenden hire moste he,
> And thoughte, "Allas! O tendre creature,
> Now wolde God ye myghte wel endure
> Al my corage, it is so sharp and keene!
> I am agast ye shul it nat susteene.
> But God forbede that I dide al my myght!"
>
> (IV.1752–61)

And certainly we *are* laughing at him. But we are also chortling at May, whether we realize it or not. For if we really thought he could "manace" her or "offenden" her this passage would not be funny; it would be frightening in either its threat or its distaste. Its humor turns on the unlikelihood of May being either overwhelmed, overcome, or overpowered by January's skill and vigor. The amusement in these lines depends on January *thinking* he is sexy and May *knowing* he is not. But we do not know what May knows; at this point she is quietly seated at her wedding feast "with so benyngne a chiere" that she seems enchanting (IV.1742–43). She has not said a word. She has not flinched a muscle. She has not sneered a lip. We, however, smile because we hold a preconceived notion that no matter what January "purtreyed in his herte and in his thoght" about his chosen one's "fresshe beautee and hir age tendre, / Hir myddel smal, hire armes longe and sklendre" signifying "Hir wise governaunce, hir gentillesse, / Hir wommanly berynge, and her sadnesse" (IV.1600–1604), a hoary old man cannot satisfy a fresh young woman.

Similarly we titter at January's nuptial night antics. His aphrodisiacs, his lulling, his petting, his protestations that "'Ther nys no werkman, whatsoevere he be,/That may bothe

werke wel and hastily'" (IV.1832–33) are foolish because we
know they are ineffectual and unconvincing. Or, again, at least
we think we know. A close look at the text reveals that May
says nothing about it at all when she sees her new husband
sitting up in bed in his shirt, chanting and croaking with the
snake skin about his neck shaking. Quite the contrary, the
Merchant says, "But God woot what that May thoughte in hir
herte" (IV.1851). Only God knows what she thought, and we
only know what she failed to do. That is, "She preyseth nat
his pleyyng worth a bene" (IV.1854).

Yet critics often cite this passage as the one in which our
sympathy for the fresh new bride begins to ebb. Once more
Cooper states the issue with terse accuracy, "one's pity is jolted
at the very moment it should be most intense . . . [this] line
associates May too clearly for comfort with an interest in sexual
gratification."[10] We must remember two things though: one,
this is a fabliau/anti-romance, and our pity is not what the
narrator wishes to elicit; and two, May actually has said
nothing. It is what she did not say that is reported to us.
Donaldson speaks to this line in reference to the Merchant:

> Strictly speaking, since the Merchant does not know what
> May thought—only God knows—her failure to praise
> January must be taken as negative narrative action: she
> did not speak praise of him, and yet, since she is not said to
> have spoken at all, she did not speak dispraise of him. On
> the other hand, the Merchant, by saying she did not praise
> his playing *worth a bean*, that is by seeming to use the very
> words with which May did not speak, has either contra-
> dicted his earlier disclaimer of knowledge or has foisted
> upon her his own thought.[11]

What we must add to Donaldson is that this foisting of
attitude would not work comically if the Merchant could not
assume it to be our evaluation of January's performance as well.
Maybe that is also why we are so quick to attribute the same
opinion to May—we already share it with the Merchant. It is
part of our preconceived notion about what sexual appeal and
performance are like between nasty old men and vigorous young
women.

Accepting that the Merchant assumes certain attitudes by his listeners clarifies two passages rarely, if ever, commented upon by critics describing May's traditional confinement for four days after her wedding. On the morning after their nuptial consummation:

> Up ryseth Januarie; but fresshe May
> Heeld hire chambre unto the fourthe day,
> As usage is of wyves for the beste.
> For every labour somtyme moot han reste,
> Or elles longe may he nat endure;
> This is to seyn, no lyves creature,
> Be it of fyssh, or bryd, or beest, or man.

(IV.1859–65)

Twenty-three lines later, and after three more references to "fresshe May," the Merchant reiterates:

> So longe hath Mayus in hir chambre abyden
> As custume is unto thise nobles alle.
> A bryde shal nat eten in the halle
> Til dayes foure, or tre dayes atte leeste,
> Ypassed been; thanne lat hire go to feeste.

(IV.1888–92)

Why are these references to May's seclusion here? Surely not merely to supply a little cultural education.

The lines concerning the need of all fish, birds, beasts, men, and we would assume women, to rest sometime from labor have a prurient tone. The most obvious work they all do in common is certainly procreative. Not to have mentioned the need for rest would have left us with a gentile reference to a cultural nicety which protects a blushing new bride from the knowing glances of a more knowledgeable public after the initiations of her wedding night. Remember, the wedding guests went home and "doon *hir thynges* as hem leste, / And whan they sye hir tyme, goon to rest" (IV.1803–1804, my emphasis) that night as well.[12] Even though we know why she blushes, decorum dictates we do not mention it. Mentioning labor, though, keeps us thinking in the graphic physical details with which the Merchant has just described that night. The effect is to suggest to us that May could hardly need rest from the work required of her that evening. Reiteration of her confinement, this time stressing that it is due to the custom of noble people, confirms our suspicion. That the Merchant fills the intervening lines between the two passages with "sike Damyan in Venus fyr" (IV.1875), languishing in his bedroom seems quite suitable in wry contrast. Still, any smile we get from these lines depends on our assumptions about May's need for rest.

Throughout the tale, the Merchant depends on his audience's comedic response in much the same way as does a standup comic. In other words, the Merchant is playing off of generally held, but not necessarily generally acknowledged, cultural attitudes. He seems to say much more than he does, and he assumes much more than we realize. In a thought-provoking study, which compares the standup comedian to an anthropologist, Stephanie Koziski concludes, "Documenting areas of tacit knowledge and bringing them to the conscious awareness of their particular audiences are important functions performed by the anthropologist and the standup comedian in their respective roles."[13] She speaks of the standup comedian as one who talks about cultural conventions so basic to a society that they are neither fully apparent or conscious.[14] Are not our assumptions about the *senex amans* and the ill-matched wedding pair just such conventions?

Claiming standup comedy to be "arguably the oldest, most universal, basic, and deeply significant form of humorous expression," Lawrence E. Mintz defines the standup comic as a "single performer behaving comically and/or saying funny things directly to an audience" without the aid of props or dramatic vehicle.[15] Admittedly, the narrative plot, the tale-telling game, the pilgrimage itself, frame the Merchant's tale in an essentially dramatic vehicle (the degree to which this vehicle is *dramatic* in the conventional Chaucerian sense is, of course, highly debatable); nevertheless, I believe it can be argued that the Merchant does function here in much the same way as a standup comic. Alone before his audience he describes in exaggerated detail the two scenes just addressed, saying "God knows what May thought about it all," and supplies the anticipated punch line. We laugh with him and in laughing validate his "foisted" thoughts.

It is in thinking about our own laughter that the anthropological studies on comedy become invaluable, for they remind us that in laughing with the comedian we agree with him or her on certain cultural attitudes to be affirmed and certain cultural attitudes to be ridiculed.[16] At first glance what we affirm in the *Merchant's Tale* is that old men in love are often silly and that an old man married to a young woman is bound to suffer. And certainly we've seen these themes affirmed before in the *Miller's Tale*. But there is something different here, for in the story of John and Alisoun the humor depends on action—a misdirected kiss, a scorched rear end, a falling tub—but in the passages we've been examining the humor depends on innuendo.[17] In other words, it depends on our recognition and acceptance of the insinuation made by the Merchant that May would not find her silly spouse's endeavors worth a bean. As a result we affirm something else as well, something that we do not consciously realize we are affirming: May has a sexual appetite that January can neither frighten nor fulfill.

If we pity May in her marriage to this hoary old knight, it is not because we believe she is innocent and January's lust will offend her; it is because we assume he will leave her eternally unsatisfied. For critics to claim that we lose sympathy with her in the later part of the tale due to her demonstrated interest in sex with Damian reveals a type of blindness akin to January's. How can we profess to have ever expected her to act otherwise? As mentioned before, the Merchant's intention to speak of the cursedness of wives in the prologue and the fabliau tradition lead us to anticipate her adultery. Moreover January admits that if he had an old wife with whom he could not find sufficient pleasure, he himself would commit adultery:

> I wol noon oold wyf han right for this cause.
> For if so were I hadde swich myschaunce
> That I in hire ne koude han no plesaunce,
> Thanne sholde I lede my lyf in avoutrye
> And streight unto the devel whan I dye.

> (IV.1432–36)

If these were not adequate clues to May's eventual adultery, Justinus warns his friend that even a young man works overtime to give his wife enough pleasure to keep her his alone.[18] An old man simply cannot expect to satisfy a woman:

> The yongeste man that is in al this route
> Is bisy ynough to bryngen it aboute
> To han his wyf allone. Trusteth me,
> Ye shul nat plesen hire fully yeres thre—
> That is to seyn, to doon hire ful pleasaunce.
>
>   (IV.1559–63)

We cannot acknowledge the incongruity of the marriage and not be surprised by anything else but adultery. If we lose sympathy for May it should be due to the rudimentary crudity of her adulterous act, not the fact of it. Now, this is not to say that May is justified in sporting with Damian anywhere, much less in a tree, while standing on her husband's back. But it is to say that our deep-seated cultural attitudes lead us to expect adultery—or at least to expect a sexually frustrated young wife. The point of the tale is not that adultery is right, but that it is probable given this mismatched husband and wife.

If May reacted otherwise, this tale would not be a fabliau.[19] It would be a domestic saint's life. And it would be devoid of humor. In "A Vocabulary for Chaucerian Comedy," Paul G. Ruggiers divides the comic tales in half in terms of plot: those that involve conflicts in which the younger triumph sexually over the older (*Miller's, Reeve's, Merchants',* and *Shipman's* tales) and those that involve unmaskings (*Friar's, Pardoner's, Summoner's,* and *Canon's Yeoman's* tales).[20] In both types, though, he finds a tendency "to move from an old law, stated at the outset . . . to a wily escape from its bondage into momentary freedom from its constraints."[21] He concludes that the norms ultimately upheld in the "comedies about adultery are clearly those of nature."[22] This is essentially the point I make in speaking about the probability of May's adultery rather than its morality.

Elsewhere in the article Ruggiers refers to this movement from bondage to freedom as a comedic "contest between opposing value systems,"[23] in which an *idée fixe,* such as an "absurdly observed convention of marriage or family held by an older person" in the comedies of adultery, is subverted by subsequent action.[24] If May did not give in to Damian's amorous plea for mercy, if she faithfully and passively accepted all January's lascivious demands, acquiesced to all his egoistic pronouncements, and doted on him in his jealous, aged infirmity, then she would have proven him right when he said, "'Noon oother lyf . . . is worth a bene, / For wedlok is so esy and so clene / That in this world it is a paradys'"(IV.1263–65). Such a validation of January's fantasies, however, might leave as many readers uncomfortable as does the pear tree incident. The comedy simply depends on proving the prideful, self-deceived braggart wrong.[25] It should surprise us very little that Chaucer would have the Merchant insinuate the elderly knight's inanity by echoing the phrase "[not] worth a bene" in reference to his love making.

I would like to return to the articles on standup comedy for a moment now to address the tale's deprecation of women. In particular, some elements of the standup comedian's performance strategy may provide a new angle on the Merchant's prologue. Mintz explains that the comedian first establishes a sense of community with his or her audience, a sense "that the group is homogeneous" so that laughter will come easily;[26] then "establishes his or her comic persona, discussing personal background, life-style, and some attitudes and beliefs. This allows the audience to accept the comedian's marginal status and to establish that the mood of comic license is operative."[27] Might this not explain what the Merchant does in his prologue?

Does he exaggerate his own marital straits to consolidate a sense of brotherhood with the other pilgrims who have been talking about demanding, impatient, and shrewish wives, and to give himself comedic license to expatiate on the cursedness of women? The opening lines of his prologue "Wepyng and waylyng, care and oother sorwe / I knowe ynogh" (IV.1213–14) undeniably link his sentiments to those of the envoy to the *Clerk's Tale*; moreover, if we accept the words of the Host intervening between those of the Clerk and the Merchant (IV.1212a-12g), the Merchant's lines "Ther is a long and large difference / Bitwix Grisildis grete pacience / And of my wyf

the passyng crueltee" (IV.1223–25) bond him to his self-proclaimed browbeaten Host. Neither should we forget, because
Chaucer reminds us of the fact several times throughout the full
text of the *Canterbury Tales,* there is a game going on.[28]

But in the middle of the Merchant's routine the act turns
crude and the tale turns mean as he moves from the incongruity
of fantasy and reality to the shock of unexpected and coarse
action for his source of humor. Until May enters her privy with
the love letter from Damian, the humor in the tale depends on
the audience's recognition of a fundamental disparity between
what January—and the narrative voice in his mock encomium on
marriage—says and what experience and cultural convention
have taught us to be true. After that, it relies on our astonish-
ment at the action: May's balancing on her husband's back to
couple with her lover in a tree; the very fact that Damian and
May are successful, no matter how rudimentarily; the timely gift
of explanation given to May by Proserpina; January's willingness
to believe that explanation.

This shift in comic strategy is the real cause of our loss of
sympathy for May. Once we see her act rather than imagine her
reactions, we are forced to accept that she has sexual desires and
intends to fulfill them, something we were not willing to
acknowledge in our protestations of her initial freshness.
Admittedly, had she and Damian met in a flowered bower in the
tenderness and bashfulness of secretive young lovers rather than
in a tree, our sympathies might well have remained with her. But
then, we would have a romance, not a fabliau, and the Merchant
would not have fulfilled his intention to speak of the cursedness
of women.

Once the Merchant begins to describe May's actions, they
have an unrefined air about them. The first thing we see her do
by her own volition, for January has sent her to Damian in the
first place, is deceptive:

> She feyned hire as that she moste gon
> Ther as ye woot that every wight moot neede;
> And whan she of this bille hath taken heede,
> She rente it al to cloutes atte laste,
> And in the pryvee softely it caste.
>
> (IV.1950–54)

Literature on the tale abounds with disapprobations of May for reading a love letter in such an uncouth place. But in all fairness to May, where else was she to get some privacy from her hovering husband? Moreover, there is no textual indication she knew that it was a love letter until she "hath taken heede" of it.[29] Besides, it may well be that more readers than May have perused their mail in the bathroom—even if it was only junk mail—and used the john to dispose of things they wished to remain undiscovered. More to the point is that the Merchant associates the inception of May's sensual longing with scatological commonplaces.

The tale's second account of January's love-making with May, which follows, is accordingly curt and crude, and decidedly without the descriptive humor of their nuptial night. She returns to their room and lies by his side until he is awakened by his own coughing:

> Anon he preyde hire strepen hire al naked;
> He wolde of hire, he seyde, han som plesaunce,
> He seyde hir clothes dide hym encombraunce,
> And she obeyeth, be hire lief or looth.
>
> (IV.1958–61)

Obviously more hindered by clothes than Damian will later be, January speaks abusively and his actions are self-centered. This time, though, the Merchant does not disavow knowledge of the young bride's reaction, rather he says he dare not tell how January "wroghte," "Or wheither hire thoughte it paradys or helle" (IV.1963–64). This implied response is much darker than the first, for it turns not on praise for pleasure but on the pain of genuine discomfort.

This pain, however, elicits no sympathy on the part of the narrator. He quickly follows by stating that any woman will find a way to get her love and that May thought to herself that no matter who cared she would love Damian, even if he owned no more than his shirt on his back (IV.1973, 1981–85). Then he editorializes with unmistakable sarcasm, "Lo, pitee renneth soone in gentil herte!" (IV.1986). Actually, the Merchant displays more pity for the now physically blind January as the tale moves to its close than he does for May. We are told that January goes to the garden this day due to the "eggyng" of his wife and that he summons her as his "white spouse" without known spot (IV.2135, 2144–46), underscoring both his blindness and her impending adultery.

Once in the garden he professes that he married her only for love and asks that she promise always to be true to him. Probably the high moment of compassion for the infirm old man in the tale, this speech remains nonetheless pure fabrication; at the beginning he clearly states he is marrying to sanctify his bodily delight and engender an heir. He chooses May because she is the youngest and prettiest he can find. The ease with which May lies in response, even before Proserpina's gift, epitomizes medieval antifeminist conventions about the deceitfulness and aggressiveness of women, especially since she delivers her defense with one hand touching her husband and one eye searching for her lover. It should be noted, too, that these are the first actual words May speaks in the tale.[30]

The Merchant's skill in story telling becomes clear as he suspends the time between Damian's climbing into the tree and the anticipated adulterous actions with the argument between Pluto and Proserpina, proving even the gods are no verbal matches for the verbal virtuosity of women. What follow quickly then are a two-line long tree tryst, "And sodeynly anon this Damyan / Gan pullen up the smok, and in he throng" (IV.2352–53); May's verbal deception of her old husband; and January's reaffirmed self-deception as he strokes his wife's stomach.

If we return one last time to the theory of standup comedy, we note that the comedian's purpose is to single out a convention of society, to hold it up for analysis either through exaggeration or ridicule so that it can be "'scrutinized, assessed, and perhaps remodeled.'"[31] If the analogy between the Merchant and the standup comedian holds, then what he holds up is the societally sanctioned marriage of young women to old men with the intent of proving it to be a bad practice.[32] But he also holds up for affirmation misogynist attitudes about the nature of women. In addition, he traps his audience in an uncomfortable bind as he changes his comic strategy between the two purposes, as he moves from verbal suggestion where the audience joins him in catching the humor of incongruity in the mismatched old husband and young woman to the surprise of unexpected action in the pear tree incident.

To recognize the humor of the initial incongruity, we must accept a healthy sexual appetite for May, but once that is acknowledged the Merchant forces us to see that appetite exercised in the crudest and most perfunctory of ways, which leaves us uncomfortable and embarrassed. To save ourselves from the implications of our original acquiescence in the culturally held attitude of young women as sexual beings, we deceive ourselves, much like January, into believing May to be innocent in her freshness and lose sympathy with her as she begins to take control of her own sexual desires. The crux comes after May has read Damian's letter and returns to the side of her sleeping husband. With the line "Who studieth now but faire fresshe May?" (IV.1955) she begins to take control of her own sexuality; from this point on January and readers alike will have to weave some thick cloaks of deception in order to maintain fantasies about her.

The fact that the Merchant can depend upon conventions of female sexuality both to show the folly of the *senex amans* and the mismatched marriage and to misogynistically deprecate it finds some explanation in his medieval society's antifeminist traditions. But that contemporary readers continue to get entrapped in his dual-purposed performance may say something about our own society's difficulty in coming to terms with female sexuality in particular and human sexuality in general.

In rural Alabama today there exists a garden reminiscent of all the rich and conflicting meanings inherent in the image of the medieval garden. Called the "Mirical Cross Garden" by its self-avowed moralist creator, it is an eclectic collection of painted wooden crosses standing among abandoned appliances—refrigerators, washers, air conditioners, Coca-Cola coolers. Painted on the sides of these wasted machines slogans such as "Sex Pit" and "Sex Used Wrong Way In Hell" remind the garden viewer of the persistent anxiety of human sexuality lingering on six hundred years after Chaucer's May returned to her sleeping husband's side and began to study the idea of a lover."[33]

NOTES

1. I would like to acknowledge the work of two English majors at Birmingham-Southern College, Deneen Senasi and Amorak Huey, who did some preliminary research for this paper and served as an impromptu jury for some of its ideas.

2. See J. S. P. Tatlock, "Chaucer's *Merchant's Tale*" (*Modern Philology* 33 [1936]: 367–81), and E. Talbot Donaldson, *Speaking of Chaucer* (New York: Norton, 1970), for representative views of the Merchant as embittered; for less dark views of the tale and its humor see B. H. Bronson, "Afterthoughts on *The Merchant's Tale*" (*Studies in Philology* 58 [1961]: 583–96), and Martin Stevens, "'And Venus Laugheth': An Interpretation of the *Merchant's Tale*" (*Chaucer Review* 7 [1972]: 118–31). Stevens (and to some extent Cooper [202—see note 5]) also argues that the text offers no proof that January is a surrogate for the Merchant. The Merchant's complaints of his wife in the prologue center not on infidelity but on her shrewish behavior and lack of patience, something Harry Bailey complains of as well, and we never take his protestations at face value, much less accuse Goodeleif of adultery.

3. Norman T. Harrington differs on this point as he argues in "Chaucer's *Merchant's Tale*: Another Swing of the Pendulum" (*PMLA* 86 [1971]: 25–31) that the ultimate effect of the tale "is not comic" (26).

4. All quotations are from *The Riverside Chaucer*, gen. ed. Larry D. Benson (Boston: Houghton Mifflin, 1987), and will be noted parenthetically as to fragment and line numbers.

5. Helen Cooper, in *The Canterbury Tales*, Oxford Guides to Chaucer (Oxford: Clarendon, 1989), says the following about the genre of the tale: "If in subject it is all fabliau, the literary treatment it is given suggests something very different. The discursive opening suggests the story should be read as an exemplum; the paraphrase of the Song of Songs suggests a mystical work; the explanation of why women always have a ready answer suggests a just-so story, a folktale *pourquoi*. Above all, the characters of knight, lady, and amorous squire, the trappings of gardens and gods, the courtly vocabulary, and the parody of a happy ending all suggest that what one is reading is really a romance. The disparity between the generic expectations aroused by the plot and its handling is the source of much of the power of the tale, and makes it one of the most startling, in literary and poetic terms, of the whole Canterbury sequence" (203). The designation of the lovers as knight, lady, squire; the garden;

and the gods are "unique to Chaucer," according to Cooper (204). On genre, see as well Thomas J. Garbáty, "Chaucer and Comedy," *Versions of Medieval Comedy*, ed. Paul G. Ruggiers (Norman, U of Oklahoma P, 1977), 173–90. See Larry D. Benson and Theodore M. Andersson, *The Literary Context of Chaucer's Fabliaux* (Indianapolis: Bobbs-Merrill, 1971) for various analogues (206–78).

6. Bronson, 30.

7. Donaldson, 31.

8. Garbáty, 176. See also Paul G. Ruggiers, "A Vocabulary for Chaucerian Comedy: A Preliminary Sketch" (*Medieval Studies In Honor of Lillian Herlands Hornstein*, ed. Jess B. Bessinger, Jr., and Robert R. Raymo [New York: New York University Press, 1976], 193–225) on the comic plot (both reprinted above) and Jay Schleusener, "The Conduct of the *Merchant's Tale*" (*Chaucer Review* 14 [1980]: 237–50), and Donaldson (35) on the *senex amans*.

9. Cooper, 207.

10. Cooper, 210.

11. Donaldson, 52.

12. See Schleusener (241) on the Merchant's innuendo in these lines.

13. Stephanie Koziski, "The Standup Comedian as Anthropologist: Intentional Cultural Critic" (*Journal of Popular Culture* 18 [Fall 1984]: 57–76), 57.

14. Koziski, 58.

15. Lawrence E. Mintz, "Standup Comedy as Social and Cultural Mediation" (*American Quarterly* 37 [Spring 1985]: 71–80), 71.

16. Citing May Douglas in "Joking," *Implicit Meanings: Essays in Anthropology*, Mintz claims that "the *experience* of public joking, shared laughter, and celebration of agreement on what deserves ridicule and affirmation fosters community and furthers a sense of mutual support for common belief and behavior" (73).

17. Schleusener argues the tale to be one far more dependant upon sarcasm than irony and notes the degree to which the Merchant depends on innuendo, allowing the audience to supply conclusions he fails to mention (240–41).

18. See Carolyn P. Collette, "Umberto Eco, Semiotics, and the *Merchant's Tale*" (*Chaucer Review* 24 [1989]: 132–38) for a very suggestive semiotic analysis of three major images of the tale, the mental mirror, the wax, and the garden. In regard to clues to May's eventual behavior in the text, note her analysis of January's assertion "A man

may do no synne with his wyf, / Ne hurte hymselven with his owene knyf" (IV.1839–40), which leads to the analogy "man:wyf=man:knyf." Collette then concludes:

> In the midst of a comparison designed ostensibly to show Januarie's blind confidence that he can control and dominate his wife utterly, we find, following Eco's lead, that Chaucer links the ideas of wife and knife to create the idea of a woman as ironically powerful, dangerous, potent. The apparent sense of the analogy, a woman, like a knife, can be manipulated, is expanded to include, a woman, like a knife is very dangerous. As readers we almost automatically sense the irony of the phrase, as semioticians we understand the dynamics of how that irony comes to exist. (135)

19. See Sherry Reames, "Fabliaux" (*Women's Studies Encyclopedia*, Vol. 2, ed. Helen Tierney [Westport, Conn.: Greenwood Press, 1990], 121–22) for a definition of *fabliau* which pays particular attention to female behavior and characterization.

20. Ruggiers, 195–96.

21. Ruggiers, 196.

22. Ruggiers, 197. Derek Pearsall, in *"The Canterbury Tales* II: Comedy" (*Cambridge Chaucer Companion*, eds. Piero Boitani and Jill Mann [Cambridge: Cambridge UP, 1986], 125–42 finds the characterization of Damian and May unusual for the fabliau and concludes her behavior indicates "a perverted cold sexuality" (138), rather than natural desire.

23. Ruggiers, 204.

24. Ruggiers, 206.

25. See Donald MacDonald, "Proverbs, *Sententiae*, and Exempla in Chaucer's Comic Tales: The Function of Comic Misapplication" (*Speculum* 41 [1966]: 453–65) on Chaucerian comedy resulting from foolish and prideful misapplication of advice.

26. Mintz, 78.

27. Mintz, 79.

28. Koziski similarly states that the standup comic "ridicules himself to make a point about [a] pervasive atmosphere" (60).

29. Priscilla Martin, in *Chaucer's Women: Nuns, Wives, & Amazons* (Iowa City: U of Iowa P, 1990), notes that "May is viewed exclusively from the outside for a long time," her thoughts being projected upon her. In discussing May's silence when the Merchant says only God knows

what she thought, Martin claims "her silence proves to be stealth," for when we "learn her thoughts, she is thinking of a lover" (49). If the implication here is that May quietly thinks of Damian the night of the wedding, I find no substantiating textual evidence; although it is quite true that the first time the narrator directly relates May's thoughts, she is thinking about Damian (IV.1982–85).

30. Note, too, that all her communication with Damian is done with letters and signs (IV.2003, 2150, 2209, 2215). See Cooper (207) about the use of speech in the tale.

31. Victor Turner, qtd. in Koziski, 60.

32. Cf. Ruggiers, "[Chaucer's] comedies about adultery, it should be pointed out, may also raise criticism of a society that tolerates the marriage of youth and age" (196).

33. The "Mirical Cross Garden" was brought to my attention by Sandra Sprayberry and Roger Casey, two colleagues doing fieldwork on Alabama folk culture.

Chaucer, Freud, and
the Political Economy of Wit
Tendentious Jokes in the Nun's Priest's Tale

R. James Goldstein

When daun Russell outfoxes Chauntecleer and makes a run for
it, rooster in mouth, all hell breaks loose. In a famous allusion
Chaucer compares the hue and cry raised by the human and
animal pursuers to one of the most appalling episodes from the
Great Revolt of 1381, the rebels' massacre of the Flemings on
Friday, June 14:[1]

> So hydous was the noyse—a, benedicitee!—
> Certes, he Jakke Straw and his meynee
> Ne made nevere shoutes half so shrille
> Whan that they wolden any Flemyng kille,
> As thilke day was maad upon the fox.[2]

What seems most remarkable about this allusion is that at no
other time in his poetic career does Chaucer refer directly and
unequivocally to an event from contemporary English history.[3]
Yet if Chaucer intends his historical hapax legomenon as a
joke, the few critics who have commented on it are uncertain
what to make of it.

Paul Strohm, for example, remarks that "the apparent
reference in the *Nun's Priest's Tale (NPT)* to the rising of 1381"
is handled "in ways that forbid us to draw solid conclusions
about his intentions."[4] Ian Bishop suggests that the allusion
"may be a literary joke at the expense of Gower," whose "crude,
onomastic humour at the expense of the rustics" in *Vox Clam-*

145

antis I, xi Chaucer may have in mind.[5] More recently, John Ganim has observed that the poet's "famous topical allusion to the Peasants' Revolt is contained in a peculiarly unfunny joke in the *NPT*."[6] But Ganim never explains in what sense the joke is "unfunny." Did Chaucer or his audience find it funny while we moderns do not? Has Chaucer's joke simply fallen flat? Did Chaucer intend to give the allusion the formal appearance of a joke without meaning it to have the effect of one?

Laura Kendrick believes "it is fitting that Chaucer's only clear reference to the Peasants' Revolt should occur at the comic climax of this implicitly rebellious, life-affirming tale," though it remains unclear precisely why it is "fitting" to allude to the brutal massacre here, no matter how rebellious in spirit the tale may seem.[7] One thing at least is clear: the joke makes no attempt to mask Chaucer's hostility to the aims of the revolt; it constitutes, in Peter Travis's words, "a subtle piece of professional violence."[8] As Travis suggests, "unless one finds human slaughter to be a sprightly witticism, no matter what one's political persuasion there is an unsettling dissonance in this casual juxtaposition of comic alarums and gross brutality" (215). In short, the lack of critical consensus on the significance of the passage suggests the need for a fresh examination of this problem.

The purpose of the following essay, therefore, will be to address the puzzling fact that Chaucer chooses to break his characteristic silence about contemporary politics by alluding to the most serious challenge to the social and political order of fourteenth-century England in a joking *comparatio* at the climax of one of his greatest comic tales. If literature is a socially symbolic act in the sense that Fredric Jameson has argued, what can the joking comparison of a fox chase to the slaying of the Flemish merchants tell us about the political unconscious of the poem?[9] What relation, in other words, does this brief and unexpected joke have to the rest of the poem, to the various contests for authority and power that it stages? To help address these questions, I will be drawing on Freud's *Jokes and Their Relation to the Unconscious*.[10]

A few points, however, need to be clear from the outset. My purpose is not to provide an exhaustive reading of the *NPT* as comedy, but to focus on the relation between a specific pattern of humor and the politics it implies.[11] In discussing the political unconscious of the tale, moreover, I do not mean to suggest that Chaucer was unaware of the class and gender issues at stake, but that his intentions cannot provide an adequate measure of the political significance of his work. Chaucer himself playfully demonstrates the principle that we may mean more than we say we do when the narrator interrupts a philosophical discussion of free will to reassure us, "My tale is of a cok, as ye may heere" (VII.3252). A psychoanalytic reading goes a step further and reveals that we also may mean more than we think we do, even (or especially) when we are not being serious, if, as Freud says, jokes are *"the contribution made to the comic from the realm of the unconscious."*[12]

Freud argues that jokes, like dreams, are governed by a psychic economy and perform a kind of work, which he calls *Witzarbeit* or "joke-work" by analogy with "dream-work."[13] Like any mode of production narrative, Freud's includes a discussion of the techniques of production.[14] Although his taxonomy of the variety of joke techniques would provide suggestive ways for analyzing the techniques of a comic poet like Chaucer, what concerns us here is the discussion of the purposes (or tendencies) of jokes.[15] Some jokes are "innocent" or "non-tendentious" since they have no other purpose than to create pleasure. But others are clearly "tendentious" (*SE* VIII.90) and may be either hostile, taking "aggressiveness, satire, or defence" as their purpose, or obscene, aiming at "exposure" (*SE* VIII.97).

Freud observes that tendentious jokes as a rule require three people to function, and he uses dirty jokes to illustrate the social dynamic of the tendentious joke: "Through the first person's smutty speech the woman is exposed before the third" (*SE* VIII.100). Jokes (unlike dreams) are thus social by definition: "No one can be content with having made a joke for himself alone. An urge to tell the joke to someone is inextricably bound up with the joke-work" (*SE* VIII.143). Indeed, this social aspect of jokes constitutes an important distinction between jokes and the comic: "I can laugh to myself at something comic, but not if a joke comes to me" (*SE* VIII.143). Like the creator of a witticism, the author of a comic narrative must have an audience.

   The social space cultivated by the work of wit implies a
micropolitics; tendentious jokes (even when inscribed in a literary text) mask their aggression under the cover of laughter at
someone else's expense. The hostile joke thus requires an "object
person" (*SE* VIII.144) in order to work. This political aspect of
the tendentious joke is clearly evident in Freud's fondness for
quoting anti-Semitic and antifeminist jokes.[16]
   The narrator of the *NPT* enjoys sharing antifeminist jokes
with his implied male audience. Freud's important recognition
that jokes can mask hostile and aggressive tendencies suggests
that when women or peasants are the butt of Chaucer's jokes,
not all the humor must be taken innocently. "But ye that holden
this tale a folye, / As of a fox, or of a cok and hen, / Taketh the
moralitee, goode men" (VII.3437–40) may thus be read against
the author's intentions.
   The best known instance of a tendentious joke against
women is the passage on the proverbial dangers of following
their advice:

> Wommennes conseils been ful ofte colde;
> Wommannes conseil broghte us first to wo
> And made Adam fro Paradys to go,
> Ther as he was ful myrie and wel at ese.
> But for I noot to whom it myght displese,
> If I conseil of wommen wolde blame,
> Passe over, for I seyde it in my game.
> Rede auctours, where they trete of swich mateere,
> And what they seyn of wommen ye may heere.
> Thise been the cokkes wordes, and nat myne;
> I kan noon harm of no womman divyne.
>
> (VII.3256–66)

Critics have found the passage extremely slippery. On the one
hand, the narrator (presumably the Nun's Priest) claims that
when he appears to blame women's counsel, he was "only
joking" ("I seyde it in my game"). On the other hand, the first-
person speaking voice that enunciates the accusation, and
perhaps the voice that goes on to rehearse the story of the Fall,
is not really "Chaucer's" voice, nor even that of the Nun's
Priest: "Thise been the cokkes wordes, and nat myne."[17] But

which words, exactly, are Chauntecleer's—only the line about cold counsel? Modern typographic conventions are necessarily misleading, since the joke depends on the undecidability created when reading the poem in manuscript or hearing it aloud. According to Derek Pearsall, Kenneth Sisam's edition "places the line in inverted commas, implying a signaled quotation, but it is not easy to be sure the signal is so explicit" (*Variorum* 221). Pearsall suggests that "the narrator's tongue-in-cheek apology is characteristically Chaucerian . . .and in ways characteristically medieval," thus leaving it unclear exactly whose apology it is (*Variorum* 222). Peggy Knapp takes these lines to be "the Priest's (or the cock's) flat antifeminism."[18] Perhaps no one better captures the difficulties that Chaucer's tendentious humor poses than one reader who remarked nearly fifty years ago, "Chaucer's new emphasis upon the ill effect of woman's counsel transforms the *NPT* into a document in the literature of antifeminism, a light and merry document, to be sure, but one none the less telling."[19] The last twenty years of feminist scholarship have made us sensitive to the oxymoronic quality of a "light and merry" antifeminism.

Indeed, critics have found that the antifeminist edge to many of the remarks in the *NPT* slices in many directions at once. Charles Muscatine suggests "the tale seems to have an irreducible core of antifeminism, but by similar tokens it is feminist too."[20] Charles Owen speaks of the Nun's Priest as "floundering in the kind of antifeminist cliché he knows to be unworthy."[21] Sheila Delany, on the other hand, reads the *NPT* as far more patriarchal and conservative than its sources and analogues.[22] Another slippery joke that the narrator directs at women concerns the truth-status of his fable, when he addresses the male members of his audience:

> Now every wys man, lat hym herkne me;
> This storie is also trewe, I undertake,
> As is the book of Launcelot de Lake,
> That wommen holde in ful greet reverence.

> (VII.3210–13)

Much of the humor of this aside rests in the commonplace distinction between *historia* and *fabula* in the Middle Ages.

From Cicero and Quintilian to Isidore of Seville and John of Salisbury, the rhetoricians agree that *historia* narrates actions that really took place, while *fabula* narrates the purely fictitious.[23] For Isidore, the talking animals of Aesopic fable provide the quintessential examples of *fabula* (see *Etymologiarum* I, xl, 1–2). Chaucer pretends that women cannot properly distinguish the elementary difference between *historia* and *fabula*, implying that every wise man realizes that both stories are fictions.[24]

The debate between Chauntecleer and Pertelote can be taken, in part, as an extended antifeminist joke, from Chauntecleer's condescending dismissal of Pertelote's medical authorities ("'Madame . . . graunt mercy of youre loore'" [VII.2970]), to his cocky mistranslation of the antifeminist tag, "*Mulier est hominis confusio*" (VII.3163–66).[25] By stressing Chaucer's tendentious presentation of women as a target for male humor, I certainly do not wish to suggest that Chaucer singles them out. A beast fable obviously makes fun of human foibles, and there is much to ridicule about Chauntecleer's behavior and, by implication, about the reader's. Yet much of the humor that the *NPT* directs at debunking human beings in general seems to illustrate not "*der Witz*" so much as what Freud distinguishes as "the comic." We might well be reminded of Chauntecleer's strut—his "chuk" when he finds "a corn," his regal posturing ("real he was") before "he fethered Pertelote twenty tyme" (VII.3174–77), his all-too-human gullibility as he stands "hye upon his toos, / Strecchynge his nekke," holding "his eyen cloos" (VII.3331–32)—when we read Freud's remark:

> The comic . . . is found in people—in their movements, forms, actions and traits of character. . . . By means of a very common sort of personification, animals become comic too. . . . One can make a person comic in order to make him contemptible, to deprive him of his claim to dignity.
>
> (*SE* VIII.189)

Readers of Chaucer may be reminded at this point of Charles Muscatine's famous warning that the tale "does not so much make true and solemn assertions about life as it tests truths and tries out solemnities. If you are not careful, it will try out your solemnity too."[26] At the risk of testing Freud's solemnities further, we should now ask what Chaucer's tendentious jokes about women have to do with the greatest popular uprising in England during the Middle Ages.

To answer this question, we must turn to the opening frame, where the narrator begins with the story of "A povre wydwe, somdeel stape in age" (VII.2821). The significance of her portrait has been the object of much critical dispute. For many readers, her simple life sets a moral standard by which we may judge the rest of the poem.[27] Others have read the widow allegorically.[28] However, exegetical and moral readings of the widow, as Derek Pearsall observes, "allow little to the strong element of burlesque in the description" (*Variorum* 140). Indeed, it is not difficult to read the following lines as a joking description of a way of life far below Chaucer's social station:

> Thre large sowes hadde she, and namo,
> Three keen, and eek a sheep that highte Malle.
> Ful sooty was hire bour and eek hire hall,
> In which she eet ful many a sklendre meel.

> (VII.2830–33)

One critic has described the sheep's proper name as "appropriately plebian."[29] The rustic name might seem droll to an urbanite like Chaucer. In any case, the author and his audience share a superior view of the entire scene, both in terms of narrative perspective and social position. This distance is clearly evident in a line like 2833 ("In which she eet ful many a sklendre meel").[30] It would be comical indeed to imagine her stuffing herself with whatever would be the opposite of a "sklendre" meal.

Much of the humor of her portrait derives from an implicit comparison of peasant life with the aristocratic world of the court:

> Of poynaunt sauce hir neded never a deel.
> No deyntee morsel passed thurgh hir throte;
> Hir diete was accordant to hir cote.
> Repleccioun ne made hire nevere sik;
> Attempree diete was al hir phisik,

> And exercise, and hertes suffisaunce.
> The goute lette hire nothyng for to daunce,
> N'apoplexie shente nat hir heed.

(VII.2834–41)

The narrator implies that consuming rich delicacies or dancing gaily would seem as out of place in this rural setting as the strenuous "exercise" of tending a farm would be in an aristocratic household. The widow and her family struggle to maintain a subsistence economy, defined by the absence of those luxuries ("poynaunt sauce," "deyntee morsel," "wyn") enjoyed daily by a bourgeois or aristocratic family. The humorous description of the widow thus depends on socioeconomic difference:

> No wyn ne drank she, neither whit ne reed;
> Hir bord was served moost with whit and blak—
> Milk and broun breed, in which she foond no lak,
> Seynd bacoun, and somtyme an ey or tweye,
> For she was, as it were, a maner deye.

(VII.2842–46)

This class-conscious form of verbal wit depends on a play of two pairs of associated words that have one member in common: *whit/reed, whit/blak*. The technique, as Freud remarks, involves the "multiple use of the same material" (*SE* VIII.33). Chaucer, the vintner's son who enjoyed a royal grant of a daily allowance of wine, drinks the white and red of Alsace and Gascony.[31]

Chaucer presents sufficient detail to represent a local unit in a rural subsistence economy. The widow's "housbondrie" (along with that of her neighbors who later join the fox chase) seems to take part in a manorial economy, or even (since there are no apparent traces of money, rent, commerce, or commodities) in a "natural" economy.[32] I do not, of course, mean to suggest that such an economy actually existed in Chaucer's day, or that he could have intended such a description. If we cannot determine, as Pearsall observes, whether the widow "is or is not a demesne servant" (*Variorum* 147), this is because the narrative frame occludes any sense of the wider social context that would provide such crucial information as landlord-tenant relations. The *NPT*, that is, mystifies both the forces and relations of the feudal mode of production. What does it mean, for example, that the widow has "hertes suffisaunce" and "no lak"? Who enjoys her surplus?[33]

Chaucer's description of material production in a peasant household, moreover, is deeply marked by gender: the male head of household has died; there are only daughters mentioned; the kind of labor implied by the description is all typically women's work.[34] In a typical peasant household, males would perform most of the agricultural work. Women's work typically included childcare and the preparation of food and clothing and such activities as milking and raising chickens.[35] It is not by accident, then, that Chaucer seems specifically to associate female labor with a natural economy; we find a similar description of a peasant household managed by a woman in the *Clerk's Tale* (IV.197–224). In the *NPT* the boundary between the social category of gender and the natural category of sex is difficult to separate in the feminine world occupied by the widow and her daughters, who consume the product of *female* animals: milk, eggs, and occasionally bacon from the sows.

In Chaucer's presentation of a timeless natural economy in the framing narrative of the widow, the only form of struggle he permits us to see is that between the fox and his victim and everyone who pursues them: the "sely wydwe and eek hir doghtres two" (VII.3375), "many another man" carrying "staves" (VII.3382), and "Malkyn, with a dystaf in hir hand" (VII.3384), not to mention the variety of barnyard animals who add to the general confusion. This moment of comic struggle and terror provides the only interruption to the idealized portrait of rural labor in the tale. If this view of rural society occludes the dominant feudal mode of production of Chaucer's time, the late-medieval conflict in feudal relations is nonetheless signalled by the reference to the Peasants' Revolt of 1381. The narrative also inscribes the emergent capitalist mode of commodity production and exchange that operates beyond the widow's yard, where the wine known to the narrator is produced, bought, imported, and resold at a profit, or where the

Flemish merchants slain by the mob were engaged in textile manufacture.[36]

As we have already seen, Freud's essay, like Chaucer's narrative, conceals a mode of production narrative in its founding metaphor of psychic economy. Freud's thesis about "psychical expenditure" is that jokes function "in lifting internal inhibitions and in making sources of pleasure *fertile* which have been rendered inaccessible by those inhibitions" (*SE* VIII.130, my italics).[37] Jokes (like dreams) thus plow the field of the unconscious, that dark place inhabited by repressed energies and desires not directly available to consciousness. Freud's metaphor of fertility also appears in his central distinction between the manifest content of dreams and latent dream-thought, though the English translation obscures the fact that Freud's metaphor *Kern/Hülle* (kernel/husk) is borrowed from patristic exegesis, which also supplied these key terms to medieval poetics (Chaucer's "fruyt and chaff").[38] Jokes, according to Freud, provide a pleasurable release for what has been repressed: "Tendentious jokes . . . are able to release pleasure even from sources that have undergone repression" (VIII.134), satisfying what Freud elsewhere calls a "compulsion to repeat."[39]

Chaucer's tendentious jokes suggest that the real target that has been repressed by the tale only to be repeated in jocular form is the class of peasant producers within the feudal mode of production. The joke-work labors to keep the peasant widow and the 1381 rebels on opposing sides. Yet as peasant producers, their class interests would in fact be aligned, though the tale's idealized portrait of a natural economy, in mystifying the dominant feudal relations of production, obscures the class interests shared by peasants against their lords. We may therefore read the repression of the class interests of the exploited producers as a symptom of the political unconscious of the text.

Because jokes and dreams are closely linked in Freud's theory, it is tempting to compare the *NPT* to the dream of a traumatic neurotic. In *Beyond the Pleasure Principle*, Freud suggests that traumatic neuroses are brought on by a frightening experience: "dreams occurring in traumatic neuroses have the characteristic of repeatedly bringing the patient back into the situation of his accident, a situation from which he wakes up in another fright" (*SE* XVIII.13). If we read the *NPT* according to this analogy, the unexpected violence of the 1381 revolt caused a fright that Chaucer transfers to Chauntecleer, who wakes up frightened by a dream of unexpected danger: "By God, me mette I was in swich meschief / Right now that yet myn herte is soore afright" (VII.2894–95); Chauntecleer, in turn, transfers *his* fright onto one of the two pilgrims of his exemplum, whose dream foretells the murder of his companion: "This man out of his sleep for feere abrayde" (VII.3008). Yet "mordre wol out" (VII.3052). Despite these transferences, Chaucer is compelled to repeat one of the most frightening events of the revolt in the form of a joking comparison of the hue and cry raised against the fox by the widow, her daughters, neighbors, and animals to the noise of the revolt. Let us look closely at the passage again:

> So hydous was the noyse—a, benedicitee!—
> Certes, he Jakke Straw and his meynee
> Ne made nevere shoutes half so shrille
> Whan that they wolden any Flemyng kille,
> As thilke day was maad upon the fox.

Chaucer's comparison uses the *historia* of Jack Straw and company as a "vehicle" for an event in the *fabula*; the "tenor" is a fictional fox chase by those who seek justice against a thief. To restate this in psychoanalytic terms, the fox who trespasses on the widow's "yeerd" and steals her property displaces, through the process of secondary revision, the traumatic experience of the rebels' violent incursion into the city. Through the joke-work performed by the political unconscious of the *NPT*, an assault by a fictive predator becomes a metaphor for the assault on London during the Peasants' Revolt.[40]

In his 1915 essay "Repression," Freud offered a telling metaphor for the mechanism of repression, which he suggests resembles "ordering an undesirable guest out of my drawing-room or out of my front hall, and refusing to let him cross my threshold once I have recognized him." His footnote adds an image more military than domestic in its architecture to

describe the censorship of repression: "a sentinel to keep constant guard over the door which I have forbidden this guest to
pass, lest he should burst it open" (*SE* XIV.153). If we read the
peasant producers as the "undesirable guest" who is banished to
the political unconscious of the *NPT*, the repressed element
returns with a murderous vengeance. When the peasants from
the countryside were admitted through the gates of London, the
Essex rebels entered through Aldgate, where Chaucer was
leasing his apartment. Was he at home on Thursday, June 13?
Did he stand guard at his threshold? The rebels, joining in
alliance with the urban underclass of apprentices and wage
laborers, in their staging of popular justice, burned Savoy
Palace, executed the Archbishop of Canterbury, and challenged
the king in person. To their further discredit in Chaucer's eyes,
they also beheaded the Flemings.

If, as Freud argues, jokes provide a form of rebellion
against "critical reason" (*SE* VIII.126), it should be clear by
now that Chaucer's tale of a cock and fox may temporarily
challenge the rule of reason—whether it takes the form of
feudal lordship or the patriarchal domination of wives and
daughters—but in the end reason remains firmly in control.[41]
The Peasants' Revolt may have led King Richard II to issue
charters of manumission to the rebellious serfs, but he revoked
them as soon as the revolt was suppressed. "Rustics you were
and rustics you are still; you will remain in bondage, not as
before but incomparably harsher." Thus spoke the voice of the
sovereign, as imagined by the chronicler Walsingham.[42] Once
Chauntecleer escapes and order is restored, life will go on as
usual back at the manor. The sovereign will enjoy the privileges of patriarchy:

> He chukketh whan he hath a corn yfounde,
> And to hym rennen thanne his wyves alle.
> Thus roial, as a prince is in his halle,
> Leve I this Chauntecleer in his pasture.

> (VII.3182–85)

In closing his tale, the narrator warns us against
misreading the fable: "Taketh the fruyt, and lat the chaf be
stille." We can never be sure what Chaucer intended by his

allusion to the Peasants' Revolt, but as we have seen, his dream of a natural economy reduces the voice of peasant protest to a bad joke or nightmare, serving to remind us that the land and its produce not only furnishes one of the most enduring metaphors for hermeneutics, it also marks the site of political struggle. Yet in testing the boundaries between history and fable, this frivolous tale "of the Cok and Hen" makes the deadly serious point that sometimes people are so persuaded by their fictions that they are willing to shed blood in their name.[43]

NOTES

1. No one to my knowledge has observed that the allusion to the slaying of the Flemings provides another instance in the tale's pattern of Friday catastrophes.

2. The *Nun's Priest's Tale*, VII.3393–3397, *The Riverside Chaucer*, Larry D. Benson, gen. ed., 3rd ed. (Boston: Houghton Mifflin, 1987); all quotations from Chaucer are from this edition.

3. Peter Travis, "Chaucer's Trivial Fox Chase and the Peasants' Revolt of 1381," *JMRS* 18 (1988): 195–220, has recently described the allusion as "the most strikingly historical passage in all of Chaucer's poetry" (216). This fine essay is the most extended discussion of the allusion to date.

4. Paul Strohm, *Social Chaucer* (Cambridge, Mass.: Harvard University Press, 1989), 164–65.

5. Ian Bishop, *The Narrative Art of the* Canterbury Tales (London: Everyman-Dent, 1988), 170. Gower's use of animal and infernal imagery to describe the revolt also appears in English chronicle reports, a point of intertextual coincidence that has been well remarked by Lee Patterson, "'No man his reson herde': Peasant Consciousness, Chaucer's Miller, and the Structure of the *Canterbury Tales*," *SoAR* 86 (1987): 457–95 (at 472 and n. 42).

6. John M. Ganim, "Chaucer and the Noise of the People," *Exemplaria* 2 (1990): 71–88 (at 77). Like many other commentators, he also considers *Troilus and Criseyde* IV.183–90 a likely candidate for

another topical allusion to the revolt, since "strawe" may well be a pun on Jack Straw, though he admits the evidence is inconclusive.

7. Laura Kendrick, *Chaucerian Play: Comedy and Control in the Canterbury Tales* (Berkeley and Los Angeles: Univ. of California Press, 1988), 105.

8. Travis, "Chaucer's Trivial Fox Chase," 216; cf. 204, where he describes the presentation of the fox chase as "not entirely free of aggression."

9. See Fredric Jameson, *The Political Unconscious: Narrative as a Socially Symbolic Act* (Ithaca, N.Y.: Cornell University Press, 1981). Although I have borrowed the idea of the political unconscious from Jameson, I shall be using the term in a sense that owes as much to Freud as to Jameson.

10. I will henceforth abbreviate the title as *JRU*. The translation of Freud's terms presents notorious difficulties. The German title, *Der Witz und seine Beziehung zum Unbewussten*, was first translated by A. J. Brill as "Wit and Its Relation to the Unconscious." See Strachey's discussion in *The Standard Edition of the Complete Psychological Works of Sigmund Freud*, James Strachey, gen. ed., 24 vols. (London: Hogarth Press, 1953–74), VIII.7 for justification of his translating *Witz* as "jokes." Henceforth Freud's works will be cited in English from the *Standard Edition* as *SE*, followed by volume and page numbers; citations of the German text of *JRU* are to *Gesammelte Werke*, Sechster Band (London: Imago, 1940), henceforth abbreviated as *GW*.

11. A few critics have found Freud's theory of jokes useful in discussing Chaucer's humor, though no one has yet turned to *JRU* for guidance with the *NPT*. Some Chaucer critics who make use of Freud's theory of jokes include Paul G. Ruggiers, "A Vocabulary for Chaucerian Comedy: A Preliminary Sketch," in *Medieval Studies In Honor of Lillian Herlands Hornstein*, ed. Jess B. Bessinger, Jr., and Robert R. Raymo (New York: New York University Press, 1976), 193–225 (at 207); Peggy Knapp, *Chaucer and the Social Contest* (New York: Routledge, 1990), 41–43; Kendrick, *Chaucerian Play*, 38, 74–75.

12. *SE* VIII.208; italics added in 2nd ed., 1912. Freud is attempting here to distinguish between *der Witz* and *das Komische* or *die Komik*. The distinction between them is not absolute, as Freud acknowledges (see *SE* VIII.203, 206–07).

13. Freud reiterates the close connection between joke-work and dream-work a number of times (*SE* VIII.28–29, 88–89, 107); he explores the link in detail in chapter VI.

14. At times Freud's economic metaphor takes on the character of the kind of joke he seeks to analyze. His condescending attitude toward women is evident in the following remark about the economies of joke-work: "They may remind us, perhaps, of the way in which some housewives economize when they spend time and money on a journey to a distant market because vegetables are to be had there a few farthings cheaper" (*SE* VIII.44). The connection between Freud's joke about household economy and the *Nun's Priest's Tale* will become clear later.

15. As a note in the *Standard Edition* explains, the substantive *Tendenz* is translated as "purpose" while the adjective *tendenziös* appears as "tendentious" (*SE* VIII.90).

16 Cf. Karen Smythe, "Sexual Scenarios in Freud's Joke-Analysis," *SubStance* 64 (1991): 16–30, esp. 17.

17. One of the most frequently debated aspects of the tale is the status of the narrator. Derek Pearsall sums up what has become a critical commonplace: "The more we try to characterize the personal qualities of the narrator, the closer we get to what we habitually admire in Chaucer" (*A Variorum Edition of the Works of Geoffrey Chaucer*, Vol. 11, the *Canterbury Tales*, Part 9, the *Nun's Priest's Tale*, ed. Derek Pearsall [Norman: University of Oklahoma Press, 1984], 41); henceforth cited as *Variorum*. Similarly, Helen Cooper, *The Structure of the* Canterbury Tales (Athens, Georgia: University of Georgia Press, 1984), calls the Nun's Priest "the poet's double" (184).

18. Knapp, *Chaucer and the Social Contest*, 89.

19. J. Burke Severs, "Chaucer's Originality in the *Nun's Priest's Tale*," *SP* 43 (1946): 22–41 (at 37).

20. Charles Muscatine, *Chaucer and the French Tradition: A Study in Style and Meaning* (Berkeley and Los Angeles: University of California Press, 1957), 238. Unfortunately, he quotes lines 3362–68 as evidence of feminism.

21. Charles Owen, *Pilgrimage and Storytelling in the* Canterbury Tales: *the Dialectic of "Ernest" and "Game"* (Norman: Univ. of Oklahoma Press, 1977), 140; cf. Owen's discussion of the tale's antifeminism in "The Crucial Passages in Five of the *Canterbury Tales*: A Study in Irony and Symbol," *JEGP* 52 (1953): 294–311, rpt. in Edward Wagenknecht, ed., *Chaucer: Modern Essays in Criticism* (New York: Galaxy, 1959), 251–70 (at 267). See also David V. Harrington, "The Undramatic Character of Chaucer's Nun's Priest," *Discourse* 8 (1965): 80–89 (at 82).

22. Sheila Delany, "'*Mulier est hominis confusio*': Chaucer's Anti-popular *Nun's Priest's Tale*," *Mosaic* 17 (1984): 1–8.

23. See *The Institutio oratoria of Quintilian*, ed. and trans. H. E. Butler (Loeb Classical Library, 1921–22), II, iv, 2; Cicero, *De inventione*, ed. and trans. H. M. Hubbell (Loeb Classical Library, 1949), I, xix, 27; *Rhetorica ad Herennium*, ed. and trans. Harry Caplan (Loeb Classical Library, 1954), I, viii, 13; *Isidori Hispalensis Episcopi Etymologiarum sive Originum Libri XX*, ed. W. M. Lindsay, Oxford Classical Texts (Oxford: Clarendon Press, 1911), I, xliv, 5; *Ioannis Saresberiensis Metalogicon*, ed. C. C. J. Webb (Oxford: Clarendon Press, 1929), I, 24, p. 54. R. T. Lenaghan discusses the rhetorical background in his important article, "The Nun's Priest's Fable," *PMLA* 78 (1963): 300–07.

24. Robert Jordan takes this aside as "jesting tribute to the integrity of authorship" (*Chaucer's Poetics and the Modern Reader* [Berkeley and Los Angeles: University of California Press, 1987], 143). Although the line about Lancelot is syntactically ambiguous as Saul Brody observes, it cannot support his reading: "Lancelot, who held women in great esteem." See Saul Nathaniel Brody, "Truth and Fiction in the *Nun's Priest's Tale*," *ChaucR* 14 (1979): 33–47 (at 41).

25. Derek Brewer is one of the few critics who does not assume the rooster's mistranslation is intentional. He takes it rather as "a joke between Chaucer and an audience that can understand both English and Latin." See Derek S. Brewer, "Chaucer: What Is the *Nun's Priest's Tale* Really About?," *Trames (Travaux et Mémoires de l'U. E. R. des Lettres et Sciences Humaines de l'Université de Limoges)*, Collège d'Anglais, 2 (1979): 9–25 (at 10). Cf. Delany, "Anti-popular," 6–7.

26. Muscatine, *Chaucer and the French Tradition*, 242.

27. See John Speirs, *Chaucer the Maker* (London: Faber, 1951), 186; Trevor Whittock, *A Reading of the* Canterbury Tales (Cambridge: Cambridge University Press, 1969), 230; A. Paul Shallers, "The 'Nun's Priest's Tale': An Ironic Exemplum," *ELH* 42 (1975): 319–37, esp. 334.

28. For exegetical readings of the widow, see Mortimer J. Donovan, "The *Moralite* of the Nun's Priest's Sermon," *JEGP* 52 (1953): 498–508, esp. 505; Charles Dahlberg, "Chaucer's Cock and Fox," *JEGP* 53 (1954): 277–90, esp. 286; D. W. Robertson, "Some Disputed Chaucerian Terminology," *Speculum* 52 (1977): 571–81 (at 579–80) and Paul Olson, *The Canterbury Tales and the Good Society* (Princeton: Princeton Univ. Press, 1986), 199.

29. Beryl Rowland, *Blind Beasts: Chaucer's Animal World* (Kent, Ohio: Kent State University Press, 1971), 142.

30. Stephen Knight comments on the "genteel connotation" of "bour" and "sklendre" and emphasizes that the jokes in the description of the widow introduce the "mock-heroic to the tale." See *Rymyng*

Craftily: Meaning in Chaucer's Poetry (Sydney: Angus and Robertson, 1973), 213.

31. Martin M. Crow and Clair C. Olson, eds., *Chaucer Life-Records* (Oxford University Press, 1966), 112–19.

32. See Marx's discussion of "natural economy" in *Capital*, Vol. 2, trans. David Fernbach (New York: Vintage-Random House, 1978), 195–96, 554–55; *Capital*, Vol. 3, trans. David Fernbach (New York: Vintage-Random House, 1981), 425, 442, and esp. 921–22, 930–32; and Engels's Supplementary Note, *Capital*, Vol. 3, 1034.

33. See Patterson, "'No man his reson herde,'" 468–69 for a discussion of "need" and "enough" as key terms in the *Miller's Tale* (I.3158–66), which he reads in the context of the seigneurial extraction of peasant surplus product.

34. See Barbara Hanawalt, *The Ties That Bound: Peasant Families in Medieval England* (New York: Oxford University Press, 1986), 141–55. On peasant widows in general, see Hanawalt, 220–26.

35. Hanawalt, 146–48. Later the tale will mark gender with the emblem of female labor: "Malkyn with a distaf in hire hand" (VII.3384); cf. Pearsall's notes to the line (*Variorum*, 246–47).

36. The Flemings were particularly active in London as weavers; see Rodney H. Hilton, *Bondmen Made Free: Medieval Peasant Movements and the English Rising of 1381* (New York: Viking, 1973), 195–96.

37. Kendrick, p.187 n. 7, has called attention to what we might call the sexist tendency of Freud's theory of tendentious jokes in *SE* VIII.148–58. See also Smythe, "Sexual Scenarios" and Jerry Aline Flieger, "The Purloined Punchline: Joke as Textual Paradigm," *MLN* 98 (1983): 941–67.

38. For Freud's use of the exegetes' trope, see *SE* VIII.161; *GW* VI.183; and esp. *SE* VIII.185; *GW* VI.211.

39. See *Beyond the Pleasure Principle, SE* XVIII.20–23. The examples he uses are the dreams of traumatic neuroses and ordinary child's play (represented by the famous *fort-da* game).

40. Cf. Larry Scanlon, "The Authority of Fable: Allegory and Irony in the *Nun's Priest's Tale*," *Exemplaria* 1 (1989): 43–68 (at 63–64) for a different interpretation.

41. Cf. Scanlon, "The Authority of Fable," 61–65. I agree with his conclusion that "Chaucerian authority is critical yet profoundly conservative, ironically self-conscious yet deferential to the status quo" (64).

42. Walsingham excerpt printed in R. B. Dobson, *The Peasants' Revolt of 1381*, 2nd ed. (London: MacMillan, 1983), 311.

43. I wish to thank Professor Britton J. Harwood for his comments and suggestions on an earlier draft of this essay.

Paradoxicum Semiotica
Signs, Comedy, and Mystery in Fragment VI of the Canterbury Tales

John Micheal Crafton

> Two Jews met in a railway carriage at a station in Galicia.
> "Where are you going?" asked one. "To Cracow," was the
> answer. "What a liar you are!" broke out the other. "If you
> say you're going to Cracow, you want me to believe
> you're going to Lemberg. But I know that in fact you're
> going to Cracow. So why are you lying to me?"
> > Freud, *Jokes and Their Relation to The Unconscious*

> Sompnia ne cures, nam fallunt sompnia plures.
> > Holcot, *Super Sapientiam Salomonis*

> But wel I woot thou doost myn herte to erme
> That I almoost have caught a cardynacle.
> > Harry Bailey, Fragment VI, *Canterbury Tales*

John Gardner, in his insufficiently appreciated *The Poetry of Chaucer*, begins the section on the *Canterbury Tales* by pointing out a most fundamental notion that the phrase "a Canterbury tale" is Middle English slang for a lie. Reading the *Canterbury Tales*, then, must be approached the way we might approach the joke from Freud cited above—the truth is a lie, and the lie is the truth. Only by keeping that notion operative will we be able to appreciate the full flavor of Chaucer's comedy from the beginning of his collection of tales to the end. This "slang" insists that the famous dichotomies of "sentence and solas" and "ernest and game" are not true dichotomies, but rather more inextricably connected like amphiboles. That is, the language of Chaucer's poetry both asserts and denies the truth of its statements simultaneously, thereby creating a type of double truth, which thinkers as far apart as Ockham and Paul de Man claim points beyond the mere surface humor of puns and ironies to a divine comedy, a higher truth, a truth beyond truth that is best apprehended in literary language. In this essay, I want to follow Gardner's lead and examine Chaucer's comedy as a function of the inherent paradoxes of language, particularly as articulated by Freud and later treatments of comedy and language. I will also argue that the comedy of Chaucer's *Canterbury Tales* is framed by allusions to medieval language theory which so ironizes the utterances of the text that we are forced to read everything "up so doun" and vice versa at the same time; that is, part of the humor of the frame and the tales depends upon the audience's awareness of just how slippery is the notion of truth and lies in Chaucer's hands. Finally, then, I will examine the comedy (especially the black comedy) of Fragment VI, the *Physician's Tale* and the *Pardoner's Tale* in the context of these theories.

I

> Freud, the very name's a laugh. . . . It is the most hilarious
> leap into the holy farce of history.
>
> Lacan, *Feminine Sexuality*

Few would argue that the earliest modern treatment of the subject of comedy and language is Freud's *Jokes and Their Relation to the Unconscious*. There, Freud not only subjects his repertoire of jokes (mostly Jewish jokes that he tells at the expense of his own Jewish identity, an identity his atheism is all too happy to dispense with)[1] to a rigorous classification, but also to an analysis of technique (the joke-work) and to an analysis of purpose. For Freud the purpose of jokes is satisfied on two levels: the first is the level of individual psychology, wherein the joke releases a certain amount of repressed or surplus energy; and the second is the level of social psychology, wherein jokes function to maintain a balance in society between order and anarchy. The most interesting recent work on Chaucer's humor has focused almost exclusively on the latter purpose. Inspired by Bakhtin's *Rabelais and His World*, much of the recent work on Chaucer and play, such as Carl Lindhal's *Earnest Games* and Laura Kendrick's *Chaucerian Play*, is committed to analyzing the ways that Chaucer's comedy addresses social class and cohesion, particularly by studying folk tradition and the various comic festivals that occurred among the social classes of fourteenth-century England. As Kendrick puts it, Chaucer intended "the *Canterbury Tales* to renew the productive forces of English society and, at the same time, through controlling play, to stabilize the late-fourteenth-century social order."[2] This latest direction in the discussion of Chaucer's comedy follows the venerable tradition of Barber, Suzanne Langer, and Northrop Frye on romantic comedy and is certainly understandable as a corrective to the psychodynamic approach of the dramatic principle that has held such a dominant position in Chaucer criticism for so long and against the exegetical criticism and its emphasis on irony as the single most powerful tool for reading every comic tale as in fact a statement of *allegoria et anagogia*.

Yet we may use the Freudian model as entre to another method of taking Chaucer's comedy as seriously as I think he meant it. It seems to me that the *Canterbury Tales* does not work so much to exemplify one or more of the *functions* of humor as it does to exemplify the *analysis* of humor in addition to its functions. In other words, the *Canterbury Tales* is Chaucer's *Jokes and Their Relation to the Unconscious* just as much as Chaucer's early poetry may well be considered his version of *The Interpretation of Dreams*. A further uncanny resemblance to Freud is that Freud's later work on jokes incorporates the earlier analysis of dreams, just as the *Canterbury Tales*, likewise the later work, incorporates the early interest on dreams in the *Nun's Priest's Tale*. More significantly, however, what Freud and Chaucer do is to trace the radically ambiguous messages of dreams, jokes, and language to their sources in the ultimate ground of concern—for Freud, the mystery of the Unconscious; for Chaucer, the mystery of God.

Freud was as much motivated by the need to demystify as he was by the need to cure; in fact, the two are really the same. The "talking cure" is simply the act of revealing to the patient something repressed, something mysterious in the unconscious. (That this method did not always work is beside the point.) Thus, in his analysis of humor he works as hard as he can to write the "science" of jokes. Having earlier demonstrated the basic grammar of dreams as relevant for interpreting jokes, he concludes, "We found that the characteristics and effects of jokes are linked with certain forms of expression or technical methods, among which the most striking are condensation, displacement and indirect representation. Processes, however, which lead to the same results . . . have become known to us as peculiarities of the dream-work."[3] Freud goes on to state that in the creation of a joke, the revision of a preconscious thought occurs in the unconscious before it manifests itself as a joke just as dreams are revised in the unconscious before they manifest themselves to the dreamer. Finally, like dreams, jokes function to release repressed desires—"wish fulfillments." In the last page of *Jokes*, Freud sums up his scientific discoveries:

> All three [jokes, humor, and the comic] are agreed in . . . regaining from mental activity a pleasure which has in fact been lost through the development of that activity. For the euphoria which we endeavor to reach by these means is nothing other than the mood of a period of life in which we were accustomed to deal with our psychical work in general with a small expenditure of energy—the mood of our childhood, when we were ignorant of the comic, when we were incapable of jokes and when we had no need of humour to make us feel happy in our life.[4]

The question now is just what is this happiness beyond humor? What is our contact to it? Our contact is the unconscious, where language is a play of opposites, where multiple meanings cohabit effortlessly, and negation does not exist. A language without repression is a language that does not say no. What points Freud toward this character of the unconscious is the repeated use of opposite meanings that he saw so frequently in symptoms. As Marie Jahoda summarizes, "Through his working life he was ... concerned with assembling confirmation of the idea of the closeness of opposites. He found it in folk wisdom, in myth and fairy tales (the ugly frog turned into the beautiful prince), in legend and poetry, in primitive ritual, but above all in language with its remnant of primitive thought."[5]

In comedy the closeness of opposites is most obviously operative in puns, *double entendres*, or what Freud calls ambiguous language. Yet Freud's concept of ambiguity is itself quite ambiguous. In Jerry Flieger's analysis of Freud's theory of humor, the problematic nature is clearly addressed.

> [T]he use of the term *ambiguity* invites comment for several reasons. First, it highlights the joke's reliance on multiple meanings and hence emphasizes the layered and articulated nature of language, acknowledging that words are never simply identical to that which they designate. So, even though Freud sometimes sounds as though he believes in an original transparent and unambiguous language (referring, for instance, to words that "have lost their original full meaning, but which regain it again in the joke" [34]), his position on joking nonetheless depends on the notion of inadequacy and even arbitrariness of linguistic designation, and of the inherently imprecise nature of language, its inability to "keep its word," to hold itself to unequivocal meaning. In other words, comic effect could be understood as either an excess of meaning, resulting from *double entendre* (too much meaning in one word), or as a paucity of meaning, resulting from play with cliché or understatement (too little meaning in a worn out word). In either case, ambiguous language is a sign of the inadequation of word to referent, the desire within meaning, the *je veux dire* that may approximate what it *wants* to say.[6]

This excess of meaning, Flieger goes on to assert, is an effect of the notion that nearly all postmodern theorists exploit, which is the notion of undecidability or paradox. That ambiguity is necessary for much verbal humor no one will doubt, but postmodern writing, such as Derrida's *Glas*, works to undermine the reader's ability to decide which of the many possible meanings should be rendered dominant; rather, in the hands of some writers we are allowed only to watch the meanings oscil-

late, denying our attempt to settle into a comfortable understanding or interpretation.

Certainly the rigorous readings of Hartman, De Man,
Derrida, Lacan, Foucault, Lyotard, Bordieu, and others echo
Freud's attempt, with greater and lesser degrees of sobriety, to
reduce concepts or even images to language of radical undecid-
ables, paradoxes that give us some glimpse of the unconscious.
Indeed, we find jokes, puns, and paradoxes throughout late
modern writing literary theory and philosophy; it is almost
epidemic. Jerry Flieger uses this fact to argue that comedy runs
throughout postmodern writing as an allegory of intersubjective
communication in order to effect, perhaps, a type of community,
a type of integration, that in a world obsessed with its own
annihilation is indeed most welcome. Geoffrey Hartman, in his
book length study of Derrida's *Glas* (published long before
Flieger pointed out a similar thesis without giving Hartman
any credit), suggests that by "reaping the page," as he called
it, of the postmodern text one saves not only the text but the
human. In fact, Hartman, in his chapter punningly titled
"Epiphany in Echoland," goes further to point out the textual
nature of our ground of being, of our human comedy, and of the
ascent through to our own Paradiso

> If thinking is for us, today, textual, then we should under-
> stand that grounding. To some extent it can and must be
> argued that we have fallen into the condition of viewing
> all things as texts, and even the "thing" itself is textual.
> Structured "like" language, Lacan says ambiguously of
> "la chose freudienne." Heidegger describes our condition,
> whether or not he is right in historicizing it, on the theo-
> logical or Platonic model of a fall.
>
> Texts are a false bottom, no doubt; a ground as treacher-
> ously sustaining as Nature was for Blake. Nature, says
> Blake, is there because of God's mercy, for otherwise we
> would still be falling . . . . Today, not to fall, means to
> accept the grounding of textual thought as well as to keep
> falling *through* the text, as Blake said we see *through* the
> eye. There is no "cure of the ground"; there is only the
> "here hear!" of the text.[7]

Flieger argues in a similar vein that the "bottom line" of Freud's theory of comedy is likewise bottomless. "If Freud's aesthetic has a bottom line, it is perhaps only that the aesthetic is a bottomless non-linearity, the antithesis of closure. . . . The comic, like every aesthetic process, is a paradox deriving from both excess and lack, an excess of desire and of opportunities of its partial satisfaction, and an unbridgeable gap stemming from the irretrievable loss of the original object."[8]

The "original object" exists nowhere, of course, except as memory traces in the unconsciousness, on the one hand; on the other, the fact of the "object" being lost is the thing itself producing existence. The original object, understood as an original plenitude or what a naive theology would designate as the God of presence, Derrida and company designate the transcendental signified and cast aside; the original object that a sophisticated fourteenth-century theology designates as the Cloud of Unknowing as presence/absence, Derrida calls *différence* and founds one of the most influential modern movements in philosophy upon it.

With Freud, Nietzsche, Heidegger, and Derrida, we as close readers all are falling through the *mise en abyme* of representation, listening to the peal of laughter made of the echoes of all puns, all jokes, fragments that we may shore against our ruins or that we may set to music whilst whistling past the graveyard.

II

Guildenstern: I think I have it. A man talking sense to
    himself is no madder than a man talking nonsense not
    to himself.
Rosencrantz: Or just as mad.
Guildenstern: Or just as mad.
Rosencrantz: So there you are.
Guildenstern: Stark raving sane.
        Stoppard, *Rosencrantz and Guildenstern are Dead*

The discussion of signs in postmodern language theory is not far at all from the medieval debates over language and the existence of the universal. However problematic, medieval theories of language are still classified into three categories based upon each category's ontological account of the sign. The first, the Realist school, stems from Plato and Augustine and asserts the existence of signs prior to things—*universalis ante rem.* The second, generally termed moderate Realism, claims an Aristotelian and Thomistic tradition and posits the existence of universals only in things—*universalis in re.* The last group, referred to by several names (the Nominalists or Termists or conceptualists) and whose heritage may stem from the so-phists, but certainly from Abelard and Ockham, allows universals only as mental or logical terms—*universalis in mente.*[9]

The first two categories accept the existence of universals outside the human mind and thus can both be called essentialist positions, whereas the third, the Nominalist position accepts no extra-mental universals. The trend in early modern medieval scholarship associated the first two with the Great Medieval Synthesis and the third with the destruction of that synthesis, with the advocacy of skepticism (and perhaps irreligion) and with the beginnings of the scientism, natur-alism, and the secularism associated with the modern world.

Yet the nature of Nominalism is always undergoing revi-sion as the nature of Ockham's work undergoes revision. David Knowles summarizes the contours of Ockham scholarship as follows: "Hailed by his younger contemporaries and their successors as the herald . . . of a new era, he was attacked in his lifetime by those who detested his opinions and later by those who reacted against his technique while preserving many of his opinions. . . . More recently still, within the past two decades, members of his own order have endeavored and still endeavor to destroy what they regard as the myth of Ockham's destructive genius, and to show him as the great logician, fun-damentally traditional in thought and doctrine, who rejuve-nated Aristotelian logic and who never intended that his daring hypotheses should do more than provide material for intellectual debate."[10] Therefore, one can easily claim Ockham as a source for any position from skeptic to faithful, from rebel to conservative, from ancient to modern. Since the Nominalists were also theologians and since the gulf between philosophy and theology was ever widening due in part to the Bishop Tempier's Condemnations of 1277, one cannot find a singular, univocal, monolithic nominalist theology. The Nominalist posited an unlimited, all powerful, and unknowable God and left the theologian without the help of philosophy for grappling with the problem. Thus Ockham could share with the Realist Wycliff antipapal positions, and the Nominalist Holcot could share with Augustine an emphasis of will over intellect.[11]

Regardless of these difficulties, the two poles of essentialism (*via antiqua*) and Nominalism (*via moderna*) still obtain and have been used most recently (on the one hand) by Gardner, Russell Peck, Holly W. Boucher, and Sheila Delany—claiming Chaucer to be some form of Nominalist—and (on the other) by P.B. Taylor, Morton Bloomfield (perhaps Robert Pratt) along with the Robertsonian tradition—claiming Chaucer as a neo-platonic Christian essentialist. Taylor claims that Chaucer's position is made clear by the comedy. That is, all of the tales that participate in Nominalism are told in a comic or satiric vein and those of essentialism in a serious or religious vein. The Robertsonian tradition has always assumed that Chaucer is a Realist throughout and any comic tale that may imply otherwise is to be read as, of course, ironic. However, we can not allow such a simple formulas to stand. In fact, it seems that while the effect of the sign theory controversy on Chaucer's tales is real, Chaucer's position is radically ambiguous—setting both positions against one another or collapsing them in ways impossible to disentangle. Like Freud, Chaucer explored the possibilities of language and comedy and was led to the same results, paradox. Chaucer's comedy throughout the *Canterbury Tales* is framed by his teasing references to language theory. We are forced to see, therefore, the *Canterbury Tales* as a text of humor that analyzes the technique of humor while it entertains with humor. Finally, Chaucer's analysis of the language of humor is operative at all levels of discourse: the frame, the fragment, and the individual tale.

At the level of the frame, we have the advantage of analyzing very different statements about the nature of language by the same character—Chaucer. Under the sign of his own name, he articulates three positions regarding his use of language at the beginning, middle, and end of the *Canterbury Tales*, each of which functions as an apologia, each with the comic refrain—"blameth not me." The first position stated toward the end of the *General Prologue* and toward the end of the *Miller's Prologue* defends his use of controversial language in the manner of Reason in the *Roman de la Rose*.[12] In the *General Prologue* he asks the reader not to "arrete" the foul language in the tales to his "villanye" because:

> Whoso shal telle a tale after a man,
> He moot reheerce as ny as evere he kan
> Everich a word, if it be in his charge,
> Al speke he never so rudeliche and large,
> Or ellis he moot telle his tale untrewe,
> Or feyne thyng, or fynde wordes newe.

(I.731–736)

To further buttress this defense, he refers to Christ's speech as "full brode" and to Plato's claim that the word be cousin to the deed.

This passage which seems to plead a simple case for Realism in art as mimesis of *natura naturata* is—as we know from P. B. Taylor's excellent analysis—comically ambiguous throughout. He asks to speak full "brode" like Jesus, but Jesus spoke in parables, not in foul language, Chaucer's meaning of *broad* here. *Brode* furthermore means plainly or openly; this seems quite opposite the parabolic language alluded to. He claims that the word is cousin to the deed, but the meaning of *cousin* is ambiguous. It may mean relatedness, implying the word and thing are ontologically connected, but *cousin* may also mean deception, the connotation worked so heavily in the *Shipman's Tale*. Finally, he says that he must tell his tale as he heard it ("everiche a word") or otherwise he will be forced to invent something and "fynde wordes newe," but, of course, the tale *is* Chaucer's invention; he never heard it. The irony is dizzying. (Taylor also suggests that "dede" may be a pun on dead, leaving us with the darkly comic, Nominalistic, quasi-deconstructionist notion of words as cousins to the dead.)

The second passage is Chaucer's defense of the Thopas stated in the headlink to the Melibee. In this passage Chaucer seems to be quite outrageously arguing just the opposite. He again says "blameth not me" if "I nat the same wordes seye / As ye had herd," for "as in my sentence / Shul ye nowhere fynden difference" (VII.959–962). In this section, then, Chaucer seems to say that he need not be a slave to the words of others; in fact, he may alter words and add proverbs to the original in order "To enforce with th'effect of my mateere" (VII.958). Though he makes reference to Christ, this time he argues that just as the four gospels differ yet the same "pitous passioun expresse"; so for him, the "sentence is al oon" (VII.950–951). Now it seems we are indeed in the world of the nominalist, wherein God's absolute power (what the Nominalists stressed in their theologies as *de potentia absoluta*) and alterity are affirmed along with the freedom of the speaker's language.[13]

The last testament of Chaucer on the notion of language is, of course, the Retraction. (Although a decidedly problematic text, we may assume it represents some persona of Chaucer.) In this text, he follows the same three-point pattern, but the Retraction is the most radically ambiguous of them all. First, Chaucer again refers to Christ, this time as the absolute source for poetry, saying if the reader finds anything enjoyable, he should attribute it to Christ as the source of all wit. Second, we hear the refrain, "blameth not me" when Chaucer says, "I preye hem also that they arrette it to the defaute of myn unkonnynge, and nat to my wyl that wolde ful fayn have seyd bettre if I hadde had konnynge. For oure book seith, 'Al that is writen is writen for oure doctrine,' and that is myn entente" (X.1082–1083). (This may sound penitent enough, but it could be a sly joke as well, for basically Chaucer is saying that if he had it to do over again, he would do exactly the same thing.) The Retraction, finally, is ambiguous, for in it could be claimed by both the Realists or the Nominalists. Either Augustine's Realist notion of the primacy of the will (as explained in *De mendacio* cited in the *Parson's Tale*) or Holcot's Nominalistic voluntarism (which elicited the Pelagian controversy between him and Bradwardine referred to in the *Nun's Priest's Tale*) could be used to explicate Chaucer's excuse that nothing in the *Canterbury Tales* was told with the *intention* of sinfulness.

Perhaps Chaucer designed the Retraction to hedge his bet, but there does seem to be a pattern of difference here among the three positions. We might say that in the General Prologue at the beginning of the journey and before the fall into fictionality, he ascribes to the belief of *universalis in re*—universals existing in things. This position dictates that there is a connection between *res* and *verba* and that one must be careful about attending to things in order to preserve this connection. In the middle of his journey when he speaks, quite literally, between two tales, in the full freedom of fictive unreality, the connection between *res* and *verba* is severed, and he is free to use words as he wishes, for universals exist only in the minds of the users. Finally in the Retraction, he is neither free from nor bound to things, but rather his responsibility is to society (the readers) and to God. His stated desire is to write for the doctrine of Christianity—to appeal to a pre-existing design— and any fault in doing that is due to a lack of knowing, not a lack of attention to the world, nor a lack of freedom. This final position is consistent with both essentialist and Nominalist positions, and the joke is therefore on the audience if it held on too steadfastly or doctrinally to either one of the two positions. Chaucer folds these two contradictory theories into each other in order to cancel them out, to create a coincidence of opposites, a laughter of negation which might then lead to prayer or meditation on both the absolute fullness and emptiness (*pace* Eckhart), a meditation that provided for many in the four-teenth-century a spiritual path around such scholastic quibbles as Ockham's *suppositio*.

III

> Knight: The condition is that I may live as long as I hold out
> against you. If I win, you will release me. Is it agreed?
> *Death points to one of the knight's hands; it contains a*
> *black pawn.*
> Knight: You drew black!
> Death: Very appropriate. Don't you think so?
>
> Bergman, *The Seventh Seal*

The second level of analysis of language theory within the tales results also in a dialectical questioning of the theories. Indeed, it seems that at least part of the sense of the grouping of the *Canterbury Tales* is informed by the tale's relation to language. This pattern is most obviously also set forth in the Chaucer's two tales of Thopas, all glitter but original, and Melibee, all sermon and quotation. Another similar pair make up Fragment V. The *Squire's Tale* is a poorly told foil to the *Franklin's Tale* on the theme of the magic of gifts and the magic of words. Also the *Monk's Tale* and *Nun's Priest's Tale* can be read as two commentaries on the theme of *fortuna*; the Monk seems to undermine the realist position as he repeats the pattern of the fall ad nauseum, but the Nun's Priest places passages from Holcot's sermon on Wisdom in mouths of chickens.[14] The *Summoner's* and *Friar's Tales* seem likewise joined with the *Friar's Tale* as a celebration of Nominalist voluntarism (appropriately since most of the early English nominalists were Franciscans) and with the *Summoner's Tale* as a critique of the Nominalist's notion of words as *flatus vocis*.[15]

In all of these pairings, a facility with language is compared to a lack thereof. The facility with language points out the comedy of the one who is inept with language, and the ostensibly naive bumbler usually introduces elements that the "smooth talker" cannot gloss over. Thematically, this structure speaks to a dualistic view of language, as both creator and destroyer, both obstacle and vehicle of truth, beauty and God. Even the final two tales underscore this theme. For the *Manciple's Tale* gives us a most tarnished view of golden Apollo and depicts language as tarnish, leaving us with the moral that it is probably better to keep one's mouth and language closed, yet the tale is told in some very fine poetry. The *Parson's Tale*, which is not told in very fine poetry, advertises the power of language, a power that underscores much of Chaucer's positive attitude toward language, the power of confession and the ability to speak away the manifold burdens of postlapsarian life, and in effect speak through to God.

Fragment VI is an appropriate selection for this kind of investigation, principally because both tales are manifestly about the difficulty of the relationship between language on the one hand and truth and/or nature on the other, and it is the discrepancy between these two that provides the comedy within each tale and provides the satiric effects we notice when comparing the tales to each other. Furthermore, we see that in each tale the narrator's stance or attitude toward story telling is informed by an extreme version of Realism or Nominalism.[16] That is, Chaucer creates caricature of a Realist and a Nominalist much in the same way that David Lodge creates caricatures of a Leavisite and a Deconstructionist in his novel *A Small World*; the representations are partially accurate, but revealed to be lacking because neither caricature finds the grail at the end of the quest. Also in each case, any validity of the informing theory is undermined by the effects of the story. This negation operates twice for each story: one, the primary audience (the Host) does not respond appropriately, and two, the narrative, following the pattern of the narrator's thought, results in such undesirable consequences that it turns us away from embracing the theory that it espouses. In so doing, Chaucer points the way toward a third position, one grounded in the effect of language on the audience, evidencing a humanistic theory of language.

In the *Physician's Tale*, we are presented a narrator whose informing theory of art is extreme Realism—the only justification for narrating is to tell the historical truth for didactic purposes. This Physician's Realism relies on two basic principles—one, avoidance of creativity and two, a principle necessarily implied by the first, strict adherence to the perceived authority, especially to law. As the *Physician's Tale* unfolds, we learn that these two principles extend outward to inform the narrator's and his characters' approaches to life in general, and this plot further negates the appeal of the narrator's *ars poetica* since the result is so undesirable.

This complex reveals itself early in this tale wherein the realist's reliance on a hierarchical ontology of the sign and contempt for poesis or art are made clear. The passage that calls our attention the loudest is Nature's boasting of her powers. Nature here, as Virginius does later, echoes the mindset of the narrator:

> . . . Lo! I, Nature,
> Thus kan I forme and peynte a creature,
> Whan that me list; who kan me countrefete?
> Pigmalion noght, though he ay forge and bete,
> Or grave, or peynte; for I dar wel seyn
> Apelles, Zanzis, sholde werche in veyn
> Outher to grave, or peynte, or forge, or bete,
> If they presumed me to countrefete.

(VI.11–18)

Nature or Realism claims that she made Virginia more beautiful than any art could capture because she is the natural principle of creation which no art can "countrefete"—counterfeit or counter make.[17] Yet, ironically, the only way that Nature can make this claim is in the language of art—"forme and peynte." In fact, Nature repeats the terms of art so much in her efforts to denigrate art that her attempts becomes absurdly humorous. Already the problematic nature of avoidance of art is made painfully clear; every attempt to avoid art leads to becoming enmeshed in art, which informs the critique that since art is a part of this world, avoiding it through any form of hyper-mimesis is in vain, thereby underscoring the point of the pun of truth and lying in language: the two are always already bound together. Secondly, the theme of governance or law as strict adherence is introduced. Nature is absolutely obedient to God as Nature's creatures are obedient to her at the point of creation. Yet, what this accomplishes is to turn Nature into a completely determined and mechanical principle (a problem that haunts Augustine and Boethius in their attempts to work out their Realist positions concerning questions of morality).

This mechanizing of the natural principle then renders the personification and boast absurd at best. The lack of creative freedom in Nature's description of her role denudes her ability to create anything superior. When she says, "I made hire [Virginia] to the worshipe of my lord; / So do I alle myne othere creatures," she undermines her efforts to create a superior person since they are all the same. Again, Nature appears humorous at her own expense. It is as if she were saying, Virginia is the most sublime emblem of virginity in the world, or at least as good as Harry Bailey. Of course, we may justify Nature's claims along theological, metaphysical, and perhaps physical lines, but there can be no doubt that her rhetoric fails. The arrangement of the words simply undercuts her claims to greatness. As with the tale as a whole, the conclusion here does not match our expectations.

In Nature's opening speech we cannot miss the Realist concern with counterfeits, or mimesis. The narrator makes this point clear a number of times in the text. Even the very first line with its citation of Livy, a historian, not a writer of imaginative narratives, attempts to step outside of narrative to assert the truth of its claims. In the approximate center of the text, the narrator eliminates all doubt about his tastes.

> This false juge, that highte Apius,
> (So was his name, for this is no fable,
> But knowen for historial thyng notable;
> The sentence of it sooth is, out of doubte).

(VI.154–157)[18]

Just as the voice of nature functions as a prosopopoeia for the attitude of the narrator, so Virginius acts out the implications of extreme Realism. In short course Virginius finds himself at the mercy of a shrewd corrupt judge, the very rhetorical Apius; Apius seems therefore aligned with art, and Nominalism, the arch-enemies of the narrator of the *Physician's Tale*. Although he is the agent in the tale who does know how to use art, it is, of course, for evil purposes, and since he is a counterfeit, a false judge, he certainly bears out Nature's negative value of counterfeits. Virginius, standing before the false judge, knows he faces deceit, but a defense or escape requires much creativity, inventiveness, and one who either avoids or repeats will not be able to counter this predicament. In fact, Virginius' attempts at appeal are in keeping with the law, attempts that Apius negates.

After he is effectively silenced in court, Virginius goes home and attempts to remedy the situation through obedience by setting up his own mock court in imitation of the false court. Even the language of the two scenes is similar. As Apius "sat in his consistorie" to deal out the death of virginity, so Virginius "setts him in his hall" to deal out death to Virginia. In this imitation of Apius, which becomes darkly comic in its repetitions, he calls his accused daughter before him, just as Apius calls for Virginius to appear before him. Moreover, Virginius begins his speech in such a way as to give the illusion of discussion or debate just as Apius effected an illusion of justice. Yet, by the end of his speech, any alternative disappears:

> O gemme of chastitee, in pacience
> Take thou thy deeth, for this is my sentence.

(VI.223–224)

The term "sentence" resonates cruelly and with black comedy in this line. We are told that the story is no fiction, that the "sentence of it sooth is." However, "sentence" is used three times in a twenty-line passage, each time referring to Apius's false law. Since the "sentence" of Apius's sentence is the lie taught him by "the feend [that] into his herte ran" (VI.130), the meaning of the word by this point becomes ambiguous. In fact, it seems quite clear that in a tale so obsessed with getting at "sentence," the goal of ever achieving pure "sentence" is shown to be impossible, thus satirizing the extreme Realist position as a single-minded quest for and strict adherence to "sentence."

Further evidence of just how unsuccessful the Physician has been conveying his story comes from the response of Harry Bailey. He says that he was greatly affected by Virginia's death, but he attributes the cause of her death to her beauty and thus misses the point of the story, indicating, perhaps, there may not be a point or if so, it is poorly related, an interpretation underscored by the fact that he says the tale is "no fors"—of no social impact. Most interestingly, the Host mocks the Physician by repeating his words, as if to say that a certain amount of imitation is harmless, and to speak in "term" (either medical or rhetorical) may in fact be appropriate. However well the Host may be at terms, he undermines his authority near the end of his address to the Physician by saying that he almost "caught a cardynacle." The malapropism is nearly always read as the Host's confusion of cardinal and cardiacle, but, in fact, Chaucer may imply behind the surface joke yet another meaning, "cardy-ne-acle," that is a non heart attack. To say that the tale gave the Host a non heart attack is much closer to what the Host himself actually says of the Physician's skill, now humorously; it has "no fors."

If the Physician is a caricature of the Realist, then in the adjoining tale, the Pardoner serves as an example (as many have pointed out) of the extreme, Nominalist who believes he is completely free to use words in any way that he desires.[19] For him there seems to be no ontological difference between a particular word and a so-called universal than there is between a relic and a pig's bone. In fact, his sermon is a kind of verbal "relic." The motivation of his discourse is not to capture the "historial thyng notable," but rather to persuade with the "moral thyng profitable."

> Youre likyng is that I shall tell a tale.
> Now have I dronke a draughte of corny ale,
> By God, I hope I shal yow telle a thyng
> That shal by reson been at youre likyng.
> For though myself be a ful vicious man,
> A moral tale yet I you telle kan,
> Which I am wont to preche for to wynne.

(VI.455–461)

The disjunction between signifier and signified is made extremely, hilariously, clear by the fact that the opening sermon is against the three tavern sins of drinking, swearing, and gambling, yet the introduction quoted above represents the narrator as a drinker, a false witness, and a gambler with words. The Pardoner does not play dice, but he most certainly gambles with his tongue and the bones in his relic bag.

It is freedom, however, that distinguishes the Pardoner's informing attitude toward language and narrative from that of the Physician's. Not only does he delight in the disjunction between the prologue and the opening sermon, but he also delights in literalizing his metaphor, a structure that Stewart Justman sees as evidence of Chaucer's siding with Nominalism. Thus, the theme of *radix malorum* is illustrated with a story of greed taking place literally at the root of a tree, certainly a visual pun. This humor reveals a speaker concerned only with the physical quality of language, treating it as chaff only (without fruit), a quality that Steven Khinoy associates with the Pardoner's relation to language in general—as singular, all letter without spirit. This attitude ironically connects the Pardoner and Physician because just as the Pardoner's freedom is perhaps an effect of his Nominalist perception of language as singular, particular, and therefore material—so also the Physician's Realist attitude focuses on the letter as sacrosanct object, because of its potential truth, and renders it concrete, material as well. (If we follow Robertson's lead, especially in his latest essay on the *Physician's Tale*, we must see both characters as professional frauds, and thus driven by a kind of *cupiditas* that does indeed cheapen their world by turning it into material possession—yet, as we can see, these diametrically opposed theories of language are both employed and both found wanting.[20])

Further, as with the narrator of the *Physician's Tale*, the Pardoner's performance undermines the success of his theory. While the *Pardoner's Tale* is told brilliantly, his freedom of the word leads to his confession and revelation of his wickedness, the result of which of course infuriates the Host. Thus, if the Pardoner's goal is to win money, he has lost; if his goal is to create forgiven and forgiving Christians, he has lost on this score too, for the Host (perhaps as we are) is in no condition to forgive anything. Since it is the Knight, the symbol of authority, who forces the kiss of peace between the two, Chaucer underscores the idea that this free-wheeling, free-wording Nominalist is not effective, does not bring good out of evil, as is

the case with Sir Ciappelletto in the *Decameron*.[21] Also, if
there really were no ontological difference between a relic and
a pig's bone, the Host would not be so moved to enshrine the
Pardoner's *coillons*.

As another echo of the structure of the *Physician's Tale*,
the major characters in the tale act out the theory of the
narrator and double the self-irony. The three revelers to a
certain extent parallel the Pardoner. They are brave gamblers
and swearers; they make great sport in tearing the body of
Christ—the Logos, the source of words and all wit according to
the Retraction. It is no accident, furthermore, (since they, as
extreme Nominalist juniors, tear at the Word) that they use an
imitation, a mocking, of the Eucharist, in attempting to
achieve the ends of greed. Also, since they pervert the sense
(signified) of the Communion, it is proper that the wine
(signifier) be perverted by using the iconographic imagery of
wine and bread for the murder weapons. Here the revelers
assume only the singularity of the wine, an assumption that
proves fatal.

In addition to the signs of the Eucharist, the gold coins
found at the tree are quite clearly signs that have more
signification than the revelers realize. Coins would be better
understood by a medieval audience as connected to sign theory
than by a modern audience, so the idea of coins functioning to
signify death would be an equation taken quite seriously by a
Realist and jokingly by a nominalist. However, we may further
see the gold coins at the root of the tree of *cupiditas* as
something like the dream image rebus which Freud argues that
the unconscious generates in dreams, as a wish fulfillment
emanating from the very strange psyche of the teller. The
Pardoner, or perhaps Chaucer, feels "cut off" from truth or
significant contact. It may be that the keener one manipulates
language, the keener one feels the anxiety of separation, a
separation resulting from the Nominalistic split between *res*
and *verba*. The speaker, therefore, desires death or, in other
words, the end of dying; he desires the unity of the signifier
and the signified (perhaps transcendental); he desires the
Lacanian Phallus of signification that as Carolyn Dinshaw has
ably argued, is central to the meaning of the Pardoner's

eunuchry. Yet the more that the Pardoner tries to please his audience, the more he tries to persuade them, the more furious the Host becomes and the bleaker the state of the Pardoner appears. The Pardoner fails to win over his audience and his narrative reveals the poverty of an extreme Nominalism.

Chaucer in presenting the caricatures of these two extremes of the philosophy of language and then undermining them even for the sake of comedy may well leave the reader with the dominant impression of skepticism, a characteristic mistakenly attributed to Nominalism or (in contemporary language) deconstructionism. Although a number of scholars have made such claims, as Gordon Leff says, we can't attribute this sense to Nominalism because "the belief in the inherent uncertainty and contingency of all existence, other than God's, was a tenet common to all Christians."[22] I believe that this dialectical manner of canceling out these scholastic methods reveals Chaucer's sympathy with moderate conceptualism, a position that may be consistent with one of the many interpretations of Ockham, but that is certainly consistent with the new humanistic rhetorical attitudes emerging from Italy during this period, the tradition in which Dante, Boccaccio and Petrarch were all trained, flourishing among the law students and the university students, those trained like Chaucer in the *ars dictaminis*. This rhetorical tradition argues, as Chaucer does in the Retraction, that the poet's words are not dictated absolutely by things, or the Realists' signs prior to existence, or by some psuedo-Nominalistic whim, but rather by the civil needs of society and by the desire to create beauty and glorify God. Therefore, Chaucer's comedy, seen as one effect of language as pun-ridden, as necessarily slippery and duplicitous, is not based upon a notion of language as word play for nihilism's sake, but rather on the notion of necessary play in thought, word, and deed; this necessary play interrupts the systems of human construction and allows the divine comedy to exist, the mystical laughter that emanates from paradox, from the coincidence of opposites, and perhaps as Chaucer's contemporaries would have thought, from the heart of the Cross.

NOTES

1. See Elliott Oring, *The Jokes of Sigmund Freud: A Study in Humor and Jewish Identity* (Philadelphia: U of Pennsylvania P, 1984) for a psychoanalysis of Freud through his selection of Jewish and marriage jokes.

2. Laura Kendrick, *Chaucerian Play: Comedy and Control in the Canterbury Tales* (Berkeley: U of California P, 1988): 161.

3. Sigmund Freud, *Jokes and Their Relation to the Unconscious. The Standard Edition of the Complete Works of Sigmund Freud*, Vol. 8, trans. James Strachey (London: Hogarth, 1955, and New York: Norton, 1961): 165.

4. Freud, 236.

5. Marie Jahoda, *Freud and the Dilemmas of Psychology* (Lincoln: U of Nebraska P, 1977): 45.

6. Jerry Flieger, *The Purloined Punch Line: Freud's Comic Theory and the Postmodern Text* (Baltimore: Johns Hopkins UP, 1991): 61.

7. Geoffrey Hartman, *Saving the Text Literature/Derrida/Philosophy* (Baltimore: Johns Hopkins UP, 1981): 66.

8. Flieger, 72. He says that although Freud divides jokes into two groups, the tendentious, whose purpose is aggression, and the aesthetic, whose purposelessness is called play, it is finally the aesthetic language that is the always already necessary component of all joking. "Even the most tendentious of jokes is always a substitutive satisfaction entailing a diversion from biological goals; therefore, it is no more subservient to serious purpose than is the innocent joke." Furthermore, the aesthetic is not entirely innocent. "Even the most innocent of jokes is in some sense purposeful since, as Freud reminds us, all jokes are based on transgression, on the articulation of something forbidden, and derive their quotient of pleasure in part from the overcoming of censorship" (70).

9. For a thorough presentation of these categories see T.K. Seung's *Cultural Thematics*. He furthermore articulates a bridge between medieval language theory and postmodernism in two later books, *Structuralism and Hermeneutics* and *Semiotics and Thematics in Hermeneutics*.

10. David Knowles, *The Evolution of Medieval Thought* (New York: Random House, 1962): 318–19.

11. See Marcia L. Colish, "The Stoic Theory of Verbal Signification and the Problem of Lies and False Statement from Antiquity to St. Anselm" (*Archéologie du Signe*, ed. Lucie Brind'amour and Eugene Vance

[Toronto: Pontifical Institute of Mediaeval Studies, 1983]: 17–44) for a detailed discussion of just how the Augustinian theory of language could accommodate lies, jokes, and fiction. Colish is particularly helpful for the Stoic antecedents to medieval Realism.

12. Robertson's *Preface* and Dahlberg's Introduction provide excellent starting places for understanding the Realist basis behind the discussion of signs in the *Romance*.

13. See Karla Taylor, *Chaucer Reads The Divine Comedy* (Stanford: Stanford University Press, 1989) for a different perspective on this passage.

14. See Robert A. Pratt, "Some Latin Sources on the Nonnes Preest on Dreams," *Speculum* 52 (1977): 538–570.

15. See Beryl Smalley, *English Friars and Antiquity in the Early Fourteenth Century* (New York: Barnes and Noble, 1960).

16. The tales in Fragment VI certainly have not been generally regarded as a comic. The criteria that Pearsall sets forth in his chapter in the *Cambridge Companion* would disqualify this fragment. In Corsa's book on Chaucer's comedy, she can find it appropriate to argue only that the tales reveal the triumph of morality and the unmasking of evil and therefore comic in the sense of medieval genre theory. The *Physician's Tale* has been regarded as comic by arguing that the narrator so fumbles his material that the audience would have to laugh (Longsworth and Robertson, "Physician").

17. Chaucer uses the term "counterfeit" thirteen times to express three meanings roughly: imitate, pose, or forge. In every case, the context of the word points to artistic incompetence (as in *BD* wherein the Black Knight makes fun of his inability to imitate the speech of his lady [1231]) or to fraud (as in *MLT* wherein a messenger forges the letter indicting Constance). In the *PhT*, the word is used in all its senses, and it seems almost as if Chaucer is indicating that the connection between fraud and artistic incompetence is one of the major themes at hand.

18. The narrator's obsession with truth and fear of counterfeits may be fruitfully read in the context of the crisis of the sign in the thirteenth and fourteenth centuries. The emergence of vernacular standards, humanism, and especially Nominalism were all very powerful symptoms of this breakdown in the faith of universals. The *PhT* is certainly influenced by these issues, but they require a much more elaborate articulation. See Vance, Taylor, Bloomfield, Boucher, Peck, Steinmetz, and Justman.

19. Williams is the most extreme about rendering the Pardoner an arch-Nominalist in his introductory Twayne book on the *Canterbury*

Tales, but he follows Gardner, Khinoy, and Justman in this tradition. See P. B. Taylor for the opposite view.

20. D. W. Robertson, Jr., "The Physician's Comic Tale," *Chaucer Review* 23 (1988): 129–39.

21. See Paul Beekman Taylor, "*Peynted Confessiouns*: Boccaccio and Chaucer," *Comparative Literature* 34 (1984): 116–129.

22. Gordon Leff, *This Dissolution of the Medieval Outlook: An Essay on Intellectual and Spiritual Change in the Fourteenth Century* (New York: New York UP, 1976): 12.

The Comedy of Innocence*

Alfred David

The *Knight's Tale* tried to exemplify the truths that lie at the heart of the fourteenth-century feudal establishment. The conflict of human passions and the dire influence of warring planets constantly threatens to dissolve the world in chaos, but behind this apparent chaos lies an eternal, immutable hierarchical order. In the social and political realm this order is represented by the institution of chivalry, which gives form and beauty to the otherwise savage pursuits of love and war. Chivalry is patterned upon the grand cosmic design of the Prime Mover who has bound all elements in a "faire cheyne of love." Man's duty is to accept his lot within the universal order and make a virtue of necessity. In Theseus's words:

> Whoso gruccheth ought, he dooth folye,
> And rebel is to hym that al may gye.
>
> (I.3045–46)

As the preceding chapter has maintained, the tale itself does not succeed fully in convincing the reader of the truth of these propositions, and in the dramatic framework of the *Canterbury Tales* they are immediately challenged. On the surface, the band of pilgrims, when we first encounter them at the Tabard, would seem to exemplify the Knight's ideal of order. For all their differences, the pilgrims seem bound by a "faire cheyne of love," united by the season and the common goal of travelling to the martyr's shrine. As though to cement their solidarity, the pilgrims have by unanimous consent submitted to another bond: the agreement to the storytelling contest. Rule and order are stressed in the legalistic language by which the bargain is sealed. The Host asks the company if they will stand by his "juggement" (I.778), they in turn ask him to pronounce his "voirdit" ("verdict," I.787), and after the scheme has been explained to them swear oaths and ask him to act as their "governour" and "juge" (I.813–814). It is all very feudal and ceremonious, and to make sure that order prevails, Harry Bailly, the Prime Mover of the contest, arranges, by pinching off the end of the Knight's straw, that the noblest of the pilgrims tells the first tale.

However, barely has the Knight pronounced God's blessing on "al this faire compaignye," when the first of many quarrels erupts to shake this microcosmic fellowship and to subvert the principle of order. The generally favorable reception of the *Knight's Tale* sustains the spirit of harmony for a brief moment:

> Whan that the Knyght had thus his tale ytoold,
> In al the route nas ther yong ne oold
> That he ne seyde it was a noble storie,
> And worthy for to drawen to memorie;
> And namely the gentils everichon.

> (I.3109–13)

The specification of the "gentils" already intimates the social comedy that is about to explode. A taste for courtly romance is, of course, a badge of class, and clearly the socially mixed pilgrim audience has responded to the *Knight's Tale* with varying degrees of enthusiasm. Harry Bailly takes personal pride in the Knight's success. He is enjoying his part as though he really were "a marchal in an halle" (I.752), officiating at some aristocratic entertainment. There will be no more drawing of lots; the Host himself will summon the contestants into the lists, and he calls next upon the Monk—the closest thing to a knight among the ecclesiastics. The Nobility having spoken, it is now the turn of an aristocratic representative of the Church.

But before the Monk has a chance to speak, the third estate breaks in with an arrogant display of feudal pride:

> By armes, and by blood and bones,
> I kan a noble tale for the nones,
> With which I wol now quite the Knyghtes tale.

(I.3125–27)

The Miller launches what turns out to be a literary Peasants' Rebellion. His noisy vulgarity is the antithesis of the Knight's aristocratic reserve, but like the Knight he is a fighter and a champion. The Knight splinters lances; the Miller shatters doors by charging through them with his skull. His generally aggressive demeanor is made more martial by his sword and buckler, and he has already taken the lead in heading the procession of pilgrims out of town. If the Knight is introduced as a *miles Christi*, the Miller is presented as something of a *miles gloriosus*.

In his Prologue the Miller casts down his gauntlet in a literary challenge. He will "quite" the Knight with a "noble tale" of his own and insists on telling it there and then. Harry Bailly is appalled and soothingly pleads with the Miller to observe his proper place:

> Abyd, Robyn, my leeve brother;
> Som bettre man shal telle us first another.
> Abyd, and lat us werken thriftily.

(I.3129–31)

But the Miller will not be silenced. The Reeve makes a last-ditch attempt to stop him by appealing to the canons of decency:

> Lat be thy lewed dronken harlotrye.
> It is a synne and eek a greet folye
> To apeyren any man, or hym defame,
> And eek to bryngen wyves in swich fame.

(I.3145–48)

But the Reeve's motives in assuming the role of public censor are suspect, and the Miller gleefully turns *that* argument *ad hominem*.

The Miller has been a rebel against the Host's judgment, against the social order, and he is about to offend against propriety by telling a thoroughly indecent story. Yet our sympathies are entirely on his side against what we recognize instinctively as the Host's snobbishness and the Reeve's sanctimoniousness, for we know without having to be told that the Miller's drunkenness, impudence, and coarseness have the license of the time and season. His rebellion is in harmony with the great annual revolution Chaucer has described in the opening lines of the General Prologue. The pilgrims have a serious purpose in journeying to Canterbury, and at the end the deeper meaning of their common goal will be spelled out by the Parson. They are seeking "Jerusalem celestial," the city of God.[1] But their pilgrimage is also a holiday, an escape from serious matters and from holy things. I have commented above on the festive spirit of the company as it is expressed even in the unsavory Summoner and Pardoner. The festive note is also in the sound of the Miller's bagpipe. The time is right for feasting and for licentious comedy.

Such comedy has the sanction of deep-rooted folk custom. C. L. Barber has shown how the "form" of Elizabethan holidays underlies the structure of Shakespearian comedy. The "Saturnalian Pattern" is, as Barber points out, an ancient one:

> F. M. Cornford, in *The Origins of Attic Comedy*, suggested that invocation and abuse were the basic gestures of a nature worship behind Aristophanes' union of poetry and railing. The two gestures were still practiced in the "folly" of Elizabethan May-game, harvest-home, or winter revel: invocation, for example, in the manifold spring garlanding customs, "gathering for Robin Hood"; abuse, in the customary license to flout and fleer at what on other days commanded respect.[2]

Renaissance festival and festive comedy go back to medieval tradition of parody, burlesque, and mock-defiance of authority. The saturnalian spirit survived in the celebration of the great seasonal feasts long after these had been integrated into the Church calendar. They were occasions for drinking, dancing, and sexual license. They could also be occasions for travesties of the solemn rituals of the Church.

One of the most ancient of these customs was the institution of the Boy Bishop who with the rest of the choir boys would take control of the service on Holy Innocents Day at the reading of the Psalm: *Deposuit potentes*—He has put down the mighty from their seats. A similar and far more riotous practice was the popular Feast of Fools usually celebrated on one of the days of the New Year season. Here the passing of the *baculus*, the celebrant's staff of authority, to the master of the feast touched off wild demonstrations and parodies of the divine service among the lower clergy. Another such institution, closely related in spirit, was the Feast of the Ass. According to one document, quoted by E. K. Chambers, at Beauvais:

> A pretty girl, with a child in her arms, was set upon an ass,
> to represent the Flight into Egypt. . . . The ass and its riders
> were stationed on the gospel side of the altar. A solemn
> mass was sung, in which *Introit, Kyrie, Gloria* and *Credo*
> ended with a bray. To crown all, the rubrics direct that the
> celebrant, instead of saying *Ite, missa est*, shall bray three
> times (*ter hinhannabit*) and that the people shall respond
> in similar fashion.[3]

An analogous institution is the Lord of Misrule who presided over the Christmas Revels at the court of the Tudors. The significance of such customs as the Feast of Fools or the Feast of the Ass and of the whole tradition of medieval parody has been given a profound explanation by Mikhail Bakhtin:

> Laughter was as universal as seriousness; it was directed
> at the whole world, at history, at all societies, at ideology.
> It was the world's second truth extended to everything
> and from which nothing is taken away. It was, as it were,
> the festive aspect of the whole world in all its elements,
> the second revelation of the world in play and laughter.

> This is why medieval parody played a completely
> unbridled game with all that is most sacred and important
> from the point of view of official ideology.[4]

Ritual thus generates ritual comedy.

The Miller in pushing himself to the fore is, therefore, claiming no more than the privilege of the Boy Bishop, the master of the Feast of Fools, and the Lord of Misrule. By challenging the Knight, the figure of authority, he follows the pattern of medieval comedy. His tale will be outrageous in the same way that the holiday revels were outrageous. Just as in his rudeness, aggressiveness, and profanity we can see an inversion of the qualities of the Knight, so the *Miller's Tale* can be looked at as a burlesque romance inverting the traditional values of feudal society. It is Chaucer's "festive comedy."

Insofar as the *Miller's Tale* has any specific target, it is the *Knight's Tale*. The two perfectly illustrate Per Nykrog's theory about the relationship between fabliau and chivalric romance: both treat essentially the same subject matter but from radically opposed points of view and in totally different styles.[5] In both tales we have two rivals competing for the favors of a lady. The wooing of Alisoun contains burlesque echoes of the wooing of Emelye. But the earthiness of the Miller's Oxford is at the opposite pole from the courtliness of the Knight's Athens, and instead of two noble kinsmen fighting over the hand of the sister-in-law of Duke Theseus, we have a pair of clerks trying to seduce a carpenter's country wife.

All this has been noted before.[6] It would be a mistake, however, to regard the *Miller's Tale* simply as a reply to the Knight's or as a travesty of chivalric ideals. The range of its comedy is much broader. It turns "up-so-doun" the idealism of the medieval world of which chivalry, as we encounter it in the *Knight's Tale,* is only one of the many forms of expression. The targets of the *Miller's Tale* could be described more generally as conventional attitudes toward sex, conventional attitudes toward learning, and conventional attitudes toward the Church. Naturally the tale has no such clear-cut divisions, and the three areas overlap; however, they will make a convenient basis for discussion, and I shall deal with each of these topics in turn.

To begin with sex. The fabliau reverses the asceticism that underlies both medieval Catholicism and the "religion of love." Though it is an oversimplification, one may say generally that the Church in the Middle Ages denigrates sex as a necessary evil and upholds celibacy as the ideal. Chivalry, even though it idealizes human love, does not do much better by the physical act of love. Chivalry envelops sex with a mystic aura and makes a cult of sentiment. The emphasis thus falls mainly on the courtship and desire. Romances are preoccupied with the psychology of divided lovers, rarely with the consummation of love, and in this respect the *Knight's Tale* is typical.

Much of the gaiety of the *Miller's Tale* comes from the inversion of these repressive attitudes. Sex is frankly presented as the *summum bonum* because it is the supreme *physical* pleasure, a natural satisfaction like food and drink, the highest expression of the joy of life. If we apply to the *Miller's Tale* Arcite's despairing question—"What is this world? what asketh men to have?"—the answer is easy: what men desire to have is summed up in Alisoun.

She embodies all the purely sensual pleasures. In her portrait she is closely identified with the objects of Nature. Her brows are black as a sloeberry; she is a more blissful sight than a peartree in bloom; her breath is as sweet as apples stored in hay. Most particularly she is compared to a series of young and graceful animals:

> As any wezele hir body gent and smal. . . .
> Therto she koude skippe and make game,
> As any kyde or calf folwynge his dame. . . .
> Wynsynge she was, as is a joly colt.

> (I.3234, I.3259–60, I.3263)

She is full of animal spirits, as fresh and wholesome as one of Nature's products, simply begging to be seen, heard, tasted, and especially to be touched. The cheap, shiny ornaments and silky materials she wears enhance her natural voluptuousness. The closing lines of the portrait make explicit the cumulative sex appeal of the imagery:

> She was a prymerole, a piggesnye,
> For any lord to leggen in his bedde.

> (I.3268–69)

For Alisoun sex can be enjoyed as though the fall of man had never taken place, as though she really did belong to the animal world that is described happily mating in such lyrics as "Lenten is comen with love to towne."

Music is used throughout the tale with sexual overtones. When Nicholas plays upon his "sawtrie" there is an implied relationship to his playing upon Alisoun's body:

> He kiste hire sweete and taketh his sawtrie
> And pleyeth faste, and maketh melodie.

(I.3305–6)

The same chord is struck when Nicholas and Alisoun hasten to bed: "Ther was the revel and the melodye" (I.3652). The imagery is humorous, but it is also intimately connected with the theme of Nature. The instinct that moves Nicholas and Alisoun is the same impulse that compels the "smale foules" that "maken melodye" in the Prologue. Like the birds, they too "slepen al the nyght with open ye," and in exactly the same sense.

The tale thus gives its blessing to any form of sexual indulgence that is simple and natural. On the other hand, it deals harshly with any violation of Nature, including all gratuitous refinements of pure sexual pleasure. Among the four protagonists, Alisoun's response to sex is the most healthy and natural, and I think it is significant that no mention is made at the end of any punishment for her. However, all three of her lovers go against Nature in some way and receive their appropriate rewards.

John's case is summed up in a line: "She was wylde and yong, and he was old" (I.3225). He is introduced as the stock character of the *vieux jaloux*, and Alisoun is justified in finding an outlet for her frustrated desires because John has sinned against Nature and common sense by marrying a young wife. This would be enough in most fabliaux to merit cuckolding. As the tale progresses, however, Chaucer alters the conventional character by making John appear almost pathetically trusting instead of jealous and suspicious. His emotions about his young bride are not represented as the senile lust of January for May but as a tenderness and protective feeling. He is more like a father than a husband. There is a strong element of fantasy in his love for Alisoun, and it is precisely this that makes him vulnerable to Nicholas's scheme. As soon as he hears of the flood, he can visualize the waves overwhelming his "hony deere." His first thought is for her: "Allas, my wyf! / And shal she drenche? allas, myn Alisoun!" (I.3522–23). He falls (literally as it turns out) not as a result of his jealousy but as a result of deluded sentiment.

The same point can be made, in a different way, of Absolon who has gazed into the well of Narcissus and fallen in love with his own image as a courtly lover. He is not really interested in Alisoun sexually but sentimentally as a stimulus to his absorption with his curls, his clothes, his breath, his serenading, and his acting. Not only does he play the part of Herod "upon a scaffold hye" (a bad case of miscasting)—he is playing a part all the time. The unnaturalness of his wooing is brought out by the emphasis on his effeminacy; the harder he works at the role of courtly hero, the more he resembles the courtly heroine. Like a lady, he is "daungerous" of vulgar speech and put off by such natural bodily functions as farting. The appropriate punishment for the courtly idealist is to discover reality by kissing his lady's ass.

Nicholas *is* genuinely interested in Alisoun's physical charms, but he too is undone by overelaborating the simple pleasures of sex. Not content with a straightforward seduction, he must turn his sexual triumph into a triumph of his art, a victory not simply of a young man over a jealous old husband, but of a clerk over a carpenter. He enjoys the execution of his plot as much as he enjoys Alisoun, and the chain of circumstances he has set in motion finally proves to be his ruin. He overreaches himself, and his cry for "water, water!" brings down the deluge even if only in the mind of John. To be branded in the rear end by fire is a punishment worthy of Dante for the false prophet of a second flood.

Thus John, Absolon, and Nicholas all bear witness to a lesson pointed out by the narrator:

> Lo, which a greet thyng is affeccioun!
> Men may dyen of ymaginacioun,
> So depe may impressioun be take.

(I.3611–13)

In context this bit of "sentence" applies to John whose passion for Alisoun causes him to visualize the terrors of the flood. However, "affeccioun" might be extended to include other obsessions that addle the brain and especially the "celle fantastik,"[7] the seat of the imagination. Absolon is under the spell of "love paramours." Of Nicholas we are told that "al his fantasye / Was turned for to lerne astrologye" (I.3191–92). Each suffers from an unnatural ruling passion that brings him to a bad end. In this respect the *Miller's Tale* is like a comedy of humors in which the characters are compelled by some idiosyncratic urge to violate a rational norm. Here the norm is represented by the simple satisfaction of man's physical appetites so richly provided for by "Goddes foyson"—God's plenty. The portrait of Alisoun is an itemization of God's plenty, personified in one delectable female body. Here is everything that man could desire. But man always wants more than what he is given. Not content with the gift of physical pleasure, he wishes to enhance this pleasure through the dangerous use of the imagination. Dissatisfied with his earthly Paradise, he seeks knowledge of good and evil. In terms of the *Miller's Tale* he becomes inquisitive about "Goddes pryvetee."

This fatal curiosity brings up the second area where the *Miller's Tale* undermines the conventionally accepted scale of values. The celebration of man's animal nature is complemented by a distrust of his higher faculties. The reverence for book learning and philosophical inquiry so characteristic of the Middle Ages is lacking in the fabliaux. The heroes are frequently clerks, but this in itself indicates a certain irreverence toward the intellectual establishment. The clerk is admired because he is clever as a lover, not because he is clever at his books. It is Nicholas's misfortune that he tries to mix his intellectual and his fleshly interests.

The fabliau respects common sense and shrewd practical wisdom of the sort that is contained in maxims or proverbs. The *Miller's Tale* is full of such nuggets as

> Alwey the nye slye
> Maketh the ferre leeve to be looth.

> (I.3392–93)

The pursuit of knowledge beyond such empirical observations lays traps for the theorist and the dreamer. One could go further and say that the fabliau opposes itself to the tendency of the medieval mind to see physical objects and everyday events as outward signs of an invisible higher reality—the exegetical impulse. In the fabliau, attempts to get to the bottom of the mysteries of life usually backfire.

In this respect also the fabliau can be contrasted with romance, and the *Miller's Tale* with the Knight's. All epic poetry—and romance is a form of epic—tries to justify the ways of God to man. It sees human action against the background of a higher order—a destiny or providence that has justly decreed that things should be as they are. Thus the pagan gods, the planetary influences, and the Boethian philosophy of the *Knight's Tale* all attempt to explain and rationalize the human condition as well as the outcome of the story.

In the *Miller's Tale* in place of the celestial machinery we have the astrology of hende Nicholas. Stargazing is for him a serious business, and no doubt he has faith in his Almagest and his astrolabe. The prediction of the second flood is only a brilliant hoax, but it has precedent in the bona fide attempts of astrologers to foretell the future, especially the advent of the ultimate catastrophe, the end of the world. However, to make the destruction of the world part of a stratagem to allow Nicholas to sleep all night in Alisoun's arms robs the idea of its terror. Doomsday jokes are probably archetypal. *Dr. Strangelove or How I Learned to Stop Worrying and Love the Bomb* is only a nuclear-age variation of the comic apocalypse. One reason Chaucer's audience delighted in the *Miller's Tale* was no doubt because it enabled them to stop worrying and to love the flood, the fire, or whatever it would be next time. Maybe Doomsday is only a prank played upon gullible men by mischievous clerks. When we laugh at the carpenter's terror, perhaps we are laughing not only at his folly but at our own in preparing daily for a judgment that may never come.[8]

Philosophy fares no better than science. The carpenter is ironically portrayed as a village Boethius who discovers in everyday happenings examples of man's fate. He takes a generally pessimistic view of life. As soon as he thinks that Nicholas is sick, John begins to fear that he might die. This depressing thought leads to a general reflection: "This world is now ful tikel, sikerly" (I.3428). Then the example clinching the point: John has that very day seen the funeral of a neighbor who was up and working only last Wednesday. The basic thesis and even the method of proof is not so very far removed from Theseus's Boethian speech at the end of the *Knight's Tale:*

> Of man and womman seen we wel also
> That nedes, in oon of thise termes two,
> This is to seyn, in youthe or elles age,
> He moot be deed, the kyng as shal a page;
> Som in his bed, som in the depe see,
> Som in the large feeld, as men may see;
> Ther helpeth noght, al goth that ilke weye.
> Thanne may I seyn that al this thyng moot deye.

> (I.3027–34)

Theseus declares that man can never fully grasp the will of the Prime Mover but must nonetheless submit to it. John blames Nicholas's supposed illness on his foolish desire to know more than is good for him:

> I thoghte ay wel how that it sholde be!
> Men sholde nat knowe of Goddes pryvetee.

> (I.3453–54)

John has stumbled upon the theme stated by the Miller in his Prologue:

> An housbonde shal nat been inquisityf
> Of Goddes pryvetee, nor of his wyf.

> (I.3163–64)

If John had taken this lesson to heart he might have escaped his nemesis. There is a superficially pragmatic quality to some of his ramblings, but in fact they are the complacencies of a garrulous old man and are forgotten as soon as the clerk lets him in on the awful secret. Nicholas's prophecy fits in well with John's outlook. He is at bottom a believer in dark and malevolent powers, ready to pounce at any moment. Finding Nicholas in a trance, he immediately concludes that the clerk has been bewitched and recites a magic charm to ward off the evil spirits.

His mind is a muddle of Christian doctrine, pagan superstition, and homespun philosophy, all of which conspire to persuade him: "This world is now ful tikel, sikerly."

The psychological effect of the *Miller's Tale* is to ridicule that picture and to prove it false. In the Knight's Tale Egeus, the old father of Theseus, describes the world as "a thurghfare ful of wo." In the *Miller's Tale* the world is a garden of delights. The original sin is, as always, to seek knowledge that we are better off without or, in terms of the tale, to pry into the secrets of God or of one's wife. Men bring their destiny upon themselves through vanity and folly. There are no secret agents or stellar influences. The even-handed justice of the fabliau is absolutely clear: the punishment always fits the crime.

Finally, I want to glance at the treatment of the Church in the *Miller's Tale*. One might wonder what the Church has to do with a fabliau, but if one looks closely, one finds its presence everywhere. Of course the Church played so pervasive a role in medieval life that it is necessarily part of any realistic picture. Nevertheless, the density of allusions to the Church, its rites, and its teachings is extraordinary. Separately these allusions seem unobtrusive and harmless enough but they work together to produce a background of bustling religious life going its daily rounds oblivious of the intrigues that are hatching in and around the carpenter's house.

Each of the characters is involved in the affairs of the Church. Nicholas is presumably at the University studying for orders. Absolon is parish clerk. John happens at the time to be employed by a religious house at nearby Osney. Alisoun, immediately after she and Nicholas have reached their understanding, is pictured on a holiday going to mass, "Cristes owene werkes for to wirche" (I.3308). Absolon is right there with the incense dish, "Sensynge the wyves of the parisshe faste" (I.3341).

The characters are associated with a number of biblical figures. Absolon's name evokes the son of David who was characterized by medieval commentators as foppish and effeminate.[9] John and Alisoun become Noah and Noah's wife of the miracle plays. Absolon's complaint beneath Alisoun's window is a travesty of the *Song of Songs*.[10] Nowhere else in the *Canterbury Tales* are the oaths so strategically placed. Alisoun vows to be at

Nicholas's will "by seint Thomas of Kent" (I.3291). Gerveys the Smith greets Absolon:

> What, Absolon! for Cristes sweete tree,
> Why rise ye so rathe? ey, *benedicitee*!
>
> (I.3767–68)

Absolon asks for his kiss "For Jhesus love, and for the love of me" (I.3717). That way of putting it—"For Jhesus love, and for the love of me"—typifies the pattern of these references. They give an additional ironic twist to the action, the final touch of absurdity.

A question arises whether such comic touches are not calculated to alert the reader's moral sense. What precisely are we laughing at? A genuinely devout reader might not find anything funny in such allusions just as he might not be amused by a plot that is, after all, about adultery. One may sympathize, therefore, with a number of recent critics who have tried to find a "moral edge" in the tale while at the same time preserving its humor.[11] Is the tale perhaps meant to show the Christian reader that sin, just like the burlesque Vice characters of the morality plays, is not only wicked but ridiculous?

Such readings are clearly possible, but they go against the grain of Chaucer's humor and the humor of medieval "festive comedy." It is a brand of humor that still survives in most Latin countries (the films of Marcel Pagnol are a good example) where the Church is regarded with the same worldly, irreverent, but in the end sympathetic eye along with everything else under the sun. The sacred is seen from its temporal and human side. No doubt there is a vast distance between the spiritual and stylistic levels of the *Song of Songs* and the *Miller's Tale*. But Chaucer's comedy also implies their common humanity. The Canticle is, after all, on its literal level also a love song. In the low style of Absolon, "Awaketh lemman myn" sounds preposterous, but part of the fun is that the sacred words lose their awe when they are brought down to the level of the fabliau world.

The natural world celebrates its Maker in its own way. When Nicholas and Alisoun are in bed,

> Ther was the revel and the melodye;
> And thus lith Alison and Nicholas,

> In bisynesse of myrthe and of solas,
> Til that the belle of laudes gan to rynge,
> And freres in the chauncel gonne synge.

(I.3652–56)

The counterpoint of the melody made by the lovers in bed and the song of the friars in the chantry beautifully illustrates the comic balance Chaucer has achieved between the sacred and the profane. Each in his own way is performing the office of praise and sending up his *Te Deum*.

This balance of sympathy exists, to be sure, only for the moment. In the background the Church looms in the sanctity of its divine power, and the characters are absurd in their petty world of ephemeral pleasures. But the whole point of the *Miller's Tale* is that it provides an escape from the eternal and permits its audience to look briefly at the temporal world as though it were all that mattered. What is remarkable about the *Miller's Tale* is its *innocence*, a quality Chaucer never quite brings off again in any of his other fabliaux. The Parson's judgments are suspended in order to let us enjoy our holiday.

Chaucer himself seems to suggest in the person of the narrator that we should not take the *Miller's Tale* too seriously, and that it belongs in a different category from the expressly didactic tales. At the end of the Miller's Prologue, the narrator's voice is heard again, offering an elaborate apology to the reader for the painful duty of having to tell this objectionable story; any reader whose sense of propriety might be offended or who prefers not to waste his time on such foolishness is advised to

> Turne over the leef and chese another tale;
> For he shal fynde ynowe, grete and smale,
> Of storial thyng that toucheth gentillesse,
> And eek moralitee and hoolynesse.
> Blameth nat me if that ye chese amys.
> The Millere is a cherl, ye knowe wel this;
> So was the Reve eek and othere mo,
> And harlotrie they tolden bothe two.
> Avyseth yow, and put me out of blame;
> And eek men shal nat maken ernest of game.

(I.3177–86)

Of course no one is taken in by this. It is an obvious come-on, and Chaucer's audience was hardly more squeamish than we are today. No doubt they enjoyed it all hugely, including the narrator's apology. The tacit understanding between the poet and his audience is that we are all men of the world able to enjoy a bit of disreputable fun, and this is basically the attitude taken by the majority of readers and critics ever since. Nevertheless, in raising the question of vulgarity and bad taste, Chaucer is sidestepping a more basic problem. The fabliaux can be defended as harmless amusement—"men shal nat maken ernest of game"—but is that the best that can be said for them? Is the *Miller's Tale* nothing more than a "jape" or a "nyce caas"—a foolish affair?

There is certainly more to be said for it than this, and it is possible to take festive comedy seriously without turning it into inverted morality. No matter how it starts out, in the end the *Miller's Tale* is something better than a sop to Momus or a holiday game. The vitality and earthiness of the *Miller's Tale*, the sheer pleasure expressed in the physical world, and the disregard for intellectual and spiritual ideals—all this is enormously seductive. These are not values entertained simply in play but genuine values. We do not merely laugh at the people and the pleasures in the *Miller's Tale*—we identify with them and love them until they may mean as much and more to us than the Knight's "trouthe and honour."

The *Miller's Tale* has its own truth, different from the Knight's—what Bakhtin calls "the people's unofficial truth."[12] The Knight's truth means fidelity to higher principle; the Miller's truth is fidelity to the vital principle of life. In the work of a major poet like Chaucer, the sheer artistry expended on the relatively simple plot of the *Miller's Tale* implies a new concept of art that goes beyond the one that sees a direct relationship between the value of a work of art and its "sentence." There is a profound meaning in the narrator's promise to tell everything that happened on the journey even if it means telling of churlishness and obscenity. His literalism is meant to seem naive, but it is also a defense of the artist's commitment not only to a moral or spiritual truth but to the representation of life as he sees it. On this plane of artistic truth the Knight and Miller and their respective tales achieve genuine equality. All creatures, no matter what superficial social or moral distinctions separate them, are equal in the eye of their creator if only they are imagined strongly enough.

In medieval life, ritual comedy is supposed to stay in its place:

> Throughout the year there were small scattered islands of time, strictly limited by the dates of feasts, when the world was permitted to emerge from the official routine but exclusively under the camouflage of laughter. Barriers were raised, provided there was nothing but laughter.[13]

However, the vitality of the celebrations is a measure of how deeply those emotions run for which laughter provides the only acceptable outlet. That is why holidays have a way of getting out of hand. Our knowledge of customs like the Feast of Fools comes largely from the efforts of bishops to reform the festivities. Some of the best accounts of May Day celebrations are to be found in Puritan tracts written against them. Once the spirit of license is set free, it transgresses the boundaries decreed for it, nor is it easily confined again.

Something like that must have happened to Chaucer as well. What starts out as "game" in the *Miller's Tale* releases creative energies more powerful than the poet may have imagined. The true Lord of Misrule is the artist himself, and the writing of fiction becomes a holiday during which the sanctions of everyday are suspended. The Miller's insistence that he be permitted to tell his tale turns out to be Chaucer's declaration of independence as an artist, the assertion of his freedom to write what he pleases. The apologetic narrator is Chaucer's old persona professing embarrassment at the turn of events. But it is really the Miller who speaks for Chaucer:

> By armes, and by blood and bones,
> I kan a noble tale for the nones.

I am not, of course, trying to maintain that the subversive spirit is foreign to Chaucer's earlier poetry. The goose and duck in the *Parliament of Fowls* and especially Pandarus strike discordant notes in their courtly surroundings; they anticipate the Miller's pragmatism, his gusto, and, in a more polite way, his concerns. However, in the *Miller's Tale* this spirit is given free play and allowed to dominate for the first time. A case could be made that the whole pilgrimage had to be invented for the sake of the fabliaux. The *Knight's Tale* of Palamon and Arcite was one that Chaucer had already told in his own person to his court audience. Many of the tales could well have been told as separate stories by Chaucer himself. But the *Miller's Tale* called for the creation of a new world of characters who make up a new audience and a new set of narrators. The *Canterbury Tales* is Chaucer's personal holiday from the business of being a noble philosophical court poet, and like all good holidays it gets out of hand. It will occupy him for the rest of his life. The *Miller's Tale* necessitates the Reeve's, and the *Reeve's Tale* leads to the Cook's, which was never finished possibly because Chaucer felt that it was time to put a temporary stop to the festivities. He makes good his promise that there will be tales of "moralitee and hoolynesse," but once the Miller has begun the game, things will never be the same. The result is a new kind of fiction, a representation of life with a Shakespearian fullness.

NOTES

*Reprinted with permission from *The Strumpet Muse: Art and Morals in Chaucer's Poetry* (Bloomington and London: Indiana UP, 1976), pp. 90–107.

   1. I am indebted here and elsewhere to Ralph Baldwin's fine study, *The Unity of the* Canterbury Tales, *Anglistica*, V (Copenhagen: Rosenkilde and Bagger, 1955), reprinted in part ST I, pp. 14–51. However, I feel that the road to "Jerusalem celestial" contains many detours and that the "unity" of the *Canterbury Tales*, at least in this symbolic sense, can be exaggerated.

   2. C. L. Barber, *Shakespeare's Festive Comedy* (1959; reprinted New York: Meridian Books, 1963), p. 7.

   3. E. K. Chambers, *The Mediaeval Stage*, I (London: 1903), p. 287.

4. Mikhail Bakhtin, *Rabelais and His World*, trans. Hélène Iswolsky (Cambridge, Mass.: M.I.T. Press, 1965), p. 84. Bakhtin's entire discussion of medieval laughter (pp. 71–96) bears closely on the thesis of this chapter.

5. Per Nykrog, *Les Fabliaux* (Copenhagen: Munksgaard, 1957), pp. 66–71.

6. See William Frost, "An Interpretation of Chaucer's *Knight's Tale*," *RES* 25 (1949), pp. 303–304, reprinted in ST I, pp. 98–116.

7. See *Knight's Tale*, 1376, where Arcite's "celle fantastik" becomes diseased through "homour malencolik," and Robinson's note.

8. Cf. Bakhtin, pp. 90–91: "It was the victory of laughter over fear that most impressed medieval man. It was not only a victory over mystic terror of God, but also a victory over the awe inspired by the forces of nature, and most of all over the oppression and guilt related to all that was consecrated and forbidden ('mana' and 'taboo'). It was the defeat of divine and human power, of authoritarian commandments and prohibitions, of death and punishment after death, hell and all that is more terrifying than the earth itself. Through this victory laughter clarified man's consciousness and gave him a new outlook on life. This truth was truly ephemeral; it was followed by the fears and oppressions of everyday life, but from these brief moments another unofficial truth emerged, truth about the world and man which prepared the new Renaissance consciousness."

9. See Paul E. Beichner, "Absolon's Hair," *MS* 12 (1950), pp. 222–223.

10. See R. E. Kaske, "The *Canticum Canticorum* in the *Miller's Tale*," *SP* 59 (1962), pp. 479–500.

11. The phrase "moral edge" is used by Kaske who confronts this problem in "The *Canticum Canticorum*," pp. 495–500. Kaske makes it a question finally of "where the greater weight of the comedy created by the allusions is supposed to fall: on the situation, characters, and mores of the *Miller's Tale* or on those of the *Canticum*." He concludes that the allusions are probably not "a parody of the *Canticum*" and that instead they provide a moral perspective from which to judge Absolon and Alisoun who are characterized as the "false" bridegroom and bride. This, argues Kaske, does not detract from the comic effect but enhances it and gives the comedy a "moral edge" without turning it into a "covert sermon." But why must "the greater weight of the comedy" fall *either* on the characters of the tale *or* on those of the Canticle? Why cannot the weight be equally distributed? Kaske does recognize examples where the "burden of laughter is kept neatly divided" (e.g. *The Owl and the*

Nightingale), but says that most readers will agree that this is not the case with the *Miller's Tale* (p. 499). This reader, at least, does not agree.

    12. Bakhtin, p. 90.

    13. Ibid.

Metamorphic Comedy
The Shipman's Tale

William F. Woods

To describe the humor of the *Shipman's Tale* as fabliau wit is
somewhat misleading if one thinks immediately—as one does—
of the Miller's or Reeve's tales, where a good part of our
enjoyment derives from the appropriate, almost inevitable ways
in which vividly drawn characters like Nicholas, or Alayn and
John act out the implications of their own portraits. The
merchant of St. Denis, his wife, and their friend, daun John the
monk from Paris, are sparely drawn, generic figures.[1] Their lack
of physical and psychological coloring forces us to seek the tale's
comic art and significance in its formal elements—the details of
its social setting, as well as the structure of its episodes, and in
particular, the dialectical play characteristic of the character
relationships and dialogue.

Indeed, the mercantile milieu of the *Shipman's Tale* must
provide the basis for its humor because the tale's real focus is not
a (nameless) merchant of St. Denis, but *merchants*—their
schemes, their fears, the little triumphs that sustain their lives.[2]
We do not find here the broad comedy of John's fall from the
rafters. What we do have is the dry irony of an insider's tale, the
knowing wit that plays upon the small absurdities of merchantry,[3] while giving form, and a sort of comic resolution, at
least, to the great ones.

In a sense, there is only one joke in the *Shipman's Tale*, and
that is the truism, restated throughout the tale with almost
infinite variety, that what it all comes down to is marketing.[4]

There is a constant comic levelling, in other words, which reduces, or "converts" everything of importance, whether it be social, sexual, or religious, by subordinating it to the over-riding purpose of mercantile exchange.[5] Our merchant, for instance, is rich, "for which men helde hym wise" (VII.2)——they infer his wisdom from his apparent success in trade.[6] His wife is "compaignable and revelous" (VII.4), but in the tale, this is chiefly important for only two reasons: such a woman is used to dressing well, and the merchant must clothe her; yet in so doing he keeps a "worthy" house, where this wife "of excellent beautee" (VII.3) and his "largesse" create mirth and cheer among the guests, thereby maintaining public confidence in his prosperity, and swelling the volume of his trade.

As the tale continues, it is increasingly obvious that the merchant's world is ordered by *quid pro quo*, and the nexus of its values is the inexhaustible plenitude of mercantile exchange, or "Goddes sonde" (VII.219), as the wife puts it. The result is twofold. On the one hand, the realignment of motives and morals along the axis of prosperous trading—an intellectual discipline, of a sort—produces a moral and imaginative tunnel-vision, a narrow view of life. This is one reason for the brevity of the tale. On the other hand, translating all values and acts into the language of profit motive—merchants' needs—creates a varied and sensitively nuanced account of a merchant's social and personal life; in other words, it gives us a look at the world as a late-fourteenth-century merchant might see it.[7] That is why, for careful readers, at least, the tale is not blighted by cynicism, and why we can retain an interest in the lives of the merchant and his wife that goes beyond a certain fascination with the cleverness of the fabliau plot. It is also the reason why the humor of the tale is not confined to the irony of displacement, whereby profit motives subsume all others, but also extends to the web of character relationships within this "profit purview," and to the larger question of how, within this specialized social context, a merchant's, or a merchant's wife's personal and spiritual needs might be served.[8]

I am going to begin my discussion of the tale by pointing out some of the ways in which the situational irony of the merchant's life is developed. That is, I will try to show how this "merchant's world" re-orients all needs and values to its core motive of profit, and how such ironic inversion creates the baseline for comedy in the tale. The corollary to such displacement of values is the transformation of social roles in the world of this tale, and I will argue that there is a sense in which the merchant and monk switch places, reacting to the pressure of their circumstances by somewhat absurdly taking on aspects of each other's roles.[9] Finally, I will try to show that the wife, too, transforms her role in the course of the tale, not in any brief, ironic fashion, but permanently, in a profound comic metamorphosis by which exile within the home and social and sexual dependency become, paradoxically, her means of dominating the market and achieving what constitutes, in this tale at least, a sense of personal worth.[10]

The merchant's world, we should admit at outset, is a cheery one—it has to be, because confidence is the only thing that sells. Consequently, every sort of human warmth and closeness is valued for its use in projecting the image of well-being, the good life. Village life, for instance, with its closely woven kinships and dependencies, is remembered here. The merchant and his friend the monk were born in the same village, and now that they both dwell in the larger commercial world, they claim each other "as for cosynage"—in kinship.[11] Never mind that this monk, "a fair man and a boold" (VII.25), makes good company in the semi-public arena of the merchant's house, a place known, in fact, for its many guests, some of whom are presumably clients. Or that daun John is "manly of dispence/ As in that hous, and ful of diligence/ To doon plesaunce, and also greet costage" (VII.43–5)—virtues that ensure his welcome in the great house in St. Denis where he comes, as outrider, to inspect the abbey's lands; where he had better be welcome if he intends to deal with the local landowners on an easy basis; and where it is very pleasant to be welcomed by the merchant's beautiful wife.

The significance of the merchant's need for "cheer" becomes clearer when he plans a business trip to Brugges, to buy merchandise. As preparation for the trip, he invites daun John "to pley/ With hym and with his wyf a day or tweye" (VII.59–60). And when he returns from his trip, having bought "al hool" his goods, he celebrates once more, this time privately, with his wife. In effect, the "pley" with daun John is prelude, and the play with the wife, postlude to the merchant's climactic performance in Brugges. "Cheer," in other words, has an internal, as well as an external, or public significance. It is necessary for maintaining a positive public image, but it is also the invocation of an ideal. It is a ritual imitation, a charmed and safe play-market, an imaginative return to a merchant's paradise where "trade" is as easy and natural as an intercourse of souls.[12]

Something of this celebratory mood is conveyed by the recurrent metaphor of birds joyfully greeting the dawn, which is applied first to the merchant (VII.38), then his household (VII.50–1) (both are glad when daun John comes calling). Such overwhelming joy can seem a bit forced, though, especially when the metaphor is repeated within the space of fifteen lines, and Chaucer makes sure we get the point:

> they were as glad of his comyng
> As fowel is fayn whan that the sonne up riseth.
> Na moore of this as now, for it suffiseth.

(VII.50–52)

Later in the tale, we hear this bird-like joy when the wife returns, "jolif as a pye" (VII.209), after plotting with daun John in the garden, and we hear it again when the merchant returns from Paris, "murie as a papejay" (VII.369), having made a buy that is sure to make him richer. "Pye" and "papejay" imply a parallelism between the wife's and merchant's roles which I will discuss presently. But the magpie and parrot also condition our attitude toward the merchant and his wife. These are birds with merry speech, every word of which is an empty, pointless imitation.

Through this bird analogy, we begin to see that the mildly pretentious "cheer" of this household is undercut by the language, the social manners, and indeed the entire lifestyle we find there. The merchant has his sums, books, bags and "thyngs" (VII.217), the monk walks in the garden saying his "thynges"— his morning prayers, presumably—and finally the entire relationship between the monk, the merchant and his wife is referred to as a "thyng" (VII.429). The dialogue is full of epithets, as people swear (fashionably, we may suppose) on every saint imaginable, as well as on a book of hours, a sundial and Jesus Christ. In the course of this litany, the oaths seem to lose definition, fading along with our sense of the characters' personal convictions. It is, moreover, a "busy" life and a hurried one—practically everything, from going to dinner, to doing business, to making love is done in haste—and as a consequence, the quality of life seems thin. In a general sense, all of these reductive "rituals" express an ongoing need for renewal, for tapping the richness of the world once again, in yet another transaction, because in this merchant's world, life *is* trade: an infinite series of exchanges, alternating either with celebration or mourning.

The humor of this social description is that of gentle satire, a knowing irony based upon an understanding of how merchants live, how they behave, and what drives them. There is a certain pleasure in recognizing the logic of keeping a worthy house full of happy guests, and even if we are distanced from the scene by any number of small insights, we have to remember that this is, after all, a successful merchant, a "goode man" of trade, who clings to his own version of the good life. Yet that is not the full extent of the tale's humor, because the characters in their matching schemes and paired relationships turn a strong light on each other's small failings. This is the humor of social transformation, the projection of an inner want—call it envy, perhaps—that causes the characters to imitate each other, exposing each of them for a while, before the final comic resolution.

The merchant deserves first consideration, because his professional practices create the background scene and the controlling mercantile metaphors that define the tale. He is introduced as a rich merchant and a "goode man," which means that he is established, predictable, a solid citizen. As we have seen, his worthy house and beautiful wife serve to maintain that public self. But when the action of the tale begins, we begin to see what being a merchant is like from the inside. On the third morning of daun John's visit, just before the merchant leaves on his trip to the marketplace at Brugges, he takes stock:

> The thridde day, this marchant up ariseth,
> And on his nedes sadly hym aviseth,

And up into his countour-hous gooth he
To rekene with hymself, wel may be,
Of thilke yeer how that it with hym stood,
And how that he despended hadde his good,
And if that he encressed were or noon.
His bookes and his bagges many oon
He leith biforn him on his countyng-bord.
Ful riche was his tresor and his hord,
For which ful faste his countour-dore he shette;
And eek he nolde that no man shold hym lette
Of his acountes, for the meene tyme;
And thus he sit til it was passed pryme.

(VII.75–88)

In contrast with the cheer of the foregoing scenes, the
merchant rises up on this third day, not "glad . . . as fowel of day
(VII.38)," but solemnly ("sadly"), as he reckons his expenses
("nedes") and balances profit and loss for the year. The
repetition of "countour-hous," "countyng-bord" and "countour-
dore" conveys the intense importance of this mercantile self-
reckoning, as well as its privacy, reminding one of the merchant
in the General Prologue: "There wiste no wight that he was in
dette" (VII.280). This counting house is the central locus for what
the merchant calls his "curious bisynesse" (VII.225). It holds his
"tresor," and is the basis of "oure good," the social, economic
and professional standing which he tells his wife to guard
carefully while he is away:

"And for to kepe oure good be curious,
And honestly governe wel oure hous."

(VII.243–44)

From "oure estaat," kept "in pryvetee" (VII.232), the merchant
issues forth to "make chiere and good visage,/ And drive forth
the world" (VII.230–1), until he either dies, or fails in business, in
which case he must "pley/ A pilgrymage, or goon out of the
weye" (VII.233–4).

The significance of this concentric self/world/out-of-
bounds view of life is partly its precariousness. The merchant
reminds his wife pointedly that among chapmen, scarcely two in

twelve thrive continually into their old age (VII.228–9). He adds
that all this creates a great necessity to inform himself about this
fickle ("queynte") world:

> "For everemore we moote stonde in drede
> Of hap and fortune in oure chapmanhede."

> (VII.237–38)

Whether or not we are sympathetic to it, there is a kind of pathos
to the merchant's account of his works and days, and oddly, this
is a source of humor in his role. For as his complaint takes shape,
its features begin to sound suspiciously like ones associated with
saints' lives.[13] He rises up early on the third day (not, like
Abraham, on his way to the mountain, but just up the stairs to
the counting house, where he solemnly reckons, not the truth of
divine justice, but the balance of his accounts). His profession is a
"curious" business—full of care—and his life in the fickle world,
beset by chance and fortune, is so hard that like the apostles,
only about two out of twelve chapmen last long in this tough
market.

The distancing irony of this "complaint" passage is extended by the merchant's relationships with his wife and the
monk. The wife has actually initiated the passage by calling for
him to come down from the counting house:

> "How longe tyme wol ye rekene and caste
> Youre sommes, and youre bookes, and youre thynges?
> The devel have part on alle swiche rekenynges!
> Ye have ynough, pardee, of Goddes sonde;
> Come doun to-day, and lat youre bagges stonde."

> (VII.216–20)

Her repeated reference to "youre" sums, books, things and bags
sets his professional life aside from their life at home and at
table, and so does her own reckoning of his accounts: he has had
enough of "Goddes sonde." It is not, perhaps, that she doesn't
wish him richer, but that she does not share his chapmanhood—
these are merchant's "thynges," after all, and she has cares of her
own. This division between husband and wife becomes more
obvious as he shifts from his complaint to his instructions for

keeping the house while he is gone. The complaint evokes the hardships of chapmen—"oure chapmanhede"—and this possessive pronoun, reiterated throughout the passage, is like a line drawn around his professional experience, isolating it in somewhat the same way as the counting house itself does. When he instructs his wife, "oure good" and "oure hous" briefly seem to refer to what they hold in common, but quickly he reverts to type. "Thou hast ynough," he says, to keep a "thrifty" household (VII.245–46). He has provided her with plenty to eat, and to wear, and even some silver—spending money—for her purse (VII.247–48). And with that he shuts the "countour-dore" and comes down to dinner (VII.249–50).

The problem with this generosity is that silver for maintaining the household is not at all the same thing as the gold in the merchant's counting house—the gold he takes with him to the Brugges or Paris markets to "drive forth the world." As the merchant reminds the monk, who has just borrowed from him a hundred gold franks,

> "But o thyng is, ye knowe it wel ynogh
> Of chapmen, that hir moneie is hir plogh.
> We may creaunce whil we have a name,
> But goldless for to be, it is no game."

> (VII.287–90)

In other words, gold constitutes professional identity, as well as the (male) power to beget more money on credit (to "creaunce") by "plowing" the "queynte world." Clearly, the merchant feels that this is not woman's work; in fact he addresses this passage to another man, the monk. We might reflect that from the merchant's rather narrow perspective, the pursuit of profit has colonized the territories of both religion and sex, insofar as the languages of saints' lives and barnyard sexuality have both offered metaphors for chapmanhood. But really, what else might we expect, in a merchant's world? The more immediate question is what results from the division of labor, power and "being" that separates the merchant and his wife?

The immediate answer to the merchant's chauvinistic professionalism is the monk, who, in a series of parallel scenes, secures the wife by anticipating the merchant's own business practices. "This yonge monk, . . . so fair of face" (VII.28), must of necessity pursue the beautiful fabliau wife. What we may not expect is the degree of symmetry with which daun John "plays" a householder, "buying" the wife on credit while the merchant is buying merchandise on credit in Brugges. This comic reversal is a version of the familiar plot device in Ovid and in folktales, where the hunter becomes the hunted. It has the effect of mirroring the merchant's "driving forth the world," but also transforming, and thereby revealing it more clearly. The monk displays an energy and rapacity in his dealings that has been lacking in the "curious" merchant, and thus he reveals new possibilities for the merchant's role. For unlike the merchant, the monk is fully capable of betraying a "business" partner (the wife). Yet it is precisely this "lack," or absence of ethical values in the monk's trading that enables the final comic resolution, because it reminds us that some solid professional and personal values still exist in this merchant's role, in his "real" world of trade, and in his mercantile marriage.[14]

When daun John arrives with game fowl, "as ay was his usage" (VII.72), he immediately takes the upper hand with the merchant and his household, who are as glad to see him "[a]s fowel is fayn whan that the sonne up riseth" (VII.51). This "noble" monk, who is a man of "heigh prudence" (VII.64), and "ful of curteisye" (VII.69) brings gifts for everyone in the house, according to their degree, because it ensures his welcome, making him in effect a part of the household hierarchy—a man worthy, indeed, to be a householder like the merchant. This parallel becomes clearer when the merchant rises early on the third day to shut himself in the countour-hous, with his merchant's "thynges," while daun John

> was rysen in the morwe also,
> And in the gardyn walketh to and fro,
> And hath his thynges seyd ful curteisly.

(VII.89–91)

But whatever a monk's "thynges" might be, his "curteisye" in the garden is applied solely in courting the wife. She comes walking "pryvely" (VII.92) into the garden, where he is walking "softe" (VII.93), so that already the stage is set for a pairing of the wife with this surrogate "lord." Then he somewhat fortuitously compares "wedded men" (like the merchant) with tired rabbits cowering in a hollow, "al forstraught with houndes grete and smale" (VII.103–5), and by laughing merrily and "waxing all red" with his own idea, he makes his intentions obvious.

This merry blushing reveals daun John as an interloper, but as the first example of unforced and genuine "cheer" in the tale, it also sets him apart from the planned merriment in the worthy house, the solemn, perhaps anxious reckoning in the counting house, and, as we soon see, the wife's unhappiness as mistress of the house. This monk is provided with more features of physical description than any other character in the tale. He is at various times fair of face, red in the face, and "With crowne and berd al fressh and newe yshave" (VII.309)—a "new face" indeed, this "monkes snowte" (VII.405), and one that supplies a certain natural, even animal exuberance that has been lacking in the merchant's household where public image is one's only defense against the shifting fortunes of the marketplace. The monk's role is the broadest, most accessible source of humor in the tale, and this is mainly because his outrageous, amoral sexuality and scheming can be felt as a relief from the artificial merriment and covert economic *Angst* that typify the roles of both merchant and wife.

Indeed, daun John's comic appeal is inextricable from his function in the plot. He is both a courtly lover and a merchant of love—a sort of domestic chapman—and although the combination is bizarrely humorous, especially for a monk, it is just such a "marriage" of the sexual and the entrepreneurial that finally resolves the differences between the merchant and his wife. Daun John displaces the merchant at mid-tale, assuming his role as lover and lord in the garden scene and during the merchant's trip to the market at Brugges. In turn, the monk's change of role develops the interior conflict between merchant and wife that surfaced in the counter-house scene, because it makes the wife a player in a negotiation involving both love and money. This negotiation between the wife and her surrogate

husband provides a model for the wife's "final solution" for her
marriage, which constitutes the comic resolution of the tale.

The flavor of daun John's role as a merchant of love is
probably best conveyed by the climax of the garden scene, where
he closes his bargain with the wife. By this point, the wife has
worked her way up to a formal bid:

> "Daun John, I seye, lene me thise hundred frankes.
> Pardee, I wol nat faille yow my thankes,
> If that yow list to doon that I yow praye.
> For at a certeyn day I wol yow paye,
> And doon to yow what plesance and service
> That I may doon, right as yow list devise."

(VII.187–92)

We note the pairing of "plesance" and "service," where
overtones of love service and services rendered mingle suggest-
ively, and the monk is quick to accept the offer:

> This gentil monk answerde in this manere:
> "Now trewely, myn ownene lady deere,
> I have," quod he, "on yow so greet a routhe
> That I yow swere, and plighte yow my trouthe,
> That whan youre housbonde is to Flaundres fare,
> I wol delyvere yow out of this care;
> For I wol brynge yow an hundred frankes."
> And with that word he caughte hire by the flankes,
> And hire embraceth harde, and kiste hire ofte.

(VII.195–203)

The comic punch of these lines is delivered when the wife's coy
"frankes/thankes"—followed by several lines of courtly
euphemism from both of them ("pray," "plesance," "gentil,"
"routhe/trouthe," "care")—is answered by the monk's jarringly
physical, and thus, unimpeachably genuine "'frankes'
/flankes." One is both dismayed and delighted: these are bad
practices, no doubt, yet clouds of pretentious posturing are being
swept aside, and real needs are being met. In a way, this passage
could stand for all of Chaucer's fabliau comedy; blunt and
"real," it flattens preposterous illusions to leave a bedrock

foundation for the stained but sustainable world that it projects beyond the endpoint of the tale.

It would be nice, from the Prioress's point of view, at least, if daun John were a "hooly man,/ As monkes been—or elles oghte be" (VII.642–43), but in fact his "routhe" and "trouthe" extend only as far as honoring his promise to produce the hundred franks. He is prepared to deliver the wife out of this particular "care," but he is no savior. He swears by his "portehors" (portable book of hours, or breviary) not to betray her, and later he says his "chilyndre" (portable, cylinder-shaped sun dial) tells him it is dinnertime:

> "Gooth now youre wey," quod he, "all stille and softe,
> And let us dyne as soone as that ye may;
> For by my chilyndre it is pryme of day."

> (VII.204–06)

These "monk's things" correspond to the books, bags, and "thynges" in the merchant's counting house. The breviary is *his* book, an account of the truth he serves, and the sundial tells him when to say mass, which is a sort of market day for clerics. But obviously, daun John's reference in these lines is not mass, or even the dinner time but rather the state of his appetite for the wife.

Daun John will not be "true," in any significant or lasting sense. His real attitude toward the wife is implied by his catching her by the "flankes," and later borrowing the merchant's hundred franks to buy "certein beestes" (VII.272). As for their secret (which he quaintly calls "conseil"), he freely informs the merchant where the hundred franks went . . ..

> "But natheless, I took unto oure dame,
> Youre wyf, at hom, the same gold ageyn
> Upon youre bench; she woot it wel, certeyn,
> By certeyn tokenes that I kan hire telle."

> (VII.356–59)

—and insinuates that he could tell more if she were foolish enough to pursue the matter. He concludes his dealings at the merchant's house by going out of town with his abbot. Daun

John is "out of business," as it were, like merchants who die or "pley a pilgrymage" to escape their creditors. But the wife remains at home, where she will apply to her marriage the same sort of buying on credit that the monk and merchant have performed in her household and in the marketplace, respectively.

When the wife enters the tale, in the garden scene, we know nothing about her except that she is accompanied by a girl child who is still "under the yerde" (VII.97)—under her authority. This child is important, not as a spy, a constraint on conduct in the garden, but as a sign of the wife's control over her household. Daun John's frequent gifts for everyone down to the "leeste page," and her own governance have made the house safe even for talk that goes against the merchant. From the beginning, then, the wife—like the merchant—has her own "apprentices," and she occupies a household "space" of her own that corresponds to the merchant's marketplace, even though she complains that she has none (VII.143–44). The household has been invaded by the monk, who will buy on credit (from the wife) and make a loan (from the merchant), just as the merchant will make a "reconyssaunce" at the marketplace in Bruges and a "chevyssaunce" in Paris. When the monk has left the story, the merchant returns to find his house transformed, in effect, into a domestic "market," whose chief trader is now his wife.[15]

In the garden scene, moreover, it is the wife who initiates each stage of the bargaining with daun John. She lures him from one promise to another until she is sure of his aid, and can reveal to him her marital and fiscal "privetee," the core of her discontent. She assumes the authority to trade in this domestic market, in other words, and this transformation in her role is conveyed by a number of images. The monk begins by comparing wedded men, and presumably merchants, to "a wery hare, / ... al forstraught with houndes grete and smale" (VII.104–05), but when we next see this metaphor, the wife has applied it to herself:

> "Though men me wolde al into pieces tere,
> Ne shal I nevere, for to goon to helle,
> Biwreye a word of thyng that ye me telle"

> (VII.136–38)

She ends her plea with an even more vivid image of dismemberment:

> "And but I do, God take on me vengeance
> As foul as evere hadde Genylon of France."

(VII.193–94)

Fears of dismemberment are appropriate for a merchant, since loss of "integrity"—one's image—can mean failure.[16] But now the wife is putting *her* integrity on the line, and her worry takes the same form. These related metaphors for loss of integrity, financial failure, and perhaps loss of self express what we might call the "evil," or the central "lack" of this merchant's world, the fear that freezes mirth, but which is finally embraced and thereby dispelled in the wife's comic resolution at the close of the tale. When her garden scene with the monk is answered by her bedroom scene with the merchant, she transforms her failure in this domestic market so that loss of integrity actually produces credit, riches, and the profoundly comic reintegration of self.

What makes this garden dialogue central to the tale's structure, however, is the way it begins with references to the merchant and his alliance with the monk, but shifts to an emphasis on the wife and her different kind of alliance with daun John. The wife's progress toward this new "wholeness" appears in the language of her complaint in the garden. Her initial emotion is dismay so deep that no kind of "pley" has any savor:

> "In al the reawme of France is ther no wyf
> That lasse lust hath to that sory pley.
> For I may synge 'allas and weylawey
> That I was born,' but to no wight," quod she,
> "Dar I nat telle how that it stant with me.
> Wherefore I thynke out of this land to wende,
> Or elles of myself to make an ende,
> So ful am I of drede and eek of care."

(VII.116–23)

We have heard this kind of language before. It was the merchant's own complaint, world-weary and tagged with features out of the martyrologies. We are not surprised, then, by her notion of telling "a legende of my lyf,/ What I have suffred sith I was a wyf" (VII.145–46). Like the merchant himself, she borrows this victim's role because it offers deeper ethical roots. But in the course of the garden scene, as daun John warms to the subject, she shifts to the language of *fin' amor*. "'My deere love," she begins, once he has denied any loyalty to the merchant, "O my daun John" (VII.158). She ends by promising him "plesance and service/ . . . right as yow list devise" (VII.191–92). Thus her move from the language of martyrdom to the language of love parallels her rejection of the merchant's alliance with the monk, in favor of her own alliance. She will befriend the monk,

> "Nat for no cosynage ne alliance,
> But verraily for love and affiance."

> (VII.139–40)

"Cosynage" was how the merchant and monk described their convenient friendship; but her deal with daun John is based on more powerful and fundamental needs, despite the preciosity of her courtly language.

The crux of this garden scene is the wife's betrayal of her marital "privetee," which refers to bedroom secrets as well as family finances. "God shilde I sholde it tellen" (VII.166), she says, magnifying her powers of resistance—and then, explosively, spilling it all:

> "A wyf ne shal nat seyn of hir housbonde
> But al honour, as I kan understonde;
> Save unto yow thus muche I tellen shal:
> As helpe me God, he is noght worth at al
> In no degree the value of a flye."

> (VII.167–71)

This sudden outburst is like the monk's "'frankes'/flankes" response at the end of the garden scene, and like the merchant's professional "complaint" which comes after the garden scene. In effect, the wife's complaint refers both to the merchant and the monk; to the "nygardye" of the one, and the "manly[ness] of dispence" (VII.43) of the other. As she says,

> ". . . wel ye woot that wommen naturelly
> Desiren thynges sixe as wel as I:
> They wolde that hir housbondes sholde be
> Hardy and wise, and riche, and therto free,
> And buxom unto his wyf and fressh abedde."

(VII.173–77)

These qualities are "women's things" that balance the professional "thynges" associated with the merchant and monk. Of the six, "hardy," "wise," and "riche" are a pretty good description of the merchant's public self, at least, and "free" (i.e. generous), "buxom," and "fressh abedde" refer unmistakeably to how the monk has presented himself up to this time. This is as close a look into the wife's heart as the tale allows us, and we must conclude that from her point of view, a satisfying marriage would have to include a man with both sets of qualities. But in the wife's marriage, he is hardy, wise, and rich (a responsible male role), and she is expected to be the responsive good wife— free, buxom, and fresh abed. He keeps the counting house, and she gets to spend . . . only what is given her; and that, of course is the problem. She has spent one hundred franks "'For *his* honour, *myself* for to arraye'" (VII.179, my italics), but since only he can say if that is a justifiable expense, she remains merely a piece of his household, of "oure good." Like the Wife of Bath, for whom this tale was originally written,[17] this wife craves "sovereignitee"—control over herself. She will not get it from the monk. But by defending herself against his combination of mercantile skill and sexual "fredom," she will succeed in uniting the six qualities within *herself*, as she replays the garden scene with her husband, in her own "countour-hous," the bedroom.

After the garden scene, the plot unfolds with an exact symmetry. The merchant goes to the market at Bruges, and later goes to Paris to borrow money. The monk borrows money from the merchant, and then returns to complete his "trade" with the wife. By the time the merchant returns to his wife, both he and the monk have borrowed on credit ("creaunced") and bought at a favorable price. What will the wife do? I am going to argue that the wife's "deal" in her bedroom is the central role transformation of the tale. By borrowing, and then selling *herself* in the right way, she paradoxically redeems her social standing, her marriage, and to a degree, the merchant's "curious" profession.

When the merchant returns, successful, from Paris, the wife meets him at the gate, next morning he embraces her "al newe" (VII.378)—that is, she admits him "agayn" (VII.381). This echoes the monk's coming "agayn" (VII.312), "al fressh and newe yshave" (VII.309) to redeem his bargain with the wife. Both passages have an overtone of renewal, and that, I believe, is the way to read this final scene. The obstacle is that daun John retains a lien on her. The merchant has paid his Lombard bankers, redeeming his debt with gold "redy in hir hond" (VII.367), but the monk still holds evidence "By redy token" (VII.390) of the wife's debt to him, and thus to the merchant. Only she is not free and clear.

But this is the moment of reversal. Unlike weary hares and fearful merchants (cp. VII.103–06), she is not "afered or afrayed" (VII.400). "Boldely" (like "boold" daun John) she defies both the "tokenes" (VII.403) of her own conduct and daun John's "monkes snowte" (VII.403–05). In effect she rejects her "old" relationships with both men and in the next few lines recreates herself as a domestic merchant by claiming an equal partnership in her marriage. Why did she accept the franks from daun John?

> For, God it woot, I wende, withouten doute,
> That he hadde yeve it me bycause of yow
> To doon therwith myn honour and my prow,
> For cosynage, and eek for beele cheere.

> (VII.406–09)

In other words, it was a gift to her in her role as part of the household, part of the facade of "cheer." The gift recalls her divided marriage, the semi-erotic overtones of "beele cheere" suggesting the wife's independent source of funding, as well as the merchant's seducing the public by maintaining an expensive image. Now, of course, her debt has fractured her own image as keeper of "oure good." Yet from her point of view (since this "transformation" is really nothing more than a shift from a man's view of the world to a woman's, from counting house to bedroom), the divisive debt is actually a source of plenty; "scoring it on her taille" will generate capital because, like a merchant's gold, it too is a "plough" for "creauncing," for "driving forth the world" and making it bear. "Taillynge" heals the division in this mercantile marriage because it rewards him for being hardy, wise, and riche, but it also provides her with a controlling interest in exchange for being free, buxom, and fresh abed.

In the following lines, the wife describes her new arrangement, restating and thus "transforming" the terms of the old one, as money given for "myn honour" (VII.408) becomes array she bestows for "youre honour" (VII.421); the uneasy external alliance of "cosynage" (VII.409) is displaced by an intimate marital bond ("Ye shal have my joly body to wedde," VII.423); and the ambiguous, manipulative "beele cheere" (VII.409) is replaced by "Forgyve it me, myn owene spouse deere;/ Turne hiderward, and maketh bettre cheere" (VII.426). The merchant accepts this arrangement, in effect, when he tells her "Keep bet *thy* good" (VII.432, my italics), for he is acknowledging (as of course he must!) that she is part owner, indeed the gatekeeper of this operation.

The comedy of this ending is essentially different from the social irony earlier in the tale.[18] When all values are subordinated to profit, oaths lose their force, the home lacks warmth, love is not fulfilling, and all trades, even merchantry, clothe themselves in precious illusion. The fading of value and the flight into pretense that we have seen in this tale are devolutions, the transformations of descent. They are versions of the Fall (hence the garden scene).[19] On the other hand, the wife's confronting her loss of integrity, or "image," by capitalizing on her sexuality and making a virtue of necessity, is a version of atonement. It is a return to wholeness like the merchant's recovery when he has, "Thanked be God," bought "al hool his marchandise" (345); like the monk's return to his abbot (perhaps); and certainly it is like the Wife of Bath's hardy, rich and wise affirmation of life:[20]

> Lat go. Farewel! The devel go therwith!
> The flour is goon; ther is namoore to telle;
> The bren, as best I kan, now moste I selle;
> But yet to be right myrie wol I fonde.

> (VII.476–79)

Like all good comedies, the *Shipman's Tale* ends with a reascent to unity. It begins with the wife's Fall in the garden, where all values are "converted" to the profit motive, and debased by the fear of fortune, change and dissolution, which drives that motive. It ends with an atonement in her bedroom, where she casts herself into the chaos of fortune, market forces and the fickle desires of men—and makes it her kingdom.

NOTES

1. Cf. V. J. Scattergood, "The Originality of the *Shipman's Tale*," *Chaucer Review* 11 (1977): 213–15. For a dissenting view, see John P. McGalliard, "Characterization in Chaucer's *Shipman's Tale*," *PQ* 54 (1975): 1–18, who argues at some length that "In the *Shipman's Tale*, as in all of Chaucer's fabliaux, the characterization is a distinguished achievement" (2).

2. See Thomas Hahn, "Money, Sexuality, Wordplay, and Context in the *Shipman's Tale*" in Julian N. Wasserman and Robert J. Blanch, ed., *Chaucer in the Eighties* (Syracuse: Syracuse University Press, 1986), pp. 235–49: "The descriptions of the Merchant's working environment at Saint Denis, and of his financial transactions in Bruges and with the Lombards of Paris . . . . are so precise and numerous that they call attention to themselves, and in doing so these features—and the larger cultural context from which they draw their meaning—would certainly have shaped the audience's response to the tale's meaning" (235–6). See also Scattergood (note 1): 211–13.

3. Cf. A. Booker Thro, "Chaucer's Creative Comedy: A Study of the *Miller's Tale* and the *Shipman's Tale*," *Chaucer Review* 5 (1970): 97–111, who presents the *Shipman's Tale* as "a series of persuasive scenes, a continual demonstration of triumphant wit" (109).

4. Cf. David Aers' brief but penetrating discussion of the *Shipman's Tale* in "Representations of the Third Estate: Social Conflict and Its Milieu around 1381," *Southern Review* (Adelaide) 16 (1983): 335–49: "Like so many of the *Canterbury Tales*, the *Shipman's Tale* plunges us into a world where market relations are the norm" (342).

5. On the commercialization of the marriage relationship in the *Shipman's Tale*, see Albert H. Silverman, "Sex and Money in Chaucer's *Shipman's Tale*," *PQ* 32 (1953): 329–36; Bernard S. Levy, "The Quaint World of the *Shipman's Tale*," *Studies in Short Fiction* 4 (1967): 112–18; Janette Richardson, "The Facade of Bawdry: Image Patterns in Chaucer's *Shipman's Tale*, *ELH* 32 (1975): 303–13; Hahn (note 2); and William F. Woods, "A Professional Thyng: The Wife as Merchant's Apprentice in the *Shipman's Tale*," *Chaucer Review* 24 (1989): 139–49. For a discussion of punning as an analogue to economic exchange, see Gerhard Joseph, "Chaucer's Coinage: Foreign Exchange and the Puns of the *Shipman's Tale*," *Chaucer Review* 17 (1983): 341–57, esp. 349–55.

6. All quotations from Chaucer are drawn from *The Riverside Chaucer*, ed. Larry D. Benson, *et al.*, 3rd ed. (Boston: Houghton-Mifflin, 1987).

7. Cf. Joseph (note 5): "In the *Shipman's Tale* our moral reservations about the merchant's arguably exaggerated concern with business affairs are surely countered by our aesthetic fascination with the complexities of a newly consolidated money economy of which he is master" (347).

8. Cf. Aers (note 4):

> Once we register this religious and ethical potential [in the merchant's role], we are well placed to understand the significance of the fact that far from being actualised the potential is stunningly transformed. For what Chaucer figures here is the way such mercantile dedication to the market involves a psychological state which transforms traditional religious orientations in a manner that can be described, in Weber's words, as worldly asceticism. . . . Religion thus sanctifies a life centred on the individualistic and socially irresponsible pursuit of economic profit, while the social milieu not only allows this but favours it and even seems to take it for granted.
>
> (323)

9. Cf. Hahn (note 2): "Although the characters all are deeply concerned with their names or reputations, desire for possession inverts and conflates the spectrum of roles in the tale" (245). Hahn provides a good brief discussion of role shift.

10. For an opposing view, see Frederick Tupper, "The Bearings of the *Shipman's Tale*," *JEGP* 33 (1934): 352–72, who concluded that the tale belonged to an antifeminist tradition, and had never been intended for the Wife of Bath: "[T]he Wife of Bath, protagonist of her sex in the Canterbury *querelle des femmes* . . . surely never at any stage of her development gave advantage to the masculine enemy by such a flagrant betrayal of the cause of womanhood as in her supposed version of the Shipman's story, where the merchant's faithless wife is no less a butt than the merchant himself" (357).

11. Cf. Richardson (note 5): "[T]he "cosynage" between them . . . is in essence real—they are akin by action if not by blood" (306).

12. Cf. Richardson (note 5):

> To be "knyt with *eterne* alliaunce" to a friend affords great joy to the man who longs for something eternal but can envision achieving it only by the hazardous manipulation of the tokens of worldly exchange. In this "bretherhede" there is apparently no buying and selling, only mutual love, and with pathetic eagerness the merchant grasps at this fulfillment of his spiritual need."
>
> (312)

Levy (note 5) calls the counting house the merchant's "own little commercial heaven" (112–13).

13. Cf. Hahn (note 2): "[I]f he is not much of a husband, [the merchant] is positively monkish in his devotion to his profession" (244).

14. Cf. Scattergood (note 1): 215–17.

15. Lorraine Kochanske Stock, "The Meaning of *Chevyssaunce*: Complicated Word Play in Chaucer's *Shipman's Tale*," *Studies in Short Fiction* 18 (1981): 245–9, argues that "chevyssaunce" can also mean "strategem," and that this alternate sense helps to distinguish the wife's merchantry from that of the merchant and the monk.

16. See John P. Hermann, "Dismemberment, Dissemination, Discourse: Sign and Symbol in the *Shipman's Tale, Chaucer Review* 19 (1985): 302–37, for a thorough discussion of this theme.

17. See William W. Lawrence, "Chaucer's *Shipman's Tale*," *Speculum* 33 (1958): 56–68, esp. 68.

18. Paul G. Ruggiers, "A Vocabulary for Chaucerian Comedy" in Jess B. Bessinger, Jr., and Robert R. Raymo, ed., *Medieval Studies in Honor of Lillian Herlands Hornstein* (New York: New York University Press,

1976), pp. 193–225, proposes two fundamental kinds of comic emphasis in Chaucer: the first refers to tales "largely aimed at giving satisfaction through cleverly arranged episodes, suspense, and a sense of something being carefully nudged toward surprise and an unexpected conflation of happenings," and the second, to tales where "the emphasis is largely upon describing the ethos of a society or group: something more communal, perhaps a community of demon types, mostly hypocrites and liars, persons wearing masks of one sort or another, who are either exposed or destroyed" (196).

It seems to me that what I call wife's "reascent to unity" at the end of the tale is also her reestablishing a mercantile community of values within her marriage, where, both in economic and sexual ways, she and her husband had earlier been devalued and thus divided from each other. But perhaps this merely implies Ruggiers' own caveat: "Seriousness is always an implied quality in Chaucerian comedy" (196)—"seriousness" being the way in which narrative devices shadow forth a "rising" toward community, as in the *Shipman's Tale*, or a falling away from it, as in the *Pardoner's Tale*.

19. Cf. Gail McMurray Gibson, "Resurrection as Dramatic Icon in the *Shipman's Tale*" in John P. Hermann and John J. Burke, Jr., ed., *Signs and Symbols in Chaucer's Poetry* (University, Ala: University of Alabama Press, 1981), pp. 102–12, who compares the garden scene to Christ's meeting with Mary Magdalen after the resurrection: "[I]t is clear that Chaucer makes of the merchant's wife a Magdalen playing a perverse version of a *Hortulanus* play, a play in which the prostitute-made-saint is replaced by a contemporary Magdalen who will contract to prostitute herself both within and without her marriage" (109). But see also Lorraine Kochanske Stock, "The Reenacted Fall in Chaucer's *Shipman's Tale*," *Studies in Iconography* 7/8 (1981–2): 135–45, who argues plausibly that "the garden encounter between daun John and the merchant's wife . . . is constructed as a parody on man's first sin in Eden" (135). See also John P. Hermann (note 13): 327–9.

20. It is probably here that my reading most directly opposes that of Robert Adams, "The Concept of Debt in *The Shipman's Tale*," *SAC* 6 (1984): 85–102, who argues that "the philosophical coloring that Chaucer introduced to this story with his puns about 'debt' served to highlight for his first readers the hollow impenitence of its conclusion" (93).

Rough Music in Chaucer's *Merchant's Tale*

Frederick B. Jonassen

At the beginning of his seminal book about Rabelais, Bakhtin states, "Of all great writers of world literature, Rabelais is the least popular, the least understood and appreciated."[1] The Russian formalist perceived this historical misunderstanding as a failure to grasp the tradition of folk humor that pervades *Gargantua and Pantagruel*, especially that humor derived from the cycle of medieval feasts.[2] Of these, Carnival is the most significant and emblematic, the source for the parody, humor, and sense of the grotesque found not only in other holidays, but in many artifacts of western culture, such as its literature. These traditions, Bakhtin claimed, inspired that irreverence, vitality, and wisdom that has come to be associated with Rabelais.

Carnival was, first and foremost, a celebration of the body in its material and physical nature. As a result, Carnival generated broad humor by bringing all that was abstract, theoretical, and without an anchor in the material world to the level of bodily functions. The most sacred beliefs of society were the special targets of Carnival degradation since these were precisely the notions that sustained and legitimized the social order through fear, if not temporal, then religious. Carnival was a temporary declaration of liberty, a licensed rebellion that undermined the power of fear through laughter. In playfully destroying what was oppressive, Carnival celebrations were regenerative in their exploration of new possibilities beyond the limitations of everyday thought and behavior sanctioned by church and state. "To degrade an object does not imply merely hurling it into the void of nonexistence, into absolute destruction, but to hurl it down to the reproductive lower stratum, the zone in which conception and a new birth take place."[3]

Given the extensive significance of festivities like Carnival, reflections of festive themes can invest literary works with a vast network of subtextual meaning that may be accessible to modern scholarship through the study of popular culture, folklore, and anthropology, as well as learned or elite literary sources. Indeed, various aspects of Carnival humor, the celebration of the body, degradation of what is high, playful rebellion, regeneration, and others, would seem quite as typical of Chaucer as of Rabelais. Chaucer's juxtaposition of the bawdy with the sacred, his renditions of fabliaux and hagiography, indeed, the contrasting themes of *sentence* and *solas, ernest* and *game*, which have become commonplaces in Chaucerian criticism, all reflect the Carnival/Lenten dichotomy of his medieval culture. As a result, a number of scholars, such as David, Kern, Payne, Cook, Kendrick, Lindahl, Ganim, and Jonassen, have been able to apply Bakhtin's ideas to the *Canterbury Tales*.[4]

Chaucer, however, was an artist of the Middle Ages rather than the Renaissance. The elaboration of his relationship to folk custom, therefore, must fully recognize the medieval context that framed his work and lifetime. Furthermore, Chaucer's is a highly original and sophisticated poetic sensibility. Interpretations of his work derived from the tradition of folk humor or custom must never reduce his art to a given scheme or pattern, even one as meaningful as the conflict between Carnival and Lent, but should instead reveal the complexity of the poet's syncretic thought and artistry, his integration of the folkloric and popular with the learned and bookish.

In *Chaucerian Theatricality*, John Ganim compares the uproar at the endings of the *Miller's Tale* and the *Nun's Priest's Tale* to the festive release of an ancient custom known as the "charivari."[5] J. A. Burrow also likened this custom to the

treatment typically afforded the *senex amans* who, like the
impotent husbands of the Wife of Bath or January of the *Merchant's Tale*, married a much younger woman: "Traditional
peasant communities in France used to express their disapproval of such mismatches through the institution of the charivari:
'a serenade of "rough music," with kettles, pans, tea-trays, and
the like used in France, in mockery and derision of incongruous
or unpopular marriages.'"⁶ Determining the extent to which
these Chaucerian works draw meaning from the charivari depends upon a close examination of the custom as well as
Chaucer's text.

"Charivari" is the French term in general use for a widespread ritual of humiliation accounts of which date back to the
fragmentary description by Nicholas Damascenus of the first
century B.C. and a passage in *The Greek Questions of Plutarch*
from the first century A.D.⁷ Historical examples of charivaris
come from England, France, Germany, Spain, Sweden, Denmark,
Persia, India, the Caucasus, Turkey, and Egypt, each country
having its own variety of names for the event. In parts of Spain
it is known as the *cencerrada,* in Italy they call it the *far companate* or *scampanate,* in Basque lands the *zinzarrotsa* or *galar-
rotsa,* and in Germany *Katzenmusik, Eselritt, Haberfeldtreiben,* and *Tierjagen.* Besides rough music, the English names for
the charivari include the skimmington ride, riding the stang,
and the stag hunt.⁸

As one might expect of a folk custom this widespread over
time, geography, and nationality, the charivari possesses a
diversity of forms and features. It appears to be universal,
however, that the charivari is meant to punish some behavior
that a community finds shameful. The classical impetus for the
charivari is a disorder within the marital bond. According to
Natalie Zemon Davis, marriages between parties who were
greatly different in age or in which one party was marrying a
second time were the most common cause of charivaris in rural
France, while in French cities, charivaris were performed
mostly to identify and mortify married couples in which the
wife committed adultery or physically beat or dominated her
husband.⁹ Although a charivari might occur at any time to
punish such vagaries, these processions became typical of

Carnival celebrations in which they not only stigmatized objectionable marriages, but also pilloried unpopular political and religious figures.[10]

A typical charivari might take place in the following way. After an individual or couple had been singled out on account of behavior deemed unacceptable by their neighbors, the people of the community would secretly conspire to meet one night in costume or disguise so as not to be recognized. They would bring with them pots, pans, kettles, rattles, horns, pipes, bagpipes and other noisemakers of all descriptions along with torches. Effigies of those who were the targets of the derision might be used, or perhaps one or more of the maskers would impersonate the culprits. The effigies or representatives of the offending parties would be made to ride a horse or donkey backwards while horns of all types would figure prominently in the procession. The noisy crowd, yelling profanities or singing obscene lyrics made for the occasion, would make its way to the place where their victims lived. Sometimes they would force their victims out of the house, make them ride backwards, and beat them or dump them in a pond or ditch. The next day, everyone who participated in the charivari would act as if nothing had happened at all. Seldom did such treatment fail to drive the targets of the charivari out of the community.[11]

Accounts of English charivaris imposed on quack physicians,[12] perjurers, unscrupulous merchants, adulterous priests,[13] incontinent widows,[14] and hen-pecked husbands[15] may be found in records dating back to the fourteenth century. These accounts of rough music are what Martin Ingram has in mind in his study of the English charivari.

> Divers règlements de la cité de Londres, à la fin du XIVe siècle, prévoyaient, par exemple, que certains malfaiteurs seraient promenés dans les rues, avec accompagnement de chants et de danses de ménestrels. Au début de l'époque moderne, certains délinquants, à Londres et ailleurs, étaient promenés à l'envers sur un cheval, c'est-à-dire tournés côté queue, ou encore accoutrés de vêtements de l'autre sexe; et il arrivait que les tribunaux infligent officiellement la *rough music* à titre de châtiment.

Various regulations of the city of London at the end of the
fourteenth century provided, for example, that certain
malefactors be led through the streets to the accompaniment
of songs and dances of minstrels. At the beginning of the
modern era, certain lawbreakers were paraded backwards
on a horse, that is to say, facing the tail, or dressed in the
clothing of the opposite sex; and so it happened that the
authorities officially inflicted the punishment under the
name of "rough music."[16]

The literary history of the English charivari is extensive. There is an account of a backwards ride in the thirteenth-
century *Lay of Havelok the Dane*.[17] Thomas Heywood dra-
matized a skimmington ride in *The Witches of Lancashire*,[18]
and the final scene of Shakespeare's *The Merry Wives of
Windsor* in which Falstaff appears with the horns of a stag
gracing his brow is quite possibly a literary rendition of rough
music, though, I suspect, in the variant known as the stag
hunt.[19] Samuel Butler wrote a well-known description of a
skimmington, which he called an *"antique* Show."[20] One year
earlier, Andrew Marvell, in his *Last Instructions to a Painter*,
characterized the skimmington as recommended by "Prudent
Antiquity, that knew by Shame, / Better than Law, Domestick
Crimes to tame."[21]

The *Roman de Fauvel*, an early fourteenth-century French
allegory, has a description of the custom, the first to use the
term "charivari," and provides manuscript illuminations of the
event.[22] In respect to the *Merchant's Tale*, this text is worth
considering in detail, since it is the most extensive literary
account of a charivari we have that Chaucer may have known.
Fauvel is actually a donkey who represents the disorder of the
age and wants to marry Fortune. She, however, spurns his
advances, and so he marries Vain Glory instead. On the night
of his wedding, the followers of the clown Harlequin celebrate
the charivari with pots, basins, cowbells, horns, drums, and
cymbals, for, as one would expect, everyone knows that Vain
Glory will not be faithful to Fauvel. In the illuminations,
masked revelers may be seen dancing and playing their various
instruments in mockery. There is, however, no ride backwards:
the revelers go no farther than to create a racket outside the

home of Fauvel on the night of his wedding, a point which should be remembered in connection with Chaucer's description of January's wedding.

Of course, Chaucer could have observed the custom on his visits to France or from popular culture in his own country.[23] There is, however, evidence in the *Canterbury Tales* that Chaucer was well-acquainted with processions in which malefactors were ridden about with loud music. The Cook, for example, refers to such events in the description of the apprentice, who remained with his master,

> Til he were ny out of his prentishood,
> Al were he snybbed bothe erly and late,
> And somtyme lad with revel to Newegate.

(I.4400–02)[24]

The most common provocations for the charivari make Burrow's linkage of the custom to the *Merchant's Tale* most viable. January is a good candidate for a charivari. First, the wedding is a match between partners who are greatly different in age, January being sixty and May probably less than twenty, a difference which is underlined by their names. Secondly, the likelihood of cuckoldry is broadly suggested, not only by the *senex amans* situation, but by numerous instances of sarcasm in the text. Old January resembles the French donkey in many respects: he exhibits a weakness for flattery, envy, low-mindedness, and newfangledness,[25] and he marries a young woman who will surely betray him.

In another connection, however, Ganim makes a suggestion upon which I would like to elaborate here and later. "In a sense, fabliau might be regarded as the literary expression of the spirit of charivari. . . . "[26] Indeed, Chaucer's fabliaux, like the charivari, often concern old men marrying young women, or cuckolding, or both. In the *Miller's Tale*, Alison betrays old John the Carpenter, and in the *Merchant's Tale*, May betrays January. The old husbands of the young Wife of Bath also fit into the category of elderly cuckolds. Other fabliau cuckoldings occur in the *Reeve's Tale*, the *Shipman's Tale*, the *Manciple's Tale*, and perhaps one was intended for the *Cook's Tale*. Furthermore, the exposure caused by these fabliaux provokes great ridicule or humiliation, as in the charivari. Certainly John the Carpenter, January, and the other cuckolds are made to appear foolish, the objects of cruel, even vicious, derision. Perhaps the plots of the fabliaux, like the conventional plots of Greek New Comedy, arose as literary enactments of the folk sentiment which took pleasure in ridiculing unconventional sexual liaisons.[27]

In the Merchant narrator's description of January's wedding, suggestions of charivari conspire to indicate that rough music is heard at the wedding, and the tale becomes, in effect, a charivari. According to David Chamberlain, in the entire corpus of Chaucer's works, only the description of Chauntecleer surpasses the description of January's wedding in respect to the elaborateness and originality of its musical allusions.[28] The description of the wedding music begins:

> Al ful of joye and blisse is the paleys,
> And ful of instrumentz and of vitaille,
> The mooste deyntevous of al Ytaille.
> Biforn hem stoode instrumentz of swich soun
> That Orpheus, ne of Thebes Amphioun,
> Ne maden nevere swich a melodye.
> At every cours thanne cam loud mynstralcye
> That nevere tromped Joab for to heere,
> Nor he Theodomas, yet half so cleere
> At Thebes whan the citee was in doute.

> (IV.1712–21)

At first, the instruments (as well as the food) are described as the "mooste deyntevous of al Ytaille." This should indicate that the instruments will have a light, delicate sound. But when the courses are actually served, the narrator calls the music "loud mynstralcye," which would appear to contradict the earlier adjective, "deyntevous." The subsequent allusions to classical and biblical music makers serve to extend and intensify the contradictory description of the music.[29]

Of the instruments it is said that neither Orpheus nor Amphion ever made such melody. These are musicians of string instruments. Orpheus, of course, was the Thracian singer and harpist whose music, as Boethius put it, could make "the

fearful deer lie down bravely with the fierce lions," could calm
the frightened rabbit or quiet the maddened dog.[30] His music,
however, could not console him over the loss of his wife, and so
he went to the underworld to beg for her return. Upon hearing
him play, "The three-headed guardian of the gate is
paralyzed . . . and the Furies . . . are touched and weep in pity.
Ixion's head is not tormented by the swift wheel, and Tantalus
long maddened by his thirst, ignores the waters he now might
drink. The vulture is filled by the melody and ignores the liver
of Tityus."[31] Hell is quieted and soothed by the harmonious
song of Orpheus, but not for long. Leaving, he looks back at
Eurydice and loses her to become later a dismembered head at
the hands of the Maenads.[32] Amphion appears in the *Thebaid*
of Statius.[33] He was the harpist whose music arranged the
rocks into the fortifications of Thebes (*Thebaid* 1.9–10, 8.232–
33, 10.873–77), a feat that implies that his music, like that of
Orpheus, was peaceful, harmonious, and regenerative.

Of the music that is actually heard, however, the narrator states that neither Joab nor Thiodamus ever trumpeted so
loudly. These are not really musicians at all, but are figures
associated with trumpeting that signals war. Thiodamus, like
Amphion, also appears in the *Thebaid*. He was a Greek prophet whose prayers were followed by trumpets blown in an
attack on Thebes (*Thebaid* 8.275–347, 10.160–553). Joab was a
general of David's army who is said to have blown his trumpet
on three occasions in the Second Book of Samuel, 2.28, 18.16,
20.22. All three involve civil wars among the Jewish people: in
the first instance, Joab defeats and kills Abner, the son of
David's predecessor, Saul; in the second, he defeats and kills
Absalom, David's own son; and in the third he defeats and
kills a rebel named Seba. Joab's loud trumpet then is a signal of
internal struggle within a nation and even within a family. As
opposed to the music of Orpheus and Amphion, the music of
Thiodamus and Joab is loud, raucous, and emblematic of violence. In particular, Amphion's music, which helped to build
Thebes, contrasts with the blaring military trumpets announcing the destruction of the city which the prayers of Thiodamus
anticipate. Thus, the classical and biblical allusions serve to

amplify the contradictory dissonance conveyed by music that is said to be both "deyntevous," and "loud mynstralcye."

As Robertson, Chamberlain, Higdon, and Gellrich have shown, Chaucer's use of musical symbolism derives from classical and medieval traditions that invest music with moral significance.[34] The Middle Ages contrasted the harmonious New Song of charity with the cacophonous Old Song of cupidity. The Old Song, however, was often reflected in domestic strife. Ideally, marriage was "that order which most readily suggested love bringing concord from difference."[35] Marital discord, therefore, was representative of cosmic disorder. In Robertson's exposition of the New and Old Songs, he discusses a leaf from the Ormesby Psalter. In the upper margin a female grotesque brandishes a pot and ladle in confronting a goat-footed husband. According to Robertson, this represents an interruption to the heavenly music figured by God's bellman of the leaf's initial.[36] The idea of Discord is also portrayed in reliefs from the Cathedrals of Notre Dame de Paris and of Amiens which depict a quarreling husband and wife.[37] Given the auspices of January's marriage, the wedding music must be of the Old Song variety, its discord suggestive of the groom's lechery and cupidity, as well as the future strife the relationship will suffer.

Aside from the Old and New Songs, the contrast between stringed and wind instruments is also traditional. In the *Metamorphoses*, Book VI, Ovid recounts the story of how the satyr Marsyas, who played reed pipes, challenged the god Apollo, who played the lyre, to a musical contest and lost ignominiously.[38] According to Emanuel Winternitz this contest:

> is a poetic condensation of an eternal conflict . . . between
> string and wind instruments. This means not only the
> difference between the serene and silvery sound of plucked
> gut strings and the bleating, shrill, guttural, exciting sound
> of a reed pipe . . . . It means in the rationalized form of the
> Greek myths the realm of inhibition, of reason, of
> measure—in the literal Pythagorean sense of measuring
> strings and intervals, and in the metaphorical sense of
> *mesure*—as opposed to the realm of blind passion: in short,
> the antagonism between Apollo and Dionysus.[39]

Several Chaucerian musical references suggest that he was very much alive to this dichotomy. Consider, for example, the contrast between the bagpipe with which the drunken, perhaps bacchic, Miller brought the pilgrims "out of towne" (I.566), or out of "tune,"[40] and the "harpe and lute, and gyterne, and sautrie" (I.268) which Phoebus Apollo played before learning he had been cuckolded in the *Manciple's Tale*. These contrasting instruments and musicians stand at the beginning and ending of the *Canterbury Tales*, as the text has come down to us.[41] There are descriptions of music elsewhere in the Chaucer canon which, like the description of January's wedding, employ similar allusions, the inexpressibility topos, and deliberate combinations of string and wind instruments. These passages usually signal moral ambiguity. Perhaps the most comparable to the description of January's wedding is that of Sarpedon's feast in *Troilus and Criseyde*:

> Nor in this world ther is non instrument
> Delicious, thorugh wynd or touche of corde,
> As fer as any wight hath evere ywent,
> That tonge telle or herte may recorde,
> That at that feste it nas wel herd acorde.

> (5.442–46)

Chamberlain comments, "The scriptural echo in 'tonge telle or herte may recorde' suggests that this musical 'feste' is another false heaven to which Pandarus is trying to lead Troilus."[42]

The wedding music of the *Merchant's Tale* likewise denotes the false heaven by which January is seduced, for the instruments at the wedding promise a string sound associated with heaven, but actually produce trumpet blasts, an infernal noise. In this respect, the music reflects the disappointment of January's expectations, who looks forward to marriage as a heaven on earth, but experiences purgatory or hell instead. It is, in any event, a difficult, if not impossible, task to accurately describe music when one is limited to words, even if these are the words of a poet such as Chaucer. Rather than attempt to convey the notion of cacophony through a direct description of the rough music at January's wedding, Chaucer's narrator makes use of contradictory allusions to alert the reader to the peculiar character of the music: contradiction symbolizes the discord of the music and the marriage.

This sense of discord deepens as the wedding takes on a surrealistic quality. Suddenly the gods Bacchus, Venus, and Hymen are present and taking part in the festivities:

> Bacus the wyn hem shynketh al aboute,
> And Venus laugheth upon every wight,
> For Januarie was bicome hir knyght
> And wolde bothe assayen his corage
> In libertee, and eek in mariage;
> And with hire fyrbrond in hire hand aboute
> Daunceth biforn the bryde and al the route.
> And certeinly, I dar right wel seyn this,
> Ymeneus, that god of weddyng is,
> Saugh nevere his lyf so myrie a wedded man.

                                        (IV.1722–31)

Perhaps the mythological figures are merely figments of January's addled brain, allegorically expressing the inebriating quality of the celebration. Or just possibly, they may be revellers in costume or disguise contributing to the rough music of the wedding, like the figures in the illuminations of the *Roman de Fauvel*. If this is the case, the disguised maskers nevertheless retain their allegorical significance, lending to the description of this charivari another syncretic layer of learning and interpretation. Bacchus, the god of drunkenness, reflects the lack of discreet judgment and control demonstrated by January. Venus, the goddess of physical love, indicates the prurience of his interests in May, especially given the phallic possibilities of the firebrand that Venus brandishes for "hir knyght," "biforn the bryde and al the route." Torches, incidentally, are customarily carried by nighttime revellers in a charivari.

The narrator then reverts to describing the music with his pervasive and repetitive inexpressibility topos:

> Hoold thou thy pees, thou poete Marcian,
> That writest us that ilke weddyng murie
> Of hire Philologie and hym Mercurie,
> And of the songes that the Muses songe!

> To smal is bothe thy penne, and eek thy tonge,
> For to descryven of this mariage.

(IV.1732–37)

The reference is to the fifth-century Latin poet, Martianus Capella, and his allegorical work, *The Marriage of Philology and Mercury*. Similar to Apuleius's narrative of the marriage between Cupid and Psyche, this poem is meant to celebrate the apotheosis of Philology by means of her marriage to Mercury.[43] Chamberlain explains, "in medieval tradition Philology signifies the quadrivium and wisdom, Mercury the trivium and eloquence," so that their union represents the Ciceronian ideal of the marriage between wisdom and eloquence.[44] Furthermore, Martianus exploits an elegant musical metaphor in conjunction with these numbers, showing that the marriage of Philology and Mercury promises:

> marital harmony ("nuptialis congreuentia") by virtue of
> the numbers 4 and 3 . . . . These numbers promise great
> harmony primarily because they embody the musical
> consonances diatessaron, diapente, and diapason.

(II.107)[45]

Here, as elsewhere in the passage, the narrator's use of the inexpressibility topos is really a peculiar play on this rhetorical convention. Consider the example of this topos provided by Curtius: "Homer and Orpheus and others too would fail, did they attempt to praise him."[46] Conventionally, this statement is highly complimentary, indicating virtue beyond the powers and skills of the greatest poets to praise. If the same phrase were applied, however, to a well-recognized rogue, it would immediately become or be taken as sarcasm: the compliment would turn into mockery. When the Chaucerian narrator states that the musical instruments at January's wedding possessed, "swich soun / That Orpheus, ne of Thebes Amphioun, / Ne maden nevere swich a melodye," he is not, I think, exalting the musical quality of the instruments as superior to those of Orpheus and Amphion, as one would normally expect from the inexpressibility topos. Rather, the narrator is indicating that the music at January's wedding has, in fact, nothing to do with the melody of Orpheus or Amphion, or any melody at all. Indeed, the succeeding inexpressibility topos alluding to Joab and Thiodamus contradicts the former by implying the music was loud rather thab soft. The suggestion that, "Ymeneus, that god of weddyng is, / Saugh nevere his lyf so myrie a wedded man," does not mean that January is happy beyond the observational experience of the god of marriage, but rather is quite miserable in his blissful oblivion to his real situation and fate as a cuckold.

The narrator's sarcasm, in effect, turns the inexpressibility topos on its head, reversing its conventional meaning. Thus, when Chaucer's narrator dismisses Martianus with a coarse innuendo, claiming, "To smal is bothe thy penne, and eek thy tonge, / For to descryven of this mariage," the narrator is not saying that even one so expert in depicting marital harmony as Martianus is unable to describe the harmony of this particular marriage. Rather, the poet is suggesting that such marital harmony as Martianus describes has nothing to do with this marriage. The Latin poet wrote of celestial euphony, not of the domestic discord symbolized by the churlish custom of rough music. The apotheosis of an allegorical matrimony was his theme, not a marriage made in hell. Martianus's idealized union of wisdom and eloquence could hardly be more ludicrously inappropriate when language itself is totally incapable of expressing the foolishness and infernal disorder of the January-May marriage. Only sarcasm, which relies on tacit understanding rather than explicit statement, will do justice to this wedding by hinting at the maliciously mirthful uproar.

The wedding description provides one more instance of the inexpressibility topos, which summarily ties together the several thematic threads that weave their way through the passage as well as the tale:

> Whan tendre youthe hath wedded stoupyng age,
> Ther is swich myrthe that it may nat be writen.
> Assayeth it yourself; thanne may ye witen
> If that I lye or noon in this matiere.

(IV.1738–41)

At last the narrator explicitly states the problem that makes the marriage fair game for rough music, "tendre youthe hath wedded stoupyng age." This situation produces, "swich myrthe that it may nat be writen." From the sarcasm already noted in this passage, the reader must realize that this "myrthe" is not some joy so beneficent that the author is incapable of describing it in written language. This mirth is instead the cruel pleasure arising from the ridicule of the charivari. Just as words would fail to describe adequately the raucous noise of rough music, words would fail to describe the viciousness of its mockery. After refusing to grant an explicit description so many times, the narrator ends by urging, "Assayeth it yourself; thanne may ye witen / If that I lye or noon in this matiere." The reader must experience the event in order to judge the truth of the narrator's claim that such mirth is impossible to describe. The poet's choice to suggest rough music by sarcastic implication rather than explicit description is the underlying inexpressibility topos of the entire passage.

The repeated refusal to be explicit manifested in this passage constitutes but one of several instances of the Merchant narrator's peculiar distrust of plain speaking. In his *Prologue*, the Merchant complains of his wife, though he doesn't provide much detail beyond wishing she were coupled to "the feend" (IV.1219). "What sholde I yow reherce in special / Hir hye malice?" (IV.1221–22) he asks. The Merchant claims that single men could never speak as he could of the woe a "wyves cursednesse" (IV.1239) may cause, making experience the uniquely effective teacher, as in the wedding description. To the Host's invitation, "Syn ye so muchel knowen of that art / Ful hertely I pray yow telle us part" (IV.1241–42), the Merchant responds, "Gladly . . . but of myn owene soore / For soory herte, I telle may namoore" (IV.1243–44). Rather than tell of his own troubles, he relates a tale about an old, ridiculous cuckold instead. Perhaps the story concerns the Merchant's personal life. Just as he uses the inexpressibility topos to avoid explicitness about January's wedding, he uses his tale to avoid direct reference to himself.[47]

Many critics have noted how Chaucer places the efficacy of language in doubt in the last few tales of his work. The

Canon's Yeoman's Tale is an exposé of how an alchemist cheats his clients, a possible metaphor for the work of the poetic artist. The *Manciple's Tale* recounts how Phoebus Apollo destroys his musical instrument and punishes the crow for telling him the truth about his wife. The *Parson's Tale* seems to abandon poetic language altogether in favor of a very plain penitential treatise on examining one's conscience for sin.[48] The *Merchant's Tale* shares with these others a sense of pessimism and doubt about language. Consider, for example, the debate between Justinus and Placebo. January ignores the honest and sensible counsel of Justinus which warns him not to marry a woman so much younger than himself. He welcomes instead Placebo's sugar-coated flattery, which only tells him what he wants to hear. From this Justinus learns that he cannot state his opposition to the marriage explicitly. He must do so by implication.

> Dispeire yow noght, but have in youre memorie,
> Paraunter she may be youre purgatorie!
> She may be Goddes meene and Goddes whippe;
> Thanne shal youre soule up to hevene skippe
> Swifter than dooth an arwe out of a bowe.

(IV.1669–73)

If January is too dense to perceive Justinus's meaning, the audience certainly is not.

January's refusal to acknowledge the truth of Justinus's words is replicated in a quite different context when he is unable to acknowledge the evidence of his own eyes. This last scene exemplifies the narrator's reticence to speak frankly about sexual matters, though he never fails to make a crude point when he must. For instance, what January does in bed, the narrator claims, "I dar nat to yow telle" (IV.1963). As in the case of the wedding, the reader must guess about what goes on. Later, however, when May is up in the tree with Damian, the narrator insists, "I kan nat glose, I am a rude man— / And sodeynly anon this Damyan / Gan pullen up the smok, and in he throng" (IV.2351–53). Only ten lines later, the narrator becomes coy again, when January looks up with his restored sight and sees Damian treating his wife, "In swich manere it may nat been expressed, / But if I wolde speke uncurteisly" (IV.2362–63). It is left to January to state, in response to May's claim that she was merely struggling with Damian, "Ye, algate in it wente! . . . He swyved thee" (IV.2376, 2378), a blunt rendition of the facts which January later abandons when May persuades him to doubt the meaning of what he himself has seen. January cannot acknowledge the plain truth of his cuckoldry, at least not openly, preferring to go along with the blandishments of his wife rather than suffer the pain and consequences of facing the truth.

Paralleling these passages which undercut plain-speaking are passages which present music in a morally questionable light. I have already noted how the narrator repeatedly makes use of the inexpressibility topos in describing the wedding, avoiding an explicit assessment of the music and mirth with which the marriage is celebrated. To the extent that the wedding music is an infernal parody of ideal harmony, it is a species of the Old Song of the unredeemed. Aside from the wedding description, however, one may note January's grisly parody of the Song of Songs on his wedding night, when he "sang ful loude and cleere," and "The slakke skyn aboute his nekke shaketh, / While that he sang, so chaunteth he and craketh" (IV.1845, 1849–50). Another variety of the Old Song is the "melodye" which Pluto and Proserpina make with the fairies while January is cuckolded in his garden (IV.2038–41).[49] Dissimulating speech and evil music come together in the name of January's ingratiating adviser, Placebo, for the phrase, "to sing Placebo," commonly meant, "to flatter."[50] Similarly, speech and music present an intriguing juxtaposition in the *Manciple's Tale.* Upon hearing from the crow in very plain terms that his wife was unfaithful, "Cokkow! Cokkow! Cokkow! . . . on thy bed thy wyf I saugh hym swyve" (IX.243, 256), Phebus killed her, broke his musical instrument, and then cursed the crow as a "traitour" (IX.271). Phebus had been happy before he knew the truth about his wife, and may have preferred his blissfully ignorant state to his miserable consciousness, a state of affairs that leads the Manciple to praise dissimulation.

The insinuating rhetoric of the Merchant narrator is quite appropriate for a tale which reflects the charivari custom, for charivaris are precisely expressions of matters known to everyone through hushed rumor. The perpetrators of a charivari organize secretly, wear costumes for disguise, and use the night for cover. Afterwards, though everyone knows what has happened, no one admits to it candidly. Instead of public accusation and rational discussion, the self-appointed defenders of village morality make use of a deafening but anonymous racket as the most eloquent means of expressing disapproval. If any words are used, they take the form of inchoate ridicule. This is the type of mirth that obtains "whan tendre youthe hath wedded stoupyng age." Indeed, "swich myrthe . . . may nat be writen," since it is the shameful and clandestine creation of oral culture, not of literary record.

In a charivari, the traditional community concentrates all its tensions, conscious or unconscious, consummated or repressed, upon the hapless individuals who are identified as offensive. These victims are no more than scapegoats at whom considerable hatred, animosity, and sometimes violence are directed, a sublimation of the frustrated drives of the community. As with all scapegoats in whom the evils of a community are concentrated, the charivari seeks to destroy the presumed violators of village mores, if not physically, at least in reputation.[51] In this way, tensions are released, and the sexual standards have been defended, at least for the time being.

The enjoyment of such mirth can itself be a source of shame with the realization that pleasure has been derived from the infliction of pain. In the *Merchant's Tale* in particular, Chaucer develops a sense of unease and discomfort among many readers over the victimization of the *senex amans*. January is an unusually hapless and pathetic figure: a deluded, old man who learns of his wife's infidelity upon recovering his sight, and then sheepishly accepts it. May and Damian, on the other hand, are themselves portrayed in rather dark shades due to their unscrupulous betrayal and duplicity.

Throughout the tale, the narrator's sarcasm and irony entice the reader to take pleasure in January's foolishness. But if the reader should enjoy this ridicule at January's expense, the reader is soon unwittingly allied to the pleasure that the rather reprehensible characters, May and Damian, have in deceiving the old man. In being privy to the narrator's sarcasm, the reader is allied even to the bitter Merchant narrator himself. In fact, the reader becomes a participant in his literary charivari, which the narrator's cunning reticence has rendered partially concealed until the end of the tale when the destruction of January's dignity is complete, and it is too late for the reader to withdraw. As Tatlock long ago put it, "One might feel half-ashamed of so greatly enjoying so merciless a tale."[52]

In any fabliau there must be a gull whose comic embarrassment, when objectively assessed, implies pain, a suffering to which each member of the audience to some extent contributes, perhaps with a sense of gladness and relief that the gull is someone else. One cannot enjoy low comedy without in some way becoming a part of the low life. It is perhaps startling for a reader to learn that the apparently innocent activity of enjoying a fabliau may elicit a pleasure akin to that that of destroying the scapegoat of the charivari, to find out that the serpent lurks in the reader's mental and psychological garden as well as January's. Given the Edenic resonances of January's garden, the serpent in the form of Damian, May as Eve, January as the old Adam, and the pear tree which, like the Tree of the Knowledge of Good and Evil, provides January with the certain knowledge of his unenviable state, perhaps the experience of enjoying the *Merchant's Tale* is rather like St. Augustine's anecdote of biting into a stolen pear, and tasting the sinful bitterness inside.[53]

NOTES

1. Mikail Bakhtin, *Rabelais and His World*, trans. Hélène Iswolsky (1965; (Cambridge, Mass.: M.I.T. Press, 1965), p. 1.

2. See Bakhtin's discussion, pp. 30–58. Bakhtin surveys the history of Rabelais criticism, pp. 59–144. Also see Samuel Kinser, *Rabelais's Carnival: Text, Context, Metatext* (Berkeley: University of

California Press, 1990), pp. 127–79, for his discussion of Rabelais criticism.

3. Bakhtin, p. 21. On the meaning of Carnival, see Bakhtin, esp. pp. 5–30; Natalie Zemon Davis, *Society and Culture in Early Modern France* (1965; Stanford: Stanford University Press, 1982), pp. 97–123; Peter Burke, *Popular Culture in Early Modern Europe* (New York: New York University Press, 1978), pp. 178–204; Peter Stallybrass and Allon White, *The Politics and Poetics of Transgression* (Ithaca: Cornell University Press, 1986), *passim*.

4. Alfred David, *The Strumpet Muse: Art and Morals in Chaucer's Poetry* (Bloomington: Indiana University Press, 1976), pp. 93–94; Edith Kern, *The Absolute Comic* (New York: Columbia University Press, 1980), pp. 40–46; Anne F. Payne, *Chaucer and Menippean Satire* (Madison: University of Wisconsin Press, 1981), pp. 2–9; Jon Cook, "Carnival and the *Canterbury Tales*: 'Only Equals May Laugh' (Herzen)," in *Medieval Literature: Criticism, Ideology and History*, ed. David Aers (New York: St. Martin's Press, 1986), pp. 169–91; Laura Kendrick, *Chaucerian Play: Comedy and Control in the* Canterbury Tales (Berkeley: University of California Press, 1988), *passim*; Carl Lindahl, *Earnest Games: Folkloric Patterns in the* Canterbury Tales (Bloomington: Indiana University Press, 1989), pp. 44–61; John Ganim, *Chaucerian Theatricality* (Princeton: Princeton University Press, 1990), *passim*; Frederick B. Jonassen, "The Inn, the Cathedral, and the Pilgrimage of the *Canterbury Tales*" in *Rebels and Rivals: The Contestive Spirit in The* Canterbury Tales, ed. Susanna Greer Fein, David Raybin, and Peter C. Braeger (Kalamazoo: Medieval Institute Publications, 1991), pp. 1–35; *idem*, "Cathedral, Inn, and Pardoner in the *Prologue to the Tale of Beryn*," *Fifteenth Century Studies* 18 (1991): 109–32.

5. Ganim, pp. 108–20.

6. J. A. Burrow, *The Ages of Man: A Study in Medieval Writing and Thought* (Oxford: The Clarendon Press, 1986), p. 158.

7. Nicholas Damascenus, in *Fragmenta historicorum graecorum*, ed. K. Müller, 5 vols. (Paris: A. F. Didot, 1841–70), vol. 3, fragment 130, pp. 461–62; Plutarch, *The Greek Questions of Plutarch*, ed. W. R. Halliday, (Oxford: The Clarendon Press, 1928), p.p 17, 41–45.

8. Violet Alford, "Rough Music or Charivari," *Folklore* 70 (1959): 505–18; Ruth Mellinkoff, "Riding Backwards: Theme of Humiliation and Symbol of Evil," *Viator* 4 (1973): 153–76; E. P. Thompson, "Rough Music: le charivari anglais," *Annales; économies, sociétés, civilisations* 27.2 (March-April, 1972): 285–312; and E. Hoffman-Krayer and H. Bächtold-Staubli, *Handwörterbuch des deutschen Aberglaubens* (Berlin and

Leipzig: Walter de Gruyter, 1927–42). Claude Lévi-Strauss provides an interpretation of the custom in *The Raw and the Cooked*, trans. John and Doreen Weightman (New York and Evanston: Harper and Row, 1969). See also the pertinent articles in Robert Chambers, *A Book of Days*, 2 vols. (London and Edinburgh: R. Chambers, 1883) and Christina Hole, *British Folk Customs* (London: Hutchinson, 1976).

9. Yves Marie Bercé, *Fête et révolte* (Paris: Hachette, 1976), makes a distinction between the charivari and the *chevauchée de l'âne*, the donkey ride, among other folk punishments. The former "consiste en un vacarme effectué sous les fenêtres d'une victime, qui, le plus souvent, est une veuf ou une veuve contractant des secondes noces," "consists of a racket made under the windows of a victim, most frequently, a widower or widow marrying for the second time" (p. 40). The latter "était réservée aux maris battus ou dominés qui, Mardi Gras . . . étaient promenés par les rues sur un âne. La victime était représentée par un mannequin de paille ou par un compère jouant le rôle. Le personnage chevauchait l'âne à l'envers. On lui ajoutait un panier sur la tête et une quenouille à la main. Cet équipage allégorique montre qu'il s'agit d'une cérémonie réparatrice, vengeresse de la suprématie masculine," "was reserved for beaten or dominated husbands who on Shrove Tuesday . . . were ridden through the streets on a donkey. The victim would be represented by an effigy made of straw or a reveller playing the part. The character would ride the donkey backwards. He would be given a basket to wear on his head and a distaff to hold in his hand. This allegorical gear shows that it concerns a ceremony of redress and vengeance of masculine supremacy," (pp. 44–45). Having noted this distinction, I will follow N. Z. Davis's practice of referring to all such customs as charivari. In any event, the "rough music" of the *Merchant's Tale* would appear to resemble the charivari rather than the donkey ride.

10. To be sure, the charivari could also punish conspicuous lechery, deviancy, or indeed any behavior the community found objectionable. Throughout the Middle Ages and Renaissance, charivaris also served to ridicule or stigmatize unpopular rulers, corrupt politicians, and unscrupulous businessmen, especially on holiday occasions such as Carnival. Davis, 1982), p. 116. See Mellinkoff, pp. 154 ff., for accounts about how the punishment was inflicted on antipopes John XVI and Gregory VIII, Beatrice, the wife of Frederick Barbarossa, and others, and Davis, pp. 117–21, for the use of the custom against local political authorities in sixteenth-century France.

11. An informant told Theo Brown, "The 'Stag-Hunt' in Devon," *Folklore* 63 (1952): 104–9, that at the end of the stag hunt, "members of the hunt told each other of a *good job done*, and everyone showed a marked

delight and expressed the hope that the objects of the hunt would soon leave the town. This was often the result; something like drumming them out as in places up the country, in those days" (p. 105). Thompson, p. 290, states, "'En général,' remarquait un autre témoin du 'riding the stang,' 'les coupables ne pouvaient par la suite supporter la haine ainsi déchaînée contre eux, et . . . quittaient clandestinement la contrée.'" "'In general,' remarked another informant of 'riding the stang,' 'the guilty would not as a result be able to endure the hatred thus unleashed against them, and would quietly leave the country.'" Also see Lynda E. Boose, "Scolding Brides and Bridling Scolds: Taming the Woman's Unruly Member," *Shakespeare Quarterly* 41 (1991): 179–213; and T. N. Brushfield, "On Obsolete Punishments, With particular reference to those of Cheshire," *Chester Archaeological and Historic Society Journal* 2 (1855–62): 31–48 and 203–34.

12. In London, 1382, a quack physician suffered the backwards ride with two urinals hung around his neck to indicate his pretenses at diagnosis, Mellinkoff, p. 160; Thomas Walsingham, *Historia anglicana,* ed. Henry Thomas Riley, 2 vols., Rolls Series 28 (London: Longmans, Roberts, and Green, 1864), vol. 2, p. 63. Also see Henry Thomas Riley, ed., *Memorials of London and London Life in the XIIIth, XIVth, and XVth Centuries,* 2 vols. (London: Longmans, Green, 1868), vol. 2, pp. 464–66.

13. John Stow relates that the punishment was inflicted on swearers of false inquests during the year 1509, and in 1559 a London carman who cheated on the number of billets (pieces of firewood) he delivered was similarly punished. As with the quack doctor, the emblems of the carman's offense, four billets, accompanied him on his backwards ride. Stow also has an account of how the ride was administered to an adulterous priest, "with a Paper on his Head, wherein was written his Trespasse." John Stow, *A Survey of the Cities of London and Westminster,* enl. John Strype, 2 vols. (London: A. Churchill *et al.,* 1720), vol. 1, pt. 1, p. 258; vol. 1, pt. 2, p. 135; and vol. 1, pt. 2, p. 134.

14. Thomas Blount, *Fragmenta antiquitatis,* ed. Josiah Beckwith (York: W. Blanchard for the Editor, 1784), pp. 265–66, records an eighteenth-century statute from Berkshire that requires an incontinent widow to forfeit her estate unless she "comes to the next Court held for the Manor, *riding backward* upon a *Black Ram,* with his *Tail* in her *Hand,*" and repeats verses acknowledging her affair.

15. In 1562 a hen-pecked husband received such a punishment at Charing Cross. Here, the offender was represented by a neighbor who was carried on a pole, the variant known as riding the stang. John Brand, *Observations of the Popular Antiquities of Great Britain,* rev. Sir

Henry Ellis, ed. J. O. Halliwell, 3 vols. (London: Henry Bohn, 1848), vol. 2, p. 193.

16. Martin Ingram, "Le charivari dans l'Angleterre du XVIe et du XVIIe siècle," in *Le Charivari*, ed. Jacques Le Goff and Jean-Claude Schmitt, Civilisations et Sociétés 67 (Paris/The Hague/New York: Mouton, 1981), p. 253. According to the *Oxford English Dictionary*, the term, "rough music," is not recorded until 1708. However, being a folk custom, the term may have been current long before appearing in a text. Besides, the existence of the German term, *Katzenmusik*, and a variety of onomatopoeic terms for the charivari, such as the Spanish *cencerrada* and the Italian *zinzarrotsa*, suggests that the notion of the noise as a sort of cacophonous music is quite ancient and widespread. See Claudie Marcel-Dubois, "La paramusique dans le charivari français contemporain," in *Le Charivari*, pp. 45–53. Also note how Robert Cotgrave's early definition of charivari reflects the noise and music of the custom: "A public defamation, or traducing of; a foule noise made, blacke *Sanctus* rung, to the shame, and disgrace of another; hence, an infamous (or infaming) ballade sung, by an armed troup, under the window of an old dotard married, the day before, unto a young wanton, in mockery of them both." *A Dictionary of the French and English Tongues* (1611; London: A. Islip, 1632).

17. The traitors Godard and Godrich are forced to ride to their execution backwards on "scabby meres," their faces tied to the hindquarters of the horses. *The Lay of Havelok the Dane*, ed. Walter W. Skeat, rev. Kenneth Sisam, (Oxford: The Clarendon Press, 1956), ll. 2449–88, 2823.

18. Thomas Heywood, *The Witches of Lancashire*, in *Heywood's Dramatic Works*, ed. J. Pearson, 6 vols. (1874; New York: Russell and Russell, 1964), Vol. 4, act III, scene 1, pp. 233–34. The stage directions allude to the custom in instructing the characters, Parnel and Lawrence, to break up the procession. "Enter drum (beating before) a Skimington, and his wife on a horse; Divers country rusticks (as they passe) Parnel (puls Skimington of the horse: and Law[rence] Skimingtons wife: they beat em.) Drum beats alar[um]. horse comes away: The hoydens at first oppose the Gentlemen: who draw: the clownes vaile bonet, make a ring Par[nel] and Skim[ington] fight." Parnel is Lawrence's wife who has previously beaten him, for which they are the targets of the skimmington.

19. See Anne Parten, "Falstaff's Horns: Masculine Inadequacy and Feminine Mirth in *The Merry Wives of Windsor*," *Studies in Philology* 82 (1985): 184–99; Christiane Gallenca, "Ritual and Folk-Customs in *The Merry Wives of Windsor*," *Cahiers Elisabéthains* 27 (1985): 27–41; and Frederick B. Jonassen, "The Stag Hunt in *The Merry Wives of Windsor*,"

Bestia 3 (1991): 87–101, for interpretations of this scene as a skimming-ton, a riding the stang, and a stag hunt respectively. On the tradition of the stag hunt, see Brown, "The 'Stag-Hunt' in Devon," and *idem*, "A Further Note on the 'Stag Hunt' in Devon," *Folklore* 90 (1979): 18–21. Richard Leighton Greene, finds an instance of rough music in *Hamlet*, "Hamlet's Skimmington," in *Evidence in Literary Scholarship: Essays in Memory of James Marshall Osborn*, ed. René Wellek and Alvaro Ribeiro (Oxford: The Clarendon Press, 1979), pp. 1–11.

20. *Samuel Butler, Hudibras*, ed. John Wilders (1667; Oxford: Clarendon Press, 1967), pt. 2, canto 2, l. 592. Butler knew that the procession was intended as a punishment for dominating wives: "For when Men by their *Wives* are Cow'd / Their *Horns* of course are understood," pt. 2, canto 2, ll. 711–12.

21. Andrew Marvell, *The Last Instructions to a Painter*, in *The Poems and Letters of Andrew Marvell*, ed. H. M. Margoliouth, 2 vols. (Oxford: The Clarendon Press, 1971), vol. 1, ll. 387–88. One may find the skimmington ride in Thomas Hardy's novel, *The Mayor of Casterbridge*. In the novel, the procession is carried out to ridicule the Mayor and Lucetta who are represented by two effigies "on a donkey, back to back, their elbows tied to one another's. She's facing the head, and he's facing the tail." Thomas Hardy, *The Life and Death of the Mayor of Casterbridge* (New York and London: Harper and Brothers, 1886; Ann Arbor: University Microfilm, 1975), p. 320. To this may be added a variant of the stag hunt, the hare hunt, in Sabine Baring Gould's novel, *Red Spider* (New York: D. Appleton and Company, 1887). Today, the tradition is carried out in a more moderate and only slightly malicious form in the midwestern U.S. under the name of "shivaree," a corruption of charivari which was introduced to America by the French in Canada and Louisiana. See the article on charivari, *Funk and Wagnalls Standard Dictionary of Folklore, Mythology and Legend*, ed. Maria Leach (1949; reissued New York: Funk and Wagnalls, 1972). For still more literary references to the custom, see Ian Donaldson, *The World Upside-Down: Comedy from Johnson to Fielding* (Oxford: Clarendon Press, 1970), pp. 39–42. For the later social history of the custom, see David Underdown, "The Taming of the Scold," in *Order and Disorder in Early Modern England*, ed. Anthony Fletcher and John Stevenson (Cambridge: Cambridge University Press, 1985), pp. 116–36; and Martin Ingram, "Ridings, Rough Music, and the 'Reform of Popular Culture' in Early Modern England," *Past and Present* 105 (1984): 79–113.

22. The *Roman de Fauvel* was written by Gervais du Bus in 1314 with interpolations that contain the reference "chalivali" (ll. 682 and 694) attributed to Raoul Chaillou de Pestain, a high-level administrator

in the service of the French king. Ed. Arthur Långfors (Paris: Didot, 1914–19). John M. Ganim, *Chaucerian Theatricality*, regards the *Roman de Fauvel* as an analogue to the *Nun's Priest's Tale*, pp. 109 and 113.

23. In other medieval French literature, the punishment of the traitor Ganelon in *La Chanson de Roland* is quite possibly a charivari (ll. 1816–29). *La Chanson de Roland*, ed. T. Atkinson Jenkins (American Life Foundation, 1977). Also in *Le Mystère d'Adam*, after the fall of Adam and Eve, when the devils conduct them to Hell, "in eo facient fumum magnum exsurgere, et vociferabuntur inter se in inferno gaudentes, et collident caldaria et lebetes suos, ut exterius audiantur," "they will make a great smoke rise from Hell and rejoicing in Hell they will yell among themselves, and they will bang their pots and pans, so that they may be heard outside" (stage directions, ll. 590). Ed. Paul Studer (1918; Manchester: Manchester University Press, 1967). Eugene Vance, "*Le Jeu de la feullée* and the Poetics of Charivari," *Modern Language Notes* (1984): 815–28, sees suggestions of a charivari in the thirteenth-century *Jeu de la feuillée*, which, he argues, is a literary charivari in terms of "disparate elements" which converge in the work "constituting a poetic performance at every level and from beginning to end" (p. 816). Richard Bernheimer, *Wild Men in the Middle Ages* (Cambridge: Harvard University Press, 1952), p. 67, describes two charivaris in which King Charles VI of France participated, in 1389 and 1393. The second was quite notorious, since four men died as a result of their costumes catching fire. The king was saved when the Duchess of Berry threw the train of her dress over him and smothered the flames. However, he lost his sanity as a result of the shock. See O. Driesen, *Der Ursprung des Harlekin* (Berlin: A. Duncker, 1904), p. 121; and J. Froissart, *The Chronicles of Froissart*, trans. J. Bourchier, Lord Berners, 6 vols. (London: Nutt, 1903), vol. 6, chapter 188, pp. 96–100.

24. *The Riverside Chaucer*, ed. Larry D. Benson *et al.*, 3rd ed. (Boston: Houghton Mifflin, 1987). All citations from Chaucer's works will be taken from this edition. See Lindahl, p. 117. Earlier, in the *Miller's Tale*, the narrator mentions that Absalom, as he borrows the hot colter with which he intends to brand Alison, "hadde moore tow on his distaf / Than Gerveys [the blacksmith] knew" (ll. 3774–75). According to the note in *The Riverside Chaucer*, p. 848, the carrying of a distaff with tow in it was statutory punishment in London for a person guilty of crimes of sex and violence. Such persons were led to the pillory carrying a distaff with tow and accompanied by revel and minstrelsy. These penalties of rough music demonstrate that the folk custom could be granted a legal status in the punishment of certain types of sexual behavior that were regarded as unlawful. The *Merchant's Tale* itself exhibits several examples of folk custom concerning marriage. Besides

the traditional situation of the *senex amans* which Burrows points out, there is the blessing of the wedding bed (l. 1819), and the four days that May remains in her bedchamber (ll. 1859–61). See R. B. Schwartz, "The Social Character of May Games: A Popular Background for Chaucer's *Merchant's Tale*," *Zeitschrift für Anglistik und Amerikanistik* 27 (1979): 43–51.

May's oath uttered just before her betrayal of January warrants some comment:

> If evere I do unto my kyn that shame,
> Or elles I empeyre so my name,
> That I be fals; and if I do that lak,
> Do strepe me and put me in a sak,
> And in the nexte ryver do me drenche.

(IV.2197–2201)

One of the more disturbing punishments of the English skimmington ride or rough music was the cucking stool. This was a device in which a pole was balanced over a fulcrum: one end of the pole had a chair or stool which extended over a pond or river as the case may be. A woman who cuckolded or beat her husband might find herself strapped to this chair and dunked in the water several times. Accounts of the cucking stool are found from the Middle Ages to the early nineteenth century. See W. Carew Hazlitt, *A Dictionary of Faiths and Folklore*, 2 vols. (New York: Scribner's, 1905), vol. 1, pp. 158–59; and John Webster Spargo, *Juridical Folklore in England Illustrated by the Cucking-Stool* (Durham: North Carolina University Press, 1944), esp. p. 34 where Spargo lists medieval references to the device dating back to 1124. See n. 51 below.

25. Fauvel's name is formed by faus, which in modern French is *fauve*, fawn or tawny-colored, the color of vanity, and vel, modern French *voile*, a veil. His name also consists of the initials F for *Flatterie*, A for *Avarice*, V or U for *Vilenie*, and V for *Variété*, E for *Envie*, and L for *Lâcheté* or cowardliness. Marcel-Dubois, p. 46. (See n. 16 for first ref.)

26. Ganim, p. 36.

27. See Paul G. Ruggiers, "A Vocabulary for Chaucerian Comedy: A Preliminary Sketch," in *Medieval Studies in Honor of Lillian Herlands Hornstein*, ed. Jess B. Bessinger, Jr., and Robert R. Raymo (New York: New York University Press, 1976), pp. 193–225, especially his discussion of the character types to be found in Chaucer: " . . . [the tales] contain a topic anchored in a tradition going back through Roman to late Greek comedy, a topic so popular it has never gone out of style since

Menander. It may be seen at a glance which tales are, in a sense, Roman comedies built around the theme of a senex and the successful rebellion against his rule," pp. 211–12.

28. "The most original and elaborate combination of musical signs in Chaucer is found in the description of Chauntecleer just before he is seized by the fox, although the wedding of old January offers a close second in elaborateness," David Chamberlain, "Musical Signs and Symbols in Chaucer: Convention and Originality," in *Signs and Symbols in Chaucer's Poetry*, ed. John P. Hermann and John J. Burke, Jr. (University, Ala.: University of Alabama Press, 1981), p. 68.

29. Chamberlain perceives contradiction in the muscial allusions, n. 78, p. 223, referring to this passage, "with its allusions to the 'melodye' of Orpheus and Amphioun (effeminizing), the 'mynstralcye' of Joab and Thiodamus (violent), the 'daunce' of Venus (erotic), and the 'songes' of Capella's muses (virtuous)." Also see n. 5, p. 217.

30. Anicius Manlius Severinus Boethius, *The Consolation of Philosophy*, trans. Richard Green, The Library of Liberal Arts (New York: Bobbs-Merrill, 1962), p. 73.

31. Boethius, p. 74.

32. For the Middle Ages, the Orpheus story was an exemplum of the failure of the musician to conquer his uncontrollable passions despite his music, as Boethius concludes, "But who can give lovers a law? Love is a stronger law unto itself . . . whoever is conquered and turns his eyes to the pit of hell, looking into the inferno, loses all the excellence he has gained" (p. 74). The love of Orpheus for his wife stands in sharp contrast to January's foolish carnal love. Likewise the beautiful music of Orpheus, inspired by his attempt to win her back from death, contrasts with the din at January's wedding. January himself is a parodic Orpheus, who, near the end of his life, looks back longingly to the pleasure a youthful wife can afford him and finds Hell instead, as he will later find the serpent Damian in his garden.

33. Publius Papinius Statius, *Thebaid*, trans. J. H. Mozley, Loeb Classical Library, 2 vols. (London: W. Heinemann, 1928).

34. D. W. Robertson, Jr., *A Preface to Chaucer* (Princeton: Princeton University Press, 1963), pp. 127–37; Chamberlain, pp. 46–48; David L. Higdon, "Diverse Melodies in Chaucer's 'General Prologue,'" *Criticism* 14 (1972): 97–101; Jesse M. Gellrich, "The Parody of Medieval Music in the *Miller's Tale*," *JEGP* 73 (1974): 176–77.

35. Lawrence J. Ross, "Shakespeare's 'Dull Clown' and Symbolic Music," *Shakespeare Quarterly* 17 (1966): 112.

36. Robertson, pp. 129–30, fig. 39. Pots and ladles often figure in the skimmington ride, the word, "skimmington," being derived from the skimming ladle, Underdown, p. 130. Horns may be suggested by the goat feet of the husband, and by the horns of a snail which startle a man in the right margin of the leaf so that he drops his sword. Perhaps, then, some aspects of the folk custom are reflected in the Ormesby Psalter.

37. Robertson, p. 130, fig. 56; Ross, p. 112, plate 2.

38. Ovid, *Metamorphoses*, trans. Frank Justus Miller, Loeb Classical Library, 2 vols. (1916; rpt. Cambridge: Harvard University Press, 1964), vol. 1, bk. 6, ll. 384 ff. Perhaps another pertinent Ovidian tale is that in which Midas preferred Pan's pipe music over Apollo's lyre music because of the rude and foolish sensibility of his donkey ears, vol. 2, bk. 11, ll. 146 ff. Midas resembles both the donkey Fauvel and January who does not discern the meaning of the music played at his wedding.

39. Emanuel Winternitz, *Musical Instruments and Their Symbolism in Western Art* (New York: W. W. Norton, 1967), p. 152. Also see Ross, pp. 119–20; John Hollander, "Musica Mundana and Twelfth Night," in *Sound and Poetry*, ed. Northrop Frye, English Institute Essays, 1956 (New York: Columbia University Press, 1957), p. 67; and Winternitz, "The Curse of Pallas Athena: Notes on a 'Contest between Apollo and Marsyas' in the Kress Collection," in *Studies in the History of Art Dedicated to William E. Suida* (London: Phaidon Press for the Samuel H. Kress Foundation, 1959), p. 187.

40. On this pun, see Samuel McCracken, "Chaucer's *Canterbury Tales*, A.565–66," *Explicator* 23 (1965): #55. On the libidinous aspects of the bagpipe, see Edward A. Block, "Chaucer's Millers and Their Bagpipes," *Speculum* 29 (1954): 209–28.

41. In *The Parliament of Fowls*, the narrator hears "instruments of strenges" of such "ravyshyng swetnesse, / That God, that makere is of al and lord, / Ne herde nevere beter, as I gesse" (ll. 197–200). In Chaucer's translation of Boethius's *Consolation of Philosophy*, Lady Philosophy accompanies her "subtil soong, with slakke and delytable sown of strenges" (book 3, meter 2). In contrast, perhaps the most extremely gross example of the cacophony of wind instruments is produced by the miller and his wife in the *Reeve's Tale*:

> This millere hath so wisely bibbed ale
> That as an hors he fnorteth in his sleep.
> Ne of his tayl bihynde he took no keep.
> His wyf bar him a burdon, a ful strong.

(I.4162–65)

Of course, stringed instruments could be used for immoral purposes, as is the case with Nicholas and Absalom in the *Miller's Tale*.

42. Chamberlain, p. 50. See Paul A. Olsen, "Chaucer's Merchant and January's 'Hevene in erthe heere,'" *ELH* 28 (1961): 203–14. Note also the description of musical instruments and their sound in *The House of Fame*, ll. 1193–1250, which begins with Orpheus and ends with Joab and Thiodamus. Note finally the description of Apollo's music-making in the *Manciple's Tale*:

> Certes the kyng of Thebes, Amphioun,
> That with his syngyng walled that citee,
> Koude nevere syngen half so wel as hee.

(IX.116–18)

43. Martianus Capella, *Martianus Capella and the Seven Liberal Arts*, Vol. 2: *The Marriage of Philology and Mercury*, trans. William Harris Stahl and Richard Johnson with E. L. Burge (New York: Columbia University Press, 1977), p. 14.

44. David Chamberlain, "The Music of the Spheres and the *Parlement of Foules*," *Chaucer Review* 5 (1970): 42.

45. Chamberlain, "The Music of the Spheres," n. 57, p. 42.

46. Ernst Robert Curtius, *European Literature and the Latin Middle Ages*, trans. Willard R. Trask (New York and Evanston: Harper and Row, 1953), p. 160.

47. There has been controversy in determining the relation of the Merchant to his tale and, as a consequence, the level of irony and sarcasm with which the tale is invested. The older school of critics emphasized the bitterness of the Merchant narrator and the trenchant satire of the tale. These include: G. L. Kittredge, *Chaucer and His Poetry* (Cambridge, Mass.: Harvard University Press, 1915), pp. 201–2; J. S. P. Tatlock, "Chaucer's *Merchant's Tale*," *Modern Philology* 33 (1935–36): 367–81; G. G. Sedgewick, "The Structure of the *Merchant's Tale*," *University of Toronto Quarterly* 17 (1948): 337–45; and C. Hugh Holman, "Courtly Love in the *Merchant's* and the *Franklin's Tales*," *English Language History* 18 (1951): 241–52. Robert M. Jordan, "The Non-Dramatic Disunity of the *Merchant's Tale*," *PMLA* 78 (1963): 293–99, dissented on the issue of identifying the Merchant with January; and Martin Stevens, "'And Venus Laugheth': An Interpretation of the *Merchant's Tale*," *Chaucer Review* 7 (1972): 118–31, downplayed the cynicism of the text. Norman T. Harrington, "Chaucer's *Merchant's Tale*: Another Swing of the Pendulum," *PMLA* 86 (1971): 25–31, and E. T.

Donaldson, "The Effect of the Merchant's Tale," in *Speaking of Chaucer* (New York: W. W. Norton, 1970), pp. 30–45, while accepting a fictional narrator, insisted upon the bitterness of the tale. More recent studies include Emerson Brown, Jr., "Chaucer, The Merchant, and Their Tale: Getting Beyond Old Controversies," *Chaucer Review* 13 (1978): 141–56, 247–62, who reaffirms the similarity between the narrative voice of the prologue and the tale, and Michael A. Calabrese, "May Devoid of All Delight: January, the *Merchant's Tale* and the *Romance of the Rose*," *Studies in Philology* 87 (1990): pp. 261–84, who perceives a relationship between pilgrim and narrator in their love or marriage to worldly goods.

48. On the connection between alchemy and poetry in the *Canon's Yeoman's Tale*, see Robert W. Hanning, "The Theme of Art and Life in Chaucer's Own Poetry," in *Geoffrey Chaucer*, ed. George Economou (New York: McGraw-Hill, 1975), pp. 15–36; and Derek Traversi, *The Canterbury Tales, A Reading* (Newark: University of Delaware Press, 1983), p. 208. Concerning language and the *Manciple's Tale*, see Britton Harwood, "Language and the Real: Chaucer's Manciple," *Chaucer Review* 6 (1971): 268–79; V. J. Scattergood, "The Manciple's Manner of Speaking," *Essays in Criticism* 24 (1974): 124–46. Donald R. Howard, *The Idea of the* Canterbury Tales (Berkeley: University of California Press, 1976), p. 304, and Chauncey Wood, "Speech, the Principle of Contraries, and Chaucer's Tales of the Manciple and the Parson," *Mediaevalia* 6 (1980): 209–29, perceive the discrediting of poetic language as a preparation for the austerity of the *Parson's Tale*. Also see A. C. Spearing, "The *Canterbury Tales* IV: Exemplum and Fable," in *The Cambridge Chaucer Companion*, ed. Piero Boitani and Jill Mann (Cambridge: Cambridge University Press, 1986), p. 175; "The attempt, embodied in exemplum and fable, to make narrative serve general truth is finally abandoned; and it is tempting to see the self-destructive cynicism of the *Manciple's Tale* as a springboard designed to project the collection towards the Parson's puritanism and its own end." Also see Spearing, "Medieval Poet as Voyeur," in *The Olde Dance*, ed. Robert R. Edwards and Stephen Spector (Albany: State University of New York Press, 1991), pp. 75–76.

49. Chamberlain, "Musical Signs," p. 73.

50. *The Riverside Chaucer*, n. for l. 1476, p. 886.

51. A rather violent description of the skimmington, with a reference to the cucking stool, is recorded in the Wiltshire Quarter Sessions Records as occurring in Quemerford near Calne in 1618, Howard Cunnington, "A 'Skimmington' in 1618." *Folklore* 41 (1930): 187–90. Thompson, p. 290, states: "Le charivari est une proclamation publique de ce qui n'a été dit auparavant qu'en privé. Aprés cela, il n'y a plus de

brouillard. La victime doit réapparaître dans la communauté le lende-
main matin, sachant qu'aux yeux de chaque voisin et de chaque enfant il
est quelqu'un de méprisable . . . . Dans certains cas le charivari pouvait
conduire à la mort, par l'humiliation (comme Hardy le suggère dans
Mayor of Casterbridge) ou par le suicide." "The charivari is a public
proclamation of that which has only been said previously in private.
After this there is no doubt. The victim would have to reappear in the
community the next morning, knowing that in the eyes of each neighbor
and child he is contemptible . . . . In certain cases the charivari can lead to
death, on account of humiliation (as Hardy suggests in *The Mayor of
Casterbridge*) or suicide." See notes 11 and 24 above.

52. Tatlock, p. 176. Also see Donaldson, p. 42, and Jay Schleusener,
"The Conduct of the *Merchant's Tale*," *Chaucer Review* 14 (1979): 237–
50, esp. 246: "The Merchant's rhetoric attacks the feelings of his
audience and forces an answering meanness to match his own. He
degrades himself in the process, but he degrades his willing listeners as
well, and wounds us with our own bad taste . . . . the effect of the
Merchant's Tale is modified by a conclusion which removes the immediate pressure of sarcasm and provides a kind of comic catharsis of bad
feeling." My only disagreement is that the conclusion, in my opinion,
intensifies bad feelings rather than relieves them.

53. St. Augustine, *The Confessions*, The Loeb Classical Library, 2
vols. (1912; Cambridge, Mass.: Harvard University Press, 1977), vol. 1,
book 2, chapter 4, p. 78: "Arbor erat pirus in vicinia nostrae vineae,
pomis onusta, nec forma nec sapore inlecebrosis . . . foeda erat, et amavi
eam; amavi perire, amavi defectum meum, non illud, ad quod deficiebam,
sed defectum meum ipsum amavi, turpis anima et dissiliens a firmamento
tuo in exterminium, non dedecore aliquid, sed dedecus appetens"; "There
was a pear tree next to our vineyard, loaded with pears tempting neither
in shape nor taste . . . it was foul, and I loved it; I loved my ruin, I loved
my sin, not that for which I sinned, but I loved the sin itself, a corrupt
soul shrinking from your firm grasp to destruction, not to seek anything
shameful but shame itself."

PART THREE

"Generic" Humor: Lyric, Poetic, Demonic, Religious, Scatological, and Tragic

Chaucer's Witty Prosody in General Prologue, Lines 1–42

Charles A. Owen, Jr.

The wit in prosody, as Alan Gaylord will also be showing with what he calls the "elvyssh" prosody of *Sir Thopas*, is almost always dependent on context and meaning, it includes not just the humorous but the ingenious, the unexpectedly patterned. Rhythm in patterns of sound can even include grammatical considerations. These observations have special relevance for poetry like Chaucer's, with its avoidance of system and its tendency to test meaning. When some twenty-six years ago I published an article on Chaucer's prosody called "'Thy drasty rymyng. . . .'" (*Studies in Philology*, 63, 533–64), the title itself suggested the indirection inherent in the subject. Part IV of that article on the decasyllabic couplet included many instances of what might be considered witty prosody from the General Prologue,[1] but none from the introductory section, before the first of the pilgrims' portraits.

I should like to concentrate on that section of 42 lines in this effort to build on what I there attempted. Let us consider first the noble opening period, lines 1–18. The obvious prosodic features include the internal rhyme ("swich-which") in lines 3 and 4; the two run-on lines, 7 and 16; the four consecutive heavily feminine rhymes on *-ages*, *-ondes* from 11–14; the spondaic effect in the first two syllables of 12; the pronounced alliteration on *str* in 13 accompanied by an *n*-dominance from 12–16, similar rhymes (-*ondes*, -*ende*) from 13–16, and near-internal-rhymes in the run-on "Of Engelonde" 16; the near-internal-identicals ("hooly" and "holpen") and the rime riche ("seeke") of the last two lines; finally the syntax-defining openings of lines 1, 5, 12, "Whan," "Whan," "Thanne." All of these features participate in the underlying ingenuity that weds sound and meaning in the passage.

In this respect we must pay some attention to the relationship between syntax and line-structure. The first four lines are subordinated by the first "Whan" and include (in line 1) the subject of the subordinate clause, (in line 2) the predicate, (in line 3) a parallel predicate, (in line 4) a clause subordinate to the predicate, the "swich-which" internal rhyme helping to establish a highly elided subordination. The words "Whan Zephirus eek" start off the parallel but shorter ($2^1/2$–line) second clause, line 5 having an almost exactly parallel subject to the first one and 6 having a predicate that runs over into 7. The third subordinate clause (introduced simply by "and") continues the grammatical acceleration, completing itself wittily in $1^1/2$ lines with the first rhyming verb in the passage "yronne." The alert reader recognizes that the half course the young sun has run is its second (April), not its first (March); in other words that we're twice as far in the Ram as we might have thought. The rhyming verb "yronne" closes a series of strikingly active verbs, a delight in and celebration of the forces in nature and simultaneously a delight in and celebration of the power in language to express these forces: water in showers pierces to the root and bathes in "licour"; the breeze's breath "inspires" (first use in English with this meaning) "the tendre croppes"; the young sun runs his fifteen daily rounds that move him also in the zodiac (only a half-course and backward at that). Is it one of the slant meanings of these lines that the sun, for all the speed of his daily running, finds himself further and further behind in the Zodiac?

The grammatical acceleration, noted in the first three clauses, appears to continue when the fourth and last parallel clause (again introduced by "and") gives a complete subject and predicate in the single line (I.9). But it turns out to have merely postponed its more vivid meanings to subordinate (I.10) and sub-subordinate lines. The first word of 12 "Thanne" makes clear that we have completed the temporal context with the strongly feminine rhyme-word "corages" and that we are about to find out what this long series of subordinations has led up to.

The length of the first two syllables, the verb-subject reversal, and the grammatical completeness, "Thanne longen folk to goon on pilgrimages,"[2] make this line (I.12) and especially the word "longen" stand out. A number of observations crowd in at this point to define the implications, liminal and subliminal, of this crucial line and this crucial word. The "corages-pilgrimages" rhyme seals the role of nature in the longing of people for movement at the same time that it helps to contrast the quickness of the birdlike ("priketh") with the implications for people in the word "longen." The ensuing two lines, grammatically dependent on "longen" even as they elide it, define it further with the rich sound of "straunge strondes/ To ferne halwes kowthe in sondry londes." There is a gradual shifting in these seven lines of the main clause, reflected in the words "specially" and "ende." The period is winding down. It carries with it in the *nd* of the rhyme (I.15 f) and the *en* and the *ond* of the run-on (I.16), sounds associated with the longing. But we are coming to the end and the purpose, up from the inner to what can be seen. "Pilgrimages," longest word in the passage and rhyming with "corages," is in part premonitory; "Caunterbury," almost as long, specifies the where:

> The hooly blisful martir for to seke,
> That hem hath holpen whan that they were seeke.

> (I.17–18)

The rime riche on "seeke" has abrupt sound and meaning: it brings us back from the longed for "straunge" and distant to the world of illness and obligation and established institutions. The consoling, the redeeming implications of "hooly blisful" and "holpen" (note the internal near-identical) only partly balance the final emphasis of "seeke."

The "corages-pilgrimages" rhyme is striking enough in sound, meaning, and position to call attention to itself when it recurs a few lines later in singular form, carrying with it "wenden" and "Caunterbury" and characterizing the I-narrator, at his first appearance, as a pilgrim of "ful devout corage." As earlier, observations and qualifications crowd in. This second verse paragraph starts with the verb "Bifil," sudden and specific. Details of time and place fill the first two lines, a day in the spring, the Tabard, Southwerk, all subordinated by the last three words that of course include the rhyme, "as I lay." The passiveness of "lay" and the seriousness of "ful devout corage" give way to the activity of the main clause, the nighttime arrival of the twenty-nine—pilgrims, it is true, "That toward Caunterbury wolden ride." The emphasis, however, given by the two successive run-ons (I.25 and 26), is on their diversity and their "felaweshipe." These characteristics absorb the attention and the energies of the narrator as in the second sentence, after two main clauses and a subordinate clause of description, we get the hyperbole, "So hadde I spoken with hem everichon" (adverb, verb, subject, verb, phrase, and rhymeword),

> That I was of hire felaweshipe anon
> And made forward erly for to ryse
> To take oure wey ther as I yow devyse.

(I.32–34)

The fellowship has thus not only taken over the narrator's "corage," but his grammar as well: the "I" and "hire" (32) become "oure" (34). The dance of the pronouns continues in 34 with "I" and "yow," in the narrator's first address to the reader.

The address to the reader continues through the third and final of the introductory verse paragraphs; the emphasis moves from "felaweshipe" to diversity ("sondry folk"); and a surprising third element is added. But I should like to put off discussion of these matters and concentrate for the moment on the development of "pilgrimage" as a rhyme word. It occurs again at the end of the first portrait, the Knight's, in a context that wittily reverses the direction of change in the case of the narrator. The portrait is concluding with surface matters, the Knight's "array." This passage of six lines (73–78) is dominated by the startling "Al bismotered" at the beginning of the fourth line. The "smot" stands out from everything else in the portrait in both sound and meaning.[3] The surface stains become in the final two lines, "For he was late ycome from his viage/ And wente for to doon his pilgrimage," the inadvertent and hence the all the more validating proof of the Knight's inner worth. It is perhaps an enhancement of this testimony to the Knight's "devout corage" that "viage," a mere surface word, replaces "corage" in the rhyme pair.

"Viage" continues in this role later in the Prologue (I.723 f) and, more importantly for the consideration of the devout, in the Parson's Prologue (X.49 f). Here, at the final moment in the collection of tales, the Host must grant the Parson his turn; there are no other pilgrims left. The Parson proposes "To knytte up al this feeste and make an ende" with God's grace showing the pilgrims

> the wey, in this viage,
> Of thilke parfit glorious pilgrymage
> That highte Jerusalem celestial.

> (X.149–51)

The Parson thus seeks to reverse what happened to Chaucer when the twenty-nine pilgrims entered the Tabard and roused him ("as I lay"). The distraction from "ful devout corage," perhaps not absolute, since there would be some religious tales, has in general prevailed throughout what we have of the journey. This pattern is repeated late in the development of the tales, when Chaucer has the Canon and his Yeoman overtake the pilgrims some four miles from Canterbury and distract them from the spiritual commitment implicit in the *Second Nun's Tale*. It is worth noting that the reversal in the Parson's Prologue occurs in a plan for the whole work that emphasizes the frame narrative as a collection of stories: there is no contest, no judgment by the Host ("Fulfilled is my sentence and my decree" X.17), no prize-awarding supper at the Tabard. The reversal to spiritual values is to occur in and through a tale.[4]

I would like at this point to return to the three introductory verse paragraphs in the General Prologue. The opening of the third provides a striking contrast with the first two. Instead of "Whan that" (with the long subordination) or "Bifil" (abrupt main verb), we get a whole half line of function words, "But nathelees whil." There follow three lines of rationalization, at the end of which comes the "yow" that determines the level of discourse: a continuation of address to the reader first indicated in the last words of the second verse paragraph. Meanwhile we have the near-identicals for the first couplet, "space-pace," rhyme-words that will be used on several other slant occasions in the Prologue. Why this long self-justification? What is the time and space he tells us he has, "Er that I ferther in this tale pace"? The answers are not simple.

If the narrator has time and space, it is because nothing is happening until the time for the "forward" to be observed, the early rising and the departure. Ostensibly the pilgrims are sleeping, and the narrator can take the opportunity (in an almost conspiritorial way) to convey to the audience everything he knows about each of them. Does the line "That slepen al the nyght with open ye" make ever so slight a resonance at this point? Certainly the narrator is sleeping as pilgrim at the same time he is addressing the audience.

Real time and space of course has the narrator before his audience (or the writer before his blank leaves) with perfect freedom to tell the audience whatever he pleases. In addition to ostensible time and space and conspiratorial converse, we get accordance to "raisoun" (rhyme word) to justify telling us "al the condicioun/ Of ech of hem" (run-on). Chaucer's awareness of the task he has set himself, twenty-some portraits one after the other, before anything in the way of "tale" has occurred, constitutes the undertext of these eight lines.[5]

"Space" returns as rhyme-word near the beginning of the Squire's portrait after we learn of his "chivachie" in Flanders, Artois, and Picardy. He had borne him well "as of so litel space/ In hope to stonden in his lady grace" (I.88). The space here includes as its major component time. Both are limited in extent as well as meaning, when we compare them as we must with his father's, the Knight's. "His lady grace" motivates most of this "lovyere's" multifarous activities, including his imitation of the "smale foweles" in line 10:

> So hoote he lovede that by nyghtertale
> He sleep namoore than dooth a nyghtingale
>
> (I.97–98)

The excesses of rhyme (identical plus rhyme) reflect the excess and hyperbole of youth. But the promise comes in as well, and unexpectedly, after the line "Curteis he was, lowely, and servysable" (I.99), as we see him, not in obeisance to his lady, but carving before his father at the table.[6]

The most striking use of the "space-pace" near-identical rhyme-pair occurs in the Monk's portrait, when after a rich series of sound-meaning enhancements ("manly man . . . abbot able . . . stable . . . men myghte his brydel heere/ Gynglen in a whistlynge wynd als cleere . . . chapel belle"), we get a grammatical sweeping away of monastic rule that is almost literally breathtaking:[7]

> Ther as this lord was kepere of the celle
> The reule of Seint Maure or of Seint Beneit
> By cause that it was old and somdel streit—
> This ilke Monk leet olde thynges pace
> And heeld after the newe world the space.

(I.172–76)

The abandonment of the subject "The reule" in favor of "This ilke Monk," earlier called "this lord," gives the grammatical equivalent for the enormity of his actions. Again space has an important temporal dimension. But literal holding of space in the sense of dominating wherever he is (sweeping away older things like grammar) recurs throughout the portrait and justifies the single line summation of him as "a fair prelaat" (I.204). Institutional arrangements contribute a further element of the undertext: Holding space and making it productive constitute the rationale for the cell of which the Monk is "kepere"—in a strictly limited sense. His contempt for "olde thynges" (including any expectation that as a Monk he would "keep to" his cell) finds reflection in the rhyming of "pulled hen" with "hooly men," "cloystre" with "oystre," and in the mocking agreement of the narrator, who rhymes "good" with "wood," repeats "cloystre" internally (I.185), reverses "swynken . . . Austyn bit" with "Austyn . . . his swink," and rhymes "be served" with "reserved" (with emphasis on the rhyming *re*), all in the course of asking two rhetorical questions for which the answers are the reverse of what rhetoric requires: "What sholde he studie . . . ? How shal the world be served?"

One further use of the "space-pace-grace" cluster, later in the *Prologue*, is worth noting, since it occurs with slant meaning

in another rhetorical question. We have been apprised of the
Manciple's skill in timing his purchases of "vitaille" so well

> That he was ay biforn and in good staat.
> Now is nat that of God a ful fair grace
> That swich a lewed mannes wit shal pace
> The wisdom of an heep of lerned men?

(I.572–75)

There follow ten lines (exactly half the portrait) on the wisdom of
the Manciple's more than thirty masters. "And yet this Manciple
sette hir aller cappe" (586). The "ful fair grace" of God prompts
us to measure the "passing" poverty of this perhaps the
meagrest personality among the nine-and-twenty.[8]

Rhetoric, grammar, meaning, all contribute to the witty
prosody that marks the first 42 lines of the Prologue and prefigures some of the effects in the portraits. At the end of the
portraits, the "clause" (rhyme-word) in which we have learned
"Th'estaat, th'array, the nombre, and eek the cause/ Why that
assembled was this compaignye . . ." turns out to have taken no
time at all:

> But now is tyme to yow for to telle
> How that we baren us that ilke nyght,
> When we were in that hostelrie alyght;
> And after wol I telle of our viage
> And al the remenaunt of oure pilgrimage.

(I.720–24)

The portraits are as it were a subordinate clause. The time they
have taken up is narrator's time. The space is writing space.
Address to the audience subsumes all forms of discourse. The
narrator can abandon narrative to explain himself whenever he
wants. He can also set and reset the clock. He can return to the
night at the Tabard, the night when the narrator established
fellowship with the pilgrims and agreed to rise early. He can
introduce the Host and the "remenaunt," the story telling, for
which the Host is responsible. "Clause, Viage, and Remenaunt,"
all emphasized prosodically, constitute in the slant terms of the
narrator what we know as the *Canterbury Tales*.

NOTES

1. See pp. 555–560, where the following points are discussed: the use of the couplet in the Man of Law's portrait, I.321 f, the use of the single line in the Squire's portrait, I.92, and in the Friar's, I.251, the identical plus rhyme in the Squire's portrait, I.97 f, the more complex sound patterns in the Monk's, the Summoner's, the Prioress's (the sudden deflation in the rhymeword mous, I.144, and the fastidious shudder in the run-on "Of grece," I.135), the Friar's (the prepared ambiguity in the rhymeword "post," I.214, and the series of rhymes in the "confessional" passage, I.218–32), and the Parson's portraits. See also two other things of mine, the Chapter on the Prologue in *Pilgrimage and Storytelling in the* Canterbury Tales, Univ. of Oklahoma Press, Norman, 1977, pp. 48–86, and the article in the Elizabeth Salter Memorial volume of the *Leeds Studies in English*, New Series, XIV, 1983, "Development of the Art of Portraiture in Chaucer's *General Prologue*," pp. 116–133. My position on Chaucer's prosody is closest to that of Alan Gaylord, as set forth in his article, "Scanning the Prosodists: An Essay in Meta-Criticism," *Chaucer Review* 11 (1976), 22–82. His later piece, "Chaucer's Dainty 'Dogerel': The 'Elvyssh' Prosody of *Sir Thopas*," *SAC* 1 (1979), 83–104, reprinted as the next essay in this collection, parallels and extends brilliantly the prosodic analysis in part II of "'Thy Drasty Rymyng . . . .'" Calling the prosody "elvyssh" anticipates my use of the word "witty."

2. Quotations are from the *Riverside Chaucer*, ed. Larry D. Benson, Boston: Houghton Mifflin, (1987). I do not always follow the modern punctuation in that edition.

3. Another example of a word that stands out wittily from its context in both sound and meaning in the Prologue occurs in the Guildsmen's portrait, "shaply," I.372.

4. The tale was in my opinion never written. What we have as a *Parson's Tale* in most manuscripts and editions is what Chaucer himself refers to in the Retraction as a "litel tretys," which the language of the Retraction strongly implies is not a part of the *Canterbury Tales*. For a full discussion, see my article, "The *Canterbury Tales*. Beginnings (3) and Endings (2+1)," *Chaucer Yearbook: A Journal of Late Medieval Studies*, 1 (1992) 190–212.

5. The number of portraits planned by Chaucer for the *Prologue* probably varied at different times in the development of his plan for the whole work. It might once have been as low as 14. For a discussion of

the number, see Owen, *Pilgrimage and Storytelling in the Canterbury Tales*, Norman, OK, 1977, 41–47, and "Development of the Art of Portraiture in Chaucer's *General Prologue*," *Leeds Studies in English*, N. S. 14, 1983, pp. 121–28.

6. Line I.99, "Curteis he was, lowely, and servysable," has resonance in the Friar's portrait, lines 249 f: "And over al, ther as profit sholde arise,/ Curteis he was and lowely of servyse."

7. Modern editors have tended to follow Skeat's punctuation, which puts line 172 in the preceding sentence with the gingling bridle and the chapel bell, rather than with the following sentence about the Monk's attitude toward the rule of "Seint Maure or of Seint Beneit," as Robinson does in both his editions (see also Norman Blake). In my view the gingling bridle and the chapel bell are beautifully placed in the whistling wind; localization to the Monk's cell (where in any event you would rarely find the Monk) confines and trivializes what is not intended to be literal. On the other hand, where this lord was keeper of the cell is very much to the point in the way the rule was observed. Only Donaldson has a dash after "streit." Robinson has no punctuation, making the causal clause a logical preparation for the change of subject. Donaldson's dash stresses the sudden sweeping away by the Monk of grammar, logic, and rule.

8. The use of the "mock" rhetorical question is not quite the same in the Monk's portrait and in the Manciple's. In the former the questions occur in what purports to be a statement by the narrator in a dialogue with the Monk; they expose by enthusiastic agreement the absurdity of the Monk's self-justification. In the latter there is no suggestion of dialogue. In both, the rhetorical pattern reflects and exposes the point of view of the pilgrim. The reader responds against the position implicit in this rhetorical pattern; he finds himself alert to more than the literal level of what he is reading.

Chaucer's Dainty "Dogerel"
The "Elvyssh" Prosody of Sir Thopas*

Alan T. Gaylord

"An ill-favor'd thing, Sir, but mine owne."
As You Like It (V.iv.62–63)

The humor in Chaucer's tale of *Sir Thopas* has always seemed clear enough: when called upon to tell "a tale of myrthe" in his own person, the actual poet gives the fictional poet a good bad joke at the expense of almost everyone, Chaucer included. Thus the genius of the Canterbury Way is marked as a public failure, put down and shut off by that Master of High Seriousness, Harry Bailly. And indeed, unlike other fragments, the *Thopas* seems to have been composed in order to have been interrupted. None (to adapt Dr. Johnson) ever wished it longer than it is.

In fact, few have wished to pay it close attention. Most have been willing to take on report that it parodies Middle-English tail-rhyme romances, and thereby to contemplate with amusement its general concept: a bad poem in a fashion Chaucer had no use for; a bit of clowning among friends, a bit of cunning among fools; a gem in a dunghill; a topaz with feet of lead. Its art, in other words, has been taken to stand in being so indisputably, and so obviously, bad. Close attention, at least of that sort granted to legitimate poetry, would seem to run the risk of falling into that drab category in which one explains complicatedly a simple joke. Accepting with gratitude the careful display of sources and analogues from the English romances which Laura Hibbard Loomis has provided,[1] the rest of us have

271

gone our way, relieved through the attentions of scholarship from any further critical work.

As a result, I wish to argue, we have missed the joke of jokes, and the last laugh remains to be laughed. In so exposing himself, Chaucer made himself invisible for centuries. There is, of course, a kind of poetic justice in this, for what we have been missing is invisible by nature: the eye of man hath not heard, the ear of man hath not seen, man's hand is not able to taste, nor his tongue to conceive, what this might be.[2] It is necessary, then, for us to feel, and certainly to hear, rather than to read, this transparent opacity. I refer to the meter of the poem, and the prosody of the poet.

Let us recall the extraordinary circumstances which surround the introduction of the tale, at what Charles Owen has called "the artistic crisis of the pilgrimage."[3] Everyone remembers that Harry turns his japes towards Chaucer, as for the first time, in an attempt to dispel the wonderful sobriety that the Prioress and her "myracle" have imposed on the company. And everyone enjoys his humorous attack on the plump, cuddly, but remote figure he finds in Chaucer, who must be rallied into mirth. What is often forgotten, however, is that this is the only link in all the *Canterbury Tales* not written in rhymed couplets; rather, it is in the same "rime royal" as the *Prioress' Tale*. It does not much feel like stanzas, and it certainly does not work to inspire wonder, awe, or tears, but there it is. Perhaps the link's three stanzas are indications of the potency of the Prioress' spell, but I think there is more to it than that.[4] I think Chaucer deliberately refrains from moving back into couplets, partly to increase the surprise when Thopas gallops off in an entirely different meter, and partly to make the restoration of the couplets, after the tale has been interrupted, more manifestly a return to normality—heightened, perhaps, by an appreciation of what the poet is about in his true business. For it is only in this way that Chaucer has any chance of calling attention to what is, within the most infrangible fiction of his work, the natural medium of his poetry. The couplets of the *Tales*, established in the General Prologue and sustained in the links, are the equivalent of that prose Molière's bourgeois gentleman discovers he has been speaking all his life. Insofar as Harry Bailly is concerned, Harry is only speaking—and verse has nothing to do with it. It is only when Chaucer has been put out of his profession, as it were (at the *Melibee*), that he no longer speaks in verse; and even as he prepares to obey Harry's injunction to "no lenger ryme," he is protesting in couplets.

Notice also that when Harry does break in as the second fitt is beginning, he says nothing about romances, or the reeling and writhing of the plot, or the descriptions of Sir Thopas, or the diction or the style of the preceding—in short, complains of none of the usual things critics have chosen for commentary. He has a single complaint, but it is definitive: "Myne erys aken of thy drasty speche! / Now swich a rym the devel I biteche!" He speaks *only* of the form and effect of the rhyme; he uses the same word twice, "drasty," meaning dregs, referring to wine, or meaning *faeces*, referring to excrement. Hence, "thy drasty rymyng is nat worth a tord!" And he has a category for it: "This may wel be rym dogerel!" Insofar as surviving written evidence can tell, Harry Bailly has here invented a word. Familiar, all too familiar, as its meaning and exemplars may be today, at the moment of the utterance of *Sir Thopas* it must be taken as indicating something extraordinary.

Like the presumed joke, the offending meter seems to stand out clearly: it is tail-rhyme, a very familiar form in the South and the Midlands, and one that in itself could hardly seem unusual to Harry.[5] What offends him is not the form, but its peculiar employment, so that what he condemns, in effect, is not the meter but the prosody. In other words, Chaucer's poetic practice is caricatured and then laughed out of court. But exactly what this prosody is, and what it reflects, are not so clear. There is a tendency to be misled by the subject matter into believing that simple-minded minstrels and the practice of popular poetry are the objects of the satire, but I think this view is wrong. I do not intend to re-examine in this essay the question of Chaucer's relationship to tail-rhyme romances, nor the associated problem of their reputation and critical reception. It has too long been assumed that these romances are worthy only of contempt, and that *Sir Thopas* takes them for broad and easy targets; I argue elsewhere that things are not all that simple, and that a poetic vehicle has been mistaken for its tenor.[6] But in this place, I propose to concentrate on what the prosody, attended to closely, will show or suggest about Chaucer's crafty art.[7] For the peculiar form of this verse, even in such a short fragment, has much to reveal. In losing his chance, Chaucer still makes his point. Bound up in the misadventures of a toy knight is the predicament of one expected to concoct a dainty thing upon demand. The metrical system which is exposed and exploded manages to intimate, through implicit comparisons, and by means of its context and occasion, something about the proper techniques of verse, and even about the proper aim of the poet.

Let us follow him, now, as he clambers onto his horse and starts into motion:

> Listeth lordes in good entent
> And I wil telle verrayment
>   Of myrthe and of solas—
> Al of a knyght was fair and gent
> In bataille and in tornament:
>   His name was Sir Thopas.
> Yborn he was in fer contree,
> In Flaundres al biyonde the see
>   At Poperyng in the place.
> His fader was a man ful free,
> And lord he was of that contree
>   As it was Goddes grace.[8]

(VII.1902–13)

Contrary to the way modern editors print these lines, I have run two stanzas together to show how Chaucer has begun with an approximation of conventional twelve-line tail-rhyme romance stanza—where the short lines carry the same rhyme four times. Even here, however, the second set is not a perfect match, for it is clear that we have a final-*e* sounding in "grace" and "place" but not in "Thopas" and "solas."[9] There seems very little chance that this is a result of scribal carelessness, for there are other signs of deliberate arrangements, as in the surprising rhyme of "gent/tornament," where there can be no question of final-*e*, along with what we might call the minstrel-rhyme of "entent/verrayment"—where Chaucer uses an old Anglo-Norman adverb (and only in this place), along with a spelling of "entent" that is unusual for him. From this point on, the rhyme will change for the short line every six lines; even though there is a general stanza-sense, or even paragraph-sense every twelve lines, the six-line units stand enough on their own to show us that Chaucer is imitating, yet also condensing, the romance-stanza.

The point about final-*e*'s has great prosodic significance. Although there is little debate these days as to whether they may be sounded in Chaucer's verse, there is general agreement that final-*e*'s had disappeared from standard speech and written prose, so the extent to which the poet employed them prosodically is not certain. Now, here in the *Thopas*, we see how conscious Chaucer is of the "*-e*" as optional device for spacing and timing his prosodic effects, playfully exaggerating their use by nonce-spellings and rhythmical emphases. We might say that final-*e*'s are the springs of the rocking horse.

Notice that the six-line stanza breaks into two halves, with lines *aab* using very few marked caesuras. Even the end-word is designed to fit into the next line—hence a strong lift as in "good entént," "verraymént," "fair and gént," "tornamént," "fer contrée" "biyonde the sée," "man ful frée," followed—in a large number of instances—by an unstressed word beginning with a vowel, in the next line; hence: "entent / and Í," "verrayment / Of myrth," "and gent / In bátaille," "tornament / (H)is náme," and so forth. After this opening, almost every subsequent short-line rhyme includes a final-*e*—a device, I think, of cadence or closure.[10]

The overriding impression one gains from this first stanza is of a Maker who has suddenly regressed into nursery rhyme; the *underriding* effect, so to speak, is a comic monotony of metrical pace. The beginning establishes a go-ahead rhythm, with little variation. The stresses occur regularly and forcefully, and what few substitutions appear (as in the first two trochees in "listeth lordes in good entent") allow the medial sense of accelerating anapaests. Also at the start, these sharply articulated stanzas may seem to suggest a logical order, gaining emphasis from the rhyme words, meant to accompany a firm narrative progression. By way of emphatic example, we can compare some lines from an extraordinary prosodic melodrama which, though not using tail-rhyme, does press anapaests into the service of what Americans would call "Paul-Revere meter." For Browning knew how to leap into the saddle and stay there to the end:

> I sprang to the stirrup, and Joris, and he;
> I galloped, Dirck galloped, we galloped all three;
> 'Good speed!' cried the watch, as the gate-bolts undrew;
>
> 'Speed !' echoed the wall to us galloping through;
> Behind shut the postern, the lights sank to rest,
> And into the midnight we galloped abreast.
>
>   * * * *
>
> Then I cast loose my buffcoat, each holster let fall,
> Shook off both my jack-boots, let go belt and all,
> Stood up in the stirrup, leaned, patted his ear,
> Called my Roland his pet-name, my horse without peer;
> Clapped my hands, laughed and sang, any noise, bad or
>   good,
> Till at length into Aix Roland galloped and stood.[11]

Here is no meter for rambling about in distractedly, for backing and filling, or for slowing down and speeding up: it has someplace to go, it gets there, and it delivers "good news from Ghent." Whereas Sir Thopas, after going "wood" in the wood with love, dashes about until:

> His fayre steede in his prikynge
> So swatte that men myghte hym wrynge,
>   His sydes were al blood.

(VII.1965–67)

Which leads to neither ogre nor fair lady, but to exhaustion:

> Sir Thopas eek so wery was
> For prikyng on the softe gras,
>   So fiers was his corrage,
> That doun he leyde hym in the plas[12]
> To make his steede som solas,
>   And yaf hym good forage.

(VII.1968–73)

As far as we can tell, he may only have been careening heatedly in circles. He needs rest, suddenly; and his horse—for all the grass about—gets a bucket of dry oats (from where?). The old saw applies, that this is perspiration without inspiration.

And so it goes: *Sir Thopas* is a tale that gallops about without ever really arriving. Everyone has noticed and enjoyed the bathos of anticlimax which lines can fall into, such as:

> Yborn he was in fer contree,
> In Flaundres al biyonde the see
>   At Poperyng in the place;

(VII.1908–10)

where "in fer contree" makes us think, if not of Lohengrin, at least of far-off lands in Greece or Asia Minor; but suddenly "al biyonde the see" is not the Mediterranean, but the Channel, and we are in flat, familiar Flanders, standing in the prosaic town of Poperyng.

This is verse, I have already said, that is slightly distorted from, and accelerated beyond, its models, and we have Harry Bailly's outrage to remind us that the mirror is crazy. He has recognized nothing—nothing!—in it that he likes. If few of us would appoint Harry as our tutor in mirth, he serves to remind us that Chaucer has been less popular or apparently entertaining than he started out to be, so that it will take a closer attention than Harry's to determine if there has been hidden, in plain sight, more than meets the eye.[13] The way for us to proceed, then, is to inspect certain further examples that seem humorous enough to warrant revisiting, noting the base of their humor, and then inquiring what we have not yet accounted for.

Let us look, first, at that *effictio* which rises out of romance diction, and reads in part:

> Sir Thopas wax a doghty swayn:
> Whit was his face as payndemayn,
>   His lippes reed as rose,
> His rode is lyk scarlet in grayn,
> And I yow telle in good certayn
>   He hadde a semely nose.

(VII.1914–19)

The "doghty" is a basic element in the conventional romance-kit, not otherwise much used by Chaucer, but what follows is all wrong, of course, because too pretty. These are lady-words for our hero, who stands out as a blushing doll of a child, even as the rhetoric rises solemnly to the feminine decorum of his nose.

His looks, however, are no bar to his masculinity. At least, we are told that:

> Ful many mayde bright in bour,
> They moorne for him *par amour*,
>   Whan hem were bet to slepe.

(VII.1932–34)

That is a basic datum, but since these damsels make no appearance, we are left to imagine them, brightly languishing in their bowers—presumably with bags under their sleepless eyes (line 1934 is one the goose from *The Parliament of Fowls* ought to approve).

Sir Thopas leaves on his quest—we are not told why—and begins an aimless campaign of pricking here and pricking there:

> He priketh thurgh a fair forest
> Therinne is many a wilde best,
>   Ye, bothe bukke and hare.

(VII.1944–46)

The "pricking" is a perfectly normal verb to ride out from the romances, yet one that obviously tickled Chaucer. The problem of its repetition when speaking of knights must have been comparable to the problem of whether to repeat, or vary, the use of "he said," when writing conversation. "Pricking" is what mounted knights do, and Thopas does it and does it, through the ferocious forests of Flanders, filled with savage rabbits.

So much pricking wearies him, but after a rest and a dream of Fairyland, he sets out again:

> Into his sadel he clamb anoon
> And priketh over style and stoon,
>   An Elf queene for t'espye.

(VII.1987–89)

Perhaps the meter has established sufficient up-and-down motion by now to guide us without question over those fences, but the image of horse and rider clambering over a stile is piquant; and equally attractive is the image of Thopas alert to bag *an* Elf queen, as if there were more than one lurking in the woods.

Once into Fairyland, Thopas encounters the obligatory giant, whose three-headedness is either part of his nature or our hero's imagination after-the-fact (since it is not mentioned at their first meeting). The giant, Sir Elephant,[14] says some discouraging words, and then:

> Sire Thopas drow abak ful faste.
> This geant at hym stones caste
> Out of a fel staf-slynge,
> But faire escapeth child Thopas,
> And al it was thurgh Goddes graas[15]
> And thurgh his fair berynge!

(VII.2017–22)

Goliath out-Davids David, who retreats to fortify himself. It is not a foul, but a "faire" escape, we are told, and "Thopas" now rhymes with "Goddes graas." One may note how much action is enclosed within this stanza—indeed, virtually sealed from view—as it gallops to its sententious ending in the short line, equating "fair berynge" with a clean pair of heels.

Once home, Thopas orders an accompaniment of "game and glee" (2030), and begins to arm himself. But first there must be sweets for the sweet. The meter leaves the field of battle and surveys the menu:

> They fette hym first the swete wyn,
> And mede eek in a maselyn,
> And real spicerye—
> Of gyngebred that was ful fyn,
> And lycorys, and eek comyn
> With sugre that is trye.

(VII.2041–46)

The stanza exemplifies much of the overall diction: child Thopas is a knight of Marzipan, a sugared dainty who smells good himself, rides through fragrant fields, and likes his "mede" in a "maselyn."[16] The meter has been refined in the refiner's fire, and comes out "sugre that is trye."

And now, fully comfited and accommodated with all he needs, from fine linen underwear to armor-plate, Thopas stands and makes a mighty vow:

> And there he swoor on ale and breed
> How that the geant shal be deed,
>   Bityde what bityde.

(VII.2062–64)

It is hard to make a solemn vow in tail-rhyme. The homeliness of "ale and breed," nicely mouthfilling though it be, sinks into bathos as it follows the accounting of "real spicerye." And the helpless banality of that tag-of-tags, "bityde what bityde," turns the sword of eloquence into a wet noodle.[17]

These are some, but only some, of the things that make *Sir Thopas* so obviously funny. Without a strong presumption of regularity of stress, the syncopation of sound and sense could not be so slyly entertaining. Without the external rhyme and the internal alliteration, the clarifications would not be so consistently confounded, the emphases so regularly misplaced. Without the pattern of the stanza, the narrative would not seem half so willfully coherent while helplessly disjunct. And without that meter, the surprises and the pratfalls would lose their timing, and the homely words of popular poetry would not so abruptly trip and tumble from their horses. No bad poet could achieve this kind of bad poetry.

There are even moments when the verse becomes strikingly attractive, achieving what Loomis calls "unexpected grace" (*SA* 487). The description of Thopas-the-chaste somewhat exceeds formula to bloom pleasantly:

> But he was chaast and no lechour,
> And sweete as is the brambel flour
>   That bereth the rede hepe;

(VII.1935–37)

while in the description of the Elf queen's court, the jogtrot is temporarily becalmed:

> Here is this queene of Fairye,
> With harpe and pipe and symphonye,
>   Dwellyng in this place.[18]

(VII.2004–06)

And for that matter, the lines about the spices and sweet drinks brought to Thopas are pleasant to hear, and rather exquisite poetry, silly as they may finally seem: if this is burlesque, it belongs more to the world of Oberon than of Bottom.

Beyond the little graces of sound and image, the meter itself does not simply and predictably rise and fall throughout. It also bobs. With no warning or apparent reason, something new is added:

> An Elf queene wol I have, ywys,
> For in this world no womman is,
>   Worthy to be my make,
>   In towne.
> Alle othere wommen I forsake
> And to an Elf queene I me take,
>   By dale and eke by downe.

(VII.1980–86)

Suddenly the horse, in full stride, pauses, pivots gracefully on one hoof, changes direction, and goes off at another tangent. The stanza does not so much wobble as flow around a corner. The three lines that follow the bob, "in towne," seem to reassert the shape, except that the rhyme scheme is out of kilter, with 1984–85 taking the rhyme from short-line 1982, and short-line 1986 rhyming with the bob.

The next stanza plays with our expectations, for the bob is delayed until the second three-line strophe appears:

> Into his sadel he clamb anoon
> And priketh over style and stoon,
>   An Elf queene for t'espye,
> Til he so longe hath riden & goon
> That he foond in a pryvee woon

> The contree of Fairye,
>   So wilde.
> For in that contree was ther noon,
>   Neither wyf ne childe.[19]

(VII.1987–94, 1996)

In this case, the rhyme scheme of the closing lines does not parallel that of the first bob-stanza. We have four bob-stanzas in a row, and the handling of the pivot is varied; the fourth time the bob appears it is not an additional ending, but a new beginning:

> The child seyde, "Al so mote I thee,
> Tomorwe wil I meete thee
>   Whan I have myn armoure.
> And yet I hope, *par ma fay*,
> That thow shalt with this launcegay
>   Abyene it ful sowre!
>   Thy mawe
> Shal I percen, if I may,
> Er it be fully pryme of day,
>   For here shaltow ben slawe!"[20]

(VII.2007–16)

The poem returns to normal, so to speak, for four more stanzas.[21] But the poet has one departing caper which follows:

> His spere was of fyn cipres
> That bodeth werre and no thyng pes,
>   The heed ful sharpe ygrounde.
> His steede was al dappel gray,
> It goth an ambel in the way
>   Ful softely and rounde
>   In londe.
> Lo, lordes myne, here is a Fit!
> If ye wole any more of it,
>   To telle it wol I fonde.

(VII.2071–80)

The bob now serves very nicely as a rounding-off, capping a previous section, and allowing the final unit to announce a semicoda. On the whole, then, the bob has worked well, even though its appearance is surprising and unusual.[22] Chaucer had virtually no models for this practice, unless he studied the somewhat similar stanza form of *Sir Tristrem*,[23] and the end result is to exaggerate further the mechanisms of poetry: for the bob is manifestly a device, arbitrary and clever, which calls attention to itself as Chaucer puts it in and leaves it out. It is not at all clumsy, and does not provide evidence of Chaucer's helpless mnemonics, even though it obviously fails to charm Harry. It is, indeed, a break in the regularity of the verse, and yet not one that restores the poem to the natural modulations of the speaking voice. For it is musical and metrical, and adds to the "daintiness" of the poet's production.

Looked at closely, then, the verse often provokes ambivalent responses. What seems luxuriously "bad" from one perspective, seems brilliantly "good" from another. This has not been said often enough for the *Thopas*. For example, the passage dealing with Thopas' arming hardly strikes me as "tedious" (a term those critics have used who prefer plot to poetry), and has wonderful moments like:

> His sadel was of rewel bon,
> His brydel as the sonne shon
> Or as the moone light;

> (VII.2068–70)

where the walrus-ivory alternately glitters or glimmers, as the poet flips the formulaic shades to let in or keep out the light, all the time providing a pleasing flow of sounds and a carefully spelled-out ("bon / shon," "moonë"), well regulated meter.

It is this evidence of polish and of care that may be remarked throughout. Even the matter of "formulaic writing" is artistically handled, and imitated only up to a point. I have already mentioned words, phrases, and elements that bespeak popular poetry, and which are to be widely discovered in all sorts of works and authors. And yet a close study of the copious lists of formulas compiled by Albert C. Baugh from metrical romances of "the matter of England"[24] suggests that Chaucer has consistently availed himself of very little of what is common and predictable in such works as *Guy of Warwick* and *Beves of Hampton*; and a further study of the sources of romance commonplaces compiled by Loomis from almost forty English romances, especially of those places she has emphasized with her italics, leads to the conclusion that, although Chaucer was highly aware of poetic and conventional diction, he was still absolutely in control. He is not building up a pastiche from—say—the notes he took while leafing through the Auchinleck MS.,[25] but is, rather, *gesturing* towards a kind of poetic effect which came with an English birthright. A keen ear, an attentive eye, a seasoned taste, a good memory, and a sense of humor—but no particular texts, particularly opened—were all he needed to construct his "rym."

   Let us go from this towards a summary of what we have, or have not, come to.

   We have contemplated the compulsive behavior of a meter, which carries everything before it. Regularity has been its most remarkable feature, far exceeding that of its relatives on the other side of seriousness. That regularity is responsible for a certain underlurch and overdrone, which suppress some of the normal variety and distinctive humanity of the narrator's voice. The meter rises to epic announcements, and sinks to nonsense. It seems always to be riding towards a meaning, a revelation, a climactic moment, and yet losing its way. It pops in and out of Fairyland, but never sees the Queen. It puts on all its artifices and armor, without being allowed to accomplish anything in poetry, love, or war. In effect, it is overwrought: full of nervous energy and artful elaboration, but always missing the point.

   Thus far, we might have expected as much from a poet who likes to make fun of his own artistic pretensions, and from a poetic offering in the midst of a fragment where the succession of light/heavy, grave/merry, ernest/game, and *sentence/solaas* has been made the subject of the links and the modality of their alternating tales.[26] And if Harry Bailly is the final judge, its most dismal failure concerns its inability to entertain. It was charged to be mirthful (1896), promised to tell "of myrthe and of solas" (1904), and then was aborted as a painful imposition on the company: "thow doost noght ellis but despendest tyme," complains Harry—a remark unwittingly appropriate to his condemnation of the meter. But suppose—and it is not hard to suppose—we might not wish to take Harry as the final judge: what should we say, then, about what Chaucer has done? In such a case, I should like to submit that close attention will discover that Chaucer, in an exceptionally playful and oblique manner, has given us ample measure of both *sentence* AND *solaas*.

Let us recall that extraordinary word that Harry attaches to Chaucer's appearance: "He semeth *elvyssh* by his contenance" (1893). Why should this be so appropriate for Chaucer? Harry seems to use it to imply "otherworldly," i.e., "not one of us"— abstracted and distracted, staring at the ground, wrapped up in himself, not quite social: "for unto no wight dooth he daliance" (1894). If we keep only this implied definition in mind, then the *Thopas* is itself an "elvyssh" tale, not because it deals with elves, but because, failing to touch the common note, it alienates the others.

Most readers, however, find it impossible to conceive of Chaucer as a timid introvert. The man who begins the General Prologue by reporting, "and shortly, whan the sonne was to reste, / So hadde I spoken with hem everichon / That I was of hir felaweshipe anon" (A30–32), may not be loudly overbearing, but neither is he shyly retiring. It seems more likely that Harry has caught him in a brown study like everyone else, for when the Prioress had finished, "every man / As sobre was, that wonder was to se" (1881–82). But we may also notice that Harry makes an association that seems arbitrary enough to betray some ulterior motive of the poet: as Chaucer is about to begin his recital of the "rym I lerned longe agoon," Harry chuckles, "Ye, that is good. . . . Now shul we heere / Som deyntee thyng, me thynketh by his cheere" (1900–01). Now "deyntee" implies not only a delicacy, but a rare delicacy, something elaborate, carefully made, crafted for delight. For some reason, Harry thinks Chaucer looks like someone who will make something oddly special—which is, of course, exactly what Chaucer does, to Harry's consternation.

Harry may have been condescending to this roly-poly alter-ego of his, but the association of "deyntee" with "elvyssh" is not untoward. If we look to see how the latter word is used elsewhere by Chaucer, we will find that it makes an interesting connection between the fairies, strangeness, and craft. Let us not be misled by the holiday meter into thinking that Chaucer is some pre-version of Clement C. Moore's "right jolly old elf, so lively and quick": elves in Chaucer's day were more dangerous than quaint, more infernal than amusing. Proserpine who lives in Hell is the Queen of Fairies [*Merchant's Tale*], and it has been the Friars' peculiar grace, with their prayers and dubious presence, to exorcise them from the land, where they had been pestilent [*Wife of Bath's Tale*]. But the implication was always that they were underground and very nearly infernal, oppressive spirits.[27] We do not need to stop for a disquisition on the place of Fairye in Chaucer's work, intriguing as that subject may be, for it is clear enough how he understands the more general adjective, "elvyssh." He only uses the term one other place, in *The Canon's Yeoman's Tale*, in speaking of the hermetic craft of alchemy:

> Whan we been there as we shul exercise
> Oure elvysshe craft, we semen wonder wise,
> Oure termes been so clergial and so queynte.[28]

(VII.750–52)

He is describing a dark and obsessed community, of the type to live "in the suburbes of a toun . . . lurkynge in hernes and in lanes blynde, / Whereas thise robbours and thise theves by kynde / Holden hir pryvee fereful residence" (657–60); their habitat is filled with the reek of brimstone and the fiery furnace, which the Yeoman repeatedly characterizes as hellish (916–17). "Elvysshe," then, combines the associations of the hellish-fairy with those of dark and dangerous mystery—as the associated terms "clergial" and "queynte" suggest. Their activities, that is, are infernally strange. Note also that "elvysshe" is related to "craft" which is related to a book-learning that exceeds the comprehension of normal men. The idea is repeated later:

> Though he sitte at his book bothe day and nyght
> In lernyng of this elvysshe nyce loore,
> Al is in veyn.

(VII.840–42)

This lore is foolish, or "nyce," not only because it is obscure and darkly occult, but also because it does nothing but ruin its practitioners:

> We blondren evere and pouren in the fir,
> And for al that we faille of oure desir,
> For evere we lakken oure conclusioun.

(VII.670–72)

"Conclusioun" is an alchemical word, referring to the achievement of the philosopher's stone, the power to "multiply" grosser materials into gold, and the consequent attainment of god-like wisdom and certitude. But it is a word, of course, capable of wider extensions. For is not *Sir Thopas* an elvish tale told by an elvish rhymer who cannot come to "conclusioun"? Is not the topaz a gem somewhat less than the philosopher's stone? Is not the tale a glittering which is not gold? In other words, has not Chaucer exercised his craft, strangely and wonderfully, in bringing us to a brilliant confusion? Has he not marshalled all the materials of that craft, common things, known to all—rhyme, meter, alliteration, diction, theme, and image—and brought them together in a way that is only strangely similar to what we have seen before? Are not those resemblances alienated and alienating, do not they make us conscious, to the point either of laughter or perplexity, of the tension between entertainment and instruction, familiarity and novelty, formula and surprise, trivial ornament and significant structure?

One sees, then, that the first joke is as it always is in Chaucer, that his wit should seem short and his art negligible. The second joke, however, goes farther and deeper. It is his own arranging, after all, that puts him on the spot before the pilgrims. But just as medieval scholastics knew that it was impossible for God to will a contradiction, so Chaucer could not proceed to tell a tale in his own person which would seem to compete, or even bear comparison, with the creations of those creators he himself has created. On the other hand, just as the Knight tells about chivalry, the Miller about lechery, and the Prioress about piety, so could Chaucer tell about poetry. And like all good poets, his telling is a showing: thus, his prosody is a way-of-doing what is significant.

It is the "elvyssh" prosody that illuminates and dramatizes the extremes that Chaucer had to navigate safely throughout his career. A topaz is a royal stone, the second gem on Aaron's breastplate,[29] and the romance is the form which is most "poetic" for a court poet. Yet the royal romance, like a royal society, was always in danger of degenerating from nobility to trite gentility, from intensity to frivolity, from exemplary probity to fashionable frippery. If it could be an instrument for enlarging the imagination, and for instructing, through the delights of fiction, noble hearts in their office, it could just as easily be called upon to provide "gamen and glee," diversion for the bored, or a kind of mental embroidery for the petty and shallow. (It is interesting to see how the exhaustion of romance is expressed in those works—most notably, but not exclusively, *The Squire's Tale*— which are not finished; and how that predicament is reflected in the interrupted *Thopas*.) Thus do we see the "royal" Sir Thopas shrink to a jabbering dwarf, the *childe* Thopas (in the antique sense of a young warrior) become a toddler amidst the green grass and the nutmeg, and the potential David take flight from a giant with a slingshot. The comic miniaturization has its moral aspects, but we must be careful not to promote the teller of *Thopas* into a Faustus or an Orpheus. The Prioress has wept large tears; now Chaucer, pattering behind, slips and falls, and finds he must try to keep afloat in what turns out to be only a flood of sugar-water. It is the Fancy, not the Imagination, which guides his strokes.

Chaucer is no more "mocking" romance, however, than the Nun's Priest is mocking epic. Both poems are in some measure about the poetic craft, about true rhetoric and false, and about the tension between ornamentation and sincerity. What saves the Nun's Priest from sinking into bathos or exploding with pompous gas is a rueful and reflexively applied sense of absurdity; and his tale is only saved to deliver its *moralitee* because mother-wit prevails. At least the erring ego can redeem itself by that: by revealing the egotism that disables even the cleverest dissimulator. Beware of flattery, says the Nun's Priest—and his tale whispers between the lines, *especially of oneself*.

If the Nun's Priest does not mock epic, his tale is *a* mock-epic—of the self-stellifying poetic ingenium. Is the *Thopas* a mock-romance? What would the term, by analogy with mock-epic, mean? If there are such things as epic pretensions, are there also romance pretensions? I should think there are, and that they would have something to do with the hero in love—carried away by his longing, questing into Fairyland where the Queen awaits his perfect heart. It would be impossible by Chaucer's day not to sense the metaphor in, the allegory behind, such a formulation. The danger of confusing the goal, or of losing the way, or of dissolving into the mirror of Narcissus, would be grave enough for any lover; but the metaphor points directly to the Maker. "Romance pretensions" refer to the imagined prowess of the poet of romance.

It is the essence of romance to undertake a Quest. Chaucer sends out Sir Thopas, who pricks toward Fairyland. But if in that "wilde" country there is a vision to see, good news to bring, or tidings to receive, both rider and writer fail to find them. The prosody suggests, as a caricature of all poetry with a set way of proceeding, that to be stiff in the saddle is to invite a fall. Indeed, riding rigidly—if with excellent style—towards a fixed goal may develop tunnel vision without ever delivering one to the Grail, let alone the giant or the queen. And it is even possible that much truth lies short of the horizon and anterior to the last great castle, just as there may be much to see before getting to Canterbury. Let others describe the raptures of the Beatific Vision, others seek an enchanted land. Chaucer stares at the ground. He listens to the company.

It is appropriate, then, that he should master a form, the tail-rhyme, which epitomizes the mingling and confusing of royal romance with the popular idiom, French wine with English sprouts. He is, after all, a poet, and he can master what he chooses. So he makes his first point, rocking compulsively away on a form so diverting that it is distracting. Here, he has played the poet-who-would-if-he-could; now, as Harry Bailly rears on his high horse, Chaucer turns back into the poet-who-does-what-he-will:

> "Namoore of this, for Goddes dignytee,"
> Quod oure Hoost, "for thow makest me
> So wery of thy verray lewednesse
> That, also wisly God my soule blesse,

Myne erys aken of thy drasty speche!
Now swich a rym the devel I biteche!³⁰

(VII.2109–14)

The return of couplets is a return to fresh air, and now, after the
Thopas, everything seems in sharper focus, more immediate and
brimming with life. We are shocked loose from burlesque, and
hauled back into the comedy. Harry's sputterings are the very
stuff of obstreperous humanity. Even as his speech surges past
line-ends, pauses, gesticulating, at caesuras, stomps in iambic
distress through rhymed couplets, in order to condemn utterly
Chaucer's credentials as a poet, so are we assured that our Poet
is once again free and functioning—as invisible but as potent as a
clear thought in a crystal cave.

NOTES

*Reprinted with permission from *Studies in the Age of Chaucer* I, ed. Roy
J. Pearcy (Norman, OK: Pilgrim Books, 1979) pp. 83–104.

1. Laura Hibbard Loomis, "Sir Thopas," in *Sources and Analogues
of Chaucer's* Canterbury Tales, ed. W. F. Bryan and Germaine Dempster
(The Univ. of Chicago Press, 1941), pp. 496–559.

2. But I will not follow Bottom, and say that man is but an ass, if
he go about to expound it; *MND*, IV.i.226–32.

3. Charles A. Owen, Jr., "Thy Drasty Rymyng . . . ," *SP*, 63 (1966),
540; this is virtually the only place where the prosody of the *Thopas* has
received close attention.

4. I shall argue elsewhere (in "The 'Miracle' of Sir Thopas?") that
the *Thopas* is also intended as a riposte to *The Prioress' Tale*: a difficult
and controversial line to follow. I think that Chaucer extends the
"influence" of *The Prioress' Tale* all the way through the link of the
Thopas, and then "quits" the "miracle" of "this gemme of chastite, this
emeraude, / And eek of martirdom the ruby bright" (B²1799–1800) with
the miraculous adventures of his own topazius of chastity. Naturally,
such presumption is punished, even though no one seems to have
noticed the crime.

5. The essential, and unsuperseded, monograph on the subject is A. McI. Trounce, "The English Tail-Rhyme Romances," *MÆ*, I (1932), 87–108, 168–82; II (1933), 34–57, 189–98; III (1934), 30–50. He wishes to defend not just some of the romances, but the form itself, which could act "as a spur to the imagination, since it had to be written in a lively fashion if it was to succeed at all" (I: 106). His examination of the stanza form is at I: 168–82. A more recent survey, Dieter Mehl, *The Middle English Romances of the Thirteenth and Fourteenth Centuries* (London: Routledge & Kegan Paul, 1969), acknowledges the work of Trounce, but spends little time on prosodic analysis of the tail-rhyme stanza; cf. pp. 55, 77, 81–82, 94, 100, 148, 173–75, 212—these contain only brief summaries of the character of tail-rhyme in individual romances. On the other hand, the more recent study of Velma Bourgeois Richmond, *The Popularity of Middle English Romances* (Bowling Green Univ. Popular Press, 1975) ignores metrical analysis altogether, conceding the slight literary merit of the verses, and attempts to defend the romances on sociological, thematic, and ethical grounds.

6. "The Moment of *Sir Thopas*: A New Look at Chaucer's Language," (forthcoming).

7. For a review of prosodic criticism of Chaucer in general, with some particular connections to the *Thopas*, along with definitions and methodological suggestions, see my "Scanning the Prosodists: An Essay in Metacriticism," *ChauR*, II (1976), 22–82.

8. I have lightly edited from, and provided modern punctuation for, the Hengwrt (or Peniarth) MS. as reproduced in *A Six-Text Print of Chaucer's* Canterbury Tales, ed. Frederick J. Furnivall, The Chaucer Society, Part III (London: Trubner, 871), pp. 190–200.

9. The scribe of the Corpus Christi MS. (1410–20) who may also have been the scribe of the Egerton MS. of Gower's *Confessio Amantis*, regularized this phenomenon by trading absurdities; hence, "solace," but "sire Thopace."

10. One interesting exception occurs at lines 2067/2070, short lines with "bright" and "light"—these are, respectively, adjective and noun, and Chaucer does not add -e's that do not exist; whereas with short lines 2031/2034, "fighte" and "brighte," he may retain the old final-e for infinitive and adverb (or feminine adjective: "Of oon that shoon ful brighte"). And I assume the latter are disyllabic.

11. "'How They Brought the Good News from Ghent to Aix'," in *Browning: Poetical Works 1833–1864*, ed. Ian Jack, London: Oxford Univ. Press, 1970), pp. 413, 414–15, lines 1–6, 49–54.

12. Note the careful, but exceptional, rhyme scheme, where "place" (cf. 1910) is now "plas," etc. I assume both "softe" and "steede" are disyllabic, for metrical reasons. "Corrage / forage" is a happy bump of rhyme.

13. I have discussed the function of Harry Bailly as critic, representative audience, and unwitting "guide to the interior" in my "*Sentence* and *Solaas* in Fragment VII of the *Canterbury Tales*: Harry Bailly as Horseback Editor," *PMLA*, 82 (1967), 226–35.

14. Thus translating, "His name was sire Olifaunt" (1998); but why could he not be named after Roland's famous hunting horn, of the triple blasts?

15. Note that the Hengwrt scribe is unique in the spelling, "graas," presumably to distinguish the word here from that "softe gras" (1969) on which Thopas earlier lay; the scribe refrained, at least, from writing the normal grace. Only the Petworth scribe, in the Six-Text display, bumbles into "Thopas / grace"—though undoubtedly the *-e* was not pronounced.

16. When he is "in town," that is; when he is "auntrous," he drinks water from the well. If he is a Franklin at home, he is a Percival on the road.

17. The only other time the phrase shows up in Chaucer is in the *Troilus*, used by Criseyde (V.750) but it is appropriate in her mouth, for she has been reciting proverbs to herself and reaching for homely truths in colloquial speech.

18. These lines are also situated exactly in the middle of the poem, which may argue some calculated care on Chaucer's part.

19. Although the last lines make sense, modern editors follow the less authoritative mss in adding a line 1995, "that to him durste or goon," which looks forward to the coming of Sir Elephant, and so makes a symmetrical three-line unit after the bob. The emendation is logical enough, but the argument of regularity is dangerous. Without the "restored line" the stanza is unique, and yet the other bob-stanzas are not all alike, except in total number of lines. At this juncture, however, almost any variation could be rationalized; and the evidence of the early mss is persuasive. Manly prints the revision, yet notes, "The irregularity of the stanza without it hardly justifies us in accepting it"; John M. Manly and Edith Rickert, *The Text of the* Canterbury Tales, IV (Univ. of Chicago Press, 1940), 499.

20. Note the near-rhymes in the stanza, the bogus *rime-riche* "thee" in line with "fay / -gay, related sounds Chaucer does not usually pair, since one is a single long-vowel, and the other a diphthong; note also

the sly rhyming of "armoure" with "sowre. *Sourly* will work, but is unusual; sorely would be the more common, and expected, word to follow "abyen it."

21. Except that the rhymes of the long-lines in the first "regular" stanza to follow are not exact "faste / caste / Thopas / gras." Chaucer will sometimes make both pairs of the long lines rhyme together, sometimes not, or sometimes make them "near."

22. As amusing corroboration, there exist the scribes' floundering attempts to respond to the novelty of the bob-line. Many mss show the bobs left out altogether; some run them into the previous line, separated by some kind of mark; and the more successful set the bobs out at the far right of the margin to stand alone (the Ellesmere MS. does this in confident, bravura fashion). Cf. E. G. Stanley, art. cit. below, pp. 419–21. I have looked over the Ad,[3] Ha[2], Ha[3], Ha[4], La, and Ry[2] mss of the *CT* in the British Museum, not for any definitive textual news, but to explore the physical solutions to the registering of verse forms which various scribes devised. In every case but Ad[3], the bob is so clumsily handled as to be disfigured or destroyed. With its complexity of structure and its unusual spellings, the *Thopas* is clearly the greatest challenge Chaucer threw out to the race of scribes: "and al is thorugh . . . negligence and rape"!

23. Here is a sample of the Tristrem stanza:

2245 Over Temes sche schuld ride,
   That is an arm of the se:
   "To the schip side
   This man schal bere me!"
   Tristrem hir bar that tide
2250 And on the quen fel he,
   Next her naked side,
   That mani man might yse
   San schewe:
   Hir queynt aboven hir kne
   Naked the knightes knewe.

(Ed. Kolbing, *Die . . . Version der Tristan-Sage: II. Sir Tristrem*, p. 62.) It is romance/epic boiled down to proto-ballad, enormously simplified from the rhetorical displays of Thomas or the passionate ironies of Gottfried, and offers little beyond the one-stress bob, set against the three-stress quatrains *abab*, to have commanded Chaucer's attention. In fact, I find it hard to imagine that this gigantic dwarf of a romance could have been anything Chaucer saw, reacted to, or used. There were undoubtedly many other more sophisticated examples of the bob at hand, and not just in northern literature, which have not survived. The fullest survey of the extant body of Middle English verse containing bob-lines is E. G. Stanley, "The Use of Bob-Lines in *Sir Thopas*," *NM* 73 (1972), 417–26. He emphasizes the "bathos and vapidity" of the bob-lines, perhaps without taking into adequate account the audience's complicity: if the Thopas is a clog-dance, it is a clog-dance danced by a genius. Furthermore, his tables suggest another area of "popular verse" Chaucer might more easily have remembered for bob-effects: the English cycle plays. In the Towneley Creation, for example, God the Father speaks in a form which employs a bob.

24. "Improvisation in the Middle English Romances," *Proceedings of the American Philosophical Society*, 103 (1959), 418–54. As just one example: it is delicious that Chaucer nowhere rhymes on "knight" in the *Thopas*; cf. Baugh, pp. 428–30.

25. I do not mean to exclude the possibility that Chaucer had studied either the Auchinleck MS., or its exemplar, or some close relative no longer extant. But we have perhaps not responded to the strong work of Loomis with appropriate attention: see Laura Hibbard Loomis, "Chaucer and the Auchinleck MS: 'Thopas' and 'Guy of Warwick,'" in *Essays and Studies in Honor of Carleton Brown* (New York Univ. Press, 1940), pp. 111–28. Her central thesis is that "*Guy of Warwick* and, to a less extent, *Libeaus Desconus*, were, of the romances named, unquestionably, his chief 'sources,' as from these he culled much of the phraseology and several of the narrative motifs used in Thopas" (*SA*, pp. 487–88). "Sources" needs more than one set of quote-marks, and "culled" implies a theory of composition that is naive. I argue this further in my forthcoming essay, "The Moment of *Sir Thopas*: A New Look at Chaucer's Language."

26. See my previously cited "*Sentence* and *Solaas* in Fragment VII."

27. For more on the "derknesse" of Fairye, see James F. Knapp, "The Meaning of *Sir Orfeo*," *MLQ*, 29 (1968), 263–73.

28. *The Works of Geoffrey Chaucer*, ed. F. N. Robinson, 2nd ed. (Boston: Houghton Mifflin, 1957), p. 215.

29. Interpretations of the name and symbolism of Thopas tend to fix too quickly on a single attribute; for a broader review of possibilities, see John Conley, "The Peculiar Name *Thopas*," *SP*, 73 (1976), 42–61. See also the variety of lapidaries printed in Joan Evans and Mary S. Serjeantson, eds., *English Mediaeval Lapidaries*, EETS, 190 (London, 1933).

30. Robinson, p. 167.

"Parlous Play"
Diabolic Comedy in Chaucer's Canterbury Tales

Robert W. Hanning

The aim of these remarks is to explore the presence of a "diabolic" element in many of the comic narratives of Chaucer's *Canterbury Tales (C T)*. The devil figures in person in one tale *Friar's Tale (FrT)* and is vividly evoked by the narrator (e.g., *Summoner's Tale [SumT]*, *Canon's Yeoman's Tale [CYT]*) or a character (e.g., *Miller's Tale [MillT]*) in others; but this is not to be a survey of allusions. I propose rather to suggest how comic actions within various tales approximate or reflect a diabolic "discourse" (comprising both language and behavior) inscribed within late medieval European culture as the result of a synthesis between theological understandings of the Devil and comedic or festive elments of popular culture. In England, as elsewhere, this synthesis achieved a particularly lively and influential development in pre-Reformation vernacular religious and moral drama and it was, I believe, in large part through Chaucer's exposure to the drama—especially the cycle drama developing briskly in his day—that diabolic discourse, suitably adapted to the poet's larger interests, comes to play a considerable role in several of the *CT*.

How does the Devil get to be a focus for comic impulses and energies in an age which, we must assume, took him very seriously indeed as the origin of evil, the corrupter of a substantial portion of the angelic host, the agent of humanity's fall, and the tempter who continues to seek the damnation of every Christian?

Put oversimply, the answer would appear to be that two major strands in the complex network of medieval Christian beliefs about the Evil One—his role as a trickster, and his status as the principle of opposition to, and perversion of, all the divine attributes—proved particularly amenable to representation in terms (and practices) drawn from the festive, parodic and comic dimensions of European popular culture.[1]

Identification of the Devil with the serpent who deceitfully tempted the first man and woman to disobey God's commandment, and thus to lose Paradise and immortality, was the basis of his position as the supreme trickster. This position was consolidated within the patristic tradition of exegesis which, seeking to explain the foundational Christian belief that God assumed human form as Jesus and underwent suffering and death to save humanity from damnation, developed the so-called "Abuse-of-Power" or "Devil's Rights" theory of the Incarnation and Redemption. As summarized by Kathleen M. Ashley, the "Abuse-of-Power" theory argued that "when the Devil beguiled men into sin he won the right to take them in death. In order to redeem mankind, the deity disguised himself in human flesh, and the disguise tricked the Devil into attempting to kill [more precisely, appropriate for his realm of death, Hell] one who was not mortal. [With the Resurrection,] this abuse of the Devil's legitimate power cancels the Devil's claim to men's souls after the coming of Christ"—except, of course, in so far as they choose death by sin without repentance.[2]

Although other explanations of the Redemption not centering on the Devil's trickery and Christ's counter-trickery (notably those of Anselm and Abelard) became received within scholastic theology from the twelfth century onward, the older theory persisted within less intellectually elite milieux, as the vivid images developed in patristic writings to illustrate it—e.g., Christ as a mousetrap or fishhook baited with human flesh to catch the Devil—became widely diffused throughout pre-Reformation Europe in writings intended for the formation of the parish clergy, and thus the edification and instruction of the laity, as part of the educational campaigns emanating from the Fourth Lateran Council of 1215.[3]

Just as early Christian traditions of the Devil as trickster led to the formulation of the "Abuse-of-Power" theory of Redemption, the equally ancient understanding of him as one seeking both to rival the divine power and subvert the divine providence issued in depictions of the Devil as the principle of inversion, negative imitation, and parody of God—the *simia Dei*, the promoter of disorder and irrationality where God has established a hierarchy of order and reason, both macrocosmic (the universe) and microcosmic (the human soul).[4] As a subset or emblem of diabolic inversion, in addition, the reign of Antichrist—the Devil's last and greatest agent in the history of the world—originally extrapolated from hints in several Scriptural passages, was widely developed as an evil parody/inversion of Christ's.[5]

The idea of diabolical inversion and parody had important ramifications for medieval Christian views of language, since God created the world through his vivifying Word; Scripture preserves in its language the true record of God's dealings with humanity (subject to interpretation in accord with the rule of charity); and, as the opening of the Johannine Gospel tells us, the Word of God took on flesh as Jesus in order to save those who heeded his message and believed in him. The diabolically sponsored inversion of the Word—the fallen language of pride and hence of confusion—was symbolized by the multiplication of tongues with which God punished the overreaching builders of the Tower of Babel, but also manifested itself as nonsense, uproar, quarreling, and scatology.[6]

Both the strands of medieval thought and belief about the Devil just summarized contribute importantly to, and are ingeniously and effectively represented in, the vernacular religious drama that developed under both ecclesiastical and civic sponsorship throughout Europe in the later Middle Ages. In the article from which I have already quoted, Kathleen Ashley argues that the lasting popularity of the "Abuse-of-Power" theory reflects a quasi-universal fascination with the trickster figure found in the folk tales and mythologies of so many human cultures, and the accompanying belief that a malevolent trickster (in this case, the Devil) must often be defeated at his own game, outwitted by another, beneficent trickster (in this case Christ).[7]

Hence it is not surprising that the plays, in seeking to make a vivid theatrical and didactic impression on their socially comprehensive audience, should present the Devil (and sometimes a diabolic surrogate) as a supreme trickster engaged (and eventually defeated) in a contest, or agon, with Christ (or his surrogates).

According to Ashley, this is exactly how we should understand the non-Scriptural part of the famous Wakefield "Second Shepherds' Play," which revolves around the sheep-stealing trickster, Mak. As she puts it, "the whole Mak section is in my view a brilliant comic rendition of the guiler beguiled doctrine of salvation as it was understood in the fifteenth century." Mak's theft of a sheep and his preventing disclosure of the theft by disguising it as a baby just borne by his wife Gil constitutes an inversion-parody of the Incarnation of Jesus, the Lamb of God, which occupies the last part of the play. The sheep itself, Ashley argues, "is . . . a comic version of the Incarnate flesh which tricks the Devil into his abuse of power. Just as Satan, the cosmic Beguiler, will be defeated by Christ through the Incarnation, so the shepherds exorcise the socially disruptive Mak by blanketing him. . . ." And when the shepherds visit the manger in Bethlehem a little later, one of them, making obvious the parallel with Mak, "presents the defeat of Satan as already having taken place: 'Thou has waryd, I weyne, the warlo so wylde; / The fals gyler of teyn now goes he begylde.'"[8] (Analogously, the "fals gyler" in the penultimate play of the Chester mystery cycle is Antichrist, who tricks the earthly kings into worshipping him as God by means of a series of sham miracles that are only exposed by the divinely assisted Enoch and Elijah.)[9]

Even more than diabolic trickery, diabolic inversion and parody find especially frequent and varied representation in pre-Reformation religious plays. The typological relationship between Old Testment patriarchs and holy men, on the one hand, and Jesus, on the other, has as its parodic reflection the lineage of the tyrants who, in their irrationality, injustice, and predilection for violence show themselves to be antitypes of the Devil (or, in the case of the Chester cycle, of Antichrist).[10] At the very beginning of the extant cycles, Lucifer, brightest of angels,

challenges the supreme power of God by an act—sitting in the
divine throne when God temporarily (!) vacates it—that can be
read as an imitation of the Deity. Thrown down into a newly
created Hell, the darkness, stench, and disorder of which
constitute an absolute inversion of Heaven, Lucifer is transformed into Satan, God's opposite. Whereas God presides over
an angelic community that moves in graceful circles, or is seated
in hierarchically arranged seats around him, the diabolic realm is
marked by the uproar of fiends engaged in angry recriminations
against each other over the responsibility for their fall—a
diabolic conversation salted with scatology and anality. (The
traditionally sulphurous stink of Hell lent itself easily to the
notion of the Devil's fart as the ultimate inversion of the Word of
God; in at least one cycle, the so-called "N-Town," The Devil's
defiance and fear are repeatedly emblematized as farting.)[11]

The "Harrowing of Hell" play in the cycles stages the ultimate confrontation between Christ and Satan, in which the
diabolic trickster discovers he has been the victim of God's
greater trick, the Incarnation. (As Jesus says to Satan in the
Wakefield "Harrowing," "My Godhede here I hid / In Mary,
moder mine, / Where it shall never be kid / To thee, ne none of
thine" (ll. 263–66; ed. Bevington, p. 603). The immediate theatrical context for this trickster-tricked reversal is one of comic
inversion and parody, both verbal and behavioral; as an emblem
of this context, Jesus (or a surrogate) ties Satan to his throne in
Hell, thus recalling and reversing Satan's eviction (while still
Lucifer) from God's throne in Heaven. As David Bevington puts
it, in the "Harrowing" the Devil "is contrasted with his divine
adversary in ways that remind us of previous episodes in the
cycles. Like Pharoah, Herod, or the Wakefield Pilate, he is a
boastful and tyrannical ranter seeking to destroy innocence and
meekness. . . . Satan's followers . . . raise the alarm in noisy panic,
shore up useless defenses against Christ's entry, and turn on one
another in an orgy of mutual recriminations" (ed. Bevington, p.
594). (The devils "raise the alarm" by repeatedly exclaiming,
"Out! Harrow!" the legally appropriate form for such a public
outcry. The implicit quibble on the verb, to harrow, allows a
reading of the play's title [and subject] as the "uproaring," as
well as the "laying waste," of Hell.)[12]

One of the major features of the pre-Reformation religious and moral plays in England was the frequent (if not constant) presence in the playing area and among the audience—there was usually no hard and fast boundary line between the two spaces—of groups of devils engaged in comically agonistic encounters with actors and spectators alike. Their largely unscripted performance (they are occasionally mentioned in rubrics, e.g., as conducting damned souls to Hell) would be a vivid reminder of the diabolic inversion, parody, and attempted negation of providential history and personal salvation—the plays' "official" subjects. (Early in *The Book of Margery Kempe* we read that Margery, during her period of greatest alienation from herself and God, had visions of devils that recall both church paintings of the Last Judgment and diabolic intervention at the plays [including the sensational representation of their home base, Hell-mouth]: "And in this tyme sche sey, as hir thowt, deuelys opyn her mowthys al influmyd wyth brennyng lowys of fyr as thei schuld a swalwyd hyr in, sum-tyme rampyng at hyr, sum-tyme thretyng her, sum-tym pullyng hyr and halyng hir bothe nygth and day. . . .")[13]

At the center of many plays, diabolic surrogates keep before the audience paradigms of diabolic inversion or parody, such as Cain's defiant refusal to offer God a tithe of his corn and the chronic insubordination of Cain's servant, Garcio (in the Wakefield "Killing of Abel"), and uproarious behavior, already mentioned, of tyrants such as King Herod, the *rex iratus*.

Tyrannical rant, like the anal-centered language of devils (and of diabolic disciples such as the Wakefield Cain and the "boy" of the heathen priest in the fifteenth-century "Mary Magdalene" play), sensationally inverts/subverts the divine Word.[14] Other instances of parodic and inverted (hence diabolically tinged) utterance in pre-Reformation English drama include Garcio's travestying of Cain's crying of a royal pardon for himself and Garcio—itself a parody of justice that refers to a widely practiced, and resented, legal abuse in fifteenth-century England[15]—the scatological parody of Mercy's aureate preaching by Nowadays, New Guise, and Nought, the devil-related "Vice" figures of the moral play, *Mankind* (e.g., ll. 45–63, 124–46; ed. Bevington, pp. 904–05, 907–08), and the hilarious, frequently scatological (and infinitely variable or extensible) dog-Latin parody of the Latin Mass in the "lesson" read by the heathen acolyte in "Mary Magdalene" (ll. 1186–1201; ed. Bevington, p. 726).

The obvious effect of most of the diabolic (and surrogate diabolic) behavior the late medieval English plays was comic. To quote David Bevington on the Wakefield "Harrowing of Hell" once more, "Because the devil is an evil schemer outwitted by his own machinations in a contest of guile, his overthrow is appropriately comic," and his diabolic legions "are comic in much the same ludicrous vein as their master. . ." (ed. Bevington, p. 594). And the ludic (as opposed to the theological or Scriptural) source for much of this comedy was the multifaceted festive dimension of late medieval popular culture.

For example, Robert Weimann has shown how the mystery and moral plays of pre-Reformation England depend, for many of their reiterated comic routines, on the traditional, unscripted performances known collectively as the Mummer's Play (or, in Alan Brody's nomenclature, the "men's dramatic ceremonial").[16] Disrespectful, nonsense-prone comic servants such as Cain's Garcio, Trowle in the Chester "Shepherds' Play," the doctor's assistant in the Croxton "Play of the Sacrament," and the heathen acolyte of "Mary Magdalen" share an origin in the doctor's assistant of the Mummer's Play of St. George.[17] And the Doctor, who revives St. George and/or his variously named opponent (The Slasher, the Turkish Knight, Turkey Snipe [from the latter], etc.), while making outrageous claims for his medical art and pharmacopeia, himself appears in the Croxton play, bringing with him, as Gail Gibson has shown, resonances of contemporaneous East Anglian medical practice and institutions.[18]

Kathleen Ashley's explanation of blanketing—the punishment administered to Mak in the Wakefield Second Shepherds' Play—as "a satiric folk ritual for banishing harmful elements at such seasons as Christmas or Shrovetide"[19] points to the fact that the medieval plays also appropriated to their needs a range of ceremonies and practices famously characterized as "carnivalesque" by M. M. Bakhtin. In particular, the parodic and scatological inversions of social norms or figures of authority that constitute an important part of carnivalesque festivity underlie the "theatricalized" diabolic discourse of nonsense and anality outlined above.[20]

Thus one main, defining feature of the late medieval vernacular theater *qua* theater is its practical, behavioral, *bodily* synthesis of the disruptive, parodic release that marks carnivalesque license and the presence of the diabolic as a disruptive, subversive force in salvation history.[21] This strongly suggests that the just-catalogued instances of diabolic discourse in the religious and moral plays appealed to their audience less because they sugar-coated the pill of religious instruction than because they established continuity between such "serious" ludic occasions and the festivals and folk-games with which they coexisted in what Charles Phythian-Adams has called "the ritual year" of provincial, pre-Réformation England.[22]

But establishing such a continuity—with its implied invitation for the audience to become very much involved, including vocally, in the performance—was an inherently risky enterprise that could, at any particular performance, contribute to an agonic exacerbation of high spirits and social tensions. The chronic possibility of riotous behavior accompanying the performance of the plays is noted in several extant records concerning them, perhaps most famously the record of Friar Melton's advice to the civic authorities of York (in 1426) to move their cycle of plays from Corpus Christi day to the day after, to prevent further disruption of the sacred feast by play-inspired disturbances.[23]

It is perhaps in this sense, among others, that term, "parlous play," used by the good angels to describe Lucifer's usurpation of God's throne in the Chester "Fall of Lucifer" play, should be understood.[24] Whether or not such a conjecture be accurate, the locution is a useful one to describe the adaptation of the drama's diabolic discourse in several comic narratives of *CT*, to which I can now at last turn.

Although many (probably all) of the plays that I have mentioned postdate Chaucer's life, there is every reason to believe that the Diabolic/festive routines—behavioral and especially verbal—they deploy were known to Chaucer and in his mind, as he compiled his frame tale collection, roughly during the last 10–15 years of the fourteenth century. At this time, religious plays—including a cycle from Creation to Last Judgment, performed at Skinners Well and lasting from four to seven days—were performed in and around London, while in the provinces—at York, Chester, Coventry, and elsewhere—civic cycles associated with the Feast of Corpus Christi were probably already in existence (albeit not necessarily in their extant form).[25]

That Chaucer should be interested in the diabolic discourse of the religious plays can be easily understood, I believe, in the light of two major dimensions of *CT*: its fascination throughout with specialized discourses—professional, religious, misogynistic, mercantile, *et cetera*—and its depiction of strife (in its varied verbalizations) as a function of social existence. The rivalries and confrontations that periodically occur among the pilgrims on the road to Canterbury are themselves a "parlous play"—play, because they are expressed through the "holiday" medium of story or possibly fanciful self-dramatization; perilous, because, despite their holiday disguise, words spoken in anger have the power to rend the social fabric of the ad hoc "compaignye."

As is well known, Chaucer twice makes direct allusion to the religious plays in the *Miller's Prologue* and *Tale*: in the former, the Miller challenges the Host's authority "in Pilates voys" (I.3124) i.e., the voice of the ranting tyrant; in the latter, as Absolon pursues his fruitless wooing of Alisoun, "Somtyme, to shewe his lightnesse and maistrye, / He pleyeth Herodes upon a scaffold hye" (I.3383–84)—i.e., in a stationary, scaffold-and-place staging.[26] In addition, the Miller identifies his tale before the fact—"For I wol telle a legend and a lyf, / Bothe of a carpenter and of his wyf, / How that a clerk hath set the wrightes cappe!" (I.3141–43)—as a parodic combination of the Mathaean Gospel infancy narrative of Mary and Joseph with the archetypal fabliau plot of an old husband cuckolded by a clever clerk with the connivance of his young wife; such a synthesis clearly alludes to the presentation in the cycle plays of Joseph's anger when he discovers that his young wife is pregnant by someone other than himself.[27]

Several scholars (Kelsie B. Harder, Beryl Rowland, and most recently and effectively Sandra Pierson Prior) have examined how elements from, and allusions to, the cycle plays contribute to the comic action of the *Miller's Tale (MillT)*.[28] A less-noticed aspect of that action, involving the comic climax, is its diabolic dimension. The climax features, first of all, an inversion of oral into anal communication. Absolon, expecting to kiss Alisoun's mouth (earlier described by the Millerian narrator as "sweete as bragot or the meeth, / Or hoord of apples leyd in hey or heeth"; (I.3261–62), is devastated when he kisses her arse instead; his return, hot "kultour" in hand, signals, however, that he expects his renewed request for a kiss (I.3797) to be met with a repetition of the inversion and is prepared to enact a terrible vengeance. What he does not expect is that Nicholas, seeking to "amenden al the jape" of inversion, will join Alisoun and Absolon in it: "out his ers he putteth pryvely / Over the buttok, to the haunche-bon" (I.3799–3803). In fact, so completely does Nicholas make one in the comedy of inversion that when Absolon, taking aim in the dark, says, "Spek, sweete bryd, I noot nat where thou art" (I.3805), he responds with an appropriately inverted word: "This Nicholas anon leet fle a fart / As greet as it had been a thonder-dent" (I.3806–07).

In fact, Nicholas's fart serves as an unconventional but revealing sign of his dual status in *MillT*. As the plot maker and "creator" of the pretended "Nowelis flood" in order to cuckold old John, Nicholas, as Sandra Prior suggests, functions within his little Oxford world as an analogue of the universe's Creator. But as we have seen in the "Fall of Lucifer" mystery plays, such imitation of God for purposes of self-aggrandizement characterizes the sin (in that case, sitting in God's throne, or "playing God,") that transforms Lucifer from the brightest angel to the devil, bound miserably in the Hell that God has newly created for him.[29] Hence his climactic inverted reply to (and on) Absolon functions simultaneously to identify Nicholas as the God of Job, speaking from the "thonder-dent" (Job 37.4, 5; 40.9), and as the devil responding proleptically, as it were, to the vengeance that punishes his overreaching (in this case, seeking to "amenden al the jape").[30]

But if Nicholas functions as an ad-hoc synthesis of God and the Devil, what about Absolon? That he has enlisted in the devil's party is suggested by his emphatic response to his humiliation by Alisoun: "'My soule bitake I unto Sathanas, / But me were levere than al this toun,' quod he, / 'Of this despit awroken for to be'" (I.3750–52).[31] He then moves quickly into the hell-like world of Gerveys's fiery smithy,[32] and when he asks to borrow a hot coulter, Gerveys replies, with obvious double significance (at least for the reader), "Ey, *Cristes foo!* What wol ye do therwith?" (I.3782; emph. added).

Despite the ambiguous role of Nicholas, at once God and Devil, at the tale's climax, there can be little doubt that the revenge-seeking Absolon's affiliation, and his agency in bringing about the climax, transforms *MillT* into a new comic myth: a re-imagining of the Fall of humanity which also serves as a Chaucerian parody of the way in which the religious plays of his day seek, by a consistent "anachronism," to make the biblical events immediate to their audience. Absolon-Satan buggers Nicholas-God (one recalls Dante's Vanni Fucci "making the figs" at God from deep in Hell, a gesture signifying, in effect, "screw you, God!"),[33] and (by a truly "diabolic" Chaucerian inversion of cause and effect) brings about the (literal and bone-breaking) "Fall of John" from the rafters to the floor of his house.

The result of John's misadventure is an uproar that brings the neighbors to the site. (The cry of Nicholas and Alisoun, "Out! Harrow!" duplicates, we recall, the exclamation of the "Harrowing of Hell" devils when Christ throws down the gates of their fortress.) In the ensuing, final moments of the tale John, on one side, and Nicholas and Alisoun, on the other, offer opposing versions of who is responsible for what has happened. The scene, in its noisy exchange of recriminations, recalls the analogous argument between Lucifer-become-Satan and his newly diabolic companion(s) in Hell after their fall. But what also marks the scene as para-diabolic is the inversion of truth and falsehood, whereby John's accurate account of what has happened is rejected as "fantasye" (I.3840) in favor of the fiction created for the occasion by Nicholas and Alisoun and cor-roborated by an alliance of Oxford scholars: "For what so that this carpenter answerde, / It was for noght; no man his reson herde. / With othes grete he was so sworn adoun / That he was holde wood in al the toun; / For every clerk anonright heeld with oother" (I.3843–47). Finally, in what I take to be a tacit acknowledgment of his appropriation of diabolic comedy from

the religious plays, Chaucer alludes to the effect of such comedy
on the audience for which it is staged: "And every wight gan
laughen at this stryf" (I.3849).

The conclusion of the *Miller's Tale* is not the only place in
CT where Chaucer alludes to the pandemonium that was an essential ingredient of so many pre-Reformation religious plays.
Near the end of the first part of the CYT, the Yeoman interrupts
his neurotic alternation between lamenting his involvement with
alchemy and obsessively rehearsing its debased materials—
"asshes, donge, pisse and cley" (VIII.807)—to describe the effect
of all the master alchemist's labors:

> Er that the pot be on the fir ydo,
> Of metals with a certeyn quantitee,
> My lord hem tempreth, and no man but he. . . .
> And yet ful ofte he renneth in a blame,
> And wite ye how? Ful ofte it happeth so
> The pot tobreketh, and farewel, al is go!
>
> (VIII.899–901; 905–907)

The violent explosion sends metals flying all over the
laboratory, to bury themselves in ceiling, walls, and floor. An
equally violent argument ensues about who is to blame for the
calamity, and the Yeoman prefaces his account of the fruitless
(but none the less violent) recriminations by characterizing them
in terms of the quarreling among demons (or their allegorical
and human surrogates) so frequently represented on the pre-
Reformation English stage:

> Withouten doute,
> Though that the feend noght in oure sighte hym shewe,
> I trowe he with us be, that ilke shrewe!
> In helle, where that he is lord and sire,
> Nis ther moore wo, ne moore rancour ne ire.
> Whan that oure pot is broke, as I have sayd,
> Every man chit and halt hym yvele apayd.
>
> (VIII.915–21)

The Wakefield and Chester "Fall of Lucifer" plays, or the
Wakefield "Harrowing of Hell," provide examples of such
diabolic discord; in fact, at the climax of the latter play, when

Jesus commands the gates of Hell to open and, as they give way before the Savior (presumably with a good deal of noise and smoke or fire), the assembled devils respond in a manner, and with words, that clearly parallel the alchemists lamenting their exploded pot:

> Ribald: Out, harro! Our baill is brokyn,
>   And brusten ar all oure bandys of bras!
>
> Belzabub: Harro! Oure yates begin to crak!
>   In sonder, I trow, they go,
>   And hell, I trow, will all to-shak.
>   Alas, what I am wo!
>
> (207–12; ed. Bevington, p. 601)

An even closer analogue to *CYT* occurs in the mid-fifteenth-century Croxton "Play of the Sacrament," when a group of Jews undertakes to torture a consecrated Host they have obtained from a church with the connivance of a Christian merchant. After several misadventures, they put the Host in an oven under which, by blowing, they have built a roaring fire (ll. 689–98; ed. Bevington, pp. 778–79). But as soon as they have sealed the oven, according to the stage direction in the manuscript, "Here the ovyn must rive asundere and blede out at the cranys" (*SD* after l. 712, ed. Bevington, p. 779), much to the dismay of the Jews, who have already responded to previous reverses—e.g., a cauldron of boiling water in which the Host is placed suddenly boils instead with blood (*SD* after l. 672)—in a manner recalling diabolic uproar: "Owt and harow, what devill is herein?" (l. 673, ed. Bevington, p. 778).

Although the episode of the exploding pot is the element of *CYT* most sensationally indebted to stage traditions of diabolic strife (and to the folk play/carnivalesque disorder that underlies such strife), it does not exhaust the tale's debt to late medieval representations of the diabolic. Indeed, it can be argued that inscribed in both the experience and the appearance of the Yeoman is a trajectory of diabolic inversion. Seeking wealth, he becomes poor and ragged—"Al that I hadde I have lost therby" (VIII.722); attempting to gain a godlike control over the processes of material creation, he transforms himself into a subhuman specimen of laboratory detritus, no more than a human bellows: "Ther I was wont to be right fressh and gay / Of clothyng and of oother good array, / Now may I were an hose upon myn heed; / And wher my colour was bothe fressh and reed, / Now is it wan and of a leden hewe. . ." (VIII.724–28). In short, the Yeoman and his fellow alchemists are walking multisensory advertisements for the diabolic presence: "And everemoore, where that evere they goon, / Men may hem knowe by smel of brymstoon" (VIII.884–85).

If the *Miller's Tale* assimilates itself to diabolic comedy through the ambiguity of a strategy of inversion that the religious plays share with carnivalesque festivity, the Reeve's angry response to the *Miller's Tale*—in which a thieving, bullying, and otherwise thoroughly vicious Miller is outwitted and beaten up by two rather dim-witted clerks who also violate his wife and daughter—enacts an analogous assimilation by evoking the "trickster tricked" component of the Abuse-of-Power theory mentioned earlier in this essay—a component that, as Kathleen Ashley suggests, brings theology into line with folk-beliefs about trickster figures and how to deal with them. Before he begins his tale (and to justify its telling) the Reeve raises the issue of reciprocity in a concretely physical, kinetic form: "I pray yow alle that ye nat yow greve, / Thogh I answere, and somdeel sette [the Miller's] howve; / *For leveful is with force force of-showve*" (I.3910–12; emphasis added). Then, to close the bracket he has thus opened, Oswald ends his recitation with this ostensible moralization: "Lo, swich it is a millere to be fals! / And therfore this proverbe is seyd ful sooth, / 'Hym thar nat wene wel that yvele dooth.' *A gylour shal hymself bigyled be*" (I.4318–21; emphasis added). The "lesson" of the tale is a generalized version of the shepherd's reaction to the birth of Christ, quoted above: "The fals gyler of teyn now goes he begylde."

One has the impression, moreover, that the Reeve's allusion (if my understanding of it be correct) represents a deliberate attempt on his part to "diabolize" his antagonist, capitalizing on an identification between Robin and Satan that may already have been suggested to some of the more hierarchically-minded "gentils" among the pilgrims by the Miller's Lucifer-like rebellion against the Host's self-proclaimed authority over the story-telling contest that is in fact Harry Bailly's creation.[34]

The *Nun's Priest's Tale* (NPT) taps into the diabolic comedy of pre-Reformation English drama for quite different purposes. The tale clearly assimilates its fable of cock, hen, and fox to the story of the Fall (a popular subject of the plays from the twelfth-century Anglo-Norman Ordo *representacionis Ade* [or *Jeu d'Adam*] on through the cycles), and its teller, with typically playful malice aforethought, gleefully evokes the narrative of Genesis 3–4 as an *auctoritee*, only to beat a hasty (if not particularly believable) retreat:

> My tale is of a cok, as ye may heere,
> That tok his conseil of his wyf, with sorwe,
> To walken in the yerd upon that morwe
> That he hadde met that dreem that I yow tolde.
> Wommennes conseils been ful ofte colde;
> Wommannes conseil broghte us first to wo
> And made Adam fro Paradys to go,
> Ther as he was ful myrie and wel at ese.
> But for I noot to whom it myght displese
> [e.g., the Prioress, whose chaplain he is?]
> If I conseil of wommen wolde blame,
> Passe over, for I seyde it in my game.
> Rede auctors, where they trete of swich mateere,
> And what they seyn of wommen ye may heere.
> This been the cokkes wordes, and nat myne;
> I kan noon harm of no womman divyne.

> (VII.3252–66)

Despite the (more or less mutually exclusive) exculpatory strategies by which the Priest, tongue firmly in cheek, seeks to control the potential damage this passage might cause him, its allusion to the Genesis story, as a matrix within which to understand the Chauntecleer-Pertelote fable, invites us to see the Fox, Daun Russell, as the devil figure. Interestingly, in this revisionist rendering of the Fall, Chaucer again pursues a strategy of "diabolic" inversion: the Eve-antitype has already tempted (or miscounseled) the Adam-antitype—and he has already been led astray by sexual desire for her (VII.3167–71: "For whan I feele a-nyght your softe syde . . . / I am so ful of joye and of solas, / That I diffye bothe sweven and dreem")—before the Devil-antitype arrives, and he proceeds to tempt not Pertelote but Chantecleer![35] And the fox/devil succeeds by appealing to Chantecleer's vanity about his singing and by stimulating the cock's sense of competition with the only singer whom the fox claims to have been better, namely Chantecleer's father. Having vividly described the father's intense perfor-mance—"And for to make his voys the moore strong / He wolde so peyne hym that with bothe his yen / He moste wynke, so loude wolde he cryen, / And stonden on his tiptoon therwithal, / And strecche forth his nekke long and smal" (VII.3304–08)—the tempter poses the ultimate question: "Lat se; konne ye youre fader countrefete?" (VII.3321).

Chantecleer "ravysshed with his flaterie," rises to the fox's bait, strikes a posture in complete imitation of his father's (VII.3331–32), and, eyes tightly shut, begins to crow, thereby allowing the fox to grab him and carry him off. Is this catas-trophe Chaucer's sly comment on the dangers of his own emula-tion of his poetic "fathers"—of his competition with Ovid, the poet over whose story of Ceyx and Alcyone he falls asleep, in order to remake it in his own "sweven in ryme" (*Book of the Duchess*); with Vergil, the "auctor" whose great epic he will retell "if he konne," but which he immediately appropriates to very different, quite subversive uses (*House of Fame*); or with all the classical poets whose steps he instructs his "litel bok" to kiss at the end of *Troilus and Criseyde*, thereby establishing (while pretending not to) his claim not only to be one of their company, but to be the equal of Dante, who had performed a similar maneuver at the beginning of his *Commedia*?[36]

In fact, *NPT* lends itself to interpretation as Chaucer's self-directed diabolic comedy, in which, using the conventions of the beast fable, he presents himself as both counterfeiter and flatterer, cock and fox. On the one hand, he strives to imitate the paternal voice, in the process overreaching both his abilities and his station and courting disaster. On the other, as himself a purveyor of flattery to those more powerful than he, he risks becoming the kind of foxy "losengour" against whom the Nun's Priest warns lords: "Many a fals flatour / Is in your courtes, and many a losengour, / That plesen yow wel moore, by my feith, /

Than he that soothfastnesse unto yow seith" (VII.3325–28). Of course, the flatterer who is also a "counterfeiter" is yet another description of the Devil, who in the cycle plays seeks to "countrefete" his Father by sitting in his throne, and earns Hell for his efforts.

Later in *CT*, in the *Manciple's Tale* (*MancT*), another bird, Phebus's crow, excels at a more universal kind of imitation: "And countrefete the speche of every man / He koude, whan he sholde telle a tale" (IX.134–35). The bird gets into trouble precisely as the Nun's Priest fears he will: badmouthing a woman "to whom it myght displese"—in this case his master, who is extremely unhappy to be told, by the crow, of his wife's infidelity with a blatantly inferior man. By the end of the tale the crow has experienced a metamorphosis, or inversion, which precisely parallels that of Lucifer/Satan in the "Fall of Lucifer" plays: his angry lord "pulled his white fetheres everychon, / And made hym blak, and refte him al his song [he "songe whilom lyk a nyghtyngale (IX.294)], / And eek his speche, and out at dore hym slong / Unto the devel . . . "(IX.304–07).

The crow's distinction as a universal counterfeiter of voices applies precisely to the author of the polyvocal *CT* as well; but it also offers a precise analogue in sound to the universal shapeshifting—i.e., body-counterfeiting—capacity for which the Devil, as trickster, was famous. (In the *Friar's Tale*, to be considered next, a "feend" tells the inquisitive summoner that devils have no "figure . . . determinat" in Hell, but on earth "whan us liketh we kan take us oon . . . ; / Somtyme lyk a man, or lyk an ape, / Or lyk an angel kan I ryde or go. . . . / For we . . . wol us swiche formes make / As moost able is oure preyes for to take" [III.1459–72].)

So in the last verse tale of *CT*, Chaucer draws some disturbing parallels between himself and the Devil, mediated through the crow, and offers a serio-comic depiction of the fate awaiting the voice-counterfeiting, tale-telling singer if he insists on communicating unwelcome truths to audiences who have potentially godlike power over him. (Perhaps *MancT* should be understood as, in effect, a third version—this time in the mode of diabolic comedy—of the story told in the F and G Prologues to the *Legend of Good Women*, in which the poet is accused of, and punished for, telling derogatory stories about women.)

The two tales of the *Canterbury Tales* that most clearly identify themselves as diabolic comedy are the *Friar's Tale* (*FrT*) and the *Summoner's Tale*. I have commented elsewhere on the Summoner's insulting (and quite carnivalesque) depiction of friars as embodiments of the Devil's fart, greedily perverting the Word of God by means of self-interested "glosyng" (interpretation/flattery).[37] So I will close the current discussion with a few comments on the much more cerebral—hence less ludic—diabolism of *FrT*, which centers on the meeting, and consequent sworn brotherhood, of a summoner and a fiend, as both travel about the country in search of gain (in the case of the former, money; of the latter, souls).

The tale functions by ironically undercutting normal assumptions about (and depictions of) human responses to the devil and his world (in the tale's term, his "pryvetee"), i.e., Hell. First, it demonstrates that summoners are more diabolical than devils, who only take what people really want to give them, while the summoner will take anything he can get, whether or not people want to give it to him. Then, by depicting summoners as driven by the desire to invade other people's "pryvetee," in order to control and profit from them, the tale suggests that its evil protagonist is as eager to go to hell as his victims are to send him there. For while some folk may wish their horses to the devil and not mean it (III.1538–65), no-one, least of all the old widow whom the summoner tries unsucessfully to shake down, will utter such a wish about the summoner and not mean it (III.1628–29)—unless, of course, he repents. But the summoner has no "entente / For to repente me" of his extortionate request. In fact, as his barrage of questions about the lives and habits of devils, addressed to his fiendly compeer suggests, he is eager to discover even the Devil's potentially profitable secrets, an eagerness that starkly emblematizes his enthusiastic cooperation in his own damnation. (As the devil, preparing to carry the summoner off to perdition, remarks, "Thou shalt with me to helle yet tonyght, / Where thou shalt knowen of oure pryvetee / Moore than a maister of dyvynytee" [III.1636–38].)

The ultimate irony of the tale, therefore, is that diabolic comedy is, in effect, a redundant genre: there is no need for devils to go about the world looking to lure people to hell as long as there are enough summoners about, whose lives demonstrate that they are champing at the bit to get there.

The foregoing remarks have sought to clarify a dimension of Chaucerian comedy by locating it within a network of late medieval thought, belief, and performative practice centered on two vivid cultural apprehensions of the Devil: as a trickster (beguiling humanity but beguiled in turn by God-become-man), and as a spirit of inversion seeking to distort and negate the creative, ordering, and salvific Truth-telling functions of the Word of God. Chaucer's manifold comedic appropriations of the diabolic throughout *CT* are also appropriations of the folk and carnivalesque elements that interacted with theological traditions in creating these apprehensions. His strategies, I have argued, parallel, and were surely influenced by, the ambivalent, risky manifestations of diabolic comedy in the late medieval English religious drama.[38]

NOTES

1. For a useful introduction to learned and popular medieval beliefs about the Devil, see Jeffrey Burton Russell, *Lucifer: The Devil in the Middle Ages* (Ithaca, 1984). Also relevant are Russell's two earlier books, *The Devil: Perceptions of Evil from Antiquity to Primitive Christianity* (Ithaca: Cornell U. Press, 1977), and *Satan: the Early Christian Tradition* (Ithaca: Cornell U. Press, 1981).

2. Kathleen M. Ashley, "The Guiler Beguiled: Christ and Satan as Theological Tricksters in Medieval Religious Literature," *Criticism* 24 (1982), 128, material in brackets added. See Ashley's notes for bibliography on the "Abuse-of-Power" theory.

3. For an excellent introduction to this material, see Leonard E. Boyle, O.P., "The Fourth Lateran Council and Manuals of Popular Theology" (pp. 30–43) and Judith Shaw, "The Influence of Canonical and Episcopal Reform on Popular Books of Instruction" (pp. 44–60),

Thomas J. Heffernan, ed. *The Popular Literature of Medieval England* (Knoxville: U. of Tennessee Press, 1985). In its section on the Passion, the Legenda Aurea (Golden Legend), an influential thirteenth-century hagiographical collection, gives four reasons why "the manner of our Redemption was fitting," of which the fourth is that "the manner of Our Lord's death was most wisely devised to overcome the Devil. . . . Christ hid the hook of His god-head in the bait of His humanity, and the Devil, seeking to take the bait of the flesh, was taken by the hook of the divinity. And of this artful taking, Saint Augustine says, 'The Redeemer came, and the deceiver was vanquished; and what did our Redeemer do to him who held us in bondage? He held out to him the mousetrap of His Cross, and placed thereon the bait of His blood.'" (Granger Ryan and Helmut Ripperger, trans., *The Golden Legend of Jacobus de Voragine* [New York: Longmans, Green, 1941, repr. New York, Arno 1969], pp. 212–13.) For more information on the patristic origins of the hook and mousetrap metaphors, see Ashley, p. 129 and note 9, and Paul Remley, "*Muscipula diaboli* and Medieval English Antifeminism," *English Studies* 70 (1989) 1–14.

4. See, e.g., J. B. Russell, *Satan* (cf. note 1, above), pp. 94–95, on Tertullian's presentation of the Devil as one who "distorts and perverts" God's creation, and as God's rival and ape (*aemulus*). Augustine (*Confessions* X.36) speaks of the Devil as "he who 'decided to place his throne in the north' [Isaiah 14.13f.] so that in the dark and the cold men should serve him who, by a perverted and twisted life, imitates you" (*Confessions* trans. Henry Chadwick [Oxford: Oxford U. Press, 1991], p. 214).

5. See Richard Kenneth Emmerson, *Antichrist in the Middle Ages: A Study of Medieval Apocalypticism, Art, and Literature* (Seattle: U. of Washington Press, 1981), pp. 74–77, on medieval representations of Antichrist's life as an imitation, inversion, and parody of Christ's.

6. On patristic and medieval ideas of fallen language, see Eric Jager, *The Tempter's Voice: Language and the Fall in Medieval Literature* (Ithaca: Cornell U. Press, 1994.). Eugene Vance, speaking of "Satan as the principle of perverse representation," says of diabolic language, "since evil 'represents' nothing [i.e., has no 'real' existence in a universe created by an all-good God], and since the devils' choice of evil is a free choice of what does not exist, their evil difference is to be understood above all as a lack, as a privation of what exists and of what is therefore good. Without evil substance of their own, the devils cannot signify anything but nonsense; they cannot be serious, much less grieve, but can only laugh, parody, and sneer." (*Marvelous Signals: Poetics and Sign Theory in the Middle Ages* [Lincoln and London: U. of Nebraska Press,

1986], p. 198). This is obviously the perspective that underlies the diabolic gibberish Dante encounters on his trip through Hell, e.g., at the
beginning of *Inferno* VII, where Pluto cries, unintelligbly, "Pape Satan,
pape Satan aleppe!"

7. Ashley, 127–28.

8. Ashley 135–36; "The Second Shepherds' Pageant," ll. 712–13, in
David Bevington, ed. *Medieval Drama* (Boston: Houghton Mifflin, 1975),
p. 407. All subsequent references to plays cited from this edition will
appear in the text, and be identified as "ed. Bevington."

9. On Antichrist as deceiver in the Chester play, see Emmerson,
Antichrist, pp. 181–87, and Martin Stevens, *Four Middle English Mystery
Cycles: Textual, Contextual, and Critical Interpretations* (Princeton:
Princeton U. Press, 1987), pp. 303–305, and Leslie Howard Martin,
"Comic Eschatology in the Chester Coming of Antichrist," *Comparative
Drama* 5 (1971), 163–76.

10. On this counter-lineage, see, e.g., Stevens, *Cycles*, 297–303.

11. See Russell, *Lucifer* (cf. note 1, above), ch. 9, "Lucifer on the
Stage," pp. 245–73; as Russell puts it, "Hell is the place where all values
are inverted: every praise is a curse, every song a cacophony" (p. 260).
On the stench of Hell, see Thomas H. Seiler, "Filth and Stench as
Aspects of the Iconography of Hell," in Clifford Davidson and Thomas
H. Seiler, eds., *The Iconography of Hell*. Early Drama, Art, and Music
Monograph Series, 17 (Kalamazoo: Medieval Institute Publications,
1992), pp. 132–40; on the Devil's fart, R. W. Hanning, "Roasting a Friar,
Mis-taking a Wife, and other acts of Textual Harassment in the
Canterbury Tales," *SAC* 7 (1985), 3–21, at 14–16; on the farting Devil of
the N-Town plays, see Russell, pp. 252, 259, 266.

12. See *Shorter Oxford English Dictionary*. 3rd ed. rev. with Addenda
(Oxford: Clarendon Press, repr. 1959), under "Harrow" (v.2) and "Harrow, haro" (interj.).

13. Sanford Brown Meech and Hope Emily Allen, eds. *The Book of
Margery Kempe*. EETS O.S. 212 (Oxford: Oxford U. Press, 1940), p. 7. See
also Pamela Scheingorn, "'Who can open the doors of his face?' The
Iconography of Hell Mouth," in Davidson and Seiler, *Iconography*, pp. 1–
19. In the Middle English poem on the Harrowing of Hell, preserved in
three fourteenth-century manuscripts, Christ, after announcing that he
will bind Satan in his throne in Hell—to prevent the Devil from going
about the world stealing souls from God—adds, "The smale deuelen
that beth hounstronge, / Hoe sulen among moncun ȝonge / Forto
hauen alle hem / That hem ne willeth stonden aȝein." This may be an
early reference to the disruptive activities of "smale deuelen" in the

plays. See William Henry Hulme, ed. *The Middle-English Harrowing of Hell and Gospel of Nicodemus.* EETS E.S. 100 (Oxford: Oxford U. Press, 1907), p.12 (I quote from the Digby Ms, ll. 123–26).

14. See the Wakefield "Herod the Great," ll. 80–144 (ed. Bevington, pp. 440–42), for Herod's ranting; the Wakefield "Killing of Abel," ll. 59–65, 87–88 (ed. Bevington, pp. 277–78), for Cain's anal-centered abuse of Abel, and the Digby "Mary Magdalen," ll. 1171–72 (ed. Bevington, p. 725), for the anal insult of the heathen "Presbyter's" boy to his master.

15. "Killing of Abel," ll. 417–36 (ed. Bevington, pp. 287–88); see Bennett A. Brockman, "The Law of Man and the Peace of God: Judicial Process as Satiric Theme in the Wakefield *Mactatio Abel,*" *Speculum* 49 (1974): 699–707.

16. Robert Weimann, *Shakespeare and the Popular Tradition in the Theater: Studies in the Social Dimension of Dramatic Form and Function,* ed. Robert Schwartz (Baltimore and London: Johns Hopkins U. Press, 1978), esp. Ch. 2, "The Folk Play and Social Custom"; Ch. 3, "The Mystery Cycles"; and Ch. 4, "Moralities and Interludes." Alan Brody, *The English Mummers and Their Plays: Traces of Ancient Mystery* (Philadelphia: U. of Pennsylvania Press, 1969), distinguishes three types of "men's dramatic ceremonial": the Hero Combat, the Sword Play, and the Wooing Ceremony. The many versions of these plays "collected" by antiquarians and folklorists postdate the medieval plays by several centuries, but it seems clear that the routines in them are of great antiquity and can hardly be said to have descended from the pre-Reformation drama. Speaking of figures named Beelzebub and Little Devil Doubt in the Mummer's play, Brody says, "there is little question that there was some exchange betwen the medieval drama and the men's ceremonial; but it is an example of infiltration and cross-influencing, the threads of which are so inextricable that it would be folly to try to untangle them" (p. 61).

17. See Weimann, *Shakespeare,* pp. 33–35, 138–43.

18. On the doctor, see Brody, pp. 55–59; Gail McMurray Gibson, *The Theater of Devotion: East Anglian Drama and Society in the Late Middle Ages* (Chicago: U. of Chicago Press, 1989), pp. 36–38.

19. Ashley, 136 and note 26. The opening scenes of Federico Fellini's film, *Amarcord,* depict another such "folk ritual for banishing harmful elements," the burning in effigy of the "Winter Witch," in an atmosphere of communal celebration and license.

20. See M. M. Bakhtin, *Rabelais and His World,* tr. Hélène Iswolsky (Cambridge, Mass.: M.I.T. Press, 1968). For recent, convincing reading of a tyrant and his diabolic discourse in terms of carnival and the carnival-

esque, see Martin Stevens, "Herod as Carnival King" (MS.; publication forthcoming).

21.   Assessing the effect of "diabolized" representation of leaders of popular uprisings in Shakespeare's history plays, Peter Womack writes, "in the popular theatre, this diabolism gives [figures such as Jack Cade and his troops] access to what might be called the privileges of *stage* devils. The stage has a space for their thorough-going inversion of truth and reason—that of comedy. They are clowns, unleashing upon the society of the drama the torrent of violent horseplay, nonsense, parodic doubletalk and metatheatrical jokes which characterise the devils and vices of medieval theatre" (p. 131; emphasis Womack's). Cf. Weimann, *Shakespeare,* pp. 133–42, on the meeting of folk festivity and diabolic inversion in the nonsense/doubletalk of comic servants, et al, in the religious and moral plays.

22.   Charles Phythian-Adams, "Ceremony and the citizen: the communal year at Coventry, 1450–1550," in Peter Clark and Paul Slack, eds. *Crisis and Order in English Towns, 1500–1700* (Toronto: U. Of Toronto Press, 1972), 57–85.

23.   See Alexandra F. Johnston and Margaret Rogerson Dorrell, eds., *Records of Early English Drama: York,* 2 Vols. (Toronto, 1979), p. 43 (trans., p. 728). In fact, the plays remained on the feast day and the Corpus Christi procession was moved forward to the eve of the feast.

24.   See Chester "Fall of Lucifer," 1.218, "You have begone a parlous playe"; R. M. Lumiansky and D. Mills, eds. *The Chester Mystery Cycle,* Vol. 1: Text (EETS SS 1; Oxford: Oxford U. Press, 1974), p. 9. See Stevens, *Cycles,* pp. 300–310 on "parlous play" in the Chester Cycle.

25.   For contemporaneous references to the Skinners Well "cycle," see E. K. Chambers, *The Mediaeval Stage* (Oxford: Oxford U. Press, 1903), Vol. 2, pp. 380–81. The circumstances (and dating) of the origins of the provincial cycles are unclear in most cases; for early records, see the apposite *REED* volumes (cf. note 23, above), and for a controversial investigation of special problems in dating and locating the Wakefield (or Towneley) cycle, see Barbara D. Palmer, "'Towneley Plays' or 'Wakefield Cycle' Revisited," *Comparative Drama* 21 (1987–88), 318–48.

26.   All quotations from, and references to, *CT* follow Larry D. Benson, ed. *The Riverside Chaucer,* Third Edition (Boston: Houghton Mifflin, 1987). The reference to Absolon's "lightnesse and maistrye" may be ironic, but it may also reflect the fact that there was a tradition of playing Herod with a certain acrobatic agility. See the one-word stage directions (?), perhaps refering to objects that Herod siezes or throws about, in the Chester "Three Kings" play; and, for the tradition of Herod

brandishing a sword and assuming contorted positions in high medieval pictorial representations of him, see Miriam Anne Skey, "The Iconography of Herod in the Fleury Playbook and in the Visual Arts," in Thomas P. Campbell and Clifford Davidson, ed. *The Fleury Playbook: Essays and Studies.* Early Drama, Art, and Music Monograph Series, 7 (Kalamazoo: Medieval Institute Publications, 1985), pp. 128–30, 135–36. In any case, since the ranting Herod was sure to dominate the stage, Absolon could certainly show "maistrye" of a certain kind (though not necessarily the kind most helpful to lovers) by playing him. See further Beryl Rowland, "The Play of the *Miller's Tale*: A Game Within a Game," *ChauR* 5 (1970): 140–46, and "Chaucer's Blasphemous Churl: A New Interpretation of the *Miller's Tale*," in Beryl Rowland, ed. *Chaucer and Middle English Studies in Honor of Rossell Hope Robbins* (London: George Allen and Unwin, 1974), pp. 43–55.

27. E.g., in the N-Town version, when Mary's attendant claims that an angel has told Mary "that Goddys sone in Trynite, / For mannys sake a man wolde be," Joseph replies bitterly, "An aungel! Allas! Alas! Fy for schame! . . . / It was sum boy began this game, . . . / And ȝe ȝeve hym now an aungel name." "Joseph's Doubt," ll. 68–77, in Stephen Spector, ed. The *N-Town Play* Vol. 1 (EETS SS 11; Oxford, 1991), p. 126. See further, Sandra Pierson Prior, "Parodying Typology and the Mystery Plays in the *Miller's Tale*," *JMRS* 16 (1986), 57–73, at 61 and note 10.

28. Kelsie B. Harder, "Chaucer's Use of the Mystery Plays in the *Miller's Tale*," *MLQ* 17 (1956), 193–98; Rowland, "Play" and "Churl" (cf. note 26); Prior (cf. note 27).

29. Cf. Prior, 64: "Nicholas actually plays both the role of *Deus artifex*, the Creator and Lord of history and director of the drama of salvation, and that of Lucifer, the God-Imitator and director of our fall."

30. As the N-Town Lucifer/Satan falls from Heaven, he exclaims, "for fere of fyre a fart I crake!" ("Fall of Lucifer," ll. 81–82; Spector, ed. *N-Town*, p. 24)—a response which could also be Nicholas's, if he knew of the red-hot coulter poised below his exposed buttocks. See note 11, above, on the farting N-Town Devil.

31. Interestingly, in the Chester "Massacre of the Innocents" play, Herod, the very tyrant at the center of Absolon's mimetic repertory, reacts with a similar locution to the arrival of devils to take him off to Hell: "I bequeth here in this place / my soule to be with Sathanas" (ll. 430–31; Lumiansky and Mills, eds. *Chester*, p. 201). This parallel has been noted (p. 39) in the course of an extremely provocative discussion of Chaucer's relationship to the mystery plays by John M. Ganim, *Chaucerian Theatricality* (Princeton: Princeton University Press, 1990), pp.

38–44; Ganim's entire third chapter, "The Poetics of Theatricality" (pp. 31–55), is highly relevant to the present discussion.

32. Cf. Prior, 62: "[Absolon] promptly goes off to Gerveys the blacksmith who, working at night before a roaring fire, is obviously Satan/Vulcan." See also Edmund Reiss, "Daun Gerveys in the *Miller's Tale*," *PLL* 6 (1970), 115–24. The alliterative poem, "Swarte smekyd smethes. . . ," printed from a fifteenth-century Ms. in Kenneth Sisam, ed. *Fourteenth Century Verse and Prose* (Oxford:Clarendon Press, 1921, repr. 1967), pp. 169–70, describes the nighttime activities and sounds of a smithy in terms very reminiscent of diabolic stage pandemonium.

33. See *Inferno* XXV.1–3 and the commentary on the passage in Dante Alighieri, *The Divine Comedy*, tr. C. Singleton, Vol. 1, *Inferno*; 2. Commentary (Princeton: Princeton, U. Press, 1970), p. 428.

34. See R. W. Hanning, "Appropriate Enough: Telling 'Classical' Allusions in Chaucer's *Canterbury Tales*," in Karl-Ludwig Selig and Robert Somerville, eds. *Florilegium Columbianum: Essays in Honor of Paul Oskar Kristeller* (New York: Italica Press, 1987), pp. 117–18; Edmund Reiss, "Chaucer's Miller, Pilate, and the Devil," *AnM* 5 (1964), 21–25.

35. In the *Ordo representacionis Ade* (or *Jeu d'Adam*), the Devil tempts Adam directly, only turning his wiles toward the woman after the man has unequivocally rejected him (ll. 113–204; ed. Bevington, pp. 85–90).

36. See Winthrop Wetherbee, *Chaucer and the Poets: An Essay on Troilus and Criseyde* (Ithaca: Cornell U. Press, 1984) on Chaucer's aspirations to be a true poet in the classical mold.

37. See Hanning, "Roasting a Friar" (cf. note 11, above), 9–16.

38. I am pleased to acknowledge the assistance of Mary Agnes Edsall and my colleague, Prof. Eric Jager, in the preparation of this essay. I would also like to thank the members of my Fall 1992 Medieval Drama seminar at Columbia University for the stimulus they have provided to my thoughts about the pre-Reformation English plays.

The Semiotics of Comedy in Chaucer's Religious Tales

Daniel F. Pigg

Among the *Canterbury Tales*, the religious tales[1] have attracted a great deal of attention on such subjects as the appropriateness of the pilgrim teller to tale, the pathos of the tales, the poet's modifications of his sources, and reading strategies that emphasize the allegorical significance of the stories. Traditionally, comedy has been characterized by the presence of incongruity, of absurdity,[2] of play,[3] and, of course, laughter as it exists within the fictive frame of the text as well as in the response it generates from a receiving audience.[4] Scholars, however, have been less conscious of the implications of comedy in these tales.

Some comment on their literary merits, and at times, either dismiss or undervalue the presence of comedy. Morton W. Bloomfield, for example, notes "The *Clerk's Tale*, the *Physician's Tale*, the *Second Nun's Tale* as well as MLT [*Man of Law's Tale*] cannot fully engage our sympathies or even sometimes our interest. They are the embarrassment of the *Canterbury Tales*."[5] Earlier, in her study on Chaucerian comedy, Helen Storm Corsa uses the phrase "simple proclamations of a simple truth" and suggests that these tales are "necessary complements to the more earthly and complex tales that outnumber them."[6] And in his attempt to develop a vocabulary for Chaucerian comedy, Paul G. Ruggiers omits the religious tales altogether.[7] Certainly, the fabliau tales have received greater attention for their obvious laughter and humor, and have overshadowed our perception of the comic potential in the religious tales. Admittedly, these tales are inscribed with alterity in terms of subject matter and of the method of presentation. They lack the trans-historical qualities of the fabliau tales, but they may help us to re-historicize one of the most important poets of the late Middle Ages. They certainly spoke to Chaucer's age, and we must recover that method of communication if we wish to understand one of the several facets of Chaucerian comedy.

Why critical studies have simultaneously privileged and marginalized certain tales is matter for conjecture. However, it is clear that the religious tales possess an overriding sense of comedy—a particularly complex one—charged with problematic issues. Further, the sense of comedy seen in these tales forms a major part of the ideological core underlying the entire Canterbury project. Certainly compilers of the Hengwrt and Ellesmere manuscripts saw the potential of the tales in that way. That Chaucer privileges the subject matter of the religious tales in the *Retraction* is revealing. Whether we read the *Retraction* seriously or as part of a larger irony of Chaucer's intention and evaluation of the enduring qualities of his works, we must come to terms with a writer whose historical location within the comic mode needs further investigation.

The religious tales present what we will term a refiguring of the semiotic properties of comedy. Beginning with the *Man of Law's Tale* and ending with the *Second Nun's Tale* (Ellesmere order), Chaucer explores the range of comedy from a religious and cosmic perspective. What begins as an earth-bound working out of comedy on linguistic and social levels moves to the celestial realm and thus mirrors the pilgrimage to Canterbury/New Jerusalem. The signs of earth become the things of heaven. The early tales (*Man of Law's Tale* and *Clerk's Tale*) set up a paradigm that is semiotically refigured in the later tales (*Physician's Tale*, *Prioress's Tale*, and *Second Nun's Tale*). The most significant aspects of semiotic refiguring involve the interconnected relationship between the tellers and the characters in the tales and the discourse that the tellers linguistically generate around the "central" characters. A movement in the later tales conflates these relationships, and thus produces a fiction of a different order. Such a semiotic process seems to stabilize the possibility of comedy throughout the collection we call the *Canterbury Tales*.

Before examining the tales, we must establish precisely what this medieval version of comedy includes and comment on the implications of tale order for this analysis.

I

As *Versions of Medieval Comedy*[8] has shown, comedy was deeply rooted in medieval society and cultural texts. A knowledge of comedy from the classical period does not directly inform the comic sense known in the Middle Ages, but rather through the works of Latin grammarians.[9] Donatus (*c.* 350) transmitted several ideas, noting that "Comedy, because it is a poem composed as an imitation of life and a likeness of character, consists in gesture and speech."[10] In his discussion of the parts of comedy, he termed the final stage "catastrophe"—"the change of the situation to a pleasant outcome, a change made clear to all through the knowledge of what has happened."[11] Later in his comments on Aristophanes, John Tzetzes (*c.* 1100–80) suggested that comedy is conscious of class and that laughter is the principal effect of language.[12] Clearly, these observations are based on classical notions of drama. Medieval writers developed their own sense of comedy, however, particularly that arising from religious contexts. The ecclesiastical sphere contributed two such concepts.

The notion of the mass as drama which moves from *tristia* to *gaudium* contains this sense of comedy.[13] Honorius of Autun envisioned an homology between theatrical representation and the celebration of the mass. That he refers to the celebrant as a "*tragicus*" (tragedian) does not indicate that the events recounted in the mass are tragic, but more about his perception that comedy in the sense that he received it was superficial, if not blasphemous.[14] Clearly, however, that he describes the departure from the mass as joyous after the overthrow of the forces of evil suggests the overall sense is comic. The mass reenacts the divine comedy in a semiotically controlled space with ritual gestures and verbal signs.

The liturgical calendar—a semiotic refiguring and arranging of the story of *Heilsgeschichte* (salvation history)—in its yearly progression marks the events of sacred history from Advent through Pentecost and beyond. That the prescribed readings near the end of the season after Pentecost turn to the fulfillment of human history in an apocalyptic sense further underscores the movement from *tristia* to *gaudium* seen in the performance of the mass.[15] Both of these sign systems contain the implicit form of comedy seen in Chaucer's religious tales, but Chaucer's comic notion is also traceable in one of his major sources: Dante.[16]

Dante's conception of comedy in the *Divine Comedy* and observations arising in commentaries on the poem influenced Chaucer's development of comic theory in a religious context. Recent studies on Dante's influence on Chaucer in *Troilus and Criseyde* by Karla Taylor[17] and in the *Canterbury Tales* by Richard Neuse[18] demonstrate the English poet's grappling with the material and ideology of his Italian exemplar. The *Epistle to Can Grande*, as A. J. Minnis and A. B. Scott note, initiated a considerable number of fourteenth-century commentaries on the poem.[19] In the *Epistle*, the writer, perhaps Dante himself, defines comedy according to its usage in the poem's title and material as:

> a certain kind of poetical narration which differs from all
> others. It differs, then, from tragedy in its subject-matter,
> in that tragedy at the beginning is admirable and placid,
> but at the end or issue is foul and horrible . . . whereas
> comedy begins with sundry adverse conditions, but ends
> happily, as appears from the comedies of Terence. . . .
> If we consider the subject matter [of the *Divine Comedy*],
> at the beginning it is horrible and foul, as being *Hell*; but
> at the close it is happy, desirable, and pleasing, as being
> *Paradise*.[20]

Guido da Pisa and Pietro Alighieri in their commentaries, and Boccaccio in his lectures on the poem echo this same notion of comedy.[21] Whether Chaucer was aware of these interpretive texts on the poem is not significant, because they are only voicing what was the perceived view of comedy in their day.

Chaucer allows the Knight to provide a similar idea:

> I seye for me, it is a greet disese,
> Whereas men han been in greet welthe and ese,
> To heeren of hire sodeyn fal, allas!
> And the contrarie is joye and greet solas,
> As whan a man hath been in povre estaat,
> And clymbeth up and wexeth fortunat,
> And there abideth in prosperitee.
> Swich thyng is gladsom, as it thynketh me,
> And of swich thyng were goodly for to telle.

> (VII.2771–79)

In the fictive nature of the Canterbury project, the Knight has already heard several tales which support his preferred view of human action: the religious or philosophical tales.[22] That Chaucer has the Knight stop the Monk's catalog of human tragedies, preferring a comic view of the world, may show the poet's privileging of the comic discursive strategy, and with his dismissal of the bawdy tales in the *Retraction*, the comedy of the religious tales seems to form the ideological core which the poet foregrounds.

Since the present reading of the religious tales relies on the order of the tales in the collection, the implications of order for interpretation must be considered. This essay can hardly reproduce the arguments for accepting either Hengwrt or Ellesmere as the correct reflection of Chaucer's intended order. Lee Patterson provides a helpful summary of this complex issue.[23] What we need to address, however, is an issue behind all of this discussion. Clearly, Chaucer left the *Canterbury Tales* unfinished. Apparently a scribe-compiler gave the manuscript its form. Medieval criticism of biblical texts devotes a great deal of attention to questions of textual production arising from discussions of Peter Lombard's *Sentences* and provides clear distinctions among the terms author, scribe, compiler, and commentator.[24] All have a place of importance. For some reason, Chaucer scholars are less willing to grant the compiler of the Hengwrt or Ellesmere manuscript a similar position. Clearly, there are problems with either form; the compilers are not as careful in producing the text as we would prefer. No doubt Chaucer saw this carelessness as a problem as well, for he complained about errors creeping into the text of his works in the poem to Adam, his scrivener. If Dolores Warwick Frese is correct, this fear loomed large in Chaucer's mind and may be seen in poetic manifestation in the *Canon's Yeoman's Prologue* and *Tale*.[25] She argues that this tale, written after the Hengwrt project, shows an intriguing relationship between alchemy and the medieval book trade.[26] We cannot determine Chaucerian intentionality—an anathema in some critical circles. What we can note, however, is that medieval readers of either manuscript order would probably not have been as bothered about this question, but be more concerned about what the tales in the order they appear in the manuscript communicate about medieval comedy, Chaucer's and the compiler's.

Most readers would likely follow Ellesmere, thus encountering the religious tales in the following order: *Man of Law's Tale, Clerk's Tale, Physician's Tale, Prioress's Tale,* and *Second Nun's Tale.* If they followed Hengwrt, the reading experience would obviously be different, and the sense of Chaucer's experimentation in comic form would not move from the temporal to the spiritual realm. As readers in the late twentieth century, we cannot reconstruct an absolute view of how medieval people read texts. What we can do is to suggest how the author and compiler work from different angles and produce at least one form of comedy through one order of the *Canterbury Tales.*

II

The *Man of Law's Tale*, the first religious tale, establishes a complex paradigm for comedy with its orchestrations of discourses that attempt to establish homologies between human and divine action. The rhetoric of the Man of Law, the depiction of Constance on literal and symbolic levels, and the emphasis on providence all interconnect to produce what Bloomfield calls a simultaneous "tragedy of victimization" and "Christian comedy."[27] What critics have not observed is how multi-layering generates comedy from the verbal level seen in the Man of Law's rhetorical and narratologically conscious statements that simultaneously establish a code for reading the action and the humorous undercurrent that threatens to undermine his credibility[28] to the verbally protected and remote sphere where Constance operates to the unvoiced, yet dominant image of providence. The Man of Law's discourse and the linguistic zone around Constance require further examination.

How we view the Man of Law as a narrator will in large measure determine how we understand the comic aspects of the tale, for he is the shaping force on the fictive level. He is at once the textual creation of Chaucer as he participates in the creation of the figures of Constance, Alla, and Maurice in the tale. Scholarship is by no means consistent in its perception of him. Some see him as a thinly veiled version of Chaucer, who considers the overall project of the *Canterbury Tales* as he attempts to balance *sentence* and *solas*.[29] Others see his vocation as a lawyer foregrounded in the tale's contemplation of legal matters, including canon law.[30] And still others see him as little more than a pious hypocrite whose religious knowledge is flawed.[31] All, however, must come to terms with his use of rhetoric and his particular manipulation of the devices of *"occupatio, exclamatio, interrogatio, sententia, comparatio,* and pathetic prayers," all of which he grafts onto the Constance story from Trivet and Gower as he moves the narrative toward a saint's legend.[32] We cannot, however, assess rhetorical forms that attempt to alter emotional appeal as comic anachronistically, for they are part of the coded construction of the tale and determine its intention. From the classical period, rhetorical figures were perceived as having the ability to construct a sense of reality and to sway audience response.[33] Clearly, Chaucer was aware of these aspects as he reconceived the tale from his sources.

The Man of Law's use of apostrophe merits special attention as it forms the basis for the narrative structure and determines the multi-layered aspects of comedy. Bloomfield notes 15 or 16 of them in the Man of Law's discourse.[34] They help to defamiliarize the action in the tale and to distance the audience to achieve comedy.[35] In an homologous sense to divine providence in the events surrounding Constance's protection, the narrator serves as a textual providence.[36] He governs the narrative in an overt way. If earthly signs point to heavenly things in partial and imperfect ways, then the verbal comedy which the narrator oversees is a sign to direct attention to divine providence. The apostrophes forecast, warn, and instruct; and on occasion, they might provoke laughter under doctrinally correct circumstances.

In this light, his apostrophe to the Sultaness of Syria after she convinces a group of her country's people to fain conversion and then to commit murder at the wedding feast of her son and Constance is suggestive:

> O Sowdanesse, roote of iniquitee!
> Virago, thou Semyrame the secounde!
> O serpent under femynynytee,
> Lik to the serpent depe in helle ybounde!
> O feyned womman, al that may confounde
> Vertu and innocence, thurgh thy malice,
> Is bred in thee, as nest of every vice!
>
> (II.358–64)

Some male hearers or readers might laugh at the antifeminist diatribe—a product of the patriarchal system that Carolyn Dinshaw observes is dominant in the tale[37]. All might laugh at the connection between Sultaness and the devil. To laugh at the demonic is sanctioned by ecclesiastical circles and may be a sign of one's spiritual security.[38] The Sultaness, although momentarily "successful," is ultimately killed by the Christian forces of the Roman emperor. Donegild, the mother of Alla, occupies a similar position later in the narrative, and she too is verbally damned: "Fy feendlych spirit, for I dare wel telle, / Thogh thou heere walke, thy spirit is in helle!" (II.783–84). They both participate in the tale's version of comedy, since justice is implicit in comedy.

While these rhetorical devices control the narrative pace, the Man of Law's greatest achievement in comedy involves his representation of Constance. Many critics point out the narrator's calculated measures to generate pathos for her. Bloomfield, however, sees the depiction as "near to laughing comedy."[39] As we will see below, the Man of Law is careful not to make Constance seem laughable. To laugh at a person closely associated with the heroic figures of saints' legends would be inappropriate.[40] Even dramatic texts that provoke laughter, as V. A. Kolve notes, never allow viewers to laugh at the Virgin or

Christ. For example in the Towneley *Second Shepherd's Play*, the raucous humor does not circulate around the Virgin and child.[41] The same is the case with Constance. In assessing Chaucer's "originality" in the *Man of Law's Tale*, Edward A. Block speculates that avoiding unnecessary details in Trivet's version, the poet purposely focuses attention of Constance and that he works "to invest [the fortunes of Constance] with an aura of romantic haziness and vagueness."[42] What Chaucer is doing more precisely is using Constance as the name for a character and a discourse. In the case of the latter, she represents the legal concept of *justitia*.[43] That she speaks only a few times in the tale contributes to this "aura" and suggests that the number of words is less important than the theological and semiotic process contained in them—perhaps a commentary on the excesses of the Man of Law himself. Clearly, Constance's few remarks establish her as a suffering servant. At the court of Alla, where she is on trial for the murder of Hermengild, the narrator comments: "For as the lomb toward his deeth is broght, / So stant this innocent bifore the kyng" (II.617–18). The lines are a paraphrase of Isaiah 53:7, which forecasts the actions of the suffering servant, later interpreted by the early Christian community as a prophecy of Christ's trial and crucifixion.[44] Her moments of speech demand further attention, particularly as they situate her position relative to divine providence—the creator of comedy.

Constance's speeches and prayers do not so much evoke our sympathy as they contextualize her situation within larger frames of historical reference—a key to religious comedy. Her prayer to the cross, after being set adrift in a "ship al steereless" (II.439) by the Sultaness and residents of Syria, establishes this tone:

> O cleere, o welful auter, hooly croys,
> Reed of the Lambes blood ful of pitee,
> That wessh the world fro the olde iniquitee,
> Me fro the feend and fro his clawes kepe,
> That day that I shal drenchen in the depe.
> Victorious tree, proteccioun of trewe,
> That oonly worthy were for to bere
> The Kyng of Hevene with his woundes newe,
> The white Lamb, that hurt was with a spere,

Flemere of feendes out of hym and here
On which thy lymes feithfully extenden,
Me kepe, and yif me myght my lyf t'amenden.

(II.451–62)

Her perplexity is increased by an inability to control the movement of the ship, a situation that emphasizes how "divine governance supplies the deficiencies of human governance."[45] In fact, the observation can be extended to every instance of imperial or regal leadership in the tale, because all rulers have some sense of blindness which impacts Constance's fortunes. As the narrator continues, he contemplates her providential care in a series of rhetorical questions, all of which are Chaucerian originals.[46] He mentions Daniel in the den of lions, Jonah in the whale, the Hebrews crossing the Red Sea, and Mary the Egyptian's being fed. These are not only suggestive of providential acts, but also of comedic structure, for in each case there is a movement from *tristia* to *gaudium*. They provide a narratological frame in which to contextualize Constance's situation.

Constance's own words validate a similar aspect in a tale which stresses homology as a structural principle. In the episode in Alla's court when the evidence seems to suggest that she is guilty of Hermengild's murder she prays:

Immortal God, that savedest Susanne
Fro false blame, and thou, merciful mayde,
Marie I meene, doghter to Seint Anne,
Bifore whos child angeles synge Osanne,
If I be giltlees of this feloyne,
My socour be, for ellis shal I dye!

(II.639–44)

Again, references to biblical figures reflect the comic dimension. The false knight is discovered, and for a brief moment Constance again experiences *gaudium*, but this instance and all, as the Man of Law notes, are transitory.

Even at the end of the tale, the Man of Law leaves readers or hearers with an expectation that there is final joy without change after death for Constance. Earthly comedies in this sense are signs of heavenly things. Still the focus for the *Man of Law's Tale* is earthly existence and earthly comedy in its semiotic dimensions. The rhetoric of the narrator activates, manages, and circumscribes the comedy of Constance. This tale's reliance on discursive forms to advance the comedy establishes the norms for religious comedy.

Similar to the *Man of Law's Tale*, the *Clerk's Tale* has received a less than favorable critical review.[47] In fact, scholarship seems to be more concerned with removing the barriers for a reading of the tale to ensue than with examining the tale for its inherent comedy. Exegetical and psychological critics have addressed the difficulties of plot and characterization,[48] while others have attempted to historicize the tale in the context of scholastic learning.[49] In his request that the Clerk tell a tale, Harry Bailly says:

> Telle us som murie thyng of aventures.
> Youre termes, your colours, and youre figures,
> Keepe hem in stoor til so be ye endite
> Heigh style, as whan that men to kynges write.
> Speaketh so pleyn at this tyme, we yow preye,
> That we may understonde what ye seye.

> (IV.15–20)

Yet the tale that ensues can hardly be termed "pleyn." While the Canterbury pilgrims may have understood the Clerk's signifiers, they may have missed the signifieds (the sense). Peggy A. Knapp sees the tale as an outgrowth of the Clerk's scholastic method.[50] In a sense his method becomes a self-reflexive end in itself. Robert Stepsis[51] and David C. Steinmetz[52] in separate studies have demonstrated the correspondence between the plot and character in the tale and nominalist philosophy to which the Clerk would have been exposed at Oxford. The aspect of the narrator in this tale and the associations of Walter, Griselda, and the testing are more problematic than their counterparts in the *Man of Law's Tale*.

The narrator of the *Clerk's Tale* occupies a more complex position relative to the fiction he creates than did the narrator in the *Man of Law's Tale*. Robin Kirkpatrick notes that the narrator is Chaucer's chief addition to his source for the tale.[53] The questions which all readers or hearers must have answered concern the narrator's relationship to the material he presents, for herein lies an aspect of the comedy. Does he approve of Walter's cruel testing? What do Walter and Griselda represent on the symbolic level? Do their presentations contain irony? Does the Clerk suggest whether he prefers the audience to interpret his tale on the literal level alone, or is he telling a tale which is incomplete if not an enigma on the literal level, therefore, mandating a multi-level reading of the text? And perhaps most perplexing of all, how can a tale with so much mental anguish be comic? The narratorial interruptions and *Envoy* suggest answers to these questions.

The narratorial comments, not in the elevated style of the Man of Law for the most part, suggest even from the beginning that Walter was not quite the monarch he should be. In a tale that concerns itself with order, as S. K. Heninger, Jr. notes, such a criticism is important.[54] In his first comment, the Clerk condemns Walter's excessive hunting because "he considered noght / In tyme comynge what myghte hym bityde" (IV.78–79). He does not seem concerned with his role as one who must serve the "commune profit" (IV.431, 1194)—a role that Griselda occupies in an exemplary way. As the person who provides stability within the social model, he must carefully reconcile his private desires with public demands. At the least, the Clerk suggests Walter is far from the ideal monarch, a sign of God. After the birth of their daughter, Walter begins his testing or perhaps intensifies it (IV.456–57). The narrator comments: "But as for me, I seye that yvele it sit / To assaye a wyf whan that it is no nede, / And putten hire in angwyssh and in drede" (IV.460–62). In regard to her second testing, he again comments: "O nedeless was she tempted in assay! / But wedded men ne knowe no mesure, / Whan that they fynde a pacient creature" (IV.621–23). And before the third testing, the Clerk, articulating the sentiments of the masses, suggests: "But natheless, for ernest ne for game, / He of his crueel purpose nolde stente; / To tempte his wyf was set al his entente" (IV.733–35). Taken together, these comments suggest the ambivalence of play.

The ernest/game axis, most often seen in the fabliau, suggests a comic world—a multi-layered one. Laura Kendrick suggests that the Clerk may be "deconstructing" the role of Griselda in the *Envoy*.[55] John M. Ganim contends the voice here is a product of carnival. He suggests "The Clerk we see now is the Clerk as a student in town, the student as participant in such celebrations as the Feast of Fools."[56] The first two stanzas are suggestive:

> Grisilde is deed, and eek her pacience,
> And bothe atones buryed in Ytaille;
> For which I crie in open audience
> No wedded man so hardy be t'assaille
> His wyves pacience in hope to fynde
> Grisildis, for in certein he shal faille.
> O noble wyves, ful of heigh prudence,
> Lat noon humylitee youre tonge naille,
> Ne lat no clerk have cause or diligence
> To write of yow a storie of swich mervaille
> As of Grisildis pacient and kynde,
> Lest Chichevache yow swelwe in hire entraille!

> (IV.1177–88)

In a sense, the *Envoy* shows that the Clerk understands well the power of signs. He turns the serious reading of divine comedy upside down by refiguring the signs. Even in game, however, there can be an underlying seriousness. To parody order usually requires a belief in the particular sign system that empowers that order. As a person trained in grammar, rhetoric, and logic,[57] the Oxenford Clerk is capable of engaging in an intellectual game— one which he obviously not only has some commitment to as a serious comment on order and obedience, but also a fiction which he creates to be viewed within a complex web of sovereignty whose ideological foundations have been undermined by the Wife of Bath. In a sense, this Clerk puts the Wife of Bath in her place (his perception of it) as she did her clerical husband. There are clearly several agendas working together here.

The aspect of comedy involving the narrator seems to be conducted on the literal level, but his characterization and testing of Griselda seem more attuned to the symbolic. The Clerk pushes the characterization of Griselda toward perfection,

especially with his continual use of the word "patient." He
darkens Walter's characterization, thus creating more of the
polarity we saw in the paradigmatic *Man of Law's Tale* between
Constance and all pagans. Neither Griselda nor Walter is a real
person. Exegetical critics usually see Walter as God and Griselda
as humanity.[58] Edward I. Condren, however, argues that
Walter's obvious cruelty prohibits his being God; instead he
represents humanity tempting the creator. Griselda is more
properly associated with God.[59] Given the understanding of
medieval hierarchy, however, Condren's notions seem unlikely.

Throughout the tale, the Clerk establishes several codes for
reading Griselda. In his first description of Griselda and her
father, he notes:

> Amonges thise povre folk ther dwelte a man
> Which that was holden povrest of hem alle;
> But hye God somtyme senden kan
> His grace into a litel oxes stalle.

(IV.204–07)

Clearly, there are parallels here to God's choice of the Virgin
Mary. While not born of nobility, Griselda possesses a nobility of
character which attracts Walter to her. Nobility is an inborn
quality. The Clerk uses a similar approach in comparing Griselda
and Job:

> Men speke of Job, and moost for his humblesse,
> As clerkes, whan hem list, konne wel endite,
> Namely of men, but as in soothfastnesse,
> Though clerkes preise wommen but a lite,
> Ther kan no man in humblesse hym acquite
> As wommen kan, ne kan been half so trewe
> As wommen been, but it be falle of newe.

(IV.932–38)

Knapp, however, senses some irony in this passage as part of the
tale's "comic overstatement."[60] Donald H. Reiman accurately
notes that the narrator emphasizes the differences between Job
and Griselda.[61] Griselda surpasses him, and thus moves further
from the realm of the human and believable. Similar to

Constance, she becomes a discourse in the hands of the skillful Clerk. In a sense she embodies those things which Walter needs to possess to become an effective ruler.

At the end of the tale when Griselda and her children are reunited, the Clerk offers some hermeneutic aid to readers and hearers. What does the verbal signifier "Griselda" have as its signified and referent? We would expect patience to be his answer, but instead he says that

> This storie is seyd nat for that wyves sholde
> Folwen Grisilde as in humylitee,
> For it were importable, though they wolde,
> But for that every wight, in his degree,
> Sholde be constant in adversitee
> As was Grisilde; therfore Petrak writeth
> This storie, which with heigh stile he enditeth.

(IV.1142–48)

The original signifier "Griselda" and its signified "patience" have no connection to an external reality; no referent can be perceived. The Clerk in the *Envoy* underlines the aspect of interpretation as a semiotic act. In terms of the new ternary model of the sign, Griselda is the signifier; constant is the signified, and the referent is the audience. The Clerk resignifies the tale so that its import crosses gender and hierarchical lines. Again, he plays a game with meaning, but this one is directed to all hearers, not just the Wife of Bath and to all humanity in a very obvious tropological way. This comedy is still one that works itself out on the earthly plane.

With the *Physician's Tale*, we encounter a very different kind of comedy—one that defers our understanding of the comic beyond the earthly plane through the process of semiotic refiguring. Perhaps this intangible quality and characters just short of the demonic prompt Harry Bailly to respond so strongly at the end of the tale. Laura Kendrick suggests, however, that the length of this "abreactive fiction," normally episodic in form, may provoke the Host's response.[62] It is a commonplace observation that his readings of the tales are hardly comprehensive, and are at times quite eccentric. Yet critics have at times responded to this tale with force equal to the Host's. Sheila

Delany suggests that Chaucer's omissions from his sources "deprive the story of convincing dramatic motivation and his characters of plausible psychological and ethical motives."[63] At the conclusion of an article in which she also considers Chaucer's diminishing of the role of and motivation for the masses, Delany contends "that if the project taught him something as an artist it was the importance of choosing material more suitable to his particular genius."[64] Robert Longsworth,[65] Emerson Brown, Jr.,[66] and D. W. Robertson, Jr.[67] find similar problems with the tale, but attribute the moral ambivalence, among other characteristics, to the Physician himself, who is at least a suspicious figure, if not a charlatan. Comedy thus arises from the Physician's calculated alterations; his words are also self-reflexive, and thus he highlights himself in unflattering ways. What is clear is that the Physician seems to be subsumed under the discursive form.

Separating the teller from the discursive voice is difficult, except in his moral tag at the conclusion:

> Heere may men seen how synne hath his merite.
> Beth war, for no man woot whom God wil symte
> In no degree, ne in which manere wyse;
> The worm of conscience may agryse
> Of wikked lyf, though it so pryvee be
> That no man woot therof but God and he.
> For be he lewed man, or ellis lered,
> He noot how soone that he shal been afered.
> Therfore I rede yow this conseil take:
> Forsaketh synne, er synne yow forsake.

(VI.277–86)

Clearly, disparity exists between the tale and the moral tag, not just in the sense that only Appius seems to fit into it.[68] Lee C. Ramsey argues that it "misses the point" because the judge, Virginius, and particularly Virginia are omitted.[69] Taking the tale and moral tag together, he argues that "Despite man's pieties and even despite his good intent, innocence does not survive in a world where personal knowledge of sin is the best qualification for a parent, guardian, or judge."[70] How then does this tale fit into the category of a religious comedy? If we extend the implications of Ramsey's point, we see that comedy, at least as we have seen it in the earlier paradigms, is impossible. The tale points to a discursive and significative failure. Earthly comedy, characterized by a linguistically generated homology and predicated upon the divine comedy, is postponed and extended into the higher sphere of which it previously was a sign. Virginia moves beyond the concepts of space and time to become a part of the larger comic system. At this point, Chaucerian religious comedy is at its least transhistorical.

Similar to the women of other religious tales, Virginia seems to be the central focus. Critics have noted that in contradistinction to the sources, Chaucer foregrounds Virginia and her fate and moves the question of political corruption to a secondary position.[71] To this end, Chaucer adds the opening discussion about Nature's selection of Virginia. She is the ideal daughter, a paragon of virtue and particularly virginity, an aspect reflected on the verbal level. She is more than a patronymic extension of her father.[72] The tendency to compare the women of the religious tales to saints or biblical persons is repeated here with the parallel to Jepthah's daughter, although as Richard L. Hoffman notes, the circumstances for each woman are opposite. Jepthah's daughter mourns her death as a virgin; Virginia mourns having to die in order to remain one.[73] Huling Ussery contends that the suggested parallel may have more to do with timing for mourning or contemplation of the action, rather than a character assessment.[74] At the very least, it creates a code for reading the tale which distances us as readers or hearers at the same time that it increases the status of Virginia. She must suffer because of who and what she is—an aspect of the tale that is difficult to accept. Seen in the context of patristic discussions of the nature of virginity, as R. Howard Bloch observes, Virginia becomes an object of desire, and even at the moment when Appius first sees her, she loses that status.[75] While these discussions do not lessen the problem of accepting the murder of Virginia, they do suggest part of the motivation. Indeed there is "no grace" and "no remedye" (VI.236). Seen in this way, the tale of which Virginia is the center is only an anticipated comedy of the future—a comedy of silence in a place where earthly signs are unnecessary. The *Physician's Tale* is, therefore, a transitional version of semiotic refiguring.

    The *Prioress's Tale*, unlike the three tales noted thus far, makes excessive use of emotionalism as an integral part of the fiction. A characteristic that Carolyn P. Collette traces to fourteenth-century piety arising from nominalist thought, the display of grief in several forms would on the surface seem to hinder a concept of comedy in the tale.[76] On the contrary, however, it is the emotional displays of the mother, of others in the abbey, and of the Prioress that raise the events to the level of sublime comedy. That the tale, framed with codes signaling the fictional moment as a religious act, has a profound effect on the pilgrims can be noted in the *Prologue to the Tale of Sir Thopas*, which follows the *Prioress's Tale*. The poet writes: "Whan seyd was al this miracle, every man / As sobre was that wonder was to se, / Til that oure Hooste japen tho bigan, / And thanne at erst he looked upon me" (VII.691–94). To balance this contemplation Harry Bailly asks Chaucer to tell a "tale of myrthe" (VII.706). Without question, the dual aspects of the narrator on one level and the litel clergeon on another are responsible for the comic dimensions of the tale.

    The Prioress has received a great deal of scholarly attention, due in part to the ambiguities in the *General Prologue* portrait and to the blatantly obvious anti-Semitism of her tale. If we concentrate, however, on the narrator in the tale we see a slightly different image emerging—one that focuses on humility, order, justice, and ritual. Unlike many of the narrators in the
• *Canterbury Tales*, she seems less concerned about speaking in her own voice. In the Prologue to her tale, the Prioress requests that the Virgin aid her "song" (VII.487). She uses the language of liturgical authority. As several critics have noted, the readings for the mass on Holy Innocents' Day and from the Little Office of the Blessed Virgin Mary provide a conceptual frame and allusions for her tale.[77] The unambiguous discourse of liturgy becomes her model, so we should not be surprised to see a polarization of characters in the tale. The Prioress attempts to refigure the relationship between the boy in the tale and herself. Her discourse parallels his discourse. On a linguistic and conceptual level, she participates in his martyrdom and his resurrection. Her verbal signs have their referents in him.

For her the Jews in league with the "serpent Sathanas" (VII.558) might contain a slight aspect of comedy—one that certainly does not translate to a modern audience. Clearly, she along with all medieval Christian people saw the activities of the devil as futilely comic, even laughable.[78] In a real sense, the murder only furthers the comedy, because rather than destroying the boy and his song, the murderers have set forward the action of the divine in continuing the song so that others may hear. Whether others are converted by the singing is unclear; in a traditional saint's life, such an action would be commonplace. Even within the pathetic, there are seeds of comedy—here realized in the "greyn" (VII.662) placed on the child's tongue.

At the end of the tale, her invocation of Hugh of Lincoln, at least in her estimation an historical person who was murdered by the Jewish people of Lincoln, lends reality to her comic vision. He is indeed in the sphere of heavenly comedy. The invocation is also significant for another reason. In the last few tales in the Ellesmere manuscript order, there is a growing sense of distrust about language and the creation of fiction generally. The Prioress thus illustrates by "fact" and fiction the shadowy aspects of comedy.

The litel clergeon in the *Prioress's Tale* occupies a position similar to the female characters in the other religious tales, and through his action the verbal comedy of the Prioress is articulated. Critics have taken different directions here, some concentrating on the Prioress herself,[79] others on the boy as an intricate part of a narrative mandating a multi-level reading.[80] Dismissing the perversities of the boy which may be slightly amusing to readers or hearers, we can focus on the events after the murder. As Sherman Hawkins notes, the wardrobe is a "pit of misery," which can be associated with "carnal concupiscence, the depth of iniquity, the shadow of ignorance and infidelity."[81] Of course, the tale does not justify any criticism against the child. Perhaps the descent, burial, and raising are only symbolic of death and resurrection, and thus parallel the comic action of *Heilsgeschichte*. The grain upon the boy's tongue furthers and brings an end to the comic vision. Some suggest the grain may be a pearl or wheat grain,[82] both well-articulated symbols in scripture and commentary. It might be a visible sign of the soul, because when the abbot removes it, the soul departs from the body. Hawkins suggests the grain is the "word of God,"[83] noting it becomes the sacraments allegorically, knowledge tropologically, and the eternal life anagogically.[84] The grain is thus a sign of divine comedy. The litel clergeon embodies the word in his song, and moves toward a union with the Word in his death.

The *Second Nun's Tale*, the last of the religious tales in Ellesmere order, completes the poet's contemplation of religious comedy. Little is known of the narrator from the *General Prologue*, and the tale does not advance our knowledge very much. She is essentially a faceless teller. Whether her lack of identity is intentional or unintentional, it serves to establish a distance as she serves as a conduit or translator for the saint's life—a text of *auctoritas*. The person and discourse we call St. Cecilia is the generative force for the tale, not the teller. In terms of semiotic refiguring as noted in the earlier tales, this tale seems in some measure to bring this concept to an end. The speaking voice is connected to the saint. We have almost reached the end of human, earthly signs, by definition partial, that signify only at some distance from their referent. The comic dimensions of this tale reside particularly in the narrator and then on Cecilia and her confrontations.

As did the Prioress, the Second Nun invokes the aid of the Virgin Mary in telling her tale. But she goes beyond the Prioress to describe the process and the reason behind her tale as a "translacioun" (VIII.25). She notes:

> And for to putte us fro swich ydlenesse,
> That cause is of so greet confusioun,
> I have heer doone my feithful bisynesse
> After the legende in translacioun.

> (VIII.22–25)

As Roger Ellis notes, "since the translation exists only to open a door previously closed to its readers, it will not, by and large, seek to draw attention to itself; nor will it accompany its version with the kind of running commentary that the Clerk created when he reworked Petrarch."[85] Yet as Paul E. Beichner notes, Chaucer moves the emphasis to the trial scene instead of the actual martyrdom.[86] The shift suggests that the concept of comedy here is related to language and the proclamation of the word that leads to conversion.

St. Cecilia is central to the tale and the concept of comedy. Anne Eggebroten has located several points in the tale which would have provoked laughter from a medieval audience, including the wedding night conversation about the "angel" who is Cecilia's protector, and the questioning of Valerian's brother, Tiburce.[87] In all cases, as she notes, the laughter is not directed toward God or Cecilia but to the questioner or one seeking knowledge.[88] Throughout the tale, Cecilia remains the dynamic force behind the growing Christian community with the conversion of her husband, his brother, Maximus, and others. All conversions by virtue of the ritual of baptism are comic as they semiotically refigure the events of *Heilsgeschichte*. The comedy reaches its greatest contest in the trial scene with Almachius.

In the trial scene, Almachius asks Cecilia to renounce her religion and to make a sacrifice to Jupiter. The central confrontation is imaged in the following short lines:

> Almache answerde, "Chees oon of thise two:
> Do sacrifice, or Cristendom reneye,
> That thou mowe now escapen by that weye."
> At which the hooly blisful faire mayde
> Gan for to laughe.

> (VIII.458–62)

As noted earlier, religious laughter is acceptable under certain circumstances and is even allowed in the *Rule of St. Benedict*.[89] In this case, it establishes a distances between Cecilia and Almachius, signals the futility of his options and the certainty of her position, and indicates that his action, while bringing about her death, will not bring an end to the new religion. As a subverbal sign, laughter cannot be overturned or thwarted by verbal signs. It is itself a victory over human words. The trial leads on to her martyrdom, which itself affords Cecilia opportunities to proclaim the word. Cecilia has won in the war of words because she is using words to reestablish relationship between human language and the divine. Both her words and actions reinforce the concept of divine comedy in a tale which is self-conscious about the production of the language of *auctoritas*. Her tale, while displaying elements of the pathetic, presents the most developed image of comedy beyond the human sphere.

The rhythms of comedy permeate Chaucer's *Canterbury Tales* and can be seen in the religious tales. The sense of play and game, most often noted in the fabliau tales, is also present in the religious tales. Perhaps the major difference is in the implications of these elements in the tales. In religious comedy they serve as signs to point readers or hearers away from the shadowy reality of earthly comedy to the quiet and sublime divine comedy. That some of these tales were written before the *Canterbury Tales* was conceived and that they were included in that project suggest that the poet had an overall shaping fantasy for his text—one that moves toward the immutable as it refigures the comic signs. Comedy helped him to achieve that end as it was at the same time that end to which he thought all human history was moving. The richness of Chaucerian comedy allows for considerable variety, making Chaucer a poet whose texts respond in a historical way to the cultural demands and expectation of his own day and to our own.

NOTES

1. I am following the standard designation for Chaucer's religious tales: the *Man of Law's Tale*, the *Clerk's Tale*, the *Physician's Tale*, the *Prioress's Tale*, and the *Second Nun's Tale*. I have omitted the *Monk's Tale* because it is a series of tragedies, and therefore does not fit into the present investigation. All quotations from the *Canterbury Tales* are from *The Riverside Chaucer*, 3rd ed., ed. Larry D. Benson (Boston: Houghton Mifflin Company, 1987).

2. Henri Bergson, *Laughter: An Essay on the Meaning of the Comic*, trans. Cloudesley Brereton and Fred Rothwell (New York: The Macmillan Company, 1917), 1–66, 132–200.

3. Johan Huizinga, *Homo Ludens: A Study of the Play Element in Culture* (London: Routledge and Kegan Paul, 1949).

4. V.A. Kolve, *The Play Called Corpus Christi* (Stanford: Stanford University Press, 1966), 124–44.

5. Morton W. Bloomfield, "The *Man of Law's Tale*: A Tragedy of Victimization and Christian Comedy," *PMLA* 87 (1972): 384–90.

6. Helen Storm Corsa, *Chaucer: Poet of Mirth and Morality* (Notre Dame, Ind.: Notre Dame University Press, 1964), 121–34.

7. Paul G. Ruggiers, "A Vocabulary for Chaucerian Comedy: A Preliminary Sketch," in *Medieval Studies in Honor of Lillian Herlands Hornstein*, ed. Jess B. Bessinger and Robert B. Raymo (New York: New York University Press, 1977), 193–225.

8. Paul G. Ruggiers, *Versions of Medieval Comedy* (Norman: University of Oklahoma Press, 1977). See in particular the "Introduction" by Paul G. Ruggiers and "Chaucer and Comedy" by Thomas Garbáty.

9. Paul G. Ruggiers, "Introduction: Some Theoretical Considerations of Comedy in the Middle Ages," in *Versions of Medieval Comedy*, ed. Paul G. Ruggiers (Norman: University of Oklahoma Press, 1977), 1–5.

10. Donatus, "A Fragment on Comedy and Tragedy," trans. George Miltz, in *Theories of Comedy*, ed. Paul Lauter (Garden City, N.Y.: Doubleday, 1964), 27.

11. Donatus, 30.

12. John Tzetzes, "First Proem to Aristophanes," trans. Lane Cooper, In *Theories of Comedy* ed. Paul Lauter (Garden City, N.Y.: Doubleday, 1964), 33–34.

13. O. B. Hardison, Jr., *Christian Rite and Christian Drama in the Middle Ages: Essays in the Origin and Early History of Modern Drama* (Baltimore: The Johns Hopkins University Press, 1965), 83.

14. Honorius of Autun, "*Gemma Animae*," in *Drama of the Medieval Church*, ed. Karl Young. 2 vols. (New York: Oxford University Press, 1933), 1:83.

15. Hardison, 83.

16. Scholarship is generally in agreement on the relationship between Dante and Chaucer. For a detailed treatment of this subject, see Howard Schless, *Chaucer and Dante: A Reevaluation* (Norman, OK: Pilgrim Press, 1984).

17. Karla Taylor, *Chaucer Reads "The Divine Comedy"* (Stanford: Stanford University Press, 1989).

18. Richard Neuse, *Chaucer's Dante: Allegory and Epic Theatre in the Canterbury Tales* (Berkeley and Los Angeles: University of California Press, 1991).

19. A. J. Minnis and A. B. Scott with David Wallace, eds., *Medieval Literary Theory and Criticism c. 1100–c. 1375* (Oxford: Clarendon Press, 1988), 439–58.

20. Dante Alighieri, *"Epistle to Can Grande della Scala,"* in *Medieval Literary Theory and Criticism c. 1100–c. 1375*, ed. A.J. Minnis and A.B. Scott with David Wallace (Oxford: Clarendon Press, 1988), 460–61.

21. Minnis and Scott, 445–58.

22. I am following the idea that he is participating in the fictive sequence as it appears in the Ellesmere manuscript.

23. Lee Patterson, *Chaucer and the Subject of History* (Madison: University of Wisconsin Press, 1991), 41–45.

24. Minnis and Scott, 229.

25. Dolores Warwick Frese, *An Ars Legendi for Chaucer's Canterbury Tales: Reconstructive Reading* (Gainesville: University of Florida Press, 1991), 194–233.

26. Frese, 194–233.

27. Bloomfield, 384–90.

28. Chauncey Wood, "Chaucer's Man of Law as Interpreter," *Traditio* 23 (1967): 149–90; Rodney Delasanta, "And of Great Reverence: Chaucer's Man of Law," *Chaucer Review* 5 (1971): 288–310.

29. Alfred David, "The Man of Law vs. Chaucer: A Case in Poetics," *PMLA* 82 (1967): 217–25.

30. Joseph E. Grennen, "Chaucer's Man of Law and the Constancy of Justice," *JEGP* 84 (1985): 498–514.

31. Delasanta, 288–310.

32. Paul M. Clogan, "The Narrative Style of the *Man of Law's Tale*," *Medievalia et Humanistica* 8 (1977): 223. The same idea was explored earlier by Michael R. Paull, "The Influence of the Saint's Legend Genre in the *Man of Law's Tale*," *Chaucer Review* 5 (1971):179–94.

33. For an detailed discussion of the role of rhetoric in the Middle Ages, see James J. Murphy, *Rhetoric in the Middle Ages* (Berkeley and Los Angeles: University of California Press, 1974).

34. Bloomfield, 385.

35. This observation applies to the rhetorical aspects and to many others as the following critics have noted: Bloomfield, 384–90; Corsa, 128–34; Paull, 179–94; Delasanta, 288–310; Clogan, 217–33.

36. I am enlarging upon an argument made by Laura Kendrick, *Chaucerian Play: Comedy and Control in the* Canterbury Tales (Berkeley and Los Angeles: University of California Press, 1988), 47. She does not comment on the aspect of a verbal homology to divine providence.

37. Carolyn Dinshaw, *Chaucer's Sexual Poetics* (Madison: University of Wisconsin Press, 1989), 88–112.

38. Kolve, 140–41 notes this kind of laughter in the *Knight of Tour-Landry*.

39. Bloomfield, 386.

40. Kolve, 140–44.

41. Kolve, 138–39.

42. Edward A. Block, "Originality, Controlling Purpose, and Craftsmanship in Chaucer's *Man of Law's Tale*," *PMLA* 87 (1972): 584.

43. Grennen, 512.

44. In Acts 8:26–40, the Ethiopian eunuch is reading this passage of Isaiah, and Philip connects the passage to Christ. The passage is taken as a clear messianic prophecy by the early Church.

45. Grennen, 508.

46. Block, 572–616; Bloomfield, 384–90; Delasanta, 296–97.

47. Dolores Warwick Frese, "Chaucer's *Clerk's Tale*: The Monsters and the Critics," *Chaucer Review* 8 (1973): 133–46 provides a survey of early critical opinions about the tale and examines aspects of the tale in light of difficulties that a modern audience may have with the tale.

48. The following are examples of exegetical readings of the tale: Edward I. Condren, "The Clerk's Tale of Man Tempting God," *Criticism* 26 (1984): 99–114; Peggy A. Knapp, "Knowing the Tropes: Literary exegesis and Chaucer's Clerk," *Criticism* 27 (1985): 331–45. The following are examples of psychological readings: Norman Lavers, "Freud, the Clerk's Tale, and Literary Criticism," *College English* 26 (1964): 180–87; Patricia Cramer, "Lordship, Bondage, and the Erotic: The Psychological Bases of Chaucer's 'Clerk's Tale,'" *JEGP* 89 (1990): 491–511.

49. The following critics place him in the midst of university debate: Robert Stepsis, "Potentia Absoluta and the *Clerk's Tale*," *Chaucer Review* 10 (1975): 129–46; David C. Steinmetz, "Late Medieval Nominalism and the *Clerk's Tale*," *Chaucer Review* 12 (1977): 38–54.

50. Knapp, 331–45.

51. Stepsis, 129–46.

52. Steinmetz, 38–54.

53. Robin Kirkpatrick, "The Griselda Story in Boccaccio, Petrarch, and Chaucer," in *Chaucer and the Italian Trecento*, ed. Piero Boitani (Cambridge: Cambridge University Press, 1983), 244–45.

54. S. K. Heninger, Jr., "The Concept of Order in Chaucer's *Clerk's Tale*," *JEGP* 56 (1957): 382–95.

55. Kendrick, 60.

56. John M. Ganim, *Chaucerian Theatricality* (Princeton: Princeton University Press, 1990), 86.

57. All of these are standards in arts training for the Bachelor's degree. See Muriel A. Bowden, *A Commentary on the General Prologue to The* Canterbury Tales (New York: Macmillan Company, 1948).

58. This is clearly the standard reading, but it is far from problematic. One might hazard a suggestion that if Walter is to represent God, then what the Clerk may be doing is defining the nature of God in a negative way, following a tradition that goes back as far as Dionysius's *Celestial Hierarchy*. See Minnis and Scott, 165–96.

59. Condren, 99–114.

60. Knapp, 337.

61. Donald H. Reiman, "The Real *Clerk's Tale*; or *Patient Griselda Exposed*," *Texas Studies in Language and Literature* 5 (1963): 366.

62. Kendrick, 51.

63. Sheila Delany, "Politics and the Paralysis of Poetic Imagination in *The Physician's Tale*," *Studies in the Age of Chaucer* 3 (1981): 53.

64. Delany, 60.

65. Robert Longsworth, "The Doctor's Dilemma: A Comic View of the 'Physician's Tale,'" *Criticism* 13 (1971): 223–33.

66. Emerson Brown, Jr., "What is Chaucer Doing with the Physician and His Tale," *Philological Quarterly* 60 (1981): 129–49.

67. D. W. Robertson, Jr., "The Physician's Comic Tale," *Chaucer Review* 23 (1988): 129–39.

68. Lee C. Ramsey, "'The Sentence of it Sooth is,'" *Chaucer Review* 6 (1972): 195.

69. Ramsey, 195.

70. Ramsey, 197.

71. The following source studies among others have made this observation: Robertson, 132–34; Ramsey, 190–95; Delany, 52–55.

72. Anne Middleton, "The *Physician's Tale* and Love's Martyrs: 'Ensamples Mo Than Ten' as a Method in the *Canterbury Tales*," *Chaucer Review* 8 (1973): 9–32.

73. Richard L. Hoffman, "Jepthah's Daughter and Chaucer's Virginia," *Chaucer Review* 2 (1967): 20–31.

74. Huling E. Ussery, *Chaucer's Physician: Medicine and Literature in Fourteenth-Century England*, Tulane Studies in English, no. 19 (New Orleans: Tulane University, 1971), 127.

75. R. Howard Bloch, "Chaucer's Maiden's Head: 'The Physician's Tale' and the Poetics of Virginity," *Representations* 28 (Fall 1989): 118.

76. Carolyn P. Collette, "Sense and Sensibility in the *Prioress's Tale*," *Chaucer Review* 15 (1980): 138–50.

77. Maria P. Hamilton, "Echoes of Childermas in the Tale of the Prioress," *Modern Language Review* 34 (1939): 1–8; Sister M. Madeleva, "Chaucer's Nun," in *Chaucer's Nun and Other Essays* (New York: Appleton, 1925), 3–42.

78. Kolve, 140.

79. The following exemplify this trend in criticism: George Lyman Kittredge, *Chaucer and His Poetry* (Cambridge: Harvard University Press, 1915), 175–78; Dom Maynard J. Brennan, "Speaking of the Prioress," *Modern Language Quarterly* 10 (1949): 451–57; Sister Brigitta McCarthy, "Chaucer's Pilgrim Prioress," *Benedictine Review* 6 (1951): 38–40; Charles A. Owen Jr., *Pilgrimage and Storytelling in the* Canterbury Tales: *The Dialectic of "Ernest" and "Game"* (Norman, Okla.: University of Oklahoma Press, 1977), 119–20. Beginning in some of these sources which address the Prioress herself, there is a growing trend toward the analysis of her anti-Semitism.

80. The following exemplify this trend in criticism: Sherman Hawkins, "Chaucer's Prioress and the Sacrifice of Praise," *JEGP* 63 (1964): 599–624; Sister Nicholas Maltman, "The Divine Granary, or The End of the Prioress's 'Greyn,'" *Chaucer Review* 17 (1982): 163–70.

81. Hawkins, 613.

82. Studies on the meaning of the grain are numerous. The following are exemplary: Hawkins, 599–624; Maltman, 163–70. The connection between the grain or pearl and the soul is perhaps nowhere more clearly seen than in *Pearl*. Without question, this sign demands a symbolic reading.

83. Hawkins, 617.

84. Hawkins, 617.

85. Roger Ellis, *Patterns of Religious Narrative in the* Canterbury Tales (Totowa, NJ: Barnes and Noble, 1986), 93.

86. Paul E. Beichner, "Confrontation, Contempt, of Court, and Chaucer's Cecilia," *Chaucer Review* 8 (1973–74): 198–204.

87. Anne Eggebroten, "Laughter in the *Second Nun's Tale*: A Redefinition of the Genre," *Chaucer Review* 19 (1984): 55–61.

88. Eggebroten, 57–59.

89. Brennan, 451–53.

The Mind Distended
The Retraction, Miller's Tale *and* Summoner's Tale

Judith Tschann

I would like to approach Chaucer's low humor from on high: from the vantage point of Saint Augustine's theory of time, and from the point of view of the *Retraction*. Chaucer's scatological tales give us an "up-so-doun" world in which a kiss is a fart and a fart is a problem in logic, so perhaps the best way to approach them is upside-down or backwards. An interpretive strategy that looks backward from Chaucer to Augustine and from the *Retraction* to the tales has at least the advantage of hindsight. This over-the-shoulder critical stance mimics the retrospective process underlying both narrative and the temporal nature of human experience, and provides a way of looking at the connection between time and narrative.

In talking about how we make sense of the world by telling time and telling stories, Hayden White says "there is nothing more real for human beings than the experience of temporality—and nothing more fateful."[1] The same might be said for Chaucerian scatology: there is nothing more real or more fateful or more mindful of our limited life in the flesh. When it is "emplotted," the scatological shows the connection between time and narrative because it "makes time human" and gives us an experience of "deep temporality" (to distort some of Paul Ricoeur's, and ultimately Heidegger's expressions),[2] an experience into the out-of-bounds, the fart of darkness. Because the

349

scatological in Chaucer's tales becomes associated with interiority and hiddenness, with escape from the body, and with spirituality, the scatological tales also suggest a connection between narrative and death and reveal our contrary desires to find out and to keep silent about our unavoidable temporal end. The *Miller's* and the *Summoner's Tales* direct our attention towards and then away from our "end." These tales give us a distinctive response to the agony of being time-conscious: a mocking exaltation, an ecstatic fart, rage, laughter and denial. They guffaw at death and cover it up, like Alisoun laughing into the pitch-dark night and shutting it out: "'Tehee!' quod she, and clapte the wyndow to" (I.3740).[3]

To see what Chaucer's low humor suggests about our time-bound life in the flesh, I would like to look briefly at the *Retraction*, then move back and forth between Augustine's eleventh book of the *Confession*, two scatological tales and the *Retraction* again, an organization which distends the mind in imitation (however perverse) of Augustine's three-fold present, and which imitates (however grossly) the ontologically retrospective nature of narrative.

I

The *Retraction* is a time-conscious text, with a curious Janus-faced look backward and forward. It looks forward to death, backward to the written word, oscillating between certainty and doubt: the certainty of dying, the uncertainty of death, the certainty of list-making ("these works I have written"), the uncertainty of being understood. The *Retraction* may be an act of penance, integrally connected as it is to the *Parson's Tale*.[4] It may be a death-bed conversion, a preparation for death, perhaps part of a will. Along with the *Parson's Tale* it closes down and rejects the fiction of the preceding tales, and depending on one's point of view, it does so either in an evolutionary and thematically integrated way, or too extremely and abruptly, thereby threatening any possible unity of the work. Whether we take the *Retraction* as sincere repentance or rhetorical device, an integral part of the *Canterbury Tales* or a disjointed add-on, whether reflecting Chaucer's intentions for the design of the *Tale* compiler's editorial decision, or whether we hear it as author's voice, pilgrim's voice or the voice of the book,[5] we can hardly ignore it. Even if (or perhaps especially if) one takes it as the work of a compiler or as collaboration between author and editor, the *Retraction* makes a difference to one's reading of the *Canterbury Tales*.[6] As a part of the received text of the *Canterbury Tales*, the *Retraction* recontextualizes Chaucer's writings, however slightly.

In his *Retraction* Chaucer (or the "voice" of the *Retraction*) revokes his "translacions and enditynges of worldly vanitees," mentioning specifically the "tales of Caunterbury, thilke that sownen into synne" (X.1085–1086). Precisely which tales the writer of the *Retraction* had in mind as tending toward sin we cannot say. Perhaps he had no particular tale in mind; perhaps all of them are worldly and revocable. Perhaps he was being more rhetorical than precise and we should not be literal-minded about revoking tales. In any case, the *Retraction* endlessly defers the question and the possible choice of works to be revoked, and subtly invites the reader to choose. Many readers, it would seem, have judged the scatological tales as tending towards sin or as worthy of being revoked. The idea of "revokable" is planted before the first scatological tale. Chaucer ("the pilgrim") of course warns us before the *Miller's Tale* that we may want to skip it—or in effect revoke it before reading it. Probably some readers have taken his advice to revoke the tale by turning the leaf and choosing another: in the fifteenth century, when individual tales were "excerpted" from the whole of the *Canterbury Tales* and written into miscellanies, patient Griselda was much more likely than wynsynge Alisoun to be included;[7] not long ago in the twentieth century, a court decided in favor of banning some of Chaucer's works from the school curriculum.[8] Throughout the centuries more than a few critics have found fault with the *Miller's Tale* and the *Summoner's Tale*, usually on moral grounds, judging them as reprehensible, not worth reading, "smutty," "vulgar . . . not fit to be read in a mixed company" and even as "discreditable sort of filth" which will "gag" the reader.[9] Chaucer's plea in the *Miller's Prologue*, "Blameth nat me" and "demeth nat that I seye / Of yvel entente" and again "put me

out of blame" (I.3172–3185), repeated in various forms throughout the *Tales*, almost seems to anticipate some readers' reactions
of "gagging" on the scatological elements in the tales. It is not
surprising that in the *Retraction* Chaucer again retreats to the
shelter of intention where no one can follow, and insofar as we
have heard "Don't blame me" and "Don't misjudge my
intentions" many times by the end of the *Canterbury Tales*, the
Retraction sounds more like an echo than a palinode. Chaucer
prays in the *Retraction* that we understand his intentions, and by
way of explanation or apology invokes St. Paul: "Al that is
writen is writen for oure doctrine," adding "and that is myn
entente." But intention resists pinning down, and Chaucer's
intentions remain as slippery and irretrievable as ever. Being
skeptical about Chaucer's "entente" is not to doubt his sincerity
or that he wrote "for oure doctrine," but to acknowledge that the
issue of intention is problematic, a kind of linguistic quicksand in
which all effort seems to work against you. Chaucer's apology in
the *Retraction* opens possibilities rather than eliminating them,
and by creating more room for doubt, the *Retraction* invites us to
look back at the tales. Rather than the quicksand of intention, it is
the room for doubt that I am interested in, and the idea of
looking back to reconsider.

In looking back at the *Summoner's* and *Miller's Tales* with
the *Retraction* in mind, I do not intend to find a hidden meaning
which makes the tales switch valence from sinful to acceptable,
or vice-versa. Rather, in looking back I want to begin to examine
the spatial and temporal roominess created by the *Retraction*, and
the questions of hiddenness and "making time human" as they
pertain to the scatological tales. In the *Miller's* and *Summoner's
Tales* these questions become the play between inside and
outside, contained and container. The recurring images of containers, inside-outside, privacy, and permeating boundaries give
us a way of talking about some aspects of the complex nature of
meaning. In an "up-so-doun" world these problems become
what and how a fart means.

As the potentially revokable tales, the scatological tales get
some extra attention or room at the very end of the *Canterbury
Tales*. The scatological tales are reaffirmed as a result of their
status as potentially retracted. Although some readers have

revoked these tales by eliminating them, "possibly-to-be-revoked" does not always mean eliminated. The revokable tales are still around, to be chosen or not chosen as readers see fit. They seem to be *sous rature* rather than erased, and because of their status as under erasure, they acquire a telicity or teleological directive, causing us to be re-readers with an end in view or an end in mind. Perhaps we always read narrative with an end in view; perhaps all narratives are teleologically driven, as many have claimed.[10] Reading the scatological tales through the *Retraction* in this palimpsest-like arrangement, however, makes explicit a possible "end in view" for the tales, that of "potentially-revocable." The end in view also becomes death, as I hope to show, even at the same time the end is laughter.

II

Friar John in the *Summoner's Tale* has a problem like St. Augustine's in book 11 of his *Confession*.[11] Both of them are burning to solve an enigma: how to divide the indivisible. In the course of his confession, and in the midst of his meditation on eternity, Augustine cries out "What then is time?" (11: 14:17).[12] The nature of time becomes at this point in the *Confession* the central paradox about our mortal existence. Augustine agonizes over this question, saying "My soul is on fire to know this most intricate enigma" (11.22:28). Friar John in the *Summoner's Tale* has been set afire too (III.2122), agonizing over his own enigma or "inpossible" (*impossibilium*), which is "To parte that wol nat departed be" (III.2214). The solution to the problem presented so ungraciously to Friar John unfolds in a manner resembling Augustine's search for an understanding of the enigma of time. Augustine sees his problem as a question of the metrics of time, that is, of measurement: How can one measure something that is continuous and indivisible? The present has no duration and therefore cannot be measured; we cannot measure the past because it is gone, and cannot measure the future because it has not yet come. The nature of the present seems the most troublesome. Augustine sees the difficulties involved in trying to reduce the present to an instant, finding, among other problems, that a continuous dynamical system resists being divided and that when one does try to divide such a system, there are ever and ever smaller units:

> Yea, that one hour passeth away in flying particles. . . .
> If an instant of time be conceived which cannot be divided
> into the smallest particles of moments, that alone is it,
> which may be called present. Which yet flies with such
> speed from future to past, as not to be lengthened out with
> the least stay. For if it be, it is divided into past and future.
> The present hath no space. Where then is the time. . . ?

(11:15:20)

His question, "What then is time?" becomes "Where then is time?" but this restating of the enigma leads to impasses as well, because time has no space. Again he says, "we measure times as they are passing," but how can we measure present time, "seeing it hath no space?" (11:21:27). Augustine determines that time cannot be reduced to a pointlike present, yet he knows that we habitually measure time, and decides finally that what we measure is time in transit: "that I measure time, I know; and yet I measure not time to come, for it is not yet; nor present, because it is not protracted by any space; nor past, because it now is not. What then do I measure? Times passing, not past? for so I said" (11:26:33).

Augustine's meditation takes on a quasi-spatial dimension, as "what is time" becomes "where is time." Although he concludes that time has no space, he nevertheless has to locate time to understand how it passes. Rejecting cosmological answers to what or where is time, Augustine determines finally that time is in the mind: "It is in thee, my mind, that I measure times" (11:27:36). Having determined where it is, he can then grapple with what it is. The answer seems to come all at once as he thinks about what he does in reciting or chanting a psalm. Language holds the answer of time for Augustine, specifically a measured use of language, song or verse. In thinking about reciting "by heart" the psalm *Deus creator omnium*, he works out his notion of the three-fold present in which we "stretch out our thought" (11:27:36). In reciting the verse, the mind attends to the present, anticipates what is to come, and remembers what was. What we think of as past, present and future are more correctly called the present-of-the-past, the present-of-the-present, and the present-of-the-future (11:20:26). The mind attending to the present is also said to be intending, the present being called a "present intention" (*praesens intentio*): "the present intent conveys over the future into the past" (11:27:36). Intention and attention are equated; the mind's intention is an active process of attending, of continuing, of relegating what is to come to what is past. This active dynamic of attending, anticipating, and remembering causes the mind to distend or extend itself, and thus the *intentio* becomes the *distentio animi*. Again we see a spatial quality to Augustine's theory, in the flowing of images and signs in the mind from a "place" of anticipation to a "place" of memory. The function of the present is to regulate this flow, or relegate the present of anticipation to the present of memory. The paradox for Augustine is that the more the mind engages itself or attends to the present, the more it distends itself. The mind that attends to the present, stretches in looking forward and backward, and the more attention it pays to the present, the more it extends beyond the present. The work of regulating the continuous transition of now to then causes the distention of the mind, or as Wittgenstein says, it causes a mental cramp.[13] Augustine's *distentio animi* is a mental cramp, a tension between anticipation and fulfillment. The *distentio animi* is an aporetic solution to his question, as Ricoeur says (1:5–22), since it both answers the questions "what is time?" and yet causes a mental cramp.

The beauty of Augustine's answer to "What then is time?" is that he sees all of human existence in a song. He extends his three-fold present to account for "a man's whole life" and "the whole history of mankind":

> And this which takes place in the whole Psalm, the same
> takes place in each several portion of it, and each several
> syllable; the same holds in that longer action, whereof this
> Psalm may be a part; the same holds in the whole life of
> man, whereof all the actions of man are parts; the same
> holds through the whole age of the sons of men, whereof
> all the lives of men are parts.

(11:28:38)

Making sense of temporal experience thus is fundamental for Augustine in understanding human existence. He establishes a reciprocal relationship between time and self, so that the enigmatic *distentio animi* not only allows for the continuity of self but also for the movement of history.

Friar John in the *Summoner's Tale* has a mental cramp as a result of the "yifte" given to him by Thomas. Like Augustine's burning enigma, the friar's problem involves metrics, dividing the indivisible, and the impossibility of something being simultaneously an instant in time yet in transit, something with a beginning and end and thus in the past, yet present and still coming. Like Augustine's answer to the question of time, Squire Jankyn's solution involves a spatial dimension. He must locate the indivisible entity and contain it in order to measure it out. Like Augustine's unseen but locatable time, the friar's gift is hidden but traceable. We can follow its whereabouts. Augustine consigns his enigma about time to the mind in order to understand it, and a similar process takes places in the *Summoner's Tale*. The particular mind in question in the *Summoner's Tale*, however, is "sike," "full of vanytee" and "frenesye," anger and distemper. Head and arse change places in this tale, with the division problem becoming a matter of "ars-metrike" (III.2222). The first location or "container" of the gift-fart is Thomas's upside-down body, his mind-arse: Thomas says that this "thyng is in my possessioun," but "hyd in pryvetee." The lord says the devil put it in Thomas's mind (III.2221), but Thomas says it is "Bynethe my buttok" (III.2142–2143). Once it leaves his possession, its whereabouts become uncertain. Friar John usually bags his gifts, and requires "a sturdy harlot" to carry his sack for him (III.1754–1755), but even though the gift is laid "amydde his hand," it eludes his grasp. It seems to be everywhere and nowhere, wasting away little by little (III.2235). But the lord relocates it in the mind, when he declares it is a "probleme" or "question," in the Middle English sense of these terms as a logical exercise. It is thus located in the friar, both in his hand and in his mind, as we shall see. The friar has received the sick man's insides, his rage and distemper, and his soul. Once the fart is inside again, relocated or re-contained in the mind and in the friar, a solution to the enigma can be found.

Before turning to the solution, we must consider first the connection established in the tale between the friar and Thomas. Perhaps most obviously, the transfer of rage from one to the other connects the two. Anger pervades the tale, in Friar John's long homily against wrath and in Thomas's growing anger towards the friar in direct response to his hypocritical preaching and attempts to extort money: "This sike man wax wel ny wood for ire; / He wolde that the frere had been on-fire" (III.2121–2122). Thomas's pent up anger explodes into the Friar's hand, and judging from the friar's immediate reaction to the gift-fart, the friar has received Thomas's anger as his gift. Friar John "sterte up as dooth a wood leoun," responding with a thunderous explosion of his own: "for Goddes bones!" (III.2153). The next fifty-some lines of the tale emphasize the friar's anger, how he looked like a wild boar, how the lord of the village exclaims over his angry appearance and how he exhorts him not to "distempre" himself. This transfer of inner feelings from Thomas to John suggests a shared identity or blurring of boundaries between their separate identities. John and Thomas refer to each other as brother (III.1944, 2089, 2126, 2133), and seem to be complementary halves of the same person. Between them they possess the attributes of St. Thomas the twin.[14] After the friar has begged Thomas to "lef [his] ire," give his gold, and "shewe" his confession (III.2089–2099), Thomas obliges by leaving, giving, and showing him everything at once in the form of a fart. He then disappears from the tale. The two brothers merge with the fart. Thomas's "yifte" is now Friar John's possession; Thomas's intestinal turbulence is now John's mental cramp.

Once the cramp is relocated inside John, Jankyn can solve the problem of dividing and conveying. Accustomed as he is to dividing up flesh, Squire Jankyn the carver sees the problem in terms of body parts. He foresees a stiff belly and a wheel of noses, with their respective holes of egress and ingress, and determines that the solution to the cramp is a fart. Jankyn's proposed fart-in-a-cartwheel is a *distentio animi* which allows what is inside to escape its container and to be transmitted to others. It both unites and divides, embodying a continuum and yet distinguishing breaks within it. The cartwheel is at once the extension of the mind-arse, the container of meaning, the conveyer, the form given to the fart, and the fart. The cartwheel like the distended mind can occupy more than one time, by extending to encompass expectation and memory, relegating future to past in the process of attending to the present. As the distended animus, the cartwheel becomes the fattened soul which John says the friars work to achieve in their program of fasting and "mak[ing] the body lene" (III.1880). The cartwheel is also a parodic holy spirit, an unholy animus, descending on the twelve disciples (Acts 2:1–13).[15] Since the Pentecost celebrates the gift of tongues, the cartwheel as a Pentecostal parody becomes associated with the "spreading of the word" that dominates the beginning and middle of the tale. As a parody of the power of the Holy Spirit, the cartwheel also becomes associated with the sacrament of penance ("Receive the Holy Spirit; whose sins you shall forgive . . ." [John 20: 22–23]).[16] The friar abuses both gifts of the Holy Spirit, the Pentecostal power of preaching and the sacramental power of forgiving sins. The cartwheel as Pentecostal parody connects or brings full circle a number of issues in the story, namely "groping," glossing, flatulence, and death, which, like Augustine's psalm, reveal a connection between language and time.

•   The friar's greedy abuse of the sacrament of penance occurs in images of breaching and invading privacy. Friar John describes the work of a confessor as "groping" a conscience, and describes confessing as showing (III.2093). Thomas's flatulent confession turns out to be a different kind of showing of sins or revealing of the hidden from what the confessor had expected: "how shrewdly / Unto my confessour to-day [Thomas] spak!" says the lord of the village (III.2238–2239), suggesting an equation between confessing and farting, and more generally between speaking and flatulence. As part of the travesty of the sacrament of penance, Thomas makes or "shows" his confession by telling the friar to:

> grope welbihynde.
> Bynethe my buttok there shaltow fynde
> A thyng that I have hyd in pryvetee.

In the habit of groping, Friar John immediately takes him up on the offer:

> And doun his hand he launcheth to the clifte
> In hope for to fynde there a yifte.
> And whan this sike man felte this frere
> Aboute his tuwel grope there and heere,
> Amydde his hand he leet the frere a fart.
>
> (III.2141–43; 2145–49)

Groping one's *pryvetee* in this way, and also inviting someone to invade one's *pryvetee* suggest a kind of mutual seduction and entrapment on the part of Thomas and John, each one trying to exploit the other's willingness, and calling to mind also a similar mutual entrapment between Nicholas and Absolon in the *Miller's Tale*. The friar's groping suggests simony as well, and abusing the power of forgiveness or failing in one's office as forgiver of sins. Though the friar greedily encourages Thomas to confess, and certainly hears the confession which makes a sound louder than any flatulent horse could produce (III.2150–2151), he cannot forgive the fart. He utters no words of absolution but only a mighty oath.

Friar John's hypocritical preaching and misrepresentation of Biblical texts abuse the Pentecostal gift of tongues. Friar John is a windy fellow and fond of glossing, which he considers a "glorious thynge." Glossing brings out the "spirit" of a text,[17] and furthermore seems to mean in this tale groping or ferreting out what is hidden. Because he is both greedy and hypocritical, Friar John's glossing turns the business of interpretation into a con job. But Friar John gets caught in his own game, and though he gropes Thomas and ferrets out his "spirit," he is unable to gloss the fart into anything other than insult and blasphemy. Squire Jankyn on the other hand may be a bit of a con man himself, talking his way through the exercise in logic and thereby turning a fart back into a gift, but for himself: "And Jankyn hath ywonne a newe gowne" (III.2293).

The abuse of Pentecostal gifts also leads to a confusion between language and other noises. According to the *Summoner's Tale*, when friars sing, they belch: "Lo, 'buf!' they seye, '*cor meum eructavit*'" (III.1934), and when they preach they fart (III.2282–2284). Thomas confesses by farting, and even the "spoke's end" at which each friar lays his nose on the cartwheel suggests a connection between the spoken word and flatulence. According to the lord of the village, language and flatulence are reducible to the same phenomenon: "The rumblynge of a fart, and every soun, / Nis but of air reverberacioun" (III.2233–34). We suspect elsewhere in Chaucer's writing, notably in the *House of Fame*, that to speak is to break wind:[18]

> Thou wost wel this, that spech is soun,
> . . . .
> Soun ys noght but eyr ybroken;
> And every speche that ys spoken,
> Lowd or pryvee, foul or fair,
> In his substaunce ys but air;
> For as flaumbe ys but lyghted smoke,
> Ryght soo soun ys air ybroke.
> . . . .
> Loo, with the strok the ayr tobreketh;
> And ryght so breketh it when men speketh.
> Thus wost thou wel what thing is speche.
>
> (*HF* 762; 765–770; 779–781)

Because it acts like language, especially in its potential for becoming meaningful, the scatological in this tale threatens the ascendancy of language over other human noises. The perverse equation between speaking and flatulence distorts the distinction between language and noise by leveling all human sounds to a single explanation ("eyr ybroken" or "reverberacioun"). The hypocrisy in the tale also upsets the conventional relationship between form (i.e., phonemes or speech sounds) and meaning, since hypocritical words don't mean what they "should" mean, adding to the confusion between glossing, confessing, singing and flatulence. All language threatens to shrivel into babel. But the tale does not degenerate into meaninglessness. The travesty of language created by the "emplotted scatological" or fart made meaningful exposes and thereby threatens the system of meaning which is language, but ultimately reinforces what it mocks. The tale does not sink into babel but rather ends with a (pseudo-) intellectual discussion of a problem in logic. Jankyn imposes structure and order, the lord and lady shore up semantic stability by agreeing with Jankyn's solution, and the world returns to its perverse status quo in which both flatulence and language are meaningful. The intellectual discussion may be a joke, but it makes excellent nonsense, which is not at all the same thing as meaninglessness.

Jankyn's solution is a proposal, a linguistic solution to an exercise in logic, something in the future and in the mind. We never actually get the second fart, only the cramp. But we tend to see it as having happened. For one thing, the deictic center, the "now" or "zero" temporal reference point, shifts forward with the last two lines of the tale, "And Jankyn *hath ywonne* a newe gowne— / My tale *is doon*; we *been* almost at towne" (III. 2293–2294; italics added), from the past tense of the tale to the present perfect (he has won the gown already) and the present tense of the pilgrimage, so that we tend to consider the whole of the story, with its proposed solution and consequences, as over and done with. We also tend to see the second fart as having happened because of the scatological reference at the end of the tale to Friar John's preaching which smelled "of fartes thre" (III. 2281–2284). Though the reference is out of chronological order (John having preached earlier that day), its position at the end of the tale supplies the "tock" of the plot that we anticipate and have been set up to perceive by the "tick" of the plot, the first fart, the mental cramp, the proposed solution, etc. Because language and flatulence are equated in the tale, the reader can hear the final reference to redolent preaching as the second fart and resolution of the tale. The mixture of times, tenses, and deictic centers at the end of this tale creates a sense of time travel for the reader, as if we were on a cartwheel of time in which past, present, and future seem to occur simultaneously. As it incarnates and spreads the word, the once and future fartwheel becomes a three-fold present of being, recalling and anticipating.

Finally, the Pentecostal parody suggests a denial of death. Death lurks in the background of this tale. The Pentecost celebrates the Holy Spirit and is a postmortem feast, following Christ's death. Christ's death brings the possibility for humankind of redeemed time, an eternal present, achieved at the expense of the body or attained through the release of the spirit from the body. The closest we get in this tale to an eternal present is the cartwheel, with its parodic release of the spirit and transcendence of time. Again there is at least a hint of death surrounding this release of the spirit. The friar has both "groped" and fished for Thomas's soul (III.1820) and has received it. The friar's business is to prepare souls for death, to effect their salvation, urge them to make the body lean and the soul fat. He seems to have succeeded. Perhaps "this olde cherl with lokkes hoore" (III.2182) breathed his last as a result of "showing" his sins, and distending his animus. We are not told that he dies, but after his loud expiration, he is no longer heard from, no longer present. He is in the past, a recollection and *probleme* in the mind of the friar and a topic for discussion in the lord's hall. Though Jankyn talks of bringing "this cherl" back to fart into the cartwheel, Jankyn's solution and the reappearance of the sick man remain in the future and in the mind. Moreover, since Thomas and John are two sides of the same person, or two sides of the same hub (III.2270), it could just as well be John as Thomas who farts for his brethren into the cartwheel, especially since the last reference to Friar John in the tale is indeed to his having farted. Besides lurking in the sick man's "expiration," death surfaces momentarily in the tale in the references to the dead child, who is supposedly seen ascending to heaven in a vision by the hypocritical friar and to whom the friars inappropriately sing or belch out a psalm of exaltation. The reference to the Office of the Dead (III.2075), to requiem masses ("trentals," III.1724), and to the suffering of souls in purgatory (III.1724–1731), and implications of the sacrament of penance as prerequisite for entering the next life also give the tale a taste of death. But the few glimpses of death in the tale are covered over quickly, and we end with the "worldes lust" rather than denial of the body, with a lord and lady eating at the bord (III.2167) rather than fattening the soul, and with Jankyn the carver looking forward to a new gown. Thus in the *Summoner's Tale* to fart means to expel the spirit and thus to die, but it also means to sing in the face of death, as the friars did, and to mock time with a death-defying retort. Time degenerates into arse-metrics, and redeemed time is travestied in a cartwheel.

Augustine's question "What then is time?" comes as part of his meditation on eternity, during which he cracks "the only joke in the *Confession*."[19] Augustine does not so much tell the joke as report it in order to censure it. The joke concerns God and time:

> "What did God before he made heaven and earth?" I
> answer not as one is said to have done merrily (eluding
> the pressure of the question): "He was preparing hell
> (saith he) for pryers into God's mysteries."

(11.12.14)

Augustine responds to the joke by commenting on the inappropriateness of treating weighty issues frivolously and of making "sport of enquirers." Augustine has probably never been accused of eluding the pressure of the question, and perhaps because he knows only too well that there is hell to pay for asking questions, he does not find the inquiry a joking matter. Augustine certainly takes seriously the danger and improprieties of delving into mysteries that are beyond human understanding, but proceeds nevertheless to enquire "boldly," not jokingly or merrily but in a serious, appropriate manner.

The *Miller's Tale* is Augustine's joke in narrative form. There is hell to pay in the *Miller's Tale* for prying into God's mysteries. There is also a moment or two of "solas" and a good laugh for the townspeople. The *Miller's Tale* makes a good joke out of "hell to pay," but the tale is surrounded by so many admonitions and so much ambivalence that it is hard to tell where the joke begins and ends. We are warned in the *Miller's Prologue* that we should not wreck a good joke by making earnest out of game, yet Chaucer "the pilgrim's" earnest and repeated warnings of nastiness ahead suggest that perhaps we ought to take the matter seriously and choose another tale. Then again his warnings whet our appetite. Then again the *Retraction* revokes tales that "sownen" into sin, and reading the tale with the *Retraction* in mind invites us to make earnest of game. Like Augustine, who saw fit to record a joke he disapproved of, the *Retraction* does not eliminate the tale even if censuring it, and in fact calls attention to it. Augustine, the *Miller's Prologue,* and the *Retraction* leave us with a tangle of warnings: Danger! Laughs ahead! Possible insights! Hell to pay! In the end we are left with not an either-or but a complement of contraries, hell and insight, the joke and the censure of the joke, the churl's tale and the revoking of it, the earnestness and the game.

The words "privee," "pryvely," and "pryvetee" occur a dozen times throughout the *Miller's Tale*, usually in the context of prying or invading, and we are specifically told in the prologue that a man should not be "inquisityf / Of Goddes pryvetee, nor or his wyf" (I.3163–3164) and again in the tale that "Men sholde nat knowe of Goddes pryvetee" (I.3454).[20] The privacy in the tale is of two sorts, divine and human, which correspond to the two plots of the flood and the kiss. Invading divine privacy takes the form of astrological predictions or seeing the future; invading human privacy means peeking into holes, breaching the body, letting the insides out. The invasion of divine privacy and the invasion of human privacy create two time schemes in the tale. The breaching of God's pryvetee by foreseeing the future creates an apocalyptic time scheme, the time of expected doom. The breaching of human pryvetee by peeking inside the body follows a rhythm of digestion (and also the rhythm of sex), the time of the body. The metabolic time and the apocalyptic time both mimic the retrospective nature of time in narrative, both being times of the end foreseen, or time in which the end determines the beginning. The two time schemes converge with Nicholas's fart. In the midst of all the privacy, the scatological intrudes like a fog horn, sounding of imminent doom, warning that the end is at hand. Let us start then at the end with the fart, looking at metabolic time first and then apocalyptic time.

The time of the body seems to be unidirectional, with an "arrow of time," as today's jargon would have it, proceeding from past to future.[21] We seem to experience time as both cyclical and unidirectional, change within changelessness, but we suppress our awareness of the end of body time which is death. We do not always suppress it, of course, but often do, acting as if the unavoidable end did not inform the moment. If there is such a thing as experienced time, with its arrow pointing steadfastly one way, and with its end obscured in a foggy future, it seems contrary to narrative, retrospective time, in which the end informs the beginning, and in which the arrow of time can be reversed. The "emplotted scatological" provides a good opportunity for showing how body time takes a turn when it is narratized.

The scatological "eyr ybroken" in the *Miller's Tale* ripples out from private to public, to be lost finally in a conspiracy of denial: fart leading to scalded toute, Nicholas's shouting for water, John the Carpenter's crashing down, his broken arm, the commotion, laughter and chaos stirred up within the community, and the cover-up by Nicholas and Alisoun who deny everything at the expense of the Carpenter. The fart as "reverberacioun," or the ripple effect of "eyr ybroken," stretches in both directions, however, backward as well as forward, leading not only to a future of greater exposure and ultimate cover-up, but also widening to encompass past events. The fart recollects the other exchanges in the window, the kiss, the love-songs and the courtly love talk of Absolon which flowed through the window earlier. The reverberation of the fart also extends backward to the beginning of the tale and the description of Absolon as squeamish of farts and fastidious of speech. The fart toward the end of the tale thus can become retroactively an organizing principle for the whole tale, a "grasping together" or emplotting of events past and to come, an organizing principle that appears more circular than linear, incorporating past and future into a widening present. The scatological explosion can also provide a peephole into the narrative process, showing how the tale is teleologically driven, how the end can determine the beginning, how Absolon's squeamishness makes sense retrospectively.

When viewed from the end, the fart is more than a fart. How does this happen? At what point is metabolic rumbling significant?—when it is in a window: when it is made into an event, emplotted, connected with other events, framed, contextualized. Like the cartwheel, the window allows one's attention to engage, saying "look here," while also extending to include other events within the frame. The window in the *Miller's Tale* is the mind engaged and distended, framing, configuring events, separating yet uniting, attending to the moment by looking forward and backward. The window as *distentio animi* focuses on a "present intention" and relegates future to the past, transforming what is coming into what has passed. The *distentio animi* in the *Miller's Tale* means simultaneously planting a kiss, remembering an insult, and imagining revenge. The window extends time for us; it is analogous to the cartwheel in creating space, giving form to a notion like love or revenge. The window is a distention of the mind because it causes one to see beyond the moment, to act and react apparently at the same time, or to predict, experience and evaluate at same time, and to connect or configure events. The window is the place or time in which change occurs within changelessness, and in which experience is a point-like instant with a beginning and end, yet in transit. It is the place in which expectation transforms into memory while one attends to the present.

The window is the central peephole into privacy in the *Miller's Tale*. We never really see anything, however, but sense that something private is happening on the other side of the window. Alisoun and Nicholas are involved in a private matter when Absolon intrudes, pouring his privee thoughts of love into the window. When "out she putte hir hole" for Absolon to kiss, we are reminded of other holes that lead to trouble. For example, Robyn the servant looks in through a hole in the wall at Nicholas, "And at that hole he looked in ful depe" (3442), thinking that he sees Nicholas in a trance. Holes, body orifices, and the window are all portals leading to confusion. These various holes allow one to think one sees what otherwise could not be seen. But what comes out or what is seen is nasty, funny, an illusion or a lie. Robyn sees Nicholas faking a trance, Absolon mistakes one end of his paramour for the other, and Nicholas fails to see that a hot coulter rather than Absolon's lips await him in the window.

The window is also the most noteworthy of the many containers in the tale, "containing" Absolon's singing and courtly love talk, Alisoun's "Tehee" and raucous, non-genteel speech, two bums, Absolon's lips, Nicholas's fart, and the hot coulter. Everything in the *Miller's Tale* moves in and out of restraint or being contained, including the Carpenter who is "in the snare" (I.3231), Alisoun who springs like a colt in the "trave" (I.3282) and who is held "narwe in cage" (I.3224), Nicholas in his attic, and later the Carpenter in his tub. Whatever escapes its container becomes dangerous: speech, farts, wives, tenants, coulters. Like the cartwheel, the window allows something inside to come out, and to be conveyed to another. It is a place for exchange, for getting in touch. It's a risky business, however, to put anything into the window. One risks shock and pain, though one may also get a good laugh out of the twilight-zone time-warp of a window, where head and arse, lips and labia, words and farts, beards, cheeks, holes, and mouths exist in a great confusion, a jumble of body parts in a frame.

Because the window frames Absolon's love talk, his songs, the misdirected kiss, fart, and scalding, so all these things are equalized in a way. In the *Miller's Tale* we get again the equation between speaking and farting. The imperative to "Spek, sweete bryd" is immediately answered with a fart, just as Absolon's squeamishness of farts is juxtaposed with his being fastidious of speech. As in the *Summoner's Tale*, music is also equated with flatulence. Nicholas, Alisoun, and Absolon are all described according to the songs they sing. Nicholas sings clerkish songs, Absolon sings courtly love songs, and Alisoun sings as loud and lively as a swallow (I.3257–3258). They sing the "Old Song" of cupidity or melody of the flesh, however, and their music suggests lust and discordia rather than charity and harmony (cp. Robertson, 126–133), a mocking counterpoint to the bell of lauds and the friars' singing:

> He kiste hire sweete and taketh his sawtrie,
> And pleyeth faste, and maketh melodie.
> . . . .
> Withouten words mo they goon to bedde,
> Ther as the carpenter is wont to lye.
> Ther was the revel and the melodye
> And thus lith Alison and Nicholas,
> In bisynesse of myrthe and of solas,
> Til that the belle of laudes gan to rynge,
> And the freres in the chauncel gonne synge.

$$(\text{III.3305–3306; 3650–3655})$$

Alisoun's singing degenerates into laughter ("Tehee") and name-calling: "Go fro the wyndow, Jakke fool," Nicholas's singing into flatulence, and Absolon's into the hiss of a scalding coulter. Words are increasingly ineffectual in the tale, which ends in riotous commotion. Alisoun and Nicholas yell "'Out' and 'Harrow' in the strete" (I.3825), John swears great oaths, trying to explain what had happened but "for noght; no man his reson herde," and the townspeople laugh. The equation between flatulence and language in the *Summoner's* and the *Miller's Tales* results in both cases in a sense of poetic justice, although the means to that end are different in each tale. In the *Summoner's Tale* the equation creates a feeling of inflation, so that a fart-made-meaningful shows parodically how meaning is created. In the *Miller's Tale*, the equation creates a sense of deflation, order and language dwindling into chaos and noise.

The window also gives us a peek into the other noteworthy container in the *Miller's Tale*, namely the human body. The *Miller's Tale* parodies the metabolic processes of the body, the intake and transformation of food, and the release of energy and waste. Food imagery figures prominently in the tale, along with the images of container-contained, and in and out. Food goes in and out of the body-container, creating a rhythm of anticipation, eating and eliminating. The process starts with having an appetite and salivating, then eating "full savorly," then eliminating. All the characters in the tale are involved with food, and Alisoun and Absolon especially are associated with food and described in food images.[22] The tale builds with a stockpiling of food, as Nicholas holes up in his attic with a few-days' supply of meat and drink, and with John gathering food and drink together in preparation for riding out the flood, and with Absolon chewing licorice and other spices and herbs to freshen his breath. After much preparation and build up of appetite, the food— literal and metaphoric—is consumed and then transformed into energy and waste. In Absolon's case, we focus on his lips. Feeling befouled after his meal, he bites his lip in anger and spends as much effort in wiping and cleaning and trying to rid himself of the foulness as he had in preparing his mouth: "Who rubbeth now, who froteth now his lippes / With dust, with sond, with straw, with clooth, with chippes" (I.3747–3748). Even though his meal is disgusting, it gives him plenty of energy to run to the smithy's and carry out his plan of revenge. Nicholas consummates his affair of the flesh or consumes his feast of pears, apples, berries, and the banquet of food that describes

Alisoun.[23] John also drinks, then works hard to set up his tubs and fill them with "breed, and chese, and good ale in a jubbe" and finally falls asleep. The end of this process is the final expense of energy in the form of waste or clean-up. Nicholas has *to pisse* and of course farts. Absolon has to clean up after befouling himself, and furthermore has to avenge his humiliation and befoulment by upending Nicholas. He repays the meal, and forces on Nicholas a kind of backward elimination or ejaculation in reverse, in repayment for the foul meal and befouled lips and for the fart and the semen which Nicholas has expended. Finally, John has a great fall like a turd from the rafters. As the scapegoat or object of everyone's derision, John the Carpenter is the waste product.

The logical but suppressed end of the time of the body is death, food becoming wind or spirit seeking escape from the body. Nicholas farts, then "wende for to dye" (I.3813). A sexual body rhythm here also follows the same rhythm of building up and releasing as in the metabolic time, and leading as well to a "little death." Nicholas had said earlier that he would die (with sexual pun on "spille") if he did not have Alisoun. He manages to "spille," both in having Alisoun and in the moment when he "wende for to dye." The metabolic process ending in individual pain and death, however, also ends in communal revelry and a sense of ongoingness. The time of the body in the *Miller's Tale* creates a feeling of change within changelessness by moving towards both individual waste and communal laughter.

The time of the body in this tale moves in synchronization with the time of doom. Apocalyptic time and metabolic time in the tale both move inexorably toward an end and are determined by that end. The apocalyptic time in the tale takes the form of prophecy and requital. Both prophecy and requital play tricks with time, involving rethinking an event from a different time, either the expected future shaping the present, or present events reshaping past ones. Foretelling the future means rethinking the present by looking back from a point ahead, or knowing an outcome and working backward from it. The known outcome of the tale is doom, though "in the end" Nicholas gets trial by fire instead of water. Water of course does figure in at the end of the tale. John goes to sleep "awaitynge on the reyn, if he it heere"

(I.3642), and awakens to the great thunderclap of Nicholas's fart and his frantic proclamation of "Water! Water!"[24] The expected end shapes Nicholas's and John's actions, and also Absolon's, whose actions are determined both by an expected end and by his desire for requital. Requital like prophecy connects two points in time, but connects backward, arising after the fact and reinterpreting the past. Prophecy and requital come together in the window, which frames both expectation and memory: Absolon's lips, their itching which was a sign of love and later becomes a sign of besmirching, and his love-talk-turned-to-fart; Nicholas's prophesied deluge turning to pleas for water; John's fears for his wife and his own cuckolding turning to public mockery and the realization of his fears. Apocalyptic time thus reveals our desire to make sense of experience by emplotting it, cutting it up into moments or events and configuring those events, shaping the plot of our experience according to an end. It shows our "desire to see the future in the instant, to be transported beyond the ignorant present" or the belief that our own time stands in "extraordinary relation to" the future.[25] The *Miller's Tale* shows the temporal nature of human experience by mocking our willing slavery to an end.

Death lurks in the background of this tale, as it does in the *Summoner's Tale*. Impending destruction forms the foundation for the flood plot. Death is the premise and the explanation of much of the action, explicitly so with the flood plot, and indirectly so with the kiss plot. Absolon is inevitably drawn into the time of doom in being drawn to the window, bringing about the trial by fire and the fall of John. John the Carpenter believes that death is around the corner. He bemoans his poor wife's fate. He fears that Nicholas may be dead, remarking on the "ticklish" unstable state of the world in which a man able to work on Monday is a corpse the next Sunday (I.3428–3430). Nicholas at least for a moment wants to escape the body. But his pain along with John's pain and ridicule and Absolon's humiliation are drowned out by the laughter of the people. One branded arse, one broken arm, one whiff of the frailty of the flesh, then it is laughed at and covered up.

The scatological elements in these two tales show a perverted kind of *distentio animi*, as arse out the window or fart in a cartwheel. The cartwheel and the window frame the shocking discovery that what is inside stinks. The emplotted scatological shows our insatiable desire to impose meaning on experience. In twentieth-century jargon it is a peak experience, a jolt of self-realization: "I am alive!" or "I hereby mark my time and place in the world," or "I express myself," or "I fart therefore I am." It is also perverse intimacy: "I will share with you from within, from my innermost secret place." The scatological tales make time human by giving us "hind" sight, by re-creating "now," by allowing one to live in the past as if it were the present, by cutting up the flow of experience into events, by grasping events together into a configuration with an end, and by imposing meaning on experience. The meaning is the end in view, an exhilarating and awful death notice.

III

Augustine also wrote a *Retractiones*, in which he set out to catalogue and correct all his works, a recounting and accounting of his life according to his writing. Although the work is not the complete register that he intended, it is nevertheless substantial, listing works in the order written, noting the circumstances of composition and publication, and amending passages. It is a unique undertaking: "No other ancient author came equipped with so detailed a list of his works."[26] Augustine's *Retractiones* does not retract in the sense of erasing or revoking; rather, it reconsiders and assesses. Augustine's *Retractiones* and Chaucer's *Retraction* both concern reconciling past and present, both look toward the future, and both turn their writing into a prayer. Because they mediate between past and future, the retractions of both writers are like the cartwheel and the window, holding onto yet refiguring past events, determining present events in light of anticipated ones, a kind of eternal present in which all times are present simultaneously. In their retractions, both Augustine and Chaucer seem to have readers in mind and a consciousness of themselves as writers mixed with a sense of responsibility and of guilt and a desire to set the record straight. Both Augustine's and

Chaucer's retractions combine a sense of private and public—prayer, confession, reconciliation with God and with the world, and a desire to be understood or to be "read right" in the future.

As always with Chaucer, however, one feels some ambivalence with the revoking and with this attempted stabilizing of texts and of the past. From yet another angle, looking at the *Retraction* from the point of view of the scatological tales, the *Retraction* is Chaucer's imploded flatus; "I take it back." Chaucer does and does not revoke. "I take it back," or "I revoke in my retraccions" (X. 1085) also means "I want to suck back in that lost, spent spirit. I don't want to let it go." Taking back can also mean holding on and refusing to let go as well as eliminating.

The *Retraction* does not change the scatological tales, but changes expectations. It gives readers a long view, time and occasion to think again, and some room for doubt. It draws the tales closer to death and in doing so heightens their ecstatic quality. It also heightens the tension between the scatological as innocent and as "implicated," since the scatological is inextricably mixed up in the tales with sin—blasphemy and adultery, for example. But the *Retraction* predisposes us to excuse the scatological tales, because we may have excused them already, or because we read knowing we will be asked to reconsider them as written with a good intention. Revoking does not mean excusing, but because of the intention stated in the *Retraction* (open-ended as it is) and the plea for understanding, we hold excusableness in mind as a possibility. Since their teleological prerogative is potentially-to-be-excused, the scatological tales are in time-out. Being in time-out creates a feeling of transcending time which also heightens the ecstatic quality of the tales.

Re-framing the scatological tales within the *Retraction* exposes the telicity and retrospectiveness of these tales. Reading the revoked through their revocation or reading the farts through their apology causes the reader's mind to distend in a way which makes evident what all narrative does: work backward from an end.[27] We narrate "after the fact," apparently being incapable of simultaneously experiencing and narrating. The *Retraction* causes us to see the hermeneutic circle between narrative and time by making a point of hindsight. In reading the scatological tales with the *Retraction* in mind, their end moves beyond the old boundaries of the narratives, stretching the retrospectiveness or the time frame. By moving the end forward in time, the reader's time frame enlarges to encompass not only the end of the story called the *Summoner's Tale* or *Miller's Tale*, but also the end of the poem called the *Canterbury Tales* and the supposed end of the writer's life. The *Retraction* recontextualizes the scatological tales by situating them in a dialectic between timelessness and death, and by extending them to be included in a recollection (and anticipation) of death. The tales which seem least time-conscious, most securely "in" time, become part of a prayer for redemption from time.

There is just enough of a tip-off in the *Summoner's* and the *Miller's Tales* to know that the stink of mortality hangs around the scatological. The scatological tales seem the least deathlike, the most lively and vital of the *Canterbury Tales*, but more than the other, non-scatological tales, they show our desire to dechronologize narrative. The scatological tales show the greatest tension between eternity and death, because they work the hardest to deny time. Reading the scatological tales within the scope of the *Retraction* exposes the relationship between time and death which narrative works to cover up and to transcend.

If I smell mortality behind a tale, have I made "ernest of game" and wrecked a good joke? In hindsight I see that I may have turned tales that are funny into tales that are now "about death" when it was not my intention to do so. If I have made humorous tales morbid, then I take it all back. But hindsight shows too that the escape of the spirit can still be a laughing matter. Reading with death as an end in view can reconfigure a joke, but the joke remains nevertheless. Death as the end foreseen does not wipe out the humor of the scatological tales, even as it exposes the mortality that hides behind narrative. Like a fart in polite company, the scatological tales in the company of the *Retraction*, or dressed up in academic prose, might be even funnier than without company or dressing.[28]

NOTES

1. Hayden White, *The Content of the Form: Narrative Discourse and Historical Representation* (Baltimore: The Johns Hopkins UP, 1987), p. 180.

2. Paul Ricoeur, *Time and Narrative*, vol. 1, trans. Kathleen McLaughlin and David Pellauer (Chicago: U of Chicago P, 1984), p. 3 and throughout. I am indebted to Ricoeur and to White for their discussions of the relationship between narrative and time, and also to Ricoeur for his discussion of Augustine. I hope that my scatological and distorted use of their ideas does not alter them beyond recognition.

3. The edition used throughout is *The Riverside Chaucer*, 3rd ed., ed. Larry D. Benson (Boston: Houghton Mifflin, 1987).

4. Of the many critical works on the *Retraction*, its connection with the *Parson's Tale*, and its relationship to the *Canterbury Tales*, see e.g. Judith Ferster, *Chaucer on Interpretation* (Cambridge: Cambridge UP, 1985), p. 156; Donald R. Howard, *The Idea of the Canterbury Tales* (Berkeley: U. of California P, 1976), pp. 216–277; Carol V. Kaske, "Getting Around the *Parson's Tale*: An Alternative to Allegory and Irony," in R. H. Robbins, ed., *Chaucer at Albany* (New York: Franklin, 1975), pp. 146–177; David Lawton, "Chaucer's Two Ways: The Pilgrimage Frame of the *Canterbury Tales, Studies in the Age of Chaucer* 9 (1987): 3–40; A. J. Minnis, *Medieval Theory of Authorship: Scholastic Literary Attitudes in the Later Middle Ages* (London: Scolar P, 1984), pp. 207–210; Glending Olson, *Literature as Recreation in the Later Middle Ages* (Ithaca: Cornell UP, 1982), pp. 155–163; Charles A. Owen, Jr., *Pilgrimage and Story-telling in the* Canterbury Tales*: The Dialectic of "Ernest" and "Game"* (Norman, Okla.: The University of Oklahoma Press, 1977); Lee W. Patterson, "The *Parson's Tale* and the Quitting of the *Canterbury Tales*," *Traditio* 34 (1978): 331–380; Olive Sayce, "Chaucer's 'Retractions': The Conclusion of the *Canterbury Tales* and Its Place in Literary Tradition," *Medium Aevum* 40 (1971): 230–248; and Douglas Wurtele, "The *Retraction*," *Viator* 11 (1980): 335–359.

5. See Howard, pp. 216–277.

6. For example, see Minnis' argument about the *Canterbury Tales* as a *compilatio*, pp. 207–210; and especially Lawton, who also accepts the possibility of the *Retraction* as the work of a compiler and who sees the *Retraction* as a fitting end to the *Canterbury Tales*. Even a critic who believes that we should ignore the *Retraction* because it does not fit Chaucer's intentions, laments in his recent book that "scholars and critics have paid little heed to this possibility [of rejecting the *Parson's*

Tale and the *Retraction*]." See Owen, *The Manuscripts of the* Canterbury Tales, p. 125; and *Pilgrimage and Storytelling* (note 4 above).

7. On the popularity of the *Clerk's Tale* in the fifteenth century, see Seth Lerer, "Rewriting Chaucer: Two Fifteenth-Century Readings of the *Canterbury Tales,*" *Viator* 19 (1988): 311–318.

8. Martha Brannigan, "Court Upholds School-Board Removal of Bawdy Classics from the Curriculum," *Wall Street Journal,* Jan. 17 (1989): p. B9 (western ed.; p. C27 eastern ed.).

9. Haldeen Braddy, "Chaucer—Realism or Obscenity?" *Arlington Quarterly* 2 (1969): 128–137, remarks that the division of the fart "does gag me" (p. 156); quoted in Roy Peter Clark, "Doubting Thomas in Chaucer's *Summoner's Tale,*" *Chaucer Review* 11 (1976): 178 n. 45; and in Peter G. Beidler, "Art and Scatology in the *Miller's Tale,*" *Chaucer Review* 12 (1977): 91. For a summary of reactions to the *Miller's Tale,* see Beidler, pp. 90–91, and p. 100 n. 2–7; for responses to the *Summoner's Tale,* see Earl Birney, "Structural Irony Within the *Summoner's Tale,*" *Anglia* 78 (1960): 204–205.

10. The "end in the beginning" has been a staple (and bugaboo) of narratologists' and others' writing for many years; for a convenient, brief statement on the history of the idea, see D. A. Miller, *Narrative and Its Discontents* (Princeton: Princeton UP, 1981), pp. xiii–xv. One difficulty that grows out of this notion is its potential intractability. If one treats it as a law, it becomes deterministic, the end of a narrative tyrannizing over the whole and allowing no possible contradictions or discontinuities. But hindsight is not the same as determinism, and the retrospectiveness of narrative is no more or less tyrannical than any hermeneutical act. See note 27.

11. On Augustine's discussion of time, see Ricoeur 1:5–30 (note 2 above), and his references, p. 231 n. 1; John C. Callahan, *Four Views of Time in Ancient Philosophy,* (Cambridge: Cambridge UP, 1948), pp. 149–204; Frank Kermode, *The Sense of an Ending: Studies in the Theory of Fiction,* (New York: Oxford UP, 1967), pp. 68–69; and for a very brief overview, James O'Donnell, *Augustine,* Twayne's World Authors Series, Latin Literature (Boston: Twayne, 1985), pp. 116–117.

12. Augustine, *Confessions,* trans. E. B. Pusey, *Great Books of the Western World* 18, ed. Mortimer J. Adler (Chicago, Encyclopedia Britannica, Inc., 1952); *Confessionum,* ed. P. Knoell, *Corpus scriptorum ecclesiasticorum latinorum* 40 (1899–1900).

13. Sometimes described as "mental discomfort," "mental torment," as well as "mental cramp." Ludwig Wittgenstein, *The Blue and Brown Books: Preliminary Studies for the Philosophical Investigations,* ed.

with a preface by Rush Rhees 2nd Ed. (Oxford: Blackwell, 1969), pp. 1, 26; Wittgenstein, *Zettel*, trans. G. E. M. Anscombe (Oxford: Blackwell, 1967), #452; on time and mental cramps, see also K. T. Fann, *Wittgenstein's Conception of Philosophy* (Berkeley: U of California P, 1971), pp. 67, 86–87.

14. See Clark, "Doubting Thomas" (note 9).

15. See Alan Levitan, "The Parody of Pentecost in Chaucer's *Summoner's Tale*," *University of Toronto Quarterly* 40 (1966): 236–246; Bernard Levy, "Biblical Parody in the *Summoner's Tale*," *Tennessee Studies in Literature* 11 (1966): 45–60; and Roy Peter Clark, "Wit and Witsunday in Chaucer's *Summoner's Tale*," *Annuale Mediaevale* 17 (1976): 48–57.

16. See Clark, "Doubting Thomas," p. 174.

17. See D. W. Robertson, Jr., *A Preface to Chaucer: Studies in Medieval Perspectives* (Princeton: Princeton UP, 1962): 331–332; and Mary Carruthers, "Letter and Gloss in the *Friar's* and *Summoner's Tales*," *Journal of Narrative Theory* 2 (1972): 208–214.

18. Cf. John Leyerle, "Chaucer's Windy Eagle," *University of Toronto Quarterly* 40 (1971): 247–265.

19. O'Donnell, p. 116.

20. Many critics have noted in passing the prominence of "pryvetee" as theme in the tale. See Traugott Lawler, *The One and the Many in the* Canterbury Tales, (Hamden, Conn.: Archon Books, 1980), for a discussion of the issue of privacy versus exposure in the *Miller's* and the *Summoner's Tales* (pp. 48–51); also Roy Peter Clark, "Christmas Games in Chaucer's *Miller's Tale*," *Studies in Short Fiction* 13 (1976): 277–287; Thomas J. Farrell, "Privacy and the Boundaries of Fabliau in the *Miller's Tale*," *English Literary History* (1989): 773–795; and especially Laura Kendrick, *Chaucerian Play: Comedy and Control in the* Canterbury Tales (Berkeley and Los Angeles: University of California Press, 1988), pp. 5–19, for her insightful discussion of the ambiguities of the sentence "of Goddes pryvetee, nor of his wyf." On exposure and unmasking according to Freud's analysis of jokes, see also Peggy A. Knapp, "Robyn the Miller's Thrifty Work," in *Sign, Sentence, and Discourse: Language in Medieval Thought and Literature*, ed. Julian N. Wasserman and Lois Roney (Syracuse: Syracuse UP, 1989), pp. 294–308.

21. For recent scientific views on the nature of time—made palatable for nonscientists, see Stephen Hawking, *A Brief History of Time: From the Big Bang to Black Holes* (New York: Bantam, 1988); Peter Coveney and Roger Highfield, *The Arrow of Time: A Voyage Through Science to Solve Time's Greatest Mystery* (New York: Fawcett Columbine,

1990); and James Gleick, *Chaos: Making A New Science* (New York: Penguin, 1987). On "experienced" time, see Peter Hartocollis, *Time and Timelessness or the Varieties of Temporal Experience* (New York: Universities P, 1983); Joseph McGrath, *Time and Human Interaction: Toward a Social Psychology* (New York: Guilford P, 1986); and Bernard S. Gorman and Alden E. Wessman, *Personal Experience of Time* (New York: Plenum P, 1977). On time in literature, the reciprocity between narrative and time, and narrative in history, see Ricoeur, *Time and Narrative*, Vol. 1 (note 2 above), Vol. 2, trans. Kathleen McLaughlin and David Pellauer (Chicago: U of Chicago P, 1985), and vol. 3, trans. Kathleen Blamey and David Pellauer (Chicago: U of California P, 1988); White, *Content of the Form* (note 1 above); Kermode, *Sense of an Ending* (note 11 above); Hans Meyerhoff, *Time In Literature* (Berkeley, 1960); and cf. Howard, *The Idea of the* Canterbury Tales, pp. 78–92 and passim.

22. Beidler, p. 94.

23. Alisoun does not figure into the story in the way that the male characters do because she does not count as a person so much as a morsel of food. She is served up as a tempting meal for men's consumption and later regret. She is the source of energy and desire and also the cause, ultimately, of pain and befoulment and the fall of man. It is not surprising that after warning about a wife's privetee, the Miller then tells a story about the body, since woman stands for the flesh or carries the burden of carnality. Alisoun seems removed from the time of the body even while embodying it. She is both removed from the process and at the center of it. As a symbol for the flesh, the female character in the story creates time and yet does not suffer it, at least not in the way that the male characters do.

24. Cf. Beidler, p. 97; and Janette Richardson, *Blameth Nat Me: A Study of Imagery in Chaucer's Fabliaux* (The Hague: Mouton, 1970), p. 169.

25. Kermode, pp. 84, 94.

26. O'Donnell, p. 125. Augustine, *Retractiones*. Patrologia latina, 32: 583–656, ed. J. P. Migne.

27. See note 10. On the retrospective nature of narrative, see especially Kermode; Ricoeur; White; and Suzanne Fleischman, *Tense and Narrativity: From Medieval Performance to Modern Fiction* (Austin: U of Texas P, 1990). Some narratives of course work against conventions, including the convention that says the end is contained in the beginning; these works posit the existence of such a convention rather than argue against it. On this point see, e.g., Fleischman for a discussion of the *nouveau roman*.

In referring to narrative, I mean written literary narrative; for a linguist's discussion of the ontologically retrospective nature of narrative language, both literary and nonliterary, written and oral, see Fleischman. Can one make up a narrative on the spot with no end in mind? One can do anything with narrative, no doubt. A linguist might respond that even in spontaneous narratizing, one is choosing from a repertoire of possibilities and in so doing also choosing an end, and might argue likewise for the impossibility of simultaneously experiencing and narrating an event.

In claiming that narrative works backward from an end, I do not mean to state a law which somehow governs all narratives. Language in general and narrative in particular defy hardening into laws, so that it makes sense only to speak of "emergent grammar" rather than a "superhard core" of rules that govern discourse. See Dennis Hopper, "Discourse Analysis: Grammar and Critical Theory in the 1980s," *Profession* 88 (1988): 18–24. All rules of grammar or of narrative continually undergo renegotiating and restructuring. Retrospectiveness as a rule of narrative is provisional and descriptive rather than prescriptive.

28.   Research for this essay was supported by a fellowship from the National Endowment for the Humanities.

Chaucer's Creative Comedy
A *Study of the* Miller's Tale
and the Shipman's Tale*

A. Booker Thro

> ... comic action ... is [the protagonist's] contest
> with the world and his triumph by wit ...
>
> [Comedy] expresses ... the delight man takes in his
> special mental gifts that make him lord of creation.[1]

Wit triumphant, reflecting a delight in man's mental gifts—this is the central action of much of Chaucer's comedy. We may go one step further, though, and observe that in Chaucer's comedy the triumph of wit is often a "creative" act, an act of imaginative invention and ingenious construction. Chaucer's men of wit concoct schemes or build illusions which are both brilliantly artful and astonishingly elaborate. Because such constructs are sometimes more complex than the situations in which they appear require, they call attention to themselves and emphasize the creative cleverness of their makers.

The riddle scene at the conclusion of the *Summoner's Tale* (III.2216–94) provides an example of Chaucer's gratuitously creative comedy.[2] We might well expect this tale to conclude with Thomas's "gesture of generosity," as this act completes the poem's main movement by debating the hypocritical pretensions of the Friar and by inspiring him to the very wrath that he has so strenuously denounced. But Chaucer is not content to stop here. For Thomas's request that his "gift" be divided equally among

379

the friars is suddenly taken quite literally posed as a scientific conundrum, and solved by the "lordes squier" in ingenious practical terms. The problem is absurd, and yet it is truly difficult. The assertion that "subtiltee and heigh wit" have inspired Thomas's riddle is playfully ironic, but few would deny that these abilities are involved in Jankyn's scheme. This posing of creative exercise and its fantastically imaginative solution appear, since they are in excess of plot requirements, to be dictated by Chaucer's enthusiastic delight in mental gymnastics.

Such instances of elaborate constructiveness abound in the *Miller's Tale* because its world is peopled with witty creators. No one in this Oxenford, except for the anomalous carpenter, can be satisfied with expressions and deeds of bare utility. Self-conscious, excessive ingenuity is the rule, whether in personal attire ("With Poules wyndow corven on his shoos, / In hoses rede he wente fetisly" [I.3318–19]), or in interior decoration ("A chambre hadde he in that hostelrye / . . . / Ful fetisly ydight with herbes swoote . . ." [I.3203–05]), whether in play ("In twenty manere koude he trippe and daunce / After the scole of Oxenforde tho . . ." [I.3328–29]) or in plotting ("This Nicholas answerde, 'Fecche me drynke, / And after wol I speke in pryvetee / Of certeyn thyng that toucheth me and thee'" [I.3492–94]). This practice of gratuitous elaboration is evidenced in Absolon's ludicrous courtship ("But first he cheweth greyn and lycorys, / To smellen sweete, er he hadde kembd his heer. / Under his tonge a trewe-love he beer . . ." [I.3690–92]) and even in his lively reaction to adversity ("Who rubbeth now, who froteth now his lippes / With dust, with sond, with straw, with clooth, with chippes, / But Absolon . . . " [I.3747–49]).

While Alisoun can sing, "skippe and make game," and the dandy Absolon performs with "lightnesse and maistrye" in many fields (e.g. I.3326–36), it is Nicholas whose brilliant contriving dominates the poem and supplies its main action. Chaucer introduces his clerk with the information that he is both "sleigh and ful privee" (I.3201), and the qualifier "hende" (skillful, expert, or clever) calls attention to his special status continually.[3] The cleverness of fabliaux clerks is usually presented implicitly in their successful cuckolding of jealous merchants. But with Nicholas Chaucer is concerned to accentuate the cleverness rather than the cuckolding, and thus causes his clerk to conceive of a strategem wholly gratuitous in its complexity to the practical needs of the situation. The disparity between what is required (the carpenter is a "sely" fellow of "rude wit" and his wife is not unwilling) and what is created emphasizes the prodigious expenditure of mental energy.

Nicholas unfolds his design without introductory explanations and in a step-by-step manner which conveys the impression of gradual and involved construction. We witness the growing structure of apparently irrelevant materials, irrelevant because we cannot yet imagine the final edifice. What is the purpose of the feigned illness, the flood illusion, and the request for "knedyng tubbes" and "vitaille" sufficient for a day? At last, after more than one hundred lines of pure fantasy, we read "'. . . noon of us ne speke nat a word'" (I.3586), shortly followed by "'Thy wyf and thou moote hange fer atwynne'" (I.3589), and all confusion is immediately dispelled. As the clerk fashions coherence and relevance out of perplexity, our curiosity and bewilderment alter to a profound appreciation.

Instances of ingenious and elaborate mental constructiveness are pervasive in the *Miller's Tale* and so attractive that ultimately they monopolize our attention. This is not to say that the poem deals exclusively with the comic celebration of creativity. It also involves its characters in farcical situations or expresses ironic attitudes toward their accomplishments. But farce and irony are generally subordinate and muted; Chaucer never permits them to obscure or seriously qualify his main emphasis upon triumphant wit. Because this has not always been recognized it will be useful to look more closely at farcical and ironic elements in the *Miller's Tale* and, specifically, to examine the verdicts of some critics who have, in my estimation, overemphasized the importance of farce and irony in the poem.

Mr. T. W. Craik's view that the *Miller's Tale* "is essentially a farce, with a farce's predominance of comic situation over everything else" seems to me both mistaken and confusing;[4] mistaken because, as we shall observe, creativity, not farce, predominates in the Tale, and confusing because it blurs necessary distinctions between farce and comedy. We must begin by clarifying these distinctions, as the main concerns and informing feeling of deflationary farce are diametrically opposed to those of the creative comedy of the *Miller's Tale*.

Farce is typically an action of continual, often rather heavy-handed unmasking resulting in a deflation of pretentiousness or a retribution for social (or marital) evils. Unmasking in the fabliau can take the form of caricature, verbal abuse (including narrator asides), or physical violence; acts or expressions which stimulate and gratify the antagonistic feelings of the audience (or reader). The underlying impetus of farce is destructive aggressiveness. As Eric Bentley points out, the form embodies a socially repressed desire to desecrate and damage traditional idols.[5]

The French fabliaux which deal with the "cocu battu" theme are usually farce forms. Their characteristic method, as we may discover by glancing at a tale called *La Bourgeoise d'Orléans*, is to "set up" a thoroughly unpleasant husband purely for the purpose of knocking him down. The burgher in this story is a greedy usurer who disguises himself as his wife's lover in order to foil her extra-marital activities. We soon witness his pretensions to cleverness deflated, however, for his wife easily sees through the disguise and takes action to foil his scheme, while the narrator mocks him with derisive interjections: "Dieus! comme il savoit or petit / De ce qu'ele pensse et porpensse; / Li ansiers une chose pensse / Et li asnes pensse tout el. / Tost avra mauves ostel . . ." ("Lord! How little he knew what she was thinking and plotting! As they say: the mule driver thinks he knows where he's going, but the mules have their own idea. Soon the burgher will not be so well lodged.")[6] Eventually the burgher is cuckolded, brutally beaten with cudgels, clubs and pestles and thrown into a dungheap "like a dead dog." Throughout the tale the emphasis is upon the destructive, vindictive deflation of the husband rather than upon the clever means whereby this deflation is effected. We are made to accord with the antagonism of the wife and narrator and to wish for the husband's defeat. The feeling accompanying this ignominious defeat is a malicious glee similar to that described by Paul Goodman in his discussion of Jonsonian humors characters: "The deflation of the humors is malicious laughter, energized by released destructiveness and made safe by contempt or indifference."[7]

While farce is the expression of destructive impulses, the *Miller's Tale* persistently focuses upon human constructiveness, upon the triumph of wit rather than the deflation of pretension. This destruction-construction opposition is implicit in Bentley's distinguishing of farce and comedy: "In farce, unmasking occurs all along. The favorite action of the farceur is to shatter the appearances, his favorite effect being the shock to the audience of his doing so. Comedy makes much of appearances: it specializes, indeed, in the "keeping up" of appearances. Unmasking in comedy will characteristically be the unmasking of a single character in a climactic scene—like that of Tartuffe.[8] The "appearances" of comedy are the creations of ingenious wit. To be fascinated by the subtlety of a masquerade, the intricacy and complexity of an intrigue or the cleverness of a deceptive utterance is to admire the maker of these constructions. The feeling which accompanies our recognition of comic creativity is glory,[9] an exulting in man's ability to make appearance real.

The major appearance fostered by the *Miller's Tale* is, of course, Nicholas's re-creation of biblical history. This illusion is structurally the center of the poem. Chaucer's intention that nothing should distract our attention from it is apparent from his avoidance of traditional farcical elements in the presentation of his "cocu battu." Carpenter John possesses none of the usual abrasive traits of fabliau husbands. In the more farcical *Reeve's Tale*, Chaucer "unmasks" Symkyn immediately and mercilessly (I.3926–85). We are made to feel that the Miller's swaggering bellicosity and complacent social pretentiousness render him eminently suitable for more violent deflation. But Chaucer's carpenter generates little animosity. There is a suggestion in line 3224 ("Jalous he was, and heeld hire narwe in cage . . .") that the husband of Chaucer's source may have been the fabliau type of avarice and jealousy, but the poet conspicuously neglects to develop his carpenter along these lines. John is built up, not as Nicholas's deserving victim, but as his foil. His mental deficiencies define the clerk's brilliance by contrast.

The carpenter is a physical creature and confronts problems in a straightforward, inflexible and heavy-handed manner

("This carpenter ... / ... hente hym by the sholdres myghtily, / And shook hym harde, and cride spitously, / 'What! Nicholay! ...'" [I.3474–77]), or "'Get me a staf, that I may underspore, / Whil that thou, Robyn, hevest up the dore'" [3465–66]). Mentally as well as physically he is a carpenter, building only with inanimate materials. His aphoristic "wisdom" is prefabricated and never fits when he tries to attach it to the vital situations constructed by Nicholas (an incongruity between the mechanical and the living which partially accounts for the humor of lines like:[10] "'I saugh him to-day a cors yborn to chirche / That now, on Monday last, I saugh hym wirche'" [I.3429–30]).

If John begins as Nicholas's foil, he ends by becoming an actual part of the clerk's creation. From line 3600 on he lives in an illusory biblical land, frantically building Nicholas's plan in accordance with "Goddes pryvetee." He has no independent existence. To contrast the carpenter at this point with the "cocu battu" of the French fabliau (and perhaps of Chaucer's source) is to perceive how completely Chaucer avoids the deflationary, farcical concerns of these tales in order to preserve his comic emphasis upon creativity.

A similar and equally striking instance of Chaucer's use of potentially farcical materials for comic purposes occurs at the moment of Nicholas's painful reversal (I.3815). Rather than underscoring the clerk's discomfiture as fitting retribution for one whose reach has exceeded his grasp, Chaucer makes it the occasion for recalling our attention to the carpenter and to Nicholas's strategem. The wondrous design has suddenly taken on a life of its own and is determined to complete its predicted course, even beyond the limits of utility. As at the conclusion of the *Summoner's Tale*, the movement of emphasis is from farcical reversal to fascinating construction, and the shifting of our response is from the malice of destructive deflation to the glory of creative triumph.

While farce is a form alien to creative comedy in emphasis and feeling, irony is an attitude within farce or comedy which adulterates or inverts its ostensible emphasis. Irony, no less than farce, can destroy the ingenious illusions of which creative comedy is made:

He made a gardyn, walled al with stoon;
So fair a gardyn woot I nowher noon.
For, out of doute, I verraily suppose
That he that wroot the Romance of the Rose
Ne koude of it the beautee wel devyse
Ne Priapus ne myghte nat sufase,
Though he be god of gardyns, for to telle
The beautee of the gardyn and the welle. . . .

(IV.2029–36)

But it does not seem that irony is thus enlisted against comic constructiveness in the *Miller's Tale*. The courtly love irony, for example, tends to undercut the decorum of the Oxford world rather than its creativity. Absolon's courtship may be foolishly parochial by courtly standards, but it is imaginatively elaborate none the less ("He sente hire pyment, meeth, and spiced ale, / And wafres, pipyng hoot out of the gleede . . ." [I.3378–79]).

More important for our discussion are the biblical analogies which relate Nicholas's creative acts to those of divine regeneration. Paul Siegel has traced this connection in such lines as "'Yet shal I saven hire and thee and me'" (I.3533), or "'Thy wyf shal I wel saven, out of doute'" (I.3561).[11] He concludes that, because of Nicholas's earthward orientation, this juxtaposition of the clerk's schemes to divine salvation ironically devalues his accomplishments: "This world of comedy is set against a religious backdrop which renders action ironically trivial by the perspective it suggests."[12]

The force and direction of irony resulting from a poem's mixed values must be determined on the basis of value contexts provided both by the poem (internal context) and by the reader's cultural associations (external context). It seems that the reader will be most likely to measure ironic situations in an "internal" context in moments when his attention is directed to the central values of the poem. The intrusion of external values and a greater complexity of response is likely to result only when the reader's attention is temporarily distracted from the poem's value center. Thus the ironic utterances of a character who consistently adheres to (and keeps our attention focused upon) the poem's main values may be expected to elicit a simpler response than do those of a character who distracts our attention from these values.

For example, when Nicholas holds Alisoun "harde by the haunchebones" and begs for her affection with courtly pleas (I.3276–81), we notice immediately the absurdity of courtly idealizations in a naturalistic context. We are made bluntly aware that naturalism is the norm here and courtly love the ostentatious intruder. However, when we encounter the description of Absolon's courtship (I.3678–3707), the problem of response becomes more complicated. There is still an ironic reminder in lines like "What do ye, hony-comb, sweete Alisoun, / my faire bryd, my sweete cynamome?" (I.3698–99) that love idealizations are ludicrously inappropriate when applied to this lady. But Chaucer gives so much emphasis to Absolon's courtly efforts that ultimately we lose sight of the poem's naturalistic context and begin to measure his courtship against an external ideal of courtly love. The irony reverses itself and, in lines like "'No wonder is thogh that I swelte and swete; / I moorne as dooth a lamb after the tete'" (I.3703–04), operates, not against courtly love, but against the parochial and physical nature of Absolon's conception of love.

While the special emphasis placed upon Absolon's courtship leads us to seek, for it, an evaluative perspective beyond that provided by the poem, one may doubt whether Nicholas's "divine" utterances (I.3533, 3556, and 3561) have this effect, as Siegel suggests. It must be remembered that, at the moment we read these lines, we are beholding the step-by-step construction of Nicholas's ingenious scheme. Just as his earlier control of Alisoun (I.3279) has irrefutably established the supremacy of natural "love" in the world of the poem, so now the clerk's elaborate manipulation of the carpenter attests the similar triumph of creative wit. It seems that these two moments are productive of like kinds of irony. In the earlier scene the fact of natural "love" is too solidly established to be undermined by the idea of courtly love, and here the fact of man's creative cleverness remains invulnerable against the idea of divinity. By the time we encounter Nicholas's "deification" we are simply too much involved in the clerk's machinations to back away and view his action in a "trivializing" religious perspective.

Consequently, the analogy results in religious parody rather than ironic devaluation of Nicholas's plotting.

While Chaucer sometimes seems to be working out an impudent parody of the annunciation (e.g. Nicholas's annunciation hymn, his claim to have received knowledge of "Goddes pryvetee," and his self-appointed role in human regeneration) there are perhaps moments when his poetry suggests a more serious purpose behind the clerk's mock apotheosis:

> Whan that the grete shour is goon away,
> Thanne shaltou swymme as myrie, I undertake,
> As dooth the white doke after hire drake.
> Thanne wol I clepe, "How, Alison! how, John!
> Be myrie, for the flood wol passe anon."
> And thou wolt seyn, "Hayl, maister Nicholay!
> Good morwe, I se thee wel, for it is day."
> And thanne shul we be lordes al oure lyf
> Of al the world, as Noe and his wyf.

> (I.3574–82)

These lines come at the conclusion of Nicholas's flood revelation and mark the summit of his creative effort. As we read them creation takes shape out of the flood. There are suggestions of regeneration: the "grete shour" dissolves into morning clarity; the "doke," pure in whiteness, now obediently follows her drake. It is a moment of reawakening and recognition ("Good morwe, I se thee wel, for it is day"), of joyful acceptance of vital possibilities ("Be myrie, for the flood wol passe anon") and of the re-establishment of order out of chaos ("And thanne shul we be lordes al oure lyf/Of al the world, as Noe and his wyf"). It is not "Noe's" world exactly (there is one pioneer too many here), yet there is in it a brightness and freshness, an exuberant gladness and vitality not unworthy of a human creator. About its reality in the mind of the carpenter there can be no question; from this moment he conducts himself as prospective scion of the new creation. But how are *we* to understand this striking picture of Nicholas's creation, which seems too evocative of serious associations for religious parody, and yet all too real and alive for reductive irony (i.e. irony undercutting the clerk's achievement)? Is it not possible that Chaucer wishes us to be genuinely impressed, even a little awed by Nicholas's accomplishment, that he wishes us to perceive the sense in which the clerk, as inspired creative man, is truly related to divinity? After all, the act of imaginative creativity attests man's divine likeness and defines his special place in the hierarchy of being. Perhaps by expressing Nicholas's creative accomplishment in terms of this biblical regeneration, Chaucer intends to call attention to man's natural distinctiveness, and to the unique and exalting character of his creative powers.

If, as we have suggested, the *Miller's Tale* points to man's affinity with rather than his remoteness from divinity, the poem may be said to mirror a pervasive expression of the contemporary culture. There is much evidence to suggest that the twelfth century inaugurated a gradual shifting of the European attitude toward man and the earthly world.[13] The creation began to take on an interest and significance of its own, apart from its symbolic metaphysical value. The earlier Middle Ages had emphasized the absolute transcendence of God and, consequently, had tended to depreciate nature as irreparably injured by man's sin. But now it came increasingly to be felt that the natural world, despite its flawed character and distinctness from God, was nevertheless essentially valuable and good as his creation and the expression of his divine plan: "There is no better illustration of this development [toward naturalism] than the words of St. Thomas, 'God enjoys all things, for each accords with his essence.' They are a complete justification of naturalism. Everything real, however slight and ephemeral, has an immediate relationship to God; everything expresses the divine nature in its own way and so has its own value and meaning for art too."[14]

There are many reflections in art and architecture of medieval man's growing belief in the intimate relationship between God and the physical world of his creation. Cultural historians have pointed to the increasing realism of the crucifix, or to a new emphasis, in Christian iconography of the creation, upon God's terrestrial endeavors.[15] But surely some of the most vivid evidence for the medieval interest in God's earthly creation is to be found in Chaucer's *Miller's Tale*. For here the companion portraits of Alisoun the created and Nicholas the creator together represent man's relation both to nature and to God and communicate the comic approbation of human vitality and wit; Alisoun, created of the orchard, the meadow, and the barnyard; Nicholas, creator of the bright morning and hopes of a living but illusory world. "Here is God's plenty," indeed; one cannot avoid the conjecture that their creator both made and beheld what he had made with the feeling that it was very good.

Thus far we have found evidence for Chaucer's interest in creativity in the elaborate forms (e.g. Absolon's attire and courtship, Nicholas's and Jankyn's schemes) constructed by his characters. The clerk's flood revelation and the squire's solving of the riddle (in the *Summoner's Tale*) are, of course, described as actions unfolding in time. But these actions take on significance as intricate constructs only after they are completed. When conceived of as schemes exemplifying creativity the actions are meaningful as finished expressions rather than as temporal flux. And yet there are some instances in which Chaucer is concerned to present us with the organic process, as well as with the completed form, of creativity. In these moments he places his creator in a persuasive situation, compelling him to implant his ingenious construct in the variably resisting mind of an actual listener. Thus an exemplary action becomes simultaneously an action imaginative of life; the act signifying creativity becomes a convincingly real creative act.

Chaucer's *Shipman's Tale* presents most of its action in such scenes of "creative persuasion." The longest and most involved of these, the wife's persuasion of the monk (VII.1288–1393) will serve to illustrate how Chaucer depicts creativity as a psychologically cogent, realistic life process. The wife has a difficult objective before her in this scene; she must convince the wily monk that she can be relied upon to exchange her favors for money. It would not be politic just to baldly propose a "deal," as he might well be reluctant to trust her under such conditions. Consequently, she decides upon a strategy of seduction. She makes the monk believe that he is needed primarily to redress her sexual deprivation.

The scene's dialogue makes us aware of the subsurface motivation of both characters. For example, when the wife insists that, if she had enough time, she would just as soon recount her husband's manifold insufficiencies, even though he is the monk's "cosyn" (VII.1333–37), we know that she is really drawing daun John out about his true attitude toward the merchant. But the monk's eager reply that he has pretended friendship to her husband only to be near her, whom he loves above all women (VII.1343–44), is obviously equally manipulative.

Daun John has the smaller speaking part; nevertheless we are made to feel the opposing pressure of his lively, flexible cunning reflected in the continually shifting persuasive tactics of the wife. Her persuasion is a cautious, inscrutably ambiguous process of advance and retreat which evidences the psychological tension of her situation. She first seduces the monk with hints of her sexual need, only to frustrate his expectations with refusals to share her intimate secrets. At the beginning (VII. 1032–47) these fluctuations in her approach are calculated to imply, without admitting, her sexual inclinations, while they compel the monk to make his position clear. Her later reluctance and gradual consent to reveal the secret (VII.1348–60) are perhaps intended to suggest (since she equates secrecy with honor and wifely duty) an uneasy yielding of her resistance to the idea of adultery.

Even when she feels confident enough to proceed to the subject of money, the wife continues to adhere to her policy of indirection. Her syntax blurs between fiscal and sexual "nygardye" and liberality (e.g. ". . . he is noght worth at al / In no degree the value of a flye. / But yet he greveth moost his nygardye" [VII.1360–62] or ". . . housbonds sholde be / . . . riche, and therto fre, / And buxom unto his wyf, and fressh abedde" [VII.1365–67]) and softens the transition from her seduction to her request for a loan. By compelling the monk to see her sexual deprivation simultaneously with her need for money, she forestalls any possible doubts about her reliability. This studied imprecision of speech has the general effect, as do her earlier ambiguous "encouragment-discouragement" tactics, of mitigating a proposition into a seductive concession, of disarming daun John's suspicions and convincing him that he is playing an active role in the transaction. The fluctuating, ambivalent emphasis of the persuasion helps convey the sense of a subtle interaction of opposing psyches and thus of her involvement in a process which is perpetually variable and alive.

While the wife's persuasion is an imitation of psychological reality, it is, at the same time, a continuous creative process. She constructs in the monk's mind successive illusions of her terrible marital secret (VII.1310), of her belief that the merchant and the monk are "cosyns" (VII.1337), of her reluctant yielding (VII.1349–59), and finally of her husband's "nygardye" (VII.1360–67). To observe this process from the monk's point of view is to behold a gradually altering image of the wife; at first she is nearly desperate, oppressed with a "dreadful" secret and unable to confide in anyone. The secret apparently has something to do with marital unhappiness (VII.1306–07; there is no mention of indebtedness); hence, her becoming reserve. Slowly this reserve melts away (her address alters from "cosyn myn" [VII.1304] to "My deere love . . . O my daun John" [1384]). She becomes familiar, confiding, even willing to ask help, and eager to express her gratitude in any way possible.

This seductive picture of a lady's increasing availability is reinforced by another more romantic and sympathetic image of a lady's distress. In creating herself into a "lady in distress" the wife exhibits both an acute awareness of the hyperbolically dramatic and a self-conscious inventiveness second only to Nicholas's. She imagines herself as a romance lady singing a woeful "allas and weylawey" (VII.1308), and as a saint about whose suffering a "legende" could be told (VII.1335). Her sorrow is superlative; she is the most wretched wife in all of France (VII.1306), while her husband is, in his treatment of her, the worst man in the history of the world (VII.1351). The wife talks ominously of "sclaundre" and "vileynye" (VII.1373), and of running away or committing suicide (VII.1311). Her remarks about going through hell or being torn to pieces like Genylon of France (VII.1326–27) contribute to this theatrical self-image. The histrionic catalogue of "drede" and "care" is instrumental in distracting the monk's attention from the wife's mercenary purposes.

The other passages of creative persuasion in the *Shipman's Tale* are set speeches followed by a reply, rather than a sustained dialogue. They both reveal the hidden motivations of the speaker and imply the presence of a wary listener. In his two conversations with the merchant (VII.1447–82 and VII.1538–54) the monk perpetuates the already established illusion of their friendship to secure his monetary ends. In the poem's concluding scene (VII.1570–1622) the wife successfully persuades her husband to overlook the indebtedness which she has incurred. Earlier she has presented herself to the monk as wholly unsympathetic with the merchant's sober pragmatism; now, chameleonlike, she re-creates herself into her husband's world, becoming fiscally his frigid disciple (VII.1609) and physically his collateral (VII.1613).

As a series of persuasive scenes, a continual demonstration of triumphant wit, the *Shipman's Tale* presents us with a curiously fragmented plot. Chaucer's wish to focus upon witty triumph apart from its motivation or consequence necessarily leads him away from a single "cause-effect" action. The passages of creative persuasion in the tale imitate temporally autonomous moments; they are both unmotivated and without consequence. Why, for example, does the wife complain of her husband's stinginess and ask the monk for money? We have already been assured by the narrator that the merchant is generous as well as rich (VII.1210–12). Equally unexpected is the monk's borrowing of money from the husband following his conversation with the wife. His agreement with her (VII.1390) has caused us to assume that he will himself provide the hundred franks. Chaucer does not give the monk any motivation for his wily plotting. Similarly, the concluding scene between the wife and her husband does not produce the result that our awareness of the monk's designs causes us to expect. The wife is compelled to admit having received the money, and even promises to pay it back on time. The husband's wrath is appeased and the monk's ruse seems to have been successful when, suddenly, she produces a strategem wholly gratuitous to the foregoing action (VII.1614), and thereby escapes her obligation.

As Chaucer permits the wife and the monk to triumph by freeing each from the consequences of the other's plotting, so he permits the merchant to triumph by transporting him from the domestic sphere to that of business and by giving him his own moment of success in the complicated transaction with the

"Lumbardes." Like the creative persuasion of the wife and the monk, the merchant's dealings depend both upon the construction of appearances and the concealing of reality: "'We may wel make chiere and good visage,/... And kepen oure estaat in pryvetee ...'" (VII.1420–22). One establishes the credit necessary for business success by showing the world both a "worthy hous" and a confident demeanor, by creating the illusion of one's unalterable fiscal stability. In making it clear that business is a complex creative endeavor, Chaucer dignifies the merchant's intense commitment to it. We are compelled to see the merchant's business dealing, not negatively as marital negligence, but positively as a clever coup. His transaction in "Flaundres" is similar to, but more momentous than, the domestic business of the wife and monk. Though heavily indebted to the Lumbardes, he persuades "certeine freendes" in Paris to loan him twenty thousand sheedls, and is thus able to meet his obligations and turn a profit of a thousand franks. The merchant proves himself "ful war and wys" in his own challenging and important world. That his success supplies him with a satisfaction equivalent to that attainable in domestic business becomes evident when we compare his reaction to triumph with his wife's:

... And hoom he gooth, murie as a papejay...

(VII.1559)

... And forth she goot a has jolif as a pye....

(VII.1399)

By giving the merchant his own separate action of fruitful "creauncing," Chaucer enables him to rank with his wife and with the monk as an exemplar, more than as a victim, of wily practices.

The view that the *Shipman's Tale* is a series of disconnected exemplary creative acts is (as we have seen in our examination of the wife's persuasion scene [1283–1393]) only half complete. If the poem's three characters are separated from one another in their larger actions they are, at the same time, intimately related to one another in moments of persuasion. In these situations Chaucer's dialogue suggests a consequentially probable, complex and perpetually varying interaction of opposing psyches. We are made to behold two living people engaged in a psychologically real persuasive movement of subtle maneuvering and wary reaction.

This unusual combination of realistic and abstractly separate actions in the *Shipman's Tale* clearly suggests that a double purpose underlies Chaucer's composition. If the poem's multi-action plot configuration indicates Chaucer's concern that literature exemplify an idea, its psychological verisimilitude reflects, simultaneously, his feeling that literature has a mimetic function. Such a double attitude toward artistic purpose is generally thought to be characteristic of that cultural period labeled "high Gothic."[16] This period is commonly described as occupying a transitional position in the gradual alteration of the medieval attitude toward the natural world. Because it had neither abandoned the supernaturalism of the earlier Middle Ages nor completely accepted the new naturalism, the high Gothic culture perceived and expressed a dual conception of reality. Truth was believed to reside not only in absolute, supramundane ideas, but also within the temporal movement of natural life. Consequently the artist of this period was faced with an objective unknown to the allegorists of earlier centuries; he regarded it as his function to represent the ceaselessly mutating character of actual sense experience, as well as the inalterable, metaphysical reality of ideas.

As illustrative of this double artistic impetus, one can point to the naturalistic individuation of symbolic human form in cathedral statuary. The cycle drama also evidences a dual emphasis, as it communicates, often naturalistically, biblical ideas in a movement of continuous presentation suggestive of organic process. Arnold Hauser has observed a similar dynamic vitalism in the spiritually symbolic Gothic church: "A Gothic church . . . seems to be in the process of development, as if it were rising up before our very eyes; it expresses a process, not a result. The resolution of the whole mass into a number of forces, the dissolution of all that is rigid and at rest by means of a dialectic of functions and subordinations, this ebb and flood, circulation and transformation of energy, gives us the impression of a dramatic conflict working up to a decision before our eyes."[17]

It seems that this view of the Gothic cathedral as the simultaneous expression of transcendent idea and vital process (or that of the cycle drama as both the ideological design of Christian reality and the "drama of movement," "dynamic life," and "changing and transitory particulars")[18] brings us very close to the kind of thing Chaucer is about in the persuasive passages of his Tale. As we have seen, there is a sense in which these passages are exemplary forms, closed and separate from the mainstream of temporal life. Taken collectively as a series of triumphant moments, they represent life selectively ordered (in the manner of an allegorical structure). Only in this way is Chaucer able to isolate and define his idea of creativity. This idea has reality for Chaucer, even as the transcendent idea has reality for the cathedral builder, and yet ultimately it is inseparable from the things of sense experience. The idea is perceived within life and communicated in terms of the vital, psychological process of creative persuasion. Like the Gothic cathedral, the persuasion of the *Shipman's Tale* is both form and process; it exemplifies idealogical reality while it represents life. Chaucer abstracts and reincarnates for our perception the idea of creative triumph.

NOTES

*From *Chaucer Review* 5 , no. 2 (1970): 97-111. Copyright © 1970 by the Pennsylvania State University. Reproduced by permission of The Pennsylvania State University Press.

1. Susanne Langer, *Feeling and Form, A Theory of Art* (New York: Scribner, 1953), p. 331.

2. All quotations are from *The Works of Geoffrey Chaucer*, ed. F. N. Robinson, 2nd ed. (Boston: Houghton Mifflin, 1957).

3. For a discussion of this word see Paul E. Beichner, "Chaucer's Hende Nicholas," *Mediaeval Studies*, 14 (1952): 151–53.

4. T. W. Craik, *The Comic Tales of Chaucer* (London: Barnes & Noble, 1958), p. 5.

5. Eric Bentley, *The Life of Drama* (New York: Atheneum, 1954), p. 226.

6. "La Bourgeoise d'Orléans," ed. Richard O'Gorman (St. Louis. 1957); *Fabliaux: Ribald Tales from the Old French*, trans. Robert Hellman and Richard O'Gorman (New York: Crowell, 1965), pp. 3–4.

7. *The Structure of Literature* (Chicago: U of Chicago P, 1954), p. 92.

8. Bentley, p. 242.

9. Glory is used by Paul Goodman to describe that feeling accompanying "the discovery that a deflatable talent is a wit" p. 94.

10. See Henri Bergson, *Laughter*, in *Comedy*, ed. Wylie Sypher (Garden City, N. Y.: Doubleday, 1956), p. 79.

11. Paul Siegel, "Comic Irony in *the Miller's Tale*," *Boston University Studies in English*, 4 (1960): 114–20.

12. Siegel, p. 119.

13. For a discussion of medieval naturalism see Lynn White, Jr., "Natural Science and Naturalistic Art in the Middle Ages," *American Historical Review*, 52 (1947): 421–35; and Arnold Hauser, *The Social History of Art*, trans. Stanley Goodman, 2 vols. (New York: Knopf, 1952), Vol. 1, pp. 232–44.

14. Hauser, Vol. 1, pp. 232–3.

15. White, pp. 430–1.

16. See, on "Gothic Dualism," Hauser, I, 235–37.

17. Hauser, Vol. 1, pp. 242.

18. Hauser, Vol. 1, pp. 239.

Felicity and Mutability
Boethian Framework of the Troilus*

John M. Steadman

For Dante, Boethius was "the sainted soul, which unmasketh the deceitful world." A luminary of the Christian church, he had died a martyr's death, and leaving his body to be buried in Pavia, had been glorified in the sun. In the company of Saint Thomas Aquinas and other theologians, he now enjoyed the vision of "every good":[1]

> Per vedere ogni ben, dentro vi gode
> L'anima santa che 'l mondo fallace
> Fa manifesto a chi di lei ben ode.

> Lo corpo ond' ella fu cacciata giace
> Giuso in Cieldauro, ed essa da martiro
> E da essilio venne a questa pace.

Dante's admiration for the *De Consolatione* is reflected in echoes of this work throughout the *Commedia*, but its influence is particularly striking in his relations with Beatrice. His continuous dialogue with the personification of sacred theology—the *divina scientia* which teaches the true blessedness of man and the way to achieve it—is analogous to Boethius's discourse with Dame Philosophy. Many of the same *topoi* would recur in the *Troilus*: the contrast between the fate of the body and that of the soul (extending even to the violent death that "drives" or "chases" the immortal spirit from its mortal vehicle), the contrast between the "false world" and the vision of "every good," and the antithesis between earthly and celestial felicity. Appropriately Dante begins his next canto with a Boethian *topos* ("O insensata cura de' mortali"). Echoing Philosophy's condemnation of humanity's preoccupation with temporal things, he contrasts the joys of heaven with worldly cares—legal studies, pursuit of wealth and power, delights of the flesh. It is within the same Boethian frame of reference and in much the same spirit that Chaucer contrasts the full felicity of heaven with the vanity of the wretched world and its transitory lust. Like Dante's worldlings, Chaucer's hero is "nel diletto de la carne involto."[2]

Since Chaucer's debt to Boethius has already received intensive analysis from others, we shall reconsider this problem only insofar as it has relevance for the flight stanzas. Curry's charge that the epilogue is inconsistent with the rest of the *Troilus* scarcely does justice either to Chaucer's artistry or to the evidence of the text. If one condemns the epilogue as inconsistent with the romantic values of the plot, one can hardly avoid finding similar inconsistencies in the moral reflections that recur throughout the poem either in the poet's own person or through his *dramatis personae*. In the last analysis, Criseyde's reflections on the instability of worldly joy, Pandarus's observations on Fortune's changes, and Chaucer's repeated allusions to fortune and chance or fate and providence represent partial and incomplete statements of doctrines that will receive clearer and fuller expression in the epilogue. Like the epilogue, they are an integral part of the Boethian context of Chaucer's romance.

The alleged inconsistency of the epilogue (it would seem) actually springs from Chaucer's conscious juxtaposition of two different but complementary points of view: the naive and worldly attitude toward earthly prosperity and adversity, and the heavenly teachings of philosophy. The former belongs to opinion, the latter to knowledge. In Boethius's dialogue these contrasting attitudes are initially represented by the narrator and Dame Philosophy. Conventional in classical and medieval thought, this antithesis underlies the epistemological structure of the *Troilus* and much of the poet's finest irony.

The flight stanzas themselves represent a fusion of Boethian *topoi* with the apotheosis motif of the poets and the pneumatology of Stoic and Neoplatonic philosophers.[3] Though

Troilus's condemnation of the world's transitory "lust" and his vision of the "pleyn felicite" of heaven are essentially Boethian, other motifs—the contemplation of heaven and earth, the comparison of the magnitude of the one with the insignificance of the other, the derision of earthly affections, and indeed the ascent motif itself—are common to all three of these traditions. Moreover, besides the commonplaces shared by the works themselves, medieval exegesis had forged additional links. Commentators had interpreted Boethius in the light of the same philosophical doctrines they had brought to the explication of Lucan and Cicero and Dante. In introducing his flight sequence into a poem already heavily permeated with Boethian thought, Chaucer was not patching an old garment with new or different material; he was adding like to like.

In one respect there is a significant difference between Boethius's flight metaphors and Troilus's ascent. The former refers essentially to the ascent of the mind in contemplation; the latter represents the journey of the soul after death. Different as they are, however, the two genres are interrelated. Like the felicity of philosophers in this life, the beatitude of separated souls after death consists primarily in contemplation. For the later Stoics, with their bent for natural philosophy, this was contemplation of the heavens. For the Neoplatonists, it was contemplation of the realm of Ideas and the vision of divine beauty or the Supreme Good. For Christian theologians, it was the beatific vision, the *visio Dei*. The fact that the two genres shared the same imagery and frequently the same doctrines made it easier to combine them in a single work. Thus the analogies between Troilus's flight and the speculative ascent enabled Chaucer to draw not only on the posthumous flight of Pompey's soul and the visionary ascents of Dante and Scipio but also on the speculative flight imagery of Boethius.

In recent years the Boethian content of the *Troilus*[4] and its broader intellectual background have been subjected to detailed analysis. In Professor Robinson's opinion, Chaucer's translation of the Consolation "unquestionably" reveals the influence not only of the Latin original but of "the Latin commentary of Nicholas Trivet and a French prose version ascribed to Jean de Meun." Whether Chaucer also knew the commentary by Pseudo-

Aquinas is uncertain. Parallels formerly cited as evidence for
such indebtedness seem to point instead to the influence of
Trivet's commentary; moreover, in Robinson's view, this was
"probably" a source of Pseudo-Aquinas's commentary.[5]

In considering the Boethian element in Chaucer's romance,
I shall not attempt a detailed analysis of sources and analogues.
Instead I shall limit this study to general observations on the
Boethian tradition, noting its relevance for the genre of
Chaucer's poem, for his treatment of character and passion, and
for the tragic end of his hero, followed by the final glimpse of
true felicity. Pseudo-Aquinas's commentary will be treated less
as a potential source than as a significant statement of the
medieval Boethian tradition. Representing a stage of development apparently later than Trivet's work, it brings us closer to
the *De Consolatione* of Chaucer's contemporaries. Finally, I shall
examine some of the principal Boethian *topoi* of the flight
episode, noting similarities and dissimilarities between the
Boethian and Lucanic traditions.

I

In the Monk's definition of tragedy, recent scholarship has
not only detected the influence of medieval glosses on Boethius's
reference to tragedy but has rightly stressed the significance of
this influence for the *Troilus*.[6] In accordance with contemporary
ideas of tragedy, Chaucer recounts his medieval tale as though it
were a true history rather than a fictitious argument, appealing
to the testimony of his nonexistent author Lollius. The tragedy of
Troilus is, he pretends, a "storie" recorded in "olde bookes," not
simply a fiction invented by a twelfth-century poet and
elaborated by thirteenth- and fourteenth-century authors. Like
other tragic protagonists, the hero stands "in greet prosperitee,"
falls "Into myserie, and endeth wrecchedly," a reversal
underlined by the poet's frequent references to Fortune's
changes and the hero's sorrows and by final reflections on
Troilus's unhappy end. Moreover, like two of the Monk's
"illustrious men"—Samson and Hercules—Troilus meets his

death through his "lemman," an end that is all the more tragic inasmuch as the hero, like the conventional suicide, seeks his own death through despair.

There is, nevertheless, one significant difference: Troilus is not "yfallen out of heigh degree." He enjoys the renown of a warrior and the wealth and dignities of a royal prince until the end; then he perishes not ingloriously on the battlefield, the very kind of death that other poets had celebrated in heroic verse. The prosperity and misery he encounters, the changes of Fortune he experiences—these are the conventional vicissitudes of a lover rather than of a tragic hero; other poets had treated such materials comically or elegiacally and on occasion Chaucer does so himself. Chaucer has taken the transiency of worldly love rather than the loss of worldly dignities and high estate as his subject matter, but he has invested this erotic content with the shape and structure of tragedy. Though the Trojan war provides a tragic context for the history of the lovers, though their end is tragic and they themselves belong to the rank appropriate for tragedy, much of Chaucer's material, as he must have realized, was the conventional matter of comedy; in particular, the triadic relation of lover, bawd, and mistress had been traditionally associated with the comic genre.[7] In placing the joys and sufferings of the lovers against the background of the imminent doom of Troy,[8] Chaucer juxtaposed a historical theme universally recognized as tragic in the highest degree and an erotic subject that might embrace not only the heroic values of chivalric romance but also the humbler values of comedy and the sentimental values of elegy.

The problem of the genres appropriate to secular erotic themes demands fuller discussion than one can accord it here. In classical or medieval literature, the subject of *amor* might occur in such diverse art forms as epic or pastoral, comedy or tragedy, elegy or satire, encomium or didactic verse treatise. The treatment of this theme varied, moreover, with genre. In tragedy it might be presented pejoratively, as a passion leading to madness or death. In epic it might serve either as a spur or as a check to heroic actions—an incentive to the pursuit of glory or a temptation to ignoble ease.

Though medieval poetic theory usually assigned warfare to tragedy (and/or epic), and love and marriage to comedy, this distinction was based essentially on the correlation between literary genre and social level. While the deeds of noble or "courtly" persons demanded the epic or tragic genre and the resources of the high style, the actions of the middle or lower classes were more appropriate for comedy and for the middle or low styles. Although Dante associates the theme of love (*Venus*) with *salus* and *virtus* as subjects meriting an "illustrious" and "courtly" tongue, the majority of medieval literary theorists, heavily dependent on late classical rhetoric and poetic, failed to give adequate consideration to the medieval vogue of courtly lyric and romance. Medieval poetics already possessed a theory concerning the genre and style appropriate for depicting the military exploits of a man in high estate and for portraying the sudden alterations of fortune that could change his prosperity into disaster. It had not, however, managed to evolve a systematic and coherent theory concerning the genre and style best suited for a description of his love affairs or for an expression of his passion. Though rhetorical treatises and *artes poeticae* might regard love (among other emotions) as an *affectus* especially appropriate to youth, they rarely developed this point, they considered it primarily in relation to personal attributes (*attributa personarum*) and to the requirements of decorum in character. They failed, on the whole, to come to grips with the problem of how to portray a lover of noble rank and how to differentiate his emotions and his behavior under the influence of *eros* from those of a man of meaner station. It was left to the poets, in large part, to raise and resolve such questions for themselves.

In contrast with the large body of chivalric romances and courtly lyrics devoted to the amours of the nobility, literary theorists tended to neglect this theme. Though their omission may prove a source of embarrassment to the modern scholar, it nevertheless left considerable latitude to the medieval poet. Since the essential factor determining the choice of the comic or tragic genre was the social level of the characters portrayed, the writer of courtly romance might combine the motifs of love and valor, incorporating elegiac or even comic elements into his account of the lover's fortunes without altering its genre. Whether it portrayed arms or amours, his *roman* retained its affinities with epic (or narrative "tragedy"), inasmuch as its protagonists were ladies and cavaliers of "gentle" birth and rank. In the same way, Chaucer's romance of Troilus's ill-starred passion remains an epic "tragedy," even though it contains elements of comedy, elegy, and encomium. As in Virgil's *alta tragedia* and as in the medieval romances of Tristan and Lancelot, the themes of love and valor and ruin are interwoven. Troilus's passion, like that of Dido and Achilles and Paris and so many other classical and medieval heroes or heroines, terminates in death.

In this context we may also recall the conventional distinction between elegy and tragedy in subject matter and style. According to one early Renaissance commentator, tragic and heroic poetry concern grave personages and arduous actions and require the high style. It is "inept" to employ the high and heroic style for miserable things or to treat great or magnificent things in the elegiac mode. The amours of hopeless or perishing lovers are appropriate for elegy, but magnificent things belong to heroic poetry:

> Est autem tam in metro quam in prosa triplex dicendi
> qualitas seu stilus seu genus. Aliud enim genus dicitur
> altiloquum seu sublime: & competit personis dignis &
> rebus arduis. Qualia sunt heroica & tragica carmina: &
> omnes de republica: . . . Oportet preterea ut sit uniforme
> generi poematis. Qui enim de rebus miseris loquens
> heroico stilo & altiloquo genere utatur: aut de rebus
> magnificis elegiaco multum ineptiret. Res enim misere ut
> amores misere depereuntium: epitaphia & eiusmodi elegis
> scribi volunt: res magnifice heroicis carminibus.[9]

Such considerations as these did not, of course, alter the genre of the *Troilus*, but they did at times bring Chaucer's tragedy close to the frontiers of comedy and elegy without actually violating them. They made it possible for him to include some of his finer comic scenes within the context of a tragic fable, to give lyric expression to the joys and sorrows of the lovers, and, finally, to introduce a tragicomic element into the account of his hero's death.

The flight episode itself brings into sharper focus the underlying ambiguities in Chaucer's ironic "tragedye." Pompey's death had been genuinely tragic, Arcita's slightly less so. By inserting the flight stanzas after the account of Troilus's death, Chaucer strengthened the link between his own "tragedye" and those of Lucan and Boccaccio. At the same time, however, he gave clearer definition to the comic values already inherent in his poem. In Chaucer's romance, with its rich comic overtones, the hero's laughter acquires a force and a relevance that it could not have achieved in the *Pharsalia* (which exhibits a fine sense of irony but little sense of comedy) or even in the *Teseida*.

Already established in the poetry of Lucan and Boccaccio, the motif of the hero's posthumous laughter reinforces Chaucer's tragic (or epic) decorum, yet it also accentuates the comic element already strongly enunciated in his work. The basis for this paradoxical relationship to two contrasting genres and literary modes is to be found in the doctrinal systems—Stoic and Platonic, Boethian and Christian—underlying all three of these flight episodes. That a tension between tragic and comic values underlies Chaucer's entire poem; that, though the tragic sense predominates in the plot, it is the comic vision that overcomes in the end; that, in the light of Troilus's final insight, secular tragedy itself vanishes into insignificance, and worldly prosperity and adversity seem equally negligible—this is a poetic heresy perhaps, but from the vantage point of Philosophy, it may be a divine orthodoxy.

II

It was difficult for a poet to take Boethius piecemeal. Though the *Consolation* would hardly meet Husserl's conditions for philosophy as *strenge Wissenschaft*, it is nevertheless a closely reasoned, tightly structured work centering upon the vision of an eternal good as true felicity and culminating in the idea of divine providence as an eternal present. To detach a single concept, such as Boethius's Fortune, from the whole and develop it in isolation from its original context could violate the integrity of this system and distort the concept thus isolated. Its full meaning depended on its relation to other concepts in the Boethian system and to the system as a whole.

By including the Boethian Fortune and the Boethian providence in his narrative, Chaucer had in effect introduced a Trojan horse into his Trojan tragedy. In isolation from Boethius's system, either or both of these concepts could have heightened the tragic element in the *Troilus*, lending greater dignity to the materials of Chaucer's tragedy and clearer definition to its tragic structure. Within the Boethian system as a whole, however, the sense of human tragedy tends to dissolve into divine indifference. Tragic values lose their gravity, for the objects of earthly fear or worldly sorrow are of little weight. Tragic structure loses its clarity, for the vicissitudes of Fortune are ultimately of minor importance; moreover, adversity is actually preferable to prosperity since it may lead to a recognition of the true good. Although Boethius's emphasis on the transiency of worldly felicity might provide a valid basis for tragic poetry, the cornerstone of his system—pursuit of an otherworldly felicity based on an unchangeable good, together with contempt of the world[10] and condemnation of earthly felicity as false—would seem to undermine the traditional foundations of tragedy, shifting its emphasis from temporal to eternal values. If the goods of fortune are valueless, their loss is hardly an occasion for tragic grief. If earthly adversity and prosperity are ultimately meaningless, the fall from high degree is scarcely a breathtaking fall. The potentialities for tragedy would appear to lie less in action than in character, in the hero's ignorance of his true good, the misery of his human condition, and his bondage to passion.

If pursued to its logical conclusions, Boethian ethics might severely limit the possibilities of tragedy. If the tragic poet accepted the doctrines of the Roman moralist, he might find the conventional tragic subjects, based as they frequently were on false conceptions of felicity and misery, inadequate for "genuine" tragedy. If he followed the philosopher and the theologian, he might run counter not only to poetic tradition but also to the feelings of the majority of his audience. If, however, he conformed to common opinions of happiness and misery, ig-noring the teachings of Philosophy, he would not be describing "genuinely" tragic events. He might achieve a conventional tragedy but not (by divine standards) a true one. The only event that could be regarded as tragic in the highest sense would appear to be the loss of true beatitude.

When combined with Christian eschatological beliefs, furthermore, the Boethian *contemptus mundi* could make the conventional tragic setting seem still more inadequate. An otherworldly criterion of felicity and misery would seem to require an otherworldly setting. The truly tragic catastrophe would appear to be not so much the fall of illustrious men from high degree as the descent into Tartarus: the fall of the angels or the *Höllensturz* of the damned. The supremely tragic fate would be not so much the death of the body as that of the soul, the "second death." Shifting its emphasis from this life to the next and from this world to the world to come, a strictly Christian tragedy would find its most appropriate subject in the theme of damnation, in the vision of the Four Last Things. Substituting eternal misery for temporal adversity, it would logically hinge not so much on the loss of secular dignities as on alienation from an eternal Good.

Though Dante might pursue these arguments to their logical conclusions in the *Inferno* and the *Paradiso*, other poets, both classical and Christian, were content to seek a compromise between poetic conventions and ethical doctrines. As a tragic poet Seneca could appeal to emotions that he condemned as a Stoic philosopher, portraying calamities that he might elsewhere minimize as insignificant, evils of fortune that a Stoic might rationalize as potentially good.

Chaucer also compromises between poetic and philosophical ideas of felicity and misery. Though he follows the conventional tragic pattern based on the alternation of temporal prosperity and adversity, he is nevertheless fully aware of their final insignificance from the point of view of Boethian ethics and Christian theology. Moreover, he is equally aware that knowledge of an eternal Good is the standard whereby transitory goods and evils must be judged and condemned. His image of false felicity is incomplete without the complementary vision of true felicity. In the flight stanzas, as in the final verses of his epilogue, he places the tragic vicissitudes of his romance in their true ethical perspective, complementing the limited vision of the tragic poet with the insights of the Boethian philosopher. Faithful to the Horatian ideal of poetry as a source of moral instruction as well as pleasure, he has reoriented his poem toward the traditional end of Aristotelian and Platonic ethics and scholastic theology: the knowledge of true felicity and of the supreme Good.

The insights of Dame Philosophy tend, then, to undermine the realm of tragic values, and it is not without reason that she dismisses the Muses as "comune strompettis of swich a place that men clepen the theatre. . . ." The sufferings of the tragic hero, like those of Boethius himself, may be real, but the causes of his anguish are illusory. He suffers through his own ignorance of true and false felicity. The goods he has lost were apparent goods; the happiness from which he has fallen was a false and deceptive happiness. By definition tragedy is concerned with the theme of mutability, with the changes of Fortune, and the alternations of happiness and misery. In the context of Boethian philosophy the tragic change of state from weal to woe belongs essentially to the realm of earthly and transitory values—to *terrena* and *temporalia*—rather than to the realm of celestial truth. In this context the office of the tragic poet would appear to be essentially negative and dehortatory: to demonstrate the transiency of temporal goods and the falsity of secular bliss, to induce contempt of the world and indifference to Fortune's gifts, and (by exploiting a contrary example) to persuade his readers to seek true felicity and substantial Good elsewhere, in a realm beyond mutability and change. As a rhetorical argument the tragic *exemplum* points beyond the realm of "faithless" Fortune to the "stable faith" of the heavens, beyond the values of tragic vicissitude to a permanent and abiding felicity. The secular tragedy is incomplete; it must find its complement, and ultimately its answer, in divine comedy. Dante was the lover of Beatrice (the "divine science") not the friend of Fortune; the movement of his contemplative journey leads him from the dark wood of this world to a stable and unchanging Good. The *Commedia* concludes appropriately with a vision of the Unmoved Prime Mover and a return to the "rational motion" of the Primum Mobile. Chaucer's "tragedye" of earthly mutability similarly ends with a vision of true felicity in a stable realm beyond change. The affirmative "comic" ending complements, but does not contradict, the negative example of his tragedy.

Both Chaucer and Dante exploit the mutability-immutability *topos* to underline the antithesis between secular and celestial values, temporal and eternal goods, but in different literary genres and in different social and political contexts. Dante's quest for a continuing city, an *urbs eterna*, leads him to the City of God, to the Church Militant (the ideal of a *pax Romana* under the harmonious jurisdiction of emperor and pope) and eventually to the Church Triumphant in heaven. Chaucer's tragedy of a star-crossed lover and a fickle mistress takes place against the conventional tragic background of the transiency of secular kingdoms. The protagonist of the *Commedia*, passing from Florence to a people just and sane, finds true felicity in a divine and enduring *polis*. The hero of the *Troilus* achieves a comparable vision of beatitude, but, unlike Dante's, it is (on the surface at least) largely free of political overtones. Troilus's insights are those of the lover, not the statesman; he learns the tragic lesson of Fortune's inconstancy not from the fall of kingdoms, but through the loss of a concubine. Unaware that fate has decreed the ruin of his city, he does know that it is separating him from his mistress: "Thus to be lorn, it is my destinee." Chaucer presents the tragic theme of worldly mutability primarily in terms of the changing fortunes of a love affair. These are closely interwoven, however, with the tragic destiny of the kingdom; and the poet repeatedly reminds his audience of the national catastrophe to which the tragic hero himself is ironically deaf and blind.

Behind Dante's vision of a greater Rome and Chaucer's romance of a Trojan lover lies another epic devoted to a Trojan hero and the destiny of Rome. In Virgil's *alta tragedia*, Dante might recognize the seeds of imperial grandeur—the planting of a Trojan colony that would eventually ripen into an eternal city, the seat of a universal empire and a universal church. Nevertheless, the *Aeneid* was also a tragedy of mutability, looking backward to the ruin of Troy and forward to the destruction of Carthage. It concerned the overthrow as well as the foundation of kingdoms. Carthage and Troy alike were subject to the rule of fate and the will of the gods. Just as the theme of Roman dominion links the *Aeneid* with the *Commedia*, the motif of the instability of kingdoms signalized by the destruction of Troy connects Virgil's "high tragedy" with Chaucer's tragic romance. In the *Troilus* the tragic theme of mutability acquires a double emphasis, from the vicissitudes of the lover and the impending ruin of the Trojan state.

If the flight stanzas undercut the tragic values of Chaucer's plot, the ultimate responsibility rests with the poet's fidelity to the Boethian system and to the Horatian ideal of the poet as moral teacher. Faced with the conflict between tragic and philosophical attitudes toward temporal prosperity and adversity, he exploits the inevitable tension between them for ironic effect. The critic should not rashly censure his "contra-dictions," without recognizing their origin in the poetic and ethical traditions Chaucer had inherited and without acknow-ledging the skill with which he attempted to combine them.

III

"What other thyng bewaylen the cryinges of tragedyes but oonly the dedes of Fortune, that with unwar strook overturneth the realmes of greet nobleye?"[11] Boethius's allusion to tragedy occurs in the midst of Dame Philosophy's apology for Fortune, and in Chaucer's translation it is followed by a gloss defining tragedy as "*a dite of prosperite for a tyme, that endeth in wrecchidnesse,*" and preceded by examples of two great kings who had suffered ignominious reversals of fortune: Croesus, who had been defeated by Cyrus, and a "kyng of Percyens" who had been taken captive by Rome.[12]

Unlike the conventional tragedy, the *Troilus* centers not so much on the overthrow of realms of "great nobility" as on the misfortunes of a lover. Instead of the loss of kingdoms, Chaucer portrays the loss of a mistress. Instead of the prosperity and adversity of a monarchy, he depicts a lover's joys and sorrows. Troilus himself has little in common with Croesus or Perses; the closest analogy among the characters in the poem would have been Priam. The really tragic subject, according to Boethius's definition, would have been the fall of Troy; nevertheless, though closely linked with Troilus's fate, this does not occur within the compass of the plot. Troilus's premature death is, it would seem, a blessing in disguise: it spares him from the more tragic fate of experiencing his city's doom. In comparison with the future tragedies of other Trojans—Hecuba and Priam, Polyxena and Cassandra, Andromache and Astyanax—his calamities seem relatively light.

Except for a slight modification in structure, substituting the alternations of fortune from woe to weal to final sorrow for the conventional tragic reversal from prosperity to adversity, Chaucer has retained the traditional form of tragedy but altered its traditional content. Against the background of the tragic subject *par excellence*, the ruin of Troy, Troilus's misery must appear less miserable than it seems in his own eyes. The ironic viewpoint of the apotheosis stanzas is implicit perhaps in Chaucer's professedly "tragic" elaboration of his theme.

Finally, in addition to portraying the mutability of fortune, tragedy aimed (in the opinion of one Boethian commentator) at the reproof of vice. According to Pseudo-Aquinas, "*tragedia est carmen reprehensivum viciorum incipiens a prosperitate desinens in adversitatem.*" Tragic poets recount in "weeping" verse (*luctuoso carmine*) ancient exploits and the crimes of wicked kings: "antiqua gesta & facinora sceleratorum regum."[13]

Here again Chaucer's tragedy diverges significantly from the traditional ideals of this genre. He refuses to describe his hero's gests on the battlefield, for his theme is love, not arms. Troilus is no *sceleratus*, nor is his love affair a crime (*facinus*). Though the poem may indeed be a *carmen reprehensivum*, the reproof is comparatively mild; the strongest rebuke is the hero's own condemnation of worldly vanity and the folly of those who pursue blind "lust" instead of seeking heaven.

In centering his tragedy upon the double sorrow of a lover rather than on the fall from high degree, Chaucer retained the conventional tragic emphasis on mutability but altered its content. Instead of the instability of worldly dignities, he stressed the inconstancy of earthly love. In Boethian terms both were transitory goods and could offer no more than false felicity.

In the *Troilus* they occupy respectively the background and fore-ground of the poem. In the poet's perspective—a viewpoint that may have been consciously ironic—the loss of Criseyde dwarfs and overshadows the ruin of Troy.

Instead of emphasizing the felicity of a kingdom, Chaucer has stressed the delights of the flesh, and the "tragic" action of his poem turns accordingly not so much on the hero's attainment and loss of a realm as on his winning and losing a mistress. Criseyde's physical presence or absence, and her fidelity or infidelity to her lover, occupy a central position not only in the structure of the plot but also in the framework of Boethian doctrine underlying the entire poem. According to Pseudo-Aquinas, a man should be indifferent to all temporal and transitory goods, neither grieving at their absence nor rejoicing in their presence. Since they cannot offer true felicity, they do not merit either grief or joy: ". . . ostendit bona temporalia esse transitoria et non consistere totaliter in eius [*sic*] totalem veram felicitatem. & per consequens non esse dolendum de eorum absentia: nec gaudendum de eorum presentia. et neminem debere extolli in prosperis: nec deprimi in adversis."[14] The poles upon which Chaucer's tragic fable turns are inevitably negated by the Boethian values he has introduced into his poem. In the eyes of Dame Philosophy the possession and loss of Criseyde would have offered no valid cause for either joy or grief.

IV

Throughout the greater part of the *Troilus*, the hero's predicament is roughly analogous to that of Boethius in the opening books of the *Consolation*. It is not until the end that he learns, through his experience of a faithless mistress, what Boethius (with the aid of Dame Philosophy) has learned through experience of faithless Fortune: the instability of temporal goods. If Chaucer gives definitive expression to this concept in the epilogue, he has nevertheless implied it throughout the poem. Against the background of Boethian commentary, the analogy between Criseyde's inconstancy and the inconstancy of Fortune must appear deliberate.

Commenting on Boethius's condemnation of Fortune as "faithless," Pseudo-Aquinas amplifies this topos with quotations from Seneca:

> . . . appellat fortunam malefidam: quia est deceptiva. . . .
> Unde Sene[ca]. Neminem adversa fortuna comminuit nisi
> quem fecunda [secunda] decipit. Et alibi Sene[ca]. Fortuna
> nemini servat fidem: nulli obesse semel contenta est: quem
> nimium fovet hunc stultum facit . . . fortune bona dicuntur
> levia: quia transitoria. Non enim perdurat circa
> hominem. . . . [15]

The same author also emphasizes woman's inconstancy: "etiam si bonam uxorem habuisti non potes affirmare eam esse permansuram in illo proposito: nihil tam mobile nihil tam vagum quam feminarum voluntas."[16] To medieval and Renaissance writers alike, Virgil's *dictum varium et mutabile semper Femina* (*Aeneid*, IV, 569) seemed axiomatic, and, in one form or another, this concept entered rhetorical manuals and treatises on poetics as an aspect of the decorum of persons. In his *Ars versificatoria* Matthieu de Vendôme cited Virgil's lines as an example of personal attributes (*attributa personae*) according to nature; in this passage he finds an *argumentum* or *locus* according to sex.[17] The same tradition survives in Renaissance poetics. According to Ascensius, women are by nature inconstant and prone to deceit, and the poet must bear these qualities in mind in order to observe *decorum personarum*:

> Decorum sexum afflagitat ut longe alia sint que viris
> attribuuntur quam que feminis . . . femine enim sunt
> inconstantes. modo nimium blande & affabiles. modo
> minaces aspere & proterve. modo iocose. modo tristes.
> modo amice. modo inimice. Sed status & genus vite in
> primis advertendum est. Viri autem constantiores &
> prudentiores ut plurimum sunt: quamvis feminis non
> desit solertia: & ad fallendum calliditas.[18]

In contrasting Criseyde's inconstancy with Troilus's constancy, Chaucer has not merely observed decorum in character but has developed this antithesis in Boethian terms as an argument against placing one's trust in a temporal, and therefore transitory, good. In treating the lovers' affections—another aspect of *decorum personarum*—he not only observes "congruity" in *affectiones* and decorum in age (youth being prone to love, manhood to the pursuit of honors and riches, and old age to avarice), but he is also conscious of the values of Boethian ethics, which regarded all passions directed toward temporal objects as injurious. Defining affection as a movement involving the senses and imagination and obstructing right reason ("affectio est motus particule sensitive sub fantasia boni vel mali animum afficiens et rectum rationis iudicium impediens"), Pseudo-Aquinas distinguishes four principal emotions under which all others can be reduced.[19] These are joy, hope, fear, and sorrow (*gaudium, spes, timor, et dolor*). Each of these passions is twofold, insofar as it is directed to a present or to an absent good or evil. Whereas joy concerns a present and hope for a future good, grief is directed toward a present and fear toward a future evil. Though potentially virtuous if ordered toward their proper ends, all these passions are injurious when directed toward earthly objects.

Chaucer has dwelt at length on Criseyde's characteristic inclination to fear, on Troilus's alternations between hope and despair and his interlude of joy in the midst of his double sorrow, and on Pandarus's sympathetic involvement in the emotions of the lovers. Without exception, these various passions are all directed toward earthly objects, transitory goods or evils. From the Boethian viewpoint of the epilogue they must stand condemned as harmful. Though the poet may communicate his own sympathy for his characters caught in their tangled labyrinth of affections, though he may engage the emotions of his readers, his final censure should come as no surprise. In the Boethian context of his story, his rejection is not inconsistent, but inevitable.

When Troilus condemns the vanity and ignorance of those who neglect the heavens for blind and transitory "lust," he is echoing a Boethian commonplace. Dame Philosophy had reproved Boethius in similar terms, and the repetition of this commonplace underscores the analogy between Troilus's despair and Boethius's grief. Different as they are, both men have been blinded by emotion, by concern for temporal things, and by the power of sensuality. In commenting on the opening passages of the *Consolation*, Pseudo-Aquinas interprets the dialogue between Boethius and Philosophy as an inner debate between passion and reason: "Boetius dolens & ipsa philosophia ipsum consolans non sunt aliud nisi animus dolens ex oppressione sensualitatis: & ratio consolans ex vigore sapientie."[20] Unlike the *Consolation*, the *Troilus* does not personify philosophy; a comparable debate between reason and sensuality occurs, however, in Troilus's soliloquy in Book IV.

In Philosophy's first reply (*Heu quam precipiti mersa profundo*), the commentator finds a double application: first, to humanity in general; and second, to Boethius himself: "Primo universaliter philosophia deplangit perturbationem mentis hominum. Secundo spetialiter convertit planctum super boe. ibi." The burden of her complaint is that, sunk in temporal cares, mankind neglects the light of contemplation, follows sense and lust instead of reason, and neglects the knowledge of its Creator for external goods and sensual delights:

> Heu quam .i. quantum mens hominum hebet .i. obscuratur
> mersa precipiti profundo id est cura rerum temporalium
> que precipitant hominem: & talis mens relicta propria luce
> .i. contemplatione tendit .i. laborat ire in tenebras externas
> .i. in ignorantias exteriores. . . . Nota quod in nobis
> est duplex virtus. rationalis & sensualis. sensus autem
> semper adversatur rationi: quia caro concupiscit adversus
> spiritum: & spiritus adversus carnem. Cum autem
> sensualitas vincit rationem: tunc homo est in malo statu
> regiminis & efficitur bestialis. . . . Valde conandum &
> laborandum est nobis ut virtus nostra concupiscibilis
> subiecta fit rationi. . . . Plures autem homines sequuntur
> sensualitatem quam rationem: insudantes bonis
> exterioribus & delectationibus sensualibus: per que
> impediuntur in speculatione & cognitione summi boni: . . .
> Item cum anima ingerit se curis rerum temporalium
> profunde precipitatur & hebet: quia a cognitione rerum
> & sui creatoris destituitur: & destituta cadit in tenebras
> externas .i. in ignorantias exteriores.[21]

From this general censure of mankind, Philosophy now turns to Boethius himself, who has turned from the contemplation of the heavens—from astronomy, natural philosophy, and metaphysics—to earthly affairs: ". . . destitutus a tali contemplatione solum de terrenis cogitabat." Bearing the heavy chains of the passions ("gravidis cathenis passionum") and bowed down by the weight of temporal losses ("pondere amissionis rerum temporalium"), he has fixed his mind on earthly goods ("bona terrena que homines stolidos efficiunt"). Just as a chain detains a creature contrary to its nature, Pseudo-Aquinas continues, the four affections detain man's soul, drawing it toward forbidden objects contrary to its nature and to reason, which naturally desires the best: "Nam ratio semper deprecatur ad optima."

To his interpretation of Boethius's verses, Pseudo-Aquinas brought his knowledge of Seneca and Saint Albertus Magnus, of Aristotle's *Ethics* ("in antiqua translatione"), and even of Hermes Trismegistus. Quoting Scripture on the lust of the flesh against the spirit (Gal. 5:17), he reduced Boethius's inner conflict to the struggle of sensuality against reason. Though Chaucer could hardly expect the same range of classical and Christian erudition on the part of his wider audience, he might expect it from a few judicious readers such as "moral Gower" and the "philosophical Strode." To these, Troilus's anguish might be subject to the same reproaches that Dame Philosophy had leveled against Boethius and against the generality of mankind; it proceeds from *cura* or *sollicitudo rerum temporalium*. In Chaucer's "woful" verses on Troilus's "double sorwe" they might perceive, beneath the poet's expressed sympathy for the protagonist's sufferings, a lament that (like Dame Philosophy's verses) implies rebuke. Like Philosophy's *planctus*, Chaucer's "tragedye"—his *carmen luctuosum*—might seem a lament for the tyranny of blind passion; like Philosophy, he too bewails the passion of the mind: "deplangit perturbationem mentis hominum." Like other tragedies, the *Troilus* might appear to be a *carmen reprehensivum viciorum*, even though the vices it portrays are more amiable than those of the conventional tragic protagonist and spring rather from concupiscence than from violence or fraud. For such readers the Boethian commonplaces of the epilogue would be consistent with the Boethian concepts expressed throughout the poem; and the fundamental antitheses of the epilogue—the opposition between earthly inconstancy and eternal stability, between love of the creature and love of the Creator, and between worldly and heavenly felicity—would seem not only "congruous" and probable, but necessary. They are precisely the sort of commentary that Strode and Gower might have expected.

V

Though Chaucer has retained the conventional structure of tragedy, he has replaced its traditional subject matter with an erotic content; instead of the fall of kings, he portrays the misfortunes of a lover. In his treatment of Boethian themes, we may detect a similar shift of emphasis. Though he retains the conventional Boethian attitude toward solicitude for temporal things ("cura rerum temporalium"), he focuses his attention primarily on the cares of the lover.[22] This in itself was hardly surprising; he was, after all, writing a love story, not a commentary on the *De Consolatione*. Nevertheless, in the context of an erotic romance, the solicitude of a lover could acquire shades of meaning belonging primarily to medical rather than to Boethian tradition. It was an essential feature of heroic love, that *amor nobilis* which medieval and Renaissance physicians classified among diseases of the head and which, left unchecked or uncured, might end in insanity or death. According to Burton,[23] "Avicenna . . . calleth this passion *ilishi*, and defines it, *to be a disease or melancholy vexation, or anguish of minde; in which a man continually meditates of the beauty, gestures, manners, of his mistris, and troubles himself about it. . . .*" In the Latin translation of Avicenna's treatise, *ilishi* is explicitly defined as "melancholy solicitude": "Haec aegritudo est solicitudo melancholica, in quâ homo applicat sibi continuam cogitationem super pulchritudine ipsius quam amat, gestuum, morum."[24]

Similar definitions occur in other medical treatises. As Professor Robertson has noted,[25] Bernardus de Gordonio followed Avicenna's opinion, defining *hereos* as "sollicitudo melancolica propter mulieris amorem. . . . Et quia [philocaptus] est in continua meditatione: ideo sollicitudo melancolica appellatur." Similarly, in his *Practica medicinae* Giovanni Michele Savonarola[26] defined *ilishi* as "sollicitudo melancolica qua quis ob amorem fortem & intensum sollicitat habere rem quam nimia aviditate concupiscit: . . . Dicitur sollicitudo quia tales facti iam melancolici ex amore inordinato sunt in continua cogitatione memoria & imaginatione: ita ut non dormiant neque bibant. . . ."

In English poetry, as in Continental literature, this idea left a long and distinguished record, ranging from "the loveris maladye of Hereos" in Chaucer's *Knight's Tale* to Spenser's account of Scudamour's ordeal in the House of Care. In the *Troilus* this concept acquires Boethian connotations in addition to its original medical significance. In the hero's double sorrows we may recognize not only the *cura* for which Philosophy reproaches Boethius—the *cura rerum temporalium* of Pseudo-Aquinas and the *insensata cura de' mortali* of Dante—but also (more specifically) the *solicitudo melancholica* of Avicenna and his successors. Like Boethius, Troilus has fallen into "a commune seknesse to hertes that been deceyved"; but, unlike Boethius, he lacks the nourishing "medicyne" of Philosophy.

Like the commentators on Boethius's *affectio*, medical discussions of *hereos* emphasize the subordination of reason to imagination, the corruption of rational judgment, and the combination of a false conception of felicity with passionate desire for a false or transitory good. Just as Boethian tradition had stressed the illusory nature of every joy based on temporary and secular good, medical tradition had emphasized the lover's mistaken belief that the enjoyment of his mistress's beauty constituted the highest felicity. For Bernardus (as Professor Robertson points out),[27] *hereos* resulted from the corruption of the "estimative" virtue ("Corruptio extimative propter formam et figuram fortiter affixam"); ardently desiring his beloved, the lover regards her as his end and his felicity; "unde cum aliquis philocaptus est in amore alicuius mulieris: ita fortiter concipit formam et figuram ad modum . . . et ideo ardenter concupiscit eam: et sine modo & mensura opinans si posset finem attingere: quae hec esset sua felicitas et beatitudo: & intantum corruptum est iuditium rationis. . . ." Again, "sicut felicitas est ultimum dilectionis: ita hereos ultimum dilectionis. & ideo intantum concupiscunt quod insani efficiuntur."

Both Bernardus and Savonarola (1384–1461) give detailed accounts of the physiological and psychological aspects of *hereos*; and, like Bernardus, Savonarola attributes its cause to the corruption of the "estimative virtue." According to the latter's treatis, "Coniuncta autem est nimia & continua operatio virtutis imaginative & cogitative circa desiderium rei comprehense. Et modus generationis est quia apprehenso obiecto a virtute imaginativa primo per sensum exteriorem sibi deportato secundum plurimum tamquam multum delectabili: deinde virtus extimativa inducit ipsum esse appetendum & ultra quam conveniat. & in hoc corrumpitur iudicium. . . . Existimativa quae est virtus altior imperat deinde imaginative. & imaginativa concupiscibili: & concupiscibile irascibili: & irascibile motive lacertorum. et sic totum corpus movetur spreto ordine rationis & discutit de nocte & die vagando spernendo frigus. calores. pericula & huiusmodi stans in continua cogitatione & concupiscentia ad rem desideratam. . . ."

Because the lover's judgment has been corrupted by imagination and sense (Savonarola explains), he overestimates the true worth of his beloved. To possess her seems, in his mistaken judgment, to be his true felicity: "unde fiiocapti super omnem rem amasiam appetunt omnia alia spernentes & existimantes suam felicitatem esse si habere possent. & sic de his quae talia sine usu rationis appetunt." Just as the Boethian commentators stress the transiency of all worldly goods, Savonarola emphasizes the transiency of the lover's delight: "O miseri qui ex tam parva ac cito transitoria delectatione tam gravia & auasi insupportabilia ut sunt non timere frigus neque vigilias continuas. sitim: famem & huiusmodi videntur facilia & delectabilia. ut ribaldones qui vitio ludi aut vini nudi incedunt."[28]

By introducing *hereos* into a Boethian frame of reference, Chaucer subjected the lover's solicitude to Philosophy's sweeping condemnation of temporal cares. Combining medical and ethical tradition, he brought together two highly specialized conceptions of solicitude and two conventional ideas of false felicity. Both traditions had stressed the distortion of rational judgment by passion. Both had regarded the lover's delights as transitory and his opinion of felicity as irrational. In the epilogue, Chaucer depicts the lover's return to right reason and rational judgment. After portraying a mistaken notion of felicity and a false opinion of the chief good, Chaucer brings his hero to a vision of eternal stability and knowledge of "pleyn felicity." Troilus's ascent to the eighth sphere is not only a progression from an imaginary heaven—an earthly paradise that cannot endure—to the real heavens but also a "rational movement" from creature to Creator. It is as much a recovery of his "estimative virtue" as a reorientation of his will. Boethius had been free "to gon in hevenliche pathes" *per rationem* and to contemplate the "wandrynge recourses" of each *stella erratica* only insofar as he had been free from solicitude for temporal things, "solutus a cura rerum temporalium."[29] Released from the body and its appetites, Troilus is likewise free to contemplate the "erratik sterres" and to "herken" their "armonye." Like Boethius's astronomical meditations, Troilus's intellectual vision is closely associated with release from the malady of temporal cares, but in his case the disease is more easily diagnosed. It is *Ilishi* or *Hereos*, the solicitude of the lover.

NOTES

*Reprinted with permission from *Disembodied Laughter: Troilus and the Apotheosis Tradition* (Berkeley, Los Angeles, and London: University of California Press, 1972), pp. 84-111.

1. Grandgent, pp. 748–749; Carlyle-Wicksteed, p. 465.

2. Grandgent, pp. 752–753; Carlyle-Wicksteed, p. 469.

3. On the problem of the sources of Boethius's doctrines—Stoic, Platonic, Aristotelian, or Christian—see Fritz Klingner, "De Boethii *Consolatione Philosophiae*," *Philologische Untersuchungen*, Vol. XXVII (Berlin, 1921); E. K. Rand, "On the Composition of Boethius' *Consolatio Philosophiae*," *Harvard Studies in Classical Philology*, XV (1904): 1–28; G. A. Mueller, "Die Trostschrift des Boetius, Beitrag zu einer literarhistorischen Quellenuntersuchung" (Ph.D. diss., Berlin, 1912); Jan Sulowski, "Les sources du De *consolatione Philosophiae* de Boèce," Sophia, XXV (1957): 76–85; Sulowski, "The Sources of Boethius' *De Consolatione Philosophiae*," *Sophia*, XXIX (1961): 67–94; E. T. Silk,

"Boethius's *Consolatio Philosophiae* as a Sequel to Augustine's Dialogues and Soliloquia," *Harvard Theological Review*, XXXIII (1939): 19–39; Howard R. Patch, "Fate in Boethius and the Neoplatonists," *Speculum*, IV (1929): 62–72; Patch, "Necessity in Boethius and the Neoplatonists," *Speculum*, X (1935): 393–404; Volker Schmidt-Kohl, *Die neuplatonische Seelenlehre in der "Consolatio Philosophiae" des Boethius, Beiträge zur Klassischen Philologie*, Heft 16 (Meisenheim am Glan, 1965); Pierre Courcelle, *La Consolation de Philosophie dans la tradition littéraire, antécédents et postérité de Boèce* (Paris: Etude Augustiniennes, 1967). See also Willy Theiler, "Antike und christliche Rückkehr zu Gott," in *Mullus: Aschendorff Festschrift Theodor Klausner* (Munster: Aschendorff, 1964), pp. 352–361.

4. See chap. iii, n. 3, *Disembodied Laughter: Troilus and the Apotheosis Tradition* (Berkeley, Los Angeles & London: University of California Press, 1972, on Chaucer's indebtedness to Boethius.

5. F. N. Robinson, *The Works of Geoffrey Chaucer*, 2nd ed. (Boston, Houghton Mifflin 1957), p. 797. The commentaries by Guillaume de Conches and Nicholas Trivet are available in the MLA Collection of Photographic Facsimiles, nos. 99 and 100. Relevant portions of Trivet's commentary have been summarized or quoted by D. W. Robertson in *A Preface to Chaucer: Studies in Medieval Perspectives* (Princeton: Princeton UP, 1963), pp. 24–27, 358–360, and passim. For the uncertainty attending the date of Pseudo-Aquinas's commentary, cf. Kate O. Petersen, "Chaucer and Trivet," *PMLA*, XVIII (1903): 174; examining over 370 parallels, Petersen (pp. 175–176) finds about 70 cases in which Pseudo-Aquinas fails to "give as close a correspondence with Chaucer's text as Trivet's comedy does." For discussion of the commentaries on the *Consolatio* from the ninth century through the fifteenth, see Courcelle, *La Consolation de Philosophie*. The authorship of Pseudo-Aquinas's commentary has been variously ascribed to William Whetley, Thomas Waleis, and "un certain Marquand" (possibly Marquand the Scot, who was rector of the University of Paris around the middle of the fourteenth century); Courcelle, pp. 322–323.

6. See Robertson, *A Preface to Chaucer*, pp. 346, 472–474, 495, 500; Robertson, "Chaucerian Tragedy," *ELH*, XIX (1952): 1–37; Walter Clyde Curry, *Chaucer and The Mediaeval Sciences* (New York: Barnes and Noble, 1960), pp. 241, 281–294; Willard Farnham, *The Medieval Heritage of Elizabethan Tragedy* (New York, 1956), pp. 129–172; Patch, "Troilus on Determinism," *Speculum*, VI, (1929): 225–243.

7. For medieval theories of comedy and tragedy, see Marvin T. Herrick, *Comic Theory in the Sixteenth Century* (Urbana: U of Illinois P, 1964), pp. 57–70; Madeleine Doran, *Endeavors of Art: A Study of Form in*

Elizabethan Drama (Madison: U of Wisconsin P, 1964), pp. 105–109; J. E. Spingarn, *A History of Literary Criticism in the Renaissance* (New York: Columbia UP, 1925), pp. 65–67; Willi Erzgraber, "Tragik und Komik in Chaucers *Troilus and Criseyde*," *Festschrift für Walter Hubner*, ed. Dieter Riesner and Helmut Gneuss (Berlin: E. Schmidt, 1964), pp. 139–163. On the mixture of comic and serious elements in medieval epic and the "principle *ludicra seriis miscere*," see Ernst Robert Curtius, *European Literature and the Latin Middle Ages*, trans. Willard R. Trask (New York and Evanston: Pantheon, 1963), pp. 428–431. As Curtius points out (p. 429), Servius found elements of the comic style in book IV of the *Aeneid*: "Est autem paene totus in affectione, licet in fine pathos habeat, ubi abscessus Aeneae gignit dolorem. Sane totus in consiliis et subtilitatibus est: nam paene comicus stilus est: nec mirum ubi de amore tractatur." For a medieval reader, the mixture of comic and tragic elements in Chaucer's poem might seem consistent with Virgil's practice in the *Aeneid*. Common to both tragedies would be the Trojan nationality of the hero and the theme of Troy's destruction, the contrast between faithful and unfaithful lover (an antithesis developed in Chaucer's account of Dido and Aeneas in the *House of Fame* and the *Legend of Good Women*), the seriocomic treatment of a love affair, and the tragic death of the faithful partner. Just as Dido's *dolor* springs from *abscessus Aeneae*, Troilus's grief is renewed by the departure of Criseyde.

    8. On the Trojan background of the Troilus, see Charles A. Owen, Jr., "The Significance of Chaucer's Revisions of *Troilus and Criseyde*," *MP*, LV (1957–1958): 1–5; Bloomfield, Morton, "Distance and Predestination in *Troilus and Criseyde*." *PMLA* 72(1957): 14–26.; Theodore A. Stroud, "Boethius' Influence on Chaucer's *Troilus*," *MP*, XLIX (1951–1952): 1–9; John P. McCall, "The Trojan Scene in Chaucer's *Troilus*," *ELH*, XXIX (1962), 263–275; Robert D. Mayo, "The Trojan Background of the Troilus," *ELH*, IX (1942): 245–256.

    9. Ascensius, "Proemium," in *Boethius: Commentum duplex.*

    10. Cf. Pseudo-Aquinas, "Proemium," in *Boethius: Commentum duplex*, on the subject matter of the *Consolatio:* "Causa materialis huius libri est philosophica consolatio ordinata ad contemptum mundanorum & ad appetitum summe felicitatis." The epilogue of Chaucer's poem is similarly directed or ordered ("ordinata") toward contempt of worldly things and toward desire for the highest felicity.

    11. Boethius, Book 11, prose 2; Robinson, *Works of Geoffrey Chaucer*, p. 331.

    12. Boethius is actually referring not to a king of Persia, but to Perses, king of Macedonia, who had been defeated by Aemilius Paulus

Macedonicus; see *Boethius*, trans. H. F. Stewart and E. K. Rand (London and New York: Loeb Library, 1918), p. 180n.

13.   Pseudo-Aquinas on Book 11, prose 2, *in Boethius: Commentum duplex*. Cf. Trivet, fol. 126: "antiqua gesta atque facinora sceleratorum regum luctuosc carmine. . . ." Defining tragedy as "carmen de magnis iniquitatibus a prosperitate incipiens & in adversitatem terminans," Trivet interprets Boethius's phrase *Quid tragoediarum clamor* as an allusion to the daily representation of fortune's mutability in the theater: "probat mutabilitatem fortune divulgari cotidianis clamoribus quia clamores poetarum cotidie in teatro recitantium tragedias nihil aliud continebant quam mutabilitatem for tune." Tragedy presents nothing other than the mutability of fortune: "Quid aliud deflet clamor tragediarum nisi fortunam vertentem regna felicia ictu indiscreto." Cf. Robertson, *A Preface to Chaucer*, pp. 346, 473, on the definitions of tragedy by Trivet and Radulphus de Longo Campo.

14.   Pseudo-Aquinas, "Proemium," in *Boethius Commentum duplex*.

15.   Pseudo-Aquinas on Book 1, meter 1, in *ibid*. Trivet, fol. 107, explains that fortune (".s. temporalium mutabilitas") is called "male fida" because a man can ill confide or trust ("male . . . confidere") in her favors.

16.   Pseudo-Aquinas on Book 11, prose 4, in *Boethius: Commentum duplex*.

17.   Edmond Faral, ed., *Les arts poétiques du XIIe et du XIIIe siècle* (Paris: E. Champion, 1958), pp. 136–137.

18.   Iodocus Badius Ascensius, "Proemium," in *Boethius: Commentum duplex*.

19.   Pseudo-Aquinas on Book 1, meter 7, in *ibid*.

20.   Pseudo-Aquinas on Book 1, prose 1, in *ibid*.

21.   Pseudo-Aquinas on Book 1, meter 2 in *ibid*. Trivet's commentary (fol. 109) similarly develops the contrast between Boethius's solicitude for temporal; things and his former contemplation of the heavens, free of temporal care. Commenting on the phrase *Heu quam precipiti mersa profundo*, he explains *cura* as "sollicitudo temporalium" and *profundo* as an allusion to the "sollicitudine rerum temporalium qua homo ab altitudine dignitatis precipitatur ad ea quae sub se sunt. . . ." Formerly, when Boethius had contemplated the heavens, he had been free from care for temporal things: "solutus a cura temporalium celo aperto .s. per agnitionem quod clauditur per ignoranciam suetus .i. assuetus ire.s. motu rationis . . . in erhereos meatus. . . ."

22. For the use of the term *care* (or *cares*) to designate the sorrows and anxieties of the lover, cf. *Troilus*, Book I, lines 505, 550, 587; IV, 579. In Chaucer's account of how Troilus lies "Ibounden in the blake bark of care, Disposed wood out of his wit to breyde" (IV.229–230), there may be a concrete allusion to the melancholy basis of the lover's malady. Cf. also the references to "colde care" (I.612) and "cares colde" (I.264; III.1202, 1260; IV.1690; V.1342, 1347). Chaucer also employs the terms *cure* and *business* as equivalents of the Latin *cura*. Thus Criseyde (III.1041–1042) diagnoses Troilus's supposed jealousy as naught "but illusioun, Of habundaullce of love and besy cure, That doth youre herte this disese endure"; and elsewhere (IV.1645) she complains that Love is full of "bisy drede." In the *Knight's Tale* (line 1928) Bisynesse and Jalousye are depicted, among other allegorical figures, on the walls of Venus' temple; earlier in the same poem (line 1007) Chaucer associates "bisyness and cure," though in reference to the diligence of "pilours" on the Theban battlefield rather than to the anxiety of lovers. In his translation of the *Consolation of Philosophy*, he renders Boethius's *cura* (Book I, meter 2) as "anoyos bysynes"; cf. also "the pleyinge bysynes of men" (Book III, meter 2), "bytynge bysynesse" (Book Ill, meter 3), "bytynges of bysynesse" (Book III, prose 5).

23. Robert Burton, *The Anatomy of Melancholy* (London, 1837), II, 207–208.

24. Burton, II, 207; c.f. *Liber Avicenne* (Venice, 1500, HEH # 100359), Book III, tractatus 4, chap. 24.

25. Robertson, *A Preface to Chaucer*, pp. 109–110, 458; cf. Bernardus de Gordonio, *Practica sive Lilium medicinae* (Venice, 1498, HEH # 87627), particula II, chap. 20. Cf. John Livingston Lowes, "The Loveres Maladye of Hereos," *MP*, XI (1914): 491–456.

26. Giovanni Michele Savonarola, *Practica medicinae* (Venice, 1497, HEH # 95857), tractatus VI, chap. 14.

27. Robertson, *A Preface to Chaucer*, pp. 49, 458–459; cf. Bernardus, particula II, chap. 20; Burton, *Anatomy*, I, 155, "*Phantasie*, or imagination, which some call *aestimative*, or *cogitative*. . . ."

28. Savonarola, tractatus VI, chap. 14.

29. Cf. Pseudo-Aquinas on Book 1, meter 2 in *Boethius: Commentum duplex.*

Select Bibliography

Primary Sources

Books

Baugh, Albert C., ed. *Chaucer's Major Poetry*. New York: Appleton-Century Crofts, 1963.

Benson, Larry D., ed. *The Riverside Chaucer*. Based on Robinson's Edition. Boston: Houghton Mifflin, 1987.

   This is the standard edition, most often used.

Blake, N. F., ed. *The Canterbury Tales by Geoffrey Chaucer Edited from the Hengwrt Manuscript*. London: Arnold, 1980.

Donaldson, E. Talbot, ed. *Chaucer's Poetry: An Anthology for the Modern Reader*. 2nd ed. New York: Ronald, 1975.

Fisher, John H., ed. *The Complete Poetry and Prose of Geoffrey Chaucer*. New York, Chicago, etc.: Holt, Rinehart and Winston, 1977; 2nd ed. 1989.

Manly, John M., ed. *The Canterbury Tales*. New York: Holt, 1928.

———. and Edith Rickert, eds. *The Text of the Canterbury Tales, Studied on the Basis of All Known Manuscripts*. 8 vols. Chicago: University of Chicago Press, 1940.

Pratt, Robert A., ed. *The Tales of Canterbury*. Boston: Houghton Mifflin, 1974.

Robinson, F. N., ed. *The Works of Geoffrey Chaucer*. Boston: Houghton Mifflin, 1st ed. 1933; 2nd ed. 1957. (3rd ed. by Larry D. Benson. See above under *Riverside Chaucer*).

Root, Robert K., ed. *The Book of Troilus and Criseyde, Edited from All the Known Manuscripts*. Princeton: Princeton University Press, 1926.

Ruggiers, Paul G., ed. *The Variorum Edition of the Works of Geoffrey Chaucer*. Norman, OK: University of Oklahoma Press, 1982—.

> Each tale is edited in a separate volume with complete critical apparatus by individual scholars under the general editorship of Ruggiers.

Skeat, Walter W., ed. *The Complete Works of Geoffrey Chaucer*. 7 vols. Oxford: Clarendon, 1894–97.

Thynne, William, ed. *Geoffrey Chaucer: The Works, 1532, with Supplementary Material from the Editions of 1542, 1561, 1598, and 1602*. 1969; rpt. 1976.

Tyrwhitt, Thomas, ed. *The Canterbury Tales, 1775–78*, 5 vols. London: Pickering, 1830.

Secondary Sources

Books

Corsa, Helen S. *Chaucer: Poet of Mirth and Morality*. Notre Dame: University of Notre Dame Press, 1964.

> Notes that in the *Book of the Duchess*, the gentlemanly obtuseness of the narrator offers a comic view which never detracts from the poem's grave simplicity or sad dignity. Finds the *Parlement of Foules* gay, comic in its subject (an hilarious council of love), happy in its tone, joyous in celebrating nature, and "of good aventure." Chaucer's human figure standing unnoticed in the noisy bird-

world is one of comic irony. Humor occurs only in the second book of the *House of Fame* where the dreamer meets the eagle who is even more comic than the situation, "though the vision of the large poet subjected in mid-air to a lecture on physics is wonderfully funny." In the tragic *Troilus and Criseyde*, book two is almost pure comedy, laughter, song, and bright gaiety. Book three's comedy is of fulfilled happiness, love achieved, agony stilled. In the whole work, comedy is laced into serious love scenes and tragic moments although books four and five have nothing of joy in them. The *Canterbury Tales*, a comedy of human existence in all its mirth and morality, encompasses various modes of humor. Each portrait, falling into one of the three estates, displays some tension, a "warring soul" full of comic potential for the "game," which always requires mirth.

Craik, T. W. *The Comic Tales of Chaucer*. London and New York: Barnes & Noble, 1964.

Offers a systematic discussion of comedy in ten humorous tales for those not very familiar with the *Canterbury Tales*. His plot summaries point out humorous elements in the *Tales*.

Kern, Edith. *The Absolute Comic*. New York: Columbia University Press, 1980.

Notes that in the literature of the comic absolute, the scapegoat is not the father blocking young love, but "a cuckolded husband who becomes the laughing stock of all concerned, while his adulterous wife triumphs and frequently is the object of tacit or open approval" (40). Compares the *Wife of Bath's*, *Merchant's*, and *Miller's Tales* to sixteenth-century charivari, a processional punishment of males whose wives defy their submissive role. Concludes "the real place of woman in society, its stress on morality concerning an event of a fundamentally carnivalesque nature and therefore belonging originally to the realm of fantasy is . . . expressive of the spirit of

Calvinism that ultimately came to supress all carnivalesque festivities or to interpret them in a manner
oblivious to the spirit of the absolute comic" (42–43). The
unjudged women win: "It is the fantasy triumph of the
meek and powerless over those in authority" (44).

Kendrick, Laura. *Chaucerian Play: Comedy and Control in the
Canterbury Tales*. Berkeley: University of California Press,
1988.

Investigates the mechanisms and meanings of medieval
mirth, especially of Chaucer's literary play by analyzing
human behavior from modern psychological, psychoanalytic, anthropological, and historical studies. Heavily
relying on art history to compare and reinforce literary
interpretation, Kendrick finds goliardic-style and other
burlesque of sacred Christian texts in paintings and
Chaucerian *fabliaux*. Especially during festivals, rebellion
against censorship leads to churlish, infantile, goliardic
parody or performance. Play may also be aggressive and
dangerous, break verbal taboos, or invert the social
order, as well as stabilize and console.

Leonard, Frances McNeely. *Laughter in the Courts of Love: Comedy
in Allegory from Chaucer to Spenser*. Norman, Okla:
Pilgrim Books, 1981.

Explores how our direct response to non-serious comedy
impinges on our understanding of serious allegory. Believes "To appreciate comedy in allegory [an "unholy
alliance"], the reader must begin by understanding that
comedy is not an evasion of morality and doctrine nor
an attack upon them, but a component of both the literal
and the figural levels that stress that the letter too is a
form of reality" (11–12). Offers extended definitions of
allegory and comedy, finding the first upward-moving,
toward human improvement, and the second practical
and down-to-earth. Generally follows chronology, trac-
ing the Chaucerian tradition of comic allegory from its
origins to its culmination in the *Faerie Queene* while

admitting neither comedy nor allegory follow any clear chronological pattern. Both get efficacy and vitality from the poet's artistry and vision but do not function in isolation from each other, co-existing in a vital tension. Although Leonard devotes little attention to the *Canterbury Tales*, she claims "From the *Book of the Duchess* through the *Canterbury Tales*, Chaucer is intent upon evoking both serious reflection and laughter" (30).

Payne, F. Anne. *Chaucer and Menippean Satire.* Madison: University of Wisconsin Press, 1981.

Claims "Menippean satire is frequently called a medley . . . of prose and verse, of tones, of attitudes, points of view, philosophies, of places high and low, fantastic and realistic, of characters divine and human, living and dead" (4). While disregarding decorum of consistency and hierarchy, and denying the possibility of ideal standards, its serio-comic utterances and parodies juxtapose extreme perceptions of intelligence. Believes Chaucer uses the free-wheeling parody of Boethius and its dialogic, unyielding presentations of the world's multifariousness, finding Menippean dialogue the dominant structural feature of his work.

Rodway, Allan. *English Comedy: Its Role and Nature from Chaucer to the Present Day.* Berkeley and Los Angeles: University of California Press, 1975.

Notes Chaucer created comedy both skeptical and complex, cosmopolitan and bourgeois, especially obvious in the eagle of the *House of Fame*, the birds in the *Parlement of Foules*, Pandarus in *Troilus and Criseyde*, and in the *Canterbury Tales* where it issues in complete comedies. Claims Chaucer's great gift is not so much a flair for satire but the zestful conveying of a three-dimensional world in a pervasive quizzical tone with frequent shifts of viewpoint. Examines the *Miller's*, *Reeve's*, and *Wife of Bath's Tales*, all implicitly satirizing bourgeois churlishness. Finds sensuous vitality, vigorous ribaldry, and technical mastery inspiring the *Miller's Tale*. In contrast to this celebration of natural life, the *Reeve's Tale* is a comic satire on aggressive roguery and vulgar pride leading to a fall. The *Wife of Bath's Tale* offers temperamental opposition to orthodoxy, a focus on life rather than mortality, persistence rather than repentance. The Prologue moves from a toughly humorous comedy of an innovating and anti-patristic kind, to satirical comedy of a conserving sort. "The vitality of her love of life is matched by the vulgarity of her life of love; and the reader is presented not with a judgment but a summing up"(75).

Steadman, John M. *Disembodied Laughter: Troilus and the Apotheosis Tradition: A Re-examination of Narrative and Thematic Contexts*. Berkeley, Los Angeles, London: University of California Press, 1972.

This well-informed, wide-ranging exploration of *Troilus* draws on classical and contemporaneous European literature and philosophy. Finds Troilus is not a tragic hero fallen from high degree but a lover experiencing conventional vicissitudes—prosperity and misery, change of Fortune—which could be treated comically as other poets and Chaucer himself do elsewhere. Claims "transiency of worldly love rather than loss of worldly dignities and high estate [are] his subject matter, but he has invested this erotic content with the shape and structure of tragedy" (89). Chaucer uses conventional matter of comedy "the triadic relations of lover, bard, and mistress [which] had been traditionally associated with the comic genre" (89). Since the social level of the characters determines the genre type, combined motifs of love and war would not alter it. Believes Chaucer "gave clearer definition to the comic values already inherent in his poem [than do his predecessors]. In Chaucer's romance, with its rich comic overtones, the hero's laughter acquires a force and a relevance that it could not have achieved in [Lucan's] *Pharsalia* which exhibits a fine sense of irony but little sense of comedy) or even in [Boccaccio's] *Teseida*" (93). Although the tragic sense predominates in the plot, the comic vision overcomes in the end, complementing but not contradicting the tragic.

Bibliography

Allen, Mark, and John H. Fisher. *The Essential Chaucer: An Annotated Bibliography of Major Modern Studies.* Boston: Hall, 1987. (1900–1984)

Baird [Lange], Lorrayne Y. *Bibliography of Chaucer Review 1964–73.* Boston: Hall, 1977.

Crawford, William R. *Bibliography of Chaucer 1954–63.* Seattle: University of Washington Press, 1967.

Giaccherini, Enrico. "Chaucer and the Italian Trecento: A Bibliography." In *Chaucer and the Italian Trecento.* Ed. Piero Boitani, Cambridge: Cambridge University Press, 1983.

Griffith, Dudley D. *Bibliography of Chaucer 1908–53.* Seattle: University of Washington Press, 1955.

Hammond, Eleanor P. *Chaucer: A Bibliographical Manual* (1908). New York: Peter Smith, 1933.

Leyerle, John, and Anne Quick. *Chaucer: A Bibliographical Introduction.* (1900–1979). Toronto: University of Toronto Press, 1986.

Peck, Russell A. *Chaucer's Lyrics and Anelida and Arcite: An Annotated Bibliography 1900–1980.* Toronto: University of Toronto Press, 1983.

Studies in the Age of Chaucer. Annotated Bibliography, Norman: University of Oklahoma Press:, 1979– .

Biography

Baugh, Albert C. "Chaucer the Man." In *Companion to Chaucer Studies*. Ed. Beryl Rowland. New York: Oxford University Press, 1979.

Bland, D. S. "Chaucer and the Inns of Court: A Reexamination." *English Studies* 33 (1952): 145–55.

———. "When Was Chaucer Born?" *TLS* 26 April 1957: 264; Amplifications: Margaret Galway (10 May 1957): 289; C. Warner and C. E. Welch (17 May 1957): 305; G. D. G. Hall (28 June 1957): 397; Margaret Galway (12 July 1957): 427.

Brewer, Derek. *Chaucer and His World*. New York: Dodd, Mead, 1977.

Crow, Martin M. and Clair C. Olson, eds. *Chaucer Life Records*. From materials compiled by John M. Manly and Edith Rickert. Oxford: Clarendon Press, 1966.

Gardner, John Champlin. *The Life and Times of Chaucer*. New York: Knopf, 1976.

Howard, Donald R. *Chaucer: His Life, His World, His Works*. New York: Dutton, 1987.

Hulbert, James R. *Chaucer's Official Life*. Menasha, WI: Collegiate Press/Banta Publishing Co., 1912.

Kern, Alfred. *The Ancestry of Chaucer*. Baltimore: Lord Baltimore Press, 1906.

Rudd, Martin B. *Thomas Chaucer*. *Research Publications of University of Minnesota* 9, Minneapolis: U of Minnesota Press, 1926.

Journal Articles

Ames, Ruth. "Prototype and Parody in Chaucerian Exegesis." *Acta* 4 (1977): 87–105.

Claims Chaucer's parody was as irreverent as it sounds and his piety as sincere. Discusses Old Testament parodies, particularly interpretations of Solomon, concluding Chaucer was neither deeply moved by the Old Testament nor convinced by current exegetical modes. "Proper" persons—the Prioress, Parson, Man of Law and Prudence—take the high line, reverent and traditional. Dubious tellers—the Wife, Miller and Merchant and their characters—are rude and shrewd questioners who impiously parody the *Canticle of Canticles*. Finds Chaucer's balance between laughter and prayer most precarious and his parodies twisting from grossness to subtlety and back again.

Andreas, James R. "The Rhetoric of Chaucerian Comedy: The Aristotelian Legacy," *The Comparatist* 8 (1984): 56–66.

Finds the comic theory of Aristotle the ultimate source for the tradition, assimilated but not superseded by Bergson, Freud, and Bakhtin. Notes the early dream visions are shot through with parody, reversal, exaggeration, and elaborate punning, standard features of comic performance. Examines characters, themes, and rhetorical devices of *Canterbury Tales* in the light of Aristotelian poetic theory.

Bloomfield, Morton W. "The *Man of Law's Tale:* A Tragedy of Victimization and a Christian Comedy." *Publications of the Modern Language Association* 87 (1972): 384–90.

Notes that "a mixture of the superficially tragic and the slightly comic . . . does not lie easy with us. What are we to feel about an incredible heroine, Constance, who is subjected to an impossibly ridiculous and coincidental series of events which one cannot take seriously, while . . . the teller apostrophizes and laments in exaggerated fashion over the happenings, attempting . . . to play on our feelings?" (384). Notes that interruptions and apostrophes, little characterization, much improbability and description distance us from emotional involvement in the *Man of Law's Tale*, and links it to the Greek romance genre and hagiography derived from it. Notes the religious significance of the exile-and-return motif, the *Contemptus Mundi* theme, and that this is a Christian comedy: God's grace conquers all for those who trust Him throughout all suffering.

Dane, Joseph A. "The Mechanics of Comedy in Chaucer's *Miller's Tale.*" *Chaucer Review* 14 (1980): 215–224.

Contends the comic effect of the denouement rests on the tale's formal structure: its stylized *solaas*. Discusses the static elements (organization of characters into two stable, parallel sets) and dynamic elements (Chaucer's manipulation of those sets) which combine to heighten the denouement, "one of the most absurdly comic situations in the *Canterbury Tales*," as we too are duped. Finds the carpenter's flood fantasy a burlesque of the Old Testament Deluge paralleling Gervase as a New Testament plowmaker. The first is punished for his faith in false doctrines while good faith between Absolon and Gervase is stressed. John's broken arm is a physical and spiritual fall while Absolon is reborn and healed from his pride and lust. Sees parallels and reversals between triadic structures (Alison-John-Nicholas and Alison-Nicholas-Absolon, Alison's functional role connecting the two.) In the dyadic, more active relationships, Alison-John relationship is legitimate, public, and dispassionate while the Alison-Nicholas relationship is adulterous, secretive, and lecherous. The Miller-narrator sublimates our expectation of "low-comedy" by glossing moral deficiencies, thus giving Chaucer free reign with the aesthetics of comic denouement.

David, Alfred. "Sentimental Comedy in The Franklin's Tale." *Annuale Mediaevale* 6 (1965): 19–27.

Claims Chaucer's irony extends to the Franklin despite sympathy for his bourgeois values. Thus, his tale bears a striking resemblance to bourgeois genre called sentimental comedy: a potentially tragic plot resolved happily through noble behavior. As he dons the symbols and not the substance of aristocracy in his garb, he adorns his tale with elevated chivalric language. Further he transforms courtly ideals of love and nobility to conform to his own values as reason, not passion rules. The tenderness and nobility of courtly sentiment touch the Franklin's heart in a tale without consequences usual in a courtly romance.

Falke, Anne. "The Comic Function of the Narrator in *Troilus and Criseyde.*" *Neophilologus* 68 (1984): 134–141.

Believes attempts to isolate a readily identifiable persona for the speaker in the *Troilus* or to separate him from Chaucer the poet fails. Rather, discusses the effect of the narrator on the audience and how he converts tragedy to comedy. At the end, both Troilus and the narrator reach a new level of understanding. Ignores whose voice speaks the commentary, while seeking the purpose of the commentary in the scope of the poem. Finds the effect of a proud young man falling to Eros amusing; the Proem to Book I seems a gently humorous hyperbolic overstatement of lovers' miseries, but is prophetic. Believes the narrator serious in his religious remarks and Chaucer the poet and Chaucer the naive narrator to be the same. From Troilus' vision in the eighth sphere, the earth seems paltry; his laugh clinches the narrator's efforts to transform his tragedy into a comedy when Troilus reaches knowledge of eternal completeness and comprehends mutability. He laughs at the grief of those who weep for his death. Movement from involvement to detachment, passion to understanding, are achieved through changes in narrative distance which offer a comic perspective. Reluctance to blame Criseyde is also a comic attribute. Unlike tragedy, comedy assumes men receive no worse than they deserve; Chaucer depicts the escape from the first to the second.

Foster, Edward E. "Humor in the *Knight's Tale*." *Chaucer Review* 3 (1968): 88–94.

> Chivalric anachronism reveals the limitations that cause unexpected and unconscious humor in the *Knight's Tale*. Examines how this humor qualifies, but doesn't reject, the Knight's "sentence." Endorses Boethian interpretations of the tale, suggesting the Knight accepts Boethianism because he despises unhappy endings. Surveys puns, dialogue, incongruous actions and style, concluding the Knight "is comic in the enviable way that idealists are often made to seem ludicrous by the demands of reality; but that, of course, does not destroy the value of his ideals" (94).

Frank, Robert W., Jr. "The *Reeve's Tale* and the Comedy of Limitation." In Directions in Literary Criticism: Contemporary Approaches to Literature. Eds. Stanley Werntraub and Philip Young. Pennsylvania State University Press, 1973.

> Claims if "the contrast between the Knight and the Miller (and Reeve) is a comedy of class and nurture, the conflict between the Miller and the Reeve arising between members of the same class, is a comic reflection of the absurd clashes created by the limitations of human vision."

Garbáty, Thomas J. "Chaucer and Comedy." In *Versions of Medieval Comedy*. Ed. Paul G. Ruggiers. Norman: University of Oklahoma Press, 1977, pp. 173–90.

> Finds Chaucer's comic theory only implied in opposition to his Boethian definition of tragedy in the *Monk's Prologue.* Although he reworked tradition as he used it, humor of situation, using control and balance, was always one of his strengths.

———. "Satire and Regionalism: The Reeve and His Tale." *Chaucer Review* 8 (1973):1–8.

Finds internal humor emerging from the text, and external humor only available to Chaucer's contemporaries who knew its historic context. Notes the Reeve comes from a small area in Norfolk which sent numerous provincial, perhaps gauche immigrants to London and would have been identified as one of them. Claims slight touches of North East Midland dialect are essential to Chaucer's satire: the Reeve "spoke a kind of backwoods patois which was not only ludicrous in polite society, but which would have been barely understood with the best intentions. . . . [He] took it on himself to mimic a provincial dialect in his own barbarous jargon."

Grennen, Joseph E. "*Makyng* in Comedy: '*Troilus and Criseyde*', V, 1788." *Neuphilologische Mitteilungen* 86 (1985): 489–493.

Examines the difficult phrase at the end of the *Troilus* that God might yet send him "myght to make in some comedye." Sees the poet as surrogate for the Creator who "makes" within his world rather than as a shaper working from some external position. Chaucer might have gotten that idea from Augustine's second homily on the Gospel of St. John, or more likely from Bradwardine's citation of it in *De Causa Dei*, informing Chaucer's conception of the way in which a "maker" works.

Hira, Toshinori. "Chaucer's Laughter." *Bulletin of the Faculty of Liberal Arts, Nagasaki University* 20 (1979): 27–42.

Examines Chaucer's role of love servant, love-renegade, and spectator, claiming as Chaucer grew older he gradually came to reject courtly conventions of love. Considers how the mercantile influence and feudalism affect Chaucer's characters and tellers: the Squire, Merchant, John the Carpenter, the Merchant in the *Shipman's Tale*, Thopas and others replace the idealism of Chaucer's age with materialistic and commercial values. Finds the bourgeoisie the favorite butts of the court audience. Claims satire is directed at Symkin's flour theft, laughter at the wiles of the wife in the *Shipman's Tale*, and ridicule at the pecuniary knight of the *Merchant's Tale* mocked by his unfaithful wife. But ultimately, as the aristocratic standards are replaced by bourgeois ones, no differences are found between human beings. Comic idealization, such as that toward Thopas' lady love, leads to satirization of courtly love. Concludes "humorous or malicious cynicism about the courtly attitudes of romances can be found in a ridiculous treatment of the practical attitude of fabliaux" (42).

Lanham, Richard A. "Game Play and High Seriousness in Chaucer's Poetry." *English Studies* 48 (1967): 1–24.

Uses Matthew Arnold's theory of high seriousness as a touchstone to examine Chaucer as a "great" poet of high seriousness. Discusses the corpus as it reveals game theory, positing that Chaucer subconsciously viewed the world *sub specie ludi*, using intricate jokes and games whose rules fix and stylize conflict revealing ambivalence toward seriousness. For Chaucer, human activity contains playful enjoyment within itself—the pleasure of pattern-following. The voyage is both pilgrimage and game as interstices between tales and the host's comments, Palamon and Arcite's contest, the Wife's agonistic rhetoric, and the Clerk's rejoinder remind us. Finds "implicit in the matrix of the *Tales*, in the game on the way to Canterbury, and in Geoffrey Chaucer's detached role within this game . . . a characteristic attitude toward human behavior. . . . [The gallery of portraits] are all, to one extent or another, trying to play a part, to establish an identity." Arnold believes this view of character precludes high seriousness which demands "a conception of human character as single, solid, substantial and important." Like Harry Bailly, the *Troilus* host, Pandarus, controls his game, courtly love, intertwining the aristocratic game of conflict with the bourgeois one of pleasure. The *Troilus*, comedy fully as much as tragedy, unites games of war, love, and rhetoric, and sees self-conscious character posing/role-playing as the means to an identity. Arnold believes this view of character precludes high seriousness which demands "a conception of human character as single, solid, substantial and important."

Levy, Bernard S. "Biblical Parody in the *Summoner's Tale*." *Tennessee Studies in Literature* 11 (1966): 45–60.

Describes relationship of *Prologue* to *Tale*, the first positing the special kind of grace or wind the Friars are said to have and the second exemplifying it. The division of the "gift" is a precise parody of the descent of the Holy Ghost upon the Apostles at Pentecost, both being a problem of distribution. Notes that the Pentecost cupola in St. Mark's, Venice, uses a wheel as a central iconographic image to separate the Apostles, much like that of the Summoner's cartwheel. The tale is an effective answer which strikes at the character of the Friar and his pretentious claims.

MacDonald, Donald. "Proverbs, *Sententiae*, and Exempla in Chaucer's Comic Tales: The Function of Comic Misapplication." *Speculum* 41 (1966): 453–65.

Claims Chaucer consciously employed proverbs, *sententiae*, and exempla to enhance comic effect. Considers advice given in *Melibee, Wife of Bath, Merchant's, Miller's Tales* showing the outcome of the advice determines the character of the advisor: having naive folly or calculating shrewdness. Reveals comedy of unconscious misapplication of monitory elements used by Chaucer to dramatize the folly of his comic victims, suggesting pride and complacency are essential to comic characterization.

Marzec, Marcia Smith. "The *Man of Law's Tale* as Christian Comedy; Or, the Best-laid Schemes." *Proceedings of the Patristic, Medieval and Renaissance Conference* 12–13 (1987–88): 197–208.

Claims Chaucer cultivates simultaneously a dual perspective—from man's, within the world, and from
God's, from above, where the order and reasonableness
can be seen. What appears to be random wanderings at
sea are really a directed, purposeful voyage; what appears to be a linear and episodic plot is really symmetrical and hierarchical. "This is not a story of how God
comes through in the clutch" but of his eternally having
planned things for the greater good. Admits the plot
offers intellectual but not emotional pleasure—a
thematic success but dramatic failure. God's providential
perspective reigns in evoking the long-range good. Thus,
that Constance's life is not particularly felicitous is
irrelevant; and the many deaths are of little import
because the victims, such as the sultan and Hermingeld,
are born into eternal life, all within the providential
schema, creating a Christian comedy.

McCall, John P. "The Squire in Wonderland." *Chaucer Review* 1
(1966): 103–09.

Argues that in the Squire, Chaucer has carefully created
ambivalence—a teller of youthful, zesty, fantasy yet also
a self-conscious narrator craftily using his literary
tools—for a delicate, humorous effect. Points to plot
irrelevancies and inconsistencies which create "a pattern
of elaborate inconsequence, incongruity, and downright
bathos" (108). In trying to do too much, the tale shows
self-conscious affectation and enthusiastic discontinuity.

Nist, John. "The Art of Chaucer: *Pathedy.*" *Tennessee Studies in
Literature* 11 (1966): 1–10.

Chaucer's genius is in his fusion of the tragic and comic
visions, encompassing both tears and laughter, avoiding
the presumption of comedy and the despair of tragedy
through the tragicomic art of humility: *pathedy.* The
pilgrims constitute "a common humanity shown to be
simultaneously sublime and ridiculous, funny and sad,

everything and nothing, by the art of the supreme medieval poet of serenity" (10).

Pearsall, Derek. "The Canterbury Tales II: Comedy." *The Cambridge Chaucer Companion*. Eds. Piero Boitani and Jill Mann. Cambridge, London, New York, etc.: Cambridge University Press, 1986, 125–42.

Reid, David S. "Crocodilian Humor: A Discussion of Chaucer's Wife of Bath." *Chaucer Review* 14 (1979): 73–89.

Describes the Wife of Bath as "absurd and grotesque, a figment of that anti-feminist gallimaufry, the *Prologue* to her tale . . . our different ethos has not given us a detached view of the real nature of the Wife's comedy. It has made her an embarrassment, so that, fearing for Chaucer's good name, we misunderstand her elaborately." In fact she is not an individual, but a comic shrew stock figure of both good fun and woman-evil execration in a pantomime of stock tricks from which she draws vitality for that absurd stock figure. Because we are involved in a comic displacement, our response is equivocal or crocodilian: "we enjoy her jolly, hearty nature. On the other, we know her to be, like Falstaff and Long John Silver, common and villainous." Their distortion, oddity, or exaggeration makes us recognize and enliven them. Claims the *General Prologue* is topsy-turvy bathos which places her on a comic stage to give her life; her own *Prologue* is farce; and she makes sense only in terms of burlesque and knockabout comedy. "Her shrew's confession is, in fact, so enormous and put with such verve that it receives a comic absolution." Finds the *Wife of Bath's Tale* a more subdued burlesque, the second part mirroring the first: male dominance (rape) being replaced by female dominance (of the hag). Believes the correct answer to the question "brings with it an ambiguous good fortune. . . . what is Cinderellalike in her *Tale* is gargoyled." The end of farcical comedy is "solely the preposterous conclusion" or the ridiculous; the comedy of the wife's marriages "is as cruel and banal as those of a Punch and Judy show, and Chaucer's urbanity is a way of feasting upon the base and ugly." Concludes the comedy of *Tale* and *Prologue*, part of courtly flyting against the Third Estate, is a coarse joke, the "Archewyf" both rogue and laughingstock because she is base, fool's gold; "obviously Chaucer meant her for a bad lot."

Reiss E. "Medieval Irony." *Journal of the History of Ideas* 42 (1981): 209–26.

> Medieval irony best describes the literary art of the best medieval writers whose surface ironies are as varied as their accomplishments; a basic irony, which we must acknowledge to understand them, underlies all their works. The ironic artist is one who focuses on the creation instead of the Creator, who writes about the world instead of salvation or perfection. Reiss claims that "Because of the ironic nature of his artistry— because it is a given that the workings of the artist are trivial—Chaucer is able to reveal traditional Christian *doctrina* at the same time as he reveals a literary *poseur*, the Man of Law."

Rudat, Wolfgang E. H. "Chaucer's Spring of Comedy: The *Merchant's Tale* and Other 'Games' with Augustinian Theology." *Annuale Mediaevale* 21 (1981): 111–120.

> Demonstrates that January's portrayal is influenced by Augustinian ideas of pre- and post-lapsarian sexuality— he must labor all night because of his sinful motives for marriage. His marriage is his fall. Discusses the parodic use of Christian notions and how Chaucer's bawdy manipulation of Christian ideas are absorbed into the Spring of Comedy permeating the *Canterbury Tales*.

Ruggiers, Paul G. "A Vocabulary for Chaucerian Comedy: A Preliminary Sketch." In *Medieval Studies in Honor of Lillian Herlands Hornstein*. Eds. J. B. Bessinger and R. Raymo. New York: New York University Press, 1977.

Lays out a vocabulary for the complex subject of Chaucerian comedy, relying on Aristotle's *Nicomachean Ethics* and *Rhetoric*, the Coislinian *Tractate*, and Lane Cooper's recreation of an Aristotelian theory of comedy. Focuses on plot and character rather than Chaucer's ironical point of view, the larger movement of the *Canterbury Tales*, their placement in the frame, or relationship between tellers and tales. Divides article into definition, plot, elements of plot, the dianoetic function, comic catharsis, reader response, comic characters, and probability.

Sarno, Ronald A. "Chaucer and the Satirical Tradition." *Classical Folia* 21 (1967): 41–61.

Explores the classical tradition of satire, especially of Horace, Juvenal, and Jerome to determine Chaucer's relation to each. Claims "Chaucer is conscious of a satirical tradition and is using it consistently in his poetry . . . [believing] the ancient writings took on a quasi-religious authority which paralleled the power of the Bible in Christian polemics" (41). Finds satire's purpose "to correct moral flaws and to entertain its audience" (43) for without the former it disintegrates into burlesque. Notes that "Chaucer's satire possesses a warm and humane tolerance for the foibles of his fellow men" much like Horace's, concluding "[h]is satires deliberately stress tolerance, because he knows that by nature men prefer to depreciate others" (47). While links to Horace are tenuous and unstated, Chaucer does mention Juvenal in *The Wife of Bath's Prologue* and *Troilus and Criseyde*. Believes the shrew described in Jerome's *Adversus Jovinianium* is the model for the Wife of Bath, concluding "Chaucer seems to be laughing at all the anti-feminine literature of the past [pointing] out the dangers inherent in a satire which treats women merely as the gate of hell and forgets they are persons with feelings too" (53). Chaucer does not write complaint literature of abstractions but of the concrete, "restoring literary satire to English by giving equal emphasis to both the good and evil polarity of human life and constantly maintaining the moralizing entertainment polarity of satire" (57). Lastly, Sarno compares Chaucer to Gower and Langland, finding the *double-entendre*, his clever wit and humane understanding, Chaucer's personal contribution to English satire.

Scheps, Walter. "Sir Thopas: The Bourgeois Knight, the Minstrel and the Critics." *Tennessee Studies in Literature* 11 (1966): 35–43.

Sir Thopas, a tail-rhyme in miniature, telescopes description and action of typical romance characteristics and forms, describing flora, birds, hunting, beasts all in 207 lines. Satire is found in the diminutive knight, use of syntax, rhetoric, and vocabulary, and the tail-rhyme stanza.

Smith, Francis J. "Mirth and Marriage in *The Parliament of Foules*." *Ball State University Forum* 14 (1973): 15–22.

Sees irony and sophisticated amusement beginning the *Parliament* which "is dotted with wry incongruities, changes tempo quickly, and proceeds from part to part by a kind of organized ramble or controlled incoherence" (15). Stresses the dream-vision experience, and objects to overly serious treatment of the work's putative design to reconcile apparently conflicting authorities. Emphasizes the refreshing spirit, mixture of familiarity with serious learning, and joyful affirmation of life and love also found in the Prologue to the *Legend of Good Women*.

Stevens, Martin. "'And Venus Laugheth': An Interpretation of the *Merchant's Tale*." *Chaucer Review* 7 (1972): 118–31.

Believes the *Merchant's Tale* comic, and the teller sympathetic but not self-revelatory. Points to the Ellesmere manuscript showing the Merchant in his prime, youthful and energetic, in dapper clothing. Contends the harangue about wife and marriage are delivered with tongue in cheek, with absurd exaggeration. The Merchant is not January, neither cuckold nor lecher, but simply a husband henpecked by an overbearing wife; she is identified with the Wife of Bath, but not May of his story, in contrast to Griselda.

Thro, A. Booker. "Chaucer's Creative Comedy: A Study of the *Miller's Tale* and the *Shipman's Tale*." *Chaucer Review* 5 (1970): 97–111.

Finds that in Chaucer's comedy the triumph of wit is often a "creative act" of imaginative and ingenious construction more complex than the situations require. Points out brilliant contriving, one more joke when we think Chaucer has offered his last. Rejects Craik's notion of farce, with its destructive impulses, finding creativity and human constructiveness dominating the *Miller's Tale*. Although irony can destroy the ingenious illusions of which creative comedy is made, it is not enlisted against comic constructiveness here. Believes that although "Chaucer sometimes seems to be working out an impudent parody of the annunciation . . . there are perhaps moments when his poetry suggests a more serious purpose behind the clerk's mock apotheosis . . . [as] creation takes place out of the flood." Additionally, finds the *Shipman's Tale* presents its action in scenes of "creative persuasion," especially in the wife's shifting persuasive tactics of "advance-and-retreat" indirection in content and syntax. Both monk and merchant triumph by freeing themselves from the consequences of the other's plotting, the latter by being transported to the world of creative business dealings. All three are intimately related through moments of persuasion. Concludes Chaucer's double attitude—idealism and verisimilitude—toward artistic purpose is a "high-Gothic" characteristic.

Veldhoen, N. H. G. E. "Which Was the Mooste Fre: Chaucer's Realistic Humour and Insight into Human Nature, As Shown in *The Frankelyens Tale*." *In Other Words:*

Transcultural Studies in Philology, Translation, and Lexicology Presented to Hans Heinrich Meier on the Occasion of His Sixty-Fifth Birthday. Dordrecht: Foris, 1989.

Sees the Franklin's ironic excuse for his weak rhetorical skill in the Prologue as granting liberty to defy conventions and rendering an intense imaginative tone unusual in this genre. He is announcing that conventional material will be treated critically. Claims conventionally the husband Arveragus is thought most free: Dorigen's love has inspired him to uphold honor and generosity has been inspired by courtly love. He secures the happy ending by having the courage of his convictions and all the others follow him. But, perhaps some ambiguity is intended, here and in the *Squire's Tale* where the Franklin similarly extols a young squire, since the young lover Aurelius has been presented with more stylistic and dramatic vividness in lively and sympathetic detail. His grief is more protracted and his motives of grief and compassion are sanctioned. Structurally and dramatically, he receives preferential treatment. Thus, a double answer, the official one (the husband) and the one from the heart (the young squire): fits Chaucer's realistic humor and insight into human nature.

Index

Abel 300, 316
Abner 236
Absalom 235
Absolon xx, 18–19, 47, 49, 52,
    53, 56, 67–69, 71, 93, 103,
    109, 111, 195, 196, 199,
    200, 204, 302–304, 317,
    359, 365–371, 380, 385,
    386
absurdity xxv, xliv, 10, 89, 200,
    270, 288, 321, 386
Abuse-of-Power theory xlv,
    296, 297, 308
Achilles 403
action 62, 83
    cause-effect 392
    and humor 133
    illusion of xxv
ad hominem humor 96
Adam xlvi, 148, 246, 252, 309,
    319, 325
adultery 44, 46, 56, 103, 133–
    135, 138, 140, 143, 200,
    231, 373, 390
Aeneid 408, 409, 412, 421
Aers 224, 225, 246
affection 113, 386, 413
Africanus 95
agon xxxvii, 45, 50, 54, 55, 298

Alayn 207
alazon 64–66
Albertus Magnus 415
alchemy 33, 257, 286, 306, 325
Alford, Violet 247
alienation 300, 406
Alisoun [Alison]
    Miller's wife 18, 19, 92, 108–
        110, 192–197, 199, 200,
        205, 234, 303–305, 350,
        365–369, 377, 380, 386,
        388, 389
    Wife of Bath 84–86
    See also wife, Wife of Bath
allegorical structure 395
allegory 5, 18, 35, 161, 168,
    233, 289, 343, 374
Allen, Hope Emily 315
Allen, Mark 431
alliance 69, 71, 107, 156, 220,
    221, 224, 305
alliteration xliv, 261, 280, 287
allusion 4, 10, 21, 24, 33, 109,
    145, 146, 157, 158, 303,
    308, 309, 409, 422, 423
    musical xxi, 108, 113, 235
    See also biblical allusions
Almagest 197
alta tragedia 403, 408

alter-ego 285

ambiguity xli, 37, 167, 238, 269, 308

amor xxvii, 221, 401, 416

Ames, Ruth 432

Amphion 235, 236

analogy 138, 142, 147, 155, 210, 289, 387, 409, 411, 413

Andersson, Theodore M. 123, 141

Andreas, James R. xxxiv, 433

Andromache 410

Angelus ad Virginem 108

Anglo-Norman 274, 309

angst xlii, 216

animals xxvii, xxxviii, 106, 111, 113, 150, 153, 155, 193

annunciation xxii, 387

antagonist xlvi, 308

anti-feminist conventions xxxix, xl, xlvi, 95, 138, 139, 148, 149, 159, 226, 313, 328

Antichrist xlv, 298, 314, 315

anticlimax 277

aphrodisiacs 118, 129

Apollo 175, 237, 238, 243, 255, 256

appetite xxxv, xxxviii, 103, 128, 133, 139, 217, 362, 368

apprentice 225, 233

Aquinas, St. Thomas 356, 388

Arcite xxiii, xxvi, xxvii, xxix, 19, 54, 92, 102, 193, 204

aristocracy 107

Aristophanes 36, 50, 75, 190, 322, 342

Aristotle xxxvii, xli, 15, 41, 47, 54, 55, 57–61, 64, 67, 415

Arnold, Matthew 15, 98

arrogance 58, 59

ars-metrik 121, 122

art 42, 60, 61, 82, 195, 388
and realism 176, 177, 178

artist 36, 37, 71, 83, 202, 203, 230, 243, 336, 394

artistic freedom 50

artistry 106, 201, 229, 398

Ascensius 412, 421, 422

ascent motif 399

asceticism 192, 225

Asia Minor 276

ass xliii, 25, 39, 90, 191, 195, 289

astrolabe 197

astrologye 196

astronomy 31, 32, 415

Astyanax 410

Atkins, J. W. H. 74

atonement 224, 225

aube 113

Auchinleck MS. 284, 294

auctoritee xlvi, 308

Augustine, St. xlvii, 170, 171, 174, 177, 246, 258, 314, 349, 350, 353–356, 358, 362, 363, 371, 375, 376, 377, 420

Aurelius xxxi, 56

authority xxvi, xlii, 26, 34, 146, 161, 176, 180, 181, 190, 191, 218, 300, 302, 308, 337

avarice 115, 252, 383, 413

Avicenna 416, 417

Bacchus 239
Bächtold-Staubli, H. 246
baculus 191
bagpipe 190, 238, 255
Bailly, Harry (Harry Baily)
    xx–xxi, 189, 190, 271–
    273, 277, 284, 289, 292,
    309, 331, 335, 338
Baird (Lange), Lorrayne Y. 431
Bakhtin, Mikhail xlii, xliii, 104,
    123, 165, 191, 201, 204,
    205, 228, 229, 246, 247,
    300, 315
Baldwin, Ralph 204
Barbarossa 248
Barber, C. L. 165, 190, 204
bargain 188, 217, 223
barnyard communication 94
bathos 277, 288, 294
battlefield xxv, 401, 410, 423
Baugh, A. C. 283, 294, 425,
    432
Baum, Paull F. 74
bawd 401
bawdy xxvii, xxviii, xliii, 79,
    230, 324, 375
beast fable xlvi, 82, 89, 150,
    309
beatitude 399, 406, 408
Beatrice 247, 397, 407
Beaumont, Francis 6, 25
Beerbohm, Max 82
behavior xxix, xxxviii, xlii,
    xliii, xlv, xlvii, 10, 45,
    141, 150, 230–232, 247,
    251, 283, 294, 299, 300,
    301, 402
Beichner, Paul E. 205, 340, 348,
    396

Beidler, Peter G. 375, 377
beliefs 16, 46, 135, 228, 295,
    308, 312, 406
bells 122
Bennett, J. A. W. 123, 315
Benson, Larry D. 4, 5, 18, 252,
    425
Bentley, Eric 61, 76, 382, 383,
    395, 396
Bercé, Yves Marie 248
Bergson, Henri xxiii, 26, 103,
    123, 341, 396
Bernardus 416–418, 423
Bernheimer, Richard 252
Bethlehem 298
betrayal 24, 50, 221, 227, 245,
    253
Beves of Hampton 283
Bevington 299–301, 307, 315,
    316, 319
biblical allusions xxii, 49, 95,
    199, 235, 236, 246, 304,
    325, 330, 337, 359, 376,
    383–385, 388, 394. *See
    also* Christ, David, God,
    Noah, religious themes,
    Saul
birds xxxiii, 20, 28, 29, 33,
    67, 86, 88–90, 131, 194,
    210
Birney, Earle 74
birth 330, 308, 403
black comedy 116, 164, 179
Blake, N. F. 270, 425
Bland, D. S. 432
blind xxxviii, 44, 48, 84, 137,
    160, 408
Bloch, R. Howard 337, 347
Block, Edward A. 255, 329, 345

Bloomfield, Morton xxviii,
    xxix, 171, 185, 321, 326–
    328, 343–345, 421, 433
Blount, Thomas 249
bob-stanza 282
Boccaccio, Giovanni xix, 13,
    81, 105, 107, 183, 186,
    323, 345, 404
body xliii, xlvii, 46, 355–357
    Alisoun's in *Miller's Tale*
        193–194, 196
    bodily orifices 364–366
    of Christ 182
    counterfeiting 310
    and death 361, 406
    and spirituality 349
    "time of the body" 368–370,
        377
Boethian framework xlviii
Boethius, Anicius Manilus
    Severinus xlviii, 29, 177,
    197, 235, 254, 255, 397–
    400, 404, 405, 407, 409–
    415, 417, 419–423
Boitani, Piero 123, 142, 256,
    345
bomolochos 64
bond xxxvi, 37, 115, 136, 188,
    222, 223, 230
Book of Margery Kempe 300, 315
Book of the Duchess xxxii, 310
Boose, Linda E. 249
bourgeois xxv–xxvi, 35, 93,
    105, 107, 152, 272
Bowden, Muriel A. 346
Braddy, Haldeen 375
Braeger, Peter 247
braggart xl, 135
Brand, John A. 249

Brannigan, Martha 375
Brennan, Dom Maynard J. 347
Breton lai xxxi
Brewer, Derek 4, 12, 160,
    432
Brockman, Bennette A. 316
brotherhood 122, 136, 312
Brown, Emerson, Jr. 257, 336,
    346
Brown, Theo 248
Brugges 103, 225
Brushfield, T. N. 249
buffoon xxxvii, 64
Burke, John J. 228, 254
Burke, Peter 247
burlesque xxxv, xlii, xlv, 14,
    19, 43, 82, 93, 94, 151,
    190, 192, 200, 281,
    290
Burney, Charles 11
Burrow, J. A. 230, 247
Burton, Robert 423
Butler, Samuel 233

caesuras 275, 290
Cain 300, 301, 316
Cambridge 102, 112, 123
Canterbury Tales xvii, xviii,
    xxvi, xxiv, xlvii, 19, 37,
    55, 61, 268, 325-327, 350-
    352; audience of 105;
    interpreted as "lie,"
    163-165; and language
    theory, 171, 172, 175;
    reference to law in, 56;
    rhyme in, 272; structure
    of, 53; as an unfinished
    work, 325. *See also*
    Chaucer, comedy,

Index

humor, individual
character names
Canon's Yeoman's Tale 42, 43,
45, 51, 52, 55, 56, 59, 61,
62, 67, 75, 134, 242, 256,
285, 294, 305
Clerk's Tale xxviii, xxx, 42,
76, 135, 153, 320, 321,
325, 330, 341, 344, 345,
375
Cook's Tale 42, 69, 102, 233
Franklin's Tale xxviii, xxxii,
42, 49, 52–54, 62, 102,
175
Friar's Tale xxvii, 42, 43, 45,
50–52, 55, 56, 61, 65, 67,
69, 71, 72, 75, 102, 120,
175, 294, 310, 311
General Prologue xliv, 64–
66, 68, 81, 84, 90, 91, 97,
105, 172, 174, 190, 211,
253, 260, 264, 268, 269,
271, 284, 337, 339, 345
Knight's Tale xxiii, xxvi,
xxvii, xxviii, xxx, xli, 25,
42, 80, 92, 106, 187, 188,
192, 193, 197–199, 203,
204, 417, 423
Man of Law's Tale xxviii,
xxix–xxx, xlvi, 33, 42,
321, 325, 328, 330, 333,
341–344
Manciple's Tale 68, 175, 233,
237, 242, 243, 255, 256,
310
Merchant's Tale xix, xx, xxvi,
xxxix–xl, xliii, 42, 44, 46,
47, 49, 50, 52, 53, 55, 56,
59, 63, 67–69, 71, 75, 84,
93, 102, 107, 116, 118,
127, 128, 132, 133, 140,
141, 228, 230, 232, 233,
237, 242, 244, 245, 247,
251, 252, 255–257
Miller's Tale xix, xx, xxi, xxii,
xxxvii, xxviii, xxxviii,
xlii, xlvii, xlviii, 18, 42,
43, 45–47, 49, 50, 52, 53,
55, 56, 59, 67, 69, 73, 81,
83, 103, 105–107, 112,
114, 116, 117, 123, 133,
161, 192, 193, 196, 197,
199–205, 224, 229, 233,
251, 253, 255, 294, 303,
305, 307, 317, 348, 350,
358, 362, 363, 364–366,
368–370, 373, 375, 376,
379–383, 385, 388, 396
Monk's Tale 79, 175, 341
Nun's Priest's Tale xx, xxiii,
xxvii, xl, xlvi, 42, 43, 49–
51, 55, 67, 71, 72, 82, 89,
93–95, 145, 153, 155, 157,
159, 160, 161, 165, 174,
175, 229, 251, 308
Pardoner's Tale xxvii, 42, 43,
45, 49, 51, 52, 55, 56, 61,
62, 69, 75, 164, 181, 227
Parson's Tale 174, 176, 242,
256, 268, 349, 374, 375
Physician's Tale 76, 128, 164,
176, 178, 179, 181, 182,
185, 320, 321, 325, 334,
336, 341, 345, 346
Prioress's Tale 321, 325, 337,
338, 341, 346
Reeve's Tale xx, xxii, xxxvii,
xxxvi, xxxix, xlvi, 42, 45,

46, 48–50, 52, 54–56, 67–
     69, 72, 76, 83, 93, 107,
     112, 114, 117, 123, 203,
     233, 254, 383
Retraction xlvii, 173, 174,
     182, 183, 268, 321, 324,
     348–351, 362, 371–374
Second Nun's Tale xxviii,
     xxxi, 42, 264, 320, 321,
     325, 339, 341, 347
Shipman's Tale xxi, xxiv,
     xxvii, xxxviii, xlii, xlvii,
     42–48, 50, 52, 55, 56, 67–
     69, 75, 76, 102, 107, 114,
     134, 172, 206, 224–227,
     233, 379, 389, 391–395
Squire's Tale 42, 175, 287
Summoner's Tale xx, xxvii,
     xlvii, 42, 49, 51, 53, 55,
     56, 59, 63, 66, 67, 70, 71,
     75, 76, 92, 102, 120, 294,
     311, 348, 352, 355, 358,
     361, 366, 368, 370, 373,
     375, 376, 379, 384
Tale of Sir Thopas xxv, 270,
     337
Wife of Bath's Tale xxii,
     xxviii, xxxii, 25, 42,
     43, 50, 54, 56, 62, 70,
     389
Canticum Canticorum 205
Capella, Martianus 240, 254,
     256
caricature xxiv, xli, 18, 176,
     180, 289, 382
caritas 83
Carnival xliii, 76, 125, 229, 230,
     232, 316
Carruthers, Mary 376

Carthage 408
cartwheel 56, 357, 358, 361,
     362, 365, 366, 372
Cassandra 410
catharsis 57–61, 76, 257
cathedral statuary 394
cathedral(s) 236, 246, 395
     of Amiens 237
     of Notre Dame de Paris 237
Cato 55, 56
cause-effect 392
Caxton, John 7
Celestina 81
celibacy 117, 192
cencerrada 231, 250
Cent Nouvelles Nouvelles 105
Chamberlain, David 236, 237,
     238, 240, 254, 256
Chambers, E. K. 192, 204,
     317
Chambers, Robert 248
chaos xxii, xl, xlvii, 187, 225,
     365, 368, 376, 387
characterization xxxvi, xli, 11,
     13, 47, 142, 225, 331, 333,
     334
charity 121, 237, 297, 367
charivari xliii, 230–235, 239,
     242, 245–248, 250–252,
     258
Charles VI 252
Chaucer, Geoffrey
     and audience 61–62, 371
     birthdate xiii, 32
     Boethius's influence on 397–
         419
     and comedy 79–99, 163–166,
         200, 228, 272, 322, 379–
         380, 383

comic attitude of xliv, 23, 31,
    230, 326, 395, 438, 445,
    446
comic conventions of 62,
    274, 277, 402–403
and comic effect 58–61, 98,
    306, 321, 371
and comic theory 70–80,
    138, 324, 442
critical reception of xxxv–
    xxxvii, 3–21, 25, 79, 331
and Dante 324, 397–398
eye for detail 66
and folk custom 230, 233–
    237
as humorist 3–20, 24–29, 122
imitation of 5, 6, 25, 81, 82
and language 172–183, 185,
    242
and lyricism 108–109, 114,
    116
persona 86–88, 95–96, 98–99,
    203, 285, 287, 289, 351,
    363, 426, 435
as poet 271–290
presence in tales 114
quality of mind 8, 17, 36–37
and scatology 349–353, 372–
    373
and seriousness 71
and social consciousness
    145–157
social and moral norms of
    103–104, 105, 200, 225,
    228, 336, 385–386, 408,
    427, 434
tone 102, 285
use of comic structure xviii,
    xxxviii, xlvii, 11, 20, 45–

    46, 53, 58, 101–122, 220–
    222, 246, 265, 330, 342,
    389
use of drama xlv, 13, 29,
    295–313, 318, 323, 329
use of law 56–57
use of plausibility 70–72
use of tradition 81, 117, 118,
    234, 237, 239, 244, 277,
    283, 297, 302, 313, 323,
    327, 350–373, 398, 406,
    409–410, 430, 432–433,
    436, 437, 442
view of marriage 76, 84, 105,
    116, 117, 127–128, 134,
    238
See also Canterbury Tales,
    comedy, comic
    technique, humor
Chauntecleer xxi, xxiii, xxvii,
    xl, 50, 51, 53, 56, 89, 90,
    94, 95, 145, 149, 150, 155,
    156, 235, 254
cheer xliii, 38, 99, 208–212,
    216, 223
Chester cycle 298, 317
chevauchée de l'âne 248
child 161, 191, 218, 258, 277–
    279, 282, 328, 330, 339,
    362
children xxx, 83, 97, 335
chivalry xxv, 10, 187, 192,
    287
Christ xxx, xxxi, xlv, 172, 173,
    182, 211, 228, 296–299,
    305, 308, 313–315, 328,
    345, 362
Christian church 397
Christian tragedy 406

Church xxiv, 33, 97, 108, 188,
        190, 192, 199, 200, 229,
        299, 306, 342, 344, 394,
        397, 408
Church Militant 408
Church Triumphant 408
churlishness 202
Cicero 150, 160, 399
circumlocutions 74
citizen 112, 211, 317
Clark, Roy Peter 375, 376,
        377
class xli, 27, 74, 76, 88, 89, 92–
        94, 105, 107, 147, 152,
        164, 165, 188, 322
classical rhetoric 402
Clerk xxii, xxx, 31, 84, 135,
        153, 331–334, 339, 341,
        344, 346
clerks xx, xxii, xxiii, xxvii, 55,
        83, 192, 196, 197, 308,
        380
cleverness xlvii, 56, 75, 208,
        380–383, 386
climax xxiv, xxix, xxx, xxxiii,
        xl, 39, 104, 146, 217, 303,
        304, 307
Clogan, Paul M. 344
clowning 271
Cobb, Samuel 9
cognition 49
Colle 94
Collette, Carolyn P. 141, 142,
        337, 347
comedy
    festive xli, xlv, 104, 190–192,
        200, 201, 203, 229, 294,
        295, 300, 301
    licentious xlii, 190

    satirical xxxix, xl, 40, 103,
        109, 115, 119
    situational 81, 83, 128, 207
    universal language of 42
    See also Chaucer, *Canterbury
        Tales,* humor
comedy of manners 115
comic characters 63–70
comic genius 83
comic tale xxv, xxxii, 42, 165,
        171
comic technique xvii, xix–
        xxxiv, xxxix, xli–xliii,
        xlviii, 12, 15, 19, 41, 44,
        70, 72, 81–82, 83, 97–98,
        105, 107, 119, 128–132,
        136, 165–167, 190, 193,
        194, 207–208, 230, 240–
        241, 280, 287, 304, 309,
        312–313, 380, 394, 400,
        436, 439, 440
community xxxix, xliii, 45, 65,
        108, 135, 141, 168, 228,
        230, 231, 245, 248, 258,
        286, 299, 329, 341, 365
compact 55, 56
complaint xxxiii, 53, 119, 199,
        213, 220–221, 273, 414
complaint d'amour 93
Complaint to his Purse 92
conception xxxvi, 17, 20, 230,
        324, 386, 394, 417
Condren, Edward I. 334, 345,
        346
confessio 52
Confessio Amantis 291
conflict 18, 153, 187, 216,
        229, 230, 237, 394, 409,
        415

"cocu battu" theme 382
Conley, John 294
consciousness 117–119, 154, 205, 244, 372
Consolation of Philosophy 254, 255, 423
consonances 240
conspiracy 55, 365
constancy 344, 412
constructiveness xlix, 380, 381, 383, 385
contemplation 110, 327, 338, 340, 399, 414, 422
contemptus mundi 406
contest xxxviii, 54, 134, 158, 159, 188, 237, 255, 265, 298, 301, 309, 341, 379
conviction 71, 211
Cook 8, 91, 96, 101, 233
Cook, Jon 247
Cooper, Elizabeth 10
Cooper, Lane 41, 52, 58, 68, 73, 75–77, 343
Cornford, Francis Macdonald 66, 73, 190
Corpus Christi MS 291
Corsa, Helen Storm 99, 185, 321, 343, 344, 426
cosmic design 187
costume 232, 239
cosyn xxv, 390, 391
Cotgrave, Robert 250
coulter 48, 56, 83, 305, 318, 366, 368
counter-trickery 296
Courcelle, Pierre 420
courting 215, 310
courtly love 28, 88, 92, 364–366, 385, 386

courtly lover 93, 109, 195, 216
courtly lyric 402
courtship 18, 192, 380, 385, 386, 389
Coveney, Peter 377
Coventry 303, 317
Crabb, George 12
cradle 45, 48, 52, 80
craft xxxiv, xlvi, 98, 285–287
Crafton, John xxxv, xl, xli, 163
Craik, T. W. xxi, xxii, xxiv, xxv, xxvii, xxviii, 381, 427
Cramer, Patricia 345
Crawford, William R. 431
creation 85, 110, 166, 177, 204, 245, 294, 303, 307, 309, 314, 327, 339, 379, 383, 384, 387, 388
Creator xlii, 304, 318, 387–389, 414, 416, 419. *See also* God
Criseyde xxix, 5, 59, 76, 85, 86, 157, 238, 292, 310, 319, 324, 398, 411–413, 421, 423
Croesus 409
crow 243, 244, 310, 311
Crow, Martin M. 161, 432
crowd 12, 232
Croxwell, Samuel 9
cucking stool 253, 257
cuckolding xx, 194, 234, 370, 380, 381
culture xxxvii, xliv, xlvi, 39, 143, 229, 230, 233, 245, 295, 296, 301, 388, 394
Cunnington, Howard 257
cupidity 237, 367

Curry, Walter Clyde 398, 420
Curtius, Ernst Robert 240, 256,
    421
custom 132, 190, 230, 231, 233,
    234, 241, 248, 250, 255
cynicism 117, 119, 208, 256,
    257

Damascenus, Nicholas 231,
    247
Dame Philosophy 397, 398,
    407, 409, 411, 413, 415
damnation 46, 50, 63, 295, 312,
    406
Dane, Joseph A. 434
Dante xlvii, xlix, 23, 62, 80, 87,
    183, 195, 305, 310, 314,
    319, 324, 343, 344, 397–
    399, 402, 406–408, 417
daun John xxiv, xxvii, 207,
    209–211, 215, 390, 391
daun Russell 145, 309
David (biblical) 199, 236, 253,
    255, 279, 288
David, Alfred xlii, 123, 187,
    247, 344, 434
David's army 236
Davis, Natalie Zemon 231,
    246, 248
De Consolatione 397, 400, 416,
    420
de Gordonio, Bernardus 416,
    423
De Meun, Jean 399
de Vendôme, Matthieu 412
Decameron 105, 189
deceived xli, 43, 48, 50, 51, 63,
    119,
decency xxxvii, 12, 189

deception xxxviii, 48, 51, 52,
    75, 138, 139, 172
decorum xxxvii, 8, 131, 278,
    385, 402, 404, 412, 413
definition xviii, xxix, xxxv,
    xxxviii, 8, 26, 41–44, 52,
    54, 75, 79, 103, 105, 142,
    147, 211, 250, 285, 340,
    400, 404, 405, 407, 410
deflation xxiii, xlviii, 269, 368,
    382–384
Delany, Sheila 149, 159, 160,
    171, 335, 346
Delasanta, Rodney 344, 345
demon types 45, 228
deprivation 389, 390
depth psychologists 58
derision 231, 232, 234, 369, 399
Deschamps, Eustace 6, 28, 33,
    92
descriptio 92
descriptive 82, 97, 137, 378
desecration 58
destiny 49, 71, 197, 199, 408
destruction xxxviii, 46, 58,
    170, 197, 230, 236, 246,
    258, 370, 383, 408, 409,
    421
device xxi, 56, 96, 215, 253,
    275, 283, 350
devil 120, 294–300, 304, 309–
    316, 318, 319, 328, 339,
    356
devil-yeoman 120
diabolic xlvi, xlvii, 295, 297–
    305, 307–314, 316, 317,
    319
diabolic discourse 295, 302–
    312

dialogue xix, xxxi, 90, 207, 210, 220, 270, 389, 393, 397, 398, 414
dianoetic function 54
diapente 240
diatessaron 240
diction 51, 73, 74, 272, 276, 279, 283, 286
Dictionary of Faiths and Folklore 253
didactic 82, 176, 201, 298, 401
didactic verse 401
Dido 403, 421
Digby MS 315
Dinshaw, Carolyn 182, 328, 345
Dionysus 237
discomfort 137, 245, 376
discord 236, 238, 241, 307
discoveries xxxviii, 47, 48, 166
disguise 232, 239, 245, 296, 303, 382, 410
dismemberment 220, 227
disorder 19, 231, 233, 237, 241, 251, 297, 299, 307
disparity xxviii, xli, xliv, 128, 136, 140, 335, 381
displacement xxx, xliii, 166, 208, 209
dissolution 186, 225, 394
divinity 314, 386, 383
dogerel xlv, 269, 271, 272
domestic strife 236
Donaldson, E. Talbot 123, 128, 140, 425
Donaldson, Ian 251
Donatus 323, 343
donkey 232–234, 248, 251, 254
donkey ride 248

Doran, Madeline 421
Dorigen xxxii, 50, 53, 54, 56, 63, 68
Dorrell, Margaret Robinson 317
Dr. Strangelove 197
drama xlvi, xlvii, 71, 76, 295, 297, 309, 313, 315–318, 323, 343, 394, 395, 421
dramatis personae 398
dreamer 26, 166, 196
dreams 50, 53, 56, 71, 89, 95, 147, 154, 161, 165, 166, 182, 185
Driesen, O. 252
drunkenness xxii, 190, 239
Dryden, John xviii, 7–9, 23, 25, 82, 92
dwarf 288, 293

earnest 82, 89, 90, 165, 247, 363
ecclesiastics 188
Edward III 82
effictio 277
effigies 232, 251
Egerton MS 291
Egeus 199
Eggebroten, Anne 340, 347
Egle 86–89, 95
eiron 64, 65
elegiac xlix, 403
elegy xlix, 10, 401, 403
Ellesmere MS 89, 293
Ellis, Roger 340, 348
eloquence 240, 241, 280
emergent grammar 378
Emily 19, 92
Emmerson, Richard Kenneth 314, 315

emotions xxiv, 16, 57–62, 194, 203, 402, 406, 413

encomium xl, xlix, 117, 136, 401, 403

entertainment 188, 287

envious 58, 114

Envoy to Bukton 85

envy 57, 58, 211, 234

epic xxix, xxx, xxxvi, 19, 82, 197, 284, 288, 289, 293, 310, 401–404, 408, 421

epilogue 36, 398, 406, 411, 413, 415, 418, 421

Epistle to Can Grande 324, 344

epithets 210

equanimity 57, 59

ernest xliv, 201, 202, 230, 284, 332, 374

eros 402

erotic content 401, 416

Erzgraber, Willi 421

eschatological beliefs 406

Eselritt 231

eternity 59, 353, 363, 373

ethics (Ethics) 41, 64, 405–407, 413, 415

ethos xxvi, xxxii, 45, 66, 71, 228

euphemisms 74

Eurydice 236

Evans, Joan 294

Eve xlvii, 246, 252, 309

Evil One 296

exchanges 211, 365

excrement 273

exegesis 154, 296, 345, 399

exegetical impulse 197

exemplar 294, 324, 393

exemplum 45, 49, 51, 53–56, 71, 140, 142, 155, 160, 254, 257, 407

existential truths 71

fabliau(x) xx, xxii–xxvi, xxxviii, xxxix, xl, xlii, xliv, xlviii, 73, 81, 89, 93, 114, 119, 133, 142, 196–197, 199–201, 234, 246, 303, 342

and anti-romance 128

as farce 382–384

humor of 18

and romance 105–107

Shipman's Tale as 207

fabrication 138

factual 46, 52, 72

Faerie Queen 4, 10

"faire cheyne of love" 187

fairy xxvi, xxxii, xxxiii, 85, 94, 167, 286

Fairyland 277, 278, 284, 289

Falke, Anne 435

Fall of Lucifer 302, 304, 311, 317, 318

Falstaff 34, 35, 122, 233, 250

fancy 12, 32, 287

fantasy 17, 59, 62, 111–119, 128, 136, 194, 342, 381

far companate 231

Faral, Edmond 422

farce xxii, xxiii, xxxvii, xlix, 19, 39, 164, 381–384

Farnham, Willard 420

Farrell, Thomas J. 374

fart xlviii, 52, 53, 83, 121, 122, 299, 304, 312, 315, 318, 349, 350, 352, 356–362,

364–367, 369–371, 373, 375

fate xxvii, xlix, 9, 50, 70, 71, 118, 197, 241, 311, 337, 371, 398, 406, 408–410, 420

fear xxii, 32, 57, 75, 185, 197, 205, 220, 225, 229, 299, 325, 405, 413

Feast of Fools xliii, 191, 203, 333

Feast of the Ass xliii, 191

Fein, Suzanna 247

felicity xlix, 397–400, 404– 408, 410, 411, 416–419, 421

fellowship 99, 188, 264, 268, 378

fertility 110, 111, 154

festivities 65, 203, 204, 230, 238

feudal establishment 187

fidelity xliii, 56, 72, 102, 114, 202, 409, 411

fiend 312

fiscal 219, 390, 393

Fisher, John H. 425, 431

Flanders xxvi, 266, 277, 278

flattery 234, 243, 288, 310, 312

Fleischman, Suzanne 378

Flemings xli, 145, 156, 157, 161

flood xx, 53, 83, 110, 111, 194, 195, 197, 288, 304, 364, 368, 372, 381, 387, 389, 394

foil 90, 175, 382–384

folk humor 229, 230

folk punishments 248

folk ritual xlii, 301, 316

folk-beliefs 308

folklore 83, 230, 247, 248, 250, 253, 257

folly 14, 74, 103, 139, 190, 197, 199, 316, 410

food 86, 153, 193, 235, 368, 369, 377

formel xxxiv, 88

formula 280, 287

fortune xlix, 47, 48, 66, 71, 72, 95, 213, 225, 233, 398, 400–402, 404–412, 422

Foster, Edward E. xxiii, xxiv, xxvi, xxvii, xxviii, xxix, 436

Fourth Lateran Council 296, 313

fox xxiv, xlvii, 51, 56, 67, 94, 145, 146, 148, 152, 153, 155–158, 160, 254, 309

Frank, Robert W. 436

freedom xxi, xxxviii, 15, 19, 44, 50, 106, 134, 173, 174, 178, 181, 203, 266

Frese, Dolores Warwick xviii, 325, 344, 345

Freud, Sigmund xli, xlii, 38, 58, 61, 63, 75, 145–148, 150–152, 154–156, 158, 159, 161, 163–169, 171, 182, 184, 345, 376

friendship 54, 84, 221, 390, 392

Frost, William 205

Frye, Northrop 58, 73, 75, 76, 165, 255

Funk and Wagnalls Standard Dictionary of Folklore, Mythology and Legend 251

furies 236

Gallenca, Christiane 250

galorrotsa 231

game 19, 40, 90–92, 103, 136,
161, 190, 191, 193, 213,
332, 333, 335, 363–364.
See also play

Ganim, John 146, 157, 230,
234, 247, 252, 253, 318,
333, 346

Garbáty, Thomas xxxvii,
xxxviii, 79, 128, 141, 343,
436

Garcio 300, 301

garden xxxiii, 45, 112, 117,
138–139, 140, 143, 199,
219–222, 224, 225, 228,
244, 246, 254, 343, 397

Gardner, John 432

Gargantua and Pantagruel 229

garrulity 52, 54, 74

Gay, John 10

Gaylord, Alan xliv, 261, 269,
271

Geffrey (of *House of Fame*)
xxxii, xxxiii, xxxviii, 4,
82, 86–88, 95, 256, 293,
395

Gellrich, Jesse M. 237, 254

generic figures 207

generosity xxxi, 45, 109, 115,
214, 380

genre xxiv, xxxv, xxxviii,
xlviii, 3, 79, 81, 101, 102,
105, 107, 119, 123, 127,
140, 141, 185, 312, 343,
347, 400–403, 410

Genylon of France 220, 391

Giaccherini, Enrico 431

giant xx, xxiii, 279, 289

gift(s) xl, 15, 16, 30, 83, 92, 122,
136, 138, 175, 196, 214,
218, 222, 355–358, 379,
407

glee 279, 288, 383

Gneuss, Helmut 421

gnome 54, 55

God xvii, xx, xxx, xxxi, 9, 55,
95, 117, 129, 130, 166,
168, 169, 171, 173–177,
183, 188, 190, 197, 199,
224, 237, 239, 255, 265,
289, 294, 296–300, 302,
304, 305, 312–316, 332,
334, 336, 340, 345, 346,
363, 364, 388, 408
See also religious themes,
biblical allusions, Christ

Godard 250

Godrich 250

Godwin, William 12

God's Plenty xviii, 9, 92, 196,
389

gold xx, 48, 52, 67, 68, 182,
214, 218, 223, 224, 287,
357

Golden Legend 314

Goldstein, R. James xl, 145

Goodman, Paul 382, 396

Goodman, Stanley 396

goose 88, 203, 278

Gorman, Bernard S. 377, 396

Gothic aesthetics 53

Gottfried 293

Gower, John 6, 33, 145, 157,
291, 327, 416, 417

gratification 71, 72, 130

Great Revolt of 1381 xl, 145

Greece 276

The Greek Questions of Plutarch 231, 247

Greene, Richard Leighton 251

Gregory VIII 247

Grennen, Joseph E. 344, 438

Griffith, Dudley D. 431

Griselda xxx, 331–335, 346, 351

grotesque xliii, 229, 237

Guy of Warwick 283, 294

Haberfeldtreiben 230

Hagen, Susan K. xxxix, 127

hagiography xliii, 230

Hamilton, Maria P. 347

Hammond, Eleanor 431

Hanning, Robert xlv, xlvi, 257, 295, 315, 319

happy xviii, xxviii, xxix, xxxi, 43, 44, 46, 99, 140, 166, 211, 241, 244, 292, 324

Harder, Kellsey 303, 318

Hardison, O. B., Jr. 343

Hardy, Thomas 251, 258

Harlequin 233

harmony 188, 190, 241, 244, 367

Harrington, Norman T. 140, 256

Harrowing of Hell 299, 301, 305, 306, 315

Hartocollis, Peter 377

Harvey, Gabriel 7

Harwood, Britton 162, 257

hating 60

Hauser, Arnold 394, 396

Havelok the Dane, Lay of 233, 250

Hawking, Stephen 376

Hawkins, Sherman 339–340, 347

Hazlitt, W. Carew 13, 29, 253

heaven xx, xliii, 17, 227, 238, 299, 318, 322, 362, 363, 398, 399, 408, 410, 419

Hecuba 410

heir 138

Hell 47, 59, 121, 139, 205, 236, 238, 241, 252, 254, 286, 299–301, 304–307, 312–313, 324, 363

Hengwrt 291, 292, 322, 325, 326

Heninger, S. K., Jr. 332, 346

Henry IV 82

Hercules 400

hereos 416–419, 423

heresy 18, 404

hero xxvi, xlviii, 48, 66, 93, 103, 110, 195, 278, 279, 288, 316, 398, 400, 401, 403–405, 407, 408, 410, 411, 417, 419, 421

Herod 112, 195, 299, 300, 316–318

heroic love 416

heroines 403

Herrick, Marvin T. 420

Heywood, Thomas 233, 250

high Gothic 394

Highfield, Roger 376

hoax 197

Hoffman, Richard L. 337, 347

Hoffman-Krayer, E. 247

Hogarth, William 12, 76

Holderness 102

Hole, Christina 248

Hollander, John 255

Holman, Hugh 256
Homann, Elizabeth Rudisill 74
Homer 240
homogeneous 135
honor 33, 68, 73
Honorius of Autun 323, 343
Horatian ideal 407, 409
horns xliii, 232, 233, 250–251, 255
horse xxv, xxxii, 48, 70, 112, 121, 232, 250, 274–277, 279, 281, 359, 405
hospitality 113
Host xxi, xxvi, 11, 31, 55, 59, 64, 94–96, 99, 135, 136, 176, 179–183, 188–190, 242, 265, 268, 303, 309, 335. *See also* Harry Bailly
House of Fame xxxii, xxxiii, 25, 26, 32, 82, 86, 87, 95, 256, 310, 421
Howard, Donald R. 257, 374, 377
Hughes, John 10
Huizinga, Johan 19, 342
human nature xxxvi, 35–37, 73
humanity xlv, 14, 17, 62, 72, 81, 92, 200, 290, 295–297, 305, 313, 314, 334, 335, 398, 414
humiliation 122, 231, 235, 258, 304, 369, 370
humor ix, xxii, xxiv, xxvi–xxviii, xxx–xxxii, xxxiv–xliv, xlvii, xlviii, l, 1, 3–6, 23–38, 63, 81, 84, 90–92, 96, 97, 128, 147–151, 171, 184, 229

and action 133
audience awareness of 136, 164–167
definition of 8–18
"festive comedy" 200
linguistic 68
low humor 349, 350
in *Merchant's Tale* 136, 137, 139
in *Shipman's Tale* 207, 211, 213, 216
Hunt, Leigh 4, 13–14, 24
Hurd, Richard 10
husbands xxiii, 50, 51, 56, 65, 69, 83, 85, 231, 232, 249, 384
Hymen 239
hypocrisy 45, 56, 59, 62, 65, 360

ideal xxix, xxxvi, 16, 37, 46, 187, 192, 244, 387
idée fixe 56, 134
illusion xxv, 45, 53, 62, 103, 119, 179, 223, 366, 381, 383–384, 392, 393
imagery xix, 70, 157, 182, 193, 194, 368, 399
imagination 7, 13, 35, 196, 279, 288, 291, 418, 423
impostor xxxvii, 64, 65, 67
impotent husbands 231
incongruity xix, xx, xxiii, xxv, xxvi, xxvii, xxxvi, xxxix, 26, 27, 34, 37, 128, 134, 136, 139, 321
indirection 15, 261, 390
indulgence 59, 194
Inferno 315, 319, 406

Ingram, Martin 232, 250
innocence xvii, xxx, xxxix, xli,
    42, 109, 118, 127, 128,
    201, 299, 333
Innocents Day 190
innuendo 55, 64, 118, 133, 141,
    241
instability 398, 409–411
instinct 18, 24, 46, 58, 62, 63,
    77, 194
instruction 288, 296, 407
instruments xliii, 233, 235, 237,
    238, 240, 255, 256
integrity 160, 219, 222, 223,
    404
intention 31, 45, 116, 133, 136,
    174, 322, 326, 351, 355,
    365, 372, 373, 383
interiority xlvii, 350
interpretation xvii, xxxv, 3,
    16–20, 33, 168, 180, 239,
    248, 297, 310, 324, 335,
    359, 415
intimacy 115, 371
invention xxxiii, 110, 111, 173,
    379
inversion xlii, xliii, xlv, 192,
    193, 297–300, 304, 305,
    307–309, 311, 313, 317
Iphigenia Among the Taurians
    57
ironical man 64
irony xvii, xxiii, xlii, xliii, xlix,
    6, 17, 24, 26, 33, 34, 42,
    45, 46, 47, 55, 62, 68, 71,
    82, 91, 141, 142, 159, 161,
    165, 173, 182, 206, 208,
    211, 213, 224, 245, 256,

    312, 322, 332, 334, 381,
    384–387, 398, 404
Iswolsky, Hélène 123, 205,
    246, 316
Ixion 235

Jack Straw 155, 158
Jager, Eric 314, 319
Jameson, Fredric 146, 158
January xx, xxiii, xxvi, xxxix,
    xl, xliii, 56, 65, 70, 84,
    103, 107, 116–119, 127–
    130, 133, 135–141, 194,
    231, 234–245, 253–257
Janus xlviii, 350
jealousy 195, 383, 423
Jekyll and Hyde 114
Jerusalem 190, 204, 265, 322
Jeu d'Adam 319
Jews 163, 236, 339
Joab 235, 236, 240, 254, 256
Johannine Gospel 296
John (carpenter) xix, xxii, xlii,
    6, 52, 72, 103, 107, 110–
    113, 133, 194, 195, 197–
    199, 234, 304, 325, 365,
    368–370, 383, 384, 387
    Friar John 353, 356, 357–359,
    361, 362. *See also* daun
    John
John of Gaunt xxxii
Johnston, Alexandra F. 317
joke xxiii, xxxviii, xliv, xlv, 39,
    80, 82, 90, 93, 97, 121,
    145–150, 154, 155, 157–
    158, 163–167, 174, 180,
    184, 206, 271–273, 287,
    361–364, 373

Jonassen, Frederick B. xliii,
    229
Jonson, Ben 37, 103
Jonsonian humors 382
Jordan, Robert 53, 75, 160, 256
joy xxi, xxiv, xxviii, xxix, xxx,
    xxxi, 13, 15, 59, 62, 86,
    99, 193, 330, 398, 411,
    413, 417
judgment 17, 72, 98, 189, 197,
    238, 265, 300, 303, 417–
    419
Jupiter 85, 341
justice xvii, xxviii, xxxviii, 80,
    83, 111, 155, 156, 199,
    212, 272, 300, 328, 338,
    368
Justinus xxvi, 50, 54, 84, 119,
    134, 243

Kaske, Robert 19, 205
Katzenmusik 232, 250
Kempe, Margery 300
Kendrick, Laura xx, 146, 158,
    161, 165, 184, 230, 247,
    332, 335, 345, 376, 428
Kermode, Frank 375
Kern, Alfred 432
Kern, Edith 247, 428
kindness xxxi, 49
Kinser, Samuel 246
kinships 209
Kirkpatrick, Robin 331, 346
kiss of peace 59, 181
kissing 48, 111, 195
Kittredge, George Lyman 4,
    23, 28, 29, 88, 256, 347
Klingner, Fritz 419
Knapp, Peggy 149, 158, 159

Knight xxi, xxii, xxiii, xxiv,
    xxv, xxvi, xxvii, xxviii
    xxx, xxxii, xli, xlii, 19,
    20, 25, 42, 43, 80, 95, 175,
    181, 185, 187–189, 191,
    192, 197–199, 202, 263–
    265, 287, 324, 325
Kökeritz, Helge 74
Kolbing, Eugen 293
Kolve, V. A. 328, 343, 345

labor 131, 153, 214
lamb 61, 109, 111, 298, 329,
    386
Lancelot 160, 403
Langer, Suzanne 74, 165, 395
language xxvii, xxxviii, xl, xli,
    xliii, xliv, xlv, xlvi, 4, 9,
    12, 15, 25, 27, 42, 55, 60,
    65, 73, 90–92, 109, 164–
    168, 170–173, 175–177,
    179, 181–185, 188, 242,
    257, 262, 266, 295, 297,
    300, 314, 323, 338, 339,
    341, 342, 354, 358, 359,
    360, 361, 368, 378
Lanham, Richard 438
largesse 208
Last Instructions to a Painter
    232, 250
laughter xx, xxiii, xxviii, xxix,
    xxxi, xxxvii, xxxviii, xli,
    xlvi, xlvii, xlviii, 10, 16–
    19, 35, 40, 41, 43, 59–60,
    64, 67, 68, 73, 75, 81, 98,
    103, 104, 120, 123, 127,
    133, 135, 141, 148, 169,
    174, 183, 191, 202, 204,
    287, 321, 323, 328, 345,

350, 353, 365, 367, 369, 370, 382
  posthumous 404
  religious 341
law(s) xxviii, xxix, xxx, xxxi, xxxvii, xlvi, 33, 42, 44, 46, 50, 56, 57, 61–63, 66, 67, 69–71, 77, 134, 176, 177, 179, 254, 327, 375, 378
Le Goff, Jacques 250
lechery 237, 287
Legend of Good Women 312, 421
Legenda Aurea 314
lemman 93, 109, 200, 401
Lent 230
Leonard, Francis McNeely 428
Lerer, Seth 375
Lèvi-Strauss, Claude 248
Levitan, Alan 376
Levy, Bernard 226, 227, 376, 439
Lewis, C. S. 5, 17, 18
Leyerle, John 376, 431
liberty 229
license xvii, xix, xlvi, 42, 46, 59, 64, 66, 76, 135, 190, 202, 301, 315
life xxiv, xxxvii, xxxviii, xlii, 8, 11, 15, 23, 36, 54, 59–62, 73, 104, 150, 197, 199, 226, 241, 257, 290, 323, 340, 349, 350, 362, 394, 395, 399, 406
lifestyle xliii, 209
Lindahl, Carl 230, 247
literature xxxiv, xliii, 15, 17, 18, 62, 71, 73, 79, 83, 92, 146, 229, 247, 252, 256, 294, 313, 314, 346, 347, 375–378, 395, 397, 402, 417, 421
  medieval 170, 401
logic 31, 170, 211, 270, 333, 349, 359–361
Lollius 400
London xix, 13, 102, 155–158, 233, 249, 303
Longsworth, Robert 185, 336
Loomis, Laura Hibbard 271, 280, 284, 294
Lord of Misrule xlii, 191, 202
love xx, xxv, xxix, xxxiii, xxxvii, xlii, xlviii, 5, 6, 18, 19, 28, 29, 48, 54, 66, 87, 90, 92, 93, 108, 133, 135, 187, 192–194, 216, 224, 237, 239, 254, 257, 276, 284, 289, 366, 370, 385, 386, 401–403, 410, 413, 416, 423
love-letter 118
lover xxiv, xxxi, xxxviii, 28, 43, 48, 83, 93, 109, 136, 138, 142, 195, 196, 201, 216, 289, 382, 401, 402, 403, 407–411, 416–419, 421, 423
low-mindedness 234
Lowell, James Russell 14, 23, 27, 29, 30
Lowes, John Livingston 4, 28, 423
Lucan 399, 404
Lucifer 298–299, 302, 304–306, 308, 311, 315, 318
luck 55, 74, 92

lust 26, 133, 194, 219, 361, 367,
    398, 399, 410, 413–415
Lydgate 4–6, 33, 80
lyre 237, 255
lyricism xxxviii, 108, 109, 114

MacDonald, Donald xxvi,
    xxvii, 142, 439
Machaut 92
Madeleva, Sister M. 347
Maenads 236
magic 52, 175, 198
Mak 298, 301
malice 69, 241, 309, 328, 384
Malkin 94
Maltman, Sister Nicholas 347
Malyne 93, 113, 114
Manly, John M. 292, 425
Mardi Gras 248
marketplace 210–211, 215,
    218
Marquand the Scot 420
marriage xx, xxvii, xxix, xxx,
    xxxiii, xxxix, xl, 44, 46,
    49, 53, 56, 62, 77, 83–85,
    89, 105, 117, 119, 128,
    133–136, 138, 139, 143,
    214–216, 219 , 222–224,
    226, 228, 236–243, 252,
    257, 402
Marriage Group 84
*Marriage of Philology and
    Mercury* 240, 256
Marsyas 237, 255
martyrdom 221, 338, 340, 341
Marvell, Andrew 233, 251
Marx, Karl 161
Marzec, Marcia Smith 439
mask 65, 76, 146, 148

maskers 232, 239
master xxxix, 8, 70, 79, 82, 89,
    191, 234, 271
maxim 54, 196
May xx, xxxvii, xxxix, 55, 56,
    63, 65, 69, 75, 84, 85, 107,
    117–119, 127–139, 141–
    143, 234–235, 239, 243–
    246, 253, 257
May Day 203
Mayo, Robert D. 421
Mayor of Casterbridge 251,
    258
McCall, John P. 421, 440
McCarthy, Sister Brigitta 347
McCracken, Samuel 255
McGrath, Joseph E. 377
Meech, Sanford Brown 315
Mehl, Dieter 291
Mellinkoff, Ruth 247–249
melody 201, 235, 236, 241,
    367
memory 169, 284, 355, 358,
    366, 370
Menander 63, 254
Merchant xix, xxiii, xxix, 44,
    83–85, 91, 101, 119, 127,
    128, 130, 131, 132–142,
    206–220, 235, 242, 246,
    256–258, 306, 390, 391,
    392, 393
Meredith, George 81, 98, 99,
    103
Merry Wives of Windsor 233,
    250
mesure 237, 332
metamorphosis xlii, 13, 209,
    311
metaphysics 415

meter xliv, xlv, 272, 273, 276, 279–283, 286, 287
Meyerhoff, Hans 377
Middle English Dictionary 96
Middleton, Anne 347
miles christi 189
miles gloriosus 65, 189
Miller xx, xxi, 8, 18, 44, 52, 63, 66, 69, 75, 83, 91, 92, 101, 105–106, 112–114, 189–193, 196–206, 238, 287, 303, 304, 308, 319, 377
mimesis 53, 172, 177, 178, 395
Minnis, A. J. 324, 344, 374
minstrels xxv, 233, 273
miracle plays 83, 199
mirth xxi, xxvi, 6, 8, 24, 25, 34, 208, 220, 242, 245
misery xlviii, 339, 401, 406–408, 411
mistress 95, 109, 401, 408, 409, 411, 417
mock heroic xxxv, 82
Molière 35, 36, 103, 271
monarchy 409
money xxiv, xxxviii, 48, 63, 70, 83–84, 115, 116, 152, 214–216, 222, 224–225, 357, 389, 390, 392
Monk xxi, xxiv, xxxix, xlii, xliii, 44, 48, 55, 70, 80, 91, 115, 116, 175, 188, 210, 215–217, 267, 269, 270, 325, 389–393, 400
monologue xviii, 84, 91
morality 50, 60, 62, 71, 122, 134, 151–153, 200, 201, 204, 208

social 63, 97, 103, 105, 187–189, 203, 332
motif xix, 398, 399, 404, 409
motivation xxiii, 180, 336, 389, 392
Muscatine, Charles 18, 111, 123, 149, 150
music xliii, 23, 60, 108, 194, 231–239, 241, 242, 244, 249–255
music makers 234
musicians 235, 236, 238
mutability xlviii, 407–410, 422
mystery plays 18, 112, 304

N-Town Play 318
Narcissus 195, 288
narrator xviii, xxxiii, xlv, xlvi, 43, 50, 82, 96, 101, 103, 114, 115, 120, 127, 128, 130, 137, 143, 147–149, 151–153, 156, 159, 176–178, 181, 185, 235, 236, 255–256, 264, 265–267, 284, 295, 326–333, 338, 339, 382, 392, 398
natural philosophy 399, 415
Nature 90, 176–178, 193, 194, 262, 263, 337, 386, 388, 389
negotiation 216
neoclassical xxxvi, 8
Neuse, Richard 19, 343
New Comedy 235
New Song 237
newfangledness 234
Nicholas xix, xxii, xlii, xlvii, 48, 55, 56, 69, 71, 91, 93, 103, 104, 108–111, 113,

194–200, 207, 256, 304,
    305, 318, 359, 364–370,
    380, 381, 383–389, 391
Nist, John 440
Noah xxii, 53, 83, 110, 112, 199
nobility 35, 188, 288, 334, 402,
    409
nonsense xlvi, 76, 297, 301,
    302, 314, 317, 361
norms 18, 103, 196
Nun's Priest 42, 43, 148, 149,
    288, 306–310
nursery rhyme xlv, 275
Nykrog, Per 123, 192

oaths xxxvii, 55, 74, 199, 211,
    224, 253
Oberon 281
obscene xvii, xxi, 42, 147, 232
old and new law 50
old hag 50
Old Song 237, 244, 367
Olson, Elder 74, 76
ordeals xxx, xxxvii, 54, 56
order 19, 44, 70, 156, 165, 188,
    229, 237, 251, 275, 297,
    313, 325, 332, 333, 338,
    346, 368, 387
organic process 389, 394
Ormesby Psalter 237, 255
Orpheus 235, 236, 240, 241,
    254, 256, 288
Ovid 215, 237, 255, 310
Owen, Charles A., Jr. xlv, 149,
    159, 261, 269, 272, 290,
    347, 374, 376, 385
Oxenford 333, 380
Oxford 9, 18, 102, 123, 140,
    160, 161, 192, 247, 249,

250, 291, 304, 314, 317,
    331, 343, 344, 376, 385

pagan gods 197
pain xxx, xxxi, xxxviii, 25, 35,
    43, 57, 60, 137, 244–246,
    367, 369, 371, 377
pairing xli, 215, 216
Palamon xxvii, xxix, xxxiii, 54,
    92, 204
Pandarus 81, 86, 98, 203, 238,
    398, 413
Paradiso 406
paradox xli, 84, 167, 169, 171,
    183, 353, 355
Paris 102, 116, 207, 210, 214,
    219, 222, 223, 225, 237,
    247, 248, 250, 393, 403,
    420, 422
Parliament of Fowls (*Parlement
    of Foules*) xxxiii, 86, 88,
    255
parlous play xlv, xlvi, 295,
    303, 317
parody xxi, xxii, xxxv, xxxvii,
    xxxviii, xlii, xliii, xlv, 43,
    49, 72, 76, 81, 82, 84, 92–
    94, 113, 140, 190, 191,
    205, 228, 229, 244, 297–
    301, 305, 314, 333, 358,
    361, 387
Parten, Anne 250
passion 20, 56, 195, 196, 237,
    313, 400–403, 405, 414–
    416, 418
pastiche 284
pastoral 401
Patch, Howard R. xxxvi, 18,
    20, 23, 420

pathos xxiii, xliii, 10, 15, 34, 45, 128, 213, 321, 328, 422
patriarchs 298
pattern 11, 14, 30, 35, 107, 147, 265, 269, 280
Patterson, Lee 157, 161, 325, 343, 374
pax Romana 408
Payne, Anne F. 230, 246, 430
pear tree (peartree) xix, xx, xxxviii, 53, 56, 84, 93, 117, 135, 139, 193, 246, 258
Pearsall, Derek xvii, xxxv, xxxviii, xxxix, 101, 142, 149, 151, 152, 159, 185
Peasants' Rebellion (Peasants' Revolt) 146, 153, 155–157, 189
Peck, Russell A. 171
penance 49, 350, 358, 362
Penelope 57
performance 12, 117, 118, 130, 135, 139, 210, 300, 302
Perses 409, 421
Pertelote xxi, xxvii, xl, 33, 50, 68, 89, 150, 310
Petersen, Kate O. 420
Petronius 82
phallic element 50
Pharsalia 404
Philebus 57
Phillips, Edward 7
philosopher's stone 287
philosophers 58, 398, 399
  Neoplatonic 398–399
  Stoic 398, 404, 406, 419

philosophy xxiii, xlii, 16, 26, 29, 30, 52, 168, 171, 183, 197, 199, 331, 375–376, 397, 398, 399, 404, 405, 407, 409, 411, 413–415, 417, 418
physicians 90, 416
piety 287, 338
Pigg, Daniel F. xlvi, xlvii, 321
pilgrim 91–92, 101, 120, 257, 263, 265, 270, 321, 351, 363
pilgrimage 85, 99, 132, 190, 204, 263, 268, 272, 322, 361
pistis 54
Placebo 50, 54, 243, 244
Plato xli, 26, 57, 62, 170, 172
Platonic 62, 168, 404, 407, 419
play 19, 24, 33, 95, 101, 103, 109, 181, 191, 195, 201, 203, 206, 236, 332, 351. *See also* word play, games, parlous play
"Play of the Sacrament" 307
pleasure 57–62, 76, 133, 134, 147, 184, 193, 194, 196, 201, 245, 246, 254, 407
  Freud and 154–155, 166
plot xviii, xx, xxi, xxii, xxiv, xxviii, xxxii, xxxvii, xlvii, xlviii, 41, 44, 47–54, 55, 59, 66, 67, 68, 72, 75, 83, 107, 111, 132, 134, 140, 177, 200, 202, 215, 216, 273, 283, 303, 331, 361, 370, 380, 392, 394, 398, 404, 409–411
Plutarch 231

Pluto 56, 117, 138, 244, 315
pneumatology 398
poetics xlviii, 154, 314, 319,
    344, 347, 402, 412
Poetics (Aristotle) 58
poet(s) 17, 29, 30, 55, 95, 97,
    240, 287, 310, 321, 398,
    401, 402, 406, 410
poetry 271–284
Politics xl, 60
Polyxena 410
Pope, Alexander 7, 10, 23, 26,
    81, 82
posthumous laughter 404
power. See Abuse-of-Power
    theory
Pratt, Robert A. 171, 425
prayers 210, 236, 286
Priam 410
pricking xxv, 278
priest 117, 148, 149, 299
Prime Mover 99, 187, 188, 198,
    407
Primum Mobile 84, 407
prince 34, 401
Prioress 8, 28, 42, 90, 218, 269,
    285, 287, 288, 309, 321,
    325, 338–340, 347
procession 189, 231, 250, 317
profane xlii, 201
profanities 232
profit 88, 208–209, 212, 214,
    223–225, 270, 312, 332,
    393
proofs xxxvii, 54, 55–57
Proserpine (Proserpina) 56,
    117, 136, 138, 244, 286
prosody xliv, xlv, 261–270,
    271–294

prosperity 207, 398, 401, 402,
    404, 405–406, 409, 410
providence 71, 72, 197, 297,
    326–329, 345, 398, 404,
    405
prudence 50, 215, 333
pryvetee 110, 196, 198, 212,
    312, 356, 358–359, 364,
    376, 380, 384, 387, 393
Pseudo-Aquinas 399–400,
    410–415, 417, 420–423
psyches 391, 394
psychological tension 390
psychologists 58
punish xliii, 231
puns xviii, xxv, xxvi, xxvii,
    xxix, 45, 96, 111, 121,
    164, 168–169, 228
purgation 60
purity 127

quadrivium 240
queen of fairies 286
quest xxiii, xxxii, 65, 176, 278,
    289, 408
Quick, Anne 431
quid pro quo 207

Rabelais 165, 229, 230, 246, 316
Raleigh, Sir Walter 16
Ramsey, Lee C. 336, 346
Rand, E. K. 419, 422
reader response 61–63
realism xxxvi, xli, 18, 34, 97,
    104, 170, 172, 176–178,
    185, 388
reality xxiv, xlvii, 105, 117,
    120, 327, 335, 339, 342,
    387, 393–395

reason xxii, xl, 46, 97, 156, 172,
197, 317, 413–415, 417,
418
rebellion 63, 190, 229, 254, 309
See also Peasants'
Rebellion
redemptive closure 61
Reeve 8, 46, 54, 69, 75, 83, 91,
97, 101, 112, 114, 189,
190, 204, 207, 308
Reid, David S. 441
Reiman, Donald H. 334, 346
Reiss, Edmund 442
relationships 207, 208, 211–
213, 222, 322
religious themes xxix, xxxi,
xxxv, xxxviii, xlii, xliv,
xlvi, xlvii, 37, 91, 102–
103, 107, 108, 117, 199,
208, 210–211, 228, 232,
295, 297, 298, 300, 302,
303, 305, 306, 308, 313,
321, 322–327, 329, 331,
336–342, 348, 385–387
religious laughter 341
religious plays 298–307
religious tales xlvi, xlvii, 102,
265, 321–348
responsibility xxxvii, 298, 371,
409
    artistic 50
    moral 47, 76
    social 174
resurrection 227, 296, 338, 339
retribution 382, 384
revelation xxxvii, 284, 387, 389
revellers 232–233, 239
revenge 48, 58, 59, 72, 305, 366,
368

reversal 48, 104, 214, 223, 265,
299, 384, 400, 410
Reynard xxi, 89
rhetoric xxxix, xlv, 52, 75, 89,
94, 117, 178, 245, 258,
267, 268, 278, 288, 326,
327, 331, 333, 344, 402
rhyme scheme 93, 281–282,
291
rhythm 261, 271, 364, 368, 369
Richard II 82, 156
Richardson, Janette 73, 227,
377
Richmond, Velma Bourgeois
291
Rickert, Edith 292
Ricoeur, Paul 349, 374, 375,
377
riddle 379, 380, 389
Riesner, Dieter 421
"rime royal" 272
rioters xx, 43, 45, 48, 51, 56, 59,
65, 75
ritual xxviii, xli, 88, 92, 167,
191, 210, 301, 302, 316,
338
    of baptism 340
    ritual comedy 203
Riverside Chaucer 226, 252
Robertson, D. W. 181, 185,
186, 237, 255, 336, 416,
417
Robinson, F. N. 269
Robyn 105, 366, 384
Rodway, Allan 429
Roland 276, 292
Roman 63, 68, 81, 253–254,
403, 405, 409
roman 403

Roman de Fauvel 232, 238, 250, 251
Roman de la Rose 28, 92, 172
romance xxxviii, xlv, 15, 41, 92–94, 102, 106, 192–193, 288, 289, 391, 416
    and astrology xlii
    comic 404
    in *Merchant's Tale* 130, 136, 140
    Middle-English tail-rhyme 93, 271, 274, 276
    in *Miller's Tale* 109
    and realism 104
    in *Sir Thopas* 273, 274, 277, 278, 283, 293
    in *Troilus and Criseyde* 398, 406, 408–409
rooster-hero 48
Rowland, Beryl 303, 318
Rudat, Wolfgang E. H. 442
Ruggiers, Paul G. xviii, xxxviii, 41, 134, 143, 228, 321, 426, 442–443
ruin 195
    of Troy 409–411
Ruiz, Juan 81
Ruskin, John 14

sacred xlii, xliii, 191, 200, 229, 230, 324, 397
saints' legends 95, 102
saints' lives 42, 213, 214
Saintsbury 16, 31, 32
salvation xxxiii, 49, 51, 52, 298, 300, 302, 324, 362
Samson 400
sarcasm 15

    in *Merchant's Tale* 137, 141, 234, 240–242, 245–246, 256, 258
Sarno, Ronald 443
Sarpedon 238
satire xxxvi, xliii, xlv, 4, 6, 10, 11, 23, 31, 33, 40, 45, 81, 103–104, 119, 122, 147, 211, 256, 273, 401
saturnalian spirit xli, 190
Saul 236
Savonarola, Giovanni Michele 418, 423
Sayce, Olive 374
scapegoat xxxvii, 45, 59, 64, 65, 245, 369
scatological xxxv, xlvii, 137, 258, 300, 301, 349–353, 360, 361, 364, 365, 370–374
schemes 207, 211, 364, 379, 385, 389
Scheps, Walter xxv, 444
Schless, Howard 343
Schleusener, Jay 257
Schmidt-Kohl, Volker 420
Schwartz, R. B. 252, 315
Scott, A. B. 324, 344
scripture 18, 297, 339, 415
Seba 236
Second Shepherds' Play 33, 298, 301
secrecy 115, 390
Sedgewick, G. G. 256
seduction 195, 359, 389, 390
self-control 60
self-righteousness 114
semiotics xlvi, 321–348
Seneca 406, 412, 415

senex (amans) 83, 117, 128, 132, 231, 234, 245
sensuality 414, 415
Sent Denys 102
sentence xliii, xlv, 82, 83, 164, 173, 179, 195, 202, 230, 284, 285, 292, 294, 327
sententiae xxxvii, 54
sentiment xlii, 192, 195
Sergeant at Law 96
seriousness xxxvi, 7, 8, 15, 16, 24, 36, 37, 44, 49, 191, 227, 264, 271, 284, 333
Serjeantson, Mary S. 294
serpent 245, 254, 296, 328, 339
service d'amour 92
sex xxiv, xxxvii, 139, 214, 364
  and marriage 105, 119
  as a commodity 116
  in *Miller's Tale* 192–195
  in *Troilus and Criseyde* 86
  in *Wife of Bath's Tale* 85
sexual appetite 133, 139
sexual comedies 62
sexual deprivation 390
sexual possession 118
sexual triumph 44, 63, 195
Shakespeare, William 5, 13, 18, 35, 40, 104, 233, 254, 316, 317
shameful xliii, 46, 66, 231, 245, 257
Shepherds' Play 301
sibyl 66
Sidney, Sir Philip 7
Siegel, Paul 385, 386, 396
signs xl, xlvii, 185
  in language theory 170, 341
  philosophical 183

religious 182, 197, 322, 327–328, 332
Signs and Symbols in Chaucer's Poetry 254
Silk, E. T. 419
silver 48, 52, 214
sin 102, 200, 243, 258, 296, 304, 336, 351, 363, 372, 388
Sir Tristrem 283
Skeat, Walter W. 426
Skimington 250–251
skimmington ride 231, 233, 251, 253, 255
Smith, Francis J. 444
social level xlviii, 64, 402
social order 146, 165, 189, 229
social roles xlii, 208
society xxxvi, 47, 81, 228
  civil needs of 183
  classes in 89, 105, 153, 165
  comic 19
  conventions in 138, 139, 143
solas (solaas) xliv, 80, 164, 284, 301, 327, 363
soliloquy 414
son-father rivalry 62
Song of Solomon 93
Song of Songs 109, 117, 140, 199, 200, 244
soul xlviii, 57, 60, 81, 258, 297, 312, 339–340, 347, 353, 356, 358, 362, 397, 399, 406, 415
Spearing, A. C. 257
Spenser 4, 7, 10, 11, 417
Spingarn, J. E. 421
spirit 359, 361, 362
  comic xxvi, 19, 67, 81
  contemporary 34

evil 198
poet's 23, 26
See also saturnalian spirit
Spurgeon, Caroline 4, 5, 7, 8, 20, 21, 24, 33
stag 231, 233, 248, 250, 251
Stanley, E. G. 293, 294, 397
Statius, Publius Papinus 235, 254
Steadman, John xlviii, 397, 430
Steinmetz, David C. 345
Stepsis, Robert 345
stereotypes 65, 81, 90
Stevens, Martin 256, 315–317, 444
storytelling 188
Stow, John 249
Strode 415, 416
Strohm, Paul 145
Stroud, Theodore A. 421
structure
  comedic xxxv, xlii, xliv, 101, 330
  in *Friar's Tale* 53, 56
  narrative 106
  in *Reeve's Tale* 112
  in *Physician's Tale* 182
  syntax and line- 262
  tragic 401, 405
suffering xxxvii, 46, 49, 50, 62, 296, 329, 362, 391
suicide 258, 391, 401
Sulowski, Jan 419
Summoner 44–45, 53–54, 91, 97, 101, 119–122, 190, 269, 312
summum bonum 193
supernaturalism 394
Supreme Good 399, 407

surprise xix, xxiii, 45, 65, 287
  and deception 50–52
  and reversal 104
  sexual 128, 139
surrogate xxx, 127, 216, 298, 299, 301
survival xxix, xxxviii, 72
Symkyn 383
symmetry 214, 221
sympathy 58, 201
  for May 133, 134, 136, 139
  of the poet (Chaucer) 13, 16, 85, 88
  of the reader 110, 119, 133
  tone of xxiv
syncopation 280
syntax xliv, 262, 390
Sypher, Wylie 67, 76, 396

Tabard Inn 95, 96, 187, 264, 265, 268
taboos 104
tail-rhyme romance xlv, 273
Tantalus 236
Tartuffe 383
Tatlock, J. S. P. 140, 245, 256
Taylor, Karla 343
Taylor, Paul B. 171–173
Te Deum 201
technique xxxvii, 152
  comic 41, 171
  in *Merchant's Tale* 116, 152
  in *Miller's Tale* 81, 83
  in *Reeve's Tale* 112
temporality 72, 349
tercels 88
Teseida 404
testimony 55, 56, 265, 400
theatrical 298, 299, 323, 391

Thebaid 236, 254
Thebes 256
Theiler, Willy 420
theology 49, 169, 171, 296, 308,
   397, 406, 407
Theophrastus 43
Theseus 54, 187, 198, 199
three-headed guardian 236
Thro, A. Booker xxii, xxiv,
   xlvii, xlviii, 225, 379,
   445
Thynne, William 7, 426
time xxxv, 72, 86, 203, 349,
   350, 352–356, 361–367,
   370–373
   and place xliv, 102, 264
   and space 266, 268, 337
   and timing xix
topaz 271, 287, 288
tortures 56
trade 210, 211, 215, 219, 222,
   326
tragedy xxviii, xxxvii, 34, 41,
   43, 70, 324, 416, 422
   of Chauntecleer 95
   in *Knight's Tale* xxx
   as "mithridatic" 76
   and plot 66–67
   in *Troilus and Criseyde*
   400–410
tragic reversal 410
tragicomic 403
Traversi, Derek 257
Travis, Peter 146, 157, 158
trick 122, 298
   Alison's 103, 104, 111
   May's 119
trickery 46, 59, 83, 105, 296,
   298

trickster xlv, xlvi, 67, 120, 296–
   299, 308, 311, 313
Tristan 403
triumph xviii, xlvii, 44, 67, 74,
   134, 185, 195, 379, 383,
   384, 386, 392, 393, 395
Trivet, Nicholas 327, 329, 399,
   400, 420, 422
Troilus xxxiv, 7, 17, 80, 86,
   397–424
Troilus and Criseyde xxviii, 5,
   25, 33, 36, 59, 76, 86, 157,
   238, 291, 310, 324, 391–
   424
Trojan horse 405
Trojan war xlix, 401
Trotaconventos 81
Trounce, A. McI. 291
Troy 86, 401, 408–411, 421
trumpet xliii, 236, 238
trust 389, 413, 422
truth xxxvii, xl, xli, xlii, 14, 68,
   185, 205, 305, 317, 394
   in Chaucer's language 163,
   164, 175–178
   in the *Knight's Tale* 187
   quest for 65
   spiritual 202, 288, 313, 407
Tschann, Judith xlvii, 349
Tyrwhitt, Thomas 426
Tzetzes, John 323

unity 12, 225, 228, 350
unmasking 47, 59, 61, 65, 76,
   376, 382, 383
   of evil 185
urbs eterna 408
Usk, Thomas 6
Ussery, Huling E. 337, 347

Vain Glory 233
valor 402, 403
values 35, 102–104, 202, 208
  aesthetic 30
  bourgeois 107
  comic 404
  demonic 47
  in the General Prologue 91
  in marriage 228
  quality of life 54
  religious 405
  romantic 59, 398, 401
  secular 67, 408
Vance, Eugene 252, 314
vanity 199, 253, 310, 398, 410,
  413
Veldhoen, N. H. G. E. 445
Venus xxix, 94, 239, 254, 402,
  423
verbal agility 52
vice 97, 200, 300, 328, 410
vicissitudes 401, 405, 406,
  409
victim xxviii, 110, 120, 221,
  258, 299, 383, 393
victimization xxviii, 245, 325,
  342
Victorians xxxvi, 13
villains 47, 83, 95
villainy xxxviii, 46, 120
violence 50, 146, 155, 236, 245,
  383, 415
  in *Miller's Tale* 112
  religious 298
Virgil 403, 408, 409, 412
virtus 402
visio Dei 399
vow xxiv, 280
Vox Clamantis 145–146

Wakefield 298–301, 306, 316,
  317
Waleis, Thomas 420
Walsingham, Thomas 156
war xxviii, xxix, 80, 187, 284,
  401
warrior 288, 401
water 88, 262, 288, 307
  force of nature xliv
  as imagery xix
  in the *Miller's Tale* 45, 52,
    104, 111, 195, 369, 370
wax 117, 141
wealth 59, 306, 398, 401
wedding xxxi, xxix, 18, 118,
  131, 143, 233–235, 236–
  243, 252–254, 328,
  341
Weimann, Robert 301, 316, 317
Wessman, Alden E. 377
Wharton, Thomas 4, 10, 11
Whetley, William 420
White, Hayden 349, 374
wife (wives) 105, 106, 115–117,
  142, 194, 209, 236, 254,
  303, 308, 311, 382
  in *Merchant's Tale* 107, 129
  in *Miller's Tale* 92, 110, 112,
    113, 133
  in *Shipman's Tale* 55, 75, 216–
    228, 389–393
  See also Alisoun, Wife of
    Bath
Wife of Bath xxiii, xxiv, xxxiii,
  6, 36, 37, 40, 51, 53, 54,
  65, 67–70, 81, 84–86, 91,
  92, 98, 222, 224, 227, 231,
  234, 333, 335. *See also*
  Alisoun

Wilders, John 251
wine xxv, xlv, 38, 152, 153,
    182, 273, 289
winning 72, 411
Winternitz, Emmanuel 237,
    255
wisdom xxvi, xxxi, 14, 24, 88,
    229, 240, 241, 268, 287,
    384
witness 180, 381, 382
Wittgenstein, Ludwig 355,
    375–376
wood xxiii, 67, 68, 276, 407
Woods, William xlii, xliii, 207
Woolf, Virginia 66, 77

word play xviii, xli, 51, 74,
    152, 167, 183
wrath 53–55, 357, 379, 392
Wurtele, Douglas 374

Yeoman xxiii, 33, 47, 55–56,
    65, 70, 120, 265, 306, 307
Yorkshire 102
youth 118, 266
    and age (marriage of) 44, 45,
        62, 82, 143
    and love 402, 413
Ysengrim 89

zinzarrotsa 231, 250